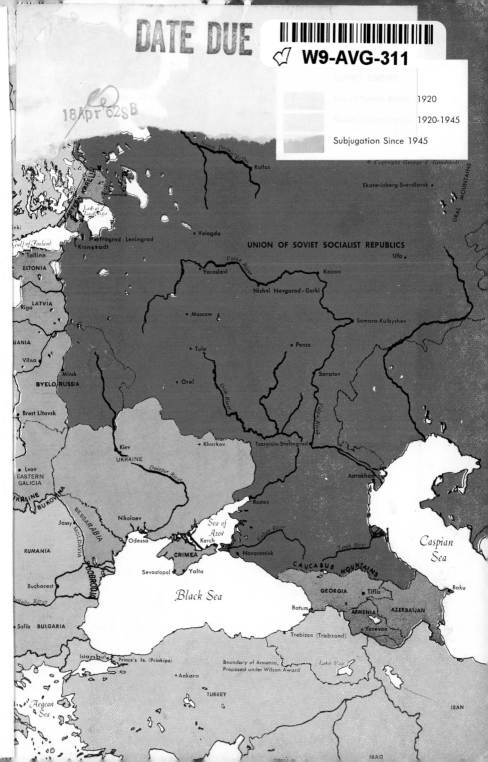

COLD WAR
AND
LIBERATION

JOHN F. O'CONOR

———————————★———————————

COLD WAR

AND

LIBERATION

A CHALLENGE OF AID
TO THE
SUBJECT PEOPLES

———————————★———————————

VANTAGE PRESS   NEW YORK   WASHINGTON   HOLLYWOOD

[Dedication]

This book is dedicated to the memory of all those, known and un-known, who have died for the cause of freedom, and to those who are now suffering for freedom—whether for their own freedom or for the freedom of others, in bondage or on the field of battle, in glory or with jeers and insults, in the prime of health or in the wretchedness of hunger and exhaustion, honorably or in forced moral debasement, alone or in the company of others, heralded or ignored, successfully or in vain.

ACKNOWLEDGMENTS

I WOULD like to express appreciation to my father, Daniel J. O'Conor, through whose generosity this work has been made possible; to many who have provided help and guidance in the research required; and for the helpful comments and suggestions of those who have read all or parts of the manuscript, including in particular three American citizens by birth; Nicholas T. Nonnenmacher, president of the Christianform, Carl Chadsey, president of Freedom Fund, Inc., and the Reverend Patrick Higgins, S.J., professor of history at Holy Cross College; two American citizens of Russian origin, Mrs. Vera M. Johnson, former reporter for *La Cause Commune*, and the Reverend Nikolai Bock, S.J., of the Russian Center, Fordham University; and one representative of Eastern Europe, Mr. Brutus Coste, secretary general of the Assembly of Captive European Nations.

CONTENTS

ILLUSTRATIONS

PREFACE

AT A PRESS conference in April, 1956, two months after Khrushchev destroyed the mythical image of Stalin as the benevolent father of Russia, and six months before the tanks of the Red Army ground across the bodies of those who destroyed his brazen image in Budapest, President Eisenhower put his finger on one of the biggest disadvantages of free government. He did not complain that the machinery of democratic procedures is too cumbersome, or that the demands of the people are conflicting or impossible to satisfy: the difficulty, he found, is in the lack of time for thinking by government officials. Such officials, the President said, "whether elected or appointed, or whether in Congress or in Executive Departments, are busy. They are always busy trying to get their desks cleared for the day. There is very little time in Government, as you know, for thinking, for contemplating, for pondering, and that has to be done."[1]

This handicap would go far to explain the free world's failure, in more than forty years, to find a means of effective assistance to the victims of communism. It could at least explain the assumption that in its own struggle with communism the choice of the free world is limited to such self-contradicting solutions as a war to prevent war or peaceful co-existence with a system based on violence, terror and subversion.

Lack of time for thinking may well be the reason why the "weapon of moral condemnation" has been described by an American ambassador as the "only alternative to action which might well bring on the third world war";[2] or why it was assumed by an American delegate to the United Nations that "when people talk about 'kicking the Russians out' " of that body, "what they really mean is that we should withdraw and, so to speak, 'take the United Nations Charter with us.' "[3] It may even explain why a secretary of state was willing to have us look war "square in the face" and go to its "brink,"[4] for the protection of those who are free but not of those who are slave. With such a disability it is possible to work out short-term solutions

11

and temporary expedients, but lasting policies and permanent goals are bound to suffer.

It does not take much time to reject the thought of "preventive war," at least if this means the use of nuclear bombs and intercontinental missiles to forestall the mere *possibility* of enemy attack. As President Eisenhower said, this would involve the destruction of cities and the slaughter of innocent peoples—it would not prevent war, it would *be* war.[5]

It does take time, however, to find the alternative—unless supine acceptance of "peaceful coexistence" is permissible when these same innocent peoples are slaughtered by their oppressors. There should be a great deal of serious thinking before such a state is described as "peace" and before we put ourselves in the position of protesting, as we have, that "we are falsely accused"[6] of assistance to the oppressed. It has been said that Soviet accusations of "subversion" by the United States will cause laughter "when our descendants read them in the history books."[7] It is more likely, however, that there will be sorrow and shame, for the United States itself is the result of such "subversive" activity. The free world cannot in conscience reject the pleas of those who are in open, continual revolt against tyranny, especially after more than forty years of proof that they, like ourselves, are unable to go it alone.

If assistance to the subject peoples means war, it would not be *preventive* war, because for such people the war *already exists*—a war which Lenin declared long ago and which he described as "most determined" and "ruthless"—a "persistent struggle—sanguinary and bloodless, violent and peaceful, military and economic, educational and administrative—against the forces and traditions of the old society."[8]

The casualties in this war already number many millions, of which uncounted victims of the civil wars in Russia, Spain and China, and of external wars in Eastern Europe, Korea and Indochina, are but a small fraction. They include, in the Soviet Union, more than fifteen million deaths from planned and accidental starvation,[9] uncounted victims of forced labor in camps with an estimated constant population of fifteen million, the victims of mass deportations, and millions of homeless refugees. They include twenty million persons "liquidated" in China and another twenty-three million whom the Chinese Communists have condemned to forced labor.[10] They include the victims of terror and deportation in Eastern Europe, and millions of exiles from East Germany and Hungary, China, North Korea and Viet Nam. The casualties of this war, which far outnumber those of any other, are the victims of that policy which Trotsky described, frankly, as "terror." "Terror," he claimed, "as the demonstration of the will and strength of the working class, is historically justified, precisely because the proletariat was able thereby to break the political will of the Intelligentsia, pacify the professional men of various categories and work, and gradually subordinate them to its own aims within the fields of their specialties."[11]

It is neither practical nor humanitarian that the free world should concern itself, or be willing to risk war, solely to assist those who have not yet been condemned to such a fate. But most important of all, it is a duty of charity and justice and, as President Truman said in the case of Korea, "a matter of basic moral principle,"[12] that practical means be found to assist every member of the great family of nations. Of each it may be said, with equal certainty, that there is "one God and Father of all, who is above all, and throughout all, and in us all."[13]

What is said here is not said to provoke hatred, or thoughts of war, but only that thinking, contemplating and pondering which has to be done to avoid war. Neither is it intended to imply judgment upon any free government or person whose policies are criticized, nor to make invidious comparisons between them. None of the policies yet adopted by the free world have succeeded either in eliminating the threat of war *or* in bringing freedom to the subject peoples, and it is therefore reasonable to conclude that none has been adequate.

It may be said, finally, that nearly every means of liberating the Communist-dominated peoples has at some time been employed. These have ranged from the League of Nations' advice to "be content to wait in confidence,"[14] to Hitler's brutal attempt to substitute one form of subjugation for another. It is the author's conviction that the subject peoples can be helped without provoking—or awaiting—world war, simply by giving due consideration to suggestions which have been made by persons within our own government, and by the subject peoples themselves, for a mutual-assistance program which would include them as well as the free nations.

> . . . let us not live in word or in tongue,
> but in deed and in truth (I John iii, 18).

INTRODUCTION

THE DESIRE for peace is universal—shared even by those who are most at odds on every other issue. It has been expressed by so-called liberals and leftists in the resolutions of international congresses and demands for world government, and by "conservatives" and "rightists" in what they term the avoidance of entangling alliances. Many have completely reversed their opinion as to how peace should be obtained—those who once opposed neutrality now seek it, and those who formerly favored it are now opposed. Nevertheless, they still want peace. Even the Communists say they want peace, but they want it only on the basis of universal acceptance of their own creed.

Most people, however, want peace only on the basis of universal freedom. In many nations the desire for peace was submerged in two world wars—thought to be fought for universal freedom. In America, at least, it has even been considered appropriate to wage war for the sole sake of the freedom of others. As President Wilson said in 1916, "America has more than once given evidence of the generosity and disinterestedness of its love of liberty. It has been willing to fight for the liberty of others as well as for its own liberty." "The world sneered," he continued, "when we set out upon the liberation of Cuba, but the world sneers no longer. The world now knows, what it was then loath to believe, that a nation can sacrifice its own interests and its own blood for the sake of the liberty and happiness of another people. Whether by one process or another, we have made ourselves in some sort the champions of free government and national sovereignty in both continents of this hemisphere; so that there are certain obligations which every American knows that we have undertaken."[1]

Wilson considered such obligations as a mandatory exception to the renunciation of war as an instrument of national policy. "The world's peace," he said, "ought to be disturbed if the fundamental rights of humanity are invaded, but it ought not to be disturbed for any other thing that I can think of . . . ."[2]

15

In the light of this policy, which has certainly never been rejected, and which indeed has been the asserted basis of every American
military venture since Wilson's pronouncement, it is difficult to explain the denial of assistance to those who are engaged in a struggle
which is more closely a war for freedom than either of the great
"total" wars in which the policy found its most earnest expression.
The explanation is made even more difficult by the fact that true
support of this other struggle for freedom requires neither war nor
a declaration of war, but at most an alleged increase in the *risk* of
war. How, it may well be asked, is it possible to explain the failure to
accept this other struggle, the struggle of the subject peoples, as the
real basis of the cold war; or the supine willingness to treat the latter,
not as a fight for the fundamental rights of all humanity, but
rather—in the words of John Foster Dulles—as an "effort, first of all,
to do away with the great danger of hot war."[3]

For the subject peoples the cold war is already hot. It is a
question not of doing away with the danger of war but of winning a
war which already exists—for only by winning it is it possible to do
away with it. The free peoples may assume that by withholding
assistance they can prevent the cold war from becoming too hot for
themselves—but they cannot evade the responsibility to assist the
oppressed—a responsibility which they themselves have so often
acknowledged. They can only ignore, they cannot erase, the death
and destruction which have been the daily toll of the cold war since
Lenin, Trotsky and their associates in terror removed it from the
arena of pamphlets, polemics and theoretical disputation by pervert-
ing a democratic Russian revolution into the dictatorship of an armed
minority.

The free world's ignorance of this war and its casualties has been
a great advantage for the enemies of freedom. A much better
definition of the so-called cold war would not describe it as an
effort to *avert the danger* of war but rather as an effort to *conceal the
existence* of war. "The new technique," said William Clayton in 1947,
when he was Adviser to the Secretary of State, "is to bore from within,
in the hope that this will not particularly disturb the rest of the world
and will not bring in powerful allies to help. The whole world sees
the intended victim writhing in the grasp of a great power bent upon
subjugation and control, but because armies are not on the march
and airplanes on the wing, some of us cross to the other side of the
street and go about our business."[4]

By this definition, the cold war and the problem of liberation did not begin after the end of World War II, but in the middle of World War I. Its end will come either with victory for communism, when the free nations will no longer be free; or in victory for freedom, when free nations will no longer withhold assistance from those enslaved peoples who can profitably use it.

There have been many opportunities for the free world to assist the subject peoples—many occasions when these peoples were close to freedom, and even slight assistance from abroad would have tipped the scales of victory. The first of these opportunities occurred in 1918, when there was a great interest in the liberation of central Europe but notably little in the cause of freedom for the former Russian Empire. Another occurred in 1956, when some of the free nations were willing to risk war for the Suez Canal, but none were willing to risk it for the freedom of Hungary. During the intervening years there were many similar opportunities, both in times of war and in times of peace. None of them required an unlimited war; many did not even involve the risk of war; but all were neglected.

In explanation of the failure of the free world to take advantage of such opportunities, many reasons have been advanced. Circumstances often suggest that the real reason is, as Lenin would say, that the free nations are not interested in the liberation of the oppressed but only in the "red gold of war profits."[5] Many have found proof of this in the supposedly secret agreements of World War I, or more recently in the British and French invasion of Egypt. The greatest confirmation of such a thesis, however, could be found in the failure itself—in the failure of the United States and its allies during two wars of "liberation" to liberate the victims of communism; and in their failure during times of peace to make the same effort, or to take the same risk of war, on behalf of these victims that they are willing to make and take in areas where their own interests are more clearly affected. There are not many, for example, even in the free world, who can otherwise explain such assertions as that made by Congress in its joint resolution on the Eisenhower Doctrine, that the use of armed force is appropriate in the Middle East because the "independence and integrity" of those nations is "vital" to our "national interest,"[6] while only a few months earlier, Vice-President Nixon had indicated that such action was not appropriate in Hungary because of the danger of a "third and ultimate world war."[7]

It would seem, however, that there is another reason for our failure to help the subject peoples—and one which is even more useful to Communist propaganda. This reason may be found not in the selfish desires of free peoples but in a persistent persuasion that the Communist regime of terrorism, purges, concentration camps and forced labor is supported by a majority of the population of the Soviet Union. This uncharitable belief has been well promoted by the promises and propaganda of the Communists, but they themselves admit that in their own terminology those who resist are not "people" —they are "enemies of the people." In the words of Mao Tse-tung, head of the Chinese Communist Party and former Chairman of the so-called People's Republic of China, "The term 'the people' has different meanings in different countries, and in different historical periods in each country." "At this stage of building socialism," he said, "all classes, strata and social groups that approve, support and work for the cause of Socialist construction belong to the category of the people, while those social forces and groups that resist the Socialist revolution, and are hostile to and try to wreck Socialist construction, are enemies of the people."[8] Under this definition it does not matter how many resist—whether nine-tenths or ninety-nine one-hundredths of the population are fighting the Communist regime. They simply do not count—they are not "people."

Thus, in spite of Lenin's promises of rule by the proletariat, his real prescription was the rule of a small, but armed, minority. He applied it even to the Communist Party, and from the very beginning, by his insistence on minority rule and rigid party discipline, split the Russian Social-Democratic Labor Party (RSDLP), making his own Bolshevik faction a minority even among Marxists. This occurred in 1903; and as Stalin later summed it up, "five out of the six [party leaders] fell out of the cart. Lenin alone remained."[9]

Leon Trotsky, who was to become one of Lenin's chief colleagues, was at that time opposed to his methods, and described them with accuracy. "In Lenin's scheme," Trotsky asserted, "the party takes the place of the working class. The party organization displaces the party. The Central Committee displaces the party organization, and finally the Dictator displaces the Central Committee."[10] After the seizure of power in Russia, Lenin himself frankly stated the manner in which it would be ruled: "Just as 150,000 lordly landowners under Czarism dominated the 130,000,000 of Russian peasants, so," he wrote, "200,000 members of the Bolshevik Party are imposing their proletarian will on the mass, but this time," he added, "in the interest of the latter."[11] Like so many others, Lenin assumed that his concept of the real interests of the masses was superior to their own.

Trotsky himself could never really accept the Leninist theories of party discipline, and because of this he eventually became one of its best-known victims. But his life was a contradiction. He was read out of the party because he insisted too long on greater repression of the people than the party dictator was ready, at the time, to enforce. Trotsky applied his belief in what he considered democracy within the party to oppose even temporary concessions to those without.

Lenin was also very glib in his promises of peace, even while plotting war. During the First World War he vigorously attacked those Socialists who loyally supported the war efforts of their own national governments. At a conference of dissident Socialists, held at Zimmerwald, Switzerland, in 1915, Lenin set his signature to a manifesto on peace. It urged the people in every land "to take up this battle for peace, and for a peace without annexations or war indemnities." "Such a peace," it said, "is only possible on condition of the condemnation of all violence against the rights and liberties of the peoples. Neither the possession of whole nations nor of separate sections of nations must be permitted to lead to forcible incorporation. No annexation, either open or masked, and no forcible economic union secured through any violation of political rights must be made. The right of self-determination of peoples must be the indestructible foundation of the creation of national relations."[12]

President Wilson also accepted this Zimmerwald slogan. In his message to Congress in February, 1918, he said there would be "no annexations, no contributions, no punitive damages. Peoples are not to be handed about from one sovereignty to another by an international conference or an understanding between rivals and antagonists. National aspirations must be respected; peoples may now be dominated and governed only by their own consent. 'Self-determination' is not a mere phrase. It is an imperative principle of action, which statesmen will henceforth ignore at their peril."[13] He added a warning, however, that "we cannot have general peace for the asking, or by the mere arrangements of a peace conference."

Lenin's insincerity and Wilson's failure to heed his own warning set the pattern for a long series of Communist victories. Since then the Communists have never ceased to exploit the world's desire for peace. At the same time the free world has never really accepted the fact that peace with Communists can only be had upon full acceptance of their—Communist—terms. This is why the Soviet Union has been able, for more than forty years, to wage a hot war against the subject peoples, while the democratic powers are content with cold-war efforts, not always effective, to prevent the extension of such war to those who are still free.

This is why the people of America have not assisted the subject peoples to assert those rights which Americans themselves were originally able to assert only because others generously provided assistance comparable to that which the United States now withholds. It is why the United States has permitted the infliction upon the present-day subject peoples of "a long train of abuses and usurpations, pursuing invariably the same Object"; and—in the words of our own Declaration of Independence—evincing "a design to reduce them under absolute Despotism." It is also why the subject peoples have not been able to exercise "their right" and "their duty, to throw off such Government, and to provide new Guards for their future security," as we ourselves were able, so long ago, to do.

Finally, this is why the American conscience has not known peace, and will never know peace until it accepts the realities of the case, assesses them objectively, and adopts the inescapable conclusion —the same conclusion which caused it to propose the League of Nations and accept the United Nations—as the basis for effective action rather than idle words.

CHAPTER I

THE COLD WAR BEGINS

"Within a few days Russia was transformed into a democratic bourgeois republic, more free—under war conditions—than any other country in the world."   V. I. Lenin[1]

DURING the night of July 16, 1918, Nikolai Alexandrovitch Romanov, last Czar of all the Russias, was shot and killed with his family, but without the benefit of clergy, trial or ceremony, in the basement of a large house in the Ural mountain city of Ekaterinburg. This act of terrorism was the contribution of the Bolsheviks to a revolution which had occurred eighteen months before, in March, 1917, and with which they had little to do. It was symbolic not of the overthrow of autocracy but of the terror and massacres which were to be the lot of the peoples of Russia under the far greater tyranny of the Czar's ultimate successors.

Of all the groups which had been seeking to give political direction to the Russian revolutionary movement, the Bolsheviks were one of the smallest, and the least representative. There were large liberal groups, or "middle of the roaders," who had spoken largely through elected provincial assemblies, the Zemstvos—and the elected national assembly, the Duma; there were the more radical groups, with socialistic programs, who preferred the elected workers' councils, the Soviets; and finally there were the Bolsheviks, who chose violence and repression.

The Zemstvos were first authorized in 1864. Their powers were limited to local matters, health and public welfare, and their election law favored the landowner, but they became a powerful voice for freedom and constitutional reform. The Duma was a result of the revolution of 1905. It was originally elected under almost universal franchise, and given full legislative powers. Its authority was later curtailed, the voting franchise restricted, and it was twice dissolved. A number of its members were arrested or deported. Nevertheless, it continued to oppose the autocracy of the Imperial Court, maintained a broad political composition, and won the confidence and support of the people. Even the Bolsheviks were represented—until their deputies were sent to Siberia during World War I.

The Soviets were first organized in Petrograd, the capital, and Moscow—also during the revolution of 1905. They were the creatures not of the Bolsheviks but of all the socialist parties, and were formed to lead a general strike for universal suffrage and the election of a constituent assembly. Revived in the revolution of 1917, they quickly spread throughout the empire. They were elected in factories, in the army, and by the peasants, but the "upper classes" and the "intelligentsia" were largely excluded, the elections were haphazard, and the Soviets became for Lenin an excellent opportunity for the creation of the first Communist fronts.

Among the liberal parties were the Constitutional Democrats, sometimes called the "Cadets," who were the strongest party in the First Duma, elected in 1906, and the Octobrists, who held the largest number of seats in the Third and Fourth Dumas, elected in 1907 and 1912. Both of these parties were organized in 1905, the Octobrists deriving their name from their support of the program promised by the government in its Manifesto of October 30 of that year—enforcement of civil liberties, elective local self-government, and full legislative powers for the Duma. This manifesto was a direct answer to demands for reform made by the Zemstvo Conference held in 1904. Among the socialistic parties were the Social Revolutionaries and the Social Democrats; and among the Social Democrats were the Mensheviks and the dissident faction of Bolsheviks.

The final revolution occurred in 1917, the third year of World War I. The Czar was forced to abdicate on March 14, 1917. A new Provisional Government was formed on the same day by a committee of the Duma; and on the following day, March 15, it received the conditional support of the Petrograd Soviet. On March 16, the Czar's designated successor, the Grand Duke Michael, made his acceptance of that role conditional upon the election and decision of a constitutional assembly.

At this time, many of the Bolshevik leaders were in exile, and they were as much surprised by these events as was the entire outside world. When they received the news, they converged upon the Russian capital from all directions, only to find that a free provisional government, conservatively oriented, was already ruling by the agreement of all parties. This was the government which Lenin asserted was "more free" than any other in the world, but which he set about immediately to destroy.

Trotsky, who was destined to be the Bolsheviks' first "Commissar for Foreign Affairs" and subsequently, as "Commissar of War," to mastermind their military conquests, was in New York. He was stopped by the British in Canada, but after a month's internment was allowed to proceed to Petrograd. Lenin was in Switzerland. The Germans eased his path by giving his party a *laisser-passer*, extra-territorial rights and a private railway car. Since Russia was on the side of the Allies, and Lenin would demand its withdrawal from the war as well as promote internal disorder, Germany was only too happy to assist him.

Having thus permitted the archconspirators to return to the scene of their crimes, the outside world with growing concern watched, but did little to oppose, their efforts to destroy the tenuous hold of democracy. It was thus privileged to behold, from positions of comparative safety, the losing struggle of the first free government to become a victim of Communist methods—a struggle which was a prototype of its own predicament today, and which offers many lessons that it could now apply with profit.

Not the least of such lessons was the early proof that communism cannot be defeated by argument, or by weak measures, or by the desire for peace. Perhaps the most important lesson, however, may be derived from the fact that the Bolsheviks did not come to power through their own devices, but because of the mistakes of others. The disagreements and conflicting claims of authority between the Provisional Government and the Soviets, particularly in matters of war and peace, led to a series of political crises which resulted in the formation and fall of several successive governments, the disorganization of the army, the discrediting of all parties, defeat at the front, and finally a state of anarchy in which the Bolshevik seizure of power was possible.

The first Provisional Government had strong representation from the Duma. Its Foreign Minister was Paul N. Miliukov, the leader of the Constitutional Democrats. Its Minister of War was Alexander I. Guchkov, leader of the Octobrists, and a man who had spent the major part of his political life in work on army reform. The Soviets, on the other hand, declined to participate. Despite its qualified support of the government's program, the Executive Committee of the

Petrograd Soviet voted against participation; and the President of the Soviet, Nikolai S. Chkheidze, rejected the offered post of Minister of Labor. As a result, there was only one Socialist represented, Alexander Kerensky, Minister of Justice. Although he was a Vice-President of the Soviet, he considered it a duty to accept a government post, and he was looked upon as a strong link between the two conflicting groups. Eventually, he was made Prime Minister. Both Kerensky and Chkheidze were also members of the Duma and of the committee by which the Provisional Government was appointed.

In spite of their differences, the Soviets and the Provisional Government were agreed on at least one thing—the paramount necessity for nationwide elections, and for a constituent assembly to determine the form of a permanent, democratic government. On this issue only the Bolsheviks differed. They purported to favor the planned elections; but, after seizing power in November, they attempted to manipulate them, arrested a number of the delegates and finally suppressed the Constituent Assembly itself.

The Soviets and the Provisional Government were also agreed on the need for unity. It was in the knowledge of this necessity that an All-Russian Conference of Soviets resolved in April, 1917, despite many demonstrations of hostility, to follow the lead of the Petrograd Soviet and give the government its qualified support.[2] Here too the Bolsheviks purported to agree, and voted for the resolution as adopted. But under Lenin's direction they continued to stir up the people with all sorts of impossible demands designed to widen the breach—complete socialization, liquidation of the army and an immediate end to the war. Their tactics were condemned in a resolution of the Petrograd Soviet, April 20, 1917:

The agitation now being waged by Lenin and his followers is dangerous to the revolution, his action in traveling through Germany was an act most injurious to the Russian nation, and the Council of Workmen's and Soldiers' Deputies should explain the injurious effect of Lenin's agitation to the workmen and soldiers and strive to paralyze his propaganda by every means in its power.[3]

In spite of all efforts, however, the Soviets and the Provisional Government were unable to overcome the early effects of divided authority. One of the very first acts of the Petrograd Soviet was intended to produce democracy in the Army and therefore, ultimately, peace. Instead it produced only chaos and destruction of the power of defense. This was the so-called General Order No. 1, which called for Soviet control of the armed forces and the election of local Soviets in each military unit. "All kinds of arms," it stated, were to be at the disposal of these groups, "and in no case should be given to officers even on their demand." The attempted implementation of this order played into the hands of intensive German pacifist and revolutionary propaganda. It resulted in contradictory orders, fraternization with the enemy, and disobedience even of tactical commands. When the mistake was realized, it was too late for it to be corrected.

Another early and unilateral act of the Petrograd Soviet was an appeal to "all peoples to take the question of war and peace into their own hands," and to "begin the struggle against the grasping tendencies of the governments of all countries." It was an effort to obtain the clarification of war aims, but it was couched in terms that were most unlikely to appeal to the governments of either side. The Allies only pressed their demands for greater war effort.

Three years of the war, however, had exhausted Russia. Six million troops had been lost, transportation was disrupted, and there were serious food shortages. The demands of the Allies were not popular; and when the new government pledged itself to meet them, it was criticized for not having obtained the much sought war-aims clarification. Miliukov was understood to advocate insistence upon Russian control of the Dardanelles—an "annexationist" goal. There were demands for his resignation—and for the resignation of Guchkov, Minister of War—and many street demonstrations, for and against the Provisional Government. These provided the occasion for one of the first of several preliminary displays of Bolshevik violence.

This early *putsch* occurred on May 4, 1917, when the Bolsheviks attempted to join the demonstrators with a parade of armed civilians. They soon discovered, however, that the people were not so anxious for peace that they were willing to obtain it at the cost of surrender to Bolshevism or its methods. The spontaneous and forceful reaction of those present was described to the State Department by the United States consul in Petrograd, North Winship, as follows:

One of the largest of the parades formed on the Petrograd side and crossed the river heading for the Nevski Prospekt. This parade consisted mostly of adherents of Lenin. Among the placards and flags it bore a large black flag with white skull and crossbones. As it approached the corner of the Catherine Canal and the Nevski, going in the direction of the Mariinski Palace where the Temporary Government was supposed to be sitting, a crowd of unarmed soldiers which had formed at the corner shouted to pedestrians to support them in dispersing this procession of armed anarchists. This appeal was immediately responded to and the crowd thus gathered halted the advancing procession. Soldiers started to tear the anarchistic banners from the hands of the Leninists and some one of the workmen fired two shots, killing one noncommissioned officer and wounding a Red Cross nurse; after this the Leninites dispersed. A very large parade of Government sympathizers immediately formed and proceeded to the Mariinsky Palace. In the evening about 9 o'clock a similar conflict took place between soldiers and another Leninist manifestation parade in which three persons were killed and seven wounded.[4]

Nevertheless, the process of disintegration continued.

On May 10, 1917, the eleventh anniversary of the first meeting of the First Duma, Guchkov gave a warning that proved to be only too correct, asserting that the nation could not survive in "conditions of dual government." Speaking in the former hall of the Duma, at an unofficial session attended by the members of that body, the Petrograd Soviet, and a convention of delegates from the front, he pointed out that loss of army discipline was destroying benefits which the revolution had brought in the form of improved morale and increased energy. In a further warning, one that is valid for the free world today, he decried demands which called for "peace at any cost," and even for "peace at the front and war within the country." "That motto," he declared to the assembled delegates, "that death-bringing motto, that doctrine of international peace at any cost and civil war at any cost, which was brought to us by persons who may or may not know what they are doing, must be drowned in the compelling voice of the whole great Russian people crying: 'War at the front and peace within the country.' "[5] Within a few days, however, Guchkov confessed that he was unable to reverse the destructive process. He and Miliukov were forced to resign, and their loss was, in itself, a severe blow to the cause of organized government.

A determined effort was then made to correct the situation. In a spirit of compromise, a new government was formed with five socialist members. It published a declaration accepting the slogan advanced by the Soviets and derived from the Zimmerwald Manifesto—"peace without annexations or contributions on a basis of the self-determination of nations"—and it agreed to promote the cause of peace among the Allies.[6] The Socialists, on their part, agreed to give more practical support to the defense of the nation. Kerensky was made Minister of War in the belief that he could reverse the effects of General Order No. 1 and persuade the army to fight. He made a tour of the front for this purpose, and the Petrograd Soviet made a strong appeal for co-operation:

Remember, comrades, at the front, in the trenches, you are guarding Russian liberty. Your blood is not defending the Tsar nor his Protopopovs or Rasputins, nor the riches of the landowners and capitalists. You are defending the revolution. . . . The front can not be defended by merely sitting motionless in the trenches. There are times when the enemy's attack can only be foiled by attacking him.

There are times when humbly waiting to be attacked is equivalent to awaiting death. There are times when an attack is the only way to save yourselves from death and to save your brothers on other parts of the front.[7]

This was strong but sound advice, and by the most ardent proponents of peace. In Russia, however, it came too late. As Guchkov had predicted, the subversive process had gone too far.

In July the Russian Army launched an offensive. It met with initial success, but discipline could not be maintained, mutinies occurred, and many soldiers refused to pursue the initiative thus gained. German counterattacks eventually brought the threat of capture to Petrograd itself.

The Bolsheviks, in the meantime, had planned another armed demonstration for June. An attempt was made to forestall this at a meeting of the first All-Russian Congress of Soviets, but without great success. While the Congress prohibited armed demonstrations, and staged a peaceful one of its own, the Bolsheviks refused to abstain from violence. Joining forces with a group of anarchists, they forced the release of several prisoners held on charges of espionage, and the government had to use troops to quell the disturbance.

Prior to this event, the authorities had been very tolerant of the Bolsheviks, and the United States consul (Winship) reported that this was "the first time that force has actually been used by the Temporary Government." He added that "the act met with universal approval from all sides" except, of course, from the Bolsheviks.[8]

Another demonstration occurred in July, after the collapse of the Russian Army's offensive. On this occasion, the Bolsheviks, or at least some of them, believed that the opportune moment for seizure of power had arrived. It is reported that there was much indecision on the part of their leaders, who were even then divided by so-called extreme and moderate factions, but they ultimately elected in favor of an uprising, which lasted for three days. Although this uprising was a failure, it greatly accelerated the spread of disorder, and did the Bolsheviks no harm. Trotsky was arrested, the party went underground, its headquarters were seized, and Lenin went into hiding. But Trotsky was soon released, and Lenin reappeared in time to direct the final revolt. In the meantime, the uprising contributed to a new government crisis in which Kerensky himself offered to resign. His offer was not accepted, and a third Provisional Government was formed in which he was designated Prime Minister.

Still another crisis occurred in September, when the retreating Russian Army was forced to surrender Riga, and Petrograd itself was threatened by the German advance. The Russian Commander-in-Chief, General L. G. Kornilov, sought to replace the Provisional Government with a military administration. He failed, and his abortive effort succeeded only in aggravating the condition which he hoped to improve. In anticipation of his attempted coup, the government had issued some 50,000 rifles to civilians, for its own defense. Many of them undoubtedly found their way into the hands of Bolshevik supporters, and the fear of renewed violence was increased.

By this time, Kerensky was losing support on every side. A fourth Provisional Government was created in October, and also a pre-Parliament, the "Provisional Council of the Russian Republic." But unity was not produced, and the head of the American Military Mission, Brigadier General William V. Judson, reported that anarchy was becoming "nearer daily."[9]

These were the conditions which Lenin had sought to promote. And as he had hoped, the Bolsheviks and their supporters were winning control of the Soviets. On October 7, General Judson predicted that the next Congress of Soviets would be Bolshevik. On the following day, Trotsky was elected Chairman of the Soviet in Petrograd.

Under Trotsky's direction the Petrograd Soviet organized a "Military Revolutionary Committee"—ostensibly for the defense of the city against German attack and "counter-revolutionary" *coups d'état* like that of General Kornilov. Through control of this committee, the Bolsheviks also obtained control of those troops in

Petrograd which were obedient to the Soviet. On November 7, they seized a number of strategic positions and announced the overthrow of the Provisional Government.

November 7, 1917, was also the day fixed for a meeting of the Second All-Russian Congress of Soviets. When it met in the evening, many delegates walked out in vain protest against the action taken by the Bolsheviks, thereby leaving them in control of the Congress. During the night the members of the Provisional Government were "arrested," and on November 8 the Congress elected an all-Bolshevik regime, with Lenin as Premier and Trotsky in charge of foreign affairs.

Kerensky was the only member of the government to escape capture. He assembled a small force to retake Petrograd, but was soon defeated. After a week of fighting the Bolsheviks were in control of both Petrograd and Moscow.

There still remained the elections—and Russia, so often considered to be the Communists' strongest redoubt, is probably the only nation in which the myth of their "popularity" has been disproven by such means while they were in open control. After the seizure of power, the Bolsheviks used various devices to influence the elections, and subsequently to prevent the meeting of the Constituent Assembly thus chosen. They succeeded only in delaying the meeting until January, 1918. In spite of the arrest of many, and the discouragement of attendance by others, the Bolsheviks and their sympathizers controlled only about one-third of the delegates present. They tolerated only one day's session, which they turned into a bedlam.

In an effort to intimidate the delegates and disrupt the proceedings, the Bolsheviks saturated the neighborhood with troops, filled the halls with Red Guards, and heckled the speakers. Lenin laid himself down on the steps of the speaker's platform and pretended to go to sleep. When the delegates refused to accept their program, the Bolsheviks withdrew and had it adopted at a Congress of Soviets. The assembly was never permitted to meet again.

Why the people permitted the Bolsheviks to seize power, even by force, is a story whose full details may never be known. Sukhanov, a socialist narrator of these events, indicates that some of the Menshevik leaders did not understand what was going on.[10] Undoubtedly, the radical spokesmen were unaware of the extent to which their demands, by making panaceas plausible, were assisting those who promised to produce them more quickly by violent means. People of

moderate views, on the other hand, were apparently intimidated by
the prevailing disorder. General Judson reported that all elements
in Russia, except the Socialists, were "cowed."[11]

The desire for an end to the war was foremost in the minds of
many. Perhaps they were unwilling at first to take up arms against
any group which promised peace, no matter what its other aims.
Possibly many reasoned that the Bolshevik regime would become
more moderate, or that it could not last. No one thought that any
political party could rule Russia alone, and when Lenin made such
a claim for the Bolsheviks, at the first Congress of Soviets, the delegates
only laughed.[12] Perhaps the people assumed that moral pressures
would suffice, and that the Bolsheviks must inevitably yield to the
force of public opinion. Even their first public act, the seizure of
power, was done in the name of the Soviets, which still represented
many political parties. Perhaps the people thought the Bolsheviks
were only preaching abstractly, and did not intend to instigate action.
At the beginning of the July uprising they had actually urged the
demonstrating crowds to go home. Sukhanov reports that Lenin
seemed noncommittal:

Lenin made an extremely ambiguous speech from the balcony. He
didn't demand any concrete action from the impressive force standing
in front of him; he didn't even call on his audience to continue the
street demonstrations. . . . Lenin merely agitated strongly against the
Provisional Government and against the Social-traitors of the Soviet,
and called for the defense of the revolution and for loyalty to the
Bolsheviks.[13]

An important factor was a growing lack of interest in the Soviets,
which made it possible for the Bolsheviks to obtain deceptive majorities in those bodies. *The New York Times* reported, in October, that
the people were becoming tired of meetings and ignored them:

The Bolsheviks think they are gaining the upper hand among the
masses. This is true and untrue. It is true so far as meetings, votes,
and resolutions are concerned. It is untrue if it means that the great
masses of the people sympathize with the Bolsheviks or are prepared
to support them actively. . . .
In the workmen's committees the Bolsheviks are strong, but
most of the workmen have ceased to attend the meetings. In the
villages the peasants ignore the elections and express disgust for all
committees.[14]

The Soviets were to a large extent superfluous in a country which was about to elect a constitutional convention, and which already had its elected Zemstvos and the Duma, to which real power could readily be transferred. The Soviets provided an outlet for early enthusiasm, but when this gave way to disillusionment, when their cumbersome, argumentative, and frequently unproductive proceedings brought weariness and neglect, they furnished a convenient front for the Bolsheviks.

One circumstance which was of great assistance to the Bolsheviks was the fact that the people of Russia did not have the advantage, that we have today, of over forty years of experience with Communist terror. Even many of the Bolsheviks did not anticipate the extremes to which they would be led by Lenin and the desire to retain control at all costs. In 1917, they had never held power, and it was less illogical to judge them by their promises.

A major source of outside help for the Bolsheviks was the vast amount of money spent by the Central Powers to create disorder in Russia. The German propaganda campaign was a matter of great concern to Elihu Root, elder American statesman, who in June, 1917, led a special diplomatic mission to Russia. He had been Secretary of State in the cabinet of Theodore Roosevelt. Root reported that Germany was "attacking Russia by propaganda and is spending millions, at least a million dollars monthly, to capture the minds of the Russian people."[15] The formal report of the Root Mission states:

Thousands of German agents swarmed across the border immediately after the revolution. They made common cause with the internationalists and extreme socialists who sought to destroy industrial and national Russia. They stirred to activity all the pro-German sympathizers in the country; they spent money like water in the secret purchase of adherents; they bought and established newspapers; they distributed literature in enormous quantities; they sent out an army of speakers to harangue the crowds in the cities and towns; they traversed the country and sought to make the simple-minded peasants believe that they had only to stop fighting and take possession of all the land in Russia to live in affluence forever after; they incited the working men to make demands far in excess of the entire profits and capital of the enterprises in which they were engaged, with a view to seizing upon the mines and factories for themselves.[16]

The Bolsheviks, therefore, could hardly take the credit for doing the job alone.

Although the Bolsheviks had destroyed the Provisional Government, and two months later the Constituent Assembly, it could scarcely be said that they had established a government of their own, or that the "Council of People's Commissars" was regarded as such. The Soviets assumed power in many parts of the country, but they exercised it autonomously, frequently ignoring the asserted authority of the Central Executive Committee. From Petrograd the United States Ambassador, David R. Francis, reported that Allied representatives were agreed that the "pretended government" had been established only by force and was "not recognized" by the Russian people.[17]

Thus the disorganization and anarchy which prevailed before the Bolshevik coup continued to develop afterwards; and control, where it existed, was established only by terror. Only two weeks after the Bolshevik seizure of power, the United States consul general in Moscow, Maddin Summers, reported that anti-Bolshevik feeling was growing because of "cruelties and atrocities."[18] In December, Ambassador Francis reported that "even extreme socialist and peace champions are disgusted with sailor and Red Guard excesses. . . ."[19]

The Left Social Revolutionaries were induced to participate, for a few months, in Lenin's regime, but they too were repelled by the Bolshevik methods. One of their leaders, Isaac N. Steinberg, who was "Minister of Justice" in this "coalition government," escaped and lived to write a book which helps to explain the long duration of the Bolshevik regime.[20] In it he points out that while many in Russia were willing to use terror to get rid of the Czars, only the Bolsheviks adopted it as a permanent principle of government.

In the summer of 1918, there was a series of anti-Bolshevik revolts and assassinations, including the attempted assassination of Lenin, which nearly unseated the new regime. The Bolsheviks maintained thmselves only by a stepped-up campaign of terror. Robert Lansing, the United States Secretary of State, described it as "barbarism" and "indiscriminate slaughter," and he sought moral condemnation by all the Allies, asking them to "register their abhorrence." He also mentioned "the earnest desire of the people of the United States to befriend the Russian people and lend them all possible assistance."[21] But he proposed no effective means of doing so.

By this time, all parts of the empire were seething with revolt against Bolshevik rule. The first great opportunity to assist the subject peoples had come, but it was neglected. How they were to be kept subject was indicated in a summary, by the United States consul in Moscow, of an order sent to all Soviets on September 2, 1918:

> Murder of Volodarski and Uritski, attempt on Lenin and shooting of masses of our comrades in Finland, Ukraine, the Don, and Czecho-Slavia, continual discovery of conspiracies in our rear, open acknowledgment of right Social Revolutionist Party and other counter-revolutionary rascals of their part in these conspiracies together with insignificant extent of serious repressions and shooting of masses of White Guards and *bourgeoisie* on the part of the Soviets, all these things show that notwithstanding frequent pronouncements urging mass terror against the Social Revolutionists, White Guards, and *bourgeoisie* no real terror exists.
>
> Such a situation should decidedly be stopped, should be put to weakness and softness. All right Social Revolutionists known to local Soviets should be arrested immediately. Numerous hostages should be taken from the *bourgeois* and officer classes. At the slightest attempt to resist or the slightest movement among the White Guards, shooting of masses of hostages should be begun without fail....
>
> .   .   .   .
>
> Not the slightest hesitation or the slightest indecision in using mass terror.
>
> (Signed)   PETROVSKI, Commissar of Home Affairs[22]

CHAPTER II

REVOLT SUPPRESSED

"Formerly, the war was conducted in the field in which the imperialists were infinitely stronger, the military field. If you count the number of guns and machine-guns they have and the number we have, the number of soldiers their governments can mobilise and the number our government can mobilise, we undoubtedly ought to have been crushed in a fortnight."   V. I. Lenin[1]

WHATEVER made it possible for the Bolsheviks to seize power in Russia, the failure of the Russian people to oust them almost immediately afterwards was not the result of any lack of popular efforts, but rather the result of failure on the part of Russia's Western Allies to give such efforts determined and effective support—in spite, it must be said, of the recognized obligations and commitments of such Allies to do so. What Winston Churchill described as the "complete absence of any definite or decided policy among the victorious Allies,"[2] produced only what the United States Secretary of State, Robert Lansing, called "desultory support ... for the principles of democratic self-determination in Russia."[3] The free world thus forfeited, during 1918-19, its best opportunities to bring an early end to Bolshevism.

Strange as it may now sound, this failure was largely due to the reluctance and dampening influence of the United States, whose assistance was considered essential even in those days, but which at first maintained that assistance was not desired, then that it was impossible, and finally that it was too late. The other Allied nations, particularly Great Britain and France, vainly urged the United States to give assistance; but when these pleas were rejected, their own leaders quailed. Even the Russian people, according to President Wilson, when they saw the attitude taken by the United States, thought there must be something wrong with the anti-Bolshevik groups.[4]

The struggle to restore free government began immediately after the Bolshevik seizure of power, and particularly after the suppression of the Constituent Assembly. It extended to all parts of the Russian

Empire, and in those areas which did not declare their complete independence of Petrograd there were efforts to create local provisional governments which would restore order until the recall of the Assembly or the conduct of a new national election.

In Siberia a Provincial Duma was elected—in November, 1917. It included representatives of the Zemstvos, municipalities, co-operative trade organizations and other national and social groups. One of its members, Pietr Vasilievich Vologodsky, had been Siberian Magistrate under Kerensky. In January, 1918, this Duma formed a Provisional Government for Siberia, whose stated purpose was to re-establish "legitimate order" and the "legitimate power of the All-Russian Constituent Assembly," and to take "all measures to counteract the further German advance on Russian territory."[5]

The Siberian Duma and its government were eventually dispersed by the Bolsheviks and forced to seek refuge in Manchuria. In April, 1918, American aid was requested through the United States consul at Harbin, and a formal appeal was wired to Washington. At the same time co-operation was sought from the Russian governor and general manager of the Chinese Eastern Railway, General Dmitri L. Horvat, whose headquarters were also in Manchuria. He declined, however, to participate, on the ground that the new government was dominated by extreme Socialists and not representative of a majority of the people.

Horvat attempted to create a more conservative government of his own; and on April 12 the United States consul, Charles K. Moser, requested permission to assist in bringing the two factions together. The consul believed that with a little encouragement both factions would agree to a coalition under Horvat's leadership, and he reported that they were already convinced that no party could succeed without the support of the Allies. "The presence of Allied troops," he stated, "would be guarantee to all classes and lead, in my opinion, to re-establishment of law and order."[6]

In south Russia a nucleus of armed resistance had been created by former leaders of the Russian Army. Among these were Generals Alexiev, Kornilov and Denikin, all of whom had served at various times as commander-in-chief under the Provisional Government. The Cossacks of the Don River region were organized by Generals Kaledin and Krasnov. The possibility of direct assistance to these armies was considered by the Allies, and by the United States, shortly after the Bolshevik seizure of power. But Turkish control of the Dardanelles

Straits blocked the movement of Allied shipping into the Black Sea, and further difficulty was presented when the Germans occupied the Ukraine and the Caucasus. Nevertheless, without assistance, the White armies of the south succeeded in driving the Bolsheviks from large areas in the vicinity of the Don and Kuban rivers. They began to grow, and soon presented a formidable challenge to the continued existence of the Bolshevik regime.

Elsewhere in the south, and in the west and northwest, the influence of Bolshevism was blocked by separatist movements or by the German invasion. In the peace treaties made between the Bolsheviks and the Central Powers at Brest-Litovsk (March 3 and August 27, 1918), independence was guaranteed to the Ukraine, the Trans-Caucasus and Finland, while the Baltic States, Poland and Byelorussia were surrendered to German occupation.

In central Russia the Bolsheviks were generally discredited. On April 7, 1918, Maddin Summers, the United States consul general in Moscow, reported that, "the *de facto* government" was "growing sensibly weaker on account of internal dissension, dissatisfaction and opposition on [the] part of workingmen and peasants and the swollen strength of the anarchists...." In a telegram to the Department of State, he reported that the anarchists were in possession of "arms, artillery and machine guns" and threatened openly "to overthrow the Soviet government." "Outside Moscow," he said, "the local Soviets are practically autonomous and ignore the central authorities who confess they cannot control them." As a result, the Bolsheviks were being forced to look for help among the hated "bourgeoisie," a fact which Summers reported was generally considered to indicate the "full failure" of the "present political experiment."[7]

In June the acting Commissar of Public Education, Mikhail Pokrovsky, went even further in conversation with the United States Ambassador. The Ambassador reported that Pokrovsky said the government admits "we are a corpse but no one has the courage to bury us."[8] The consul at Moscow, DeWitt C. Poole, reported that "the Bolshevik government could hardly be expected to survive, were it not that the disorganization of the country has so far assumed the proportions of a terrible catastrophe that no other party cares to attempt the management of affairs without direct foreign assistance."[9]

Direct foreign assistance did come at this time, but from an unexpected quarter. There had been formed, during the war, a contingent of Czecho-Slovak troops, composed of defectors and prisoners taken from the armies of the Central Powers, and Czech residents of the Russian Empire, all of whom sought freedom for their own country through an Allied victory. The independent development of the Czech force had been greatly encouraged after the Russian revolution, and in September, 1917, it was organized into a corps of two divisions—an army-in-exile fighting under the banner of the Czecho-Slovak National Council.

When the Bolsheviks agreed to a truce with the Germans, in December, 1917, an effort was made by Thomas G. Masaryk, President of the Czech Council, to move the Czechs in Russia to the western front. Permission was obtained for their departure via the Trans-Siberian Railroad, eastward through Vladivostok. Later, when they were scattered in small groups across the long route through Siberia, the Bolsheviks tried to stop them. The Czechs then decided to fight their way through, and joined forces with the people. They won control of the entire railroad, and soon a new military front, facing west, was established along the Volga River.

Encouraged by this unexpected intervention, the people acted quickly. Free government was restored in eastern Russia and Siberia, from the Volga to the Pacific.

At Samara (now Kuibyshev) a government was established under the leadership of Victor N. Chernov, a Social Revolutionary who had been elected President of the Constituent Assembly before its dissolution by the Bolsheviks. He was the leader of the party which had won the elections, and had been a member of the Petrograd Soviet Executive Committee. In May, 1917, he was appointed Minister of Agriculture in the second Provisional Government.

In Siberia a number of free governments were immediately formed. The Provisional Government created by the Siberian Duma also returned, and by July, 1918, its authority was widely accepted. Its composition was changed and all radical theories of government were rejected. The popular enthusiasm with which it was at that time received was described by the United States consul at Tomsk. His report, like the previous report from the consul at Harbin, recommended prompt Allied recognition and assistance:

The government created last January by the popularly elected Siberian territorial parliament in Tomsk has assumed power and its authority has been accepted throughout western Siberia from near Irkutsk to the Urals, except in Ekaterinburg. Conventions of peasants and Cossacks held at Omsk voted to support new government. The new ministry is composed of representatives of all moderate parties including the Constitutional Democrats.... Complete order is maintained with popularly elected Zemstvos and city councils in operation and organization new army proceeding as rapidly as limited equipment permits. Fourth of July government issued declaration independence Siberia until federation can be effected with other Russian states after expulsion Germans and usurping Bolsheviks and convocation All-Russian Constituent Assembly. Government is pro-Ally and declaration of war on Central powers delayed only by desire to ascertain whether united Allied support can be obtained in the matter of munitions.... Recommended prompt recognition and support with munitions and money....[10]

In the meantime, the Allies themselves had already been convinced of the need for such assistance, and were endeavoring to persuade the United States.

In January, 1918, the Allied Ministers in Jassy, the temporary capital of Rumania, recommended that Chinese, Japanese or American troops be sent to Russia through Siberia. They were close to Russia, and their report indicated a great demand for foreign assistance in all areas. "It is confirmed to us on all sides." they said, "both from Russian and Rumanian sources that the only remedy for the anarchy reigning in Russia lies in the sending immediately to that country of Japanese or American troops." They expressed the opinion that three or four divisions would suffice to "ruin the authority of the Bolsheviks" and to rally "with the defenders of order those who to-day are hiding and dare not voice their opinion." A real Russian army "could quickly be formed round this nucleus."[11]

The conclusions of this report were supported by the British Government. In a memorandum to the Department of State, the British Ambassador in Washington advised that, according to all the information which his government had "been able to collect," the Russians "would welcome some form of foreign intervention in their affairs."[12] The United States Government took an opposing view, however, and in its reply the State Department expressed the opinion that foreign aid would neither be welcome nor useful. "The information in the possession of the American Government," it said, "does not lead it to share the opinion... that any form of foreign intervention in the affairs of Russia would be welcomed by the people of that country. It is believed on the contrary... that any foreign intervention in Russian affairs would, at the present time, be most inopportune."[13] The State Department's memorandum, which was dated February 8, 1918, went on to express a vain hope to which the United States still clings, after more than forty years of expectation:

The American Government is not indifferent to the effect which the unfortunate condition of Russia at the present time is having upon the plans of the Allies, but *it has not lost hope of a change for the better to be brought about without foreign intervention.* (Italics added)

During the next few months, the British view was confirmed by frequent reports of American Foreign Service personnel,[14] but the United States continued to maintain that intervention would be resented.[15] When the Czech intervention, and the popular reaction, proved how wrong this was, the United States added an additional argument, stating that any substantial effort in Russia would jeopardize the supply of Allied armies in Western Europe.

In July the Allied Supreme War Council made an urgent appeal to President Wilson. The United States then finally agreed to "limited" intervention for the stated purpose, primarily, of rescuing the Czechs, and secondarily to promote "modest and experimental plans" of assistance to local efforts at self-government. The position was described in an *aide-mémoire* to the Allied ambassadors:

Military action is admissible in Russia, as the Government of the United States sees the circumstances, only to help the Czecho-Slovaks consolidate their forces and get into successful cooperation with their slavic kinsmen and to steady any efforts at self-government or self-defense in which the Russians themselves may be willing to accept assistance. Whether from Vladivostok or from Murmansk and Archangel, the only legitimate object for which American or Allied troops can be employed, it submits, is to guard military stores which may subsequently be needed by Russian forces and to render such aid as may be acceptable to the Russians in the organization of their own self-defense. For helping the Czecho-Slovaks there is immediate necessity and sufficient justification. Recent developments have made it evident that that is in the interest of what the Russian people themselves desire, and the Government of the United States is glad to contribute the small force at its disposal for that purpose. It yields, also, to the judgment of the Supreme Command in the matter of establishing a small force at Murmansk, to guard the military stores at Kola, and to make it safe for Russian forces to come together in

organized bodies in the north. But it owes it to frank counsel to say
that it can go no further than these modest and experimental plans.
It is not in a position, and has no expectation of being in a position,
to take part in organized intervention in adequate force from either
Vladivostok or Murmansk and Archangel.[16]

The war with Germany was looked upon as the main struggle for
freedom, and the concessions thus made "to the judgment of the
Supreme Command" were accompanied by the flat assertion that the
United States could not even sanction intervention in principle, much
less participate:

It is the clear and fixed judgment of the Government of the
United States, arrived at after repeated and very searching reconsiderations of the whole situation in Russia, that military intervention
there would add to the present sad confusion in Russia rather than
cure it, injure her rather than help her, and that it would be of no
advantage in the prosecution of our main design, to win the war
against Germany. It can not, therefore, take part in such intervention
or sanction it in principle.[17]

In accordance with the policy thus adopted, the United States
urged the withdrawal of the Czechs to the east of the Ural Mountains,
and kept its own troops in Siberia east of Irkutsk. No effort was made
to furnish arms or other military equipment to the Russian forces,
and the right was reserved to withdraw all American troops if the
Allied plans "should develop into others inconsistent with the policy
to which the Government of the United States feels constrained to
restrict itself."[18]

When this negative decision was made, intervention would in
fact have been most timely. The Bolsheviks were at the point of
defeat, and their morale was at a low ebb. On July 6, 1918, the very
day on which the President and his Secretaries of State, War and
Navy were making their decision,[19] a widespread revolt was launched
in central Russia. A few days later, the Red commander on the Volga
front, General Muraviev, decided to defect, urging peace with the
Czechs and war with the Germans. In August Lenin himself was
critically wounded by an assassin.

During the same period, important advances were being made by
the anti-Red armies in the south and east. In the south the Cossacks
were threatening Tsaritsyn (Stalingrad), while Trotsky and Stalin

argued about the method of its defense. General Krasnov was approaching the cities of Saratov and Penza in his drive to make contact with Samara. The Czechs and free Russians at Samara were at the same time pushing across the Volga to meet him, and winning new victories in the north, at Ekaterinburg and Kazan. Taking Kazan on August 6, 1918, they came within 500 miles of Moscow and captured $200,000,000 in gold reserves of the Russian Imperial Bank. Anticipating the fall of Ekaterinburg, the Bolsheviks in desperation murdered the Czar and his family, and other members of the house of Romanov —to prevent their release and possibly to forestall a German plot to restore the Czar.

In July, 1918, the tide of war on the western front turned definitely in favor of the Allies, but the United States position did not change. Its decision was made known on July 17; and finally in August small Allied expeditionary forces—British, French, American and Japanese—were landed in Vladivostok, Murmansk and Archangel.

This limited assistance soon deflated the early optimism of the Czechs and free Russians. On September 10, Kazan was retaken by the Bolsheviks, and by the end of the month the military situation at Samara was also critical. The American vice consul in Samara reported urgent need for rifles, ammunition and military advisers. The troops, he said, were tired from weeks of constant fighting against superior forces; and because of the lack of weapons, further recruiting was impossible.[20] Moreover, because of the widespread feeling of discouragement, the initial spirit of co-operation between political factions soon gave way to the renewal of dissension. The United States consul at Tomsk, John A. Ray, reported on September 30:

General impression derived from trip in various cities western Siberia is that political situation has suddenly grown extremely serious since it has become known that Allies have not sent strong military forces to Vladivostok. In order to dispel discouragement of Russian public, I recommend that some American troops be sent immediately into western Siberia, coupled with promise [of] adequate military aid.[21]

No such promise came, of course, and on October 8 Samara too was lost.

In the meantime, an effort had begun to unify the various anti-Bolshevik governments. In a conference at Ufa (September 8—23, 1918), an agreement was made for the merger of the Siberian and

Samara governments into a new all-Russian Provisional Government. At this conference there were representatives not only from these governments, but also from the Regional Government of the Urals, the temporary government of Estonia, a number of Cossack and Central Asian governments, various political parties and organizations, and the provisional government established in north Russia after the Allied landings at Archangel. The leader of the latter group, Nikolai V. Tchaikovsky, and Pietr Vologodsky, Chairman of the Council of Ministers of the Siberian government, were named to the five-man directorate. General Alexiev, who had assumed political leadership in the south, was named as an alternate member and invited to come to Siberia. Many expected that he would assume the direction of all the anti-Bolshevik armies. It was agreed that the capital of the new government would be at Omsk, in western Siberia.

The forces of disintegration, however, were already too strong, and the agreement was not fully carried out until November. By that time General Alexiev had died; a *coup d'état*—with rumored support of Allied personnel—had crushed the spirit of the government of Northern Russia; and violence and attempted coups were plaguing the government of Siberia. The use of troops, badly needed at the front, was required to preserve order in the rear.

Under these circumstances, the new All-Russian Government submitted to military leadership. The Minister of War and Navy, Admiral Alexander Kolchak, was appointed Supreme Ruler, and although he was widely respected as a sincere patriot, the change in form of government led to further loss of popular support. It took place on November 18, only two weeks after the new All-Russian Government had been formally installed.

The morale of the Czechs was also destroyed. Although it was the Czechs for whom the United States had expressed its main concern, and whose safety was its asserted principal object, they were nonetheless disillusioned by its failure to support them in the positions they had fought so hard to attain. A United States consul on special duty in Russia and Siberia, J. P. Jameson, reported that the Czechs held the United States "alone responsible for Allied failure to aid them on Volga front." "America," he stated, "was the most popular nation with the Czechs and the majority of Russians months ago but now reverse is true."[22]

In November, 1918, the end of the war with Germany brought new opportunities for Allied assistance in Russia. With the opening of the Black Sea and the Baltic, it was possible to give aid directly to the armies in the south, and to move transports and warships to Petrograd itself. Even more important, as far as the attitude of the United States was concerned, it was no longer necessary to send supplies and troops to the western front.

Still the attitude of the United States remained unchanged. Instead of bringing new efforts to assist the people, the end of the war—or at least the destruction of the original enemy—produced an opposite reaction, a strong desire for peace and a weakening of the resolve to save democracy. As far as the United States was concerned, the important goal now was not to commit its troops to new battles, in new areas, but to bring them home from those in which they were already engaged.

The disillusioned Czechs also expressed a desire to go home. They were withdrawn from the front and assigned to duty guarding the Trans-Siberian Railroad.

Only the British and French attempted to continue support, and even their efforts were limited and unpredictable. Plans drawn up at Jassy, involving the use of twelve Allied divisions then in the Balkans, were discarded, and a delegation of representative Russians who came to Paris to plead for its implementation was summarily ordered to leave the city.

In lieu of the Jassy plan, the British and French revived an agreement, made in 1917, for the division of Russia into British and French "spheres of influence." The Baltic area and all territory east of the Don River—the Caucasus, Kuban and Transcaspia—were assigned to the British, and all territory west of the Don—Poland, the Ukraine and the Crimea—were assigned to the French. Under this agreement the French sent an expeditionary force to the Ukraine and the Crimea, but it was withdrawn in April, 1919. Instead of twelve divisions it consisted of four—two French and two Greek—with smaller units of Rumanians, Poles and Serbs. It succeeded only in antagonizing the Ukrainians with demands for submission to General Denikin, and in producing mutiny and Bolshevik leanings in some of the French forces.

The British moved a fleet into the Baltic Sea, where it was of assistance in preserving freedom in the Baltic states, but not in Petrograd. They also sent troops into the Trans-Caucasus and Trans-caspia, and military supplies and advice to General Denikin.

With the assistance that he did receive, Admiral Kolchak was

able, in the spring of 1919, to launch a new attack. A report from the
United States consul at Irkutsk, Ernest L. Harris, revealed an enduring *esprit de corps,* and a promising development of law and
order, but continuing need for assistance from the United States:

The campaign of the Siberian army against the Bolsheviks is pro-
gressing favorably. Kolchak government is stronger than ever before
and growing in power. This power is now practically absolute in
Central and Western Siberia and that while Kolchak is not a strong
man he is at least a good man and a Russian patriot of the best type.
He is supported by the Zemstvo in Central and Western Siberia, and
cities and villages are beginning to pay taxes regularly to Omsk
Government. Kolchak is not surrounded by monarchists and reac-
tionists as is generally supposed. His chief advisers in all civil matters
are right Social Revolutionists. . . .
. . . Kolchak today does not ask for foreign soldiers to assist him in
fighting Bolsheviks. He can do that himself and is doing it successfully. He does want clothes and munitions of war and Siberia needs
economic assistance. . . . Russia is now in a fair way to master
Bolshevism with her own resources, but at this moment success
practically depends upon our decisive policy as adopted right here
in Eastern Siberia.[23]

This report clearly indicated that a second chance for the overthrow
of Bolshevism was at hand. It was forwarded to the American Commission at the Paris Peace Conference, with full State Department
endorsement of the views expressed.

By the end of April, 1919, Kolchak was again approaching the
Volga River. In May his government was formally recognized by the
government at Archangel as the National and Provisional Government of Russia. Soon after, his leadership was formally acknowledged
for the south by General Denikin.

At the same time, Allied and Russian troops in north Russia were
advancing in several directions. One column, from Murmansk, was
moving in the direction of Petrograd. By May it had penetrated as far
as Lake Onega, and was continuing its advance. Another column,
from Archangel, was pushing up the Dvina River, with the object
of meeting Kolchak's forces at Kotlas.

In June, 1919, the British commander in the north, General William E. Ironside, stated that he expected to reach Kotlas, Vologda
and Petrograd "in the course of the summer." He pointed out that the
link-up at Kotlas would make it possible to supply the armies of

Admiral Kolchak directly from Archangel, which was only "eight days from England." This would obviate the necessity of using the long route by sea to Vladivostok and back again by rail through Siberia. The only thing lacking was the "indispensable assistance" of American supplies.[24]

In August, a joint British-Russian attack destroyed the entire Bolshevik force on the Dvina River, and it was reported that no effective resistance remained to bar the way to Kotlas.[25] But by this time, withdrawal had already been agreed upon and the last American contingents were on their way home.

Even more promising results were obtained in the south and west. On October 13, 1919, the armies of General Denikin arrived at Orel, scarcely 200 miles from Moscow. Eight days later a Russian army in the northwest, under General Yudenich, reached the outskirts of Petrograd.

Once again, however, the free world failed to seize the opportunity for victory. The armies of freedom virtually melted away with victory in sight. The Allied force in north Russia was withdrawn, Kolchak was belatedly promised assistance which he did not receive, and Denikin's appeals to the United States were ignored. Yudenich, poorly supported, was driven out of Petrograd.

In Paris the Allied heads of government were so impressed by Kolchak's success that they had begun to worry about what he would do after taking Moscow.[26] The British suggested that conditions be imposed upon the shipment of further supplies. President Wilson seconded this proposal. He asserted, moreover, that the United States did not believe in Kolchak, and that he had always been of the opinion that the proper policy of the Allies and associated powers was to clear out of Russia and leave it to the Russians to fight it out among themselves.[27]

Accordingly, on May 26, the Allied Powers advised Admiral Kolchak that assistance would be continued only if they could be "satisfied that it will really help the Russian people to liberty, self-government and peace." They said that they would be "disposed to assist the Government of Admiral Koltchak and his Associates with munitions, supplies and food," and to establish itself "as the government of all Russia," if they were given "definite guarantees" that the policy of the Russian Government "has the same objects in view as that of the Allied and Associated Powers."[28]

If the Allied note did not seem to encourage hopes of assistance

with no strings attached, the long list of conditions and guarantees at
at least seemed to indicate that there was no longer any reluctance to
interfere in Russia's internal affairs. Among the conditions which the
Allies and the United States imposed were assurances by the Provisional Russian Government that elections would be held for a
constituent assembly; that no attempt would be made to revive
special privilege; that the independence of Finland and Poland would
be recognized; that Russia would join the League of Nations; that
the status of the Baltic nations and other border areas would be
settled in consultation with the League; and that the debts of previous
Russian governments would be acknowledged.

Kolchak's government passed the test. His reply was considered
to be satisfactory, and in June, 1919, he was informed that the Allies
and the United States were "therefore willing to extend to Admiral
Koltchak and his associates the support set forth in their original
letter."[29]

Actually, however, the withdrawal of Allied support was already
well under way. In April the French had removed their expeditionary force from south Russia. In the process they destroyed a large
part of the Russian Black Sea fleet to prevent it from falling into the
hands of the Bolsheviks. Plans for the withdrawal of Allied forces
from north Russia were not changed. American troops were withdrawn from that area in the months of May through August, and the
last Allied contingents departed in September and October.

The United States rejected Admiral Kolchak's request for a loan,
and even private lending was discouraged. The shipment of rifles,
ammunition and clothing for sale to his government was subsequently authorized, but little if any arrived in time to be of effective
assistance. No request for Congressional action was made lest it
interfere with Senate ratification of the European Peace Treaty.

Without adequate military supplies, Admiral Kolchak had not
been able to equip an army large enough to cover the vast distances
involved. His front was fanned out in a wide arc west of the Ural
Mountains, more than 3,500 miles from Vladivostok, his sole source
of supply. He was eventually forced to withdraw, and after a number
of defeats, Omsk, the seat of government, was lost on November 15,
1919. Early in January, 1920, Admiral Kolchak abdicated in favor
of General Denikin.

In June, 1919, when the Allied promise to support Admiral
Kolchak was made, his drive to Moscow had already been stopped,

and the best opportunity to help had passed. This was not true of General Denikin, however. His advance was just getting under way in August, when the last American troops were being withdrawn from north Russia. There was ample time to give him quick and effective assistance. A contrary course, however, was followed, and upon learning of the intended withdrawal of an American mission, sent to study conditions in the areas under his control, General Denikin directed a personal appeal to President Wilson:

I regret to learn that you are withdrawing your South Russian Mission. This fact might be understood as meaning that the cause for which we are fighting does not meet with sympathy in the United States. You have seen the program of Admiral Kolchak; you also know the aims of the Armed Forces of South Russia; in them there is no hint of return to reaction. We need freedom; we are against any sort of tyranny. Let the people decide their own future. The Bolsheviks will not allow them to do this. They have destroyed everything —religion, family and the idea of possession and they have trampled upon every right except force.... The crimes of the Bolshevists against the people of all nations far exceed the crimes of Germany which brought America into the war. With us it is not a civil war or a class war; we are struggling against an artificially produced disease which will without doubt spread far beyond the borders of Russia and across the ocean if action be not taken. If the League of Nations is worthy of its high destiny it should make a stand against Bolshevism which is striving to destroy all moral and material worth and culture in the world.

...We believe in the justice of our cause, but moral and material assistance is also of great importance to us. South Russia for a long time was cut off from the world and its inhabitants suffer from lack of clothing. Last winter typhus raged and this winter it may spread with greater force. We need mostly linen, boots and overcoats and in this matter the United States might assist us greatly by sending us clothing for the military and civil population from her great military stores. Your assistance would play a great part and would hasten the restoration of a general peace.

Signed, General Denikin[30]

The need for such supplies was confirmed by the United States High Commissioner in Constantinople, Admiral Mark S. Bristol. In a telegram to the Secretary of State, September 1, 1919, he indicated that in spite of the promises made to Admiral Kolchak, United States assistance, and even contacts, in south Russia were almost nonexistent.

He reported, moreover, that there was "general bitterness in Denikin circles because America lends no aid." "The British," he said, "are assisting with war material for which they get a good price and considerable praise, but we have done nothing beyond sending a shipload of Red Cross supplies. Our military mission, which never amounted to anything because it was headed by a captain instead of a general, has been withdrawn and in all south Russia there remains a solitary vice consul, not of career, to represent the United States of America."[31] Admiral Bristol suggested an economic commission for south Russia with authority to ship a hundred million dollars' worth of goods during the next few months.

Both appeals were made in vain. A special agent, Admiral N. A. McCully, was appointed for south Russia, and authorization was given for the sale of such surplus supplies as "clothing, shoes, cloth, etc.," to the extent available. But the authorization applied only to those items "for which a ready market is not found in the United States."[32]

By December, 1919, General Denikin's armies were also in full retreat and the army of General Yudenich had been annihilated. The Allied powers (Great Britain, France and Italy) decided to terminate all forms of assistance. In the United States, Secretary of State Lansing presented a program of economic assistance, but it came too late.

In March, 1920, General Denikin withdrew into the Crimea. By that time Admiral Kolchak had been captured and executed, and the Russian army in the north was destroyed. The Allied troops were withdrawn from Siberia, leaving only Japanese occupation forces, which remained in Vladivostok until 1922.

Still the Russians were not wholly defeated. In south Russia General Peter N. Wrangel succeeded to the command of General Denikin. During 1920, he launched a new attack against the Bolsheviks, with considerable success, driving northward from the Crimea and westward into the Kuban region. On July 31, Admiral McCully made an optimistic report on the results. Wrangel's forces, he revealed, had "grown enormously since June 1 and are in excellent spirits. They are well equipped, well disciplined and are led by capable, experienced, and resolute leaders." For General Wrangel himself, the Admiral had high praise. "In every serious operation Wrangel is with his men at the front. He has succeeded in completely breaking up the Red organizations as they existed in the South of Russia on June 1, and has captured in prisoners a force equal to the force with which he began operation. He has won the good will of the civil populations, and has taken steps to let remainder of Russia know about this, and about his Land Law, and his Liberal Programme." "Wrangel," the Admiral said, "believes himself invincible, and his officers and men also believe it. As a matter of fact in his military history he has never been beaten in any operation undertaken by him. . . ."[33]

General Wrangel, however, received little or no material assistance from any of the free powers. The British withdrew even moral support, insisting that he negotiate a surrender and seek amnesty from the Bolsheviks. The United States hastened to correct the mere rumor of economic assistance—a rumor which the Secretary of State said produced "considerable embarrassment."[34] From the French, General Wrangel received moral support, and de facto recognition, but this was not enough. By the end of the year, he too had been defeated.

In spite of all their defeats and their many sufferings, the efforts of the White leaders were not made in vain. While the Bolsheviks were "consolidating" their control of Russia, additional Red uprisings were breaking out in central Europe—uprisings which the Bolsheviks persistently supported and to which they would have given effective assistance if they had not been required to devote their every effort to the suppression of resistance at home. Accordingly, although the White armies failed to save their own country, they played a tremendous part in saving those of others.

When the war ended, in November, 1918, there was a socialist revolution in Germany, complete with Councils of Workmen's and Soldiers' Deputies, just as there had been in Russia the year before. The German Communists, therefore, felt they had an opportunity similar to that of the Bolsheviks—a belief in which they were encouraged by propaganda from Moscow. Such propaganda was carried out under the direction of Karl Radek, one of Lenin's closest associates, and facilitated, after the peace of Brest-Litovsk, by the arrival in Berlin of a Bolshevik ambassador.

In January, 1919, just prior to the scheduled elections, the Communists attempted to overthrow the German Provisional Government, and in April a Communist "republic" was proclaimed in Munich. In March, 1919, a Communist regime was successfully installed in Hungary, under the leadership of Bela Kun.

Between the Bolsheviks in Russia and the Communists in central Europe, there remained only a thin shell of resistance—offered by the new, independent border states (Estonia, Latvia, Lithuania, Byelorussia, Poland and the Ukraine). All of these states had been a part of the Russian Empire and had fallen under German occupation. When the occupation ended, their hastily organized national defense was no match even for the Red Army, and the Bolsheviks attacked immediately.

By the spring of 1919, when Admiral Kolchak began his offensive from Siberia, the Bolsheviks had driven deep into the Baltic States and the Ukraine, and they were attempting to follow the retreating Germans through Poland. It looked as though they might quickly obtain control, after World War I, of even more of Europe than they were able to seize later, after World War II.

The Bolsheviks were forced, however, to give up this offensive because of the advance of Admiral Kolchak. Later in the year, they proposed to send a Red Army expedition to Hungary, but they were forced to give this up because of the advance of General Denikin. Finally, in 1920, they nearly captured Warsaw, but Europe was saved again, this time by the advance of General Wrangel. In August, 1920, while Wrangel's army was creating its greatest diversions in the south, the small army of Poland, fighting almost without assistance, won an unexpected victory. It may well be said, therefore, that the free world was saved only by efforts in which it had itself refused, or failed effectively, to participate.

While the British and French had given some assistance, there were no illusions as to its inadequacies. Winston Churchill, the British Secretary of State for War, enumerated these in a memorandum made in September, 1919. His list included not only the "complete absence of any definite or decided policy," but also the "withdrawal of all support" from Admiral Kolchak, "the practical cessation of any serious pressure along the whole Western or European Front," "the lack of any moral support or vigorous concerted action" in favor of General Denikin, and perhaps most important of all, "the feeling of being abandoned by the great Allied Powers."[35]

In the case of the United States, the President apparently recognized the destructive effect of his own policy. According to the notes of a meeting of Allied leaders in Paris, May 9, 1919, he described the policy and its results in Siberia as follows:

The position was that the United States Government did not believe in Koltchak. The British and French military representatives in

Siberia, however, were supporting him. Koltchak had become irritated by the presence on the railway of United States soldiers, whom he regarded as neutrals. Moreover, the impression had got abroad among the peasants of Siberia that the United States was the standard of a free Government which they ought to imitate. When they saw the attitude of neutrality taken up by the United States soldiers, they thought there must be something wrong with the Government of Koltchak.[36]

According to the United States chargé d'affaires at Archangel, Felix Cole, the Bolsheviks in north Russia were actually citing American troop withdrawals to promote this kind of thinking. They assert, he said, "that the withdrawals prove that America, the most liberal and democratic of the Associated Powers, disapproves of the 'reactionary and monarchistic' Provisional Government." Such propaganda, he added, "is strengthened by the rapidity with which the withdrawals follow one another."[37]

In December, 1919, after the White armies were largely defeated, Secretary of State Lansing frankly admitted that the peoples of Russia had received only "desultory support" in a task of tremendous magnitude. In a memorandum to President Wilson, he described some of the difficulties they had faced and asserted that they were fighting for the same principles for which the United States and its Allies had fought:

> The difficulties besetting the leaders of the anti-Bolshevik forces are very great. From a military point of view, they must operate independently over vast stretches of territory which are separated from one another and imperfectly provided with the means of communication. The military equipment which has been furnished them from the outside is not comparable in quantity with that which the Bolsheviki found at their disposal or have been able to produce in the munition factories of central Russia.... One must admire the courage with which these leaders have met the obstacles in their path and the steadfastness which they have shown up to the present time in their opposition to German imperialism, while fighting with but desultory support from the Allied and Associated Powers, for the principles of democratic self-determination in Russia.[38]

The Secretary also indicated that there was a *duty* on the part of the United States to give material support to the struggle for these principles:

When the necessities of our self-defense call thus for measures which instincts of humanity and loyalty also dictate, there seems to me a manifest duty imposed upon the United States which it will perform with the same vigor and determination with which it has performed every duty in the past.[39]

His analysis was correct, but his prediction, unfortunately, has not yet been fulfilled.

CHAPTER III

THE FIRST SOVIET "PEACE" CAMPAIGN

"Anglo-Franco-American imperialism was unable to attack us because we first offered it peace."   V. I. Lenin, 1920[1]

THE PEOPLES of Russia had every reason to expect the aid of America in their fight for freedom. In April, 1917, when the President asked Congress for a declaration of war against Germany, he had said that the *whole world* must be made safe for democracy. Praising the democracy of the Provisional Russian Government, which was then only one month old, he called it a "fit partner for a League of Honour,"[2] and in the months which followed he promised to give it every possible assistance not only during the war but also after the war.

In May, 1917, the President sent the Root mission to Petrograd. Its stated purpose was "to express the deep friendship of the American people for the people of Russia" and to find "the best and most practical means of cooperation" in the "struggle for the freedom of all peoples." In a message directed to the Russian peoples, the President said that we were "fighting for the liberty, the self-government, and the undictated development of all peoples, and every feature of the settlement that concludes this war must be conceived and executed for that purpose."[3]

These assurances were renewed when the mission arrived at its destination. In an address to the Russian Council of Ministers, the leader of the mission, Elihu Root, repeated the President's remarks and emphasized the need for mutual assistance. "We are going to fight," he said, "and have already begun to fight for your freedom equally with our own and we ask you to fight for our freedom equally with yours. We would make your cause ours and our cause yours and with common purpose and the mutual helpfulness of firm alliance make sure the victory over our common foe."[4]

In July, 1917, when the President welcomed the new Russian Ambassador, he confirmed the statements of Mr. Root. "The mission," he stated, "which it was my pleasure to send to Russia has already assured the provisional Government that in this momentous struggle and in the problems that confront and will confront the free Government of Russia that Government may count on the steadfast friendship of the Government of the United States and its constant co-operation in all desired appropriate directions."[5]

Assistance in the Russian struggle with Bolshevism might also have been expected from the Germans. General Ludendorff, a member of the German High Command, indicates in his memoirs that such assistance would have been both possible and profitable: "We could have deposed the Soviet Government, which was thoroughly hostile to us, and given help to other authorities in Russia, which were not working against us, but indeed anxious to co-operate with us. This would have been a success of great importance to the general conduct of the war."[6]

Initially, the Germans did supply arms and ammunition to the Cossack leader, General Krasnov. Krasnov eventually sent an emissary, the Duke of Leuchtenberg, to seek German recognition and further assistance. But the Germans sided with the Bolsheviks in the Peace of Brest-Litovsk. Their reply to Krasnov was reported to the United States by its consul at Moscow:

After being kept in expectancy until supplementary treaties with the Bolsheviks were agreed to Ludendorff gave Leuchtenberg a categorical refusal on the ground that the Germans had promised the Bolsheviks to help none of the factions opposing them.[7]

The Allies and the United States made no such agreement, but the factions opposing the Bolsheviks were deprived of their assistance just as effectively. If, as Churchill stated, there was "a complete absence of any definite or decided policy" among the Allies, and if, as he further said, "some were in favour of peace and some were in favour of war," and if, as he concludes, "in the result they made neither peace nor war,"[8] no small part of this was due to the ceaseless stream of Bolshevik peace proposals which began on the very first day of the seizure of power and continued unremittingly through and after the war.

In the President's request for a declaration of war, he had also made a great point of the fact that the arrival of democracy in Russia had clarified the issue as a struggle between autocratic powers on one side and a pure alliance of democracies on the other. After the Bolshevik seizure of power, however, there seemed to be less concern for such considerations. The character of the war on the eastern front had changed once again—from a war to preserve democracy in Russia to one for the imposition of a Communist regime in Germany—but the United States and its Allies were most anxious to keep Russia in it, whether or not the Bolsheviks prevailed.

The Bolsheviks, on the other hand, were not yet prepared for war, and sought to extricate themselves from an impending defeat by offering peace to Germany. At the same time, they demanded peace negotiations by all parties—and published declarations on peace to the peoples of all nations—on the assumption that by such means they could produce the same unrest that had occurred in Russia, and thus promote the world revolution they so confidently predicted. This campaign did not produce any revolts in the Allied nations, but it may well have contributed to the postwar demand for withdrawal of troops from Russia. It likewise did not persuade the free nations to negotiate for peace with Germany, but it did end in their negotiating with the Bolsheviks—and in the delay of foreign assistance for the restoration of freedom in Russia.

As it turned out, of course, the only ones who really wanted peace were the Allies, who advocated war. The Bolsheviks agreed to peace with Germany only after a new German advance had threatened to wipe them out entirely, and they renounced their treaty as soon as possible after the German defeat. Thereupon they attempted to follow the withdrawing German armies in a march across Europe. The Germans, on the other hand, negotiated with the Bolsheviks and agreed to a treaty only because they wanted to use troops employed in Russia for a big drive on the western front.

The Bolsheviks' first appeal, the so-called Decree on Peace, was made on their first day of power, and published by press and radio. It called for an armistice and immediate negotiations by "all warring peoples and their Governments."[9] When no reply was received, it was brought to the attention of the Allied Powers by notes delivered to their ambassadors in Petrograd on November 21, 1917.

On November 27, the Germans agreed to talk. Trotsky again invited the Allies to participate, and it was announced that talks were delayed for five days, until December 2, 1917, in order to give them a chance to "define their attitude."[10] At the same time, the "Council of People's Commissars" announced that the Allies had replied to the first bid "by a refusal to recognize the Soviet Government" and insisted that the Bolsheviks required no such recognition "from the professional representatives of capitalist diplomacy." All they sought was acceptance of the "great opportunity for peace offered by the Russian Revolution."[11]

On December 6, Trotsky again asked the Allies to participate, this time stating that negotiations were suspended for one week—until December 12. The Allies still refused, and the Bolsheviks made an armistice with the Germans on the 15th.

On the 19th, the commissars issued a new appeal, "to the toiling, oppressed, and exhausted peoples of Europe," in which they frankly explained that one of the aims of peace negotiation was "to assist with all means at our disposal the working class in all lands to overthrow the sway of capital and seize State power."[12] This announcement at least seemed to vindicate the aloofness of the Allies, who could hardly be blamed for refusing to participate in their own destruction, or for rejecting proposals intended to promote a worldwide revolt.

It was soon demonstrated, however, that the free nations were not averse to dealing with the Bolsheviks if their own ends could be promoted. When they saw an opportunity to negotiate with the Bolsheviks separately, and for a continuation of the war on the eastern front, they attempted to come to terms. In the case of the United States, plans for aid to the people were put aside.

Such aid had been suggested by the Secretary of State, Robert Lansing, on December 10, 1917. In a long memorandum to the President, he recommended material assistance and open recognition of any group which demonstrated a reasonable ability to restore order and carry on the war:

My dear Mr. President: I have been considering the Russian situation and, although our information is meager and to an extent confusing, I have reached the following conclusions:

That the Bolsheviki are determined to prevent Russia from taking further part in the war.

That the longer they continue in power the more will authority in Russia be disorganized and the more will the armies disintegrate, and the harder it will become to restore order and military efficiency.

That the elimination of Russia as a fighting force will prolong the war for two or three years, with a corresponding demand upon this country for men and money.

That with Bolsheviki domination broken the Russian armies

might be reorganized and become an important factor in the war by next spring or summer.

That the hope of a stable Russian Government lies for the present in a military dictatorship backed by loyal disciplined troops.

That the only apparent nucleus for an organized movement sufficiently strong to supplant the Bolsheviki and establish a government would seem to be the group of general officers with General Kaledin, the hetman of the Don Cossacks.

These conclusions present the problem as to whether we ought to take any steps to encourage the Kaledin party, and if so the nature of those steps.

I think that we must assume that Kaledin and his Cossacks know less about us and our attitude than we know about them, that through Bolshevik and German sources they are being furnished with false information and very probably have been told that we have recognized the Bolshevik Government and so are coming to the conclusion that further resistance is useless. Of course to have this group broken up would be to throw the country into the hands of the Bolsheviki and the Germans could freely continue their propaganda which is leading to chaos and the actual disintegration of the Russian Empire.

A possible way of checking this is to get a message through to Kaledin (probably via Tiflis and courier) telling the true state of affairs, and non-recognition of the Bolsheviki and our readiness to give recognition to a government which exhibits strength enough to restore order and a purpose to carry out in good faith Russia's international engagements.

Whether such a communication is advisable is, I think, worthy of consideration, but if it is to be sent it ought to be done without delay as I am convinced that German intrigues and Bolshevik false representations will speedily impair the morale of Kaledin's followers unless something is done to give them hope that they will, if their movement gains sufficient strength, receive moral and material aid from this Government. It seems to me that nothing is to be gained by inaction, that it is simply playing into the Bolsheviki's hands, and that the situation may be saved by a few words of encouragement, and the saving of Russia means the saving to this country of hundreds of thousands of men and billions of dollars. I do not see how we could be any worse off if we took this course because we have absolutely nothing to hope from continued Bolshevik domination.[13]

As a result of these suggestions, a decision was made to support General Kaledin, but it was decided to do it secretly. It would thus be possible to preserve "the attitude" it seemed "desirable to take with the Petrograd authorities"—that is, to avoid any provocation which might cause the Bolsheviks to take an even firmer stand in favor of peace with Germany. Instructions to this effect were sent, on December 12, 1917, to the United States representative on the Inter-Allied Council on War Purchases and Finance:

> The Russian situation has been carefully considered and the conclusion has been reached that the movement in the south and southeast under the leadership of Kaledine and Korniloff offers at the present time the greatest hope for the reestablishment of a stable government and the continuance of a military force on the German and Austrian fronts. While there can be no certainty of the success of Kaledine it is not improbable that he may succeed. From Moscow and Tiflis come very favorable reports as to the strength of the movement and as to the weakening power of the Bolsheviki.
>
> In view of the policy being pursued by Lenine and Trotsky which if continued will remove Russia as a factor in the war and may even make her resources available to the Central Powers, any movement tending to prevent such a calamity should be encouraged even though its success is only a possibility.
>
> It would seem unwise for this Government to support openly Kaledine and his party because of the attitude which it seems advisable to take with the Petrograd authorities, but it is felt that the Kaledine group should be shown that the Allied Governments are most sympathetic with his efforts. Without actually recognizing his group as a *de facto* government, which is at present impossible since it has not taken form, this Government cannot under the law loan money to him to carry forward his movement. The only practicable course seems to be for the British and French Governments to finance the Kaledine enterprise in so far as it is necessary, and for this Government to loan them the money to do so. In that way we would comply with the statute and at the same time strengthen a movement which seems to present the best possibility of retaining a Russian army in the field.
>
> You will, after conferring with the Ambassador, take this matter up with proper British and French authorities....
>
>   .   .   .   .
>
> I need not impress upon you the necessity of acting expeditiously and with impressing those with whom you talk of the importance of avoiding it being known that the United States is considering showing sympathy for the Kaledine movement, much less of providing financial assistance.[14]

This strange proposal was in conformity with the attitude of the British and French. The British had already authorized secret advances for the purpose of promoting resistance in south Russia, and on December 22, 1917 they agreed with the French to support "the provincial governments and their armies"—in the Cossack lands, Finland, Siberia, the Ukraine and the Caucasus—also secretly. The agreement stipulated that it was "essential" to proceed as quietly as possible "so as to avoid the imputation as far as we can that we are preparing to make war on the Bolsheviki."[15]

Thus it came about that support of what the government of the United States described as "the greatest hope for the re-establishment of a stable government" in Russia was to be given, if given at all, in a furtive and underhanded manner—a procedure that could only stigmatize the anti-Bolshevik movement as a thing of questionable, and even shameful, character. In such an arrangement, Secretary Lansing's advice was disregarded, and his objectives wholly frustrated.

The people could still be told that the United States, which they regarded as "the standard of a free government," had recognized the Bolsheviks, and they could still come to the conclusion that further resistance was useless.

A secret war with the Bolsheviks, while the Central Powers were openly attacked as enemies of peace and democracy, necessarily carried an implication that the Bolsheviki were in some way less autocratic and less violent than the rulers of Germany and Austria-Hungary. The result was that the proposal was of greater assistance to the Bolsheviks than to the groups which sought freedom. The policy was similar to that which today impels assertions that assistance to the subject peoples, even of the most limited character, must be given only by so-called private groups. In each case direct assistance to the people has been prevented by fears that aid in the restoration of self-government would be regarded as "subversive activity."

It seemed, moreover, that the proposal for assistance to Kaledin was primarily designed not for the purpose of assisting the peoples of Russia, but to obtain their assistance for the Allies. The Allies thus appeared to be assigning greater importance to their own desire to prevent a separate Russian peace than to the desires of the people.

On December 28, 1917, Trotsky announced that talks with Germany had been suspended for a third time, "in order," as he said, "to give to the Allied countries a last possibility to take part in further negotiations." He took care to point out that they would "thus secure themselves against all the consequences of a separate peace,"[16] and he dwelt with evident satisfaction upon their desire to avoid this event. "A separate peace," he threatened, "signed by Russia, would without doubt inflict a heavy blow on the Allied countries, chiefly on France and Italy. . . . To bring their own Governments to immediately present their peace programs and to participate on their basis in the negotiations, this has now become a question of national self-preservation for the Allied nations."[17]

Secretary of State Lansing was not ready, however, to be thus intimidated. On January 2, 1918, he sent another memorandum to the President, pointing out that the Bolsheviks could not be regarded as speaking for the Russian peoples. "I think," he said, that "in considering this address it might properly be asked by what authority the Bolsheviks assume the right to speak for the Russian people. They seized the Government at Petrograd by force, they broke up opposition in the army by disorganizing it, they prevented the meeting of the Constituent Assembly chosen by the people because they could not control it, they have seized the property of the nation and confiscated private property, they have failed to preserve public order and human life, they have acted arbitrarily without pretense of legality, in fact, they have set up over a portion of Russia a despotic oligarchy as menacing to liberty as any absolute monarchy on earth, and this they maintain by force and not by the will of the people, which they prevent from expression."[18]

The Allies, on the other hand, and the President, had already been impressed with the need for negotiation. In their agreement to support the anti-Bolshevik provincial governments, the British and French had also agreed that they "should at once get into relations with the Bolsheviki through unofficial agents, each country as seems best to it."[19] In accordance with this agreement, the British replaced their Ambassador in Petrograd with a "Special Representative in Russia," R. H. Bruce Lockhart. They also announced their intention "by means of unofficial channels" to keep in touch with the Bolsheviks' new agent in London, Maxim Litvinov.[20] France dealt through a member of its military mission in Petrograd, Captain Jacques Sadoul. (Lockhart was eventually arrested by the Cheka—and exchanged with the British for Litvinov; Sadoul went over to the Bolsheviks.)

In the United States, Secretary Lansing's memorandum must have crossed in the mails with President Wilson's request for an opinion, not about the authority of the Bolsheviks to speak for the people, but "as to the most feasible and least objectionable way (if there is any)" to establish "unofficial relations" with them.[21] Such a way was quickly found. The State Department had originally issued instructions, in December, 1917, that all American representatives, including "Red Cross members in uniform," were to "withhold all direct communication with Bolshevik government";[22] but by January 3, 1918, the Ambassador reported that he was using the head of the American Red Cross Commission, Lieutenant Colonel Raymond Robins, for just this purpose.[23] The State Department approved.[24]

Although such arrangements might not have given the Bolsheviks as much prestige as the maintenance of embassies, they supplied the essential element of recognition—implicit acknowledgment that the Bolsheviks could and should be dealt with as representatives of the people. That the Bolsheviks would do their best to have them so interpreted had already been indicated by the American Ambassador, David R. Francis. "Trotsky," he reported, "gives widest possible circulation to any favors requested by even subordinates of Allied missions, hoping thereby to convince Russian people that his government is recognized by Allies as that would be most effective argument for its recognition in Russia."[25]

It was just this sort of propaganda which Secretary Lansing's first proposal was designed to deflate. The effect in Russia was the same as that which was later foreseen by his nephew and eventual successor, John Foster Dulles, as the consequence of recognition of the Chinese Communists. As Dulles said in 1957, "the many mainland Chinese, who by Mao Tse-tung's own recent admission seek to change the nature of their government, would be immensely discouraged" and their free government on Formosa would "feel betrayed by its friend."[26]

In March, 1918, the President even went so far as to address a personal appeal to the people through the All-Russian Congress of Soviets—hoping thereby to forestall its ratification of the separate peace with Germany. The message, as read to the assembled Bolsheviks, was a futile effort to reach the people through their oppressors and to win favor by expressing sympathy over the lesser of their misfortunes. It found him promising freedom to those who were most effectively destroying it and offering help in the struggle with autocracy to men who, in the words of his own Secretary of State, were setting up in Russia "a despotic oligarchy as menacing to liberty as any absolute monarchy on earth":

May I not take advantage of the meeting of the Congress of the Soviets to express the sincere sympathy which the people of the United States feel for the Russian people at this moment when the German power has been thrust in to interrupt and turn back the whole struggle for freedom and substitute the wishes of Germany for the purposes of the people of Russia. Although the Government of the United States is unhappily not now in a position to render the direct and effective aid it would wish to render, I beg to assure the people of Russia through the Congress that it will avail itself of every opportunity to secure for Russia once more complete sovereignty and independence in her own affairs and full restoration to her great rôle in the life of Europe and the modern world. The whole heart of the people of the United States is with the people of Russia in the attempt to free themselves forever from autocratic government and become the masters of their own life.[27]

No comparable effort was ever made to reach the people through their own representatives, who were even then seeking the President's assistance in their own behalf. If the United States really wished to help the people in the way the President described, it would have been aiding the so-called counterrevolutionary movement in Siberia, but when the Soviets charged that American officials were doing just that, the Secretary of State denied it.[28] The Minister in China, Paul S. Reinsch, who had suggested such support, was informed that "strict neutrality" was "desirable and must be observed." "Although," his instructions read, the "Allied governments have not recognized the Soviet they are interested in stimulating its opposition to the Central powers. *No Allied commission for organizing representative or other government in Siberia is deemed advisable.*"[29] (Italics added)

The Soviet reply to the President's message merely indicated, accurately enough, that it would help to speed the day when Bolshevism could be imposed upon other countries besides Russia. It was in the form of a resolution of the presidium of the Soviet Central Executive Committee:

The Congress expresses its gratitude to the American people, above all the laboring and exploited classes of the United States, for the sympathy expressed to the Russian people by President Wilson through the Congress of Soviets in the days of severe trials.

The Russian Socialistic Federative Republic of Soviets takes advantage of President Wilson's communication to express to all peoples perishing and suffering from the horrors of imperialistic war its warm sympathy and firm belief that the happy time is not far distant when the laboring masses of all countries will throw off the yoke of capitalism and will establish a socialistic state of society, which alone is capable of securing just and lasting peace as well as the culture and well-being of all laboring people.[30]

Lenin, however, was interested in more than the production of such Communist propaganda, or the mere denial of aid to the cause of freedom. For him the great advantage of these "unofficial" relations was the opportunity to obtain decisive material assistance for his own cause, and he came very close to getting it.

Some technical assistance in the planning and organization of the Red Army was actually provided by the American and other Allied military attachés. A limited approval of such activity was given to the United States Ambassador in May, 1918. "This Government," Lansing wired, "is not prepared to enter into formal engagement with the Soviet government which it does not recognize, nor is it now in position to give effective military support. There is however no objection to military attaché's lending such assistance as you deem in accord with the spirit of the Department's instructions to you."[31]

The Bolsheviks' main approach, however, was disguised as a bid for "economic support" which would allegedly help them to remain at war with Germany. On May 14, 1918, just prior to Robins' departure from Russia, Lenin gave him a plan for "Russian-American Commercial Relations."[32] It is interesting to note that the United States Ambassador, who had moved to Vologda, was not advised of this plan. He reported on May 16:

Associated Press representative here and Groves after talking to Robins at the station understand that he had definite proposition to the United States from the Soviet Government and was hastening to America in expectation of receiving favorable reply and definitely stated expected to return promptly if Soviet government survived, but Robins, with whom I talked fully, made no mention of such mission nor of returning.[33]

Robins subsequently submitted to the President a "Statement of Recommendations," suggesting that an economic commission be sent to Russia as quickly as possible. Among its purposes, the commission was to "encourage and assist in the organization of a voluntary revolutionary army," and in the development of "the necessary organization for its economic support."[34]

In this memorandum, which was dated July 1, 1918, Robins
asserted that intervention had been requested by the "responsible
head of the Soviet Government," and frankly stated that it should
be undertaken to promote the war with Germany rather than with any
idea of giving assistance to the people of Russia:

America's democratic war aims are such as to make allied intervention by force in Russia inconceivable unless desired by the great
mass of the Russian people. Thus far there has been no expression of
any such desire, but there is now presented in the invitation coming
from the responsible head of the Soviet Government for America's
cooperation in economic reconstruction, the opportunity for taking
a vitally important preliminary step toward complete economic and
military cooperation in the creation of an effective Eastern front. This
suggestion should be considered solely as a war measure, uninfluenced
by altruistic concern for the Russian people.

.   .   .   .

It is my sincere conviction, if this suggestion is acted upon and
such economic reorganization is accomplished as is needed to equip
and support a revolutionary army, that such an army can and will be
formed and that in such event the assistance of armed forces of the
Allies will be gladly accepted by the Soviet Power. This Power can
not be expected to countenance Allied intervention until convinced
that the intervening force will not be used to destroy it.[35]

It was not, apparently, considered to be of any consequence that
such an army would be used to crush any efforts to restore self-government. On the contrary, it was stipulated that the proposed commission
must be "willing to deal with the leaders of Revolutionary Russia
actually in power, without regard to their principles or formulas of
economic, social, or political life, so long as such leaders sincerely
desire to recreate forces in Russia which will be used in resisting the
force of German arms."[36]
The inducements offered in this proposal were precisely the
same as those which eventually produced all-out assistance to the
Soviets in World War II: denial of Russian resources to the German
armies, and creation of an eastern front. But there was also the currently familiar promise of reform—a "new look"—to be fostered by
increased personal contacts. According to Robins, the advice of the
commission, "re-inforced by the uncompromising facts of life," would

"lead inevitably to the modification, adjustment, and softening of the hard and impossible formulas of radical socialism...."[37]

If this proposal had come a few months earlier, it might have been accepted. Churchill reports that the British had been making every effort to obtain "a formal invitation from the Bolshevik leaders," and that it "would have been all important in overcoming the reluctance of the United States."[38] The Robins recommendations represented just such an invitation, and the President returned them to the Secretary of State, with the comment: "I differ from them only in practical details."[39]

The United States was not prepared, however, to intervene in full force on the side of the Bolsheviks any more than it was prepared to do so on the side of the people. But at the same time it was not considered impossible to trade United States recognition, and some form of material aid, for Soviet resistance to Germany.[40] The limited forces sent to Siberia and north Russia might easily have been sent to the Bolsheviks, and the happenstance that they were not so employed was largely due to the fact that they would have been insufficient to enable Lenin to stop the Germans, and to the fortuitous incidents in which the Czechs had already been forced to intervene on the side of freedom.

The "limited" intervention which did take place in Siberia and north Russia was certainly not due, in Robins' words, to any "altruistic concern for the Russian people," and the policy which produced his proposal was not abandoned. On the contrary, it continued to be reflected in the assertion that "the purpose of landing troops is to aid Czecho-Slovaks," and that there was "no purpose to interfere with internal affairs of Russia."[41]

Earlier, in April, 1918, the President had expressed interest in the democratic movement in Siberia, requesting the Secretary of State to provide him with all available information. "I would very much value," he wrote, "a memorandum containing all that we know about these several nuclei of self-governing authority that seem to be springing up in Siberia. It would afford me a great deal of satisfaction to get behind the most nearly representative of them if it can indeed draw leadership and control to itself."[42] This interest, however, appeared to be fully abandoned when the United States denied Soviet charges of assistance to the "counterrevolutionary" movement in Siberia. This occurred on May 9, only a few days before the Czech intervention.

As the end of the war approached, another series of peace proposals was launched, by a new foreign commissar, Georgi V. Chicherin.
His assistant, Maxim Litvinov, later stated that no less than twenty
were made during the period from 1918 to 1921.[43] The new campaign
began with a letter to President Wilson in which Chicherin gratui-
tously gave his "consent to join the negotiations"[44]—negotiations to
which the Bolsheviks had not been invited. They were never invited
to participate in the discussions at Paris, but the Allies were induced
nevertheless, with the encouragement of the United States, to take an
attitude of compromise, to attempt to impose it upon the Russian
peoples, and finally to delay and withhold effective assistance to the
anti-Red armies.

On December 2, 1918, the Bolsheviks broadcast a most urgent
demand[45] for peace, and for good reason. They had "learned that a
British fleet is moving in the Baltic Sea towards Russian shores, that
the ships of the Entente countries have been directed from Constantinople to the harbors of Crimea and the Southern Ukraine, and that
the troops of those same countries have already crossed the borders of
Bessarabia." There was a note of desperation in the plaintive appeal
of those who had promised to assist a general uprising in the free
nations "with all the means at our disposal." "The Russian Socialist
Soviet Republic," it opined, "has never menaced or tried to invade
the Entente countries; it only demanded to be left in peace. . . ."

It was Litvinov who finally drew a response, with a note handed
to the Allied ministers in Stockholm on December 23. He called their
attention to "a formal offer of peace" made by the Sixth All-Russian
Congress of Soviets, and asserted that it reflected the "sincere desire
of the Russian toiling masses to live in undisturbed peace and
friendship with all the people of the world."[46]

At the President's request, a special assistant to the United States
Embassy in London, William H. Buckler, went to Stockholm to get
the proposal in person. He reported on January 18, 1919:

I saw Litvinoff on January 14th, 15th and 16th, explaining I
was merely a private telephone without authority to make proposals
of any kind. He agreed that our talk should be confidential.

The Soviet Government, he declared, is anxious for permanent
peace. . . . They detest the military preparations and costly campaigns
now forced upon Russia. . . . the Soviet Government is prepared to
compromise on all points. . . .

. . . Litvinoff and his associates fully realize that for a long time

Russia will need expert assistance and advice especially in technical and financial matters and that she cannot get on without foreign machinery and manufactured imports. If peace were once made, Russian Bolshevist propaganda in foreign countries would cease at once. . . . Russians realize that in certain western countries conditions are not favorable for a revolution of the Russian type. No amount of propaganda can produce such conditions. . . .

. . . .

. . . Russians have no imperialistic designs on Finland, Poland or Ukraine and wish only to give them full rights of self-determination . . . .

. . . Insofar as the League of Nations can prevent war without encouraging reaction, it can count on the support of the Soviet Government.[47]

These assertions fell upon the ears of those who were anxious to believe. By the time Buckler's report was received, President Wilson and the British Prime Minister, David Lloyd George, had already made their decision—to invite the representatives of all groups in Russia, including the Bolsheviks, to a separate, all-Russian, peace conference.

The military experts, on the other hand, advised firmer action. The Council of Ten[48] was informed that Allied troops could "easily defeat" the Bolsheviks, and "at very slight cost." It would only be necessary to use modern weapons not possessed by the Bolsheviks, such as "armoured cars and bombing aeroplanes."[49] In Parliament, the British Secretary of State for War, Lord Alfred Milner, posed a question about aid to the subject peoples that is still embarrassing after the Second World War. "How can we," he asked, "simply because our own immediate purposes have been served, come away and leave them to the tender mercies of their and our enemies, before they have had time to arm, train, and organize so as to be strong enough to defend themselves?"[50] There was no adequate answer, but in the great clamor for peace, considerations of this nature were easily waved aside.

In the discussions at Paris, Lloyd George boldly indicated his disbelief that the Bolsheviks were as dangerous as the Germans. According to the secretary's notes of a meeting held in January, 1919, he doubted whether anyone believed this, and if they did, whether they were willing to make the sacrifice required to act accordingly. "We could say," he pointed out, "that Bolshevism was a movement as dangerous to civilization as German militarism has been, and that we must therefore destroy it." But, he asked, "did anyone seriously put forward this policy? Was anyone prepared to carry it out?" For his own part "he believed that no one could be found to do so.... To set Russia in order by force was a task which he for one would not undertake on behalf of Great Britain, and he questioned whether any other Power would undertake it."[51]

President Wilson did not think that force could accomplish the task in any event: "We should be fighting against the current of the times," he said, "if we tried to prevent Russia from finding her own path in freedom. Part of the strength of the Bolshevik leaders was doubtless the threat of foreign intervention. With the help of this threat they gathered the people around them."[52]

There was opposition to such views, but it was overruled. The Italian Minister of Foreign Affairs, Baron Sonnino, opposed all ne- gotiation with the Bolsheviks and suggested that help could be given to the people "with soldiers to a reasonable degree or by supplying arms, food, and money." His idea "was to collect together all the anti- Bolshevik parties and help them to make a strong Government, pro- vided they pledged themselves not to serve the forces of reaction...."[53]

This is precisely what the conferees decided to do in June, five months later, but in the meantime Baron Sonnino had been out- ranked and outnumbered. Lloyd George said he wanted to "put one or two practical questions," and the minutes of the ensuing discussion show little recollection of promises formerly made to the "free Government of Russia":

Mr. Lloyd George said ... The British Empire now had some 15,000 to 20,000 men in Russia. M. De Scavenius had estimated that some 150,000 additional men would be required, in order to keep the anti-Bolshevik Governments from dissolution. And General Fran- chet-d'Esperey also insisted on the necessity of Allied assistance. Now Canada had decided to withdraw her troops, because the Canadian soldiers would not agree to stay and fight against the Russians. Similar trouble had also occurred amongst the other Allied troops. And he felt certain that, if the British tried to send any more troops there, there would be mutiny.

M. Sonnino suggested that volunteers might be called for.

Mr. Lloyd George, continuing, said that it would be impossible to raise 150,000 men in that way. He asked, however, what contributions America, Italy and France would make towards the raising of this army.

President Wilson and M. Clemenceau each said none.

M. Orlando [President of the Italian Council of Ministers] agreed that Italy could make no further contributions.

Mr. Lloyd George said that the Bolsheviks had an army of 300,000 men and would, before long, be good soldiers, and to fight them at least 400,000 Russian soldiers would be required. Who would feed, equip and pay them? Would Italy, or America, or France, do so? If they were unable to do that, what would be the good of fighting Bolshevism? It could not be crushed by speeches. *He sincerely trusted that they would accept President Wilson's proposal as it now stood.*[54] (Italics added.)

No replies to the last group of questions were recorded, but the proponents of "peace" had won the day. President Orlando observed, for Italy, that "there remained the use of moral force."[55]

Invitations were then extended for the proposed peace conference, with the stipulation that there must be a "truce of arms amongst the parties invited."[56] When the decision was reported to Washington, a mild but prescient reproach was sent to Paris by the Acting Secretary of State, Frank Polk:

Have you considered recognition of the Omsk Government? The call for a conference will probably destroy morale of all parties opposing Bolsheviks. Recognition of that Government would make it possible to give it some assistance and would undoubtedly strengthen it so that it could withstand the crisis created by the recent action of the [Paris] Peace Conference. I realize that Kolchak is probably a reactionary and there is some question as to how he forced himself into power. I am not recommending recognition, but merely suggesting it for your consideration. If that is not deemed wise, it seems to me that some statement should be made in order not to entirely discourage the Omsk Government and the followers of Denikin. It might be possible to use suggestion of recognition of these groups as a bait to tempt them to attend the conference.[57]

Protests received from the field were less restrained. The chargé at Archangel, DeWitt C. Poole, tendered his resignation. The consul general in Siberia reported that in Ekaterinburg, where the murder of the Czar occurred, the general feeling was "one of being deliberately deserted and betrayed"; the people of Novonikolaevsk felt that agreement with Bolsheviks was "disgraceful"; in Tomsk, that "nothing would result"; in Krasnoyarsk, "all expressed surprise and disappointment"; in Irkutsk, the merchants held meetings of protest, the Cadets "bitterly disapproved," and the Socialists pointed out that an armistice would only be useful "if Bolsheviks will leave their irreconcilable position."[58]

The invitation to the conference was rejected by the provisional Russian governments in Siberia, Archangel and south Russia. The Bolsheviks purported to accept it, but agreed to negotiate only with the Allies—their "only real adversaries." At the same time, as Churchill reported, they assumed the offensive "in many directions" and "on several fronts."[59]

On February 14, the Allied leaders met to determine the next step. Churchill had succeeded Lord Milner as Secretary of State for War, and he urged strong action. His report, as recorded in the minutes of the conference, clearly showed that the Bolsheviks were already winning the cold war. "Great Britain," he pointed out, "had soldiers in Russia who were being killed in action. Their families wished to know what purpose these men were serving. Were they just marking time until the Allies had decided on policy, or were they fighting in a campaign representing some common aim? The longer the delay continued, the worse would be the situation of the troops on all the Russian fronts. The Russian elements in those forces were deteriorating rapidly because of the uncertainty of the support they might expect from the victorious Allies. The Allied troops were intermingled with these Russian troops, which were weakening and quavering, and they were themselves becoming affected."[60]

Churchill's stand brought him into disagreement with President Wilson, who asserted that "the Allied and Associated Powers ought to withdraw their troops from all parts of Russian territory" because they "were doing no sort of good" and "did not know for whom or for what they were fighting." They "were not assisting any promising common effort to establish order. . . ."[61]

Churchill's reply was prophetic:

. . . complete withdrawal of all Allied troops was logical and clear policy, but its consequence would be the destruction of all non-Bolshevik armies in Russia. These numbered at the present time about 500,000 men and though their quality was not of the best, their numbers were nevertheless increasing. Such a policy would be equivalent to pulling out the linch-pin from the whole machine. There would be no further armed resistance to the Bolsheviks in Russia, *and an interminable vista of violence and misery was all that remained for the whole of Russia.*[62] (Italics added)

He agreed that none of the Allies could send conscript troops, but expressed the belief "that volunteers, technical experts, arms, munitions, tanks, aeroplanes, etc. might be furnished."[63]

Wilson wanted to know what use would be made of such forces. "In some areas they would certainly be assisting reactionaries. Consequently, if the Allies were asked what they were supporting in Russia they would be compelled to reply that they did not know."[64]

Four months later, however, when it was too late, such assistance was agreed upon by all parties. In the meantime the future wartime Prime Minister of Great Britain fared no better than Baron Sonnino.

President Wilson next sent a secret mission to Moscow to obtain a statement of the Bolshevik conditions for peace. It was led by William C. Bullitt, a man who was destined in later years to become America's first ambassador to the Soviet Union. He talked with Lenin, Chicherin and Litvinov, and soon obtained a proposal—which the Bolsheviks asserted they would not make to the Allies, but which the Allies would have to make to them. It included an armistice "on all fronts," the withdrawal of foreign troops, and the termination of all military assistance to "anti-Soviet Governments."[65] Bullitt reported, however, that he found the Bolsheviks "full of a sense of Russia's need for peace," and "disposed to be most conciliatory."[66]

The need for "initiative" had now returned to the Allies, and they next proposed the distribution of relief supplies in all parts of Russia. This project, they asserted, "would involve cessation of all hostilities" and "a complete suspension of the transfer of troops and military material."[67]

The new proposal proved to be just as unacceptable as the other. The Bolsheviks refused to discuss the end of hostilities unless "we discuss the whole problem of our relations to our adversaries, that is, in the first place, to the Associated Governments"—i.e., the Allies and the United States. They were, however, "always ready to enter into peace negotiations" and they were "ready to do it now."[68] The free Russian governments expressed their gratitude for the offer of relief, but asserted that such supplies, in the hands of the Bolsheviks, would simply "prolong their domination." They could only point out that feeding the starving population would not solve the main problem—"the struggle for the liberation of Russia from her oppressors."[69]

By the time the Allies were through trying to make peace, the time for giving effective aid to freedom had nearly passed. Admiral Kolchak, however, was at the peak of his advance, and the Allied leaders were still unaware of the damage they had done. They abandoned their peace efforts, not because they were convinced of the folly of compromise, but because they felt assured of early victory. Bullitt later testified that "everyone in Paris, including, I regret to say members of the American commission, began to grow very lukewarm about peace in Russia, because they thought Kolchak would arrive in Moscow and wipe out the soviet government."[70] They thought, in short, that they were winning the cold war.

CHAPTER IV

THE FIRST ROUND OF SOVIET AGGRESSION

The Price of Nonintervention

As A result of the desultory support given by the free nations to principles of self-determination in Russia, the Bolsheviks were able not only to trample upon the rights of their own people but also to ignore those of many non-Russian nations of the former Czarist empire—nations whose right to separate existence they promised and pretended to recognize, and to several of which they had already "granted" actual independence. In their purported recognition of the rights of these peoples the Bolsheviks even outdid many of the free nations, which professed to support the principle of self-determination but refused to accept the fact that, insofar as the non-Russian peoples were concerned, the revolution was more than a rebellion against autocracy—it was a revolt against Great Russian colonialism.

In this respect the greatest mistake was made by the United States, which entered the First World War as the champion of self-determination, but which later asserted—in a widely published pronouncement of the Department of State—that it "strongly recoiled" from any settlement involving the "dismemberment of Russia" (see Appendix B-2: note to the Italian Ambassador). By insisting that the "true boundaries" of Russia should with few exceptions "properly include the whole of the former Russian Empire," and that any questions of Russian "sovereignty" should be "held in abeyance" until the passing of the Bolshevik regime—an event which it refused to help bring about—the United States ignored its own principles and at the same time spurned the friendship and proffered cooperation of many nations and peoples who would otherwise have been staunch and invincible allies in the cause of freedom.

If the promise of peace, or the belief that Bolshevism would not last, could lull the Allies into a state of inactivity—as it did; and if the promise of economic Utopia could deceive any of the Russian people—as it probably did; then something more was required to

73

attract the non-Russian peoples of the Empire—peoples who wanted self-rule or independence regardless of the kind of regime that might be established in Russia proper, and who would never willingly accept submersion or domination of their political, social, religious or cultural life by foreign formulas offered by the Great Russians, no matter how benevolent or alluring they might be made to appear.

These peoples included not only those who won their independence temporarily—Estonians, Latvians, Lithuanians, Poles and the peoples of the Trans-Caucasus (Georgia, Armenia and Azerbaijan)—but also countless others who did not. They included millions more of White Russians (Byelorussians); Little Russians (Ukrainians); Moldavians; Tatars; Karelians; and the peoples of the Volga-Ural—land of Bashkirs, Chuvash, Kalmucks, Komi, Mari, Mordovians and Udmursk. They included the Cossacks with lands widely spread from the Don, the Kuban, the Terek and Astrakhan to Orenburg and the Ural Mountains, and even to the maritime provinces of eastern Siberia. They also included many others in Siberia—Samoyedes, Ostiaks, Buryats, Tunguz, Yakuts and Tchuktches; and in Central Asia—Kazakhs, Kara Kalpaks, Kirgiz, Tadzhiks, Turkmen and Uzbeks; and in the North Caucasus—Balkars, Chechenzi, Circassians, Daghestani, Inguish, Kabardines, Karachai and Ossetians. None of these could ever be convinced of the virtues of any political scheme which did not include the promise of self-determination, of autonomy or independence—a promise which could lead to separation, but not subjection, and which, if carried out, would have insured the provision of anti-Bolshevik regimes for approximately one-half the population of the former Russian Empire.

Immediately after the March revolution, many of the non-Russian nations presented their demands for self-rule to the new Provisional Government. The Czar's government had promised an autonomous state to the Armenians, in the Armenian parts of Turkey; and in April, 1917, the Provisional Government proclaimed such autonomy, pending the peace treaty, for the areas then occupied by the Russian Army. A limited form of self-rule was also granted to Finland, whose elective Diet and earlier constitutional status were restored; to Latvia and Estonia, where the election of local legislative councils was approved; and to the Ukraine, which won acceptance for its own elected Rada and General Secretariat.

The Russians, however, were as divided on the problem of nationalities as they were on other issues raised by the revolution, and such concessions to separatism were rigidly opposed by many. In July, 1917, on the eve of a Bolshevik uprising, four cabinet ministers resigned because of the concession made to the Ukraine, and in the middle of this crisis the Finnish Diet was dissolved for attempting to assert complete independence.

The Provisional Government was unable, however, to prevent the development of a movement which was gaining headway in all parts of the Empire, and efforts to oppose it contributed to the dissension and anarchy in which the Bolshevik seizure of power was possible. Another Rada was formed in Byelorussia, and steps were taken to form a federal republic in the North Caucasus. In Petrograd a Soviet of Nationalities was convened, demanding a federal form of government in which the states would be permitted to secede with the approval of the Constituent Assembly. In Kiev the Ukrainian Rada convoked a Congress of the Peoples of Russia which also declared for a federal republic. Finally, in October, the Provisional Government formally recognized the rights of all non-Russians in a declaration which promised that "Measures guaranteeing to the nationalities the right of self-government will be enacted by the Constituent Assembly."[1]

When the Bolsheviks destroyed the Provisional Government, they purported to grant the immediate right of full self-determination. The first such announcement was applied to all nations of the world, and was contained in the so-called "Decree on Peace" published on November 8, 1917:

If any nation whatsoever is retained within the frontiers of a certain state by force, if it is not given the right of free voting in accordance with its desire, regardless of the fact whether such desire was expressed in the press, in people's assemblies, in decisions of political parties, or rebellions and insurrections against national oppression, such plebiscite to take place under the condition of the complete removal of the armies of the annexing or the more powerful nation; if the weaker nation is not given the opportunity to decide the question of the forms of its national existence, then its adjoining is an annexation, that is, seizure—violence.[2]

The same decree abrogated "absolutely and immediately" secret treaties made by the previous government, which were alleged to have been "intended in the majority of cases for the purpose of . . . retaining or increasing the annexations by the Great Russians."[3]

The annexations by the Great Russians were also renounced in another document—the "Declaration of the Rights of the Peoples of Russia"—issued on November 15, 1917. This declaration stated that the rights of the non-Russian nationalities would be based upon the principles of "equality and sovereignty" and of "free self-determination, even to the point of separation and the formation of an independent state."[4]

In December the Bolsheviks denounced the "subduction" of Armenia from Turkey, but at the same time promised to give all Armenians "the right of free self-determination of their political fate." Other nationalities in the south and the east—"Mohammedans of Russia, Volga and Crimean Tartars, Kirghisi and Sarti in Siberia and Turkestan, Turcos and Tartars in the Trans-Caucasus, Chechenzi and mountain Cossacks"—were urged to assert their long-suppressed desires: "Organize your national life freely and unimpeded."[5] These pronouncements were made in the "Appeal to all Mohammedan Workers in Russia and the East," December 7, 1917.

Still another declaration appeared in January, 1918, the "Declaration of the Rights of the Laboring and Exploited People," subsequently incorporated in the first "Constitution of the Russian Socialist Federated Soviet Republic." In this document the previous declarations were endorsed by the Third Congress of Soviets. The Congress, it said, "welcomes the policy of the Council of People's Commissars, which has proclaimed the absolute independence of Finland, has commenced the withdrawal of troops from Persia [Iran] and given Armenia the right to self-determination. . . . The III Congress of Soviets limits itself to the establishment of the fundamental points of the federation of the Soviet republics of Russia, allowing the workmen and peasants of each nationality to decide themselves at their Soviet Congress if they desire to take part in the federal government and in other federal Soviet institutions and on what conditions."[6]

These declarations were taken at their word in many places. Full independence was declared by the Latvian National Council (November 19, 1917), the Ukrainian Rada (November 20, 1917), the Finnish Diet (December 6, 1917), the Estonian National Council (February 24, 1918) and the Federal Democratic Republic of Transcaucasia (April 9, 1918). The Cossacks resumed the practice of electing their Krugs and Hetmen, and formed a Southeastern Federation of Cossack Territories extending from the Ukraine to the Caspian Sea, and from the Caucasus Mountains north to the cities of Voronezh and

Saratov. Under German occupation complete independence of Russia was also declared by Lithuania (February 16, 1918) and by Byelorussia (March 25, 1918).

Many of these peoples hoped that after democratic rule was restored in Russia a federal union might still be created. This was the case, for example, in the Ukraine, whose leaders were reported by the United States consul general in Moscow to be "firmly attached to the idea of a Russian federal republic."[7] In confirmation he enclosed the text of a note addressed by the Ukrainian government to all belligerent and neutral powers. It stated in part:

Striving to bring about the creation of a federal league of all the republics that have arisen until now on the territory of the former Russian Empire, the Ukraine republic in the person of the General Secretariat enters into independent international relations until such time as a general Russian federation shall be formed and the international representative functions shall be apportioned between the governments of the Ukraine republic and the federal government of the future federation.[8]

In Byelorussia, prior to the German occupation, the Central Rada called for a "democratic republic, united with Great Russia, and with other neighbor republics of the empire, on a federal basis."[9] A federal union was also sought by the provisional government of Siberia and the Southeastern Federation.[10] The United States consul at Moscow, De Witt Poole, who was twice detailed to south Russia to make contact with the resistance, reported that the Southeastern Federation considered itself a "temporary nucleus" for the "reconstruction of Russia on federal lines."[11]

Such dreams, however, were not to be realized. A few of these peoples were able to secure temporary freedom—in precarious independence—but for most there was to be only a Red-created shell of autonomous government—the form of liberty without its substance.

The pattern of this difference was very simple: where outside help was provided, the Bolshevik promise was enforced—elsewhere it was not. Finland, with the aid of Germany, was able to enforce it permanently. The Baltic States and Poland, with assistance from the Allies, were able to enforce it until 1939. The other nations, ignored or abandoned by the Allies, were able to do so only briefly or not at all, and their early subjugation added millions to the victims of Bolshevism. The failure of the Allies to recognize their claims, which were based on the principles for which the First World War was fought, and to which even the Bolsheviks paid verbal homage, prevented joint action and was in large part responsible for the failure of efforts to save Russia itself.

The independence of Finland was recognized by the Bolsheviks on January 4, 1918, but preparations to impose a Bolshevik regime were already under way. Finland was at that time occupied by some 40,000 Russian troops, requests for their withdrawal were ignored, and a red *coup d'état* was carried out on January 29, 1918. The lawful government was forced to flee from Helsinki to Vaasa, and "civil war" ensued.

Finland's independence had already been recognized by many nations—France, Sweden, Germany, Austria-Hungary, Greece, Norway, Denmark and Switzerland—but its appeals for help found little response in the free world at this time. Neutral Sweden hesitated. The Allies landed at Murmansk, not to aid the Finns but to prevent the Germans from establishing a base for submarines. The Germans, on the other hand, responded readily; and with their aid, peace and the duly elected government were restored by the end of May.

Further south the Red aggression was at first delayed by German occupation. In their treaties with the Germans the Bolsheviks renounced all claims of sovereignty in the Baltic States, Poland and most of Byelorussia. Red Guards and Russian troops, where they still remained, were to be withdrawn, and those civilians who had been arrested or deported to Russia were guaranteed a safe return.[12] After the defeat of Germany, however, and the withdrawal of the German armies, the Bolsheviks immediately attacked these nations—moving in with ready-made "Soviet governments." In the Baltic States they quickly captured Riga and Vilna, the capitals of Latvia and Lithuania.

By this time, however, the Allies were supporting the demand for independence in the Baltic area. Their intentions were demonstrated by *de facto* recognition of the nuclei of self-government—at an early date, and by major powers. The Estonian National Council had been recognized by Great Britain, France and Italy in May, 1918. The Latvian National Council was recognized by Great Britain on November 11, 1918—Armistice Day—a week before the Provisional Latvian Government was established. In Lithuania a Provisional Government was formed on November 11, 1918, and recognized by the Allies in the following year.

When the Bolsheviks attacked, the Allies first ordered the German occupation forces to remain and assist in the defense. They were entitled to make this demand under Article 12 of the Armistice Agreement, but the Germans themselves attempted to destroy the new national governments. The Allies then reversed their position and asked for immediate German withdrawal. In these circumstances, independence was won by the people themselves with the aid of British supplies, the British Navy, volunteers from Finland, Sweden and Denmark, and the free Russian army of General Yudenich.

A different fate awaited Byelorussia, whose independence was supported by no strong power. First formed in Minsk, in early 1918, its national government had been driven underground by the Bolsheviks, then dominated by German occupation authorities, and finally forced into exile when the Germans withdrew. Although recognized *de jure* by many small nations—Austria, Czechoslovakia, Estonia, Finland, Georgia, Latvia, Lithuania, Poland and the Ukraine—and *de facto* by Bulgaria, Denmark, France and Yugoslavia, there was no one but Poland to defend it. The motives of the Poles, moreover, were not untainted by their own national ambition. They sought a political union of Poland, Byelorussia and the Ukraine[13]—a desire not shared by Ukrainians or Byelorussians. It was further frustrated by division among the Poles themselves, some of whom wanted a federal union, with all of Byelorussia included, while others demanded outright annexation, which involved only the western section.

The Poles expelled the Bolsheviks from Byelorussia in 1919, and permitted the national government to return—but it was disarmed and divided. In 1920, the Poles were expelled by the Bolsheviks and nearly lost their own country. Finally, Byelorussia was partitioned. It remained in that condition until 1939, when it was taken over altogether by the Soviet Union at the beginning of World War II.

The independence of Poland itself was supported by many strong powers, including the United States. It received substantial military assistance and, accordingly, in spite of its narrow escape, was successfully defended by its own national army.

When Germany collapsed, the Allies actually depended upon the Poles to stop the Red advance into Europe—and requested them to do so. Operations in Byelorussia, on the other hand, were not approved. In December, 1919, an "ethnic" eastern boundary of Poland was suggested by the acting British Secretary of State for

Foreign Affairs, Lord Curzon. The Allies requested that Polish forces east of this line be withdrawn, but the Poles refused and Allied assistance waned.

Thereafter, in June, 1920, the Red Army gained the ascendancy. The British then suggested a conference in London. It was to include the Bolsheviks and all those western border nations whose independence the British then supported and with whom the Bolsheviks had not yet executed peace treaties—Poland, Lithuania, Latvia and Finland. The Bolsheviks, however, rejected the offer. They were already in separate negotiations with the three last-mentioned nations, and they confidently expected Poland to succumb. They continued their attack across the "Curzon line," threatening Warsaw.

In the meantime, the Bolsheviks pursued their own political-diplomatic offensive, creating a puppet government headed by a Polish Communist—Felix Dzerzhinsky. He was also head of the Soviet secret police. In "peace" negotiations with the legitimate government, they demanded reduction of the Polish army to 50,000 men, the formation of workers' and soldiers' councils (Soviets), and a Polish "workers' militia" supplied with arms exclusively by the Bolsheviks. This was to have 200,000 men.

The Allies then sought ways to give renewed military assistance. Their efforts were handicapped, however, because the Germans, who assumed a neutral attitude, prohibited the shipment of arms across Germany to either side. Some arms and ammunition were shipped through Danzig, and the French were able to send a military mission, headed by General Maxim Weygand. Perhaps the most important assistance, however, came from the Russian General Wrangel. He had emerged from the Crimea in June, and while the Red armies to the north were advancing westward against Poland, he was forcing them to divide their forces, cutting up their units in the south. At the end of July he launched another diversionary attack on the eastern shores of the Black Sea.

In the following month, August, 1920, the Poles won a decisive victory. It is still described as the "miracle on the Vistula." Warsaw was saved and the Bolsheviks driven back to Minsk. In October they agreed to an armistice, and the final peace treaty was made on March 18, 1921. During the same period, treaties were also made with the "bourgeois" regimes in Lithuania (July 12, 1920), Latvia (August 11, 1920) and Finland (October 14, 1920), and their independence conceded. A similar treaty had been made with Estonia on February 2, 1920.

The fate of the Ukraine was similar to that of Byelorussia. Unlike Byelorussia, however, its free government was first recognized by the Bolsheviks and promised peace. On December 4, 1917, the Council of People's Commissars had addressed a letter to the Ukrainian Rada, acknowledging its rights in the usual magnanimous terms:

Having regard to the fraternal kinship and community of interests of the working classes in their struggle to realize Socialism, and also to the principles constantly proclaimed by the resolutions of the democratic revolutionary organisations ... the Council of People's Commissaries again recognises the right of all the nations formerly oppressed by the Czarist regime and by the Russian bourgeoisie, to complete self-determination, even if this involves their separation from Russia.

We, therefore, the Council of Commissaries of the Russian People, recognise the Democratic Republic of Ukrainia, and acknowledge its right to separate from Russia or to enter into negotiations with the Russian Republic with a view to establishing federal or other relations with it.

The Council of Commissaries of the Russian People further recognises, without any limits or conditions, and in all respects, the national rights and independence of the Ukrainian Republic.[14]

Two weeks later, however, another message was delivered, still "recognizing" the "national rights and the national independence of the Ukrainian people," but at the same time insisting that Russian troops remain, that the Ukraine assist in the Bolshevik war with General Kaledin, and that the "Red Guards" be rearmed. "Does the Rada," it was inquired, "promise to stop all its attempts to disarm the Soviet regiments and the workers' Red Guard in Ukraina and to give back immediately arms to those from whom they were taken away?" If not, and if a satisfactory reply were not received within forty-eight hours, then "the Council of People's Commissars will consider the Rada in a state of open war against the Soviet regime in Russia and in Ukraina."[15]

Even the most radical Ukrainians were unwilling to accept such demands. The ultimatum was rejected with the support of an all-Ukrainian Congress of Soviets (convened at Bolshevik request). Dis-

82   COLD WAR AND LIBERATION

senters went to Kharkov and organized a "government" of their own, but its members did not even speak Ukrainian.[16]

On December 25, 1917 (Christmas Day), the Red Army attacked while Moscow issued fraternal "greetings" to the "true Government" at Kharkov:

> Greeting the organization in Kharkov of a truly popular Soviet regime in Ukraina, seeing in this Workers' and Peasants' Rada the true Government of the People's Ukrainian Republic, the Council of People's Commissars promises the new Government of the brotherly Republic complete and all possible support in the struggle for peace and also in the transfer of all land, factories and banks to the working people of Ukraina.[17]

Unable to fight Germans and Bolsheviks at the same time, the Ukraine sought peace with the Germans and sent its own delegation to Brest-Litovsk. It did not go, however, with any intention of betraying its people to German domination. The tenor of its negotiations is indicated in the *History of the Peace Conference at Paris*, prepared under the auspices of the British Institute of International Affairs. As this account states, "the Ukrainians at once made recognition of their independence the principal condition among their exaggerated [sic] demands on the Central Powers." Ukrainian grain supplies were a strong bargaining point, and the author relates that within ten days the Germans asserted: "The Ukrainians no longer treat with us: *they dictate!*"[18]

In the treaty, which was signed on February 9, 1918, the Germans agreed to evacuate the occupied areas, and the sovereignty of the Ukrainian National Republic was recognized *de jure*. Ten days later the Bolsheviks, in their own treaty with the Central Powers, agreed to make peace with the Ukraine, to cease all agitation and propaganda and to withdraw their troops and Red Guards.

In the meantime, however, the Bolsheviks had continued their attacks, captured Kiev, the Ukrainian capital, and forced the Rada to seek German military assistance at the price of German occupation. A military pact was made with Germany on February 18, and the Bolsheviks were driven out of the Ukraine, but the Rada was soon replaced with a regime more amenable to German exploitation.

After the defeat of Germany by the Allies, the Ukrainians threw out the puppet regime, installed a new temporary government and held elections for a Constituent Assembly. At the same time another independent government was organized in the Ukrainian areas of Austria-Hungary (Eastern Galicia, Bukovina and the Carpatho-Ukraine). Here the western Ukrainians (Ruthenians) raised an army of 150,000 men and voted to unite with the east. The union was proclaimed at Kiev on January 22, 1919.

New troubles lay ahead, however. The Red Army returned from the north with another "Soviet Government of the Ukraine." An Allied expeditionary force moved in from the south, demanding submission to General Denikin in the east. In the west a Polish army moved into eastern Galicia, the Rumanians into Bukovina, and the Hungarians into the Carpatho-Ukraine. The outcome was that the Bolsheviks recaptured Kiev, on February 6, and soon dominated large areas. The Allied expeditionary force retired in April, in confusion, and the Ukrainians, both east and west, were disillusioned and embittered.

Without the support of the free nations, constructive efforts to form a democratic Ukrainian government were given little chance for success. They deteriorated, as they had in Siberia, into quarrels and disorders. The troops were unpaid, unfed, unarmed and afflicted with typhus. The government was weakened, the countryside was terrorized by bandits, and there was a wave of anti-Semitic pogroms. Finally, the Ukrainians themselves fell apart when those in the east sought alliance with the Poles, at the expense of those in the west, and those in the west sought alliance with General Denikin, at the expense of those in the east.

The Bolsheviks, nevertheless, did not find invasion in this area a pleasant experience. During the period from April to June, 1919, there were more than 300 separate uprisings and revolts in the occupied areas.[19] On August 30, the Ukrainian army recaptured Kiev. It was immediately lost, however, to General Denikin, and a few days later it was back in the hands of the Bolsheviks.

At this time, Denikin was engaged in his nearly successful march to Moscow. His ultimate withdrawal was made necessary only because his armies were overextended, and he probably would have crushed the Bolsheviks if on his left flank there had been a friendly and powerful Ukraine. Instead there was a chaotic nation, partially controlled by the Bolsheviks, whose army was neglected and unsupplied, and whose people were antagonized to the point of declaring war on Denikin himself. This they did on September 24, 1919.

For similar reasons it seems unlikely that Kolchak's drive would have failed, earlier in the year, if the French expeditionary force which was at that time in Odessa had armed and co-operated with the Ukrainians to make an effective threat from the southwest. The tremendous resources of more than thirty million people were excluded from the fight for freedom, and they themselves were finally antagonized, simply because of the failure to consider their right of self-determination. The fact that an undetermined quantity of munitions supplied to General Denikin, for use against the Bolsheviks, was used against the Ukraine did not appear to be as much a matter of concern to the free world as the fear that it might be used for the purpose of assisting "reactionaries."

In December, 1919, the Ukrainian army was decisively beaten by General Denikin, who in his own turn was soon defeated by the Bolsheviks. The Ukrainians then came to agreement with the Poles, and with their help Kiev was again retaken in May, 1920.

The victory, however, was of short duration. The Ukrainians were alienated, the Allies opposed the venture, and it collapsed in the retreat to Warsaw. The Ukraine was divided between east and west, and so remained until the Bolsheviks took all in 1939.

Further south, in the Trans-Caucasus, the Allies supported claims to independence but failed to furnish the required assistance. The peoples of this area, on the other hand, had given unique assistance to the Allies during the war. In the First World War the enemy in the region of the Trans-Caucasus was the Ottoman Empire, which included Turkey, and when the Russian troops were withdrawn by the Bolsheviks the defense was continued by the armies of the newly formed and independent Transcaucasian Federation (Georgia, Armenia and Azerbaijan). This resistance delayed the capture of Baku until September, 1918, and thus prevented the Central Powers from obtaining large quantities of oil that was badly needed for the last great German drive in the west. When the federation was defeated and dissolved, in May, 1918, Georgia was occupied by the Germans, but the three member nations declared their separate independence and the Armenians continued to resist the advance of the Turks. The repeated and unsuccessful efforts of the Turkish Army to annihilate the Armenians were later described by the Germans as the cause of its collapse.

The independence of the Trans-Caucasus had been at least partially accepted by the Bolsheviks in the Peace of Brest-Litovsk. Russian claims to the Armenian parts of Turkey were renounced, and the

Bolsheviks agreed to refrain from interference with the establishment of self-government in certain areas formerly dominated by Russia. The applicable clauses provided that Russia would "do all in her power to have the provinces of eastern Anatolia promptly evacuated and returned to Turkey." The territories of Ardakhan, Kars and Batum were to "be cleared without delay of Russian troops," and Russia would "not interfere in the new organization of internal juridical and international juridical relations of such territories." Instead, it would "allow the populations of these territories to establish new governments in agreement with neighboring states, especially with Turkey."[20] Following the German occupation of Georgia, a supplementary treaty provided that "Russia agrees to Germany's recognising Georgia as an independent state."[21]

After the war, *de facto* recognition of all three states was extended by the Allies, and their independence was assured by the presence of British occupation forces until the middle of 1919. For the protection of Armenians in Turkey, the Allies were also authorized, under the armistice agreement with the Ottoman Empire, to occupy six Turkish-Armenian vilayets (approximately 96,000 square miles) in the event of any disorders.

The Republic of Georgia was eventually recognized *de jure* by all the major powers, except the United States, and by fourteen smaller powers, including the Bolsheviks. Similar recognition was extended to Armenia when the Treaty of Sevres, providing for its independence, was executed by the Allies, Armenia and the Ottoman government in August, 1920. The United States was not a party to this treaty, but President Wilson accepted the task of determining the the Turkish-Armenian boundary. He subsequently awarded to Armenia some 40,000 square miles of prewar Turkey, in the vilayets of Erzoroum, Trebizond, Van and Bitlis.

The concern of the United States for the welfare of the peoples of the Trans-Caucasus was largely manifested in the contribution of vast sums for the postwar relief of poverty and starvation. But in the case of Armenia there was also strong official and popular support for effective measures to protect its political independence. Of all the claims to independence made by the nations of the former Russian Empire, the claims of Armenia, Finland and Poland were the only ones to receive prompt recognition from the United States. Yet Armenia was allowed to fall unaided.

The Armenians themselves were willing, if necessary, to accept a protectorate—temporary rule from abroad—to preserve their free-dom; and in 1917, the president of the Armenian Delegation in Paris suggested a procedure similar to that followed by the United States in Cuba and the Philippines.[22] At the Peace Conference in February, 1919, the Armenians requested that a mandate be given to one of the Great Powers "to aid Armenia during the first years of its existence, in establishing its Government and in the organization and develop-ment of its economic and financial systems."[23]

Shortly thereafter, the President was urged to accept this mandate on behalf of the United States in a number of petitions sponsored by the American Committee for the Independence of Armenia. One of these, which spoke in the name of "all the denominations of the Protestant Church and the Holy Catholic Church in the United States of America," was signed by 25,000 clergymen—obviously cognizant of the fact that Armenia is one of the oldest of the Christian nations: "Heartily sympathizing with the aspirations of the Armenian people and speaking for them and for the Christian people of America," we do ask you, they said, "to do your utmost to secure and insure the Independence of Armenia, including the six Vilayets, Cilicia and the littoral of Trebizonde in Turkish Armenia, Russian Armenia and Persian Armenia; to exert your great influence to the end that the Peace Conference may make requisite arrangements for helping Armenia to establish an independent Republic, and to obtain adequate reparation for the terrible losses the Armenian people have suffered during the war."[24]

Similar petitions were made by 100 bishops, forty-five state governors, and 250 college and university presidents. The sponsoring committee was itself composed of the most distinguished members. The names of many of them, such as Charles Evans Hughes, William Jennings Bryan, James Cardinal Gibbons, Henry Cabot Lodge, Nicholas Murray Butler, William T. Manning, Oscar S. Straus and Stephen S. Wise, are even more highly respected now than they were at the time.

During the summer of 1919, an American mission, under the leadership of General James G. Harbord, was sent to the Near East to study the possible assumption of a mandate in all of the Trans-Caucasus and parts of Turkey. It reported that the cost during the first five years would be $756,014,000, and that initially (during the first three years) 60,000 American troops would be required. No rec-ommendation that the mandate be either accepted or rejected was made, but the mission offered its own prophetic comment on the effects of a failure to accept. "If we refuse to assume it," the mission's report asserted, "for no matter what reasons satisfactory to ourselves, we shall be considered by many millions of people as having left unfinished the task for which we entered the war, and as having betrayed their hopes."[25]

It is interesting to note that America's stock of goodwill in the Middle East was at that time very high. The mission reported that "without visiting the Near East" it was "not possible for an American to realize even faintly the respect, faith and affection" with which our country was regarded throughout that region. "Whether it is the world-wide reputation which we enjoy for fair dealing, a tribute perhaps to the crusading spirit which carried us into the Great War, not untinged with hope that the same spirit may urge us into the solution of great problems growing out of that conflict, or whether due to unselfish and impartial missionary and educational influence exerted for a century," this faith in America, the mission said, "is the one faith which is held alike by Christian and Moslem, by Jew and Gentile, by prince and peasant in the Near East."[26]

While the Harbord mission was making its investigation, Great Britain announced its intention to withdraw from the Trans-Caucasus. Plans to replace the British troops with a French force were deferred when, on September 9, 1919, a resolution was presented in the United States Senate for the use of American troops:

Whereas the withdrawal of the British troops from the Caucasus and Armenia will leave the Armenian people helpless against the attacks of the Kurds and the Turks; and

Whereas the American people are deeply and sincerely sympathetic with the aspirations of the Armenian people for liberty and peace and progress; Therefore be it

Resolved, etc., That the President of the United States is hereby authorized to use such military and naval forces of the United States as in his opinion may seem expedient for the maintenance of peace and tranquility in Armenia until the settlement of the affairs of that country has been completed by treaty between the nations.

Sec. 2.   There is hereby appropriated out of any moneys in the Treasury not otherwise appropriated the sum of $ to enable the President to execute the foregoing resolution.[27]

In the Senate, however, there was opposition, and subcommittee hearings were not concluded until October, 1919. On November 3, the chairman, Senator Warren G. Harding, made a statement which indicated that there would be plenty of moral support for the independence of Armenia, but that something less than a mandate would be recommended for its actual defense:

I have long had it in mind to recommend that we send a naval force to Batum with a force of Marines sufficient to guard the lines of communication and to contribute to the morale of the struggling Armenian forces. There never has been any serious doubt about granting recognition to the Armenian Republic, and there never has been any serious objection to permitting the organization of an Armenian military force in this country; that is to say, a force of volunteer Americans of Armenian origin, or Armenians in this country.[28]

In the meantime, the Allied High Commissioner for Armenia, Colonel W. N. Haskell, called attention to the dangerous predicament of this most threatened nation. Colonel Haskell, who was an American Army officer, reported that the Armenians were "surrounded by enemies and have not enough arms munitions or energy to protect themselves. . . ." "In the name of the future of these regions," he asked that the British Government be requested to revoke the evacuation order "until the question of the method of occupation shall have been decided."[29]

In spite of this warning, however, the British withdrew to Batum. In December, 1919, the Allies agreed upon a policy of assistance to border communities, "with non-Russian populations," and which had "been struggling for freedom and self-government," but they would only commit themselves to such assistance "as may be found desirable in the circumstances of each case as it arises."[30]

Finally, on April 23, 1920, the United States gave *de facto* recognition to Armenia. On May 14, the Senate suggested the use of a warship, with Marines—"ostensibly," as Senator Harding said, "to protect American lives and property," but with the actual intention of giving at least incidental relief to the struggling Armenians. The real purpose, Senator Harding said, was to maintain communication with the Armenian capital:

It was thought that the United States was going as far as it reasonably could to express its felicitations on the recognition of a new Republic there, and then for the relief of those peoples to ask the President to send a warship with marines to the port of Batum, ostensibly for the protection of American lives and property in that port and along the railway to the port of Baku. The real object, however, of the landing of marines is to guarantee the maintenance of a communication line through the port of Batum to Erivan.[31]

By this time the Bolsheviks were already in the Trans-Caucasus. On April 27, they had occupied Baku and organized a Soviet "government" for Azerbaijan. They had also attacked the Republic of Georgia, where they were repulsed and forced to agree once more to its independence. The peace treaty with Georgia, made on May 7, 1920, provided in part as follows:

Article I.   Based on the right proclaimed by the Russian Socialist Federated Soviet Republic of all peoples to fully dispose of themselves to the extent of and including total withdrawal from the State of which they form a part, Russia recognizes without reservations the independence and the sovereignty of the Georgian State, and voluntarily renounces all sovereign rights which belonged to Russia with respect to the Georgian people and territory.
    Article II.   Based on the principles proclaimed in the foregoing Article I, Russia agrees to renounce all intervention in the internal affairs of Georgia.[32]

In Armenia the Red Army was still engaged in hostilities, and an internal uprising had been instigated. There was also the threat of the Turks. Under these circumstances the Senate proposal was obviously inadequate. Since it was admittedly equivocal in its announced purpose, it was also subject to the same criticisms which were applicable to the secret support of General Kaledin. The President could not even be sure whether the Senators were trying to deceive the Bolsheviks by disguising the use of Marines as an effort to protect American citizens, or whether they were trying to deceive him by describing an ineffective gesture as an effective means of support for Armenia. He insisted on a mandate and a sincere, open approach:

The sympathy with Armenia has proceeded from no single portion of our people, but has come with extraordinary spontaneity and sincerity from the whole of the great body of Christian men and women in this country by whose freewill offerings Armenia has practically been saved at the most critical juncture of its existence. At their hearts this great and generous people have made the cause of Armenia their own. It is to this people and to their Government that the hopes and earnest expectations of the struggling people of Armenia turn as they now emerge from a period of indescribable suffering and peril, and I hope that the Congress will think it wise to meet this hope and expectation with the utmost liberality. . . .

. . . Our recognition of the independence of Armenia will mean genuine liberty and assured happiness for her people, if we fearlessly undertake the duties of guidance and assistance involved in the functions of a mandatory.[33]

Several Senators opposed this request with every argument at their command. Peace and the fear of war were uppermost in their minds, and it was obvious that the terror which had "cowed" the subject peoples was already beginning to take effect in the free world. Speaking against the mandate on May 31, Senator Reed stated:

. . . we have great Russia to reckon with. Russia controls, and for many years has controlled, a large section of this territory. To-day she is engaged in a war within her own borders, in a war with Poland, the result of which is that practically all her energies are there concentrated; and yet it appears, from the articles I have read, that she has still time and energy to send men, if not to send troops, into this very country. Is there a sane man on this earth who believes that Russia will forever be in trouble; that 180,000,000 people, who have maintained a civilization and a strong central government for centuries of time, is now wiped out; and that it is no longer a potential factor in the world's business?

Is there a sane man anywhere who believes that when Russia has reestablished peace within her own borders she will not create a central government of strength and power? Again, is there a sane man who believes that such a power will submit to the ravishment of the lands of Russia, and that England will be permitted to keep the Caucasus without a fight?

It follows, therefore, as day follows the night, that this territory which was Russian, Russia will again demand, and our little army of 60,000 troops will be instantly in peril. . . .[34]

On the following day, Senator McCormack added his fears to those of Senator Reed. "Senators," he warned, "will have noticed how the armies of Bolshevist Russia, the other day, came down the Caspian and along the shores through Daghestan past Baku and occupied the Persian port of Enzeli, flanking the greater part of the eastern frontiers of the proposed Armenia. Here is a promise that the American troops who finally were brought out of Russia, because of the insistence of Senators in this Chamber, may yet be returned to wage the same undeclared war they waged before."[35]

American troops, it seemed, were now to be withheld—not because of a desire to refrain from "interference"—but because they were deemed inadequate. The price of nonintervention in 1918 was thus already being paid in 1920. In July, 1920, the Reds invaded, and by the time the Treaty of Sèvres was executed, August 10, 1920, Armenia was under attack from the north and northeast by the Bolsheviks, and from the south by the Turks.

The Turkish invasion was instigated by the followers of Mustafa Kemal, who were leading Turkey in a successful revolution of its own. The Kemalists repudiated the Treaty of Sèvres, and on the very day it was executed Armenia was forced to sign a truce with the Bolsheviks, ceding several Armenian-populated regions to the newly established Communist regime in Azerbaijan.

The senators, however, had won their battle. The American mandate was rejected, and American troops did not return to the "undeclared war." The victory, of course, was a Pyrrhic one—they succeeded only in deferring a task which was later to require the deployment of many times the number of American troops in every part of the world. In the meantime, the price of this deferment was paid by the subject peoples.

Armenia's case next came up in the League of Nations, where it fared no better than it had in the United States Senate. Speaking in the Assembly, the British Secretary of State for Foreign Affairs described in one sentence what the free nations have done for the subject peoples in a period of forty years:

We give them words of encouragement, we express our horror at their position and our sympathy with their misfortunes, but so far we have not been fortunate enough to find a method of giving them effective aid.[36]

He apparently voiced the sentiments of a majority of the free nations, then and now, when he asserted that "the machinery of the League, as embodied in the Covenant, was not contrived to deal with the sort of situation with which we are confronted in Armenia."[37] The conclusion was the same as that which was reached in November, 1956, by the United Nations, with new machinery and a new covenant, when the free world was still being confronted with the same "sort of situation" in Hungary.

A Norwegian delegate, Dr. Fridtjof Nansen, suggested that 60,000 troops be sent to Armenia's defense. This would have been a force comparable to that suggested by the Harbord mission, but the proposal mustered small support. Finally, a resolution was adopted in which the Council was asked to persuade some power to assume the "task of taking necessary measures to stop the hostilities between Armenia and the Kemalists."[38]

This vague resolution was forwarded to the free nations verbatim, as a request for volunteers, and the replies were many and varied. It did not appear to call for any action against the Bolsheviks; and, in the light of prevailing attitudes, the words "necessary measures" could be interpreted, and were interpreted, in many different ways.[39]

Some small nations accepted the resolution as a request for military intervention and offered to co-operate to the extent of their ability. Panama, for example, stated that it was ready to "contribute effectively to the costs of any expedition," Denmark that it would participate in tasks which were not beyond its strength, and Peru that it was willing to collaborate "with all means in its power."

Other states, however, were less ready to co-operate. Some, like Honduras, offered "moral support." Others replied that they were too "far away." Australia asked for a clarification; and Nicaragua ambiguously reported that it "accepts" the resolution.

For the United States, President Wilson stated that he was "without authorisation to offer or employ military forces" and that "material contributions would require the authorisation of the Congress, which is not now in session and whose action I could not forecast." Considering the Senate's recent action, this was a generous understatement. All the President could offer was his "personal mediation," a contribution which was of no help in getting Armenia out of her difficulties, but which proved to be of immense value in getting big powers out of an embarrassing situation. Great Britain, for example, replied soon after that it would "second" the President's efforts with "moral and diplomatic support."

The replies of Spain, which offered to "co-operate in any action of a moral or diplomatic nature," and of Brazil, which stated that it would "assist, either alone or in conjunction with other Powers, in putting an end to Armenia's desperate position," were also taken as offers of mediation. Accordingly, France replied that she "follows with the greatest sympathy the work of the three mediatory Powers." Sweden also suggested that the President's offer was preferable to intervention on its part, and Uruguay expressed its pleasure at the proposal for "joint moral action."

While these replies were being submitted, Armenia capitulated. A rescue force of 40,000 men was proposed by the Rumanian delegate, but this also failed to draw support. The Assembly finally adjourned, noting that offers of mediation had been made, and resolving that it should "continue to cooperate with the Council."

In February, 1921, the Red Army attacked again in Georgia, not only from the north but also from Azerbaijan in the east, from Armenia in the south and along the Black Sea coast in the west. This time the small republic was quickly overwhelmed, and its government fled into exile. The Armenians, in the meantime, had rebelled and organized a new government, but still no assistance came from the free world. The Armenians were suppressed again, this time for good, in August.

The larger share of Armenia had been assigned by the Bolsheviks to the Turks, and the free nations now busied themselves with the negotiation of a new treaty. For two years they endeavored to persuade the Turks to provide a "National Home" for the Armenians, but eventually even this effort was abandoned. In July, 1923, the new treaty was signed at Lausanne, Switzerland, but there was no mention made of Armenia, or of the Wilson Award, or of the "National Home."

In the meantime, in the lesser known nations of the east, in Trans-Caspia, Turkestan, Central Asia and eastern Siberia, the Bolsheviks were permitted to repeat their aggressions. These were accomplished in the usual fashion, with wars and massacres too numerous to describe.[40] Most of these peoples, cut off from the outside world, were unable even to make appeals, and those who did so received a weak response or none at all.

The free world was afraid even to give membership in the League of Nations to those states which were threatened with Bolshevik aggression. As a result, admission was denied, in the first year, to the Baltic States, Georgia, Armenia, Azerbaijan and the Ukraine. By the time the First Assembly was in session, in November, 1920, Azerbaijan and the Ukraine had fallen, but there was extended discussion of the applications made by others. In the discussion on Armenia, the delegate of South Africa, Lord Robert Cecil, who was rapporteur for the committee concerned, expressed the general reluctance to admit states which the League might be called upon to defend.

"I feel," he said, that "the one thing we must not do with regard to Armenia is to hold out prospects of assistance which we do not intend to fulfill. That is the reason why I was unable to vote for her admission to the League.

"Under Article 10," Lord Cecil continued, "we are bound to preserve against external aggression the territorial integrity of every Member of the League, and to consider what it appears are the best steps to be taken for that purpose. It seemed to me very doubtful if all the members of the League intended to fulfill that obligation if Armenia was admitted, and I am quite certain that nothing could be more disastrous to this Assembly, or to any other institution, than to pretend you are going to do something you have no real intention of carrying out."[41]

When these words were spoken, on December 16, 1920, Armenia had already surrendered. This capitulation, like the fall of Azerbaijan and the Ukraine, supplied the majority of the League with a convenient, if specious, explanation for the denial of admission. In the case of the Baltic States and Georgia, however, no such ready solution was yet available, and the delegates of some of the smaller nations were unwilling to accept this travesty of the League's high purpose. The delegate from Colombia was palpably disturbed.

"The circumstances," he stated, "which are given as a reason for the refusal of the admission of the Baltic States consist of the presence of the Bolshevist State beside them. But the Bolshevist Government was the first to recognise these States! It negotiated with them, it recognised their independence because they had known how to defend it. It is said that the Bolshevists have not the right to recognise these States because they themselves are in need of recognition. Men are waiting for this monster to develop, and it is hoped that it will succeed in establishing itself as a Government which respects the right of other nations.

"I, on the contrary," he continued, "believe that it is the duty of the League of Nations to come to the help of all these States under Article 10 of which M. Viviani (France) has just reminded you. Otherwise, the League of Nations, which has just been created, and which has just, as it were, established its bank, will go bankrupt before opening its doors. This would mean bankruptcy for us and for the Great Powers, through fear of the Bolshevists. For it is Bolshevism which is troubling us here, and preventing us from approving the proposal and giving these States the moral assistance which the Assembly of the League of Nations owes them."[42]

Dr. Nansen, for Norway, had similar comments. "It has been objected," he said, "that there is a great deal of Bolshevism in that part of the world, and therefore it is doubtful whether we ought to have anything to do with that region; but I say that if we wish to fight Bolshevism we ought to have no hesitation and no doubt with respect to admitting Georgia into the League, because admitting her is a way of fighting Bolshevism and certainly not of helping it. To help Georgia to be a safeguard against Bolshevism is perhaps one of the most important things for us to attain in that part of the world."[43]

A British delegate defended the position of the majority: "Surely it is well to be prudent. It is well not to undertake risks, to assume responsibilities which we may feel ourselves inadequate to discharge. Is anything lost by such a course?"[44] The answer to this question was eventually supplied by history, but Dr. Nansen gave it immediately.

"I am afraid," he replied, "that if that should be the principle when we are considering the admission of new countries we shall not be able to admit any country into this League.

"I see greater danger, in refusing the admission of Georgia than in admitting her. I think that there is danger that this small nation, seeing no help from the League of Nations, may be pressed into the arms of those whom we do not wish to see politically her friends. We shall give support to all those forces that are now so strong in that part of the world if we refuse to allow Georgia to come into the League."[45]

The Baltic States were finally admitted in the following year, 1921, but when the Assembly met, Georgia had fallen. Its liberation was approached in the same way as its admission, and the situation was referred to a committee. In 1922, the committee reported that, in the view of some of its members, "it might be dangerous to suggest political or military action which it would be impossible for the League of Nations to undertake." Objection was made to any resolution which "might be considered provocative in relation to the Russian

Government."[46] Finally, more than eighteen months after Georgia had fallen, the following resolution was adopted by the Third Assembly:

The Assembly, having considered the situation in Georgia, invites the Council to follow attentively the course of events in this part of the world, so that it may be able to seize any opportunity which may occur to help in the restoration of this country to normal conditions by any peaceful means in accordance with the rules of international law.[47]

The interpretation of this jargon was supplied by the delegate from Belgium, in a statement addressed rhetorically to the people of Georgia:

The resolution gives you hope. That hope, and the knowledge that the justice which you claim will be yours, must banish all the promptings of despair from your hearts. Abstain from premature and violent action, which can only bring you to greater misery. Only keep the flame of liberty burning in your hearts and be content to wait in confidence.[48]

If waiting can bring contentment then the people of Georgia, as well as all of the subject peoples, must surely be happy.

CHAPTER V

FROM WAR TO "PEACE"

"Breathing Space" for the "Revolution"

AFTER the Bolsheviks had subjugated the larger part of the former Russian Empire, Lenin revived his efforts to obtain foreign economic assistance, informing the party that time out must be taken from military conquest in order to develop strength for its resumption at a later date. One of his talks on this subject was given on November 26, 1920, less than a fortnight after the last of Wrangel's army had left the Crimea, and a week before the surrender of Armenia. On this occasion Lenin pointed out that the peace made with Germany in 1918 had given the Bolsheviks a "breathing space"—a temporary respite from war—without which they could not have mobilized the force required to withstand the intervention of the free nations or to subjugate the peoples of Russia. "We made," he said, "a tremendous concession to German imperialism, and by making a concession to one imperialism we at once safeguarded ourselves against the persecution of both imperialisms.... It was just this period, which history accorded us as a breathing space, that we took advantage of in order so to consolidate ourselves that it became impossible to defeat us by military force."[1]

Now, Lenin said, both sides were getting a "breathing space," and it would be used by the Bolsheviks to build an even greater force, sufficient to subjugate all the people of the world:

Formerly, the war was conducted in the field in which the imperialists were infinitely stronger, the military field.... Nevertheless, we held our own in this field, and we undertake to continue the fight and are passing to an economic war....

Economically, we have a vast deal to gain from concessions.[2]

This was the same thesis advanced by Khrushchev nearly forty years later, when he called for "economic competition between socialism and capitalism," and stated that "the chief economic task of the

U.S.S.R." was "to overtake and surpass the most advanced capitalist countries in per capita output." As Khrushchev said, "Lenin taught that at different periods different aspects of Marxism come to the fore. Now . . . the economic aspect of Marxist theory, questions of practical economics, come to the fore."[3]

In the light of the estimates of Red Army strength at the time Lenin spoke, his deference to the military power of the free world might not seem to have been justified. Such estimates run as high as four and five million men. But at the same time, the Russian economy was ruined, and there was no way to provide arms, equipment and clothing for so large a force. Stores inherited from the Imperial Army, or from Allied aid to previous governments, were nearly exhausted, and the Bolsheviks needed to develop their own means of production.

Lenin further acknowledged that, in order to accomplish his purpose, the Bolsheviks would need the assistance of the free nations themselves. It would be necessary, he said, to "learn from them how to organise model enterprises," to "procure the last word in technology in the matter of equipment," and even to grant economic "concessions." For this, another "respite in war" was required, and Lenin was pleased to note the increasing quiescence of the free powers:

We have not one-hundredth of the forces of the combined imperialist states, and yet they are unable to stifle us. They cannot stifle us because their soldiers will not obey; their workers and peasants, fatigued by the war, do not want a war against the Soviet Republic.[4]

This unflattering opinion of the free peoples and of the morale of their armed forces might also seem unjustified, particularly in view of its source. But it was to some extent confirmed by the Allied leaders themselves. As recorded in the minutes of the discussions at Paris, the British Prime Minister, Lloyd George, had complained of just such an attitude as Lenin described—on the part of all the Allied troops. The "Canadian soldiers," he had said, "would not agree to stay and fight against the Russians." Similar trouble had also occurred amongst the other Allied troops. And he felt certain that, if the British tried to send any more troops there, there would be mutiny."[5]

President Wilson had stated that the reason "British and American troops were unwilling to fight in Russia" was "because they feared their efforts might lead to the restoration of the old order, which was even more disastrous than the present one."[6] He proved to be wrong on the latter count, and in connection with the first it might have been more accurate to say that the attitude of the troops was the result of the half-measures taken by their governments—which had failed to clarify their own aims or to support fully the cause of freedom. As Churchill stated, the soldiers did not know whether they were fighting for a common aim or "just marking time until the Allies had decided on policy." As the President himself confessed, they "did not know for whom or for what they were fighting."[7]

Under such conditions, a certain kind of military superiority was bound to be with the Bolsheviks—they could shoot every tenth or fifth man of each unit that refused to fight against its own freedom.[8] But now the Bolsheviks were running out of ammunition. Lenin had a plan by which they could acquire the means to produce it and at the same time paralyze any revival of interest in assisting the subject peoples. This twin result would flow from the lure of profits and trade—"a certain indirect guarantee of peace." "The states that might war on us," Lenin said, "will not war on us if they take concessions."[9]

These states, Lenin added, would be subjugated in their own turn, but only after the "economic war" had been won: ". . . as soon as we are strong enough to defeat capitalism as a whole, we shall immediately take it by the scruff of the neck."[10] Bolsheviks, he asserted, "have not forgotten that war will again return," and he frankly conceded that peaceful coexistence for any extended period was impossible:

As long as capitalism and socialism exist, we cannot live in peace: in the end, one or the other will triumph—a funeral dirge will be sung either over the Soviet Republic or over world capitalism.[11]

One of Lenin's close associates, Karl Radek, explained the proposed concessions to capitalism for the benefit of Communists in America. Writing in *The Communist*, then the official party organ in the United States, he described the plan as a revival of the proposal made through Colonel Raymond Robins in 1918—the proposal which Robins himself had described as designed to assist the Bolsheviks in the "economic reorganization" required to "equip and support a revolutionary army."[12] Radek stated that the approach made through Robins had been only one of several made to foreign nations at that time:

As early as the spring of 1918 the question of an economic

compromise faced the Soviet Government. When Colonel Raymond Robins, unofficial American representative in Russia, left Moscow for Washington on May 2, 1918, he took with him a concrete proposal of the Soviet Government containing the conditions of economic concessions. At the same time Bronski, assistant to the People's Commissar for Commerce and Industry, submitted in his first meeting with the representatives of the German Government practical proposals for the co-operation of the Soviet Government with German capital. Like proposals were communicated to Bruce Lockhart, the English representative to the British Government.

It may be granted that at that time, in the midst of the world war, there was ground for hope that a revolutionary explosion might do away with the necessity for such concessions, but the principal thing is that the policy of granting these concessions had already been arrived at.[13]

The only difference was that the lure of peaceful trade and private profits was now substituted for the hope of help in war with Germany.

The resumption of trade was the first requirement, and when Lenin spoke in November, 1920, the progress made in this direction was already substantial. The Allies had lifted their blockade and the United States had relaxed its own trade controls. Only one big obstacle remained—the problem of title to private property which the Bolsheviks had taken without compensation.

Normally, such property would be subject, in the courts of the free world, to the valid claims of lawful owners, and if these were to be enforced the Bolsheviks would have little to sell. An answer to the problem was soon worked out, however, in negotiations with Great Britain. The rights of the owners could be safely ignored if the free nations would simply give *de facto* recognition to the Bolshevik regime. Such recognition would effect a validation, binding on the courts, of all Soviet laws and decrees, including the seizures, regardless of the manner in which they were made.

It soon developed, however, that while many nations were willing in this fashion to waive the rights of the subject peoples, they were not willing to forget their own. They insisted upon compensation for property taken from foreign nationals and upon the payment, or at least recognition, of the foreign debt of previous Russian governments—all of which were repudiated by the Bolsheviks.

Nevertheless, in March, 1921, a trade agreement was made by Great Britain, *de facto* recognition was extended, and an official

British agent was stationed in Moscow. A few other nations took similar action. But still there was no substantial increase in trade. The Bolsheviks needed to borrow in order to buy, and no nation would lend to them because of their record of repudiation and confiscation. Even private loans and credits were discouraged by the belief that these too would be dishonored.

To meet these problems the British Prime Minister, David Lloyd George, suggested an international Economic and Financial Conference to which the Bolsheviks would be invited. In January, 1922, the invitation was extended by the Allied Supreme Council, which also announced the conditions upon which foreign capital might be made available and *de jure* recognition extended. These included the renunciation of aggression, termination of subversive propaganda, respect for the rights of foreign investors, recognition of the Russian foreign debt and compensation of foreign nationals, but no mention was made of the rights or freedom of the subject peoples.

Conferences were then held at Genoa and The Hague. They produced no general settlement, but the Germans were induced to conclude their own bilateral agreement with the Bolsheviks at Rapallo—dropping all claims against the Soviet regime. Settlements with the Bolsheviks on a bilateral basis were thereafter made by many other nations, and private credit became available when the Soviet regime established a high reputation for prompt payment of its own bills.

Within a few years, diplomatic relations and *de jure* recognition had been extended by many nations, and their courts confirmed the fact that it was no longer possible for them to question the validity of Bolshevik "laws" and "decrees." In an early test in England, after *de facto* recognition, the court stated:

This immunity follows from recognition as a sovereign state. Should there be any government which appropriates other people's property without compensation, the remedy appears to be to refuse to recognize it as a sovereign state.[14]

A similar ruling was made in 1937 by the Supreme Court of the United States in which it stated that the effect of recognition was "to validate, so far as this country is concerned, all acts of the Soviet Government here involved from the commencement of its existence."[15]

Presumably, these decisions applied, not only to the seizure of land, grain, mines, factories, savings, insurance, and other accumulations of capital, but also to homes, wearing apparel, the necessities of life, and even to the property of the Church—monasteries, schools, places of worship, relics, ikons and chalices torn from the bleeding hands of murdered priests. All such seizures were made pursuant to "laws" and "decrees" which were validated by these decisions.

Presumably, the decisions also applied to decrees and laws providing for acts of violence against the person. Presumably, such action also became valid in the eyes of the courts of the free world, with the result that the Bolsheviks and the henchmen of the Cheka were given permanent immunity from punishment—and their victims were denied redress—for countless murders, imprisonments, condemnations to forced labor, and all the other injustices of rule by terror perpetrated in accordance with the so-called laws of the Soviet Union. This was the meaning of recognition, generously granted, at the expense of the Russian peoples, by the mere fiat of free-world statesmen who were anxious to seem realistic, understanding or tolerant, and incidentally to ease the path of commerce and trade.

It was eventually demonstrated that such action was not even useful for the development of the limited amount of trade in which the Bolsheviks were willing to indulge. The highest prewar exports of the United States to the Soviet Union were made in 1930, without the benefit of either recognition or trade agreement, and exports during the early years of the Soviet First Five-Year Plan—that is, from 1928-31—exceeded in each year the exports made to the Soviet Union in any prewar year after recognition was extended or the trade agreement signed.

The Bolsheviks were only interested in priming the pump for the development of their own heavy industry, which was to be used for the production of armaments, not exports, and they were not about to purchase from the free world any more than the minimum required for this purpose. The situation was much the same as that described many years later by Secretary of State Dulles as prevailing in China:

The problem as I see it is this, that China has only a limited amount of foreign exchange with which to buy goods abroad, and the question is how high, in terms of strategic value, are the goods you are going to let China buy? It is, I think, highly doubtful that the total volume of China's foreign trade will be increased. ... instead of buying commodities of less strategic value they will concentrate their buying upon goods of higher strategic value, because their great effort today is to build up their war potential and their heavy industry that supports it.[16]

The only thing necessary on the part of the free nations was a desire, or at least a willingness, to contribute to this effort.

Initially, the Bolsheviks sought to accomplish their purpose by inviting investment of foreign capital. "Concessions" were offered in the form of rights to exploit the natural resources, and to operate mines, plants and other projects, subject always to a condition requiring the concessionaire to spend large sums in fixed installations and permanent improvements. For example, an agreement for the operation of manganese properties in Georgia required the expenditure by the operator of at least $1,000,000 for mine development and plant construction, $2,000,000 in railway equipment and construction, and another $1,000,000 for the construction of port facilities, with a yearly capacity of 1,200,000 tons of ore.[17] After termination of the agreements, which were not of long duration, these improvements were property of the Soviet Union.

Under the First Five-Year Plan, beginning in 1927, Stalin adopted a new procedure, offering quicker profits and less risk to the contractor. Contracts were made only for technical assistance, engineering and management advice, and the contractor would be paid directly for his services. Sometimes the contracts were accompanied by large but unrepeated orders for essential items, such as construction equipment and heavy machinery, but only when these could not be readily produced in the Soviet Union.

The terms of these contracts have been summarized by the United States Bureau of Foreign and Domestic Commerce:

At the outset of the first Five-Year Plan, the Soviet Union initiated the practice of negotiating contracts with foreign firms for the provision of technical assistance. Under such a contract, the firm agreed to place at the disposal of a specified Soviet agency, for a named consideration, all of its manufacturing skill and experience, blueprints, drawings, formulas, and engineering data to the extent necessary to enable the Soviet agency to manufacture a certain product or apply a particular process in a factory or mine in the Soviet Union, using native materials and labor. The contract might involve engaging the services of the firm, or of men selected by the firm, to erect plants, install machines, and introduce processes in the U.S.S.R., and otherwise assist Soviet engineers and workers to initiate a new form of manufacture.[18]

Under such an arrangement, the major investment, in labor and materials, was made by the Soviet Union; but as in the case of the earlier form of concessions, purchases could be held to a minimum.

Stalin launched the program with a great amount of publicity and a massive exchange of business delegations with the well-developed nations. During 1928-9, 133 special Soviet delegations, representing almost every important industry, came to the United States for on-the-spot study and to negotiate contracts.[19] More than 150 American firms were represented during 1929 in United States delegations to the Soviet Union.[20] An "American Business Delegation" of 100 was organized by the American-Russian Chamber of Commerce.

As a result, the Soviet Union was soon receiving the best business and technical advice available in every country, and a very large contribution was made by the United States. Two Americans in particular rose high in the confidence and trust of Stalin. One of these was John Calder, reputed to be one of the only two Americans permitted to discuss construction directly with the Red dictator. According to *The New York Times*, he ranked second among Americans in the trust and admiration of the Russians.[21] Calder was engaged to supervise construction of tractor plants at Stalingrad and Cheliabinsk, and later became adviser to Soyoustroy, the central Soviet agency for handling new construction. In this capacity he was given supervision of Stalmost, which controlled the Soviet steel-building program.

Even more favored than Calder was Hugh L. Cooper. He was selected, after a reported three-year world-wide search, to supervise the design and construction of the highly advertised dam and hydroelectric project at Dnieperstroi. He had already designed or advised in the construction of many similar projects in many other countries, including installations in the United States for the Missouri Electric Power Company, Toronto Power Company, Pennsylvania Water & Power Company and the plant at Muscle Shoals, Alabama.

With other American engineers, Cooper endeavored to popularize employment on Soviet projects, and to advertise the advantages of trade with the Soviet regime. For this purpose he became president of the American-Russian Chamber of Commerce; and according to its *Handbook of the Soviet Union*,[22] the campaign was eminently successful. The *Handbook* reports that, at the beginning of 1931, the Soviet Union had 134 technical-assistance contracts with foreign engineering firms, of which two-thirds were German or American. In addition, there were thousands of foreign engineers, foremen and skilled mechanics engaged under individual contracts of employment. In April, 1932, the number of such individuals engaged in heavy industry alone was 6,800. Many more were devoting full time to designs and plans in the home offices of the contracting firms.

In 1930, Ralph Budd, then president of the Chicago, Burlington & Quincy Railroad, and a former president of the Great Northern, was engaged to submit recommendations for the reorganization and improvement of Soviet railway transport. A delegation of thirty-five Soviet railway executives also came to the United States to study the American system. In the following year, 1931, half the locomotives and freight cars produced and sold by United States companies were sold to the Soviet Union.[23]

Top-grade American engineering firms were also employed in the development of the coal, coke and steel industries. Their tasks included the design and construction of plants at Kuznetsk, Zaporozhstal and Magnitogorsk. The latter, an integrated steel-development project, was supposed to become the largest in Europe and the equal of anything in the United States.

The Austin and Ford companies provided the design, supervision and technical assistance required for construction and start-up of the Maxim Gorky auto plant and its adjoining workers' city. Even now, when they are bragging of their own technological achievements, the Soviets make no attempt to conceal the assistance that was thus received. As Henry Ford II was told in 1959 by a Soviet First Deputy Premier:

... during that time [prior to United States recognition of the Soviet Union] your grandfather decided to recognize us. He helped to build our industry. He was smarter than your government.[24]

Industrial know-how, machinery, and equipment required in other fields were also obtained from the biggest and best—E. I. DuPont de Nemours & Co., International General Electric Company, Radio Corporation of America, Newport News Shipbuilding and Drydock Company, Electric Auto-Lite, Freyn Engineering Corporation, Stuart, James & Cooke, Sperry Gyroscope Company, and many others.

As a result, the Soviet industrial base was constructed very cheaply, insofar as foreign purchases were concerned. In the peak year 1930, Soviet imports from the United States were less than $115,000,000.[25] This figure, reached at the height of the First Five-Year Plan, was exceeded even by American exports to Yugoslavia, in 1951 and 1955. It is exceeded annually by American exports to Switzerland.

During the peak period, 1927-31, United States shipments to the Soviet Union consisted primarily of goods of high strategic value or required only for the production of the means of production. This included such items as metal-working machinery, forging machinery, foundry and moulding equipment, mining and quarrying equipment, stationary engines, water wheels, turbines, excavators, road making machinery, cranes, hoists, conveying equipment, pumps, locomotives and freight cars[26]—all no longer needed once the Soviet Union acquired the ability to produce them itself. By 1933, when the need for foreign equipment and technical assistance had tapered off, exports from the United States to the Soviet Union had fallen from the 1930 peak of $114,400,000 to a low of $8,997,307.[27]

The purpose of this program was stated by Stalin himself. In 1931, addressing the first conference of the "All-Union Communist Industrial Executives," he said:

The job we are doing, if it succeeds, will overturn the whole world and free the whole working class. For that we must learn and learn and learn and master the technique of industrial management and overcome our backwardness.

This is our duty not to the U.S.S.R. alone, but to the workers of the whole world, who now regard us as their vanguard, their "shock brigade" in the battle against capitalism, their fatherland.[28]

By 1934, at the 17th Congress of the Communist Party, he was able to boast of the progress he had made:

New industries have been created: machine-tool construction, automobile, tractor, chemical, motor construction, aircraft, harvester combines, the construction of powerful turbines and generators, high-grade steel, ferro-alloys, synthetic rubber, nitrates, artificial fibre, etc., etc.

During this period thousands of new, up-to-date industrial plants have been built and put into operation. Giants like the Dnieprostroi, Magnitostroi, Kuznetskstroi, have been built. Thousands of old plants have been reconstructed and provided with modern technical equipment. . . .

. . . .

The foundations have been laid for the Urals-Kuznetsk Combine, which unites the coking coal of Kuznetsk with the iron ore of the Urals. Thus, we may consider that the dream of a new metallurgical base in the East has become a reality.

The foundations for a powerful new oil base have been laid in the regions of the western and southern slopes of the Ural range. . . .[29]

The purpose was also revealed and fulfilled in the tremendous growth of power of the Red Army. Colonel Robins himself was able to observe it—the success of the plan which he had first carried from the hands of Lenin to the desk of President Wilson. In 1933, he revisited the Soviet Union, had a one and one-half hour interview with Stalin, and reported:

In 1918 I saw the first May Day celebration after the Bolshevist revolution—out at Khodinka Field, now Moscow's airport—on the personal invitation of Leon Trotsky. Fifteen hundred tattered soldiers of the Red Army, a few thousand "Red Guards" of the armed proletariat and an inchoate throng of workers streamed past the reviewing stand.

This year, after fifteen years, I watched in Red Square a parade of 15,000 picked troops of the Red Army with perfect discipline, equipment and every new device of mechanized warfare, while hundreds of bombing planes roared overhead in battle formation, and pursuit ships maneuvered in complicated acrobatics.[30]

In 1935, the Vice Commissar of Defense, Marshal Mikhail N. Tukhachevsky, reported on recent additions to the equipment of his once tattered soldiers. In two years, he said, the air force had been enlarged 330%, and in four years the number of light tanks had increased 760%, medium tanks 792%, heavy artillery 210%, army radio installations 1,560%, submarine tonnage 435%, coast guard vessels 1,000% and light torpedo craft 370%.[31] This was the same Tukhachevsky who, at the age of twenty-five, following the defection of General Muraviev, had been appointed commander of the First Red Army on the almost-broken Volga front, and who as field commander in the battle for Warsaw had seen the Red Army, for all its millions of men, unable to defeat the Poles. The number of the "picked troops" armed with the weapons he now described was 1,300,000.[32]

In the United States, meanwhile, the policy of the government had shifted from cold indifference to active encouragement of every kind of trade. Following the exchange of diplomatic relations (November, 1933), a formal trade agreement was made in 1935. So great had become the desire to ship goods to the Soviet Union that it was required to guarantee annual purchases of at least $30,000,000. Subsequently, this figure was raised to $40,000,000.[33]

Interest in trade, however, was not the only emotion prevalent in the free world at this time. Seeing the great expansion of Soviet industry, many became enthusiastic about it for its own sake, assuming that it would contribute to the welfare of the people, and forgetting or ignoring its cost in human suffering. Some were even willing to pass over those hideous excesses which hindered rather than contributed to its success. Mass arrests, show trials, forced labor, summary executions and all the other devices of a regime which subordinated the right and dignity of individuals to the alleged interests of the state—or of a new world order—came to be regarded by many as a deplorable, but inevitable, concomitant of Russia's economic development and the supposed advancement of the material welfare of its people.

Many came to believe, as Walter Duranty wrote in *The New York Times,* that the Red terror was "not a Bolshevik initiative but a necessary reply" to violent opposition—"a measure not of attack but of self-defense."[34] The Soviets, after all, were "fanatically devoted to their cause," and it was apparently considered that if human eggs were broken in the process of making the Marxist omelet, it was merely because their leaders were "altruists" who desired "the greatest good for the greatest number." There thus came about a growing popular tolerance of Communist excesses from which the free world has never fully recovered.

This was also the time of the great growth of Communist fronts, when hundreds of well-intentioned political and social groups were captured by the Communists, and when many persons innocently joined the countless others created by them. It was a time when liberal thinkers thought they could co-operate with Communists for the attainment of professed humanitarian ends without approving or adopting their less justifiable means, or furthering their more sinister aims. It was a time when Americans could applaud when told by people like George Bernard Shaw that the Soviet Union had been "saved by American machinery" and "American efficiency engineers" —that it already had become "one of the biggest industrial powers of the world, thanks to America."[35] Perhaps they could even agree with him when he said that Stalin was "distinguished by the fact that he is a Nationalist, a man who says . . . 'I will work for the salvation of Russia and let the other countries look after themselves.' "[36]

Before the disillusionment of such beliefs began, in 1939, the Soviets had sought and obtained approval for the construction, by American shipyards, of a Soviet battleship and other naval vessels. The arrangement also provided for the sale of plans of construction.[37] The United States even took pains to insure the high caliber of the design of these vessels—prohibiting the use of plans which were obsolete or untested.[38] This project was abandoned only after it was discovered that it would interfere with the United States' own naval-construction program.

What the Soviets really wanted, however, they had obtained during the First Five-Year Plan and they obtained again for nothing during World War II. United States lend-lease to the Soviet Union over a four-year period (1941-45) amounted to $9,477,666,000. Of this total, more than four and one-half billions represented munitions and another $3,000,000,000 was for "industrial materials and products."[39]

Even before this tremendous gift of lend-lease material, the Soviets claimed to be the strongest single power in the world. In March, 1939, Marshal Kliment Voroshilov, than Commissar of Defense, gave another run-down of the percentage growth and development of the Red Army. This report, covering the preceding five-year period, was summarized by the American *chargé d'affaires*. Numerical strength, he reported, had "slightly more than doubled" and "the fire power of the Soviet Army corps was superior to that of the army corps of any European army. . . ." Tanks had increased 191%, light artillery 34%, medium artillery 26%, heavy artillery 85%, anti-aircraft artillery 169% and airplanes 130%. Bombing planes "capable of speed far in excess of 500 kilometres an hour were not a rarity," and the bomb load capacity had increased from 2,000 tons to "slightly more than three times that amount."[40]

The Allied military experts could no longer talk of modern weapons, "armoured cars and bombing aeroplanes" as "equipment the Bolsheviki entirely lack,"[41] but Stalin, on the other hand, could now boast that "in case of war, the rear and front of our army . . . will be stronger than those of any other country. . . ."[42] He may have been bragging then, but his claim has since been conceded, even by the United States.[43]

Whether bragging or not, the Bolsheviks had come a long way since the day in 1920 when Lenin had said: ". . . from the military standpoint we were a nonentity. . . ." "We have not one-hundredth of the forces of the combined imperialist states. . . ."[44] This form of Soviet weakness was gone, never to return, and after nineteen years of waiting the Soviets were ready for a new round of aggression.

CHAPTER VI

ADVENT OF WORLD WAR II

The Second Round of Soviet Aggression

WHILE the Communist regime in Russia was building a base of arms production, and equipping the Red Army, the so-called bourgeois states were also recovering from the effects of the First World War, and by 1939 both sides were ready for the resumption of hostilities. The bourgeois states, however, had become more tolerant of the Soviets than of each other, and were preparing for a new war among themselves. The Soviets, on the other hand, were looking forward to a new opportunity for applying Lenin's maxim—"to take advantage of the antagonisms and contradictions existing among the imperialists":

... we must take advantage of the antagonisms and contradictions between two capitalisms, between two systems of capitalist states, inciting one against the other. As long as we have not conquered the whole world, as long as, from the economic and military standpoint, we are weaker than the capitalist world, we must adhere to the rule that we must know how to take advantage of the antagonisms and contradictions existing among the imperialists.[1]

In the nineteen years since Lenin made this statement, the Soviet regime had won a large degree of acceptance in the community of free nations. It had diplomatic and trade relations with all of the major powers, it was a signatory of the Kellogg-Briand antiwar pact, it had nonaggression pacts with the Baltic States, Finland, Poland, Germany, Turkey, Persia, Afghanistan and France, and it had been admitted to active and prominent membership in the League of Nations—an organization the Communists had once condemned as "nothing but an insurance policy in which the victors mutually guarantee each other their prey."[2] In short, while the non-Communist states fell apart, and talked of war, the Soviet regime in Russia appeared to have become the most devoted champion of disarmament, peace and justice among nations.

111

The original plans of the Bolsheviks, however, had by no means been given up—they had only been postponed. "We must not forget," Stalin had said, "what Lenin said about very much in our work of construction depending upon whether we succeed in postponing war with the capitalist world, which is inevitable, but which can be postponed. . . ." It could be so postponed, he said, "either until the moment when the proletarian revolution in Europe matures, or until the moment when the colonial revolutions have fully matured, or, lastly, *until the moment when the capitalists fight among themselves over the division of the colonies.*"[3] (Italics added.)

At the beginning of 1939, the "moment when the capitalists fight among themselves" had obviously been on its way for some time. It is not difficult to imagine what the Soviets were thinking in 1935, when the Italians invaded Ethiopia, or in 1938, when Hitler's armies marched into Austria and parts of Czechoslovakia. But in 1939, as the Axis powers prepared to move again—in Czechoslovakia, Lithuania and Albania—the Soviet leaders made no attempt to conceal their elation.

On January 21, 1939, the fifteenth anniversary of Lenin's death, a commemorative issue of *Pravda*, the Communist Party newspaper, announced that his advice was being followed to the letter. Its editorial asserted that the party was "putting into effect Lenin's directions regarding the necessity of utilizing the internal contradictions between imperialistic plunderers in the interests of the Soviet people and in the interests of the international proletariat."[4] One writer boldly stated that the period of postponement was drawing to a close. "The time is not distant," he said, "when the crimson banner of Marx-Engels, Lenin-Stalin will flow over the entire world, for the great truth of bolshevism and the tremendous force of Marxian-Leninist ideas are irresistible."[5] The author of this statement was Emelyan Yaroslavsky, director of the "League of the Militant Godless," whom the United States consul general and counselor to the American embassy, Alexander Kirk, described as one of the party's "leading theoreticians and historians." Yaroslavsky, Kirk reported, was speaking "for the Party as a whole."[6]

In March, 1939, Stalin called the Eighteenth Congress of the Communist Party and declared that a "new imperialist war" was "already in its second year."[7] Then, on the eve of the complete Nazi subjugation of Czechoslovakia, he asserted that the democratic nations were appeasing the Nazis because of their "fear of the revolution which may break out if the non-aggressive countries are drawn into a war and that war becomes world-wide." His tone made it clear that when he spoke of the fears of the free nations he was describing his own hopes. "Bourgeois politicians," Stalin said, "know that the first Imperialist War has made the revolution victorious in one of the greatest countries. They fear that a second Imperialist War may lead to the triumph of the revolution in one or more countries."[8]

The possibility of new revolutions, however, was only one of the fears arising out of World War II. Another foreseeable effect, of which the experience of WorldWar I gave ample warning, was the weakening of the non-Communist nations under the very shadow of the Soviet Union's new-found power and aggressive threat. A third possibility, and the most to be feared, was that the free nations would again seek Soviet help in war with Germany, and with the same result—that they would once more fail to fulfill their pledges of freedom for all peoples, forming even closer ties with tyranny and thereby dooming new movements, and wasting further opportunities, for the restoration of freedom in the Soviet Union.

The third possibility was the one most fully and disastrously realized. As the free nations had once come to Lenin and Trotsky, they now came to Stalin and Molotov, vainly seeking to persuade them to recreate an eastern front and avoid a separate peace. Again the Soviets rejected all advances, this time allying themselves with Hitler; and in the first stage of the war they succeeded, with the sole exception of Finland, in subjugating the rest of the former Russian Empire. In the second stage of the war—the Nazi invasion of the Soviet Union—the Communists were again shaken in the seat of their power, and the people were once more enabled to rise in rebellion. But the free nations still preferred to ally themselves with one tyranny against another, rather than with the people against both. In spite of adverse reaction to the massive purges recently completed by Stalin, the political repression, and the religious persecution, the belief persisted that the so-called new experiment in Russia was altruistic in its ultimate purpose, and therefore less to be feared than the corresponding "new world order" which the Nazis planned to impose with similar methods. The errors of World War I were thus compounded in World War II, the peoples of the Soviet Union were further weakened, and remained in subjection, while their oppressors were strengthened and allowed to proceed to new and even greater aggressions.

As in the First World War, the free nations were forewarned of Soviet intentions by their own diplomatic personnel in Russia, who gave them timely information that the Soviet leaders were only interested in their own expansion. One of those who gave such warning was Sir William Seeds, the British Ambassador to the Soviet Union. He decried the "innocents at home" who thought the Soviets were "only awaiting an invitation to join the Western democracies,"[9] and he advised that if the Soviets could be assured of their own safety they "would do everything in their power to keep out of the resulting struggle." In fact, he said, they would "feel considerable satisfaction at the prospect of an international conflict from which all the participants would be likely to emerge considerably weakened" and in which the Soviet Union would have the "opportunity of greatly strengthening its own position."[10]

A British embassy memorandum prepared in February, 1939, also pointed out that the Soviets would prefer the collapse of both the free and Fascist nations, and that they could gain from the defeat of Germany only if it would "lead to Soviet preponderance in Eastern Europe":

Although at the outset of a European conflict it seems likely that the Soviet would confine itself to a comparatively passive role, it would be liable to depart from this initial attitude in the light of subsequent developments. From a Soviet point of view perhaps the most satisfactory outcome of such a conflict would be the military, financial and political collapse of both sides. Such an eventuality would furnish the Soviet Union with an unrivalled opportunity to fish in troubled waters and to extend its influence by the methods so dear to it. Another solution eminently satisfactory from a Soviet point of view would be the collapse of Germany. Besides relieving this country of what is undoubtedly regarded here as a serious menace, it would lead to Soviet preponderance in Eastern Europe.... From the Western Powers, even though victorious, the Soviet Union would clearly have nothing to fear.[11]

Similar observations were made by Alexander Kirk who, in May, 1939, was transferred from his post in Moscow to Berlin. There his comments were considered of sufficient importance by the British Ambassador to Germany, Sir Nevile Henderson, to be made the subject of an official report to his own government. Kirk, he said, "spoke with great earnestness about the unwisdom of counting upon any effective support from Russia, in the event of war, *whatever she might say or promise*. Stalin was considering purely his and Russia's own interests which would be to sit still and do nothing while Europe destroyed itself and communism spread."[12] (Italics added.)

Other experts in the State Department were of the same belief, as was indicated in a memorandum prepared by Loy W. Henderson, then Assistant Chief of the Division of European Affairs. Henderson, who later became a Deputy Under Secretary, had spent five years in the Moscow embassy. His comments were based largely on the split between Germany and Poland which occurred after the latter's refusal to join the Nazis in war with Russia. This event, he said, removed the principal fears of the Soviet regime and thereby also eliminated any interest it might have in alliance with the free world—except upon a basis which would give it "hegemony over Eastern Europe":

So long as Germany and Poland were collaborating and there appeared to be a possibility that they might join in an attack upon the Soviet Union, the Soviet foreign policy with regard to Europe was based upon Soviet demands for so-called collective security, which in essence would have meant a Europe divided into two camps, in one of which the Soviet Union would have been playing a leading role.

The break which took place between Poland and Germany last March, followed by British guarantees to Poland and Rumania, has changed the whole international outlook so far as the Soviet Union is concerned. At present for the first time the Soviet leaders are in no immediate dread of either a German-Polish combination or of a great four-Power European settlement.

As a result of this change the Soviet Union has no longer any deep interest in the policy of collective security. It feels itself relatively safe from a dangerous European attack so long as Poland, supported by Great Britain, is at loggerheads with Germany. It is not anxious to enter into any European arrangement at the present time which may restrict its ability to maneuver. If it does come to terms with Great Britain, it will do so only on a basis which will give it what amounts to hegemony over Eastern Europe, and which will render impossible for at least many years to come a united Western Europe.[13]

Nevertheless, in spite of all such warnings, the British and French persistently sought Soviet aid, and they urged the Baltic States and Poland to do likewise. The Soviets, however, wanted "defensive" military bases in these countries, and their proposals were little more than poorly disguised attempts to make any German move an excuse for permanent Soviet occupation. They were thus met with stiff opposition from the free governments of these small nations, which had not forgotten the attacks of 1918-20, and were well aware of the real Soviet intentions. In fact these governments were certain that for them, at least, an attempted alliance with tyranny meant the end of independence. Their warnings, accordingly, were added to those of the Allied representatives in Moscow. The Baltic States requested that there be no mention of them in any pact, on either side, and the Poles consistently refused to accept any arrangement which would authorize the use of the Red Army in Poland.

The Soviets themselves left little doubt of their purpose. In March, 1939, they advised the governments of Estonia and Latvia that any collaboration with the Nazis, voluntary or involuntary, would serve as an excuse for invasion. The note to Estonia, which contained the usual assurances of the high Soviet regard for the independence of peoples, made it plain that the inevitable course of events would be the occasion for renewed Soviet aggression:

... the Soviet Government has invariably attached, and continues to attach great importance to the integrity and independence of the Estonian Republic, as well as of the other Baltic Republics, a condition which is consistent with the vital interests of the Soviet Union as well as with the interests of the peoples of these republics. Accordingly, it must be clearly understood that any agreement whatever, whether or not concluded "freely" or under duress, which will result in any diminution or restriction of the independence and sovereignty of the Republic of Estonia, or its submission to the domination, political, economic, or otherwise, of a third nation, or the extension to such nation of any exclusive rights or privileges whatever, whether on the territory of Estonia or in its seaports, will be considered by the Soviet Government as intolerable and as incompatible with the necessary implications and spirit of the above-mentioned treaties and agreements [Peace Treaty, February 2, 1920; Non-Aggression Pact, May 4, 1932] which at the present time govern its relations with Estonia, and even as a violation of these agreements with all the consequences which may flow therefrom.[14]

The French Foreign Minister, Georges Bonnet, asserted that in the light of this demand Soviet proposals made to France and Great Britain, for joint action in the event of "aggression" by Germany, were exposed as little more than requests for the approval of aggression by the Soviet Union. His comments were reported to the

State Department by William C. Bullitt who, after serving as Ambassador to the Soviet Union (1933-36), had become Ambassador to France:

> Bonnet went on to say that in view of this note of the Soviet Government to Estonia the word "aggression" in the Soviet Government's proposal to France and Great Britain wore a sinister aspect. It could be interpreted to mean that at any time that the Soviet Government should decide to march troops into Finland, Estonia, Latvia, Poland or Turkey because of some event which it chose to consider aggression, although the state concerned might not consider it aggression, the French and British Governments would be obliged to support a Soviet invasion of the state that the Soviet Union chose to invade. In other words, the Soviet proposal meant carte blanche for the Soviet Union to invade the states named in the Soviet note with French and British consent and support.[15]

At this time, however, the free nations were unwilling to agree to such a price, and M. Bonnet continued with the statement that neither his government nor that of Great Britain had any intention of doing so. According to Bullitt's report, the French Foreign Minister asserted that "France and England could certainly not consent to giving the Soviet Union support for an extension of bolshevism in Eastern Europe"—"the entire moral position of France and Great Britain was based on their defense of the freedom of peoples."[16]

The French analysis was confirmed by the British representatives in Moscow. From there, the British Ambassador reported discreetly that the Soviet Union desired "to have some international warrant for going to the assistance of the Baltic States, even perhaps without the assent or contrary to the wishes of the Governments concerned."[17] The report of the British Military Mission, made by Admiral Sir Reginald Drax, stated more bluntly:

> The Soviet aims in Poland and Rumania were, of course, not stated to us, but they made fairly clear the fact that they coveted certain ports and islands in the Baltic, which we were to grab for them! When we had annexed and fortified them, and accepted all the odium for so doing, the Soviet Fleet would graciously join us there. . . . Their plan is very suggestive of duplicity and bad faith, which is only to be expected from the type of men who govern Russia today. They can probably be relied on for shiftiness in negotiating a treaty and dishonesty in executing it. I therefore feel that, in the

long run, it may well prove fortunate that they allied themselves to Germany and not to us.[18]

As this report indicated, the Soviets had by this time made a "Non-Aggression Pact" with Germany, on August 23, 1939. There was also a "Secret Additional Protocol," which confirmed the worst suspicions of the Western Allies and the well-grounded fears of the border nations. In this protocol, only a week before the Nazi invasion of Poland, eastern Europe was divided into German-Soviet "spheres of influence." Finland, Estonia, Latvia, half of Poland and part of Rumania were assigned to the Soviet sphere:

1.   In the event of a territorial and political transformation in the territories belonging to the Baltic States (Finland, Estonia, Latvia, Lithuania), the northern frontier of Lithuania shall represent the frontier of the spheres of interest both of Germany and the U.S.S.R. In this connection the interest of Lithuania in the Vilna territory is recognized by both Parties.

2.   In the event of a territorial and political transformation of the territories belonging to the Polish State, the spheres of interest of both Germany and the U.S.S.R. shall be bounded approximately by the lines of the rivers Narev, Vistula, and San.

The question whether the interests of both Parties make the maintenance of an independent Polish State appear desirable and how the frontiers of this State should be drawn can be definitely determined only in the course of further political developments.

In any case both Governments will resolve this question by means of a friendly understanding.

3.   With regard to South-Eastern Europe, the Soviet side emphasizes its interest in Bessarabia. The German side declares complete political *désintéressement* in these territories.[19]

It was obvious from this agreement that the Soviets had been negotiating with the Nazis, as well as with the British and French, for the best price in terms of the subjugation of peoples and the enslavement of nations. The Nazis, of course, had been the highest bidder.

The "secret" provisions of the pact were no secret to the free nations, or at least to the United States. On August 24, 1939, the day after the public announcement, the American Ambassador in Moscow, Laurence A. Steinhardt, reported them, with astonishing accuracy, to the Department of State. "I am informed in strict confidence," he related, "that a full 'understanding' was reached last night between the Soviet and German Governments in reference to territorial questions in Eastern Europe whereby Estonia, Latvia, eastern Poland, and Bessarabia are recognized as spheres of Soviet vital interest. Apparently, Finland was not mentioned."[20] This information was, of course, correct except as to Finland.

Nevertheless, the urge for an alliance with the Soviets continued unabated. After the partition of Poland by Germany and the Soviet Union, Winston Churchill, who was then First Lord of the British Admiralty, stated on October 1, 1939:

We could have wished that the Russian Armies should be standing on their present line as the friends and allies of Poland, instead of as invaders. But that the Russian Armies should stand on this line was clearly necessary for the safety of Russia against the Nazi menace.

At any rate the line is there, and an Eastern Front has been created which Nazi Germany does not dare assail.[21]

The British Secretary of State for Foreign Affairs, Viscount Halifax, also seemed to condone the Soviet advance. Speaking in the House of Lords, he said: ". . . it is right to remember two things: Firstly, that they [the Soviets] would never have taken that action if the German Government had not started it and set the example that they did set when they invaded Poland without any declaration of war. In the second place, it is perhaps, as a matter of historical interest, worth recalling that the action of the Soviet Government has been to advance the Russian boundary to what was substantially the boundary recommended at the time of the Versailles Conference."[22] A comparable attitude today would tolerate the seizure of a Soviet bridge to Syria, across Turkey, as this would merely advance the boundary of the "Armenian Soviet Socialist Republic" to what was substantially the boundary recommended for Armenia by President Wilson in 1920.

In May, 1940, after the Soviet war with Finland, a new British Ambassador, Sir Stafford Cripps, was sent to the Soviet Union with special instructions to improve relations. In October, 1940, after the Soviet seizure of the Baltic States and Bessarabia, he offered a British commitment to make no peace with Germany without consulting the the Soviets, and to make no agreement with third powers directed against the Soviet Union. It is believed that he also offered *de facto* recognition, until the end of the war, of the new Soviet annexations.[23] The Soviets, however, were now looking for more, and the British offers were again rejected.

Although the United States was not involved in the war, its policies were also designed to attract the friendship of the Soviet rulers rather than of the subject peoples. This accounted for hesitation in the support of Finland's resistance to Soviet demands, and for the fact that the provisions of the Neutrality Act were not invoked against the Soviet Union.[24] Cordell Hull, who was Secretary of State at that time, says in his memoirs that "we still wanted to refrain from making Russia a legal belligerent." "I could not but feel," he relates, "that the basic antagonisms between Communist Russia and Nazi Germany were so deep, and Hitler's ambitions so boundless, that eventually Russia would come over to the side of the Allies. We had to be careful not to push her in the other direction."[25]

Accordingly, while Poland and the Western Allies were required to purchase goods on a "cash-and-carry" basis, it was still possible for the Soviet Union to obtain American arms on credit, delivered in American ships. It was thus made to appear that those who could be relied upon for loyalty were given less consideration than those who could not, and that the feelings of the Soviet aggressors took precedence over those of the Western Allies, who were fighting either in self-defense or for the defense of others.

While such efforts to win over the Soviets were fruitless for the free nations, they were not devoid of value for the Soviets, or without their effect upon the fate of eastern Europe. One most notable effect was the failure of the British to include a provision for defense against Soviet aggression in its guarantee to Poland. This omission, fatal for Poland, was not generally known at the time.

In April, 1939, an official communique, issued in London, announced that a permanent agreement would be made between Poland and Great Britain to provide for "mutual assistance in the event of any threat, direct or indirect, to the independence of either."[26] An unpublished "Confidential Summary of Conclusions" made it clear, however, that the guarantee was directed only against Germany. It provided that "If *Germany* attacks Poland His Majesty's Government in the United Kingdom will at once come to the help of Poland."[27] (Italics added.)

The formal agreement was not signed until August 25, 1939, two days after the announcement of the Nazi-Soviet Pact, but still there was no provision for the possibility of aggression by the Soviet Union. As publicly announced, the agreement provided for mutual aid in the event that either party should "become engaged in hostilities with a European Power in consequence of aggression by the latter." But a secret protocol stated: "By the expression 'a European Power' employed in the Agreement is to be understood Germany." In the event of hostilities with a "European Power other than Germany," it was agreed only that the "Parties will consult together on the measures to be taken in common."[28]

With this attitude on the part of the free nations, it would seem a foregone conclusion that no action would be taken when the Soviet invasion of Poland did occur. The Nazis invaded Poland on September 1, 1939, and the British and French declared war on Germany on September 3. On September 7, the United States was asked to inform the Soviet Union that France and Great Britain would also consider a Soviet attack as an act of war.[29] The Soviet attack was made on September 17, and on the 18th it was condemned as a "flagrant aggression,"[30] but no declaration of war was ever made. The British and French embassies in Moscow advised against it because of "the danger of precipitating complete military and economic cooperation between Germany and Russia."[31] The desire to placate the Communists had prevailed.

At the same time, the Soviets did everything possible, short of refraining from aggression, to encourage this result. Rumors of the "Secret Protocol" were denounced as "malicious inventions,"[32] and Molotov was vehement and categorical. "There are wiseacres," he said, "who construe from the pact more than is written in it. For this purpose, all kinds of conjectures and hints are mooted in order to cast doubt on the pact in one or another country."[33]

To create the illusion that they had no predatory intentions, the Soviets delayed their advance into Poland until the German armies had reached the Bug River and the approximate limits of the Curzon Line. They asserted that they were acting only in "self-defense," and for the "protection" of Byelorussian and Ukrainian minorities. They thus put the odium of aggression on Germany, as they had earlier sought to put it on Great Britain.

The reasons for this delay were only gradually admitted to the German Ambassador—after repeated Nazi requests for prompt Soviet occupation of the assigned areas. The first such request was made on September 3, 1939, the day on which France and Great Britain declared war on Germany. On the 5th, Molotov replied that "excessive haste" might "injure our cause and promote unity among our opponents"[34] [meaning, presumably, that it might bring a declaration of war against the Soviet Union]. On the 9th, Molotov promised action "within the next few days"[35] and sent his "congratulations" on the "entry of German troops into Warsaw."[36] Finally, on the 10th, he frankly explained the Soviet position, and the German Ambassador reported as follows:

... Molotov came to the political side of the matter and stated that the Soviet Government had intended to take the occasion of the further advance of German troops to declare that Poland was falling apart and that it was necessary for the Soviet Union, in consequence, to come to the aid of the Ukrainians and the White Russians "threatened" by Germany. This argument was to make the intervention of the Soviet Union plausible to the masses and at the same time avoid giving the Soviet Union the appearance of an aggressor.[37]

Thereafter, the conversations were dominated by Molotov's explanations of how this appearance would be avoided. One method was to let the Germans do most of the work; and on September 14, the German Ambassador reported that Molotov had in effect so indicated:

For the political motivation of Soviet action (the disintegration of Poland and protection of "Russian" minorities), it was of the greatest importance not to take action until the governmental center of Poland, the city of Warsaw, had fallen. Molotov therefore asked that he be informed as nearly as possible as to when the capture of Warsaw could be counted on.[38]

On the 15th, the Nazis protested. The German Ambassador was instructed to propose a "joint communiqué" in which both governments would assert their desire to "bring about a new order" in "the former Polish state" by the creation of "natural frontiers and viable economic organizations." The hope was expressed that the Soviets had "given up the idea ... of taking the threat to the Ukrainian and White Russian populations by Germany as a ground for Soviet action." The "assignment of a motive of that sort," according to the German Foreign Minister, would be "out of the question in practice," "directly contrary to the true German intentions," "in contradiction to the arrangements made in Moscow," and "in opposition to the desire for friendly relations expressed on both sides."[39]

Molotov, however, said a joint communique was unnecessary,

and the German Ambassador reported on the 16th that "the Soviet Government intended to justify its procedure as follows":

The Polish State had disintegrated and no longer existed; therefore, all agreements concluded with Poland were void; third powers might try to profit by the chaos which had arisen; the Soviet Union considered itself obligated to intervene to protect its Ukrainian and White Russian brothers and make it possible for these unfortunate people to work in peace.[40]

The report also indicated that Molotov had decided to meet head on, and brazenly minimize, the natural Nazi resentment:

Molotov conceded that the projected argument of the Soviet Government contained a note that was jarring to German sensibilities but asked us in view of the difficult situation of the Soviet Government not to stumble over this piece of straw. The Soviet Government unfortunately saw no possibility of any other motivation, since the Soviet Union had heretofore not bothered about the plight of its minorities in Poland and had to justify abroad, in some way or other, its present intervention.[41]

Rarely has the free world been favored with such a first-hand account of the real basis of a public explanation of aggression.

There was, of course, even less concern for the feelings of Poland, and on the day of the Soviet invasion the Polish Ambassador received a note from the Commissariat of Foreign Affairs containing all the prearranged formulae. "The Polish-German War" had "revealed the internal bankruptcy of the Polish State"; the government of Poland had "disintegrated" and "ceased to exist"; and its agreements with Russia had "ceased to operate." "Left to her own devices and bereft of leadership," Poland had "become a suitable field for all manner of hazards and surprises, which may constitute a threat to the U.S.S.R." Accordingly, the Soviets could no longer observe their "neutral attitude" or "view with indifference" the "defenceless" condition of "kindred Ukrainian and White Ruthenian people." The Red Army had been ordered to take their "life and property" under its "protection," and the Soviet government proposed "to extricate the Polish people" themselves "from the unfortunate war into which they were dragged by their unwise leaders."[42]

By the end of September, 1939, Polish resistance had crumbled;

and on the 28th, the two aggressors published a new agreement in which they openly defined "their respective national interests in the territory of the former Polish state." This agreement also included another "Secret Additional Protocol" redefining the assigned "spheres of influence" in the rest of eastern Europe. The net effect was to give Germany a larger share of Poland, while the Soviets received the greater part of Lithuania. The secret protocol also laid the basis for a joint reign of terror. "Both parties," it provided, "will tolerate in their territories no Polish agitation which affects the territories of the other party. They will suppress in their territories all beginnings of such agitation and inform each other concerning suitable measures for this purpose."[43]

In the meantime, the Soviets had turned their attention to the Baltic States, where they now insisted upon the acceptance of "Mutual Assistance Agreements." With the Nazis and Soviets co-operating, further resistance seemed futile, and the three states were soon persuaded to comply (Estonia, September 28, 1939; Latvia, October 5, 1939; and Lithuania, October 10, 1939). Occupation rights and strategic bases, so stoutly withheld a few months before, were now peacefully surrendered in the vain hope that free government might be allowed to continue.

In this new gambit both aggressors insisted upon preserving the appearance of international rectitude—with the bizarre result that the Nazis even rejected their allotted share of Lithuania. The Soviets insisted that it be transferred from Lithuania directly to Germany, while the Nazis requested that it be ceded to them by the Soviet Union. The Soviet Union, the Nazis urged, would acquire it "legitimately" in exchange for the Vilna territory which the Soviets were at that time transferring from Poland to Lithuania. The German Ambassador in Moscow reported:

It seemed to me more logical that the Soviet Government should exchange Vilna for the strip to be ceded to us and then hand this strip over to us. . . .

Molotov's suggestion [for a transfer direct from Lithuania to Germany] seems to me harmful, as in the eyes of the world it would make us appear as "robbers" of Lithuanian territory, while the Soviet Government figures as the donor.[44]

It was indeed a gullible world in which there could be such "honor among thieves." In the end, Hitler sold the strip to Stalin for $7,500,000.

The extra effort required for such pretense was not wasted. The free world acquiesced, and Secretary of State Hull records that because the three Baltic States "nominally" retained "their governments and independence, there was no diplomatic step we felt called upon to take."[45] This was a significant victory for the Communists, for if even diplomatic steps are barred because "nominal" independence is retained, they can dominate the world with impunity. All Soviet satellites are nominally independent—with governments "of their own," but not of their own choosing. Even the "governments" of the Ukraine and Byelorussia, which are parts of the U.S.S.R., have been treated as "independent" and have been given seats in the United Nations.

Actually, there was little practical doubt of what the Soviets were up to in the Baltic States. They had just seized eastern Poland, and it was known that they had used the terms of the secret protocols with Germany to convince Lithuania that further resistance was useless. The United States Minister in that country reported on October 13, 1939 that the Lithuanians were informed of the protocols almost at the beginning of negotiations for their surrender:

They discovered shortly after the conference began in Moscow that originally they had been included in the German "sphere of influence." However, Germany had seen fit to trade Lithuania and the region of Latvia as far north as Riga in this matter of influence spheres in exchange for the territory of Poland between the Bug and the Vistula rivers. . . . On being apprised of this, the Lithuanian delegation set their course and fully cooperated with the Russian Government.[46]

Documents captured from the Germans[47] indicate that the Finns were likewise advised—perhaps in the expectation of producing the same reaction.

When the Soviet Union made similar demands upon Finland, President Roosevelt was induced to intercede, but the Secretary of State continued to advocate a conciliatory attitude.[48] The result was a mild suggestion from the United States that the Soviet Union make no demands "which are inconsistent with the maintenance and development of amicable and peaceful relations between the two countries, and the independence of each."[49] The Soviets replied by denouncing "the tendentious versions" of their demands being "disseminated by circles evidently not interested in European peace." Their "sole aim," they asserted, was "a strengthening of friendly cooperation."[50] Two weeks later, however—on November 30, 1939— the Soviets invaded.

Following the pattern set by Lenin, the Soviets produced a ready-made Communist regime and called it the "Democratic Government of Finland." It was headed by a Finnish Communist, Otto Kuusinen, who was then a secretary of the Executive Committee of the Communist International. In 1941, he was appointed to the Central Committee of the Communist Party of the Soviet Union, and has since become one of its secretaries and a member of its Presidium.

The United States now reacted with strong words of condemnation. Two days after the attack, the President asserted:

> The news of the Soviet naval and military bombings within Finnish territory has come as a profound shock to the Government and people of the United States. Despite efforts made to solve the dispute by peaceful methods to which no reasonable objection could be offered, one power has chosen to resort to force of arms. It is tragic to see the policy of force spreading, and to realize that wanton disregard for law is still on the march. All peace-loving peoples in those nations that are still hoping for the continuance of relations throughout the world on the basis of law and order will unanimously condemn this new resort to military force as the arbiter of international differences.[51]

But there were no actions to match these words. A "moral embargo" was imposed upon the shipment to the Soviet Union of items useful in aerial warfare, and a small amount of military equipment was released for sale to Finland. Finland also received a $10,000,000 credit for the purchase of agricultural products; but as Secretary of State Hull reports, these were but "modest steps," and "far too small" for successful resistance.[52]

The other free nations, however, were by now convinced that stronger action was necessary. When the Soviet Union refused to respond to a League of Nations inquiry, it was expelled. This action was taken on December 14, 1939, two weeks after the attack, and the other League members were requested to give military assistance to Finland. Many promised volunteers and military equipment, and the British and French prepared to send a joint expeditionary force. As a result, the Soviets soon settled for less than the destruction of Finnish independence, and again avoided a declaration of war by major powers. Peace was made with Finland on March 12, 1940, and no more was heard about the "Democratic Government" of Otto Kuusinen, or the "treaty" which it had made with the Soviet Union.

Soon, however, the free nations of Europe suffered the collapse for which the Soviets had been waiting. In April, 1940, Norway was occupied by the Nazis, and the fall of France followed in June. The French-British expeditionary force was now out the question, and further Soviet demands were made upon Finland[53] and also on the Baltic States.

The fall of the Baltic States was speedily accomplished. Ultimatums were delivered to Lithuania, on June 14, 1940, and on June 16 to Latvia and Estonia. Alleging a military alliance "directed against the Soviet Union" in "violation" of the Mutual Assistance Agreements, the Soviets demanded "governments" that would be "capable and willing to warrant" their "honest execution."[54] Shortly thereafter, the free governments were expelled, Soviet regimes were "elected," and in the first week of August all three nations were made parts of the Soviet Union.

This action was also denounced by the free nations, but it was now more difficult to intervene, and only diplomatic steps were taken. The United States asserted that the independence of the Baltic States was being "deliberately annihilated."[55] Their annexation was not recognized either by the United States or Great Britain, and foreign credits were blocked to prevent acquisition by the Soviets. Still the United States continued to treat the Soviet Union as a nonbelligerent under the terms of the Neutrality Act.

The next Soviet move was made in Rumania, where the provinces of Bessarabia and northern Bukovina were occupied. Rumania, like the Baltic States, was forced to yield peacefully. It was also compelled, by the Nazis, to give slices of territory to Hungary and Bulgaria. In place of the guarantee received the year before from Great Britain and France, it now received a guarantee, of what remained of its territory, from Germany and Italy.

The Nazis then suggested that it was time for the Soviet Union to join the Axis. They proposed a new four-power pact (Germany, Italy, Japan and the Soviet Union), with more secret protocols and further assignments in Europe, Asia and Africa. The Soviet Union was offered a southward expansion, "in the direction of the Indian Ocean,"[56] but its rulers were not willing to be thus diverted from their designs in Europe. They asked for further information about Axis plans nearer home—in Greece, the Balkans, Central Europe, Sweden and the approaches to the Baltic Sea,[57] and in the quarrel which followed the free nations obtained the opportunity to turn Lenin's own advice against him—"when thieves fall out, honest men come into their own."[58]

Hitler indicated that the Soviets were looking in the wrong direction—the new partners must "stand not breast to breast but back to back, in order to support each other in the achievement of their aspirations."[59] He also said that there must be no more war with Finland,[60] which had been forced again, as in 1918, to seek the aid of Germany.

The Soviets countered with a list of conditions for acceptance. German troops must be withdrawn from Finland; Bulgaria must be added to the Soviet "sphere of influence"; and the Soviet Union must have rights in the Bosporus and the Dardanelles. To provide against probable Turkish objections, Germany, Italy and the Soviet Union should agree to jointly take "the required military and diplomatic measures."[61]

These conditions were too much for Hitler, and his plans to "liquidate" the Soviet Union were prepared within a month. The Soviet counter-proposal had been presented on November 25, 1940, and the first order of "Operation Barbarossa," the Führer's directive to "crush Soviet Russia," was dated December 18.

If the free nations had at this point been prepared to assist the subject peoples instead of the Communists, their task would have been easy. The Nazis and the Soviets were soon attempting to annihilate each other, and in the invaded areas the people rebelled against both tyrannies. But the free nations were not so prepared, either organizationally or psychologically. They had no contacts with the people, they did not believe that the Communists were their "real adversaries," and they did not trust the advice of Lenin, that two adversaries could be defeated by simply "inciting one against the other." One of them—the Axis—had to be singled out for defeat, and the other—communism—assisted to victory. It was proven in the end, however, that Lenin was the wiser. The remedy prescribed by the free nations was worse, and less curable, than the ailment.

In the meantime, prior to the Nazi invasion, the people in the

Soviet "sphere" had already experienced the usual methods of Soviet subjugation. Liquidations and deportations were carried out on a huge scale, and "elections" were held in which the new Soviet regimes received "overwhelming support." By June, 1941, nearly two million people had been deported to remote places in the Soviet Union, including more than 1,600,000 men, women and children from Poland alone.

Even this horror had its purpose, however, for the free nations, lulled during a period of nineteen years into a feeling of complacency, were again undeceived. The warnings of the diplomats had been confirmed, and there was no one who could now validly plead ignorance of the real aims and methods of communism. In February, 1940, after less than seven months of the war, the President himself pointed this out to members of the American Youth Congress, a group which he knew to be exceedingly prone to Soviet deception:

And I, with many of you, hoped that Russia would work out its own problems and their government would eventually become a peace-loving, popular government with free ballot, a government that would not interfere with the integrity of its neighbors.

That hope is today either shattered or is put away in storage against some better day. The Soviet Union, as a matter of practical fact, as everybody knows, who has got the courage to face the fact, the practical fact known to you and known to all the world, is run by a dictatorship, a dictatorship as absolute as any other dictatorship in the world.

It has allied itself with another dictatorship and it has invaded a neighbor so infinitesimally small that it could do no conceivable, possible harm to the Soviet Union, a small nation that seeks only to live at peace as a democracy and a liberal forward-looking democracy at that.[62]

In the beginning of the war, therefore, the free world was again made acquainted with real Soviet intentions. But once more, as in World War I and the period which followed, its own wishful thinking and inordinate self-interest made it an easy prey for Soviet blandishment—and this time far more quickly.

CHAPTER VII

THE WINNING OF WORLD WAR II

A Pledge of Freedom Compromised

On June 22, 1941, the Nazis invaded the Soviet Union and its "spheres of influence" in eastern Europe, shattering the line which Churchill said they did not "dare assail" and threatening to eliminate the existence of the Soviet regime as well as its chances of becoming preponderant in any part of Europe. Immediately, Molotov denounced this "unheard of attack," this "perfidy unparalleled," this bombing of "our cities—Zhitomir, Kiev [both in the captivated Ukraine], Sevastopol [in the subjugated Crimea], Kaunas [erstwhile capital of once-free Lithuania], and some others [recently or long since attacked and reduced to subjection by the Soviet Union]...."[1] Also, he opined, there were "enemy air-raids and artillery shelling from Rumanian and Finnish territory," recent targets of the Soviets' own frustrated aggressive intentions.

Crying out for vengeance against those who had "enslaved Frenchmen, Czechs, Poles, Serbians, Norwegians, Belgians, Danes, Dutchmen, Greeks and peoples of other nations," the despoilers of Estonia, Latvia, Lithuania, Poland, Finland, Rumania, Turkestan, Georgia, Armenia, Azerbaijan, the Ukraine, Byelorussia and a host of other nations and peoples, pretended to comfort the victims of the bloodthirsty Communist rulers of Russia with assurances that the enemy was not "the German people," not the German "workers, peasants and intellectuals whose sufferings we well understand," but "the clique of bloodthirsty fascist rulers of Germany...."[2]

Molotov's defiant words were hypocritical, but they acknowledged a truth which the free world still fails to discern. While he purported to repent of an alliance with the enemies of the people of Germany, the free nations persisted in seeking alliance with the enemies of the peoples of Russia. As a result, millions of tons of arms, once withheld from support of the democratic movements in Russia and Siberia, from Kolchak, Denikin, Yudenich and Wrangel, from Byelorussia, the Ukraine, Turkestan, Georgia, Armenia and Azerbaijan, and more recently from Poland, Finland, the Baltic States and Rumania, were speedily made available to their Red oppressors. Europe was liberated from Nazi subjugation, and the world was delivered from the threat of Nazi aggression, but only at the price of Soviet subjugation and a renewal of the threat of Soviet aggression.

In 1941, the Prime Minister of Great Britain was the same Winston Churchill whose desire for vigorous action against the Bolsheviks had led him into argument with President Wilson, in 1919. Now, however, the need of an eastern front had returned, and he was an arch-advocate of alliance with the Soviets. In 1939, prior to taking office, he had insisted that his predecessors "call upon Poland not to place obstacles in the way of a common cause"[3] with his former foes. In 1941, with the reins of Empire in his hands at last, he was able to offer these foes immediate aid, and to call for similar action by the entire free world. "We shall give whatever help we can," he said. "We shall appeal to all our friends and Allies in every part of the world to take the same course. . . ."[4]

The response to this appeal was tremendous. From the United States, to which it was chiefly directed, there came a special mission to Moscow and an initial lend-lease credit to the Soviet Union of $1,000,000,000. The total eventually exceeded $9,000,000,000. The British also gave immediate help, in the form of materials, planes and weapons, and even the Soviets were willing to accept an alliance, without conditions.

The Germans, however, were well prepared, and their advance was rapid. Within a few months they overran the Ukraine, encircled Leningrad and drove within a few miles of Moscow. During this period, the Soviet regime faced annihilation and its attitude changed accordingly. Gone was the Molotov mockery of 1939—the laughter and scoffing at "rabid warmongers" who would have others pull their "chestnuts out of the fire." Gone was the suggestion that the British and French "do their own fighting without the Soviet Union" and demonstrate "what fighting stuff they are made of. . . ." No longer did Molotov deride those who "positively demand that the U.S.S.R. get itself involved in war against Germany on the side of Great Britain," or inquire if they had not "taken leave of their senses."[5]

Now it was Stalin's turn to seek a second front, in France or in the Balkans, or in the alternative, twenty-five to thirty British divisions in Russia itself.[6] Equipment was also needed, and from Great

Britain Stalin demanded immediate shipment of 30,000 tons of aluminum and a monthly minimum of 400 aircraft and 500 tanks. Without such help, he said, "the Soviet Union will either suffer defeat or be weakened to such an extent that it will lose for a long period any capacity to render assistance to its allies. . . ."[7] "Now," he agreed, "the Soviet Union and Great Britain have become fighting allies"; and, he said, "I have no doubt that in spite of the difficulties our two States will be strong enough to crush our common enemy."[8]

There was a similar reversal of attitude toward the United States. In 1939, according to the Soviets, the United States had been suffering from a "new economic crisis," while the defenses of the Soviet Union were "stronger than those of any other country."[9] But now the United States could help with an initial contribution of $1,850,000,000— 3,000 pursuit planes, 3,000 bombers, 20,000 anti-aircraft guns, $50,000,000 in plant and equipment and large quantities of explosives and aviation gasoline[10]—as well as a declaration of war and the use of American troops on the Russian front.[11]

Then, if ever, when even the Soviet rulers wanted Allied troops in Russia, was the chance to offer aid to the subject peoples. But the free world did not want to aid the subject peoples against the Soviets; it wanted the subject peoples to aid them in war with the Nazis. Moreover, the free world still had no contact with the subject peoples. It had no adequate knowledge of their sufferings, their desire for freedom or their resistance to communism. It was not even aware that millions of Red Army troops were at that time surrendering to Germany, or that the Nazis themselves were being welcomed "with joy as liberators."[12]

Fifteen years later, the Soviets conceded that whole nations within the Soviet Union had been deported during the war "for inimical activity."[13] The free world, however, was not prepared to give them assistance. It had no armies of its own to send to Russia, even at Stalin's request. It did have millions of refugees, the potential source of free national armies, but it did not have the cadres required for their training—or the desire to use them in any event. In 1944, the British suggested an invasion of eastern Europe through the Balkans, but by that time Stalin had changed his mind, and the United States was still of the opinion that there were no troops to spare.

Moreover, as viewed from the free world, the changed Soviet attitude was truly alluring, and if the free nations were not convinced of its sincerity they were at least willing to take advantage of it to cover up their own inconsistency. At a meeting of the Inter-Allied Council in London, September 24, 1941, the Soviet Ambassador, Ivan M. Maisky, warmly endorsed the stated aims and "common principles" of the United States and Great Britain. These had been published, the month before, in the Atlantic Charter (see Appendix C-1). The Soviet government, Maisky said, "proclaims its agreement with the fundamental principles of the declaration of Mr. Roosevelt, President of the United States, and of Mr. Churchill, Prime Minister of Great Britain—principles which are so important in the present international circumstances."[14] He blandly asserted that "in all its policy and in all its relations with other nations," the Soviet Union had "consistently and with full force denounced all violations of sovereign rights of peoples, all aggression and aggressors, all and any attempts of aggressive states to impose their will upon other peoples." The Soviet Union, the Ambassador said, "has untiringly and resolutely advocated, and advocates today, the necessity of collective action against aggressors."[15]

Stalin himself went further and declared that it was *impossible* for the Soviet Union to have aggressive intentions. It was interested only in the liberation of subject peoples, Hitler's as well as its own:

We have not nor can we have such war aims as the seizure of foreign territories or the conquest of other peoples, irrespective of whether European peoples and territories or Asiatic peoples and territories, including Iran, are concerned. Our first aim is to liberate our territories and our peoples from the German Nazi yoke.

We have not nor can we have such war aims as the imposition of our will and our regime on the Slavic and other enslaved peoples of Europe who are waiting for our help. Our aim is to help these peoples in their struggle for liberation from Hitler's tyranny, and then to accord them the possibility of arranging their lives on their own land as they think fit, with absolute freedom. No interference of any kind with the domestic affairs of other nations![16]

In the case of Poland, the Soviets took specific remedial action— an open reversal of policy. In 1939, according to the note to the Polish Ambassador, the exiled government of Poland had "in fact ceased to exist." Now it became the object of special Soviet solicitude. In 1939, according to the same note, the Polish-Soviet agreements had "ceased to operate." Now it was the "Soviet-German treaties of 1939" which had "lost their validity." Diplomatic relations were renewed, mutual assistance agreed upon, and an "amnesty" was granted to all Polish citizens "deprived of their freedom . . . either as prisoners of war or on other adequate grounds."[17] Finally, a Polish national army was to be formed on Russian soil. It was to have its own commander, its own laws and decrees, and its own military courts, all specifically provided for in a pact made in Moscow.[18]

Extensive promises and concessions were also made to the subject peoples of the Soviet Union, particularly in the matter of religious freedom. In propaganda drives the shibboleths of communism and atheism gave way to inspiration drawn from old traditions. A national anthem was substituted for the "Internationale." The Orthodox Church was allowed to elect a Patriarch.

Even the Communist International, apparatus of world revolution, was "dissolved."

However, when the immediate threat had passed, the old Soviet attitude returned. By December, 1941, the Nazi drives bogged down. The Japanese attacked eastward against Pearl Harbor, instead of westward into Siberia. Stalin was even able to launch a modest counteroffensive against the invading German armies. He accordingly renewed his claims to all lands acquired in the recent Soviet aggression. The release of Polish prisoners slowed to a trickle, and went into reverse. The newly formed Polish Army was harassed with restrictions and privations. Eventually, it was allowed to leave Russia, and the Soviets formed another with officers more sympathetic to their own postwar plans. Relations with the Polish government-in-exile steadily deteriorated, and were severed by the Soviets in April, 1943.

The free nations, however, did not openly change their attitude. The Soviet demands were not accepted, but their good intentions were still ostensibly assumed. It seemed as though each new demonstration of Soviet arrogance only served to increase the determination of the free world to prove its own confidence in Soviet good will. Reports tending to disturb such confidence were dismissed as Axis propaganda and even regarded as evidence of Nazi weakness. "The Nazis," said the President, "must be frantic indeed if they believe that they can devise any propaganda which would turn the British and American and Chinese governments and peoples against Russia— or Russia against the rest of us."[19]

President Roosevelt made this statement in February, 1943, in a nation-wide radio address. Its theme was thereafter elaborated upon by the State Department. In another broadcast (April 1, 1943), Joseph

C. Grew, Special Assistant to the Secretary of State, called upon Americans to follow the more credulous example of the British:

... the British people resent and ridicule the Nazi attempt to split the Soviet Union from themselves and us. The inconsistency of this Nazi attempt is shown by the fact that the Germans talk about "the Bolshevik menace" only when it suits their purposes. We too should remember that the bogey of Bolshevism is raised by Goebbels only when the Germans are losing. . . .

Whoever fights Germany is our friend and our ally and is deserving of our respect, confidence, and trust.[20] (Italics added.)

Apparently unconscious of the absurdity of this last proposition, the State Department sought to ridicule those who could not accept it. Three days later, in still another radio address, Assistant Secretary Adolph A. Berle reported that "Vague rumors" were being "spread of huge imperial plans supposed to be harbored by Soviet Russia." "I make two piles on my desk every morning," he said. "One of them is for the type of letter that says, 'Beware of Russia'—coming usually from some misguided person who has heard some propaganda scare story. The other pile is for the type of letter or report which says that there is a plot or conspiracy among public officials to hamstring Russia —again, usually from well-meaning but misguided people...." "Of course," Mr. Berle concluded, "the briefest look at the facts swamps both kinds of propaganda. Soviet Russia, when she is victorious, as she will be, and when she has cleared her lands of Nazi troops, as she will, faces a titanic job in rebuilding her own country. She will not, in our judgment, become the victim of any urge to seize great additions to her already huge empire."[21]

As we now see the facts, it is obvious that Mr. Berle's look should not have been so brief. The rumors were not vague, and within a few weeks the Soviets had broken with the Poles in a way that was far from reassuring.

The cause for this break arose out of the concern of the Polish government-in-exile for the fate of Polish army officers imprisoned in the Soviet Union in 1939. Nearly all of them had disappeared; and in April, 1943, the Nazis announced the discovery of the bodies of several thousand in a mass grave in the Katyn Forest. The Nazis accused the Soviet Union of this atrocity; the Soviet Union accused the Nazis; and the Poles requested an impartial investigation by the International Red Cross. Sumner Welles, who was then Acting

Secretary of State, has described the Polish request as "altogether well taken,"[22] but the Soviets took it as evidence of a "hostile attitude" of collaboration with Hitler. Hitler had also invited such investigation, and Molotov asserted that the Poles, by doing likewise, had "actually discontinued allied relations with the U.S.S.R.," and therefore "the Soviet Government has decided to sever relations."[23]

In the meantime, the Soviet Union was also laying the foundations for a Polish Communist puppet regime. The formation of such a regime was predicted on April 28, 1943, in a renewed warning of Soviet plans for eastern Europe—made, not by "some misguided person," but by the American Ambassador to Russia, Admiral William H. Standley:

We should in any event be prepared, I think, for some move of this sort whether it be in the form of a committee or of a Free Polish Government, and we should realize that an organization of this kind on Soviet soil must be completely under Soviet domination. In addition, a development of this kind is possible in the case of any Slavic or bordering country outside the 1941 Soviet frontiers which does not agree to the policy of the Soviet Union.

Within the Soviet Union can be found the nucleus of any European Government and especially of those governments in which the Soviet Union has strategic or geographic interests.[24]

After the war, Congress made its own investigation of the Katyn Forest massacre, and of the official reaction in this country. The Select Committee found that the United States government was well aware of what was going on, but was deferring to "military necessity." "It is apparent," the committee reported, "that American authorities knew of the growing tension between the Soviets and the Poles during 1942-43—and they likewise knew about the hopeless search for the Polish officers. . . ." But "at the same time," the committee said, "all of these factors were brushed aside, on the theory that pressing the search would irritate Soviet Russia and thus hinder the prosecution of the war to a succesful conclusion."[25] As the committee concluded, "there unfortunately existed in high governmental and military circles a strange psychosis that military necessity required the sacrifice of loyal allies and our own principles in order to keep Soviet Russia from making a separate peace with the Nazis."[26]

The Western Allies were soon to witness the practical results of this mistake. As the war progressed, each victory over the Nazis was accompanied by a victory for communism—and for each gain for freedom in the west there was a corresponding victory for Soviet slavery in the east. In 1943, the Western Allies invaded Italy and began the liberation of western Europe. At the same time, the tide of war turned in Russia, and by the end of the year the Soviets had returned to Kiev. This was the capital of the rebellious Ukraine, where the people had clearly manifested their intention to be rid of both "isms"—communism as well as nazism. In 1944, the Western Allies landed in France, and reached the German Siegfried Line. But in the same year the Soviets reinstalled their own regimes in the Baltic States and eastern Poland. They also occupied new areas— Rumania, Bulgaria and parts of Yugoslavia, Hungary and Czecho-slovakia.

Additional warnings were then sounded by still another Ambassador to Moscow, W. Averell Harriman. On January 10, 1945, he reported that the communization of eastern Europe was extending far beyond the boundaries even of the Hitler-Stalin pact:

The relative lull in military activities on the Eastern Front has in effect given the Soviet Union a chance to pursue its political objectives in areas liberated by Russian Army. As a result the pattern of Soviet tactics in Eastern Europe and the Balkans has taken shape and the nature of Soviet aims has been clarified. It has become apparent that the Soviets, while eschewing direct attempts to incorporate into the Soviet Union alien peoples who were not embraced within the frontiers of June 21, 1941 [established under the Nazi-Soviet Pact], are nevertheless employing the wide variety of means at their disposal —occupation troops, secret police, local communist parties, labor unions, sympathetic leftist organizations, sponsored cultural societies, and economic pressure—to assure the establishment of regimes which, while maintaining an outward appearance of independence and of broad popular support, actually depend for their existence on groups responsive to all suggestions emanating from the Kremlin. The tactics are endless in their variety and are selected to meet the situation in each particular country, dependent largely on the extent and strength of the resistance to Soviet penetration. It is particularly noteworthy that no practical distinction seems to be made in this connection between members of the United Nations whose territory is liberated by Soviet troops and ex-enemy countries which have been occupied.[27]

By May, 1945, when the Nazis surrendered, the Soviets had occupied all of eastern Europe and parts of Germany and Austria. They had established puppet regimes in Warsaw, Belgrade, Sofia and Bucharest. Where they had no puppet regimes, they were ruling by occupation forces and their own secret police.

By this time, however, the Nazi threat was gone, and it was no longer necessary to trust "whoever fights Germany." Still the desire to trust the Soviets persisted. Several Congressmen became alarmed that relations with the Soviet Union might be undermined by a "group within the State Department"; and on May 31, 1945, they made a joint request for official assuagement of this fear. "Have old anti-Soviet prejudices," they asked, "clung to by a group within the State Department despite unity achieved among the Big Three at the Crimean Conference [Yalta], caused a shift since Roosevelt's death from American friendliness toward our Russian ally?"[28] They were assured by the Acting Secretary, Joseph C. Grew, that there had been no such shift. He conceded that there had been "differences of opinion," but they were "of the nature inevitably arising in the relations between any two friendly states."[29]

At the same time, the Assistant Secretary, Archibald MacLeish, criticized those who had "even spoken openly" of "inevitable conflict of interest," and who "have debated the question whether Russia, our present ally in the war, is our enemy or our friend. . . ." He himself had this to say:

. . . the United States and the Soviet Union are both young, strong, self-confident countries, with their own business to attend to; countries which, however they may differ in philosophy, and however they may differ in practice, aim in their several and dissimilar ways at what they believe to be the betterment of the lot of their own people and not at the conquest of the earth.

There is no necessary reason, in other words, in the logic of geography, or in the logic of economics, or in the logic of national objectives, why the United States and the Soviet Union should ever find themselves in conflict with each other, let alone in the kind of conflict reckless and irresponsible men have begun now to suggest.

. . . there is no necessary or logical reason why an answer to Poland or to any other difference should not be found.

What underlies the current talk of inevitable conflict between the two nations, in other words, is nothing real: nothing logical.[30]

These statements were made in spite of the Soviets' known aggressions and the most flagrant current violations of their freshly made wartime pledges. Less than a month before the Congressmen's letter, and only three weeks before the comments of MacLeish, the Soviets had publicly admitted the arrest of sixteen democratic Polish political leaders, including some of the very same men who had been suggested by democratic elements as candidates for the proposed new Polish Provisional Government.[31] They were "tried" in Moscow, and twelve were "convicted" during the period June 18-21, 1945, only a week before the statement of Acting Secretary Grew that the only differences with the Soviet Union were "of the nature inevitably arising in the relations between any two friendly states."

Many reasons were advanced for this official attitude, but they were for the most part contradictory. The basic reason, as found by the Select Committee to Investigate the Katyn Massacre, was pretty obviously the illusory assumption of military necessity, an assumption which traded the interests of the subject peoples for the vain hope of freedom from aggression.

Prior to the Nazi invasion of the Soviet Union, it was argued that opposition to communism would drive Russia into the arms of Germany, but it could just as well have been argued that opposition to Nazism would drive Germany into the arms of Russia. It was indicated, in fact, that some nations were driven into the arms of Germany, not because of Allied opposition to communism but because of the lack of it.

Warnings of such a reaction were reported in March, 1939 by the British Foreign Secretary, Lord Halifax. "It is becoming clear," he said then, "that our attempts to consolidate the situation will be frustrated if the Soviet Union is openly associated with the initiation of the scheme. Recent telegrams from a number of His Majesty's Missions abroad have warned us that the inclusion of Russia would not only jeopardise the success of our constructive effort, but also tend to consolidate the relations of the parties to the Anti-Comintern Pact, as well as excite anxiety among a number of friendly Governments."[32]

One of such reports came from the British Ambassador in Rome:

There are in fact indications here that reports of war appearing daily in the press and British and French efforts to form a democratic *bloc* against totalitarian States in association with Soviet Russia are affecting Italian opinion. Members of my staff tell me that Italians who were expressing themselves in unrestrained language about Germany a few days ago are beginning to talk bitterly about England associating herself with Soviets. It is also said that it was this factor which turned the scale at the meeting of the Grand Council and led to the resolution [reaffirming Italy's adherence to the Rome-Berlin axis] reported in my telegram No. 204.[33]

The Ambassador in Rome also reported that the Hungarian Minister was of the opinion that "if Great Britain linked up with Soviet Russia on European security, she would be cutting her own throat as this would automatically indispose a large number of other countries who, whatever else they were, were violently anti-Soviet...."[34] Similar views, he thought, were entertained by Spain and Yugoslavia.

If the free nations had aided no totalitarian state they would have had the support of *all* peoples. Mussolini might never have been able to declare war on France; the Soviets and Nazis would have weakened or destroyed each other; and the subject peoples of Europe and the Soviet Union might have been assisted to re-establish democracy. All of this is hindsight, but the free nations could have followed the course required, without clairvoyance, by simple adherence to their own stated principles. Instead, alliance with the Soviet Union brought them into conflict even with "liberal" and democratic Finland; and on December 7, 1941, the British declared war on this small country— to whose defense they had been ready, in 1940, to send an expeditionary force. In 1944, even the United States severed diplomatic relations with this most friendly country—a step which it still refuses to take against the Soviet Union.

It is no longer possible to drive free nations into the arms of Fascists and Nazis, but it is still possible to force the subject peoples into the arms of Communists. It is also possible to drive free peoples into "neutralism," because they cannot understand a policy which opposes Communists as undemocratic and yet accepts them as representative of the subject people. Under such circumstances, so-called neutrals can hardly be blamed for assuming that opposition to communism is grounded more on self-interest than on principle.

Churchill argued that Russia wished to keep Germany out of the Balkans, and that its interests therefore fell "into the same channel as the interests of Britain and France."[35] But Britain and France also wished, or should have wished, to keep the Soviets out of the Balkans —as well as out of every other area. Their own interests therefore coincided as much with Germany's as they did with those of the Soviet Union, and actually coincided with neither.

Roosevelt contended that the Soviets were "less dangerous" than the Nazis, because "The only weapon which the Russian dictatorship uses outside its own borders is communist propaganda. . . ."[36] This absurd statement, made in September, 1941, ignored the President's own previous complaint that the Soviets were running a "dictatorship as absolute as any other dictatorship in the world," that they had in fact allied themselves "with another dictatorship" and had finally, in the case of Finland, "invaded a neighbor so infinitesimally small that it could do no conceivable, possible harm to the Soviet Union. . . ."

The Department of State explained that "any defense against Hitlerism, any rallying of the forces opposing Hitlerism, from whatever source these forces may spring," was to the benefit of "defense and security."[37] But this argument was answered in the same statement, released in June, 1941, which conceded that the "principles and doctrines of communistic dictatorship are as intolerable and as alien . . . as are the principles and doctrines of Nazi dictatorship."

The arguments on the other side were far more compelling. The chief one was stated by Roosevelt himself, in 1943. "The issue of this war," he said, "is the basic issue between those who believe in mankind and those who do not—the ancient issue between those who put their faith in the people and those who put their faith in dictators and tyrants."[38] Because the United States and Great Britain *did* put their faith in dictators and tyrants, instead of in the people, they found themselves squarely on the wrong side of this issue and were led into the actual deception of the free peoples, the compromise of their own principles, and the betrayal of those who really wished to be their allies—the subject peoples.

In defense of their strategy, the spokesmen for the free powers found it necessary to repeat the assurances of the Soviets and to describe them in official releases as champions of peace, freedom and self-determination for all the peoples of the world.

Churchill had at first seemed willing only to forget the past. On the day of the Nazi attack, he said:

No one has been a more consistent opponent of Communism than I have for the last twenty-five years. I will unsay no words that I've spoken about it. But all this fades away before the spectacle which is now unfolding.

The past, with its crimes, its follies and its tragedies, flashes away.[39]

Before the end of the war he seemed fully convinced that a "new look" for the future had also arrived. Speaking to the House of Commons in May, 1944, he asserted that "profound changes" had taken place in Russia.[40] The "Trotskyite form of communism" had been "completely wiped out." The victories of the Russian armies were attended by a "great rise in strength of the Russian state and a remarkable broadening of its views"; the "religious side of Russian life" had had "a wonderful rebirth"; and the "discipline and military etiquette of the Russian armies" were "unsurpassed."

Churchill further indicated that the Soviet Union had given up all plans for aggression. "The terms offered by Russia to Rumania," he asserted, made "no suggestion of altering the standards of society in that country and were in many respects, if not all, remarkably generous." Russia had been "very patient with Finland," and, he said, the "Comintern has been abolished—that is sometimes forgotten."

President Roosevelt was eloquent and enthusiastic. Addressing the International Students' Association in September, 1942, he painted a rosy picture for the future of Russian youth. "Today," he said, "the embattled youth of Russia and China are realizing a new individual dignity, casting off the last links of the ancient chains of imperial despotism which had bound them so long."[41] In the following year, April, 1943, the Assistant Secretary of State, Adolph A. Berle, asserted over the radio that there were "four great freedom-loving powers in the world." These, he said, were "the United States, Great Britain, Russia, and China."[42]

The attitude of public opinion produced by such statements was most embarrassing to Churchill when the British were forced to move against a Communist uprising in Greece, and even caused a small rift in Anglo-American relations. In August, 1944, Churchill warned the President that the Communists would attempt to take over in Greece,[43] but the United States did not appear to be concerned. In fact, it publicly commended the Greek government-in-exile for granting ministries to six representatives of the Communist-controlled "National Liberation Front" (E.A.M.).[44] As was stated four years later (February, 1948) by Loy W. Henderson, then Director of the Office of Near Eastern and African Affairs: "Unfortunately, for some time many loyal Greeks as well as friends of Greece abroad were duped as to the real character of the EAM control."[45]

Within two months after the return of the Greek government to

Athens, the representatives of E.A.M. resigned and the Communists organized an armed uprising. When Churchill ordered its suppression, he was immediately attacked—in Great Britain as well as in America. He himself records[46] that his action was "violently condemned" by the "vast majority of the American Press" and "censured" by such powerful British newspapers as the *Times* and the *Manchester Guardian*. There was also a "great stir" in the House of Commons, and in America the State Department issued a "markedly critical pronouncement." Even the President was unable to accept the shift; and on December 13, 1944, he wrote that neither he nor the United States could support the intervention in Greece because of the "adverse reaction of public opinion."[47]

In a House of Commons address, on December 8, 1944, Churchill opined that "we are told that we seek to disarm the friends of democracy."[48] For this, however, he had no one but himself to blame. It was an attitude that was scarcely surprising in the light of the assertions made by free-world leaders, including himself, who were thought to know what was actually taking place behind the Soviet lines.

There were many other unfortunate effects of this wartime alliance. For example, the inclusion of the Soviet Union made a contradiction, and a means of deception, of every wartime declaration, including even the United Nations Charter. In the Declaration by United Nations[49] to which there were twenty-six original and twenty-one subsequent signatories, nearly all of the free nations were joined *with* the leaders of the international Communist conspiracy in a "common struggle" *against* the "forces seeking to subjugate the world." The alliance thus included those against whom it was in theory directed, and the free nations united themselves with the most determined opponents of their stated goals—to enforce the Atlantic Charter, to "defend life, liberty, independence and religious freedom," and "to preserve human rights and justice in their own lands as well as in other lands."

With similar incongruity, the Soviets were again included, in 1943, in declarations on General Security, on Austria, on Italy, on German Atrocities, on Iran and on Co-operation in War and Peace.[50] With dedicated aggressors the free powers were thus joined in calling for an international organization of "peace-loving states," and in demanding "political and economic security" for Austria and its neighboring states. With the most undemocratic of all governments they asserted that "the Italian Government should be made more democratic" and that "Freedom of speech, of religious worship, of political belief, of the press and of public meeting" should be "restored in full measure to the Italian people." With the authors of the Red terror and Stalin's brutality, they condemned the "brutalities of Hitler" and his "government by terror." With the leaders of the Communist Party, the free powers agreed to punish the "men and members of the Nazi Party"—for their "atrocities," for their "massacres" and for their "executions." With those who sought to take advantage of their own "antagonisms" and incite them "one against the other," they agreed to "banish the scourge and terror of war" and to eliminate "tyranny and slavery, oppression and intolerance"; with those who were already plotting to annex Iran, they agreed to insure its "independence, sovereignty and territorial integrity"; and with their own greatest enemy, they became "friends in fact, in spirit and in purpose."

The Soviets were also included, in 1944, in the conference at Dumbarton Oaks. There, with known aggressors, all signers of the Declaration by United Nations agreed to adopt "collective measures for the prevention and removal of threats to the peace and the *suppression* of acts of aggression."[51] (Italics added.)

In 1945, the Soviets were included in the Declaration on Liberated Europe (Appendix C-2), and again it was with known aggressors that the United States and Great Britain purported to provide for "internal peace" in all the liberated states, for the "relief of distressed peoples," for "broadly representative governments," and for "free elections."

To the rulers of the Soviet Union the value of such joint declarations was tremendous. They would "prove" to the free peoples that the Communists had good intentions, and to the subject peoples that the promises of the Western Allies were as illusory as Communist promises. At the same time, the Soviets were insuring themselves against the thing they dreaded most—Allied assistance to the subject peoples during a Soviet war with Germany. As Lenin had advised, "by making a concession to one imperialism" they were safeguarding themselves "against the persecution of both imperialisms."[52] This time the concessions were made to the free powers instead of to Germany, but they did not even have the temporary reality of those made at Brest-Litovsk. They were all paper promises, with but small chances of enforcement.

Another continuing effect of the alliance with the Soviet Union was the prevention of contacts between the free nations and the subject peoples. This eliminated all possibility of assistance to the fight for freedom inside Russia, and it led to the forcible repatriation of vast numbers of anti-Communist Russians liberated from the Nazis or otherwise found outside the Soviet Union by the Western Allies.

The State Department reported, in March, 1946, that those subject to forcible repatriation included all Soviet nationals who were members of the Red Army, or who had collaborated with the Axis:

(1)   Those who were captured in German uniforms;
(2)   Those who were members of the Soviet armed forces on or after June 22, 1941 [date of the Nazi attack on the Soviet Union] and were not subsequently discharged therefrom;
(3)   Those who on the basis of reasonable evidence have been found to be collaborators with the enemy, having voluntarily rendered aid and comfort to the enemy.[53]

This meant the return, regardless of their individual wishes, of nearly all ordinary prisoners of war.

The inclusion of collaborators and those taken in German uniforms insured the return to Soviet vengeance of those most opposed to communism, who had chosen to fight it by serving in the German armies, and whose crime of co-operating with one tyranny against another was in substance identical with the Allied strategy of alliance with communism against nazism. It is estimated that the number of those who were thus treated as enemies—because they had chosen the wrong tyranny—was in the neighborhood of 1,000,000. If the free world could so treat these people, when they were offered no other means of resistance to communism, it can well imagine how its own *freely made* choice of co-operation with the Communists was regarded by the subject peoples.

The Yalta agreement was originally interpreted to require the similar forced return of civilians and non-collaborators—of whom there were likewise many millions in Germany as a result of Nazi forced-labor programs and voluntary flights from the Soviet Union. This understanding was later evaded or ignored by the Western Allies, but not before many persons had been victimized.

Prior to the German surrender (May 7, 1945), orders for the forced repatriation of all such persons of Soviet nationality liberated after February 11, 1945 (the date of the Yalta agreement), were issued

(April 16) by Supreme Headquarters Allied Expeditionary Force (SHAEF):

> After identification by Soviet Repatriation Representatives, Soviet displaced persons will be repatriated regardless of their individual wishes.[54]

This was the opposite of the policy applied to citizens of other nationalities, concerning whom the same SHAEF order stipulated that those who did not wish repatriation would *not* be repatriated unless guilty of war crimes:

> These persons, unless they have been identified as Soviet citizens by Soviet Repatriation Representatives, will not be returned to their countries of nationality or districts of former residence unless they have committed war crimes, trial for which requires their presence there.[55]

After the German surrender, arrangements for the exchange of liberated nationals were agreed upon by the Red Army and SHAEF commands in a meeting at Halle, Germany. This plan, accepted on May 22, 1945, likewise called for the exchange of all liberated Soviet prisoners of war and civilians, regardless of their wishes:

> All former prisoners of war and citizens of the U.S.S.R. liberated by the Allied Forces and all former prisoners of war and citizens of Allied Nations liberated by the Red Army will be delivered through the Army lines to the corresponding Army Command of each side.[56]

Soon, however, as General Eisenhower reports, the "terror" induced by these arrangements "was impressed upon us by a number of suicides. . . ."[57] An effort was then made to evade or to violate an agreement that should never have been executed. On May 27, 1945, an exception was provided, unilaterally, for former residents of the Baltic States, eastern Poland and other areas annexed by the Soviet Union during the war. This action was based on the assertion that the British and United States governments had not recognized any territorial changes brought about by the war,[58] and that the residents of the annexed areas could not, therefore, be regarded as Soviet citizens unless they claimed such status. This assertion, however, was only partly true, because the annexation of eastern Poland had been agreed upon at Yalta, and the "cession" of Bessarabia and northern Bukovina had been confirmed by the Big Three in the Rumanian armistice agreement.

Other Soviet nationals, the residents of prewar Soviet territory, were given the benefit of the doubt if they denied Soviet nationality— that is, they were not surrendered unless actual proof to the contrary could be furnished by Soviet repatriation officers.[59] Eventually, such protection was given to all who did not claim Soviet nationality— making actual denials unnecessary.[60] By these means it is reported that some 35,000 Ukrainians, Byelorussians, Kalmuks and others were saved, but such a figure represents only a small fraction (0.6%) of the total repatriated from areas controlled by the free nations.

Between May 22 and September 30, 1945, 2,272,000 displaced Soviet nationals were turned over to Soviet control by the Western Allies.[61] Whether or not they went voluntarily, under the pledges which the free nations had made all of these people were entitled to be repatriated to a land of freedom, and many no doubt assumed that that was what they were getting. That was what they had so frequently been told, and it was the significance of pledges made by the free powers to establish freedom from all kinds of oppression, in all parts of the world.

In January, 1941, when the Soviets were still allied with Hitler, and when lend-lease aid to Hitler's victims was proposed, the President promised freedom—the "four freedoms"—everywhere in the world:

In the future days, which we seek to make secure, we look forward to a world founded upon four essential human freedoms.

The first is freedom of speech and expression—*everywhere in the world.*

The second is freedom of every person to worship God in his own way—*everywhere in the world.*

The third is freedom from want—which, translated into world terms, means economic understandings which will secure to every nation a healthy peacetime life for its inhabitants—*everywhere in the world.*

The fourth is freedom from fear—which, translated into world terms, means a world-wide reduction of armaments to such a point and in such a thorough fashion that no nation will be in a position to commit an act of physical aggression against any neighbor—*anywhere in the world.*[62] (Italics added.)

The Atlantic Charter (Appendix C-1) was also universal in its terms. It proclaimed "the right of all peoples to choose the form of government under which they will live," and expressed hope for "a peace which will afford to all nations the means of dwelling in safety within their boundaries, and which will afford assurance that all men in all the lands may live out their lives in freedom from fear and want." The use of force, it said, would have to be abandoned by all the nations of the world. In the meantime, however, until a "permanent system of general security" should be established, the disarmament of those "nations which threaten, or may threaten, aggression outside of their frontiers" was "essential."

This last statement, as well as the President's "fourth freedom," implied that no world-security organization could be established until the power of all nations dedicated to aggression had been destroyed. It could not be understood to apply only to Axis nations (Germany, Italy and Japan), because they were engaged in actual, not threatened, aggression. Moreover, if there were any doubts on this score they were dispelled by explanatory statements of the President and Secretary of State.

In the announcement of the Charter, the Secretary of State asserted that its principles were "universal in their application" and that its "basic principles" must be "completely restored throughout the world." (See Appendix C-1.) President Roosevelt subsequently said that this Charter "applies not only to the parts of the world that border the Atlantic but to the whole world...."[63] The "world," he said on still another occasion, "can rest assured that this total war—this sacrifice of lives all over the globe—is not being carried on for the purpose or even with the remotest idea of keeping the Quislings or Lavals in power anywhere on this earth."[64]

Because the free world was dealing with a Communist regime, and seeking its assistance, it was impossible to fulfill this pledge.

In 1943, the Under Secretary of State, Sumner Welles, called attention to the failure to fulfill pledges made in World War I. "Twenty-five years ago," he said, "we also had held up before us the concept of a free world in which peace and justice and international decency would prevail. Just because that concept held up to mankind at the close of the last war was not transplanted into reality, the world today is undergoing this far greater holocaust."[65] Yet even as he spoke, another failure, and perhaps a greater holocaust, was being made inevitable by repetition of that same mistake. Once again the free nations had withheld assistance from the subject peoples in an effort to obtain Soviet help against German aggression. The only result was a situation in which they now assumed that the denial of such assistance would win them a reprieve from Soviet aggression.

Even if the Soviet rulers were representative of a majority of the peoples under their control, as was so often implied, their support by the free nations was in conflict with the pledges of the Atlantic Charter. As President Roosevelt stated, the "right of self-determination included in the Atlantic Charter does not carry with it the right of any government to commit wholesale murder or the right to make slaves of its own people or of any other peoples of the world."[66] A hint of the extent to which the Soviet regime was doing just this was given by the Communists themselves, a decade too late, when Khrushchev made his "secret" address in 1956 to the Twentieth Congress of the Communist Party:

We refer to the mass deportations from their native places of whole nations, together with all Communists and Komsomols without any exception; this deportation action was not dictated by any military considerations.

Thus, already at the end of 1943, when there occurred a permanent breakthrough at the fronts of the Great Patriotic War benefiting the Soviet Union, a decision was taken and executed concerning the deportation of all the Karachai from the lands on which they lived.

In the same period, at the end of December, 1943, the same lot befell the whole population of the Autonomous Kalmyk Republic. In March, 1944, all the Chechen and Inguish peoples were deported and the Chechen-Inguish Autonomous Republic was liquidated. In April, 1944, all the Balkars were deported to faraway places. . . . The Ukrainians avoided meeting this fate only because there were too many of them and there was no place to which to deport them. Otherwise, he would have deported them also.

Not only a Marxist-Leninist but also no man of common sense can grasp how it is possible to make whole nations responsible for inimical activity, including women, children, old people, Communists and Komsomols, to use mass repression against them, and to expose them to misery and suffering for the hostile acts of individual persons or groups of persons.[67]

CHAPTER VIII

THIRD ROUND OF SOVIET AGGRESSION

"International Warrant" in Eastern Europe

Prior to the execution of the Nazi-Soviet pact, the Soviets had consistently advocated strong measures to contain the Axis aggressions; and in 1938, their Foreign Minister, Maxim Litvinov, took a firm stand against diplomatic recognition of the "annexation of other people's territory"—whether it was accomplished by "direct seizure" or "camouflaged by the setting up of puppet 'national' governments." Speaking in the Council of the League of Nations, he told the wavering delegates of the free powers that "It must be clear that the League of Nations has no intention of changing its attitude, whether to the direct seizure and annexation of other people's territory, or to those cases where such annexations are camouflaged by the setting-up of puppet 'national' governments, allegedly independent, but in reality serving merely as a screen for, and an agency of, the foreign invader."[1]

At the close of the war, however, the "liberating" Soviet armies brought with them to eastern Europe a veritable host of such puppet regimes. These were the Soviet-created nuclei of European governments which had been described by Ambassador Standley in 1943— designed to form the basis of camouflaged Soviet rule in Bulgaria, Czechoslovakia, Germany, Hungary, Poland and Rumania, and to restore the openly Soviet regimes installed in the Baltic States in 1940 and withdrawn in the face of the Nazi invasion in 1941.

The leader of the Bulgarian group was Georgi Dimitrov, the former secretary general of the Executive Committee of the Communist International. He had once advised its delegates to follow the example of "the ancient story of the taking of Troy,"[2] but he could now ignore this advice and return to Bulgaria, not in a Trojan horse, but in the company of the Red Army and with the assistance of the Western Allies. He was soon to be made Prime Minister of the Bulgarian Communist puppet regime, but would fall later into disfavor and die under medical treatment in Moscow. With him were

150

Vasil Kolarov, to succeed him as Prime Minister, and Vulko Chervenkov to succeed Kolarov; also Ivan Mihailov, a future deputy premier,
and Georgi Damyanov, who would become Minister of Defense and
subsequently Chairman of the Bulgarian National Assembly.

In the Czech contingent there was Clement Gottwald, who was
to become Prime Minister and later President of the puppet regime
in Czechoslovakia; also Vaclav Kopecky, to become a deputy prime
minister, Ludvik Svoboda, Minister of National Defense, and Zdenek
Nejedly, Minister without Portfolio. For party posts there were
Rudolph Slansky, to be Secretary General, and Maria Svermova, his
assistant. Both were destined for the purge in 1951, Slansky by
execution.

For Germany there were two original members of the Spartacus
League, the forerunner of the German Communist Party and instigator of the abortive revolt in 1919. One of the two, Wilhelm Pieck,
had in that year been a delegate to the founding Congress of the Communist International, and was the keynote speaker at its Seventh
Congress in 1935. He was now to become and remain the President of
the so-called Democratic Republic of East Germany. His associate,
Walter Ulbricht, a member of the Comintern Central Committee, was
slated for the post of deputy prime minister and a lasting term of
party leadership.

The Hungarian group was slated for experience that even Moscow did not anticipate. One of its members was Matyas Rakosi, future
Prime Minister and head of the Communist Party in Hungary. In
1953, he would resign as Prime Minister to placate a rebellious people;
and in 1956, as party first secretary, to placate Tito, the rebellious
dictator. Finally, he would be read out of the party.

Another Hungarian Muscovite was Imre Nagy, who would succeed Rakosi as Prime Minister, undergo the purge, and finally be
restored as a concession to violent revolt. When the revolt was
crushed, he too would be read out of the party, and then executed.

Still another member was Erno Gero, to be boosted into party
leadership and out again within four months, and also read out of the
party. Others were Mihaly Farkas, future Minister of Defense, and
the chief of the secret police, Jozsef Revai, who as party theoretician
would one day inveigh against Nagy's "revisionism," and Zoltan Vas
and Zoltan Szanto, who would attain high office only to be deported
later, with Nagy, to Rumania.

The nucleus of the Polish puppet regime, the Union of Polish

Patriots, had been created even before the severance of relations with the legitimate government-in-exile. It included, according to the report of the Select Committee on Communist Aggression, four Soviet nationals, one collaborator, five Communists, one Communist sympathizer, and three who joined under duress. One of the members was a colonel of the Soviet secret police (NKVD).[3]

Even prior to the formation of this group, the Soviets had sent agents into Nazi-occupied Warsaw to organize the Polish Workers' (Communist) Party. There they were joined by Wladyslaw Gomulka, who soon became Secretary General and, after the arrival of the Red Army, Deputy Premier and Minister of the Recovered Territories. His future also included "confession of error," purging, imprisonment and final re-emergence as the "popular" brand of "independent" Communist who would make deals for the acceptance of a "Polish road to Socialism" but not for the withdrawal of Soviet troops.

The Moscow group of Polish Communists included Boleslaw Bierut, who was parachuted into Poland in 1943 to assume the post of chairman of the party, and eventually become President of Poland under Stalin. There was also Aleksander Zawadski (colonel of the NKVD), who was to be President of Poland under Khrushchev and Gomulka. For other government posts, there were Hilary Minc, Jacob Berman, Zenon Nowak and Stefan Jedrychowski, all scheduled to become deputy premiers; Roman Zambrowski, future Minister of State Control; Stanislaw Skrezeszewski, future Foreign Minister; Jerzy Sztachelski, future Minister of Health; and Edward Ochab, future Minister of Public Administration. Ochab would eventually succeed to party leadership in March, 1956, only to turn it over to Gomulka in October of the same year.

Another member of the group was Stanislaw Radkiewicz, the future Minister of State Security. In this capacity he would seek out and destroy the members of the wartime Polish underground, incarcerate Gomulka, and eventually be transferred to other posts as a result of the post-Stalin "new look" and revelations made to the free world by a defecting colonel of his own secret police.[4] Finally, in 1957, he and Berman would be suspended from party membership by the victorious and "rehabilitated" Gomulka.

In the Rumanian contingent there was Ana Pauker, whose husband's execution as a Trotskyite had neither affected her own party loyalty nor prevented her from assuming Soviet citizenship. She was slated to assume control of Rumania under the title of Foreign Minister and eventually fall from favor, another victim of the purge. Her troupe included Vasile Luca, Dumitru Putrescu, Petre Borila, Emil Bodnaras and Iosif Chisinevschi. Bodnaras and Borila were to survive as deputy premiers, Luca and Chisinevschi to share the fate of Ana.

Many of these "native" Communists had acquired Soviet citizenship, and even positions in the Soviet government. Their return was indirectly aided by the free nations through military assistance to the Soviet Union. A different situation prevailed in Albania and Yugoslavia, which had no Moscow nuclei, and whose Communist governments were organized on the spot by Marshal Josip Broz (Tito). In these nations the Communists were assisted by the free powers directly.

Marshal Tito himself, however, was no less of a Soviet-trained Communist than his European counterparts who spent the war in Moscow. Taken prisoner by the Russian Army in World War I, he had joined the Bolsheviks in time to help destroy the last remnants of freedom in eastern Siberia. He stayed in the Red Army until 1924, and the beginning of World War II found him serving the cause of international communism as the devoted secretary general of the Communist Party of Yugoslavia.

After the Nazis turned against the Soviet Union, Tito organized the "Anti-Fascist Assembly of the National Liberation of Yugoslavia," a Communist-controlled "national" political organization, and a new Communist Party of Albania, with its corresponding National Liberation Council. In 1943, he organized a Communist "government" of Yugoslavia, with himself as Premier, and in 1944, a similar "government" of Albania—also called "National Liberation Committee"—with Enver Hoxha as Premier.

While these organizations received military assistance from the Western Allies, the non-Communist resistance movements were given only limited support and eventually cut off entirely. In the case of Yugoslavia there was a government-in-exile in London, headed by King Peter. It was recognized by the major powers, and even by the Soviet Union. Its Minister of War, General Draja Mihailovic, was the leader of a strong, non-Communist internal-resistance movement. Tito accused him of collaboration with the Axis, and although the charges were refuted by American observers,[5] many came to believe that this was true. Mihailovic was eventually abandoned even by his own government; and in 1946, he was tried and executed by the triumphant Communist regime.

For Albania there was no recognized exile organization. The government of King Zog was abandoned by the free powers after the Italian invasion, and some recognized the annexation. There were, however, strong resistance movements within the country, one representing the supporters of the King, and the other the National Union (Balli Kombetar). The latter group was led by Midhat Frasheri, who had long sought to establish a liberal and democratic form of government in Albania. During the war a British military mission was sent to Albania to make contact with the Zogist group, but its recommendation for help was never followed. After the Communists prevailed, in 1944, the leaders of both groups were forced to flee the country. They continued the fight from abroad through the Free Albania National Committee, which was formed in Paris in 1949. Since there was no recognized Albanian government, the Communists simply installed themselves as the "Democratic Government of Albania," and demanded recognition. The Western Allies could do little but send missions and observers, and ask the Communists to conduct a free election.

King Peter's government of Yugoslavia was doomed by a decision made at the Teheran Conference. There, on December 1, 1943, the Big Three agreed that Tito's Partisans should be supported by commando operations, and "with supplies and equipment to the greatest possible extent."[6] This made the defeat of non-Communist resistance movements inevitable. Thereafter, the fate of the Yugoslavs was determined by British insistence upon compromise and confidence in Communist promises. In June, 1944, the British induced King Peter's government to make an agreement with Tito, abandon Mihailovic and call upon all Yugoslavs to join the Partisans. Finally, on November 1, 1944, it was prevailed upon to agree to a merger. By this time the Red Army and Partisan forces had taken Belgrade.

The vague terms of the November agreement left everything, unfortunately, to the discretion of Marshal Tito. This was the conclusion of the United States, as expressed by Secretary of State Edward R. Stettinius, Jr., in a memorandum to the British Embassy on December 23, 1944:

... the language of the texts is so vague that the real test would seem to be an evaluation of the good will of the parties. . . . Stripped of its generalities the agreement provides for a thoroughgoing recording of administrative, legislative, electoral and institutional precedures, in which one group [Tito's], even though it may be the strongest in the country, would have practically complete and exclusive power. The gesture toward the Government in exile, in the person of Dr. Subasic [the Prime Minister], seems hardly more than a concession considered sufficient to acquire recognition by other Governments, on grounds of an apparent continuity.[7]

These conclusions were repeated in a briefing-book paper prepared for use at the Yalta Conference:

The Tito-Subasic agreement, now awaiting the King's approval in London, would transfer the effective powers of government to the Tito organization, with just enough participation of the Government in exile to facilitate recognition by other governments. The Soviet and British Governments have firmly advocated an acceptance of this agreement. This Government [the United States] has refused to exert influence on the King, and has pointed out that while the language of the agreement is in line with our ideas, the real test will be the good will of the new administration in its execution.[8]

The same paper also called attention to the totalitarian methods of the Partisans:

All indications point to the intention of the Partisans to establish a thoroughly totalitarian regime, in order to maintain themselves in power.[9]

. . . reports of American observers tend to refute the charges against Mihailovich of collaboration with the Germans, and indicate that the Partisans, with the help of Allied military supplies, are fighting the nationalists and otherwise establishing a repressive political hegemony in Yugoslavia. The Allied observers attached to the Partisans do not have the freedom of movement which would enable them to evaluate the real situation.[10]

Under the heading *Partisan Excesses*, the paper continued:

Official and unofficial reports received from Yugoslavia point to the probability that large-scale executions and confiscations of property of persons opposed to the Partisan movement are taking place.[11]

In the meantime, the stage had been set for establishment of Soviet hegemony in the rest of eastern Europe, and the free nations were already seeking to undo by persuasion the damage they had done by military assistance. Their efforts resulted only in vain importunities, and finally in the granting of that "international warrant" which the British Ambassador had said the Bolsheviks were seeking in 1939.

One such effort was the proposal of Winston Churchill, made in October, 1944, to divide the wartime "predominance" in eastern Europe on a percentage basis. Under this arrangement, the Soviets would have a "ninety percent predominance in Rumania" and a seventy-five percent predominance in Bulgaria; the British would be given "ninety percent of the say in Greece"; and the two powers would "go fifty-fifty" in Hungary and Yugoslavia.[12] However this proposal may have been intended, whether as an expression of "interest and sentiment," as Churchill said it was, or as a method of prescribing "the numbers sitting on commissions," as he said it was not,[13] it obviously involved the submission of Bulgaria and Rumania to Soviet control.

Churchill states that his proposal was accepted by Stalin with a "large tick" of his blue pencil, but the United States had already expressed its disapproval of arrangements which might lead to a new division of spheres of influence in eastern Europe, and did not participate. Its seemingly more principled position led to an even worse arrangement, under which the Soviet Union was given full predominance in all three of the former enemy states—Bulgaria, Hungary and Rumania. This was made effective in the armistice agreements, signed with Rumania on September 12, 1944, with Bulgaria on October 28, 1944, and with Hungary on January 20, 1945.[14] Under these agreements the "general direction" of the Allied Control Commissions (enforcement bodies) in each of the three states was placed in the hands of the Soviet military authorities. As the State Department's Yalta Conference briefing-book paper asserted, the United States government had "not taken exception to the Soviet view that the actual operation of the Commissions should be in the hands of the Soviet military authorities, at least in the period before the surrender of Germany."[15]

The United States position was based on the supposition that the Soviet Union had a "more direct interest" in these nations, and upon the fact that they lay in the Soviet theater of military operations.[16] It was logical enough in the case of Rumania and Hungary, which were at war with the Soviet Union, and which lay in the natural path of Soviet military operations—if it could be assumed that the Soviets would respect the right of self-determination. The mistake lay only in the making of such an assumption. Bulgaria, on the other hand, was not at war with the Soviet Union until September 4, 1944, when the Soviets unexpectedly declared war and invaded without provocation. In this case there was no logical basis for agreeing to Soviet control on any assumption.

As a result of these attitudes, the Soviets were permitted to "take the lead" in the negotiation of the armistice agreements,[17] and when peace offers were made to the Western Allies by Rumania and Hungary they were referred to the Soviet Union. In the case of Bulgaria, which was not at war with Russia, talks with the Western Allies were actually begun. But after the Soviet declaration of war these negotiations were also transferred to Moscow, and the armistice agreement with that country provided for the same Soviet domination as the others.

The Western Allies did expect that there would be "prior consultation" in the control commissions before the issuance of "policy directives," and that their representatives would therefore be informed of what was going on. They would thus be able to refer objections to their own governments, which could then at least disassociate themselves from actions of which they did not approve.[18] It was soon discovered, however, that even this right would not be observed. In the Yalta Conference briefing book the State Department reported that prior consultation did not take place in Bulgaria, and that "the Soviet rôle in the Control Commission" had "even exceeded the proportions assigned. . . ."[19] In Rumania, where the Soviet chairman "accepted the principle of prior consultation," it was not observed in practice, and the State Department cited the following example of a now familiar Soviet form of oppression:

Notwithstanding this apparent improvement there is now before us a new example of the Soviet unilateral method; namely, the orders issued to the Rumanian Government to prepare lists of racial Germans in Rumania for deportation to Soviet Russia for labor service. This matter is now being taken up in Bucharest, and representations will also be made in Moscow, both as to the substance of the order, and as to the unilateral procedure adopted.[20]

The Western Allies also expected that *after* the German surrender there would be equal participation in the operation of the control commissions, and at Potsdam the Soviets did agree to a revised procedure. The new agreement provided that directives on "questions of principle" would be issued only with the concurrence of all members, and that conferences would be regularly called "for the purpose of discussing the most important questions,"[21] but it proved to be only a paper concession. The actual operation of the Commissions continued to be so bad that their termination was cited as a benefit to be derived from the ratification of peace treaties in 1947.[22] This meant, in effect, that the free powers had concluded that withdrawal of their own representatives, and complete abandonment of these nations, was preferable to the rule of the so-called joint authority of the control commissions.

The conduct of the Soviets, however, was not based entirely on the one-sided nature of these Commissions. The agreements themselves required the dissolution of all organizations conducting propaganda hostile to the United Nations, and since the Soviet Union was one of the United Nations, this meant all organizations conducting propaganda hostile to the Soviet Union. It therefore also meant, in effect, all organizations conducting propaganda hostile to communism—political, social and religious—and therefore all effective opposition. The Rumanian agreement was the most specific in this regard:

> The Rumanian Government undertakes immediately to dissolve all pro-Hitler organizations (of a Fascist type) ... as well as other organizations conducting propaganda hostile to the United Nations, *in particular to the Soviet Union*, and will not in future permit the existence of organizations of that nature.[23] (Italics added.)

The suppression of anti-Soviet opposition could not, of course, have been prevented merely by the omission of reference to the Soviet Union, or even of the reference to the United Nations. As Ambassador Harriman reported, "Any political figure ... who disagrees with Soviet policies is conveniently branded as a 'Fascist.' "[24] But as long as the provision remained, and the Soviets were included among the United Nations, it is difficult to see how the representatives of the free powers could even raise an objection to the destruction of almost *any* organization in these strictly non-Communist countries.

The results of Soviet control of these countries are well known.

Under the ostensible rule of so-called coalition governments, in which the representatives of democratic parties were allowed nominal participation, but in which Communists occupied the positions necessary for administrative and juridical suppression of opposition, there was instituted a ruthless campaign of forcible communization and the liquidation of all non-Communist organizations, leaders, and institutions.

In Bulgaria the Communists immediately arrested the non-Communist Council of Ministers and installed a new government in which they assumed the key ministries of interior (police) and justice. The conferees at Yalta were fully apprised of the situation by the briefing-book paper on Bulgaria:

> The country is ruled—aside from the Soviet Chairman of the Allied Control Commission—by a coalition government known as the "Fatherland Front," composed of representatives of the Communist Party and the Agrarian and Union-Zveno parties, in which it appears that the Communists are steadily gaining the ascendency, aided covertly by Russian occupation authorities. . . .
>
> Bulgarian foreign relations are in effect under the supervision of the Control Commission, meaning, for practical purposes, the Soviet authorities. Thus far we have not learned much about these relations. . . .[25]

So-called people's courts were established for the trial of "war crimes," and the Select Committee on Communist Aggression states that, according to official Communist figures, 11,667 persons were put on trial during the first six months. Although the Soviet "war" with Bulgaria had lasted for only a few days, 2,850 of those tried were executed. The committee adds that those convicted included "not only Nazi collaborators but almost every prominent Bulgarian politician, officer, civil servant, judge, teacher, journalist, businessman, churchman, in a word, all potential opponents. . . ."[26]

In Rumania the army was diverted, in accordance with the terms of the armistice agreement, from war with the Soviets to the invasion of Hungary and Slovakia. Soviet troops, meanwhile, were used for the occupation of Rumania itself, and Communists were gradually moved into key government positions. As in the case of Bulgaria, there was a warning of Soviet intentions in the Yalta briefing book:

> The strong influence of the Soviet Union in Rumania has been

the cause of some alarm, especially in British circles which fear that it will block the British plans to restore their pre-war political and economic position in Rumania. Prominent Rumanian leaders, including Mr. Iuliu Maniu, the Peasant Party Chief, whose devotion to democratic principles throughout his long career is well known, have made known to the official American representatives in Bucharest their fear that the Soviet Union's present policies in Rumania are aimed at the eventual domination and annexation of that country. . . .[27]

These fears were discounted, however, and the report continued:

The Department does not believe that the evidence at hand supports their view, although there have been some indications of Soviet intervention in internal Rumanian affairs and of a Soviet policy of stripping Rumania economically.[28]

The Department was soon disabused of this skepticism. Shortly after the Yalta Conference, the Communists attempted to assassinate the Prime Minister. When this failed, a Soviet deputy commissar came to Bucharest and ordered the young King Michael to install a Communist-front government. This deputy was Andrei Vyshinsky, former chief prosecutor for Soviet purge trials, and subsequently Foreign Minister and chief of the Soviet delegation to the United Nations. The King at first rejected his demands, but a demonstration by the Red Army soon made it obvious that resistance was useless. In the new Soviet-sponsored government the Communists received four posts, including the Ministry of Justice, and the "non-Communist," Petru Groza, was installed as Prime Minister. In 1952, he was made Chairman of the Presidium of the Grand National Assembly, a post which he retained until his death in 1958.

A similar procedure was followed in Hungary, where the Communists were immediately placed in control of the police and transportation. In the first elections, in November, 1945, the Communists received only 17% of the votes, but the chairman of the Allied Control Commission, Klement Voroshilov, ordered the creation of a coalition government. Under this arrangement the Communists received four ministries, including the Ministry of the Interior (police). Voroshilov later became President of the Supreme Soviet of the Soviet Union.

The final coup occurred in May-June, 1947, when, in the words of the ousted United States Minister to Hungary, "the Communist leaders, aided by the intervention of the Soviet occupation forces, forced the resignation of the Smallholder Prime Minister and seized effective control of the Government."[29] This coup was followed, in August, 1947, by a rigged election in which the Communists won 22% of the vote.

After the acceptance of the armistice agreements, the next opportunity for the use of persuasion (or for acquiescence in further aggression) occurred at Yalta. At this conference, February 4-11, 1945, the Soviets were induced to renew their pledge of allegiance to the Atlantic Charter in a Declaration on Liberated Europe (see Appendix C-2). This was another paper concession, made up of unenforceable promises to set up interim regimes "broadly representative of all democratic elements," and to provide the earliest possible free election of governments "responsive to the will of the people." The free powers, on the other hand, agreed to surrender Poland, Yugoslavia, Outer Mongolia, southern Sakhalin, the Kurile Islands, Darien and a "preeminent" interest in the Chinese-Eastern and South-Manchurian Railroads.[30]

The agreements on Yugoslavia and Poland were expressed in terms which indicated compromise, and the desire of the free powers for democratic rule, but the grants in the Far East were outright concessions, stated as the necessary price ("conditions") for Soviet participation in the war with Japan. They were made on the assumption that Soviet assistance was indispensable, thereby repeating and compounding the errors made in seeking such assistance in war with Germany, in 1918 and again in 1939.

In the case of the grants in Outer Mongolia and Manchuria, there was a provision requiring the "concurrence" of China; but if China had any objections, they were obviously not going to receive much consideration. The "top secret" document also stated:

The Heads of the three Great Powers have agreed that these claims of the Soviet Union shall be *unquestionably* fulfilled after Japan has been defeated. (Italics added.)

In the case of Yugoslavia, where a merger with Tito had already been agreed upon, the free powers put their faith in what the briefing paper called "the good will of the new administration." It was provided that the merger "should immediately be put into effect,"[31] and the reluctant King was forced to accept it. The United States and Great

Britain thus put themselves in the anomalous position of opposing the efforts of a monarchy to preserve democracy.

One change, intended as an improvement, was made in the proposed composition of the Yugoslav government. It required that Tito's legislature, the so-called Anti-Fascist Assembly, be enlarged to include those members of the last Yugoslav parliament who had not "compromised themselves by collaboration with the enemy." That parliament, however, had itself been dissolved as unrepresentative in 1939, and with Tito deciding who was a collaborator, the change, like the original parts of the agreement, depended entirely upon his improbable consent to the end of his own personal rule in Yugoslavia.

In the new government all but five of the twenty-eight principal positions went to representatives of Marshal Tito, and Tito himself became Prime Minister and Minister of War. By the time elections were held, most of the opposition had been discouraged by the red terror, and those who refused to be discouraged were denied the right of expression. The result was a single slate, elected by more than 90% of the votes cast—an unconvincing unanimity in a state whose "diverse national and social elements," and whose "cleavages and controversies" had been the subject of State Department comment less than a year before.[32] The Department itself was not convinced, and stated as much in a press release:

... the people of Yugoslavia are entitled to expect the effective implementation of the guarantees of personal freedom, freedom from fear, liberty of conscience, freedom of speech, liberty of the press and freedom of assembly and association contained in the agreement between Marshal Tito and Dr. Subasic underlying the Yalta Declaration and to have an opportunity to express their will in a free and untrammeled election. In view of conditions existing in Yugoslavia, it cannot be said that those guarantees of freedom have been honored nor that the elections conducted on November 11 provided opportunity for a free choice of the people's representatives.[33]

In Poland, as in Yugoslavia, a full-fledged Communist regime was already installed when the Yalta Conference took place, and the free powers were induced to accept a Soviet pledge as vague as the agreement between Tito and Dr. Subasic, and as unenforceable as the "Declaration on Liberated Europe." It provided that the Communist puppet regime should be "reorganized on a broader democratic basis with the inclusion of democratic leaders from Poland itself and from Poles abroad," and it differed from the arrangement on Yugoslavia primarily in the manner of its acceptance. The recognized government of Poland was not even consulted, and those to be included in the "reorganized" regime were to be designated by a tripartite commission meeting in Moscow. Even this group was to consult, not with the recognized government, but "in the first instance in Moscow with members of the present Provisional [Communist] Government and with other Polish democratic leaders from within Poland and from abroad." The regime thus "reorganized" would be "pledged to the holding of free and unfettered elections as soon as possible."[34] This was two years later for the Communist type of election, and never for the "free and unfettered" type.

The results of the agreement on Poland were similar to the results of the agreement on Yugoslavia. The Soviets delayed the work of the commission while they arrested and imprisoned the most likely democratic leaders from Poland itself. These included the Vice-Premier of the government-in-exile, who as chairman of the underground parliament (Council of National Unity) had remained in Poland throughout the Nazi occupation, the Commander-in-Chief of the Home (underground) army, three members of the Home Council of Ministers, and representatives of all the major political parties. Communists were finally appointed to the positions of President, Prime Minister, Deputy Prime Minister, and six other strategic ministries;[35] and the Select Committee on Communist Aggression reported that "Out of 21 Cabinet posts, all but 3 positions were held by the Communists or Communist followers."[36]

By these means the free powers were induced to accept formal participation, without real influence, in the subjection to Communist domination of nearly all the countries of eastern Europe. The one exception was Czechoslovakia, where this function was performed by the government-in-exile itself.

Although the Western Allies had assisted and assented to Soviet occupation, they made no specific agreement with respect to Czechoslovakia's future government. Such an agreement was made in April, 1945, between Eduard Benes, the President of the recognized government-in-exile in London, and the leader of the Moscow group of Czech Communists, Clement Gottwald. It corresponded roughly to the agreement made between Marshal Tito and Dr. Subasic, but it was in no respect vague, calling for a drastic program of socialization,

the suppression of several important parties on charges of Nazi collaboration, and the surrender to the Communists of specified key
cabinet positions.

In the first Czech government thus created, two Communists
were appointed Deputy Prime Ministers, and one of them, Clement
Gottwald, became the real head of the cabinet. In addition, the Communists were given control of the ministries of interior (police), information, agriculture, social welfare and education, and the posts of
Prime Minister and Minister of Defense were occupied by close collaborators.[37] By the time the Red Army was withdrawn, at the end
of 1945, the Communists were well entrenched; and by 1948, they
were strong enough to seize power openly, with the aid of Soviet
pressure from abroad.

The next occasion for Big Three agreement occurred at Potsdam in July-August, 1945, where the Soviets obtained formal approval
of their control of East Germany. This was assured by agreement that
"supreme authority" should be vested in the four occupying commanders, "each in his own zone of occupation," to be exercised upon
"instructions from their respective Governments."[38] All possibility of
Western intervention was removed by the power of veto in the Allied
Control Council and by the failure to provide for any other form of
central administration.

The value of a central and independent government under conditions of joint occupation was demonstrated in Austria, which became the lone exception to the almost universal pattern of surrender
to Soviet control. The Soviet armed forces were the first to enter this
country, and they immediately authorized the creation of a provisional government, with the usual Communist control of key positions.
They also agreed that its membership should be "broadened," but in
this case the Western Allies were able to insure the "broadening" by
refusing to accept the authority of the proposed government in their
own occupation areas until *after* significant phases of the operation
had been completed. These included the addition of several new
ministers and under-secretaries, the admission of Western Allied
forces into Vienna, and the transfer of police control and election
preparations to a commission of five Austrians in which there was
only one Communist.

In further contrast to the procedure in the satellites, the chairmanship of the Allied Council was rotated, the Soviets were not
permitted to dominate, and the conduct of really free elections was

insisted upon. As a result, the police and the courts remained free of Communist control, the elections were held under acceptable conditions, and the vote against the Communists was overwhelming, even in the Soviet zone.

Another blow was dealt to Soviet intentions by the decision that all actions of the newly elected government, except those involving constitutional changes, would stand unless disapproved by unanimous vote of the Allied Council. The veto power was thus made to work against the Soviets instead of in their favor.

Even so, there were many Soviet attempts to communize the eastern zone, and they failed only because of the firm if not always successful resistance of the Austrian government, the Austrian police and the representatives of the free powers. Finally, in 1954, the Soviet representative summoned the Chancellor, Julius Raab, and other members of the Austrian government to his office, ordering an end to "hostile and subversive intrigues." He openly threatened force, stating that if the "necessary measures" were not taken, the Soviet "authorities" would "be compelled . . . to take the corresponding measures themselves."[39] The Chancellor, however, replied that his government could not obey the orders of only one occupying power, or act in violation of Austrian law. Because he spoke with the authority of more than moral force or persuasion, he had the last word; and in the following year the long-awaited Austrian treaty was accepted. The Red Army was withdrawn.

Another nation to be spared was Finland. In its case there was no occupation, and no Allied assistance to the Communists—and there was also the Soviets' early experience of stiff resistance and expulsion from the League of Nations. Both cases proved that other nations might have been spared by more courageous action on the part of the free nations, and by the adoption of any one of various proposals made during the war.

One of such proposals was the request by Stalin himself, in 1941, for British and American expeditionary forces in Russia. Another was the proposal for Allied invasion of the Balkans, originally made by Stalin in 1941, and revived by the British in 1944. Under the British proposal the Allied operations in Italy would have been continued northward through Trieste, Yugoslavia and Austria into Hungary and Czechoslovakia. The plan was favored by the British High Command, by General Mark Clark, commander of the Fifth U.S. Army in Italy, by Marshal Tito, and eventually even by Stalin,[40] but it was opposed by the United States. General Eisenhower reports that it produced one of his "longest-sustained arguments" with Churchill,[41] and it was finally ruled out by President Roosevelt himself.[42]

Still another such proposal was implied in the State Department's suggestion for an "Emergency High Commission For Liberated Europe."[43] One of the indicated purposes of this proposed commission was to "assist, where conditions require, in the maintenance of internal order, such assistance to include where other means fail *the joint use of force*."[44] (Italics added.) Presumably, this meant the use throughout eastern Europe of an arrangement similar to that adopted for Austria. The proposal was abandoned partly because of anticipated objection to the further use of American troops abroad[45]— the same objection which had been made to aid to Russia after World War I—and partly because of President Roosevelt's reluctance to accept responsibility for the internal affairs of Europe[46]—an attitude hardly consistent with the statement on the "four freedoms," or with the Atlantic Charter and the multitude of other wartime declarations.

The adoption of any one of these proposals would have provided an opportunity for direct military operations in aid of the subject peoples. Such aid might also have been provided by furnishing weapons and ammunition to the numerous anti-Communist resistance movements in eastern Europe—and in the Soviet Union—instead of to the Communists. But when the free powers became aware that conciliation was ineffective, and that Soviet pledges were meaningless, the Soviets had already received billions in lend-lease and the best opportunities for aid to the people had passed. The free powers turned instead to verbal protests—which were ignored, and to threats of diplomatic steps—which were never carried out.

The United States originally took the position that it would refuse to recognize any regimes which did not fulfill the pledges made in the Atlantic Charter. This position was firmly stated in a public address made on October 5, 1945 by Secretary of State James R. Byrnes. "We do not seek," he said "to dictate the internal affairs of any people. We only reserve for ourselves the right to refuse to recognize governments if after investigation we conclude they have not given to the people the rights pledged to them in the Yalta agreement and in the Atlantic Charter."[47]

Three weeks later this policy was reaffirmed by the President. In his Navy Day address, October 27, 1945, President Truman asserted: "We shall refuse to recognize any government imposed upon any nation by the force of any foreign power. In some cases it may be impossible to prevent forceful imposition of such a government. But the United States will not recognize any such government."[48] He repeated this statement in his next annual message on the State of the Union, January 14, 1946.

The United States, however, had already agreed to recognize the new Polish government—prior to elections—and had done so, July 5, 1945, on the strength of promises alone.[49] Its threat to withhold recognition of the others was to die in its own birth.

In August, 1945, the King of Rumania appealed for three-power assistance in the formation of a more democratic government. The United States responded immediately with a public announcement that diplomatic relations with the existing regime were impossible:

The Government of the United States has already expressed the hope that the political situation in Rumania would develop in such a way as to permit it to establish diplomatic relations with Rumania, which were not, however, possible at the present time in view of the fact the provisional government as it was constituted under Groza was not adequately representative of all important elements of democratic opinion.[50]

In the same month, the United States voiced objections to the unrepresentative character of the regime in Bulgaria, and to the conditions under which it intended to hold its first elections, at that time scheduled for August 26.[51] As a result, the Bulgarian elections were postponed until November.

A special fact-finding mission was sent to both states, but there was no substantial improvement; and in November, 1945—after receiving the mission's report—the State Department issued another protest and a new press release:

From the elections now scheduled for November 18, 1945, important democratic elements are excluded through the operation of a single list of candidates. Moreover, there are indications that the free expression of popular will is being further restricted by threats of coercion and later reprisals.[52]

Finally a compromise was made. In December, 1945, it was

agreed at a Moscow conference of foreign ministers (U.S., U.S.S.R. and U.K.) that the two regimes would be recognized after they had been "broadened" by the addition of two non-Communist ministers each. In Rumania they were to be designated by a three-power commission acting in consultation with the King, and in Bulgaria they were to be selected by the local regime itself—with the "friendly advice" of the Soviet Union.[53]

The Secretary of State conceded his own defeat. In a radio report on the conference, December 30, he stated: "The agreements regarding Rumania and Bulgaria do not go as far as I should have liked, but I am hopeful that they will result in a substantial improvement in the democratic character of these Governments."[54] President Truman endeavored to reassure him with an apparent promise that the commitment would not be honored unless the Soviets went much further than they had in fact agreed to go. He relates in his memoirs that he wrote a long handwritten letter to Mr. Byrnes, which he read to him on January 5, 1946, and in which he stated that he was "not going to agree to the recognition of those governments unless they are *radically* changed."[55] (Italics added.) The Soviets, however, did not even go as far as they had promised, and recognition was extended nevertheless.

In Rumania the designated candidates were assigned to purely nominal positions and they were ignored in all important matters. Nevertheless on the strength of such appointments and the mere *promise* of free elections, the United States and Great Britain recognized the regime in February, 1946. As a result, they were soon making new complaints. In May, 1946, the United States delivered a note which stated that the two additional ministers were given no opportunity to participate fully in the government: "Full cabinet meetings are rarely called and important pending legislation frequently is not discussed in them; in many instances Ministers are not given adequate time to study draft laws and in some other important cases decree laws are published without having been submitted to these Ministers for their study."[56] This protest was completely ineffectual and subsequent protests regarding the conduct of "electoral preparations" were rebuffed as "incompatible with the attributes of a free and sovereign state."[57]

In Bulgaria, the Moscow agreement made it possible for popular political leaders to win a promise of *three* important posts, and a further pledge of free elections, but the "friendly advice" of the Soviet

Union was to veto the whole arrangement. Another unsatisfactory election was held in October, 1946, and complaints in the Allied Control Commission were rejected as "rude interference in the internal affairs of Bulgaria."[58] Recognition was extended, however, after the execution and ratification of the peace treaties in 1947.

The pledge of nonrecognition was even more readily forsaken in dealings with the other Soviet satellites. In the case of Yugoslavia, recognition was promised in the very same document (December 22, 1945) which protested that the "guarantees of freedom" had not been "honored," and that the elections offered no "opportunity for a free choice of the people's representatives."[59]

The first postwar governments of Hungary and Poland were recognized on the strength of their promises to conduct free elections, and the postwar government of Czechoslovakia was recognized on the basis of its apparent continuity with the wartime government-in-exile. In each case, however, new governments were thereafter imposed, by the use or threat of violence, in a manner which would normally require a new act of recognition.

In Hungary the first promised elections were promptly held (November 4, 1945) and found acceptable. The Communists were thoroughly defeated, but at the command of the Soviet High Commissioner a "coalition" government was installed with four Communists in key positions. It was recognized by the United States, nevertheless; and in 1947, such recognition was extended to an entirely Communist-dominated regime imposed by Soviet-supported *coup d'état*. Since the coup itself was described as a "most flagrant interference in Hungarian affairs," and a "realignment of political authority" which "nullified the express will of the majority,"[60] such recognition could hardly be deemed consistent with the earlier pledge to withhold recognition from governments imposed "by the force of any foreign power."

A new Communist- dominated regime was established in Poland after the first so-called election, held in 1947, and another in Czechoslovakia after the *coup d'état* in 1948. Both were recognized immediately, in spite of public, official condemnation of the methods employed. In the case of Poland the "elections" were found to be accompanied by "wide-spread measures of coercion and intimidation," and the United States protested that the provisional government had "failed to carry out its solemn pledges."[61] In the case of Czechoslovakia the coup was described as a "suspension of the free exercise of parliamentary institutions and the establishment of a disguised dictatorship of a single party."[62]

Thus, the firm stand announced in 1945 was fully abandoned, and in the end recognition was actually withheld only from the Soviet annexation of the Baltic States—where no separate recognition was called for—and from the Communist regime in Albania—where the first elections were found to be free and fair by a majority of the State Department observers.[63] Recognition was withheld from the Albanian regime only because of its refusal to reaffirm the validity of prewar treaties and agreements—a consideration which seems far less important than the rights of the people so readily waived in the case of the other satellites. The effect was that the United States, which started out with the intention of recognizing no regime imposed by the force of a foreign power, ended up by withholding recognition only from that regime which it was unable officially to assert had been so imposed.

Actually, the first elections in Albania, as well as all succeeding ones, were far from free and fair. The Select Committee on Communist Aggression reports that there were provisions for nominal opposition, but that in fact "no opposition appeared, because of the prevailing terror."[64] Only three opposition candidates dared to present themselves, of whom one was executed and the other two imprisoned.[65]

Since 1945, there have been similar "elections" in all of the satellites, universally regarded as forced endorsements of Soviet puppet regimes. They have offered only single slates of candidates, or purely nominal opposition, and it is sufficient merely to read the reported results (all nearly unanimous) to discover their fraudulent nature. The following were among the percentages reported as voting in favor of the "candidates" presented by the Communists:

Albania	1945—93%		1950—98.1%		1958—99.97%
Baltic States					
Estonia	1940—92.9%				
Latvia	1940—98.7%				
Lithuania	1940—99.2%				
Czechoslovakia		1948—80%	1954—97.89%	1957—99.2%	
Czech Lands	1946—31%				
Slovakia	1946— 7%				

Bulgaria	1945—86%		1949—97.6%	1957—99.5%	
East Germany			1950—99.7%		
Hungary	1945—17%	1947—22%	1949—92.1%		1958—99.6%
Poland		1947—80%	1952—99.7%		1958—97%
Rumania	1946—69%	1948—90.8%	1952—98%	1957—98.88%	1958—99.62%
Yugoslavia	1945—90%		1952—93.2%		

Another threatened diplomatic step, never carried out, was the refusal to execute treaties of peace with governments which had not been democratically chosen. Such a refusal would have applied in Bulgaria, Hungary and Rumania (with whose Communist governments such treaties were made), and had been indicated as a likely course of action by the Secretary of State. Thus, in the case of Bulgaria, he stated in a press release, August 18, 1945, that free elections were a necessary precondition for both recognition *and* a treaty: "In the opinion of the United States Government the effective participation of all important democratic elements in the forthcoming election is essential to facilitate the conclusion of a peace treaty with a recognized democratic government."[66]

The execution of such treaties not only carried the implication that the required pledges with respect to free elections had been carried out; it also implied that the guarantees of freedom contained in the treaties themselves were being observed. There was such a provision in each treaty:

Bulgaria [Hungary] [Rumania] shall take all measures necessary to secure to all persons under Bulgarian [Hungarian] [Rumanian] jurisdiction, without distinction as to race, sex, language or religion, the enjoyment of human rights and of the fundamental freedoms, including freedom of expression, of press and publication, of religious worship, of political opinion and of public meeting.[67]

If the treaties were to be executed, it would have to be with full knowledge that they were being violated in their inception, in the most gross manner, and even while public protests were being made of the conditions created by the violation. It is difficult to conceive of any more effective means of destroying the moral influence and prestige of the United States, in these nations and elsewhere.

Nevertheless, the treaties were concluded, and even while signing the ratifications President Truman remarked that the "governments" of the three countries had "disregarded the will of the majority of the people" and "resorted to measures of repression against them."[68] He acted in the vain hope that the end of the international warrant for Soviet occupation would be followed by the withdrawal of Soviet forces.

Whether or not the fate of eastern Europe would have been different if recognition had been withheld, or if the peace treaties had not been executed, is a question which can never be answered, because the original intention was not carried out. But the experience of this period does prove that the Soviet campaign of repression could not be changed by less effective steps. Every other available means was employed to exert the purely moral force of world opinion—through diplomatic protests and publication of the protests, through representations in the Allied Control Commissions, through negotiation, and even through exposure and appeal in the United Nations—but with no threat of corrective action and therefore with no effect.

In the case of Poland the State Department called frequent attention, through protests and press releases, to innumerable violations of human freedom and crimes against humanity—to the "political murders,"[69] to the "administrative persecution ... by arrests, censorship restrictions ... interference and other oppressive acts";[70] to the "compulsory enrollment," to the "dismissal" of opposition party members from their employment, to the "searches of homes" and "attacks by secret police and members of the Communist Party," to the "suspension and restriction" of opposition party meetings and "party activities," to the "suppression of the party press";[71] and to "widespread measures of coercion and intimidation."[72] In 1947, the United States Ambassador, Arthur Bliss Lane, resigned in order, as he says, that he might "be enabled to speak and write openly"[73] in his own personal account.[74] But there was never any indication that any effective steps would be taken to secure correction.

In Rumania the protests were equally numerous and related to the same means of silencing and of crushing the opposition to communism—to the "monopoly" of state broadcasting facilities by "parties within the Government," to the "organized bands of hooligans" that "have broken up meetings";[75] to the "restrictions on registration" and on the exercise by opposition parties of the right "to print, publish and distribute their political publications" and "to organize associations, hold meetings, and be allowed premises for this purpose";[76] to the "arbitrary arrest without warrant or charge of hundreds of Opposition Party and non-party persons and the indefinite detention of such individuals in prisons and concentration camps";[77] to the "arrest of Mr. [Iuliu] Maniu and the suppression by the Government of the National Peasant Party, of which he is the leader";[78] and finally, to "All manner of chicanery, and extreme physical violence"... "inequitable distribution of newsprint, the denial of freedom to print, publish and distribute and... various other artifices"..."official censorship"..."intimidation... preventing voters from reaching the polls...multiple voting...distortion of the final returns"...a "brutal campaign to eliminate all political opposition"..."nationwide manhunts...on a mass scale resulting in the arbitrary arrest and incarceration of thousands of opposition and non-party persons."[79] But here too there was no suggestion of any positive effort to aid the people.

In the case of Hungary one protest recited that "exclusion from the electorate" had "reached 70 percent in some districts" and that "charges on which potential voters have lost their suffrage rights border on the grotesque."[80] The cause of freedom was so well pleaded that the United States Minister, Selden Chapin, was accused of complicity in the "crimes" of Cardinal Mindzenty, and after his forced recall he spoke freely of the Soviet method of subjugation, the "open terror," the "star-chamber trials on trumped-up charges," the "kidnapping," and "all the usual paraphernalia of totalitarian discipline and justice."[81] Still there was no offer of any material form of assistance.

Following the coup in Czechoslovakia, a joint declaration of condemnation[82] was published by the United States, Great Britain and France. In the Security Council of the United Nations, the American representative, Warren R. Austin, described how the coup was accompanied by "the swift and ruthless purge of the non-Communist leaders," the "complete seizure of control over broadcasting facilities," and the "elimination of non-Communist newspaper editors." He added a summary of the methods employed in all Soviet satellites, where, he said, "the general pattern was the same":

Like Czechoslovakia, all these countries have been occupied by the Soviet armies. The chief steps were the acquisition by the Communists of key posts in the Cabinet; control of the police; control of the armies; control of the media of mass communications; and finally control of or subversion of the judiciary. In none of these countries did the Communists enjoy popular support sufficient to warrant their commanding position in the government. . . .

Is it not significant that the top Communists in Hungary such as the Deputy Prime Minister, Rakosi, and the economic czar, Vas, Foreign Minister Pauker in Rumania, Prime Minister Dimitrov and Foreign Minister Kolarov of Bulgaria, and the entire leadership of Czechoslovakia, including Premier Gottwald, Cabinet Ministers Fierlinger, Kopecky, Nejedly, and the Secretary General of the Communist Party, Slansky, have all spent years of active work in Moscow and have been in close association with both the Soviet Communist leaders as well as the Communist leaders in other countries and that some of them have even become Soviet citizens?

To complete the similarity of the patterns in all those countries, is it a mere coincidence as I pointed out on Tuesday that the Soviet Deputy Foreign Minister Vyshinsky appeared in Bucharest at the crucial moment and another Soviet Deputy Foreign Minister, Zorin, was present in Prague at the time of the February coup?[83]

Again there was no threat of positive action.

Without such action all pleas were unavailing, and the condemnations were easily passed over. No matter how heinous the crime, or how loud the complaint, the Communist response was defiance. When the United States offered witnesses for the defense of General Mihailovic, the answer was simply that his "crimes" were "far too big and horrible that it could be or should be allowed to be discussed whether he is guilty or is not."[84] In the Bulgarian National Assembly, the Communist Prime Minister, Georgi Dimitrov, boldly described the impermanence and futility of protests made at the time of the "trial" and execution of Nikola Petkov, Bulgarian political leader— a trial in which it had been pointed out by the State Department that the defense attorneys "were seized by the militia," that the court had "refused to permit the appearance of numerous witnesses," and even that the "presiding judge" had "actively participated in the prosecution."[85] Dimitrov asserted:

. . . you said "The court will not dare to sentence him to death. It would be too horrible. Both Washington and London will rise against it. . . ." What happened? . . . The court . . . fulfilled the will of the people and sentenced the traitor to death.

Then you said: "If they execute the death sentence, the glass of patience will overflow. The whole world will rise against it, and all its wrath will fall on the back of the Bulgarian people."

... it was executed.

What happened then? Who rose against it in the country? Where were the demonstrations, the mutinies with which we were threatened? Nothing like that happened.

And what happened abroad? ... No one raised a hand in defense of Petkov. Some people in the West shouted for a while, but soon quietened [sic] down.... The whole incident was soon forgotten.[86]

This, unfortunately, has been the experience of the subject peoples since 1917.

CHAPTER IX

THE FOURTH ROUND OF SOVIET AGGRESSION

The United Nations, Containment and Korea

It is sometimes said that cold-war issues should be avoided by the United Nations, because their consideration imposes a "severe strain" on the organization[1] and only "increases international tensions without producing constructive results."[2] Such an approach, however, would restrict the United Nations to the maintenance of peace between those nations which are peaceful, and to the protection of the security of those which are not attacked. It is a disingenuous way of saying that the world's second attempt to create a permanent system of general security has been frustrated by the work of a few men, and that the United Nations is unable to accomplish the first task stated in its charter—"to take effective collective measures for the prevention and removal of threats to the peace" and to bring about the peaceful "settlement of international disputes or situations which might lead to a breach of the peace."[3]

A similar attitude was taken after the organization of the League of Nations, when many were of the opinion that even membership should be denied to those nations which were threatened by Soviet aggression. The excuse made then was stated by a British delegate: "We have to consider the future of the League. Could anything be more disadvantageous to our Society than that we should now embark upon responsibilities which we are patently unable to discharge, and which in the course of a few months it may become evident we are unable to discharge?"[4]

When the League was formed, however, the Soviet Union was not included. It was therefore possible, if not practical, to restrict the goal of the first world peace organization to something less than world-wide security—to ignore the depredations of the Red Army and to occupy the minds of the delegates with problems of recontruction, public health and the non-Russian boundaries of those small states, such as Finland, Poland and Lithuania, which had been able to win a temporary reprieve from Soviet attack. Later, when the Soviet Union was admitted to the League, with a permanent seat in the Council, it was no longer possible to ignore the Red aggressions. After five years it was expelled, and the League called upon all member states to give military assistance to Finland. This response to aggression bore fruit in the execution of a peace treaty, and the preservation of Finnish independence, but its full potential was never really exploited. The free nations were at that time preoccupied with the aggressive plans of the Nazis, and within a few months the collapse of western Europe brought the League itself to an untimely end.

In the case of the United Nations, on the other hand, it has never been possible to exclude the cold war, because the aggressor has been in it from the beginning. Whenever attention is turned to other problems, such as the enforcement of human rights, emancipation of non-self-governing territories, or aid to underdeveloped nations, the delegates from some Communist-dominated regime are always on hand, making a mockery of every honest effort, aggravating, instead of helping to correct, the weaknesses of the free nations, and endeavoring to convert all practical proposals into programs for the dissemination of subversive propaganda. And always there are the absent millions, the subject peoples, whose failure to obtain representation gives the lie to frequent claims of "realism" and "universality." The real issue in the United Nations, therefore, is not *whether* it should deal with the cold war, but *how* it should deal with it—whether it should comply with the provisions of the charter calling for measures of compulsion, or whether it should disregard these provisions and rely solely upon the force of world opinion.

When the United Nations was formed, it was at first assumed that the aggressive tendencies of the Soviets would be curbed simply by committing them to the principles of the charter. This, at least, is the explanation for their inclusion given by former President Truman. At a Senate hearing on proposed charter amendments, April 18, 1955, he stated: "We knew at the time the United Nations was created that we were having difficulties with the Soviet leaders and that our difficulties might increase. We were determined, nevertheless, to go ahead with the creation of the United Nations and to get the Soviet Union into it, committed to the principles of international peace which are expressed in the charter. Without such a commitment on their part, we believed that the United Nations would not be successful."[5] Because of this assumption the United Nations became at its inception another incongruous alliance, like those of the wartime declarations, spreading false confidence in Soviet intentions and creating harmful inferences regarding the sincerity of the free nations.

It was soon discovered, moreover, that there was even greater damage to be done by including Communists in the United Nations than there was in admitting them to the League, or in joining them in the purely promissory declarations of World War II. The United Nations is an agency of enforcement, but unlike the League it allows the big powers to exercise the veto in disputes to which they are parties. The presence of the Soviet Union, therefore, insures the obstruction, and some say paralysis, of every attempted measure for the prevention of aggression.

This problem was referred to by Acting Secretary of State Dean Acheson in 1947, when he asked Congress for assistance to Greece and Turkey. His reference, however, was cautious and oblique. "Even if the project were not blocked," he said, "by the objections of certain members of the United Nations, much time would have been lost, and time is of the essence."[6] By 1954, the charges were specific, and Secretary of State Dulles freely asserted that inclusion of the Soviet Union had forced the free world to look for security *outside* the United Nations:

... the veto power has been so misused by the Soviet Union, which has cast 58 vetoes, that the Security Council is not dependable.

Because of this paralysis of the Security Council, certain nations, which were bound together by ties of fellowship and of common danger, have organized for their collective security under Article 51 of the United Nations Charter.[7]

Article 51 is that provision of the charter by which the members have reserved to themselves "the inherent right of individual or collective self-defense," and it applies only "until the Security Council has taken the measures necessary to maintain international peace and security." Its invocation, therefore, on a permanent basis, does not imply a resort to United Nations machinery; it indicates a return to conditions prevailing prior to, and without the existence of, any organization for world security.

In the search for its own safety under this article, the non-Communist world has made many pacts involving many free nations. There is the Organization of American States (the Rio Pact), made effective in December, 1948, between the United States and twenty republics of Latin America; the North Atlantic Treaty Organization (NATO), made effective in August, 1949, for the defense of the United States, the United Kingdom, Canada, Iceland, Western Europe and, later, Greece, Turkey and West Germany; the Security Treaty between the United States, Australia and New Zealand (the ANZUS Pact), made effective in April, 1952; the Southeast Asia Treaty Organization (SEATO), made effective in February, 1955, for the defense of the United States, the United Kingdom, France Australia, New Zealand, Pakistan, the Philippines, Thailand, Cambodia, Laos and Viet Nam; and the Central Treaty Organization (CENTO) originating in the Baghdad Pact, which was made effective April-October, 1955, for mutual co-operation between the United Kingdom, Turkey, Pakistan, Iran and (originally) Iraq.

There are also bilateral agreements between the United States and Japan (April, 1952, superseded by the agreement of June 23, 1960); the United States and the Philippines (August, 1952); the United States and South Korea (November, 1954); the United States and the Republic of China (March, 1955); and between the United States and Pakistan, the United States and Iran, and the United States and Turkey (made in March, 1959). In addition there is the unilateral "Eisenhower Doctrine" put forth in January-March, 1957, and containing an expression of inflexible intention to come to the aid of any victim of Communist aggression in the Middle East.

There is, however, no separate pact or "doctrine" for the defense of the subject peoples. They are still forced to depend upon the United Nations as the only organization, and its charter as the only pact, designed to fulfill the Atlantic Charter pledge of a wider and permanent system of *general* security. And in spite of the Soviet obstruction, and the denial of representation to more than 300,000,000 subject peoples, there has been ample evidence that the United Nations can fulfill this pledge.

Experience has shown that the success of the United Nations is not primarily dependent upon what the Soviet delegations do or fail to do, but upon the intentions and determination of the free nations to support the charter principles. Vetoes, like resolutions, are only verbal, and in spite of the exercise of the former, or the failure to adopt the latter, where the free powers have been ready to act, not talk, the objectives of the United Nations have been accomplished. In fact, as Secretary of State Dulles observed, "It sometimes seems that world opinion is more powerful when it is sensed than when the United Nations tries to formulate it in an Assembly resolution."[8]

This is only true, however, when it is "sensed" that world opinion will be expressed by means more effective than resolutions, and that membership in the United Nations will be regarded as an assumption, not a delegation, of responsibility. This was the basis upon which Secretary Acheson was able to make his request for American aid to Greece and Turkey (March 24, 1947). As he stated at that time, "By membership in the United Nations neither the United States nor any other country has absolved itself of its responsibility for fostering through its own action the same objective as the Charter sets for the United Nations."[9]

It was also the basis for the concurrent announcement of an even broader American policy, the "Truman Doctrine," or so-called policy of containment. In his own request for aid to Greece and Turkey, the former President stated that support of free peoples and support of the principles of the United Nations are one and the same thing:

I believe that it must be the policy of the United States to support free peoples who are resisting attempted subjugation by armed minorities or by outside pressures.

> .　　.　　.　　.　　.　　.　　.　　.

The world is not static, and the *status quo* is not sacred. But we cannot allow changes in the *status quo* in violation of the Charter of the United Nations by such methods as coercion, or by such subterfuges as political infiltration. In helping free and independent nations to maintain their freedom, the United States will be giving effect to the principles of the Charter of the United Nations. (See Appendix C-2.)

The President did not define the areas in which such resistance would be given, and his reference to the possibility of changes in the *status quo* carried only the barest hint (if any) of aid to the subject peoples. Nevertheless, under the circumstances, the decision was of great significance. It was the first public assertion that the United States would give effective help to others for defense against Communist aggression, and it thus changed attitudes and policies which had persisted, not only since World War II, or since the formal recognition of the Soviet regime in 1933, but since the first Bolshevik seizure of power in 1917.

And although the statement did not promise aid to the subject peoples, it did not leave them entirely without hope. "Indirect" as well as "direct" aggression, and the seizure of power by "armed minorities" as well as by "outside pressures," were all specifically condemned. It was thus indicated that the peoples of eastern Europe and of all parts of the Soviet Union, even of Russia itself, would henceforth be recognized as victims of aggression. Accordingly, the subject peoples were able at least to hope that they would eventually receive the same assistance as the free peoples in other parts of the world.

It is true that the decision was very late. If the youngest daughter of the Czar, Anastasia Nicolaievna Romanova, were still alive, as some believed,[10] she would have been at that time no longer seventeen years of age but a middle-aged woman of forty-five. Millions like her had already lost their lives, homes, families and fortunes, and had long been forgotten. Many nations had perished, many governments had been destroyed, and a new mass emigration had swelled the ranks of the first. But this did not prevent action now to give aid to those who remained, and to new generations born in bondage or in exile. Even if nothing had survived, the same enduring oppression remained.

It was also true that the decision would not be consistently applied, and that many new victims were to be added to the already overextended rolls of the unassisted—witness Hungary, which was to fall not once but twice unaided; Czechoslovakia, to be abandoned within a year; China, to which effective aid was even then being denied; and Guatemala, which was to be saved by exiles while the United States pleaded, not for their assistance, but for the right to convoke an "Organ of Consultation."[11] But these failures, too, could be corrected. They were not due primarily to any dearth of stated principles, or even to any defect in the charter of the United Nations, but merely to the free world's refusal, as yet, fully to apply or enforce them. It might still be induced to do so with real universality.

The Truman Doctrine was first announced in 1947, as the basis for aid to Greece and Turkey, but the value of the support for which it called had been proven the year before, when the Soviets had belatedly but voluntarily ended their wartime occupation of the northern part of Iran. At that time the Soviets had already set up "republics" in the Iranian parts of Kurdistan and Azerbaijan, the troops of the free nations had been withdrawn, and there was no apparent compulsion for Soviet withdrawal. On the surface there was only a complaint to the United Nations, made by Iran, the uncompromising demands for evacuation made by the free powers, and the "force of world opinion"—a force which Mr. Dulles maintained was "far more persuasive than military force."[12] World opinion, however, was not effective in the case of eastern Europe, and it seems more probable that the Soviet withdrawal was the result of effective military assistance, in the form of arms and other equipment, given to Iran throughout the occupation and thereafter—at a time when it was not being made available for resistance to Soviet aggression in other areas. Similar assistance had produced a previous "voluntary" Soviet withdrawal, in 1921, and because of its repetition the men in the Kremlin undoubtedly "sensed" that world opinion would be expressed by more forceful means than resolutions and protests.

In May, 1920, when the Bolsheviks invaded the Trans-Caucasus, they had also invaded Iran, set up a "Soviet Socialist Republic" in the province of Gilan, and announced their intention to use it as a vehicle for "the liberation of other peoples of the East."[13] At that time, however, the British were offering extensive military assistance, and although withdrawing troops from the neighboring Trans-Caucasus, they retained others in Iran to assist in its defense. Accordingly, when Iran appealed to the League of Nations, it was not even necessary for that body to come to a decision. One of the organizers of the Iranian Communist Party, A. Sultan-Zade, relates that "events developed . . . with such rapidity that the Persian revolution, not being able to withstand the pressure by the British and the Shah's troops, suffered a defeat."[14] The Soviet Foreign Minister soon announced that the "revolution in Persia" had been postponed:

On October 22, 1920, the Central Committee of the Communist Party of Iran adopted the resolution that the revolution in Persia must still pass through the stage of the bourgeois revolution. An end was thus put to the efforts to introduce the communist regime in Persia, efforts which had started with the local soviet government in Gilan.[15]

In February, 1921, the Bolsheviks made a treaty with Iran which said, in effect, that if the British would withdraw, they would do likewise. The British did withdraw in May, and the Bolsheviks, with typical perfidy, then launched a new attack. But it was only a trial balloon. The Soviets did not give it their full support, and when it collapsed they finally withdrew, in September, 1921. At the Third Congress of the Communist International (June-July, 1921) a representative of the Iranian Communist Party indicated that the threat of outside aid was still decisive: ". . . only after the victory of the social revolution in a number of European capitalist countries, can the Iranian Communists, jointly with the toiling masses, raise the question of the seizure of political authority, and the creation of workers' and peasants' soviets."[16]

During World War II, the Soviet Union obtained a new opportunity to realize its aspirations in the Middle East. To forestall a possible Nazi penetration, Iran was jointly occupied by British and Soviet troops, and the Red Army returned to the northern provinces under the same "international warrant" which brought it into eastern Europe. There were also the usual joint declarations, designed to insure the application of the principles of the Atlantic Charter. These included an Anglo-Soviet-Iranian treaty, made in January, 1942, in which the occupying powers agreed to withdraw their troops within six months after the termination of hostilities, and the "Declaration on Iran" in which the Big Three agreed to respect its "independence, sovereignty and territorial integrity."

In the case of Iran, however, the free powers intended to enforce these agreements with more than mere words. In March, 1942, Iran was made eligible for lend-lease military assistance, and this was supplied not only for "urgent war needs" but also "for the use of post-war armies." For this reason, in December, 1944, the Secretary of State, Edward R. Stettinius, Jr., asked for a "high priority" on military shipments to Iran. This was long after the threat of Nazi invasion had passed, but very shortly after Soviet pressure had forced the resignation of the Iranian Prime Minister:

The Department desires to urge that high priority be given to shipment of these military supplies for the Iranian Army . . . the Iranian case differs in several essential respects from that of many other countries. American policy in Iran is based specifically on the Declaration on Iran. . . . Protection and advancement of our interests in Iran require that we give the military mission the tools with which to work. Furnishing the Iranian Army with essential supplies is in line with the Department's basic policy toward Iran, which envisages strengthening the Iranian security forces to the point where they can maintaain order after the withdrawal of Allied forces. The United States can contribute substantially to world security by assisting to create a strong Iran, free from internal weakness which invites foreign intervention or aggression. To carry out this policy requires strong and well-equipped security forces.

Iran is perhaps the most prominent area of the world where inter-Allied friction might arise. Such friction would grow out of the chaos and disorder in Iran which would result from a weak Iranian Army. It is in our interests to prevent this from happening.[17]

It is significant that the Secretary of State considered that "the Iranian case differs ... from that of many other countries," and his request certainly showed a different attitude than was taken with respect to other threatened nations. In a Yalta Conference briefing paper, the State Department asserted that a similar distinction was made by the British: "The British, however willing they may be to make concessions to the Russians in Eastern Europe, will probably refuse to consider concessions in the Middle East, which is so vitally important to Empire communications."[18]

The same divergence is apparent in other statements of policy made at that time. Whereas Iran was considered a "test case" for the application of the wartime pledges, the Soviets were allowed to "take the lead" and "exert predominant political influence" in eastern Europe. In July, 1944, the American Ambassador in Teheran was informed that the President "considered Iran as something of a testing ground for the Atlantic Charter and for the good faith of the United Nations";[19] and in January, 1945, Churchill wired Roosevelt as follows:

This may be something of a test case. Persia is a country where we, yourselves and the Russians are all involved: and we have given a joint undertaking to treat the Persians decently. If the Russians are now able not only to save their face by securing the fall of the Persian Prime Minister who opposed them, but also to secure what they want by their use of the big stick, Persia is not the only place where the bad effect will be felt.[20]

In the case of Bulgaria and Rumania, on the other hand, Churchill stated that "particular respect" should be shown to "Russian views" and to "the Soviet desire to take the lead."[21] A similar attitude was taken by the United States with respect to all the Balkan nations, and Poland. A Yalta briefing paper on these nations stated: "It now seems clear that the Soviet Union will exert predominant political influence over the areas in question. While this Government prob-ably would not want to oppose itself to such a political configuration, neither would it desire to see American influence in this part of the world completely nullified."[22]

The United States gave early notice of its special interest in Iran's independence during a conference with Molotov and Litvinov on Soviet lend-lease requirements. According to the report of the President's special assistant, Harry L. Hopkins,[23] this was apparently done without any direct conversation at all by the President leaving several pertinent memoranda on his desk where they would be sure to be seen by the two Soviet emissaries. These related to an offer by the State Department of its "good offices" to Iran and Turkey in their difficulties with the Soviets. Although Molotov did not appear to be "much impressed," the Army's history of operations in Iran states that the "unspoken fact" of lend-lease assistance "gave substance to the President's casual gesture"[24] of displaying the documents.

Subsequently, at Yalta, Potsdam, and the 1945 London Con-ference of Foreign Ministers, the United States and Great Britain repeatedly insisted upon a complete Soviet withdrawal, and they continued to insist when the case was brought to the Security Council in January, 1946. The Soviet occupation forces were finally withdrawn in May; and in the light of the previous events, Mr. Dulles' assertion that this would not have taken place under the threat of "com-pulsion"[25] does not appear to give the whole picture. It may well be true that the Soviet Union would have resisted a direct attempt to expel them with a hastily organized United Nations force, as they later resisted such an effort in Korea, but the compulsion in Iran consisted in the assured and timely supply of more practical forms of assistance, arms and other military equipment—on a continuing basis—for the protection of freedom and independence.

There were other possible reasons, of course, for the Soviet with-drawal, based on other possible means of Soviet subjugation. On June 21, 1946, exactly one month after the withdrawal took place, the American Ambassador reported that the overthrow of the Iranian government was still "easily possible." In a radiogram to the Secretary of State, he asserted: "There persists, in spite of Soviet troop with-drawal, real danger of Iran becoming newest puppet of Soviet Union. Overthrow of government by leftist elements is easily possible, and without effective security forces, the numerous Soviet stooges and ruthless adventurers now in Iran could easily make it successful."[26]

At that time there was a strong Communist party in Iran (the Tudeh), and although it was later outlawed, its "growing activities," and "the toleration of those activities by the Iranian Government," became a cause of such "great concern" in 1953 as to make it "difficult," as Secretary Dulles said, "for the United States to grant assistance."[27] In August, 1953, there was an attempted *coup d'état* by the anti-British Nationalist Party of Mohammed Mossadegh; and when it failed, still another plot was discovered among a group of army officers. The goal of this conspiracy, described, according to *The New York Times*, by "United States diplomatic authorities" in Teheran as Moscow's "ace in the hole," was a "People's Democratic Republic of Iranistan."[28]

Additional threats appeared in 1958, after the overthrow of the pro-Western government of neighboring Iraq. By that time, however, Iran and its other free neighbors, Pakistan and Turkey, had been assured of continuing assistance under the Baghdad Pact. Great Britain participated in this pact as a party, and the United States became a member of the Military, Economic and Counter-Subversion Committees. In 1959, effective military assistance to these three nations was further guaranteed under bilateral agreements of co-operation made with the United States.

The Soviet Union did not use the veto in the case of Iran, but the success of the United Nations cannot be attributed to that circumstance. In this and every subsequent United Nations effort, the key to success or failure was not the evasion of the veto but rather, as a realistic appraisal would show, the existence or absence of some form of compulsion. Where compulsion was employed, world opinion prevailed in spite of the use of the veto or other forms of Soviet obstruction; and where it was not employed, the United Nations failed to attain its objectives even though expressed in resolutions successfully adopted by nearly unanimous votes. This was demonstrated in Greece, where the Communists attempted to seize power by force, and where the United States was at first opposed to the use of compulsion.

In December, 1944, when the British suppressed a Communist uprising in Athens, the United States had refused to give even moral support, and the State Department issued what Churchill describes as a "markedly critical pronouncement."[29] It was perhaps due to this attitude that a second violent attempt to seize power was begun in 1946, after the Communists were defeated in the elections. A guerrilla war was launched from bases in Albania, Yugoslavia and Bulgaria, and it grew to such proportions that even the British were unable to cope with it. In February, 1947, they announced their intention to withdraw, and it appeared that Greece would soon fall.

The United Nations appointed a commission of investigation, with which the Soviets seemed at first to co-operate, but when damaging evidence was produced they began to obstruct the commission's efforts in every possible way. The borders of the satellite nations were closed, the Communist members of the commission harassed and provoked the Greek witnesses; and when the commission reported, over Communist dissent, that "Yugoslavia, and to a lesser extent, Albania, and Bulgaria" were supporting the "guerrilla" warfare,[30] the Soviets vetoed all further proposals.

When the case was moved to the General Assembly, where the veto did not apply, a resolution was adopted calling upon the three indicted satellites "to do nothing which could furnish aid and assistance to the said guerrillas."[31] This resolution was adopted by a vote of forty to six (the Soviet bloc), with eleven abstentions. It was ignored, nevertheless, and in December, 1947, the guerrillas proclaimed a "Provisional Democratic Government" of "Free Greece."

It was obvious under such circumstances that the Soviets would not be restrained by the force of world opinion, and no one seriously contended that they could. When the British announcement was made, the United States reversed its attitude; and in March, 1947, the President told Congress that action by the United Nations would not be sufficient:

We have considered how the United Nations might assist in this crisis. But the situation is an urgent one requiring immediate action, and the United Nations and its related organizations are not in a position to extend help of the kind that is required.[32]

The President, therefore, requested direct, effective military assistance by the United States. A week later his views were confirmed by the Acting Secretary of State, Dean Acheson: "...as the President said, the United Nations and its related organizations are not now in position to extend help of the kind that is required. Even if some organ of the United Nations should decide to recommend assistance to Greece and Turkey, it would have eventually to turn primarily to the United States for funds and supplies and technical assistance."[33]

In May, 1947, such assistance was authorized. Its effect was described in the following year (February, 1948) by Loy W. Henderson, at that time Director of the Office of Near Eastern and African Affairs: "... there can be little doubt," he said, "that, if American aid had not been extended last year, democratic Greece would by now have been overwhelmed by the tide of red totalitarianism.... Possibly, also, other neighboring nations would have been drawn down in their turn by the vortex of the Greek collapse."[34] Henderson added that there was still "no assurance of victory," but Soviet support of the guerrilla movement remained covert, limited and indirect. The open resistance of the free world, on the other hand, produced an unexpected result when Marshal Tito was encouraged to show his own defiance, and declare his "independence" of the Soviet Union. In 1949, he closed his borders to the guerrilla fighters and the war soon ended. A cease-fire was announced in October, and the "Provisional Democratic Government" was no longer heard from.

Permanent aid to Greece was assured in 1952, when it was included in the North Atlantic Treaty Organization. Having thus found the means to provide for its own security, the free world refused nevertheless to apply them in aid of the subject peoples. In February, 1948—when the Communists openly seized control in Czechoslovakia —the United States, Great Britain and France jointly issued a strong public condemnation; but in spite of the recently made pledge of assistance against "armed minorities" and "outside pressures," no effective action was suggested. As a result, although world opinion was deeply shocked, the United Nations, which had been so successful in Iran and Greece, was a failure in Czechoslovakia.

The Soviet part in this affair was played by Valerian A. Zorin, then Vice Minister of Foreign Affairs and subsequently to become (in 1955) the first Soviet Ambassador to West Germany, and later (1957), as head of the Soviet delegation to the United Nations Commission on Disarmament, a chief exponent of the unenforced ban on the testing of nuclear weapons. He arrived in Prague at the climax of a series of violent demonstrations in which the streets of the city were flooded with Communist action committees, regiments of Communist-controlled police and troops of armed factory militia. Opposition demonstrations were forestalled by mass arrests and deportations; and on February 25, after five days of terror and intimidation, the President of Czechoslovakia, Eduard Benes, was forced to accept a new government. It was composed chiefly of Communists, and the other parties "represented" were completely Communist-dominated.

On the following day, the free powers published their joint declaration, in which they took note of the "suspension of the free exercise of parliamentary institutions and the establishment of a disguised dictatorship of a single party."[35] They only succeeded in calling attention to their own inconsistency, for on the same day a new request was made for *effective* aid to Greece and Turkey, and in support of which Secretary of State Marshall asserted: "A world in which it is possible for indirect aggression to deprive nations of their inherent right to pursue their peaceful national existence would be a world completely devoid of the ideals which the American people have so recently fought to preserve."[36] The talk was the same, but the deeds were different.

Accordingly, when the delegate of the ousted Czech government requested a United Nations investigation, the result was a foregone conclusion. The request was rejected by the Secretary General, Trygve Lie, on the ground that it was not filed by the representative of a government of a member state. This action prejudged the issue, and it cast doubt upon the ability of any victim of completed aggression to obtain redress in the United Nations, but it was based on the "realities" of the situation, i.e., the certainty that no real corrective action would be taken by the free world. The Secretary General would hardly have acted as he did if there had been any probability that Czechoslovakia would receive effective assistance.

When the alleged deficiency in the request made by Czechoslovakia was cured by a similar request from Chile, the investigation was vetoed by the Soviet Union. The issue, however, was again prejudged by the free nations themselves when they accepted the credentials of the representative of the new "government," thereby ousting the delegate of the victim. Nine years later, upon the death of one of the principal conspirators in this aggression, Antonin Zapotocky, they observed an *honorary* "minute of silence." This demonstration and other encomiums were given in tribute to his long service as "Prime Minister" and "President" of the aggressor's puppet regime[37]—the "disguised dictatorship" which the free nations thus held out as the representative of the people.

These actions were not compelled by any Soviet veto, and they indicated that world opinion, instead of influencing, was itself being influenced by the actions of the Soviet Union. They also encouraged a new Soviet aggression. Within a few months after the coup in Prague, the Soviet military authorities in East Germany imposed a complete land and water blockade upon the western sectors of Berlin. If there was any doubt about the purpose of this action, it was speedily removed by false Soviet radio announcements that the free powers were preparing to withdraw. According to these reports, the western sectors had already become the scene of widespread riots, looting, incendiarism, exhaustion of water supplies, starvation of infants and indiscriminate firing upon civilians.[38]

When this situation was presented to the Security Council, in October, 1948, the Soviet Union vetoed a resolution calling for termination of the blockade. It was terminated, nevertheless, in May, 1949. The reason, as Mr. Dulles later asserted, was that the "prestige" of the Western Allies was involved, and they could not "acquiesce" in a Soviet seizure "without jeopardy to their position in all of Western Europe."[39] As a result, the determination to remain in Berlin was manifested by an airlift, a counterblockade and the serious consideration of more forceful measures. Under such circumstances, a majority resolution, even though not adopted, was more effective than the veto which killed it.

The converse of this situation occurred when the General Assembly called for enforcement of the human-rights clauses included in the peace treaties with Bulgaria, Hungary and Rumania. This action was inspired by widespread protests against the persecution of Cardinal Mindzenty in Hungary and several prominent Protestant clergymen in Bulgaria. The free nations, however, were not prepared to take any of the effective steps called for by the United Nations Charter; and as a result, although the veto was avoided and numerous resolutions adopted, world opinion was ignored.

In accordance with a resolution adopted by the General Assembly in April, 1949,[40] the free powers attempted to initiate the enforcement machinery of the peace treaties themselves. This called for an appeal by the "Heads of Mission" to each satellite regime, and a request for arbitration. The appeals, however, were rejected on the ground that the Soviet "Heads of Mission" did not join, and the request for arbitration was blocked by Communist refusal to participate in the appointment of arbitrators. The General Assembly then obtained a ruling from the International Court of Justice that such participation was obligatory. This too was ignored. Finally, in November, 1950, the "governments" of these nations were condemned for "wilful refusal" to "fulfill their obligation," and the member states were invited to submit "all evidence which they now hold or which may become available in future in relation to this question."[41] There were no sanctions, however, and all that the Assembly obtained was the submission of voluminous evidence of its own failure to get results.

By this time, the Soviets had been encouraged to engage in armed conflict with the United Nations itself; and in June, 1950, the Communists launched a full-scale invasion of South Korea. As Secretary of State Dulles pointed out, this action was most probably the result of a Soviet "miscalculation" of free-world intentions:

> Many believe that neither the First World War nor the Second World War would have occurred if the aggressor had known what the United States would do. It is even more probable that the Korean war would not have occurred if the aggressor had known what the United States would do. The Communists thought, and had reason to think, that they would not be opposed except by the then small and ill-equipped forces of the Republic of Korea. They did not expect what actually happened.[42]

This statement seems to contradict his assertion that in Iran the Soviet Union "would never have ordered retreat under the threat of any such compulsion."[43] It was the more accurate analysis, however, supported by the fact that United States conduct prior to the Korean War was hardly consistent with an intention to resist aggression. The occupation forces had been withdrawn, and authorized military assistance was limited to that required to "maintain internal security and to deal with external pressures short of an all-out attack."[44] There was also a public statement by Secretary of State Dean Acheson which indicated that the Pacific "defensive perimeter" of the United States did not include Korea.[45]

Korea's troubles actually began in 1945, when the Soviet Union was authorized to occupy the territory north of the thirty-eighth parallel. They were aggravated in December, 1945, at the Moscow Conference of Foreign Ministers. At that conference the Big Three decided that Korea should be governed by a five-year, four-power trusteeship (the United States, Great Britain, China and the Soviet Union) and by a provisional government formed by a Soviet-American commission in consultation with the "Korean democratic parties and social organizations."[46] Because of its provision for a trusteeship, the agreement was opposed by nearly all Koreans except the Communists, and when the Soviet delegation insisted that those parties and organizations which opposed the agreement should be excluded from the consultations, it meant in effect that only Communists should be consulted in the formation of the new Korean government.

The United States refused to accept the Soviet demands, and in September, 1947, brought the case to the United Nations. The General Assembly promptly abolished the trusteeship, ordered an election and created a temporary commission to supervise and expedite the withdrawal of the occupation forces.[47] This action was taken by a vote of 43-0 (with six abstentions). It thus represented the almost unanimous opinion of the free nations, but the Soviets refused even to admit the commission to their zone of occupation. The elections were therefore confined to the American zone, an independent government was formed, and in December, 1948, it was proclaimed by the General Assembly as the lawful government of the new Republic of Korea:

The General Assembly . . .

Declares that there has been established a lawful government (the Government of the Republic of Korea), having effective control and jurisdiction over that part of Korea where the Temporary Commission was able to observe and consult and in which the great majority of the people of all Korea reside; that this Government is based on elections which were a valid expression of the free will of the electorate of that part of Korea and which were observed by the Temporary Commission; and that this is the only such Government in Korea.[48]

At the same time, a new commission was created to make renewed efforts for the unification of the country and the withdrawal of all occupation forces.

This action was also rejected by the Soviets, who refused to accept the authority of either the government or the new commission. The commission itself was systematically vilified, threatened by radio and anonymous letter, and, like its predecessor, denied access to North Korea. At the same time, the Soviets created a separate, competing government of their own, for which they claimed jurisdiction in both north and south. This "government," of the so-called Democratic People's Republic of Korea, immediately launched a campaign of subversive activity and armed incursions across the thirty-eighth parallel, and finally, in June, 1950, its full-scale invasion of the southern zone.

When this occurred, the Soviet delegate in the Security Council, Yakov A. Malik, was conducting a one-man boycott. The Council, freed of his veto, promptly demanded the withdrawal of all invading forces and called upon the member states to give military assistance. Sixteen of them complied by sending army, navy and air forces to fight alongside of the then small army of the new republic.

As a result, the Soviet delegate came back to the Council; and in August, 1950, took his scheduled turn as chairman. In this capacity, he devoted himself, in the words of the United States representative, Warren R. Austin, to a "month of continued, complete sabotage of parliamentary law."[49] On August 8, Ambassador Austin exclaimed:

We are now struggling for a week in a procedural quagmire. It must be apparent to all of us and to the world that the Soviet represent- ative, who under our rules of procedure is acting as president of the Security Council this month, will not abide by our rules of procedure or by the expressed will of this Council.

The record shows that he has made every effort to stop our work and keep us from our business.[50]

These tactics, however, were not effective to stop the defense of South Korea, or even to keep the United Nations from its business. In order to prescribe a definite procedure for action when the Security Council was unable to "discharge its responsibilities," the General Assembly adopted a resolution providing for its own immediate con- sideration of any matter upon which the Council failed to act. This document, called the "Uniting for Peace" resolution,[51] asserts the authority of the Assembly to recommend all appropriate collective measures, including "the use of armed force when necessary," amend- ing the assembly rules to permit an emergency special session upon the request of a majority of its own members, or upon the vote (not subject to veto) of any *seven* members of the Security Council. It also provides for the establishment of a permanent Peace Observation Commission, to investigate aggression, and calls upon all member states to maintain permanent, properly trained, and equipped forces which can be promptly made available to prevent it. As its preamble indicates, the resolution is based upon a clear recognition of the individual as well as collective obligations of member states: ". . . the failure of the Security Council to discharge its responsibilities . . . does not relieve Member States of their obligations or the United Nations of its responsibility under the Charter to maintain inter- national peace and security."

In the meantime, the General Assembly also dealt with immediate problems in Korea. On September 15, 1950, shortly before the session began, a large amphibious landing at Inchon made it possible for the United Nations to break out of the Pusan perimeter, recapture Seoul and cut off the Communist troops in South Korea. When they began to move into the north, the General Assembly "recommended" another election and created a new commission (UNCURK) to represent the United Nations "in bringing about the establishment of a unified, independent and democratic government."[52]

In November, 1950, the United Nations was confronted with another act of defiance when Korea was openly invaded by the Chinese Communists. This massive new attack forced the United Nations armies to withdraw once more to the south, and the General Assembly vainly attempted to negotiate a cease-fire. Its offers were rejected with categorical demands for the evacuation of Korea, the admission of the Chinese Communist regime to the United Nations, and the termination of American assistance to the free government of China.[53] The Assembly then issued its own call for continued military assistance (February 1, 1951)[54] and recommended a universal embargo on the shipment of war materials and strategic goods to any area under the control of the Chinese or North Korean Communists (May 18, 1951).[55]

In June, 1951, a new United Nations offensive brought a Communist offer of peace. This was made by the Soviet delegate, Yakov Malik, who suggested in a New York radio broadcast that the conflict in Korea could be settled, and that discussions should begin for a mutual withdrawal from the thirty-eighth parallel. The United Nations offensive was then brought to a halt. This was an unfortunate reaction because, according to the testimony of General James A. Van Fleet, commander of the United States Eighth Army, the Chinese Communists were at this time demoralized. It was his stated opinion that a continued United Nations advance would have resulted in the capture of all their heavy equipment, together with 200,000 to 300,000 additional prisoners.[56]

From this time on, all hope for attainment of the real objective of the United Nations—the reunification of Korea—was based on the force of world opinion, which again proved wholly ineffective. Armistice negotiations were begun on July 10, 1951, but they did not bring peace or a political settlement. They did not even bring a cease-fire until after two years of fighting for limited objectives had produced world-wide antipathy to all forms of military assistance.

When the Communists finally accepted a cease-fire, in July, 1953, they conceded no more than the minimum required to obtain a "breathing space," and even as so restricted, the agreement has since been violated in almost every respect. The attempt to limit the importation of military equipment, and thus to preserve the relative strengths of the opposing armies, met with such flagrant and repeated violations by the Communists that the United Nations Command finally had to declare itself "relieved of corresponding obligations."[57]

It was impossible to obtain effective inspection or enforcement of the arms limitation provisions because of the inclusion of an equal number of Communists and non-Communists on the "Neutral Nations Supervisory Commission" and its teams. This gave the Communist members a veto power, which they used effectively; and in 1954, the non-Communist representatives (Switzerland and Sweden) protested that the controls had "merely become a face-saving device devoid of any real significance."[58] In 1955, their governments suggested that the commission be abolished,[59] and finally, in June, 1956, the United Nations Command suspended the commission's operations in South Korea. In announcing the suspension, the United Nations Command also recommended the withdrawal of the teams from North Korea, pointing out that the Communist representatives had "refused to agree to inspections in North Korea which [their] side opposed," or else "delayed inspection until evidence of the violations could be removed."[60] The decision to abrogate the restrictions themselves was taken in 1957, after four years of scrupulous observance had left the United Nations Command with "obsolete and outmoded" equipment, much of which was no longer replaceable under a literal application of the agreement.[61]

In November, 1957, the United States called attention to the fact that the Communists were also still in violation of the agreement for exchange of prisoners. In the Political and Security Committee of the United Nations General Assembly, the United States representative, Walter H. Judd, pointed out that the Communists had never given "a satisfactory accounting for 2,720 personnel of the United Nations Command," including 450 Americans, or made any report at all on thousands of civilians abducted by them during their occupation of South Korea.[62]

Another provision of the Armistice Agreement recommended "a political conference" to deal with the problem of reunification, and to arrange for the withdrawal of foreign troops. This was also nullified, if not literally violated, by the Communists. When the conference was finally held, at Geneva in 1954, the Communist delegations (the Soviet Union, Communist China and North Korea) refused to consider any proposals involving free elections or United Nations supervision, and the result was another impasse. The delegates of the sixteen participating free nations reported that the Communists had not only rejected "every effort to obtain agreement," but had even gone so far as to "repudiate and reject the authority and competence of the United Nations" itself.[63] This was seven years after the efforts at reunification had begun. Continuing efforts have been equally fruitless, despite the annual adoption of Assembly resolutions.[64]

It is important to note, however, that the failure to accomplish reunification was not due to Soviet obstructive tactics in the United Nations, the veto, or to any other defect in the machinery of that body. The United Nations had successfully adopted many resolutions on reunification, and even called for the use of force. Its failure was the result of decisions not to use this force effectively, which were made *outside the United Nations* by the free powers themselves. It is true that the Security Council was able to call for military assistance only because of the fortuitous absence of the Soviet delegate. It is also true, as Secretary Dulles asserted, that "the General Assembly is primarily a deliberative body and includes so many members that it cannot serve effectively as an executive or enforcement agency."[65] But the major obstacles to a successful occupation of North Korea were not created by these bodies.

According to the account of former President Truman, the suggestion for a limitation of operations north of the thirty-eighth parallel appears to have been first made in the *National* Security Council (of the United States) on June 29, 1950. Thus, he records that four days after the invasion occurred, and nearly three months before the scheduled beginning of the next (fifth) session of the General Assembly, it was agreed "that we should clearly limit such operations."[66] In September, 1950, the National Security Council recommended, and the former President approved, a policy prohibiting the extension of operations across the parallel if there was any threat of forceful opposition by Communist China or the Soviet Union.[67] Orders were then issued that such operations were to take place only in the event that "at the time of such operations there has been no entry into North Korea by major Soviet or Chinese Communist Forces, *no*

*announcement of intended entry, nor a threat to counter our opera-
tions militarily in North Korea....*"[68] (Italics added.)

By making the advance contingent upon events known or foreseeable only by the enemy, these conditions put the United Nations
forces at a tremendous disadvantage, causing their mission across the
thirty-eighth parallel to be an uncertain one, even for some time after
the crossing of that arbitrary line had begun. Threats of intended
entry by the Chinese Communists were actually received on October
3, 1950, when the crossing of the parallel was already taking place, but
it does not appear that explicit authority to continue the advance in
spite of them was issued until October 9.[69] This hesitation was not
properly attributable to any United Nations body. Considerable
attention was given to the fact that a new Assembly resolution on
reunification,[70] which the President regarded as "clear authorization"[71] for the crossing of the thirty-eighth parallel was not adopted
until October 7, but it did not give any more specific authority to
do so than similar resolutions which had been adopted annually since
1947.[72]

An even more serious obstacle was the decision to prohibit air
and naval action against Communist bases in Manchuria and other
parts of China. This decision was also made outside the United
Nations, by the United States in consultation with those members
having troops in Korea.[73] Because these nations were opposed to such
action, it was apparently not considered necessary to consult the
United Nations itself, or even to consider the wishes of the government of Korea, the nation most directly concerned, which was supplying more than half the troops, and whose troops it was planned to
station closest to the Manchurian border. Pursuant to the limitations
thus imposed, the President at first went so far as to prohibit the bombing of bridges across the Yalu River (between Korea and Manchuria),
and then relented to the extent of granting authority to bomb the
"Korean end" of the bridges.[74] According to the testimony of General
George E. Stratemeyer,[75] who was in charge of air operations, and
General Mark Clark,[76] who was subsequently United Nations Commander, this was almost an impossibility, particularly in view of the
fact that the bombers were not permitted to "violate" Manchurian
airspace. The result was that Chinese Communist armies entered
Korea with virtual impunity.

The General Assembly has been criticized for its efforts to negotiate a cease-fire prior to the complete liberation of Korea—efforts obviously prompted by the desire of many members to terminate the struggle. The fact remains, however, that these efforts were begun only after open Chinese intervention, and were the only practicable course of action while the restrictions on operations over Manchuria were in effect. The United Nations Commander (General Douglas MacArthur) reported that these restrictions gave the Chinese Communists an "unprecedented military advantage"[77] and created a situation in which "military stalemate" was inevitable:

Assuming no diminution of the enemy's flow of ground forces and material to the Korean battle area, a continuation of the existing limitation upon our freedom of counter offensive action, and no major additions to our organizational strength, the battle lines cannot fail in time to reach a point of theoretical military stalemate. Thereafter our further advance would militarily benefit the enemy more than it would ourselves.[78]

Although he added that the "exact place of stabilization" was "of necessity a fluctuating variable," and would "constantly move up or down," General MacArthur's report clearly indicated that the restrictions made reunification of Korea a practical impossibility.

It has subsequently been asserted that such restrictions would not be imposed again. But the decisions made in Korea reflected a more serious restriction—unjust as well as impractical—by which all effective United Nations action has been reserved for the exclusive protection of free peoples. This discriminatory policy continues and grows more fixed as every new opportunity to aid the subject peoples is neglected. Moreover, because it permits the oppressors to usurp the rightful places of those peoples in the United Nations organization, this policy actually confronts the United Nations with a much greater threat than the Soviet veto. While it is possible now for the free members of the United Nations to overcome Soviet obstructive tactics and, when necessary, to fulfill their obligations under the Charter by their own independent action, if they continue to permit the Soviet Union to appoint and control the delegations of subjugated nations, new Communist aggressions may ultimately result in Soviet control of the United Nations itself. In that event, the Soviets will no longer be concerned with retention of the veto, and the free members will no longer be capable of independent action, because the Soviets will dominate the earth under the "international warrant" of the free world's own organization for alleged general security.

Such control of other countries' delegations is simply another form of Soviet aggression against the United Nations, less bloody perhaps than that employed in Korea, but possibly more effective. Its existence was noted at the organizing conference (April-June, 1945) by Senator Arthur H. Vandenberg, who was a member of the United States delegation. The particular occasion, "a row over the Conference Chairmanship," seems relatively insignificant, but the Senator's conclusion was prophetic. "It clearly indicates a Russian purpose," he said, "to carry this same Sovietizing idea into the ultimate organization of the Peace League itself."[79]

In pursuance of this purpose, the Soviet Union originally demanded membership for each of its sixteen so-called soviet socialist republics.[80] This would have given it sixteen delegations, sixteen votes and sixteen speeches on every resolution. At the Yalta Conference, however, these demands were scaled down to three, and the United States and Great Britain agreed to support separate memberships for the Soviet Union and two of its "republics"— the Ukraine and Byelorussia.

When this decision was announced, it was widely accepted, because of the size of the Soviet Union, and because many people assumed that the Soviets could never win control of enough delegations to make any real difference. An editorial in the *New York Herald Tribune* commented that a difference of two or three votes in the General Assembly would be of "no possible practical significance." It added the warning, however, that "an Assembly 'packed' by a solid block of as many as sixteen Russian votes would obviously be inadmissible."[81] But the "inadmissible" has now been nearly realized, and the possibilities for exceeding it are extensive. As Senator Vandenberg stated at the time, "Every new surrender makes it more difficult" to "stop this Stalin appeasement."[82]

When the United Nations began to operate, the Soviet Union actually controlled the votes of six members (its own and those of the Ukraine, Byelorussia, Poland, Yugoslavia and Czechoslovakia).[83] By the end of 1955, with the admission of Albania, Bulgaria, Hungary and Rumania, the total had increased to nine, excluding Yugoslavia. With pressure mounting for the admission of Communist China, Outer Mongolia, North Korea and North Viet Nam, and with the

Soviet Union bidding, sometimes successfully, for an unknown degree of influence in the governments of certain "neutral" nations of the Middle East, Asia, Africa and even the Western Hemisphere, sixteen Soviet votes are no longer considered inadmissible—and they are deemed by some inevitable.

There is little comfort, moreover, in the fact that the membership of the United Nations has increased from fifty-eight to almost one hundred, a development which would normally decrease the Communist proportion of the total. There are many small members, and also potential members (dependencies of existing members, approaching independence) that are exposed to, and even threatened with, Soviet domination. With Czechoslovakia as a precedent, they could easily provide additional votes for the aggressor.

If all of the nations which have so far been attacked by the Soviet Union had succumbed, and if the most immediate Soviet threats were successful, the United Nations line-up prior to the 1960 session of the General Assembly would have shown a nearly equal division between the free and captive members, as follows:

The Soviet Plan for Control of the United Nations

(CAPTIVE)	(FREE)
U.S.S.R.*	France*
China*	United Kingdom*
	United States*
Communist-ruled	
Albania	Argentina
Bulgaria	Australia
Byelorussia	Belgium
Czechoslovakia	Bolivia
Hungary	Brazil
Outer Mongolia**	Canada
Poland	Chile
Rumania	Colombia
Ukraine	Costa Rica
Yugoslavia	Denmark
	Dominican Republic
Previously attacked	Ecuador
Austria	El Salvador
Burma	Ethiopia
Cambodia	Ghana
Finland	Guinea

(Captive)	(Free)
Greece	Haiti
Guatemala	Honduras
India	Iceland
Indonesia	Ireland
Iran	Italy
Korea**	Liberia
Laos	Libya
Malaya	Luxembourg
Philippine Republic	Mexico
Viet Nam**	Morocco
	Netherlands
Currently threatened	New Zealand
Afghanistan	Nicaragua
Ceylon	Norway
Cuba	Panama
Germany**	Paraguay
Iraq	Peru
Israel	Portugal
Japan	Spain
Jordan	Sudan
Lebanon	Sweden
Nepal	Tunisia
Pakistan	Union of South Africa
Saudi Arabia	Uruguay
Thailand	Venezuela
Turkey	
United Arab Republic	
Yemen	

* Permanent members of the Security Council.
** Not members of the United Nations at present.

Anticipation of such a division gives the Communists a real incentive to capture the votes of those newly independent states admitted or becoming eligible for admission during the 1960 session of the General Assembly—Cameroun, Central African Republic, Chad, the two Congos, Cyprus, Dahomey, Gabon, Ivory Coast, Malagasy, Mali, Mauretania, Niger, Nigeria, Senegal, Somalia, Togo and Upper Volta. Control of their votes, along with those listed above, could tip the scales heavily against freedom. And even if the ultimate goal was thwarted by United Nations intervention in the Congo, it was nevertheless easily discernible in Khrushchev's angry reaction—his proposal to saddle the organization with a tripartite executive body in all respects comparable to the hamstrung "inspection" teams employed in China, Korea and Indochina, and possibly even to the three-power, Soviet-run Control Commissions employed in Bulgaria, Hungary and Rumania.

The opportunities for Soviet control are even greater in the Security Council than they are in the General Assembly. There the Soviet Union is a permanent member with veto power. The six non-permanent members, of which three are elected annually for two-year terms, represent a majority; and in the absence of a veto, the vote of any seven members is sufficient for action.

The extent of the threat to this body was demonstrated by the vote recorded on the first Soviet attempt to seat the Chinese Communists. This move was made in January, 1950, when the Soviets controlled only five delegations to the United Nations. Nevertheless, it was defeated by the narrowest of margins. It was opposed by three permanent members, the United States, France and the Republic of China, but the United States and France took the position that the question was "procedural" and that their votes would not be vetoes. The Soviet Union, of course, voted for its own proposal, and the other permanent member (Great Britain) abstained.

The non-permanent members at this time were Yugoslavia, India, Norway, Egypt, Cuba and Ecuador. The first two voted with the Soviet Union, and Norway abstained. This made the vote six to three against admission,[84] but if the two abstaining delegates had voted, and if Egypt had voted as it did in later years, the poll might have been six to five in favor of admission. A shift of only one more vote would have given the Communists another permanent seat, and another veto.

It was later indicated that the United States would use the veto, if necessary, to prevent the seating of the Chinese Communists,[85] but there is still much confusion with respect to this question; and it may well be found that such a stand has been prejudiced by the position taken in 1950. The confusion can be avoided, but only if it is acknowledged that there is an issue of aggression in China, direct or indirect—as there is in all of the Communist-dominated nations— and if it is also accepted that the primary purpose of the United Nations is the suppression of aggression, as the Charter states. It seems obvious that a regime imposed by aggression cannot be accepted by such an organization unless first accepted by the people and that, until such time, their overthrown government is to be defended by the United Nations rather than unseated.

When such an issue is raised, there is more than a problem of credentials (which is plainly procedural) or of the right of the nation itself to membership (which ought to be considered as a separate issue). There is a question, first of all, as to whether an aggression has taken place, and if so there is the further question of the proper collective measures to be taken for the protection of the victim. These are the most substantive questions with which the United Nations can deal; and so long as the power of veto remains in the Charter, any realistic acceptance of the obligations which it imposes leads inevitably to the conclusion that the veto is applicable and that the individual members have a duty to use it if necessary for the Charter's enforcement.

The importance of the non-permanent members of the Security Council has also been dramatized by the struggle of the Soviet Union to perpetuate the so-called Eastern European seat. Under this arrangement, which provided that one seat in the Council should go to an Eastern European nation, the Soviets were assured of virtually continual control of at least one of the non-permanent members, and it so worked out during the first six years. During that time Poland, the Ukraine and Czechoslovakia were successively elected.

During the next two years, however, the free nations resisted the Soviet influence, electing Greece (the only free nation in Eastern Europe) and Turkey (which had already occupied the seat assigned to the Near East). In each case there was a fierce contest with candidates of the Soviet Union (Byelorussia and Poland).

In the next election, held in 1955, thirty-five consecutive ballots were cast without the successful choice of any candidate, and the issue was finally resolved by the drawing of lots between the two leading contenders. By this means, Yugoslavia was chosen for a one-year term, with the understanding that it would resign at the end of the year in favor of the Philippines. When the year expired, however, the Soviet Union ignored the understanding and attempted to elect Czechoslovakia. In this case, the Philippines won on the first ballot, and in the following year Japan was elected. The understanding on the "Eastern European seat" appeared to be terminated.

This incident proved that the free world could still win more than empty resolutions on a cold-war issue, but the victory was of value only to the free nations. The subject peoples of the affected area were made to feel this even more acutely by the concurrent admission, in December, 1955, of four new Eastern European nations— all on the basis of a nearly unanimous[86] acceptance of the regimes imposed upon them by the Soviet Union. The weakening of Soviet influence in one respect was thus offset by its expansion in another.

Moreover, by 1959, when the controversy over the "Eastern European seat" was again raised, it had become apparent that the free world had lost ground even on this issue. After fifty-one unsuccessful ballots Poland and Turkey were selected for one-year terms each, and the Polish delegate maintained that the United States had abjured all further "discrimination against Eastern European countries." The United Nations can either be made effective in spite of the obstructive tactics of those opposed to its principles, by a consistent demonstration of willingness on the part of the free nations to fulfill their individual obligations under the Charter—as in Iran, Greece, Berlin and the first stages of Korea—or it can be allowed to become the tool of aggression by the substitution of the aggressor's representatives for those of the victims—as in the case of Czechoslovakia and the other captive nations of eastern Europe. In the creation of an effective organization for *world* security there is no middle course.

In this respect, the remarks of President Lincoln are even more applicable to the United Nations than they were to the United States:

I believe that this government cannot endure, permanently half slave and half free.

I do not expect the Union to be dissolved—I do not expect the house to fall—but I do expect it will cease to be divided.

It will become all one thing, or all the other.

Either the opponents of slavery will arrest the further spread of it, and place it where the public mind shall rest in the belief that it is in course of ultimate extinction; or its advocates will push it forward, till it shall become alike lawful in all the States....[87]

CHAPTER X

THE FALL OF CHINA

A Lesson in Mutual Assistance

In March, 1947, when President Truman requested authority to give military assistance to Greece, he described its condition as a tragic consequence of "four years of cruel enemy occupation, and bitter internal strife." The "retreating Germans," he pointed out, "had destroyed virtually all the railways, roads, port facilities, communications, and merchant marine. More than a thousand villages had been burned. Eighty-five percent of the children were tubercular. Livestock, poultry, and draft animals had almost disappeared. Inflation had wiped out practically all savings." It was because of these conditions, he said, that a "militant minority" of Communists, "exploiting human want and misery, was able to create political chaos" and make "economic recovery impossible."[1]

Precisely similar conditions prevailed in postwar China, many parts of which had been occupied by the Japanese since 1937, or for nearly eight years, and whose richest region, Manchuria, had been seized in 1932 and held for more than thirteen years. The resulting conditions in China were also described by the President, as follows:

Communications throughout the country were badly disrupted due to destruction during the war and the civil conflicts which had broken out since. This disruption was preventing the restoration of Chinese economy, the distribution of relief supplies, and was rendering the evacuation of Japanese a slow and difficult process. The wartime destruction of factories and plants, the war-induced inflation in China, the Japanese action in shutting down the economy of occupied China immediately after V-J Day, and finally the destruction of communications combined to paralyze the economic life of the country, spreading untold hardship to millions, robbing the victory over the Japanese of significance to most Chinese, and seriously aggravating all the tensions and discontents that existed in China.[2]

In China there was also a "militant minority" of Communists

endeavoring to create political chaos and prevent economic recovery. As stated by General Marshall, who served as the President's special representative to China in 1945-6, this was "their announced purpose —to force an economic collapse."[3] In the case of Greece, the Communists were covertly assisted by the puppet regimes of Albania, Bulgaria and Yugoslavia; in the case of China, they were covertly assisted by the Soviet Union and its puppet regime in Outer Mongolia.

The official descriptions showed many other parallels. In a request for aid to Greece, in 1947, President Truman stated that it was "threatened by the terrorist activities of several thousand armed men, led by Communists, who defy the Government's authority at a number of points, particularly along the northern boundaries." The Greek government, he pointed out, was "unable to cope with the situation."[4] In a request for aid to China, in 1948, General Marshall pointed out that it was threatened by "Communist armies," also in the north, which "in the opinion of virtually every American authority" were "impossible to conquer" and against which "the present Chinese Government may not be successful in maintaining itself. . . ."[5]

According to the Director of the Office of Near Eastern and African Affairs, Loy Henderson, a "relatively small number of guerrillas" in Greece were able to "benefit greatly from the mountainous terrain."[6] In China, General Marshall stated, there were "thousands of miles of communications bordered by mountains affording easy retreats for guerrilla forces, numerous vulnerable river crossings and tunnels easily subject to destruction."[7]

The Communists, General Marshall asserted, had "brought about terrible destruction and virtually wrecked the economy of China."[8] In Greece, Henderson pointed out, the "instruments employed to block reconstruction and recovery" included "sabotage of railroad lines, mining of roads" and "destruction of key power facilities."[9]

It was conceded by President Truman that the government of Greece was not "perfect"—that it had "made mistakes," and that, in fact, it was "operating in an atmosphere of chaos and extremism." Nevertheless, he maintained, it represented "85 percent of the members of the Greek Parliament" duly elected in "a fair expression of the views of the Greek people."[10]

The government of China also had its critics. According to General Marshall, it was dominated by a "group of reactionaries"[11] who were failing "to do anything constructive for the common people."[12] Nevertheless, its National Assembly adopted what he called "a democratic constitution . . . in all major respects . . . in accordance with the principles laid down by the all-party Political Consultative Conference."[13] In the elections which followed, according to the State Department's White Paper on China, the "extreme right-wing faction" won so heavily that the "Government was faced with the difficult and embarrassing necessity of persuading successful candidates to withdraw after they had won, in order to comply with the commitment on broadening the Government."[14]

In both Greece and China, the United States had urged agreement with the Communists and their inclusion in the government, but Greece was in the British zone of military operations and here the parallel ends. Greece was saved by timely British intervention followed by an American military-assistance program. China was lost by the withholding of such assistance until it was too late. Whereas in 1945, the British had intervened to suppress a Communist rebellion in Greece, the United States for a long time actually prohibited the suppression of such rebellion in China. Thus, American policy in China was precisely the opposite of the more successful policies followed in Iran, Greece and Turkey.

While military assistance was being provided to "create a strong Iran, free from internal weakness which invites foreign intervention or aggression,"[15] two special ambassadors were sent to China (General Patrick Hurley in August, 1944, and General George C. Marshall in December, 1945) to induce the acceptance of Communists in government. In 1946, while the United States was insisting that no confidence should be placed in the Soviets' mere agreement to withdraw from Iran,[16] it was actually *demanding* agreements with the Communists in China. In 1947, when an "urgent appeal" for military assistance to Greece was answered with "immediate and resolute action,"[17] only a "fact-finding" mission was sent to China and Korea "to make an appraisal of the over-all situation in that region."[18] In 1948, when billions were made available for the security of western Europe, only a small fraction of that amount, concededly inadequate, was belatedly provided for the defense of China.

The result was that Communist power in China increased rapidly; and by the end of 1949, the year before the invasion of South Korea, the national government was overthrown and forced to flee to Formosa. The United States policy was by that time so obviously wrong that it was attributed to misleading reports, known Communists in government, and even treason on the part of high officials. It must be acknowledged, however, that it was only the natural extension of policies theretofore followed in eastern Europe, and that some of the beliefs on which it was based are still influencing cold-war policies in all areas today.

If the Chinese Communists were regarded as "liberals," "agrarian reformers," and not really Communists at all, similar claims had been made on behalf of Lenin's Communists in 1918, Stalin's Communists in 1925-6, and are even now being made on behalf of Khrushchev's Communists and the so-called "national Communists" of the satellite nations. If there was insistence upon the inclusion of Communists in the government of China, similar "coalition governments" had actually been foisted on the nations of eastern Europe, and wholly Communist delegations and Communist officials still find ready acceptance in all departments of the United Nations. The urge for a settlement with the Communists of China had its counterpart in the wartime alliance with the Soviet Union, and it persists today in perennial proposals for conferences between the "heads of government," in negotiations for disarmament and in the denial of assistance to the subject peoples. Even the plan of some American officers,[19] surreptitiously prepared, to give direct wartime assistance to the Chinese Communists, did not differ in principle from the delivery of billions of dollars of lend-lease to the Soviet Union, or from the exclusive military assistance given to the Communist resistance in Yugoslavia and Albania, or from more recent assistance to the Communist rulers of Yugoslavia and Poland. All of these policies have hurt the cause of freedom somewhere; all of them have advanced the cause of communism everywhere; and those which persist are no less dangerous, and will be no less of a betrayal of freedom-loving peoples than the similar policies which have already produced acknowledged calamities.

Communist aggression in China actually began in the early 1920s, shortly after the Bolshevik seizure of power in Russia, and it succeeded only because it was able to take advantage of a similar period of national weakness in China—when China, like Russia, was struggling against invasion from abroad, and when the people of China were likewise endeavoring to replace an autocratic form of government with a democratic one. In China, as in Russia, the only accomplishment of the Communists was the destruction of a popular revolution for which they could claim no credit at all.

This revolution was inspired by the teachings of Dr. Sun Yat-sen, the founder and leader of the Kuomintang, or Chinese National Party, and it was based on his three "People's Principles"—national independence, political democracy, and a fair standard of living for everyone. Like the Russian democratic revolution, it was handicapped by internal dissensions, invasion and communism; but it ultimately failed only because of the refusal of the free nations to give assistance except when they themselves desired the aid of China, during World War II.

In January, 1912, Dr. Sun became the first President of the Republic of China, but in the following month he was forced to resign. The new government was soon dominated by military rulers of the northern provinces (the Chinese "warlords"), further revolts failed, the Kuomintang was outlawed, and in 1915 the Parliament itself was dissolved. In the meantime, the First World War began. The Japanese seized the German concessions in Shantung and presented the Chinese with extensive demands for economic and political hegemony (the "Twenty-one Demands"). These included recognition of Japan's "special interests" in southern Manchuria and Inner Mongolia, and the use of Japanese advisers in the political, financial and military affairs of all China. They were only partly resisted by the existing regime in Peiping, and they presaged worse to come.

In spite of these reverses, Dr. Sun persisted in his efforts, and in September, 1917, he established a new revolutionary government in the south, with headquarters at Canton. In 1921-22 the "Great Powers," including Japan, agreed to refrain from seeking special privileges in China (at the Washington Conference), but by this time the Bolsheviks had prevailed in Russia and were preparing their own foreign threat, disguised as support and technical assistance for the Kuomintang. Their main effort was a Communist Party of China, organized in 1920-21 under the direction of Grigori Voitinsky, secretary of the Far-Eastern Bureau of the Communist International. Pursuant to the resolutions of the Communist International, adopted in 1920, the Chinese Communists determined to form a temporary alliance with the Kuomintang—for the acknowledged purpose of gaining "access to the masses"[20] and, as an early Soviet report states, of associating themselves with "the only democratic elements who . . . could be expected to succeed."[21]

In 1923, Chiang Kai-shek, the future President of China, was sent to Moscow to study Soviet military and political organizations at first hand. In his book, *Soviet Russia in China*, he relates that in the early years of the revolution, even before the Communists came into the picture, Dr. Sun repeatedly sought foreign assistance from the free nations, "but all his efforts were in vain." "Not only," he says, "did the Western Powers turn a deaf ear to his appeals, some of them were actually in collusion with the warlords for selfish ends."[22] It may be that this early rebuff was partly responsible for Dr. Sun's decision to seek aid from the Soviet Union, and it is certain that it delayed the unification of China, but the Chinese people could not be turned against the free nations by indifference any more than by exploitation. The Communists themselves complained that it was difficult to excite opposition to any of the "imperialist countries" except Japan. As the same Russian report, referred to above, states: "Not only was this the psychology of the masses, but it was true also of the leaders of society, the Kuomintang, and other revolutionary organizations, which singled out Japan as the enemy but remained silent about the other imperialist countries."[23]

In 1924, the Kuomintang was reorganized along Communist lines, Soviet advisers were accepted, and the Communists were admitted to membership and high office. They were unable, however, to win control, or to force the acceptance of Communist policies, and in 1927 they were ousted. In the meantime, Dr. Sun died (March 12, 1925), and in July, 1926, his successor, General Chiang Kai-shek, began a military expedition against the northern warlords. Hankow and Shanghai were soon captured and the headquarters of a new National Government established at Nanking. In 1928, Peiping was also taken, and the government of the Kuomintang was recognized *de jure* by the major powers.

The new Chinese government was now faced, however, with three enemies: the warlords, who still controlled Manchuria and the northwest provinces; the Communists, who had taken advantage of the expedition to stage uprisings at Nanchang and Canton; and the Japanese, who had launched another attack in Shantung (the Tsinan incident). It was impossible to cope with all three at once. The warlords soon declared their allegiance, or were defeated. The Communists were vigorously attacked and forced to take refuge, first in the southern province of Kiangsi, where they set up a Soviet regime, and finally in the northwest province of Shensi, where they established headquarters at Yenan. But the aggressions of the Japanese grew steadily worse. They invaded China again and again—Manchuria in 1931, the "Shanghai War" in 1932, and the "Battle of the Great Wall" in 1933. Finally, in 1937, they began an all-out assault, capturing Peiping and Nanking. The Chinese government was moved to Chungking.

Under these circumstances, the government was forced to make a truce with the Communists. It did so on the strength of their promise —made in September, 1937—to support the war effort, to abandon violence and to discard the Soviet system. As reported by a subcommittee of the House Committee on Foreign Affairs, this promise was expressed in the following clear and unequivocal terms:

(1)   The Communist Party shall strive for the realization of Sun Yat-sen's three principles of the people, which answer the present-day need of China.

(2)   It shall abandon the policy of armed insurrection against the Kuomintang regime, the policy of Red propaganda, and the policy of land confiscation.

(3)   It shall abolish the Soviet Government and institute a system of democracy, so that the nation may be politically united.

(4)   It shall abolish the Red army as such, and allow it to be incorporated into the National army and placed under the command of the National Military Council. The Red army, thus recognized, shall await orders to proceed to fight on any front.[24]

General Chiang relates that he "really believed that the Chinese Communists had repented and were sincere in their expressed readiness to join the rest of the nation in the fight against aggression."[25] He took their pledge, he states, "as evidence of the effect of the Government's moral influence." This mistake, he adds, led to "tragic consequences," but he expresses the hope that his own "bitter lesson," a "matter of great humiliation . . . to recount," will not be "without some value to the free world." Unfortunately, this hope has not been fulfilled.

The perfidy of the Communists was soon again apparent to General Chiang, however. They had been demanding victories over Japan, and a "declared war" against it, but they did not intend to give the government any real support. On the contrary, they intended to follow Lenin's tactics, and to "take advantage of the antagonisms and contradictions between two capitalisms . . . inciting one against the other."[26] The occurrence of war in the Far East had been predicted by the Communists in 1922, in the "Resolutions and Theses of the Fourth Congress of the Communist International,"[27] and now that it had occurred they intended to take the fullest advantage of it.

In January, 1941, after the fall of France, and not many months before the Japanese attack on Pearl Harbor, Mao Tse-tung, the leader of the Chinese Communists would publish his own restatement of the Lenin strategy in a magazine called *Chinese Culture*. "The significance of China's revolution," he would write, "is greatly magnified today, because it is happening at a time when the political and economic crises of capitalism have brought the world step by step toward the second imperialist war. . . ." Moreover, he was to state, "the Soviet Union has reached the transitional period from Socialism to Communism and has the ability to lead and to assist . . . all the revolutionary peoples of the world. . . ."[28] In the meantime, in the autumn of 1937, he revealed the Communists' intentions more clearly in a speech to the troops at Yenan:

The war between China and Japan is an excellent opportunity for the development of our party. Our determined policy is 70 percent self-development, 20 percent compromise, and 10 percent fight the Japanese. . . .

The first stage is to compromise with the Kuomintang, with the view of maintaining our existence. The second stage is to fight for a balance of power vis-à-vis the Kuomintang to achieve an equilibrium. The third stage is to infiltrate deeply into central China, to establish bases there, in order to launch counteroffensives against the Kuomintang, with the view of taking away from the Kuomintang its leading position.[29]

This was one promise which the Communists fulfilled. Instead of co-operating with the government forces, they began to attack them, and to instigate revolt. Orders from the government itself were disregarded, while its good name was used to extend the influence and control of the Communists. At the same time, there was little Communist activity against the Japanese; and in October, 1940, the American Ambassador reported that this was even conceded by the Communists. "It is generally conceded," he said, "even in local Communist quarters, that the Chinese Communists have engaged in little military activity against the Japanese forces in the past 18 months, contenting themselves largely with the establishment of military bases, mobilization of the people, and defense measures against Japanese mopping-up campaigns."[30]

In April, 1941, the Soviet Union made a nonaggression pact with

Japan, in which both parties agreed to "maintain peaceful and friendly relations." They also agreed to "respect the territorial integrity" of
each other's puppet regimes in China—the "Mongolian People's Republic," in the case of the Soviet Union, and "Manchukuo" (Manchuria), in the case of Japan.[31] The agreement made no mention of
Japan's new puppet regime at Nanking (under Wang Ching-wei),
but neither did it make any mention of Soviet efforts to set up a puppet regime in Sinkiang (under Sheng Shih-tsai). The agreement was,
of course, supported by the Chinese Communists.[32]

In June, 1941, after the Nazi attack on the Soviet Union, the
Communist attitude changed, and new assurances of support for the
government were given in October. But in 1943, when the war in
Europe began to turn against the Nazis, the attacks against the
government were renewed. In the meantime, anti-Japanese activity
was held to a minimum throughout the war. It has been summarized
in a report prepared by the Legislative Reference Service of the
Library of Congress, under the direction of the House Committee on
Foreign Affairs:

The Communists were almost entirely remote from direct observation
by the foreign press, and made the most of the opportunity to issue a
stream of accounts of heroic exploits. Actually the story seems rather
different. The Communists filled any vacuum of control that they
could reach, behind or beyond the Jap lines. They avoided battle
with the diligence they had learned in years of guerrilla warfare. The
Japanese according to their own account suffered nearly a million
casualties in the whole of the war in China, and less than 10 percent
of these occurred in fighting the Communists.... *The art of playing
two opponents against each other, subjecting them both to serious
losses while building one's own strength, was practiced more effectively by Chinese communism than by any other country or group in
the Second World War.*[33] (Italics in original.)

This was the background of the postwar struggle which took
place between the national government and the Chinese Communists
at the end of World War II, and in which the United States endeavored to "mediate," to impose its own policy of negotiation and
compromise upon the national government, and finally, after recognizing the mistake it had made, to wash its hands of the whole
affair. It has been argued that in eastern Europe the free world had
no alternative to a policy of compromise, because of Soviet occupa-

tion. The same cannot be said of China, however, where the United States was alone responsible for the acceptance of Japanese surrender in all areas except Manchuria, and where the established government had been described in the wartime declarations as one of the major free governments of the world. Yet the United States sought to force the adoption of the same policies which it had followed in eastern Europe, threatening to withhold, and actually withholding, military and economic assistance if its prescriptions were not adopted.

Against the same background, on the other hand, the Chinese officials were not optimistic about the chances of peaceful settlement, nor were they overly enthusiastic about United States proposals for the inclusion of Communists in the government. The United States, however, was the only source of needed foreign assistance; and in January, 1945, Ambassador Hurley was able to report that in response to the "suggestions" of President Roosevelt, General Chiang had "shown himself ready to grant concessions to the Communists far beyond what he had been willing to grant in the past":

... the G[eneral] issimo is now prepared to make all the concessions requested in the five points except that he does not want a coalition government or a coalition military council. He will, however, give the Communists representation in the government, in a war cabinet and in the military council which, in my opinion, would have been accepted by the Communists if offered at the time Chou En-lai was here. The G[eneral]issimo's position was that while he would be willing to give representation and recognition as a political party to the Communists he would be adverse to a coalition government. He explained to me that he would not like a situation created similar to that existing in Yugoslavia and Poland.[34]

An apparent agreement was finally obtained in 1946, by General Marshall. His achievements were summarized by President Truman in December of that year:

Events moved rapidly upon General Marshall's arrival. With all parties availing themselves of his impartial advice, agreement for a country-wide truce was reached and announced on January 10th [1946]. . . .

    .   .   .   .

Events moved forward with equal promise on the political front. On January 10th, the Political Consultative Conference began its sessions with representatives of the Kuomintang or Government Party, the Communist Party and several minor political parties participating. Within three weeks of direct discussion these groups had come to a series of statesmanlike agreements on outstanding political and military problems. The agreements provided for an interim government of a coalition type with representation of all parties. . . .[35]

In spite of the fact that General Marshall has borne the brunt of the criticism on this issue, it is a fact that his policies differed little from those followed by General Hurley under the aegis of President Roosevelt. General Hurley had been well aware of the Communists' desire for the "destruction of the National Government," but he was nevertheless "in favor of every concession that we can get from the National Government for the participation in that government by the Communists."[36] His program called for the immediate "unification of all military forces in China," the "recognition of the Chinese Communist Party as a legal political party," and for the "representation of all parties in the administration of the Chinese Government."[37] General Marshall's program was the same. It also called for the "unification of Chinese military forces," in a "single, non-political, national army made up of troops drawn from the presently existing Communist and Central Government armies,"[38] and for "the formation of a genuine coalition government."[39]

Both programs were accepted by the Chinese government. General Hurley reported that Chiang's program "gives the Communists what they have demanded," and more, in fact, than he himself recommended, because it did not "require submission of Communist troops to the National Government."[40] Under General Marshall's persuasion an agreement was made for the unification of the armed forces, and for the formation of a coalition government. The Communists, however, refused to participate, because they were not given control of key ministries, such as the Ministry of Defense, or the power to veto government action.[41] They refused to send delegates to the National Assembly convened in November, 1946, and they refused to participate in the elections held in November, 1947, the first general elections in the history of China.

Nevertheless, the government was blamed for the failure to reach a peaceful settlement. President Roosevelt had expressed the opinion that "the fault lay more with the Kuomintang and the Chungking Government than with the so-called communists";[42] and in 1948, General Marshall opined: "There was constant insistence on the part of the Generalissimo and his high military and political group that the only way the issue could be settled was by force. I had endeavored to persuade them time after time that it was not within their capability to settle the matter by force."[43]

This attitude on the part of the United States led, after the defeat of Japan, to a determination that no major program of military or economic assistance to China should be undertaken until after an agreement with the Communists had been made. General Marshall was authorized to so advise the Chinese government in his original written instructions from President Truman in December, 1945:

Particularly, you may state, in connection with the Chinese desire for credits, technical assistance in the economic field, and military assistance (I have in mind the proposed U.S. military advisory group which I have approved in principle), that a China disunited and torn by civil strife could not be considered realistically as a proper place for American assistance along the lines enumerated.[44]

The Chinese Prime Minister, T. V. Soong, had already been informed by President Truman (in September, 1945) that "it should be clearly understood that military assistance furnished by the United States would not be diverted for use in fratricidal warfare. . . ."[45]

General Marshall was also instructed to use the "influence" of the United States to obtain the inclusion in the government of the "so-called Communists":

We believe, as we have long believed and consistently demonstrated, that the government of Generalissimo Chiang Kai-shek affords the most satisfactory base for a developing democracy. But we also believe that it must be broadened to include the representatives of those large and well organized groups who are now without any voice in the government of China.

. . . To the extent that our influence is a factor, success will depend upon our capacity to exercise that influence in the light of shifting conditions in such a way as to encourage concessions by the Central Government, by the so-called Communists, and by the other factions.[46]

The intention to withhold assistance from any Chinese government which did not include the Communists was even more specifically stated in June, 1946. At that time the State Department announced that the purpose of the United States was to help "the Chinese nation as a whole" and to avoid "support of any factional military group."[47] "Too much stress," it asserted, "cannot be laid on the hope of this Government that our economic assistance be carried out in China through the medium of a government fully and fairly representative of *all important Chinese political elements, including the Chinese Communists.*"[48] (Italics added.)

This policy culminated in an exchange of notes (see Appendix D-1) which can find few parallels in the history of relations between any two friendly countries. In this exchange President Truman again made it clear that China could expect no aid from the United States until it had reached an understanding with the Communists, and he in effect accused the governing party, and General Chiang himself, of complicity in the most serious crimes and failure to carry out agreements.

In his first note, August 10, 1946, President Truman complained of "cruel murders" and "assassinations of distinguished Chinese liberals," which, he insinuated, had been instigated by the Kuomintang government. "Regardless of where responsibility may lie," he said, "there is increasing belief that an attempt is being made to resort to force, military or secret police rather than democratic processes to settle major social issues." He would be "less than honest," he asserted, if he did not point out his own conclusion that "the selfish interests of extremist elements, both in the Kuomintang and the Communist Party, are obstructing the aspirations of the people of China."

Since the Kuomintang was the government party and the party of which General Chiang was the leader, such a communication from the President of the United States was both a personal and official affront. Its rude tone and accusing statements were mitigated only by the obvious ignorance in which it was written. The "hopes of the people," the President went on, "are being thwarted by militarists and a small group of political reactionaries who are obstructing the advancement of the general good of the nation *by failing to understand the liberal trend of the times.*" (Italics added.)

This "liberal trend" was fortunately reversed by the President himself within the short space of seven months. But in the meantime, although aid to China was already largely terminated, his previous threats to withhold it were renewed. "It cannot be expected," he said, "that American opinion will continue in its generous attitude towards your nation unless convincing proof is shortly forthcoming that genuine progress is being made toward a peaceful settlement of China's internal problems."

It is difficult to imagine the feelings which must have been experienced by General Chiang upon the receipt of this note. But if he felt any resentment, or despair, he did not show it. He replied with patience and forbearance, commending the efforts of General Marshall, and making a vain effort to impress the President with the impossibility of obtaining a peaceful settlement with those who insist upon violence:

General Marshall has labored most unsparingly to achieve our common objective; namely, peace and democracy in China, since his arrival. Despite all obstacles, I, too, have done my utmost to cooperate with him in the accomplishment of his task.

The desire for peace has to be mutual, therefore, it means the Communists must give up their policy to seize political power through the use of armed force, to overthrow the government and to install a totalitarian regime such as those with which Eastern Europe is now being engulfed.

The minimum requirement for the preservation of peace in our country is the abandonment of such a policy.

President Truman, however, was unmoved by such logic. He replied briefly, and with a terse reminder that there would be no assistance in the absence of an accommodation with the Communists:

With reference to the final paragraph of my policy statement of 15 December 1945, I hope it will be feasible for the United States to plan for assisting China in its industrial economy and the rehabilitation of its agrarian reforms. This can be rendered feasible, I believe, through the prompt removal of the threat of widespread Civil War in China.

In the meantime, the threat to withhold assistance had been carried out. United States aid in the transportation of government troops to north China (excluding Manchuria) was terminated when Marshall's mission began. Shortly thereafter, the United States suspended a credit of $500,000,000 which had been earmarked for China by the Export-Import Bank. In July, 1946, a complete embargo was placed on shipments of military supplies, and it stood for nearly a year. In August, 1946, an agreement was made for the sale to the

Chinese government of all United States surplus property in China, and on seventeen Pacific islands and bases; but guns, munitions, military aircraft and other combatant materials were expressly excluded.

The State Department has explained that it was necessary for the United States to take a neutral position as long as it was "mediating" between the government and the Communists,[49] and there was also an agreement with the Soviet Union to adhere to "the policy of non-interference in the internal affairs of China."[50] The Soviet Union, however, was not bound by such "neutralism," and it did not observe the agreement. While the United States was withholding assistance from the government, the Soviet Union was giving extensive aid to the Communists, directly in Manchuria, and "indirectly" through its puppet regime in Mongolia.

By the end of World War II, the Communist armed forces in China had greatly increased in numbers. General Chiang states that, in 1934, when they were driven into the northwest, "there were only some 5,000 armed Communists left" and they "no longer constituted a serious threat."[51] But by the end of World War II, the State Department reported that they claimed a strength of 500,000 regular troops and two million militia, and that they were in control of large portions of north China as well as disconnected areas to the east and south. They were, however, "poorly equipped,"[52] and this deficiency was made up by Soviet assistance.

During its six-day war on Japan (August 8-14, 1945), the Soviet Union occupied Manchuria, where it remained until May of 1946. This period of occupation was used to turn over large areas to the Communists, delay the entry of government troops, and to make available to the Communist armies the arms and equipment of 700,000 to 1,000,000 surrendering Japanese. The Soviet occupation troops also prevented the government from using the port of Dairen and parts of the Manchurian railroad. Before the government troops arrived, they flooded the coal mines, removed the best industrial installations and equipment, destroyed the remainder and took with them $3,000,000 in gold bullion and over 500,000,000 Manchurian yuan.

Moreover, several invasions of China were launched by the puppet regime of the "People's Republic of Outer Mongolia"—in August, 1945, June, 1947, and January, 1948. The first of these enabled the Communists to occupy Kalgan, where they received training and equipment from a "Soviet-Mongolian military mission."

At the same time, the long negotiations, and the repeated "cease-fires" declared in 1946 (January, May, June, August, and November), were used by the Communists to obtain the time to organize, train, equip and to attack. They attacked wherever they found temporary superiority, and they observed the cease-fires only where necessary to gain political advantage or avoid annihilation. The original cease-fire agreement provided for enforcement by means of inspection teams, but these were made ineffective by tactics similar to those later used by the Communists in Korea and Indochina. Although the teams were composed of three members, one American, one Communist and one from the Chinese government, the Communists acquired a veto power by insisting on the "principle of unanimity."[53]

The result was that by 1947, as the State Department's White Paper says, "the strategic initiative passed from the Government to the Communists."[54] Government troops in Manchuria were isolated, and the Communists became so well entrenched in central Chiana that, as the same report states, "only a major Government offensive" could have dislodged them.[55] Such an offensive was just what the United States had prohibited, during 1946, and refused to assist in 1947-8. The government of China did attempt such an offensive in 1947, and in July of that year orders were issued for the complete suppression of the Communist rebellion, but military supplies were depleted, the Chinese had no means to replenish them, and the United States still refused to supply them.

In September, 1947, a United States fact-finding mission reported that outside assistance was urgently required. "The present industrial potential of China," the report explained, "is inadequate to support military forces effectively. Hence outside aid in the form of munitions (most urgently ammunition) and technical assistance are essential before any plans of operations can be undertaken with reasonable prospect of success."[56] The chairman of the mission, General Albert C. Wedemeyer, urged that such assistance be given "as early as practicable,"[57] but it was nearly six months (February, 1948) before the required legislation was submitted to Congress. Even then the proposed authorization called only for economic assistance—$510,000,000 to provide "minimum imports of essential civilian type of commodities" and $60,000,000 for "key reconstruction projects."[58] Spending was to be spread over a fifteen-month period, that is, until at least the middle of 1949 (by which time China was defeated).

In the meantime, actual military asistance was minimal. In May,

1947, the embargo was lifted, but during the balance of the year only scattered and small-scale aid was provided. This included a number of small naval vessels, a quantity of small arms and ammunition turned over by the departing Marines and the sale of surplus ammunition and 150 aircraft.

In 1948, Congress appropriated $275,000,000 in economic aid, for a one-year period, and $125,000,000 for military assistance. This compared with $150,000,000 requested the preceding year, for the Greek Army alone, which faced an estimated 30,000 guerrillas, and $6,800,000,000 requested in 1948 for the European Recovery Program.

A large part of the military supplies ordered under the appropriation for China did not arrive until late in the year, too late to be effective.[59] As the American Ambassador indicated in July, the appropriation itself came too late. "Even under the most hopeful conditions," he asserted, "such aid would probably require some two years or more from next January to accomplish its objective. . . ."[60]

The United States Army Intelligence Division stated that by 1949 the national government had suffered such "overwhelming losses" that its military position was "beyond possible recoupment." Even so, this conclusion was based on the assumption that China would be "acting alone."[61] In November, 1948, General David Barr, commander of the United States Military Advisory Group in China, reported that it had been "obvious" to him "for some time that nothing short of a United States organization with the authority and facilities available . . . on V-J day including a United States fed and operated supply pipeline could remedy the situation."[62] The inference, of course, was that even at this late date authority and facilities equal to that effort would have provided a remedy.

In 1949, Senator Pat MacCarran made an eleventh-hour proposal for a credit to China in the amount of $1,500,000,000, but this was also rejected. Nanking fell in April, and the national government was forced to return to Canton, where it had begun its long and fateful career thirty-two years before. By the end of the year it had fled to Formosa, and the number of subject peoples was increased by more than 450,000,000. Once again the wartime pledges had been ignored, and President Truman's new pledges—"to support free peoples who are resisting attempted subjugation by armed minorities or by outside pressures"[63]—had fared no better.

The inevitable results were new wars and far greater expenditures. For the United States alone these included approximately

$18,000,000,000 on war in Korea,[64] $4,000,000,000 on war in Indo-china,[65] and in the neighborhood of $1,000,000,000 annually for military assistance and defense support in the entire Far East and Pacific Area (Korea, Formosa, Japan, the Philippines, Viet Nam, Cambodia, Laos and Thailand). The failure to aid China is now regretted by the free powers, which see the need for assisting all *free* peoples, but the same mistake is being repeated in persistent refusal to aid the subject peoples.

In the case of China, the United States reversed its policy towards the Communists more completely than it had in the case of any other nation—so much so that in the last stages of the war it even began to express fears that the Chinese government would actually adopt the course of action which the United States had for so long attempted to impose upon it. Thus, in January, 1947, General Marshall was still castigating the "dominant group of reactionaries who have been opposed, in my opinion, to almost every effort I have made to influence the formation of a genuine coalition government,"[66] but by March, 1948, he had concluded that this matter was "for the Chinese Government to decide, not for the United States Government to dictate."[67] In August, 1948, he ruled that even the implication of support for the inclusion of Communists must be avoided. "The United States Government," he asserted, "must not directly or indirectly give any implication of support, encouragement or acceptability of coalition government in China with Communist participation."[68]

There was a similar change in the views of President Truman. In December, 1946, he had acclaimed the "statesmanlike" agreement of "the Kuomintang or Government Party, the Communist Party and several minor political parties" to form "an interim government of a coalition type with representation of all parties."[69] In March, 1948, he stated that "we did not want any Communists in the Government of China or anywhere else if we could help it."[70] General Barr asserted that his Military Advisory Group should be withdrawn if the government accepted a coalition with the Communists. "I do not believe," he wrote, "that the United States should advise or assist in any way such a government, with its Communist dominated Armed Forces, and recommend that in this event, JUSMAG be withdrawn. . . ."[71]

Nevertheless, in spite of these reversals, there was no comparable reversal in the attitude towards military assistance. This has been the case, unfortunately, with every so-called "awakening" to the aims and purposes of the Communists. When the free world was considering assistance to the armies of Admiral Kolchak, the belief was expressed that the "Lenin wing of the Communist Party" was "as moderate as any Socialist Government which can control Russia."[72] This view was soon discarded, but Kolchak was allowed to fall nevertheless. During Stalin's regime it was said that "none but the ignorant fail to recognize the many advances made for the Russian people by the communist government."[73] This view was later condemned as the complete reverse of the truth, but still without effective action on the people's behalf.

There were many of course who came to regret their advice on China—that the program of the "so-called Communists" was a "moderate one," that their "chief interest" was "to improve the economic position of China's farmers,"[74] and that there was a "definite liberal group" among them "who would put the interest of the Chinese people above ruthless measures to establish a Communist ideology."[75] But the same persons refused, nevertheless, to support a policy of effective assistance to those people. Today we are again advised that the Communists are reforming, even in the Soviet Union, that they are different from those of the Stalin era, and that the "Russian people are getting more personal security, and labor is getting increased freedom of choice."[76] These views too will be discarded, but the Russian peoples will not benefit, the peoples of eastern Europe will not be released, free government will not be restored to China, and the rest of the world will never be safe, unless there is also a change from the policy which has allowed the victims of communism to go unaided for more than forty years.

CHAPTER XI

PARTITION IN INDOCHINA

Colonialism, Imperialism and United Action

In 1927, when the Communists were expelled from the Kuomintang, many Soviet agents in China were forced to return to Moscow. One of these was Nguyen Ai Quoc, a translator for the Russian consulate in Canton. He was also a graduate of the Communist International's Moscow school for revolutionaries, a member of the presidium of the Krestintern (Peasant International) and organizer of the Association of Young Annamite Revolutionaries. As an unknown Annamite, his pleas for the freedom of French Indochina were ignored at the Paris Peace Conference, but as the Communist "Ho Chi Minh" he was destined to lead his countrymen in an eight-year war (1946-54) against France and its supporters which would cost them nearly $12,000,000,000[1] and prove that communism cannot be contained, even by the maximum expenditure of men, materials and equipment, when these are directed only to the protection of the free world and its interests.

Because the people of Indochina were forced to make a choice between colonial domination by the French, of which they had years of bitter experience, and the promises of the Communists, of whose real methods they had no knowledge, Ho Chi Minh was able to win the minds of more men with a false message than the victors in two world wars for democracy were able to convince with the combined moral force of all their wartime declarations. As a result, the free world nearly lost this war completely, and more than 12,000,000 people were given up to Communist domination. In the end, the French were not able to retain their position, and in 1956—two years after "peace" with the Communists and a belated grant of independence—it was still felt, in the words of a former ambassador to Thailand, that the "prospects for the three states of Indochina are not bright."[2] Moreover, the reputation of the free powers was so badly damaged that there are many places, even today, where the promises of the Communists carry more weight than our own. On the other hand, more than 17,000,000 people of Indochina were preserved from Soviet domination, and the free world had an opportunity to discover that even those who are most earnestly seeking their freedom may be driven into the arms of the Communists, or induced to stand aloof, when their pleas are not heard.

French rule was imposed upon the various little kingdoms of Indochina by successive steps during the second half of the nineteenth century—Cambodia in 1863, Cochin China in 1867, Annam and Tonkin in 1884, and Laos in 1893. It became a turbulent rule, marked by many periods of small wars and revolts. One such period occurred shortly after Ho Chi Minh's departure from Canton, and the Communists made the most of it to win supporters. Assuming the leadership of strikes, demonstrations and acts of terrorism, the Communists succeeded in establishing temporary "Soviet" regimes in two provinces of Annam before the outbreaks were finally suppressed.

Ho Chi Minh himself became the chief of the Southern Bureau of the Comintern; and in 1930, he went to Hong Kong to organize the Indochinese Communist Party. In 1931, he was arrested by the British, but he was never turned over to the French, who sentenced him to death *in absentia*. He was released in 1933 and disappeared.

After the outbreak of World War II, and the fall of France, Ho Chi Minh turned up again as general secretary of the League for the Independence of Viet Nam. This organization, commonly known as the Viet Minh, combined the twin purposes of permanent revolt against the French and wartime resistance to the Japanese occupation, but it was Communist-dominated and therefore had a third purpose— the substitution of the rule of Moscow. It competed with other, non-Communist, national parties which were equally opposed to French rule and seeking true independence. They were assisted by the free Chinese and united under the name of the Viet Nam Revolutionary League (Dong Minh Hoi).

In the meantime, as the Communists predicted, World War II had brought the "moment when the capitalists fight among themselves over the division of the colonies."[3] During the period in which France was controlled by the Nazi-dominated Vichy regime, the French administration of Indochina was tolerated by the Japanese; but after the Allied landings in Normandy, and the establishment of the pro-Allied government of General Charles De Gaulle, the Japanese attempted to take over. In March, 1945, they substituted their own administration, interned the French troops and proclaimed the "independence" of the former French protectorates. At the same time, they purported to recognize the sovereignty of the hereditary rulers—Bao Dai, Emperor of Annam and Tonkin; Norodom Sihanouk, King of Cambodia; and Sisavang Vong, King of Luang Prabang (Laos). Shortly before V-J Day, they also proclaimed the "independence" of Cochin China, a former French colony. This action prepared the way for the reunion of all parts of the former Annamese Empire (Viet Nam)—Cochin China, Annam and Tonkin.[4]

To the minds of the Communists, the Japanese action prepared the way for the creation of some new Soviet satellites. It brought to hand still another of the predicted "moments" of opportunity—the "moment when the colonial revolutions have fully matured"[5]—and they were thus put on notice that the time had come to complete the task assigned in 1922; to "call upon" the masses in "the colonial and semicolonial countries on the Pacific Coast" to "take up an active struggle for national liberation and to teach them to regard Soviet Russia as the bulwark of all the oppressed and exploited masses."[6]

National liberation was actually obtained without the aid of this "bulwark." The Japanese surrendered in August, 1945, and each of the states of Indochina immediately made its own declaration of independence. In Cambodia the Prime Minister, Son Ngoc Thanh, conducted a plebiscite in which the people voted to end the French protectorate. In Laos another Prime Minister, Prince Petsarath, announced that the "juridical bonds tying us to France by treaties and agreements have been broken off in fact, because France has not met her engagement to defend us against external forces."[7] An independent provisional government was appointed by the "Free Laotians." In Viet Nam a provisional government (the National Liberation Committee) was created by the Viet Minh. The Emperor, Bao Dai, abdicated in its favor, and on September 2, 1945, a declaration of independence was made.[8] It began with the following direct quotations from the Declaration of Independence of the United States and the French Declaration of the Rights of Man:

All men are created equal. They are endowed by their Creator with certain inalienable rights, among these are Life, Liberty and the pursuit of happiness.

All men are born free with equal rights, and must always be free and have equal rights.

Although five of the fifteen members of the Viet Nam government were Communists, and Ho Chi Minh became the President, many honest people supported or participated in it. It was welcomed by the majority as a democratic manifestation of their demand for independence, and even the former Emperor accepted the nominal post of Supreme Political Advisor.

It may be that this was a mistake. It may be that the people of Viet Nam would not have been able to rid this government of its Communist elements even if the French had not endeavored to re-impose colonial rule, and even if there had been no war. But if the making of similar mistakes is any criterion, there are few in the free world who are in a position to criticize. The government offered by the Viet Minh represented precisely the type of "coalition" government to which the United States was seeking agreement in China, and the number of Communists it contained was less than the number included in the "governments" accepted by all of the western powers for the nations of eastern Europe. There was, moreover, no question of Communist domination of the governments of Laos and Cambodia, but the newly won independence of all three states was nevertheless destroyed by the French, with the assistance or acquiescence of the other free powers, in spite of their wartime pledges, and in the fullest confirmation of the worst Communist predictions.

The original attitude of the United States was one of silent acquiescence. At the Yalta Conference, President Roosevelt made the sweeping statement that "France had done nothing to improve the natives since she had the colony,"[9] but he declined to oppose the French return because it "would only make the British mad."[10] While withholding effective assistance from the Chinese, because of their failure to understand "the liberal trend of the times," the United States granted billions of dollars in postwar assistance to France, with no apparent concern for the bitter struggle created by its efforts to re-establish colonialism in Indochina. Subsequently, when the people of Indochina found themselves caught between the predatory designs of the Chinese Communists and the stubborn reassertion of French domination, they had nowhere to turn for assistance. The United States, which was the logical source of such aid, provided extensive assistance in the war against communism, but nothing for the struggle with colonialism. It may well be that any other course would have made the French as well as the British "mad," but there was no apparent fear of incurring the similar displeasure of the Chinese, of the Indochinese, or of any of the other peoples of the East.

An example of what the free powers might have done for Indochina was provided by the allegedly reactionary Kuomintang government of China, which, prior to the French return, was given the responsibility of accepting Japanese surrender north of the sixteenth parallel. The Chinese were opposed to the Viet Minh, being well aware of Ho Chi Minh's identity, and having in fact imprisoned him for a time during the war. But their opposition was based upon the Communist domination of that organization, not upon its demands for independence. Moreover, the Chinese expressed their opposition by supporting other anti-Viet Minh nationalist parties, and when it became apparent that the Viet Minh regime was backed by a majority of the people, they gave it their support. Ho Chi Minh was persuaded to reduce the number of Communists in his cabinet; and before withdrawing, the Chinese insisted upon a French agreement in which the native government was accepted.

A much different situation prevailed in the south, where similar responsibility was given to Great Britain, and where the French were at once allowed to oust the native administration of Cochin China. The government of Cambodia surrendered peacefully, but both states became the scene of long and bitter guerrilla warfare in which many of those who fought for freedom were induced to accept the aid of the Communists and the Viet Minh.

The effects of the French policy were reflected in the fate of the Cambodian Prime Minister, Son Ngoc Thanh, who was deported to France for trial as a collaborator with the Japanese. After his release in 1951, he founded a nationalist newspaper in Pnom Penh; but when he was accused of stirring up disorder, and his newspaper was suppressed, he fled from the city, joined the Free Cambodians, and eventually became involved with the Viet Minh. As president of the Cambodian Committee for National Liberation, he became the leader of an active guerrilla movement, which was not dissolved until after the Geneva Conference in 1954—when full independence was granted.

In the north, to which the French returned in 1946, an even worse result was obtained. The independent government of Laos was suppressed, and the Free Laotians were driven from the country.

Many returned in 1949, when partial independence was conceded, but others allied themselves with the Viet Minh, and received its active assistance. During a Viet Minh invasion in 1953, they were established in the northern province of Sam Neua as the "Laotian People's Government"; and in the settlement made at Geneva, they were assigned two provinces, Sam Neua and Phong Saly. From there they continued to attack the legitimate government. Pursuant to an agreement made in 1957, two "Pathet Lao" battalions were to be incorporated into the national army and a "coalition" government formed, but subversion continued. When the attempt at coalition was abandoned in the following year, the Viet Minh launched new incursions, the Pathet Lao renewed its rebellion, and the fate of Laos is still uncertain.

In Viet Nam the French agreed at first to recognize the government of the Viet Minh, but no real settlement was made. The Viet Minh was supported in the suppression of other, non-Communist, national groups, but at the same time its own seemingly less extreme demands were not met. Hostile incidents and demonstrations were provoked by the presence of the French troops; the French dealt harshly with them; and tension mounted rapidly. In November, 1946, the French bombarded the port of Haiphong, completely destroying the Vietnamese quarter. In December they demanded the disarming of the Viet Minh militia. The result was open warfare which did not end until French resources were depleted and the United States had been led to the "brink" of war with Communist China. When it did end, following the Geneva agreements, Viet Nam was divided between the Communists in the north and an independent government in the south.

At the beginning of the war it looked as though the French would win. The Viet Minh were driven into the mountains and claims were made that they had been annihilated. It soon became apparent, however, that they had not lost their popular support. By means of guerrilla tactics the Viet Minh were able to dominate large parts of the countryside, particularly at night, and after the victory of the Communists in China, they received extensive foreign aid. They then launched a series of major offensives, gaining control of nearly all of northern Tonkin except the delta area of the Red River. Transportation between the French-held areas became possible only by air or by sea.

In 1951, the Viet Minh organized a "Joint National United

Front" of Free Laotians, Free Cambodians and their own Lien Viet. In 1953, they invaded Laos, nearly reaching Thailand, and in 1954 they invaded Cambodia. Finally, on May 7, 1954, they won a tremendous victory at Dien Bien Phu, annihilating the French fortress, taking 10,000 prisoners and accounting for an additional 6,000 casualties in killed and wounded. These victories were, of course, largely due to the assistance of the Chinese Communists, but it cannot be denied that the force of the Chinese intervention was offset by the intervention of France and the aid of the United States. The scales were tipped by the number of people alienated by the French and whose favor had been successfully curried by the Communists, at least in the beginning.

During the period of occupation by the free Chinese, the Viet Minh made every effort to preserve the appearance of genuine democratic government. Members of all parties were included, the open branch of the Communist Party was dissolved, and Ho Chi Minh promised the most desirable democratic reforms. In January, 1946, he held a nation-wide general election. In the south it was conducted secretly, amid assertions in the French press that the Vietnamese were incapable of holding a free election.[11] More typical Communist methods were employed for a short time after the withdrawal of the Chinese. Many of the opposition leaders were arrested or forced into exile, and the Communist representation in the cabinet was increased. But when open warfare with the French began, the Viet Minh government was "broadened" again, and the real Communist control was not openly displayed until after the victory of the Communists in China.

Thereafter, the Viet Minh moved openly into the Communist camp. Hastening to recognize the Chinese Communists, their government was itself recognized, in January, 1950, by Communist China and the Soviet Union. Soon it was recognized by all the satellites, and plentiful supplies of arms and ammunition began to arrive from the Communist arsenals in China, Russia and eastern Europe. In 1951, the Indochinese Communist Party was revived under the name of the Viet Nam Workers' Party (Lao Dong). Its platform called for a strengthening of "the Party's leadership in government organisations of all levels," and boldly stated that the existing "strength" of the "People's Rule" was the result of "assistance rendered by the Soviet Union, China and other People's Democracies."[12]

In the meantime, the French had themselves endeavored to win over the people by granting "internal sovereignty" to the three states of Indochina as "independent" Associated States of the French Union. In Viet Nam they had organized a competing and allegedly independent government headed by the former Emperor, Bao Dai. A series of agreements, promising or purporting to grant such independence, were made at Ha Long Bay in 1948, at Paris in 1949 (the Elysée Accords), and at the Pau Conference in 1950. Finally, in 1953, a new series of negotiations were initiated for the purpose of "completing" the "independence and sovereignty" thus granted.

Few of the Indochinese were satisfied with these arrangements, however, as they left the French in substantial control of economic matters, foreign policy, defense and even a large part of the internal administration. In April, 1953, the King of Cambodia complained to *The New York Times*: "Cambodian justice does not apply to the French and our police cannot touch them. In economic matters they have our hands and feet tied: we cannot import and export freely and we have no freedom of taxation."[13]

As a result, the French-sponsored regime in Viet Nam was not popular, and even those who refused to be associated with the Viet Minh regarded the war as a foreign war, conducted and controlled largely by outsiders. In September, 1953, an unofficial national congress, held at Cholon, demanded unconditional independence. In October even the official National Congress—summoned by the French-sponsored government of Bao Dai—demanded real independence. Calling for "the transfer to Vietnam of all powers still residing in the French authorities," the Congress asserted that "independent Vietnam cannot participate in the French Union in its present form." The "French Union," it said, "as defined by the French Constitution of 1946 is hardly compatible with the statute of an independent country."[14]

The difficulty, if not its cause, was recognized by the United States in March, 1950, when Secretary of State Dean Acheson asserted that "the solution of the Indochina problem depends both upon the restoration of security and upon the development of genuine nationalism. . . ."[15] He also said that "United States assistance can and should contribute to these major objectives,"[16] but the demands of the genuine nationalists were not met and United States military assistance was channeled through the French high command.

The trouble was that the French were always talking about "independence" for Indochina, but never quite able to face its reality.

"Independence" was continually being "granted," or "recognized," only to be withdrawn by the elaborately worded conditions and qualifying clauses of the declarations and agreements by which the "grant" or "recognition" was extended. At the same time, the United States was induced to fully endorse the French position, ostensibly accepting each new promise as making independence an accomplished fact. This mollified the French, but it failed to convince the people of Indochina.

An example of the French approach was furnished in March, 1945, when the "independence" of Indochina was proclaimed by Japan. The provisional French government of General de Gaulle then issued its own declaration, stating that Indochina should have a "liberty of its own" and "economic autonomy."[17] This liberty, however, was to be "within the framework of the French Union," and the "French Union" turned out to be another term for French domination. Indochina was to have its own land, sea and air forces, but they were to be organized "within the system of general defense of the French Union." In fact, the Indochinese were considered privileged to "have access to all ranks on an equal footing with the personnel coming from the mother country or other parts of the French Union." Indochina was to have its own elected assembly, which could "vote taxes," but "French interests" were to be represented and the assembly would only "deliberate" on bills. "Commercial and good-neighbor treaties which concern the Indochinese Federation" were to be submitted to the assembly, but only "for examination." Indochina was also to "have its own Federal Government," but it was to be "presided over by the Governor General [appointed by France] and composed of ministers responsible to [and selected by] him."

In the agreement with the Viet Minh (March 6, 1946),[18] the French recognized the "Republic of Viet Nam as a free state, having its own government, parliament, army and treasury," but it still belonged "to the Indo-Chinese Federation and to the French Union." The "relief forces" were to be composed of a maximum of 15,000 French troops, to be progressively withdrawn within five years. These troops would share responsibility with 10,000 Vietnamese troops having "Vietnamese cadres" and operating "under the military control of Vietnam." But the forces "as a whole" were to be "placed under supreme French command with the assistance of Vietnamese representatives." Moreover, it was stipulated in a "Modus Vivendi" that the government of Vietnam would "call upon French nationals

by priority each time it requires advisers, technicians or experts."
This "priority" would "only cease to operate in case of impossibility
on the part of France to furnish the requested personnel."[19]

In 1948, the French made a new agreement, with their own
"Central Provisional Government."[20] This also recognized the "independence" of Viet Nam, and its right "to bring about freely its unity,"
but the "Government" was a French puppet regime, and the
President, General Nguyen Van Xuan, had spent most of his life in
France. He did not even speak Vietnamese. The agreement provided
that the "independence" of Viet Nam was to have "no limits," but it
was a case of "no limits other than those emanating from its membership in the French Union."

In 1949, the "principles laid down" by this agreement were
"confirmed and determined precisely" in an exchange of letters with
Bao Dai.[21] In spite of his previous abdication, Bao Dai was again
described as "Emperor of Vietnam" and he was to "associate the
activity of his diplomacy with that of the French Union." The new
government was to "fully exercise all the attributions and
prerogatives arising from internal sovereignty," but "the modalities
of the transfer" of powers "formerly exercised by the French
authority" were to be determined by additional "particular or provisional conventions." These would be "passed with the French High
Commissioner." Still another "particular agreement" was to fix the
strength of the Vietnam national army "and that of the army of the
French Union stationed in Vietnam."

It was further provided that "All civil, commercial and penal
matters" were to "come within the full and unreserved jurisdiction of
Vietnam." Civil and commercial cases, however, between "non-Viet-
namese subjects of the French Union," or between the Vietnamese
and such subjects, and also "penal action taken in the case of breaches
of the law perpetrated by or impairing" such subjects, and penal
action "prejudicing the French State," were to be "submitted to joint
jurisdictions." This would be in accordance with the provision of a
"judiciary convention" under which "French law will be applied
every time a Frenchman is implicated." Vietnamese law would be
applied in other cases, if it should "seem applicable to the solution of
the conflict."

It was at this point that the United States purported, in February,
1950, to recognize the "established" independence of these states—
that is, as "independent states within the French Union." In the

official announcement it was variously asserted that such recognition was "consistent" with the "fundamental policy of giving support to the peaceful and democratic evolution of dependent peoples toward self-government"; that the agreements had "provided the basis for the evolution of Viet Namese independence within the French Union"; that their ratification had "established the independence of Viet Nam, Laos, and Cambodia as associated states within the French Union"; and that the "full implementation" of the agreements, and of additional agreements not yet ratified, would "promote political stability and the growth of effective democratic institutions. . . ."[22] Thus, the United States, like the French, appeared to believe that "independence" could be both "established" and in the process of "evolution" at one and the same time.

After further agreements were made at Pau, in December, 1950, the United States Minister asserted that "the French colonial regime" was "ended." There remained only the temporary necessity of re-taining some French "technical experts":

The French colonial regime ended with the signature of the so-called Pau accords on December 16. . . . A relatively large number of French Government technical experts are being held temporarily, at the request of the Indochinese, in certain posts until Indochinese can be trained to take their places. In the case of many positions that will be a matter of only a few months.[23]

Eighteen months later, however, this "temporary" situation still prevailed. In June, 1952, Secretary of State Dean Acheson asserted:

I do not think it is generally realized to what extent these new states in fact control their own affairs. Only a limited number of services related to the necessities of the war remain temporarily in French hands.[24]

These "necessities of war" had not been dissipated when the French government made a new declaration, in July, 1953. Yet it then stated that the time had come to "complete the independence and sovereignty of the Associated States" and "to adapt the agreements made by them . . . to the position which they have acquired . . . in the community of free peoples."[25] Secretary of State Dulles asserted in the United Nations General Assembly that the French were now going to "perfect" the independence of Indochina:

The pretext, until now, has been that the Associated States of Indo-china were mere colonies and that the Communist war was designed to promote "independence" rather than to expand by violence the Soviet camp.

It is no longer possible to support such a pretext. The French Government by its declaration of July 3, 1953, has announced its intention of completing the process of transferring to the Govern-ments of the three Associated States all those remaining powers that are needed to perfect their independence to their own satisfaction.[26]

As a result, he said on another occasion, the character of the war had been transformed, and the United States could therefore "in good conscience, contribute substantially" to its successful conclusion. The French had "made clear their intention":

Now, the French, by declaration of July 3, have made clear their intention to grant full independence to the Associated States of Indochina as these States desire it. They are in the process of im-plementing that declaration, and there is every evidence that they are doing so in complete good faith. Thus, the character of the war be-comes transformed. The United States can, in good conscience, con-tribute substantially, in money and matériel, to the successful con-clusion of this war. It has become genuinely a "war for independence," and the aggressive character of the Communist warfare now stands exposed.[27]

By this time, however, the United States was already contributing substantially, on the strength of previously expressed "clear" French intentions; and in the following year, when the French requested direct American intervention, Secretary of State Dulles asserted that "clear assurance of complete independence" had not yet been ob-tained.[28]

There was a similar unwarranted complacency with regard to the progress made in filling the need for native, national armies—a development which was hindered by the reluctance to give real in-dependence. Like the "independent," native governments, the national armies remained under the galling domination of French personnel and French control of the purse strings, while the United States and France expatiated upon the opportunity afforded to the people "to play the constantly greater role in their own defense to which they rightly aspire."[29]

The commencement of an effort in this direction was announced in February, 1951, by the United States Minister, Donald R. Heath. He added a warning, however, that it would take "a good many months" to create Vietnamese troops "equal in numbers and training to the rebel troops, who are trained and equipped by the Chinese Communists."[30] By June, 1952, Secretary of State Dean Acheson reported that much had been accomplished, and the units of the national armies had already "distinguished themselves in battle."[31] In July, 1952, an assistant secretary asserted that the "main effort" was being devoted to this program:

The main effort of the United States and France in recent months has been to develop national armies in the three Associated States, and, since this decision was taken in November of 1950, there has been created a total of 52 battalions for the three states. As indication of the great progress which the people of the Associated States are making and the great interest they have in developing their own national armies, it is interesting to note that 20 out of 52 battalions have either none or not more than five French officers attached to them. All of the other officers are Vietnamese. The Chief of Staff of Vietnam's national army is a Vietnamese, and in the past year approximately 1,000 new Vietnamese officers were graduated from training schools in addition to substantial numbers of technicians and noncommissioned officers.[32]

By the end of 1953, however, it was discovered that this "progress" had not been sufficient. After a tour of Indochina, Vice President Nixon stated that a major problem was the delay in the training and organization of native troops, a delay which he attributed to the failure of the French to trust the Vietnamese soldier, and to their insistence upon control of the Vietnamese national army by French *noncommissioned* officers.[33] In April, 1954, he indicated that the problem still existed, asserting that the United States might have to send its own troops to Indochina:

. . . the problem is not one of materials and wasn't four months ago. More men are needed and the question is where to get them. They will not come from France, for France is tired of the war, as we were tired of Korea. Therefore, additional manpower must come from Viet Nam, Cambodia and Laos, particularly Vietnam. The French, however, while slow in training the native soldiers, resent the idea that the United States or others should send men to do the job.

.   .   .   .

It is hoped the United States will not have to send troops there, but if this Government cannot avoid it, the Administration must face up to the situation and dispatch forces.[34]

Because real independence was not given to the Indochinese, and because there was no adequate independent national army, there was an ever-increasing need for outside military assistance. The French were required to organize a large expeditionary force of nearly 250,000 men, including foreign legionnaires, North Africans, Senegalese and approximately 80,000 French nationals. By 1953, they were spending at the rate of approximately $1,200,000,000 annually. The contribution of the United States, in materials and equipment, was even greater; and by 1954, it was paying approximately 80% of the total bill.[35] Its assistance for the period 1950-54 has been estimated at $2,300,000,000, including $1,200,000,000 in military supplies and materials, $1,000,000,000 in budgetary aid to France and the Associated States, and $100,000,000 in economic aid.[36] Another source indicates that the total of American assistance used in Indochina, including sums diverted from those supplied for use in Europe, exceeded $4,000,000,000 for the period 1948-54.[37]

Even this vast contribution proved insufficient, however, and in March, 1954, the French requested direct United States intervention in the form of an aerial bombardment of Communist forces at Dien Bien Phu. Such an intervention, "which might not be confined to Indochina," had often been threatened by the United States, but like "independence," and the "national" armies, it was subject to conditions which were always on the verge or "brink" of fulfillment, but never quite realized.

The first condition put forth was that there would have to be an "open" intervention by the Chinese Communists—an event which President Eisenhower had attempted to forestall in April, 1953, during the negotiations for an armistice in Korea. Such an armistice, he stated, should not only bring about a termination of hostilities in that country, but also "an end to the direct and indirect attacks upon the security of Indochina and Malaya. For any armistice in Korea," he said, "that merely released aggressive armies to attack elsewhere would be a fraud."[38] The armistice, however, did not bring an end to such attacks, and it did become a fraud, but the only immediate result was a series of vague threats, never carried out.

Five weeks after the armistice in Korea was concluded, Secretary of State Dulles bluntly stated that the attacks in Indochina had not been ended. There was, he said, a "single Chinese-Communist aggressive front" extending "from Korea on the north to Indochina in the south"; and "Communist China has been and now is training, equipping, and supplying the Communist forces in Indochina." But he only threatened that if the Chinese Communists sent their "own army" into Indochina, there would be "grave consequences" that would not be confined to the immediate battle area:

There is the risk that, as in Korea, Red China might send its own army into Indochina. The Chinese Communist regime should realize that such a second aggression could not occur without grave consequences which might not be confined to Indochina. I say this soberly in the interest of peace and in the hope of preventing another aggressor miscalculation.[39]

In January, 1954, Secretary Dulles repeated this threat in slightly different language. "The way to deter aggression," he said, "is for the free community to be willing and able to respond vigorously at places and with means of its own choosing. ... I have said in relation to Indochina that, if there were open Red Chinese army aggression there, that would have 'grave consequences which might not be confined to Indochina.' "[40]

In February, 1954, the threat was repeated by an assistant secretary, with emphatic assurance that it was not idly made:

In a recent speech Mr. Dulles made this very definite statement: "I have said in relation to Indochina that, if there were open Red Chinese Army aggression there, that would have grave consequences which might not be confined to Indochina."

The free world cannot afford another blood-letting such as Korea.

This is not sabre-rattling. It is very clear, thoughtfully considered policy. *We mean it*.[41] (Italics added.)

In March, 1954, the threat was further explained and reconfirmed by Secretary Dulles:

President Eisenhower, in his address of April 16, 1953, explained that a Korean armistice would be a fraud if it merely released aggressive armies for attack elsewhere. I said last September that if Red China sent its own army into Indochina, that would result in grave consequences which might not be confined to Indochina.

Recent statements have been designed to impress upon potential aggressors that aggression might lead to action at places and by means of free-world choosing, so that aggression would cost more than it could gain.[42]

.   .   .   .

Today, if aggression were resumed, the United Nations Command [in Korea] would certainly feel free to inflict heavy damage upon the aggressor beyond the immediate area which he chose for his aggression. That need not mean indulging in atomic warfare throughout Asia. It should not be stated in advance precisely what would be the scope of military action if new aggression occurred. That is a matter as to which the aggressor had best remain ignorant. But he can know and he does know, in the light of present policies, that the choice in this respect is ours and not his.

In relation to Indochina, the United States has publicly stated that if there were open Red Chinese Army aggression there, that would have "grave consequences which might not be confined to Indochina."[43]

Finally, in April, 1954, it was conceded that the Communists were "saving themselves" only by "technicalities." In a statement to the House Committee on Foreign Affairs, Secretary Dulles expressed the opinion that they were "skirting very close to doing the kind of thing against which President Eisenhower gave the warning.... They are not openly and flagrantly committing a new aggression," he said, "but they are only saving themselves from that charge by technicalities...."[44] He added that the "technicalities" did not in any way reduce the danger, or the cause for concern: "I believe it is a cause of grave concern, and that our concern should not be mitigated by the fact that the means are perhaps technically evasive of the congressional definition of aggression."[45]

As evidence of the extent of the Chinese Communist intervention, Secretary Dulles had pointed out earlier that the Viet Minh forces were "largely" trained and equipped in Communist China; that they were receiving military and technical guidance from "an estimated 2,000 Communist Chinese" in "key positions"; and that Chinese Communist supplies were "pouring into Viet-Nam at a steadily increasing rate."[46] To the Committee on Foreign Affairs, he gave a detailed description of the activities at Dien Bien Phu:

First, a Chinese Communist general named Ly Chen-Hou is stationed at Dien Bien Phu at the headquarters of General Giap, the Viet Minh commander. Under this Chinese Communist general, Ly Chen-Hou, there are nearly a score of Chinese Communist technical advisers at the headquarters of General Giap. Also there are numerous other Chinese Communist technical military advisers at the division level. There is a widespread system of special telephone lines installed, and these were installed and are maintained and operated by Chinese personnel. There are a considerable number of 37 millimeter anti-aircraft guns, radio-controlled, in the Dien Bien Phu area which are shooting through the clouds to bring down the French aircraft. These guns are operated by members of the Chinese military establishment.

In support of the battle there are approximately 1,000 trucks, about one-half of which have arrived since the first of March, all coming from the Red China area, and all driven by Chinese Army personnel. The foregoing is additional to the fact, of course, that the artillery, the ammunition, and the equipment generally come from Communist China.[47]

The United States, however, never did directly intervene. Instead, five new conditions were created—described by one source at least as "most unlikely to be fulfilled."[48] First advanced in April, 1954, they were summarized by Secretary Dulles in a statement made in June: "These conditions were and are (1) an invitation from the present lawful authorities; (2) clear assurance of complete independence to Laos, Cambodia, and Viet Nam; (3) evidence of concern by the United Nations; (4) a joining in the collective effort of some of the other nations of the area; and (5) assurance that France will not itself withdraw from the battle until it is won."[49]

The first three conditions thus enumerated should have presented no problem. In the case of number one, "an invitation from the present lawful authorities," the French had already made three separate appeals for direct American intervention.[50] Two aircraft carriers armed with atomic weapons were ready, and actually moving from the Philippines.[51]

Condition number two, a "clear assurance" of independence, had been described as already fulfilled on numerous occasions. Even though it was not, the raising of such an objection at this time seemed at best to be an eleventh-hour scruple. The suspicion that it might be an alibi was supported by the Vice President's assertion that Viet Nam was not ready for independence. "The Vietnamese," he said, "lack the ability to conduct a war by themselves or govern themselves."[52] On May 7, 1954, Secretary Dulles again asserted that the French had "pledged full independence,"[53] but he was only willing to admit that the second condition had been "advanced."[54]

Condition number three, "evidence of concern by the United Nations," was actually fulfilled after Thailand made a complaint in May, 1954. On June 3, its complaint was placed on the agenda of the Security Council by a vote of 10 to 1. But in this case also, Secretary Dulles would only concede that "some progress has been made."[55]

In the case of the fourth and fifth conditions, however, there were practical difficulties which made fulfillment highly improbable, if not actually impossible. The fourth, which called for "a joining in the collective effort of some of the other nations of the area," was given a hollow note by the inclusion of France and Great Britain as "nations of the area." This was in fact inconsistent with the spirit of the second condition regarding assurances of independence, since neither of these nations could be so regarded except by recognition of their colonial interests.

France, moreover, was already participating to the fullest extent possible. In its case an improbable commitment was required by virtue of the fifth condition—that it would not "withdraw from the battle until it is won." Such a commitment would have been inconsistent with its prior agreement at the Berlin Conference (January 25-February 18, 1954) to negotiate with the leaders of the Viet Minh and Chinese Communist regimes regarding "the problem of restoring peace in Indochina"[56]—an agreement to which the United States was also a party. This negotiation was scheduled to begin at Geneva on April 26, 1954, and it resulted in the settlement by which the war was ended and the northern half of Viet Nam turned over to the Communists.

The fourth and fifth conditions were in fact never fulfilled, because the British, who were also a party to the Berlin agreement, were opposed in principle to direct intervention at this time. Over the week end of April 10-14, Secretary Dulles made a flying trip to London and Paris and obtained what he "thought was an agreement on united action." But after his return, "it developed," as he says, "that the British and the French preferred to wait and see what came out of the Geneva armistice talks...."[57] Sir Anthony Eden, the British Foreign

Secretary, maintained that his government had gone no farther with Mr. Dulles than to state its readiness "to take part" in "an examination of the possibilities."[58] He gave what he described as three good reasons for this position:

Her Majesty's Government have also been reproached in some unofficial quarters for their failure to support armed intervention to try to save Dien Bien Phu. It is quite true that we were at no time willing to support such action, for three reasons which seemed to us to be good and still do. First, we were advised that air action alone could not have been effective. Secondly, any such military intervention could have destroyed the chances of a settlement at Geneva and; thirdly, it might have led to a general war in Asia.[59]

The necessity of the five new conditions was in effect denied by Secretary Dulles himself, in June, 1954. At that time, while the negotiations were in progress at Geneva, and scarcely a month after the fall of Dien Bien Phu, he renewed his threat of direct intervention in the event of "overt military aggression" by the Chinese Communist regime. In such an event, he now said, the situation would be "different," because the interests of the United States would be directly affected:

If the Chinese Communist regime were to show in Indochina or elsewhere that it is determined to pursue the path of overt military aggression, then the situation would be different and another issue would emerge. . . . Such an aggression would threaten island and peninsular positions which secure the United States and its allies.

If such overt military aggression occurred, that would be a deliberate threat to the United States itself. The United States would of course invoke the processes of the United Nations and consult with its allies. But we could not escape ultimate responsibility for decisions closely touching our own security and self-defense.[60]

It is not likely that the "other nations of the area" would appreciate this difference. The statement indicated simply enough that the scruples and hesitations of the United States applied only where the interests of others were exclusively concerned. Moreover, it also appeared to indicate that the peoples of Indochina, and perhaps others in southeast Asia, were not considered as "allies," an attitude hardly conducive to their participation in joint efforts for the "containment" of communism, or other actions likely to provoke the wrath of their powerful Communist neighbors.

In July, 1954, an agreement was reached at Geneva. The war was brought to an end with a Korea-like division of Viet Nam, a stipulation that free elections would be held in two years' time (July, 1956), and with the long-sought "clear assurance of complete independence." Independence was also guaranteed to Laos and Cambodia, and many predicted that the result would be Communist domination of the whole area.

In the case of Viet Nam, at least, such predictions seemed to be justified, not only by the arbitrary division of north from south and the moral and physical effects of the war, but also by the legacy of corruption and maladministration inherited from previous regimes. Many expressed the fear of a further Communist expansion through methods of infiltration and subversion, or by virtue of the popularity acquired by the Viet Minh during the period of French rule. Senator Mike Mansfield, a member of the Committee on Foreign Relations, who had been conducting annual study missions to Indochina, reported in October, 1954, that "the state of affairs throughout Vietnam offers scant hope for an outcome in accord with the objectives of our policy. Unless there is a reversal of present trends," he said, "all of Vietnam is open in one way or another to absorption by the Vietminh. Even now," he added, "there is little to stand in their way."[61] In April, 1954, even before the opening of the Geneva conference, Senator John F. Kennedy asserted that "Despite any wishful thinking to the contrary, it should be apparent that the popularity and prevalence of Ho Chi Minh and his following throughout Indochina would cause either partition or a coalition government to result in eventual domination by the Communists."[62]

The disproval of such predictions soon demonstrated, however, that even some of the best friends of Viet Nam had underestimated its people's aspirations and their ability to attain them. Such predictions also failed to take into account the personal qualifications of Viet Nam's newly appointed Premier, Ngo Dinh Diem, who accepted office in June, 1954, after many years of adamant refusal to serve a government dominated either by the French or by the Communists.

The new Premier had in fact refused so often to take part in such puppet regimes that his record appeared by some standards to be largely negative, but it was a record of action based on principle rather than expediency. It was also starkly symbolic of the passivity produced in millions of people, inside and outside the Iron Curtain, by the free world's failure to offer acceptable or practicable means of resistance to communism. In 1933, Diem had resigned as chief minister in the prewar Bao Dai government, because of French domination and French refusal to consider suggestions for democratic reform. For similar reasons, in 1945 he had rejected the post of Prime Minister in Bao Dai's Japanese-dominated regime, and the Ministry of Interior in Ho Chi Minh's Viet Minh regime. And in 1948 and 1949, he had likewise rejected offers to lead the postwar French-dominated governments. Repeatedly, however, he had urged the grant of real independence, and advised the former Emperor that he could not participate in a regime which did not have such status.

Diem's family had a similar record. His brother, Ngo Dinh Khoi, a former governor of the province of Quang Ngai, had been dismissed by the French because of his nationalism, and killed by the Viet Minh because of his anti-Communism. Another brother, Ngo Dinh Nhu, had taken a leading role in organizing the unofficial congress at Cholon. One of the signers of the manifesto by which this congress was convened was still another brother, Ngo Dinh Thuc, the Roman Catholic Bishop of Vinh Long.

When he finally accepted the leadership of the Vietnamese government, Ngo Dinh Diem refused to sign the settlement made at Geneva because of its provision for Communist domination of the northern half of his country—a course also followed by the United States. He likewise refused, in the absence of conditions of free choice in the north, to participate in the elections for which the settlement provided. But he conducted free elections in the south and established a democratic government which has been eminently successful, in spite of the intrigues and even the armed resistance of powerful dissident national groups, of the Communists, and of Bao Dai himself. Because of the Premier's firm adherence to principle, it was the conclusion of an assistant secretary of state that "the entire free world has become the richer for his example of determination and moral fortitude."[63]

Under Diem's leadership the free republic of Viet Nam has already made great progress. With the support and assistance of the United States, it has initiated programs for the improvement of irrigation, roads, public health, adult education and bona-fide agrarian reform; the corruption and maladministration of previous regimes has been rooted out; nearly a million refugees from the Communist-ruled north have been successfully absorbed. The accomplishments have been such that, in May, 1955, Secretary of State Dulles concluded: "One can only hold free Viet-Nam with a government that is nationalistic and has a purpose of its own and is responsive to the will of its own people, and doesn't take orders from anybody outside, whether it be from Paris—or Cannes, for that matter [where Bao Dai took up residence]—or from Washington. And we have got to coordinate our policies to the acceptance of the fact that it is really a free and independent country."[64]

The time to make such statements, of course, is before, rather than after, Communist aggression makes them a necessary tactic of the cold war, just as the time to aid the subject peoples is before, rather than after, the free nations are forced to seek their assistance also—in a third world war.

CHAPTER XII

THE COLD PEACE

Second "Breathing Space" for the Revolution

The postwar aggressions in the Far East were directed, of course, by what Secretary of State Dulles described as "that farflung clandestine political organization which is operated by the leaders of the Communist Party of the Soviet Union"[1]—a group far removed from China, Indochina, Korea and other Soviet targets. The Communist Party of the Soviet Union is itself directed by the Central Committee, and the Central Committee in turn appoints a Presidium—formerly called the Politburo—and not to be confused with the Presidium of the Supreme Soviet. Although the Soviet Constitution provides that the Presidium of the Supreme Soviet shall be the "highest organ of state power," it is the Presidium of the Central Committee which actually governs the affairs, not only of the Communist Party, but also of the other 96.1% of the people.[2]

After the ousters of Molotov, Malenkov and Kaganovich, in July, 1957, there were fifteen members of the Presidium of the Communist Party. Since that time four more have been ousted (Marshal Georgi K. Zhukov, Marshal Nikolai Bulganin, Alexei I. Kirichenko and Nikolai I. Belyayev), one has been retired (Kliment Y. Voroshilov) and four have been added, so that the membership now stands as follows: Averky B. Aristov, Leonid I. Brezhnev, Yekaterina A. Furtseva, Nikolai G. Ignatov, Nikita S. Khrushchev, Frol R. Koslov, Alexei N. Kosygin, Otto V. Kuusinen, Anastas I. Mikoyan, Nuritdin A. Mukhitdinov, Nikolai V. Podgorny, Dmitri S. Polyansky, Nikolai M. Shvernik, and Mikhail A. Suslov.

At the top of the Presidium is the head of the Party Secretariat; but like all dictators the head of the Party Secretariat must have those to whom he looks for support and to whom he must sometimes account. This is the normal function of the Presidium. According to Party statutes, the Presidium itself must report to the Central Committee, whose work it is organized to "direct"; and the Central Committee in turn must sometimes report to a Congress of the Communist Party—to "verify the correctness of its policy."

When the period of immediate postwar aggression drew to a close, the time for such a report seemed to have arrived. The "proletarian revolution" in Europe had not occurred, the "colonial revolutions" were not maturing in the manner prescribed, and the opportunities to take advantage of the wartime occupation agreements had been exhausted. Communist uprisings had failed in the Philippines, India, Burma, Malaya and Indonesia. Furthermore, the Soviets had miscalculated in Korea. Each new attack seemed only to increase the free world's resistance, and a shift in tactics was called for. It is not difficult to imagine what the party secretary would say at such a time. He would call for peace—peace *at all costs*—so that the Soviet Union could prepare for new aggressions.

This was what Lenin had done in 1918, 1919, and again in 1920. He made what he called a "tremendous concession to German imperialism"—in order to avoid the "persecution of both imperialisms"; he offered "peace" to "Anglo-Franco-American imperialism"—so that it would be "unable to attack us"; and when the Red Army was defeated at Warsaw, he called for a "breathing space"—in order "so to consolidate ourselves that it became impossible to defeat us by military force."[3] Now, it would be argued, it was necessary to "consolidate" new gains in Europe and the Far East. Lenin called for a "breathing space" to permit the development of socialism "in one country"; Stalin required another to permit its development in several.

Once the decision had been made, the report could easily be prepared by anyone able to cull the necessary material from Stalin's prewar reports—just as the report he now made was destined to be a similar source of material for those of Khrushchev, his iconoclastic successor. There would be the customary laudation of past "accomplishments," some explanations of "unavoidable" failures, and a new call for "peace." A brief outline—with corresponding statements of Stalin, Khrushchev and Lenin shown in brackets—might read as follows:

Comrades: (*Applause.*) The second imperialist war has rung the death-knell of imperialism in Europe and Asia, and the dictatorship of the proletariat has triumphed in many countries. (*Loud applause.*)

[Stalin—1930: ... the imperialist war and its aftermath have intensified the decay of capitalism ... the imperialist war and the victory of the revolution in the U.S.S.R. have shaken the foundations of imperialism *in the colonial and dependent countries*. ...]

[Khrushchev—1956: The defeat of fascist Germany and imperialist Japan during the Second World War was an important factor stimulating the liberation struggle in the colonies and dependent countries.]

But the immediate opportunities for socialist expansion have been exhausted. The reactionary forces have been defeated in all those capitalist (war-torn) and formerly colonized countries in which the conditions for successful transition to socialism existed. We must now wait for another decisive moment to renew the attack. (*Prolonged applause*.)

[Stalin—1927: We must not forget what Lenin said about very much in our work of construction depending upon whether we succeed in postponing war with the capitalist world, which is inevitable, but which can be postponed either until the moment when the proletarian revolution in Europe matures, or until the moment when the colonial revolutions have fully matured, or, lastly, until the moment when the capitalists fight among themselves over the division of the colonies.

Therefore, the maintenance of peaceful relations with the capitalist countries is an obligatory task for us.]

[Khrushchev—1956: As far back as the eve of the Great October Socialist Revolution Lenin wrote: "All nations will arrive at Socialism—this is inevitable, but not all will do so in exactly the same way, each will contribute something of its own in one or another form of democracy, one or another variety of the dictatorship of the proletariat, one or another rate at which socialist transformations will be effected in the various aspects of social life. ..."

... There is no doubt that in a number of capitalist countries the violent overthrow of the dictatorship of the bourgeoisie and the sharp aggravation of class struggle connected with this are inevitable. But the forms of social revolution vary.]

The antagonisms and contradictions of the capitalist nations are already leading them to new wars among themselves—which we will use to good purpose. (*Loud and prolonged applause*.)

[Stalin—1930: The most important result of the world economic crisis is that it has laid bare and sharpened the contradictions inherent in world capitalism.

It is laying bare and sharpening the *antagonisms between the most important imperialist countries,* the struggle for markets, the struggle for raw materials, the struggle for export of capital.]

[Khrushchev—1956: The contradictions and rivalry between the colonial powers for spheres of influence, sources of raw materials, and markets for the sale of goods are growing. The United States is out to grab the colonial possessions of the European powers.]

But we must be on our guard. In order to save themselves, the imperialist lackeys are plotting a new war against the Soviet Union—as if their miserable bands of slaves could oppose our glorious Red Army. (*Laughter, applause.*) With their spies, wreckers, and assassins, these foreign drivelers are making amusing attempts to undermine the strength of our Party, even in the citadel of the Revolution. (*General laughter.*)

[Stalin—1930: . . . every time that capitalist contradictions begin to grow acute the bourgeoisie turns its gaze towards the U.S.S.R. as if to say: "Cannot we settle this or that contradiction of capitalism, or all the contradictions taken together, at the expense of the U.S.S.R., the land of the Soviets, the citadel of the revolution. . .?"

Hence the tendency to adventurist assaults on the U.S.S.R. and to intervention. . . .]

[Khrushchev—1956: The inspirers of the "cold war" began to establish military blocs, and many countries found themselves, against the will of their peoples, involved in restricted aggressive alignments—the North Atlantic bloc, Western European Union, SEATO . . . and the Baghdad pact. . . . We know from history that when planning a redivision of the world, the imperialist powers have always lined up military blocs.]

Therefore the main task of the revolution at the present time is to consolidate the gains of Socialism in the new democracies, and to defend them against imperialist attack. The international proletariat stands ready, as always, to support us in this assignment. (*Stormy applause.*)

[Stalin—1930: . . . intervention is a two-edged weapon. . . . the Bolsheviks are far stronger today economically, politically and in the sense of the defensive preparedness of their country. . . . And what about the workers in the capitalist countries who will not permit intervention against the U.S.S.R., who will fight against intervention and, if anything happens, may strike at the rear of the capitalists?]

[Khrushchev—1956: Now there is a world camp of socialism, which has become a mighty force. In this camp the peace forces find not only the moral, but also the material means to prevent aggression. . . . The labour movement in the capitalist countries has today become a tremendous force. The movement of peace supporters has sprung up and developed into a powerful factor.]

The imperialists will not be able to attack us because we will make use of the enmities between them, and because the Soviet Union will first offer them peace. (*Thunderous applause.*)

[Lenin—1920-21: We were victorious . . . not because we were stronger, but because, although weaker, we made use of the enmities that existed among the capitalist states. Now, too, we shall either utilize the enmity that exists among the various trusts, or . . . we shall be unable to exist in the capitalist environment. . . .

Anglo-Franco-American imperialism was unable to attack us because we first offered it peace.]

Long live Lenin! (*Ovation. All the delegates rise to their feet. Loud cheers. A chorus of cheers: "Long live Stalin!" The delegates, all standing, sing the "Internationale," after which the ovation is resumed. Shouts of "Hurrah for Stalin!" "Long live Stalin!" "Long live the Central Committee!"*)[4]

Stalin determined to make his report in October, 1952. It was then more than thirteen years since the last (Eighteenth) congress of the Communist Party—which was held in March, 1939, on the eve of World War II, and when as Stalin had indicated, the world was ripe for aggression. Now, after six years of indecisive warfare in Indochina, and five years of unsuccessful efforts to undermine the Marshall Plan, NATO and Mutual Defense Assistance, it appeared to be no longer ripe. Accordingly, in preparation for the Nineteenth Congress (October 5-14, 1952), Stalin issued a long directive in which he explained the "contemporary movement for peace."[5] Its purpose, he said, was "to raise masses of people in the struggle for the maintenance of peace and for the prevention of a new world war. Consequently, it does not pursue the purpose of overthrowing capitalism and the establishment of socialism—it limits itself to the democratic purposes of struggle for the keeping of peace."

Stalin was careful to point out, however, that the new "movement for peace," like Lenin's "breathing spaces," meant *postponement*, not abandonment, of plans for world revolution. It might even lead to victory for the revolution in one or more countries, or at least, with the aid of external pressures, to the ouster of governments friendly to the Western powers:

It is possible that in a certain concatenation of circumstances the struggle for peace will develop in certain places into a struggle for the overthrow of capitalism.

But it is most probable of all that the contemporary movement for the maintenance of peace, in case of its success, will lead to the prevention of a given war, to its temporary postponement, to the temporary maintenance of a given peace, to the retirement of a war-like government and the replacement of it with another government prepared to keep the peace temporarily. This, of course, is good.

It is even very good.

But for the ultimate victory of "socialism"—for real "peace"—this contemporary movement would not be enough—it would eventually be necessary to "destroy imperialism":

But all this is insufficient in order to destroy the inevitability of wars in general between the capitalist countries. It is insufficient since, with all these successes of the movement for peace, imperialism never-theless, will continue to remain in force—consequently there remains in force the inevitability of wars.

In order to destroy the inevitability of wars, it is necessary to destroy imperialism.

As a part of his "movement for peace," Stalin also promised a breathing space for the subject peoples—expanded opportunities for education, reductions in working hours, improved housing conditions and the doubling of real wages:

... it is necessary first of all to reduce the working day at least to six and then to five hours. This is necessary in order that members of society should receive the sufficient free time necessary to receive om-nilateral education .... it is necessary further to introduce universal obligatory polytechnical education necessary in order that members of society should have the possibility of freely selecting a profession and not to be shackled for their whole life to any one particular profession . . . . it is necessary further to radically improve housing conditions and raise the real wages of workers and employees a minimum of double if not more both by the means of a direct increase in money wages as also especially by the means of a further systematic lowering of prices for the objects of mass consumption.

Several "liberalizing" gestures were promptly made: a committee was appointed, with Stalin at its head, to revise the party program; the words "Bolshevik" and "Politburo," with their unpleasant associations, were dropped from the Communist vocabulary; the "Presidium" was enlarged; and for the first time Stalin permitted the report of the Central Committee to be made by a deputy general secretary, Georgi M. Malenkov.

Three and one-half years later, Khrushchev reaffirmed these tactics in a directive to the Twentieth Party Congress (February 14-25, 1956).[6] Stating that the "peace initiative of the Soviet Union" had become "one of the most important factors exerting a tremendous influence on international events," he substantially repeated statements made by Stalin on the "contemporary movement for peace":

Comrades, I should like to dwell on some fundamental questions concerning present-day international development which determine not only the present course of events, but also the prospects for the future.

These questions are the peaceful co-existence of the two systems, the possibility of preventing wars in the present era, and the forms of transition to socialism in different countries.

Let us examine these questions in brief.

The peaceful co-existence of the two systems. The Leninist principle of peaceful co-existence of states with different social systems has always been and remains the general line of our country's foreign policy.

It has been alleged that the Soviet Union advances the principle of peaceful co-existence merely out of tactical considerations, considerations of expediency. Yet it is common knowledge that we have always, from the very first years of Soviet power, stood with equal firmness for peaceful co-existence. Hence, it is not a tactical move, but a fundamental principle of Soviet policy.

.   .   .   .

We have always held and continue to hold that the establishment of a new social system in one or another country is the internal affair of the peoples of the countries concerned. This is our attitude, based on the great Marxist-Leninist teaching.[7]

Khrushchev deviated a little on the subject of war *between* the capitalist states. It was true that the "reactionary forces" would "continue their drive towards military gambles and aggression, and may try to unleash war," but this was no longer "fatalistically inevitable." The increasing possibility of Soviet attack was forcing the imperialists to compose their differences:

The possibility of preventing war in the present era. . . .
There is, of course, a Marxist-Leninist precept that wars are inevitable as long as imperialism exists. This precept was evolved at a time when 1) imperialism was an all-embracing world system, and 2) the social and political forces which did not want war were weak, poorly organized, and hence unable to compel the imperialists to renounce war.

.   .   .   .

In that period this precept was absolutely correct. At the present time, however, the situation has changed radically. . . .
. . . Today there are mighty social and political forces possessing formidable means to prevent the imperialists from unleashing war, and if they actually try to start it, to give a smashing rebuff to the aggressors and frustrate their adventurist plans.[8]

War *with* the capitalist states, on the other hand, was a different matter. In those countries where capitalism was "still strong" resistance to communism was still "inevitable," and in this case, therefore, the necessity of war remained:

Forms of transition to socialism in different countries. . . .
.   .   .   .

Leninism teaches us that the ruling classes will not surrender their power voluntarily. And the greater or lesser degree of intensity which the struggle may assume, the use or non-use of violence in the transition to socialism, depends on the resistance of the exploiters, on whether the exploiting class itself resorts to violence, rather than on the proletariat.

In the countries where capitalism is still strong and has a huge military and police apparatus at its disposal, the reactionary forces will of course inevitably offer serious resistance. There the transition to socialism will be attended by a sharp class, revolutionary struggle.[9]

In the meantime, Khrushchev's peace offensive also contained the promise of "concessions" and a better life for the subject peoples. There was to be a "seven-hour day for all factory, office and other workers and a six-hour day for workers of the coal and ore mining industries." Where it was "expedient," there was to be "a five-day working week (with an eight-hour day and two free days)." Private housing was to be "developed on a larger scale side by side with Government construction."[10] There was to be "a substantial improvement of the educational facilities and equipment of the public schools." Tuition fees were to be abolished, nursery schools and kindergartens provided, and "in the suburbs" boarding schools with "bright, spacious classrooms, good dormitories, well-equipped dining rooms" and "thoughtfully furnished centers for all kinds of extracurricular activities." In the boarding schools, tuition fees would be graded, and parents "with larger incomes" would pay all or part of the cost.[11]

A new note of plausibility was added to such promises by the "secret" exposé of Stalin's "absolutely insufferable character."[12] According to Khrushchev, his former chief had "discarded the Leninist method of convincing and educating," and "abandoned the method of ideological struggle for that of administrative violence, mass repressions and terror." He "had acted on increasingly larger scale and more stubbornly through punitive organs, at the same time often violating all existing norms of morality and of Soviet laws." "Mass arrests and deportations of many thousands of people," and "execution without trial and without normal investigation" had "created conditions of insecurity, fear and even desperation."[13] The implication, of course, was that such methods were inappropriate and would be discontinued.

These "new" policies did bring the immediate postwar period of open Soviet aggression to a close—and they did provide a temporary "relaxation of international tensions"—but they did not bring the promised peace or freedom to the subject peoples. If there was any "peace" for them at all, it was the kind of "peace" which Secretary of State Dulles described as the "peace" of the "orthodox Communists" and which, as he said, the Communists ultimately intend to impose upon the world:

> To the orthodox Communists ... peace is a negative, barren concept. It means a state of enforced conformity where all men think alike, believe alike, and act in accordance with a pattern imposed by their rulers. ...
>
> If that system of conformity can be made world-wide, then, they argue, there will be an end to war. ...
>
> One thing is clear about this kind of peace: the international Communists cannot establish it without first resorting to war. This they admit. ...
>
> .   .   .   .
>
> When we hear talk of peace from the Communist camp, we must always look behind this talk to the nature of the Communist system. It is not a peace system but a force system, for only force can suppress the aspirations of men's souls.[14]

In the meantime, the Soviets expanded their capacity for launching new threats and new aggression. By 1958, it was no longer necessary for them to boast, as they had in 1939, that their military organizations were "stronger than those of any other country"—this was conceded by the free world itself. Thus, in January, 1958, a panel of the Rockefeller Brothers Fund Project, said to be composed of "some of the best and most experienced minds" in the United States, reported that "Unless present trends are reversed, the world balance of power will shift in favor of the Soviet bloc. If that should happen," it added, "we are not likely to be given another chance. . . ."[15] Another more official but classified report,[16] by an advisory committee to the President, asserted that the military budget of the United States would have to be increased to $46,000,000,000 annually—exclusive of a required annual expenditure of $5,000,000,000 for an adequate civilian shelter program. Its members were said to be "appalled, even frightened, at what they discovered to be the state of the American military posture in comparison with that of the Soviet Union."[17]

At the same time, the Communist "peace" offensive was used to divert the free nations from taking the steps required for their own security—to produce such a "relaxation of international tensions" that, as Secretary Dulles asserted, free peoples "would no longer be willing to support the military programs, the economic assistance programs," or "the inconveniences of alliances which require people to coordinate their policies with each other."[18] In this the Soviets succeeded in varying degrees. They delayed and prevented the formation of defensive alliances, they secured reductions in the military and economic assistance programs, and they even obtained the "retirement," in Stalin's words, of a number of "warlike" governments—all for the price of very few concessions. The "peace" initiative ebbed and flowed, and the hopes of the free world alternately rose and fell, but after five years the President was still seeking "evidence of a genuine intention to resolve" the "basic problems."[19]

Still another purpose of the "peace" offensive was to inhibit free-world assistance to the subject peoples. The Communists *professed* to fear invasion and atomic attack; they described the free powers as "warmongers" and accused them of "adventurist," "provocative assaults"; they complained of "aggressive blocs and pacts" between "imperialist powers"; and they condemned "big U.S. military bases aimed against the U.S.S.R." and "built in countries thousands of miles from the borders of the United States." But what they were really afraid of was effective support of resistance behind the Iron Curtain. It is for this reason that they complained about "interference in the internal affairs of other countries," "slanderous campaigns" and "inflammatory radio broadcasts," and that "unprecedented law, promulgated in 1951, called the Mutual Security Act, which openly proclaims that the United States Government undertakes to give administrative and financial support to spies and diversionists engaged in subversive activities against the Soviet Union, Hungary and the other peoples' democracies."[20] It was for this reason that they insisted upon "peaceful coexistence."

To the Communists the acceptance of "peaceful coexistence" means the toleration and acceptance of Communist domination, wherever it exists. It means that there shall be no help to those who are trying to overthrow it—no "smuggling" or "support" of "spies," "assassins," "wreckers," "bourgeois nationalists," "fascists," "reactionaries," "Mensheviks," "Social-Revolutionaries," "Trotskyites," "Yugoslav Ustachi," "Banderites and Petliura men," "Horthyists," "Gestapo agents," "Zionist spy organizations," or any of the other "counter-revolutionary" agents of "international imperialism" who are seeking to "overthrow the socialist order" and "impose their will" upon the people. It means, in short, that the free nations must assume that the oppressed peoples of the world do not need or want assistance. For "peaceful coexistence" it was necessary, as Khrushchev asserted, for the free nations to "recognize what has historically taken place, i.e., to recognize that the U.S.S.R. exists as a Socialist state, to recognize that China exists as a Socialist state, to recognize the existence of other Socialist states," and even, as he put it, to recognize "that these states are developing in accordance with the will and wishes of their peoples. . . ." If, as he said, the United States would base its policy on this, "instead of relying on some internal forces of the Socialist states supposedly capable of liquidating the Socialist system, it will be easy to reach agreement on all disputed issues."[21]

In the attainment of this aim, the Communists were eminently successful. Although the United States continued to rely on such internal forces to change the Soviet system, it assumed that they could work unaided, and new hopes were aroused for the voluntary "democratization" of communism. Although such hopes were belied by the unconcealable suppression of revolts in Hungary and Tibet—and even the most neutral nations became alarmed for their *own security* —the free powers, which actually had no plans to assist the subject peoples, were induced to make new and emphatic denials that such assistance was contemplated, or even possible—thus dispelling by unimpeachable authority any hopes which might have been inflamed by the denunciation of the policy of "containment."

The net result was that while the Soviets increased their power to terrorize their own people and threaten others, the free nations were once more convinced that their grievances could be settled at the conference table—by negotiation—and that the problems of the subject peoples, if any, would take care of themselves.

At the beginning of the new "movement for peace," if the Soviets did not actually deceive the free world regarding a change in Communist intentions, they at least kept it guessing—speculating about the chances for its own relief from fears of a third world war. After the publication of Stalin's "keynote" article, free-world diplomats in Moscow pointed to the "significant" omission of any reference to war between the Soviet Union and the United States. Secretary of State Dean Acheson established the pattern for many subsequent analyses of the "new look" by stating that a change was being made, that he could not yet tell what kind of a change it was, and that its true nature could only be determined from the deeds, not the words, of the Soviets:

These events, I believe, show that the Communist world is being forced to adjust its tactics to the new situation created by the growing strength of the free world.

Just how the Kremlin will adjust its tactics is not yet clear. It will become clear only from the actions of the Communist world, not from words—not even the words of Stalin or the resolutions of a Party Congress.[22]

The British Foreign Secretary, Sir Anthony Eden, spoke cautiously of a "change of emphasis."[23]

In December, 1952, Stalin stepped up the tempo of the "contemporary movement for peace" by answering a series of questions put to him by a correspondent for *The New York Times*. Among other things, he stated that war with the United States "cannot be considered inevitable"; that the Soviet Union was "interested in ending the war in Korea"; and that he would look with favor on proposals for a conference between himself and the new President-elect, General Dwight D. Eisenhower.[24] Immediately, there was a new welter of speculation as to whether the Soviets were making a "serious approach to the West," and as to where and when the meeting with the Soviet leaders would take place. *Newsweek* commented that "Dulles' pre-election speeches on liberating the satellites must have given them food for thought."[25]

In January, 1953, the "movement" was somewhat retarded when a "terrorist group of doctors" was accused of endeavoring, "through sabotage medical treatment," to "cut short the lives of active public figures" and "undermine the health of leading Soviet military personnel."[26] It was "established" that they were "in the service of foreign intelligence agencies," and the assistant prosecutor announced that the "imperialists, headed by the United States of America, that chief center of reaction and aggression," were "intensifying the preparation of a war against the Soviet Union and the peoples' democracies." In "developing subversive activity," he said, they "are trying to make use of routed anti-Soviet groups, morally corrupt people, the bearers of survivals of capitalist ideology and morality," and "persons infected by bourgeois nationalism."[27] This was Stalin's way of announcing that the free nations could not be friends of the Soviet peoples and friends of the Communists at the same time.

After Stalin's death (March 5, 1953), the "peace offensive" was renewed by the next Soviet Premier, Georgi M. Malenkov. In his first major address, Malenkov stated that there was "no disputed or unresolved question that cannot be settled peacefully by mutual agreement of the interested countries." "This applies," he said, "to our relations with all states, including the United States of America." "States interested in preserving peace," the new Soviet Premier declared, "may be assured, both now and in the future, of the firm peaceful policy of the Soviet Union."[28]

In still another surge of what is frequently described as "cautious optimism," the United States again asked for "deeds." Its representative in the United Nations, Ernest A. Gross, warned that the "Soviet Government, both under its past and present leadership, has talked much about 'peace.' I hope," he said, "that in Prime Minister Malenkov's speech the word 'peace' is used as it is understood by the rest of the world. There are many ways by which this can be put to the test by deeds."[29] President Eisenhower asserted that "Recent statements and gestures of Soviet leaders give some evidence that they may recognize this critical moment"; but that "We care nothing for mere rhetoric. . . . We care only for sincerity of peaceful purpose attested by deeds."[30] Secretary of State Dulles maintained that while the "vigorous position" of the Eisenhower administration was "beginning to bear some fruit, . . . how much that fruit will turn out to be still remains to be tested. It is still in words primarily rather than in actual deeds."[31]

The "deeds" thus requested were soon supplied in a flood of new "concessions." Some of them were real, such as the armistice in Korea, the "settlement" in Indochina, the withdrawal of Soviet troops from Austria, the return of a number of German and Japanese war prisoners, loans on easy credit terms to some of the less-developed free nations and the repatriation of Polish deportees, victims of Soviet aggression in 1939. Others were merely temporary, such as the "voluntarization" of collective farming, the tolerance of criticism and the rehabilitation of "national" Communists. Most, however, were paper "concessions," frauds or meaningless gestures helpful in the fabrication of pro-Soviet propaganda, but bringing no real relief either to the free nations or the subject peoples. In this category were the denunciation of the "cult of personality"; the return to "collective leadership"; mass "amnesties" which did not apply to political prisoners, or those accused of "anti-State activity"; price "reductions" and wage "increases," rendered nugatory by currency devaluation and the unavailability of desired consumer items; unfulfilled promises to de-emphasize the development of arms production and heavy industry in favor of the production of consumer goods; "reconciliation" with

Marshal Tito; "withdrawal" of territorial demands on Turkey, "relinquishment" of oil "rights" in Iran; exchange of diplomatic relations with Israel, Greece and other free nations; increased participation in international organizations, such as the ILO and UNESCO; "cuts" in the military budget; and periodically alleged unilateral reductions in the size of the Soviet and satellite armed forces.

One of the first of such "concessions" was the release, in April, 1953, of the "terrorist group of doctors" and the condemnation of those responsible for using "investigation methods which are inadmissible and strictly forbidden by Soviet law." A more scrupulous regard for civil rights, "guaranteed by the U.S.S.R. Constitution," was promised for the future, and the possibility of "foreign reactionary" complicity in the crimes of "spies and saboteurs" was minimized. It was explained that the "exploiting classes" had long since been "liquidated," and therefore "foreign reactionary forces cannot have any considerable social support inside the Soviet country...."[32]

The hopes of such "foreign reactionary forces" for the liquidation of the Soviet system were soon aroused, however, by the occurrence of popular uprisings in Czechoslovakia and East Germany. They were still further inflated by the subsequent purge of Beria, one of the new first deputy premiers. Nearly all of Beria's career had been devoted to the work of the NKVD and its predecessors, the Cheka and the GPU. As Minister of Internal Affairs under Malenkov, he was still in charge of its activities, and he was regarded as a chief exponent of terrorism and oppression. Although the uprisings were speedily suppressed, and Beria was ostensibly purged for alleged anti-Soviet activities of his own—for seeking to "activize bourgeois nationalist elements," and for promoting a "capitulatory policy" which would lead to the "restoration of capitalism"[33]—the State Department interpreted both events as new signs of impending change. The United States Ambassador was called home for consultation; and at a meeting with the French and British foreign ministers, Secretary Dulles revealed his elation. "We meet at a time of great opportunity," he said. "In East Berlin, East Germany and other satellite areas, the people are moved with new hope. Freedom is again in the air. Free elections is the slogan which now captures the imagination of the captive peoples." "Within Russia itself," he exulted, "Beria, the leader and the very symbol of the police state, is himself put under arrest. A new convulsion is under way. The old system may remain and may continue to threaten, but inherent weakness is disclosed."[34]

There was little cause, however, for such enthusiasm. The uprisings were not inspired by new hope of freedom, but by new forms of repression. On the day before the riots in Czechoslovakia, the currency had been devalued in such a way as to wipe out savings and lower real wages by at least 10%. The revolt in East Germany was similarly provoked by the announcement of a 10% increase in work quotas. Furthermore, the harsh and efficient methods by which both revolts were suppressed clearly indicated that the "police state" had survived the passing of its "symbol." In East Germany these methods were still in evidence five months after the event, when they were described in a press release issued by the Office of the U.S. High Commissioner for Germany, Berlin Element:

> The number of persons involved, the severity of the sentences, and the deliberate creation of a "witch hunt" atmosphere of conspiracy, terror, and espionage indicate recognition of Soviet Zone authorities that the passive resistance of the population has not been broken and their consequent determination to try to break it with raw terror. . . .

> .   .   .   .

> It is, as already suggested, a simple matter for the Soviet Zone security organs to lay hands on persons opposed to the regime since, as the June 17 uprising showed, nearly the entire population falls into that category. . . .
> . . . the Soviet Zone regime is giving the lie to its claims of popular support won by the "new course" and demonstrating anew that its weakness is such that it can maintain itself only by continuous application of brutal terror methods.[35]

Elsewhere, the "new look" was the same. In the satellites there was a mass exodus from the collective farms, but it brought the warning that collectivism was still the "ultimate goal." Those who left the farms were denounced as "idlers" and "skulkers," and the new President of Czechoslovakia, Antonin Zapotocky, told them threateningly: "In the future you will have to reestablish the cooperative from which you escape today."[36] In Poland work norms were actually increased, in 1953, by amounts ranging from 4% to 40%.

These facts, however, did not seem to affect the optimism of the free world, where it was apparently assumed that the subject peoples could throw off the yoke of communism with their bare hands. In his press conference statement on the uprisings in East Germany, Secretary of State Dulles asserted:

There has now developed extensive unrest within the satellite countries of Europe. It demonstrates that the people do retain their love of God and love of country and their sense of personal dignity. They want to run their own affairs and not be run from Moscow.

The unquenchable spirit of the peoples was dramatized in East Berlin, where unarmed youths tore up paving stones from the streets to hurl in defiance at tanks. Such a spirit can never be repressed, and this love of freedom is more and more manifesting itself through the captive peoples.

The cry everywhere is for "free elections." The people want to be governed by those whom they select as responsive to their needs and their desires, rather than to be ruled by those who take their orders from aliens and who give their orders with a view to achieving their own ambitions without regard to the welfare of the people concerned.[37]

In July, 1953, at a Three-Power meeting of foreign ministers, the free powers "resolved to make a new effort to bring to an end the division of Germany."[38] For this purpose they proposed a meeting of the Big Four foreign ministers at which, they stated, agreement should also "finally be reached on the Austrian Treaty."[39] There were no indications, however, that the Soviets intended to make concessions on either of these matters, and they responded with the "totally unacceptable" condition that the free powers abandon their proposed agreements on West German rearmament and a Western European Defense Community (EDC). According to the Soviet note, November 3, 1953, the ratification of these agreements, and their entry into force, would "make impossible the restoration of Germany as a unified state and thereby also render pointless the consideration of the German question. . . ."[40] In reply the United States asserted that "A defenseless Western Europe appears to be the price demanded by the Soviet Government for participation in a conference."[41]

In the Far East there was even less evidence of a change in the Communists' intentions. In Korea they displayed, as Secretary Dulles said, a "wooden inflexibility,"[42] and "their continued actions elsewhere in Asia" were "far from reassuring."[43] There was still the risk that Red China might send its own army into Indochina.

New hopes of a settlement arose on November 26, 1953, when the

Soviets dropped their conditions for a European conference. Secretary Dulles then claimed a "substantial diplomatic and moral victory for the West":

I think the latest Soviet note certainly represents a victory for Western diplomacy in the sense that the refusal on the part of the Soviets to have any meeting, except upon grossly unacceptable pre-conditions, had created a public opinion adverse to them. I believe that the fact that they have now felt it necessary to reverse themselves does represent a very substantial diplomatic and moral victory for the West.[44]

The result of this "victory" was a meeting of the Big Four foreign ministers at Berlin (January-February, 1954). It was their first since 1949, and the free powers went with great expectations. Secretary Dulles related afterwards that "We went to Berlin in the hope that Soviet policies would now permit the unification of Germany in freedom, or at least the liberation of Austria." "Those two matters," he said, "would, in relation to Europe, test the Soviet temper. We hoped to achieve those two results and we were determined to let no minor obstacles deter us."[45] On the sixth day of the conference, he told the delegates that the "United States credits the Soviet Union with a sincere desire to achieve security in Europe."[46]

By the time the conference was over, however, Secretary Dulles had reversed his belief:

The obstacles we incurred were . . . not minor but fundamental.

The Soviet position was not at first openly revealed. It was masked behind ambiguous words and phrases. But as the Conference unfolded and as Mr. Molotov was compelled to respond to our probing of his words, the Soviet purpose became apparent.

.   .   .   .

It amounted to this:

To hold on to East Germany;

To permit its unification with West Germany only under conditions such that the Communists would control the election machinery through all Germany;

To maintain Soviet troops indefinitely in Austria;

To offer Western Europe, as the price of Soviet "good will," a Soviet-controlled Europe which would exclude the United States except in the nominal role of an "observer" along with Communist China.[47]

"Gone," he said, "was the post-Stalin 'new look.' "[48]

In March, 1954, Molotov suggested Soviet membership in NATO. This astonishing proposal was dismissed by the British as "a Trojan horse,"[49] and by the United States as a "maneuver" to "undermine" security and "gain admittance within the walls of the West."[50] Secretary Dulles gloomily asserted that there was "no evidence that basic Soviet policies" had "changed." "The Soviet menace," he said, "does not reflect the ambitions of a single ruler and cannot be measured by his life expectancy. There is no evidence that basic Soviet policies have been changed with the passing of Stalin. Indeed," he added, "the Berlin conference of last February gave positive evidence to the contrary. The Soviet Communists have always professed that they are planning for what they call 'an entire historical era.' "[51]

In April, 1954, the Big Four met again at Geneva, this time with representatives of the Communist regimes of China, Korea and Indochina. There were also representatives of the free governments concerned, including most of those with troops in Korea. When this conference was over, the sixteen free nations negotiating on Korea reported that the Communist delegations had "rejected our every effort to obtain agreement." "We believe," they said, "that it is better to face the fact of our disagreement than to raise false hopes and mislead the peoples of the world into believing that there is agreement when there is none."[52]

The Indochina phase of the conference was only slightly more successful, leading to a settlement to which the United States was "unable to subscribe,"[53] and which the President asserted "contains features which we do not like."[54] A United States delegate, Under Secretary of State Walter Bedell Smith, remarked that "it's rarely possible to gain, at the conference table, what could not be gained or held on the battlefield." In reply to a question as to why the Communists had been willing to make any kind of peace in Indochina, he indicated that they were only moved by force: "With the Communists, probably what tipped the scales was the potential military situation. . . . They saw definite signs of the closing of allied ranks, the quick formation of a collective security arrangement to comprehend the Associated States, possibly an increased order of military operation."[55]

By this time the "new look" had completely evaporated, and in the free world reaction set in. Immediately after the conference, the free powers formed an organization for the collective defense of Southeast Asia—The Southeast Asia Treaty Organization. In Europe, the projected Defense Community was shelved, after more than two years of procrastination, but new agreements were speedily made for the creation of a substitute—the Western European Union. Like the earlier agreements, the new ones also provided for rearmament of West Germany.

The principal difference between the old and new agreements was that the latter provided for direct participation by the United Kingdom in the planned defense organization—a strengthening factor—and the Soviets were informed that no further conference would be held until they were ratified. It was also stated that "a basis of agreement" should be "carefully prepared and established in advance" if new negotiations were to be undertaken "with a reasonable prospect of success." This time the conditions for a conference were imposed by the free nations:

In order to establish such a basis and to deal with the foregoing questions in due order, the United States Government proposes the following:

(1) Agreement to sign the Austrian State Treaty;

(2) Clarification by the Soviet Government of its position on the question of free elections in Germany which are the essential first steps to German reunification;

(3) Exchanges through diplomatic channels on any other European question of common interest which might suitably be examined at a later four-power meeting, in particular, questions relating to European security;

(4) A meeting of the four-power Ministers as soon as it should appear that there is a real prospect of finding solutions and after ratification of the Paris agreements by the countries concerned;

(5) Should it thereafter appear useful, a wider conference of European and other interested powers to consider the remaining aspects of European security.[56]

Secretary Dulles asserted that "we do not want to talk with the Soviet representatives when their only purpose is to divide the free nations and prevent their taking necessary measures for their own security."[57]

As a result, the "new look" was re-energized, and it became the "new, new look." There was a corresponding revival of the hopes of the free world.

In February, 1955, Premier Malenkov "resigned" his post, and the new Premier, Marshal Nikolai A. Bulganin, asserted that his government would "consistently continue to pursue" that "policy of peace and general security which has been justified and proven by practice." "The Soviet Union," he said, "is a peaceful country. She does not threaten anyone. . . ."[58] A new Minister of Defense, Georgi K. Zhukov, stepped forward and reminded President Eisenhower of a ten-year-old wartime invitation. "I was invited twice by General Eisenhower to visit the United States," he said. "I know our relations will get better. Then I hope to be able to visit the United States."[59]

In April, 1955, the Chinese Communist Prime Minister, Chou En-lai, extended the "new look" to the Far East. Attending the conference of Asian and African nations at Bandung, Indonesia, he added his smiles to those of Khrushchev and Bulganin and startled the world with his "conciliatory" attitude. "China," he said, "will not and should not have any demand for territory. . . . We are ready to restrain our government and people from crossing even one step across our border. If such things should happen, we would like to admit our mistake." "As to relations between China and the United States," he said, "the Chinese people do not want to have war. . . . We are willing to settle international disputes by peaceful means."[60] He also offered a "peaceful settlement" of disputes on Korea and Formosa.

Secretary Dulles analyzed his mood as follows:

> The Bandung conference, as we had hoped, seems to have exerted a restraint on the Chinese communists. . . . There seems now a chance that the Communist Chinese may be deterred from pursuing the course of violence which has characterized their actions in relation to Korea, to Tibet, to Indochina, and, more recently, in relation to the Taiwan (Formosa) Straits.[61]

Further concessions were made by the Soviet Union, but all were overshadowed by its agreement in April, 1955, to execute an acceptable Austrian treaty. When this occurred, Secretary Dulles told the Senate Committee on Foreign Relations: "There is, I believe, an air of expectancy in the world today. A series of small but perhaps significant signs suggest that the time may be nearing when those who have been seeking the conquest of freedom will in fact put their foreign relations on a more tolerable basis." "Developments in relation to Austria," he said, "may be indicative of a change of mood which may extend to other areas."[62] The Secretary was even more positive of its extension to other areas in his statements to the American people. In a joint radio-television report, with the President and other cabinet members, he said:

This is the first time a segment of the Red Army will have turned around and started to go back. Now that is bound to have a tremendous impact in the other countries where the Red Armies are in occupation. It is going to create a desire—a mounting desire—on the part of these people to get the same freedom from that type of occupation that the Austrians have got. And, furthermore, this joy at their freedom which was so manifest by the Austrian people, that is going to be contagious and it is going to spread, surely, through the neighboring countries, such as Czechoslovakia. For the first time there will be an open door to freedom on the part of Hungary.[63]

In the meantime, the European nations had ratified the agreements on West German sovereignty and the Western European Union. Accordingly, on May 10, 1955, the free powers proposed a new conference. It was to be held at "the summit of the nations," and the "Heads of Government" as well as the foreign ministers were to participate. The other stated conditions—"a reasonable prospect of success" and a "basis of agreement . . . carefully prepared and established in advance"[64]—were waived by the terms of the note of proposal:

We recognize that the solution of these problems will take time and patience. They will not be solved at a single meeting nor in a hasty manner. Indeed, any effort to do so could set back real progress toward their settlement. Accordingly, we think it would be helpful to try a new procedure for dealing with these problems.[65]

The Soviets readily accepted this invitation. Prior to his departure, Premier Bulganin held his first press conference—at which no questions were permitted. He assured a group of sixty-five representatives of free and Communist newspapers that his delegation was going to Geneva to "find a common language," to "achieve a relaxation of international tension" and to strengthen the "confidence in the relations between states."[66]

By this time, it is reported, President Eisenhower was "exuding a spirit of hope and confidence."[67] On his way to the conference, July 15, 1955, he expectantly reciprocated the assurances of Marshal

Bulganin: "I say to you—I say to all the world—if the words that he expressed are as truly reflective of the hearts and minds of the men in the Kremlin as we are sure they are reflective of the hearts and minds of all the people in Russia, as in the hearts and minds of all the people in the world everywhere, then there will be no trouble between the Russian delegation and our own at this coming conference."[68]

At the conference itself, the President appeared convinced. A wedding present was purchased for Zhukov's daughter, and the war-time "friendship" was renewed; pictures were taken on the lawn. On the third day the President stated: "I should like to say, for my part, I have talked individually, I think, to each member of the Delegation of the Soviet Republic, which now we find differing from the other three of us on a particular point in a suggestion. And I want to make clear I believe they are earnestly desirous of finding peace, as are we."[69] At the final session he was still optimistic. "In this final hour of our assembly," he said, "it is my judgment that the prospects of a lasting peace with justice, well-being, and broader freedom, are brighter. The dangers of the overwhelming tragedy of modern war are less."[70]

Upon his return to the United States, the President urged the people not to be discouraged:

... we must never be deluded into believing that one week of friendly, even fruitful, negotiation can wholly eliminate a problem arising out of the wide gulf that separates, so far, East and West. A gulf as wide and deep as the difference between individual liberty and regimen-tation, as wide and deep as the gulf that lies between the concept of man made in the image of God and the concept of man as a mere instrument of the State. Now, if we think of those things we are apt to be possibly discouraged.

But I was also profoundly impressed with the need for all of us to avoid discouragement merely because our own proposals, our own approaches, and our own beliefs are not always immediately accepted by the other side.

> .   .   .   .

As a matter of fact, each side assured the other earnestly and often that it intended to pursue a new spirit of conciliation and co-operation in its contacts with the other. Now, of course, we are profoundly hopeful that these assurances will be faithfully carried out.[71]

Secretary of State Dulles subsequently asserted that "the only specific thing that came out of that conference" was an agreement on the reunification of Germany,[72] and this, he conceded, was soon "repudiated by the Soviets."[73] At the time, however, in spite of the fact that the Soviet delegation had refused even to discuss the fate of the captive nations, Secretary Dulles could say: "We hope that the situation created by Geneva will lead to a freeing of the satellite countries."[74]

It was not long before the free world was again disillusioned. Even before the follow-up meeting of foreign ministers (October-November, 1955), which the President said would be the "acid test,"[75] the Soviet Union had recognized the "sovereignty" of the East German puppet regime—thus putting another obstacle in the way of reunification. In a speech to the East German delegates at Moscow, Khrushchev reaffirmed his adherence to the doctrines of Marx and Lenin: "We are in favor of a relaxation of tension, but if anybody thinks that for this reason we shall forget about Marx, Engels, and Lenin, he is mistaken. This will happen when shrimp learn to whistle." "And," he added, "I might say that shrimp do not whistle very often."[76] One week later, an arms deal with Egypt was announced.

By the time Secretary Dulles was ready to leave for the second meeting, he appeared to have forgotten the hopes expressed in connection with the first. On October 18, he asserted:

It is quite true that hopes were aroused in many quarters from the meetings of the Heads of Government which went beyond the practical possibilities. I do not think that either the President or I ever shared those extreme hopes. Now, what has happened since then has been a disillusionment to some.[77]

When he returned, he reported that "no specific agreements were reached," and "no positive results were achieved." "It would of course be foolish," he said, "to attempt new negotiations if everything remains as it was when this last Conference came to an end."[78] The "new look," it seemed, was gone again.

In the meantime, the process of Communist "democratization" had also been reversed. Heavy industry and the manufacture of armament had regained their accustomed priority; housing had been cut;

and the drive against religion was pursued with renewed vigor. In the Soviet Union the requirements of the annual state loan ("voluntary" bond purchases) were doubled. The annual reduction in consumer prices was omitted for the first time since 1949.

In April, 1955, the "new course" Prime Minister of Hungary, Imre Nagy, had been replaced and dismissed from party posts for "putting the brakes on the motor of Socialist building" and hampering "the development of the farmers' collective movement."[79] He later related that after his ouster the "abuse of power and the use of illegal devices . . . exceeded even the malpractices of the period from 1950 to 1952."[80]

In December, 1955, Khrushchev told the members of the Supreme Soviet that "we never renounced and we will never renounce our ideas, our struggle for the victory of communism,"[81] but in 1956, the "new look" programs were revived—at the Twentieth Party Congress. As Khrushchev expounded upon the Soviet Union's "peace initiative" and the "denunciation" of Stalin, the free world was thrown into a new round of hopeful speculation. Secretary Dulles stated that the Soviets were now revising "their whole creed, from A to Z":

For 30 years, Soviet foreign policy and Soviet policy generally has been based upon two principles; namely, intolerance of any non-Communist system . . . and also upon the policy of using violence as a means of getting their results.

.   .   .   .

Those policies have gradually ceased to produce any results. . . .
The result is, they have got to review their whole creed, from A to Z. It is a tremendous process for them, because they have got to undo the teaching of many years and get onto a new basis.
What that new basis is going to be, I do not know. . . .[82]

In June, 1956, the full text of Khrushchev's "secret" denunciation of Stalin was published by the State Department. The Secretary of State renewed his predictions of relief for the subject peoples:

. . . there are signs that a new day may be dawning. The Soviet rulers now profess to renounce the doctrine that violence is a necessary part of their foreign policy. They are debasing Stalin, who for 25 years was treated as a demi-god. . . . The Russian people are getting more personal security, and labor is getting increased freedom of choice.
Obviously, there is a rising demand on the part of the captive

nations to have more independence and on the part of the subject people, within and without Russia, to have more freedom from fear and to enjoy more of the fruits of their labor.... Only that can explain the extraordinary exertions being made by the Soviet rulers to make it seem that they are offering a change. Out of all this may come—not this year, or next year, but some year—a government which is responsive to the just aspirations of the people and which renounces expansionist goals.[83]

Within three weeks, this "rising demand" was expressed in a popular uprising in Poznan, Poland. Because of the presence of many foreigners at the Twenty-fifth Poznan International Trade Fair, it was impossible for the Communists to conceal the suppression of this revolt. They endeavored, nevertheless, to soften the reaction of world opinion by various means. At public trials of the rioters, an unaccustomed leniency was shown. In China, Chou En-lai made an advance announcement of his intention to "enlarge the democratic base of our system of government."[84] In spite of an obvious Soviet distaste for the "liberalism" of the newly released "national" Communist, Wladyslaw Gomulka, he was allowed to assume the leadership of the Polish Communist Party.

When, however, these "concessions" were followed by nationwide revolt in Hungary, all pretense was discarded. In November, 1956, the Hungarian Communist regime was forcibly restored by the Soviet Army, and the entire population was afflicted with the most severe reprisals. The protests of the free nations and the resolutions of the United Nations General Assembly were dismissed as rude attempts at "interference" in Hungary's "internal affairs." By January, 1957, Khrushchev was again praising Stalin as "an example of a good Communist."[85] At the same time, the "new look" in foreign affairs was also once more destroyed. New arms deals were made with Egypt and Syria, and Communist "volunteers" were offered to Egypt in its war for the Suez Canal. It was stated that 50,000 Soviet citizens and 250,000 Chinese applied for service. Because of the increasing Soviet threat in the Middle East, the United States soon made a standing offer of assistance (in the Eisenhower Doctrine) to all nations of that area.

The "peace offensive" publicity was continued, nevertheless. On November 17, 1956, within two weeks after the suppression of the revolt in Hungary, the Soviet Union issued a "Declaration Concerning the Question of Disarmament and Reduction of International

Tension."[86] It was sent to President Eisenhower with a new appeal for "negotiations" and for the "adoption of urgent measures directed towards the prevention of war, cessation of the arms race and the solution of questions in dispute by peaceful means."[87] In his reply the President suggested Soviet compliance with the United Nations resolutions on Hungary, and "deliberations within the framework of the United Nations," but it was not long before the hopes of the free world rose once more. In spite of frequent assertions to the contrary, the "lesson of Hungary" soon seemed forgotten.

In March, 1957, disarmament negotiations were resumed. On April 30, the Soviet delegate offered to apply the Eisenhower plan of aerial inspection to a large part of Siberia and the western fringe of Russia—in exchange for Soviet inspection of nearly all of western Europe, the western half of the United States, and Alaska. Although this proposal was considered to be heavily weighted against the free powers, it produced the immediate conclusion that Soviet leaders were at last making a genuine effort to reach agreement. It was reported that the United States delegate, Harold Stassen, "exuded confidence about possible agreement in part with the Soviet proposals,"[88] that an atmosphere of "restrained optimism" prevailed, and that the Soviet Union "seemed willing to discuss the issues seriously."[89]

As evidence of Soviet "sincerity," the point was made that the new proposal was not accompanied by the usual type of Communist propaganda.[90] This apparent oversight was soon cured, however, when Khrushchev granted a series of "personal interviews" to foreign news correspondents, commentators, and even the radio and television networks of the Columbia Broadcasting System. In the first interview, held on May 10, 1957, with the managing editor of *The New York Times*, the Soviet dictator called for new talks, condemned the "selfish" political leaders, "stupid generals," "capitalists" and "rich men" in the United States, who were "balancing on the brink of war," and reaffirmed the Soviet desire for peace. "Ideological problems," he admitted, "will always exist between us. But that should not prevent us from having good neighborly relations." "For our part," he said, "we will do whatever is in our power not only to postpone war but not to have war at all." He was careful to point out, however, that if the Soviets were "confronted with conditions such as Dulles likes to put forward such as the liberation of East European countries from 'slavery,' it might take 200 years before we ever come together."[91]

In June, 1957, Khrushchev appeared on a radio-television program broadcast throughout the entire United States:

Let us live in peace. Let us develop our economy. Let us compete. Let us trade with each other. Let us exchange experience in agriculture, in industry, in the field of culture, and as far as the question of which system will come out on top, let history, let our peoples decide that. . . .
We believe that our Socialist system will be victorious, but that does not mean under any conditions that we want to impose that system on anyone. We simply believe that the people of each country themselves will come to realize that that system is best for them. . . . We have no intention of imposing our ideas on anybody.

.   .   .   .

. . . our proposal is to put an end to all these tests, to abolish hydrogen and atomic weapons, to limit armed forces, etc. Let us have the real steps in that field instead of empty polemics, all sorts of verbal exercises and debates.[92]

In October, 1957, Khrushchev gave still another interview, to a *New York Times* correspondent, insisting that it be publicized in three separate installments: "We have always supported the peaceful coexistence of states belonging to different social systems, the peaceful coexistence of Socialist and capitalist countries. The fight for peace is the cornerstone of our foreign policy. . . ." "If the United States displays a readiness," he said, "there are no questions upon which agreement could not be reached. To live without war on a basis of peaceful competition—such is the foundation of coexistence."[93] An offer was made to put the Soviet earth satellites, and all pilotless missiles, under international control.
In the meantime, it appeared that President Eisenhower was being convinced again. At a press conference on May 15, 1957, shortly after the submission of the Soviet proposal on aerial inspection, he said:

. . . I think that the reason that the Soviets are taking a different tone is because they, as well as all the rest of the world, are feeling the pinch of building, supporting, maintaining these tremendous military organizations. They are bound to feel the pinch. . . .
. . . And because they feel that pinch, and because they see, just

as well as anybody else, where the world is really pushing, I believe they are now growing more serious.[94]

When the chairman of the Joint Chiefs of Staff, Admiral Arthur W. Radford, asserted that we "cannot trust the Russians on this or anything," the President seemed to rebuke him. "I think our first concern," the President said, "should be making certain we are not ourselves being recalcitrant, we are not being picayunish about the thing."[95] As a result, his requested appropriations for the Defense Department were cut in Congress by almost $2,400,000,000, and his original request for mutual security appropriations was cut by more than $1,000,000,000. In December it was reported that the United States planned to cut military assistance to South Korea by more than two-thirds.[96]

The emphasis of the Soviet "peace" policy then shifted from "concessions" to threats. After final passage of the appropriation bill (August 1, 1957), by which the United States defense cuts were made, the Soviets announced successful testing of their own "super-long-distance intercontinental multi-stage ballistic rocket" (August 26, 1957). In the meantime, they had been developing their aggressive aims in the Middle East—partly by threats, partly by subversion, and partly by gestures of good will. In April, 1957, there was an attempted *coup d'état* in Jordan which the State Department ascribed to the "intervention of international communism," by which it said it meant "the agents of the fountainhead of international communism, namely, the Soviet Union."[97] In August, 1957, the Syrian Army was taken over by pro-Soviet officers, and the United States sent its Deputy Under Secretary of State, Loy Henderson, to make an appraisal of the situation. Upon his return he reported increasing Soviet efforts, through border incidents, propaganda and subversive activity, to overthrow the governments of the neighboring countries, Turkey, Iraq, Jordan and Lebanon.[98] On the day following his return (September 5, 1957), the Soviets insisted that disarmament discussions be indefinitely postponed. *Pravda* stated that the Commission on Disarmament was "not fulfilling its direct task" and demanded "open discussion in the United Nations."[99]

Still, hope lingered on. Secretary Dulles commented: "We cannot believe that that sweeping, almost contemptuous, Soviet rejection is final."[100]

But Syrian troops were massing on the southern Turkish border.

When the Red Army engaged in atomic "maneuvers" in the Trans-Caucasus, and the Soviet Union made a number of threatening statements regarding Turkey's plans for "aggression" against Syria, Secretary Dulles compared the crisis to "the period of the Korean War."[101] He may well have prevented such a war by stating that in the event of an attack the Soviet Union would not again be given a "privileged sanctuary."[102] Or it may have been prevented by what the Soviets described as a violation by their own Minister of Defense, Marshal Georgi K. Zhukov, of "the Leninist party principles of guiding the armed forces." Two months afterwards, when this charge was made the basis of Marshal Zhukov's dismissal, and of his expulsion from the Central Committee, that body stated that he had "pursued a policy of curtailing the work of party organizations, political organs and military councils," and of "abolishing the leadership and control of the party, its Central Committee and Government over the Army and Navy."[103]

There were comparable internal changes. In Communist China, for example, the Chief of State, Mao Tse-tung, had but recently abjured the use of violence and force in a statement of his much-publicized "policy of letting a hundred flowers blossom and a hundred schools of thought contend":

It is not only futile but very harmful to use crude and summary methods to deal with ideological questions among the people. . . .

The bourgeoisie and petty bourgeoisie are bound to give expression to their ideologies. . . . We should not use methods of suppression to prevent them from expressing themselves, but should allow them to do so and at the same time argue with them and direct well-considered criticism at them.[104]

This alluring policy was announced in February, 1957; but by June, when the "official" text was released, a campaign of "rectification" had already begun. Those who took advantage of the opportunity to criticize were purged or imprisoned, and Mao Tse-tung explained: "Demons can be wiped out only when they are let out of the cage, and poisonous weeds can be got rid of only when they are let come out of the soil."[105]

In the Soviet Union a new round of purges—at the very top of the Communist hierarchy—was used to "prove" the adoption of a more benevolent Soviet attitude. Thus, at the end of June, 1957, Molotov, Malenkov and Kaganovich were purged for "stubborn resistance" to efforts of the party to "do away with the consequences of the personality cult" and to "eliminate the violations of revolutionary law."[106] It was also charged that they were opposed to "consumerism." These men, the Central Committee said, carried on "an entirely unwarranted struggle against the party's appeal... to overtake the United States in the next few years in per capita output of milk, butter and meat." For Molotov there was the further crime of sabotaging the Soviet Union's "peace initiative": "He opposed the fundamental proposition worked out by the party on the possibility of preventing wars in the present conditions, on the possibility of different ways of transition to socialism in different countries, on the necessity of strengthening contacts between the Soviet Party and progressive parties abroad." Accordingly, in the free world this episode was hailed as another encouraging sign of "evolutionary" improvement in the Soviet government. Secretary Dulles commented: "The whole affair showed how powerful must be the forces for change which are at work within Russia and how perplexed the rulers must be as to how to cope with these forces and at the same time maintain absolute power."[107]

It did not seem, however, that Khrushchev was any more "perplexed" than Stalin had been before him. The way for the elimination of these potential competitors had been well paved; and like the competitors of Stalin, they had already been gradually demoted to the accompaniment of their own frequent self-denunciation, and in well-planned harmony with the current themes of Soviet "new look" propaganda. When Malenkov "resigned" as party first secretary, in March, 1953, his action was ostensibly taken in pursuance of the "new" policy of "collective leadership"—it was "Stalinist" for one man to be both Premier and party first secretary. When he "resigned" as Premier, in 1955, he "confessed" to "guilt and responsibility for the unsatisfactory state of affairs that has arisen in agriculture."[108] Molotov also "confessed" to error in 1955, denouncing his own expressed beliefs on the "building of a Socialist society in the U.S.S.R." as "theoretically mistaken and politically harmful."[109] In June, 1956, when he "resigned" as Foreign Minister, it was significantly noted in many quarters that he had been the author of the infamous "Molotov-Ribbentrop pact" and other "Stalinist" expressions of Soviet policy.

Subsequently, when Marshal Zhukov was purged, in November, 1957, it was "established" that the "cult" of his "personality" had been "cultivated in the Soviet Army" with his own "personal participation." With the help of "sycophants and flatterers," he had been "praised to the sky in lectures and reports, in articles, films and pamphlets, and his person and role in the Great Patriotic War were over-glorified." By such actions he had "minimized" the efforts of the Soviet people, the armed forces, the commanders, the fleets and even the "inspiring role of the Communist Party of the Soviet Union."[110] All of these charges were made less than a month after Khrushchev's complaints that Soviet "pride" had been hurt by President Eisenhower's failure to invite this Soviet Marshal to the White House.

During 1958, even the "new, new look" Premier, Marshal Nikolai Bulganin, was purged. In March he "resigned" as Premier, paving the way for the assumption of this post by Khrushchev, who, of course, was also party leader. In September he was "relieved" of his duties as a member of the Presidium; and in November he was finally denounced as having "sided" with the "anti-party group" of Molotov, Malenkov and Kaganovich. His "confession" came in December, at a meeting of the Central Committee.

Thus, Khrushchev succeeded in acquiring the same unrivaled position as Stalin formerly occupied, and it was clear that the "new look" and the pose of "liberal" communism had been a fraud perpetrated on many of the Communists themselves. In the satellites, where there had been no comparable struggle for succession, but where the "new" look called for the "rehabilitation" of so-called national Communists, the "Stalinist" leaders also "resigned" from various posts—but only to create the façade of collective leadership. A number of party chiefs gave up the post of Prime Minister, and a number of Prime Ministers gave up their open role as party chief, but in most cases there was no real change in control.

In Czechoslovakia President Gottwald conveniently died, nine days after Stalin, and party leadership passed to Antonin Novotny. The post of Prime Minister went to Villiam Siroky, and the former Prime Minister, Antonin Zapotocky, became President. After the death of Zapotocky in 1957, his place was taken by Novotny, and the Prime Minister, Siroky, stated that it had become "politically expedient" once more to combine the functions of President and party leader. The party paper *Rude Pravo* asserted that this "clearly stresses the leading role played by the Communist Party. . . ."[111]

In Hungary the arch-Stalinist Matyas Rakosi accused himself of supporting "the evil of the personality cult," and "resigned" as

Premier in July, 1953. He remained, however, as party first secretary until July, 1956, a few months before the revolt. Even after the revolt it was still improper to attack "Rakosiism,"[112] and few could distinguish it from the policies of Janos Kadar who acted as both Premier and party leader from November, 1956, when the revolt was suppressed, until January, 1958 when he "resigned" as Premier in favor of Ferenc Muennich. Muennich, at 73, had spent most of his adult life in Moscow; and his deputy, Antol Apro, was an acknowledged "Stalinist."

The Premier of Poland, Boleslaw Bierut, resigned in March, 1954, but as party secretary he retained control of both party and government until his death in 1956. In the near-revolt which occurred in October of that year, party leadership passed to Wladyslaw Gomulka. His views on "collective leadership" were soon made apparent by orders for a purge of the "liberal" group of Communists which had brought him to power, and by his own explanation that "We do not wish our Party to have factions or groups.... We are not so much concerned with the number of Party members as with their political and ideological quality."[113]

In Albania Enver Hoxha resigned as Prime Minister (in July, 1954), but he remained in full control as head of the party.

In Rumania the party leader, Gheorghe Gheorghiu-Dej, resigned as party secretary (in April, 1954) but retained his post as Prime Minister. In 1955, he demonstrated the artificiality of this procedure by giving up the post of Prime Minister to become party first secretary again.

In Bulgaria the party secretary, Vulko Chervenkov, "resigned" in March, 1954, but he remained as real ruler in the post of Prime Minister. In 1956, he was "demoted" to Deputy Prime Minister because of his "Stalinism," but whatever his real status, there was no doubt that "Stalinist" methods of selection still prevailed. After Bulgaria's fifth postwar general election (December, 1957) it was reported that the vote in favor of the regime was 99.92%. As usual, there were no opposition candidates.[114]

In November, 1957, all of the satellite rulers were required to confirm the "identity" of their "views" and to denounce the sins and "opportunist trends" of the "revisionists." This was accomplished by a joint declaration issued at the Moscow celebration of the fortieth anniversary of the Bolshevik seizure of power and subscribed to by all of the ruling Communist parties except Yugoslavia. "The revisionists," it said, "try to exorcise the revolutionary spirit of Marxism, to undermine faith in socialism among the working class and the working people in general. They deny the historical necessity for a proletarian revolution and the dictatorship of the proletariat during the period of transition from capitalism to socialism, deny the leading role of the Marxist-Leninist party, reject the principles of proletarian internationalism and call for ... transforming the Communist party from a militant revolutionary organization into some kind of debating society."[115]

During the deliberations on the text of this declaration, Mikhail A. Suslov, a leading member of the Presidium of the Soviet Communist Party, rejected "revisionism" in terms described by *The New York Times* correspondent as meaning that "wide-scale repression must go on for many years." "Revisionism," Suslov said, "is expressed in the willful ignoring of the doctrine that a sharp class struggle is inevitable during the transitional period."[116]

By the middle of 1958, it was reported by *The New York Times* that in the new campaign against "Titoism" fifty "high-ranking party functionaries" had been ousted from office in Bulgaria, Rumania and Czechoslovakia.[117] The Bulgarian Communists had again expelled "all former Kostovites who were readmitted to the party during the relaxations of 1956."[118] In Czechoslovakia the "liberalizing proposals originating in intellectual circles" had been so "beaten down" and "repressed" that there was no longer any "discernible Left, Right or middle."[119] In another satellite, East Germany, one-fifth of the Central Committee was purged.[120]

But the "peace" campaign was not forgotten. At the same fortieth-anniversary celebration, which has been described as reviving the Communist International,[121] Khrushchev asked for a new summit conference. In a speech to the Supreme Soviet, November 6, 1957, he told the visiting Communist leaders: "We would like a high-level meeting of representatives of capitalist and Socialist countries to take place, so as to reach an agreement based on the consideration of true reality and mutual understanding about the exclusion of war as a method of settling international problems, to stop the cold war and the armaments race and to establish relations among states on the basis of coexistence. . . ."[122] The attention of the delegates was also directed to the meeting of the NATO heads of government scheduled to be held in December, 1957. This, Khrushchev said, "bodes no good for the cause of peace."

During the week before the NATO conference, Bulganin delivered a flood of notes to the member nations, and to all members of
the United Nations, urging an "immediate agreement of non-aggression," the substitution of a "European collective security pact" for
the existing "military groupings," and again protesting the "peaceful intentions" of the Soviets. At the same time, he threatened dire
consequences for those nations accepting United States ballistic
missiles or missile-launching bases. In the note addressed to United
Nations members, he complained that it was "proposed to turn the
territory of several NATO states into bases for the installation of
American nuclear and missile weapons." "The state which is the
leader of this bloc," he said, "is consistently trying to expand the
network of its bases and does not take into account the fact that the
installation of these brings about a great danger to the countries
where they are situated." "As is known," he added, "the Soviet
Government takes a most resolute stand for the healing of the international situation."[123]

In January, 1958, even before the NATO nations had replied
to the first series of notes, a new series was distributed, again to all
NATO members and members of the United Nations. This time a
summit conference was demanded. To insure the widest possible
publicity, a summary was broadcast over the Moscow radio:

The Soviet Government proposes to call in the course of the
next two or three months of 1958 a conference of leading statesmen
on a high level in which the heads of government will participate. . . .

.   .   .   .

It would be in the interest of a cessation of the cold war and
the arms race if the conference dealt with the problem of the conclusion in some form or another of a nonaggression pact between the
partner states of the North Atlantic alliance and the members of the
Warsaw Pact. . . .

.   .   .   .

The ending of the cold war and the expansion of international
cooperation would undoubtedly favor a solution of the German
question. . . .[124]

At the NATO meeting (December 16-19, 1957), the assembled
heads of government denounced the "Soviet tactics of alternating
between peace-propaganda statements and attempted intimidation

by the threat of nuclear attack,"[125] and in his report Secretary Dulles pointed out that "the attitude of the Soviets toward the free world has, for years, alternated between threat and blandishment."[126] Nevertheless, a number of NATO states declined to accept bases for ballistic missiles, and others were noncommittal. In January, 1958, the British Prime Minister proposed a "solemn pact of nonaggression,"[127] thus supporting the Soviet demand for an agreement which had already been made—and often broken, of course—in the execution of the United Nations Charter. *The New York Herald Tribune* stated that "in the opinion of observers in this country," the British Prime Minister's proposals "put the Western world 'one up' on the Kremlin for the moment. . . ."[128] This opinion, however, did not appear to take into account the proposals for such a pact continually made by the Soviet Union, at least since the "heads of government" meeting in 1955. It certainly did not take into account the fact that similar "nonaggression pacts" had been made with the Soviet Union by the Baltic States, Poland and Finland—prior to the execution of the Nazi-Soviet nonaggression pact of 1939—and with well-known consequences.

At the same time, in response to Soviet demands, the United States agreed to participate in preparatory talks for a new summit meeting, provided that it could be "ascertained" that such a meeting "would, in fact, hold good hope of advancing the cause of peace and justice in the world."[129] As before, it was insisted that the agenda should include "some significant and urgent topics, as to which agreement seems probable."[130] It was further stipulated that the conference should be "held not as a spectacle, not to reaffirm generalities," and should not be "merely ceremonial or social." A meeting, it was said, "which merely repeated promises already given or hopes already expressed, would not, in the opinion of the Government of the United States, be warranted." Among matters suggested for discussion as "principal causes of international tension" were "the world-wide ambitions of International Communism," the "enforced partition of Germany and external interference in countries of Eastern Europe which result in a denial to the peoples of their right freely to choose their own governments." Consideration was also proposed of "effective measures of disarmament including steps to curb the production of nuclear weapons and the means of their delivery."

Thereafter, the Soviets announced unilateral termination of all nuclear-weapons tests, and the United States was induced to declare its own temporary moratorium. In the Security Council the Soviets sought to bring an end to "flights by United States military aircraft armed with atomic and hydrogen bombs in the direction of the frontiers of the Soviet Union," and through the Polish Foreign Minister, Adam Rapacki, they renewed their proposals for a "denuclearized zone" in central Europe. Strong complaints were also made against "American-English intervention" in Lebanon and Jordan. This was described as "a flouting of the rights of small peoples" in "circumvention of the United Nations" and "undertaken at the request of irresponsible rulers who do not enjoy the support of their peoples and act against their will."[131]

At the same time, however, the Soviets continued to threaten the free world and even added new menaces. In August, 1958, the Chinese Communists resumed their attacks on Formosa. Thereafter, they subdued Tibet (March-April, 1959) and made or renewed claims to large parts of India, Bhutan, Sikkim, Kashmir and Nepal; and in August, 1959, occupied several parts of the border areas. The Viet Minh made new incursions in Laos and stepped up subversive activity in the Republic of Viet Nam.

Meanwhile, in November, 1958, Khrushchev issued his ultimatum on Berlin, stating that the free powers would have to end their "illegal occupation" of that city.[132] He threatened to make a separate treaty with East Germany, and repeatedly asserted that any subsequent Allied effort to force a passage and thereby violate the "sovereign status" of the "German Democratic Republic" would be "fittingly rebuffed"—if necessary by Soviet armed force. While calling for general disarmament and the renunciation of all nuclear weapons, he announced, at the Twenty-first Congress of the Communist Party (January-February, 1959), the beginning of "mass production" of intercontinental ballistic missiles,[133] and continued to flex his atomic muscles by launching new rockets and sputniks around the sun, at the moon, with dogs and even a "dummy space man," prior to each major East-West meeting.

But the free world, nevertheless, continued to put its hopes on such meetings. New conferences, technical and political, were begun on the suspension of nuclear testing and general disarmament. Ten weeks of futile meetings "preparatory" to the summit were held in May-August, 1959 by the "Big Four" foreign ministers. Where Marshal Zhukov had repeatedly failed, cordial invitations to the White House were successively won by Anastas I. Mikoyan, Frol R.

Kozlov and, finally, even by Khrushchev himself. For purely prop-aganda purposes the "summit" was no longer necessary—the defunct "spirit of Geneva" had been replaced by the "spirit of Camp David."

The result was that when the NATO Military Committee met at the end of 1959, the speakers revealed that most member govern-ments had failed to co-operate in the implementation of resolutions made in 1957 with respect to the integration of forces and stockpiling of atomic weapons. A new summit meeting was agreed upon.

As President Eisenhower later said, it was not thought that the second summit would produce "revolutionary gains." But, as he added, the free world "did feel that there was a good chance of some amelioration of some of the tensions."[134] In fact, there was no doubt that false hopes were again aroused. As the British Prime Minister said, "The eyes of the world were on the heads of government and the hopes of the peoples of all countries rested on them."[135]

But what actually happened? In preparation for the conference the Communists launched an intense collectivization drive in East Germany. The purpose, it was said, was "to show the West, on the eve of the summit conference, that the entire population is united behind us and our policy of peace."[136] According to *The New York Times*, "pressure unparalleled since Stalin's time" was used. The result was that collectivization was completed, raising the total from 52% to 100% in three months' time, and East Germany became the first European satellite to achieve this goal. New thousands, of course, fled to the West, and the feelings of those who remained were in-dicated in a farmer's letter to a Socialist parliamentary deputy: "A man is usually tough, but when men start to cry you can imagine what's going on here."[137]

And when the meeting finally took place, there were no discus-sions about the desire for freedom behind the iron curtain, for the withdrawal of troops from the captive nations, or even about the reunification of Germany. Nor were there any conversations about peace with freedom and justice, or about the termination of Soviet subversion and threats of aggression in the free world. After raising a great cry about the flight of an unarmed reconnaissance plane at an altitude of 70,000 feet over the territory of the Soviet Union, Khrush-chev obtained a promise that such flights would be discontinued and then "torpedoed" the conference—walking out allegedly because of the United States' refusal to apologize and punish those responsible for these same flights. It could only be assumed that his walkout was a new form of threat—a gesture supporting his declared intention to retaliate against nations providing bases, or that he had suddenly realized the free nations were not yet as intimidated as he had thought, and "negotiation" with them therefore useless.

The free world, however, immediately founded new hopes on his promise to come to a new conference, six or eight months later, "in a new, more favorable atmosphere."

Stalin's new "movement for peace" thus continued to show its effect—an effect reflected, over the years, in repeated public assertions of the "inevitability" of Communist "reform." The periodic statements of Secretary Dulles had shown the steady growth of this conviction. In 1953, he had expressed only hopes of such reform. "We put our hopes," he said, "in the vast possibilities of peaceful change. Our hope is that the Soviet leaders, before it is too late, will recognize that love of God, love of country, and sense of human dignity always survive."[138] In 1954, he was more optimistic. "Developments," he then said, "clearly portend the change, at some time, of the absolute rule which international communism asserts over the once free nations of Europe and Asia."[139] In 1956, he asserted, "Out of all this there may come—not this year, or next year, but some year—a government which is responsive to the just aspirations of the people and which renounces expansionist goals."[140] By 1957, he was "almost certain" that there would be an "evolutionary change—probably evolutionary." "Already," he said, "there is a trend in the Soviet Union to somewhat greater personal freedom, somewhat greater freedom of expression, somewhat greater enjoyment by the people of the fruits of their labor."[141] And in December of that year he was "absolutely confident." At a luncheon in Paris, he asserted:

. . . I remain absolutely confident that if we follow in this course, the time will come—I do not say when it will come, one year, five years, ten years, twenty years. I do not know. But the time will come when, inevitably, the Soviet rulers will have to change their attitude toward their own people, toward the rest of the world.[142]

But it then began to appear that the change would always be just getting started, and never finished. Thus, in June, 1958, more than five years after the period of "relaxation" was supposed to have begun, Secretary Dulles was still saying that it was "already" beginning. "Already," he said in a statement to the Senate Foreign Relations Committee, "there has been some relaxation of Stalin's brutal police-state methods. And in that less frightening atmosphere, individualism tends to grow."[143] And in 1959, when he told the same committee that Communist methods "must inevitably be altered," it was the same old story. "Already," he still said, "there are indications that the Soviet leaders are beginning to realize this. . . . They are beginning to heed demands by workers and peasants for more leisure and for a greater share in the fruits of their labor."[144]

Nor was Secretary Dulles the only victim of this "new look" delusion. For example, in October, 1957, President Eisenhower and Prime Minister Macmillan jointly announced that "Even despots are forced to permit freedom to grow by an evolutionary process, or in time there will be violent revolution." "This principle," they insisted, "is inexorable in its operation. *Already* it has begun to be noticeable even within the Soviet orbit."[145] (Italics added.) And in December, 1957, the same hopeful attitude was expressed by all the NATO heads of government. "*Already*," they said, "there is evidence of the growing desire for intellectual and economic freedom. If the free nations are steadfast, the totalitarian menace that now confronts them will eventually recede."[146] (Italics added.)

Even Winston Churchill, who had so accurately predicted Soviet intentions after both world wars, was impressed. It was he who in 1953 had first suggested a conference "at the summit of the nations"[147] and who, in 1956, after the Soviet denunciation of Stalin, proposed that the Soviet Union and its satellites be included in NATO.[148] In 1957, after the ousters of Molotov, Malenkov and Kaganovich, he expressed his disbelief "that Russia desires war." "On the contrary," he said, "I think she is moving toward a different state of affairs and will aim at taking her part in this broad and easy composition of the human race."[149]

In the meantime, through the "relaxation of tensions" which such beliefs produced, the Soviets also won a relaxation of restrictions on trade in strategic materials. In 1954, the second year of the peace offensive, the free nations' embargo list applying to the European Soviet bloc was substantially reduced. In the fourth year, 1956, the United States announced the relaxation of its own "nonstrategic" trade controls, for the purpose, it said, of "promoting President Eisenhower's aim urged at Geneva."[150] In the fifth year, 1957, the "differential" between the Chinese and Soviet embargo lists was removed; and in the sixth year, 1958, both lists were again substantially reduced. Items thus freed were all kinds of nonmilitary vehicles, civil aircraft, tires, ball and roller bearings, aluminum, copper, floating docks, passenger and cargo ships with speeds of 20 knots or less, most types of fuel and lubricating oil (except jet engine fuel), stationary electric generators, turbines and Diesel engines, forging machines and hammers up to ten tons, and most types of machine tools.[151]

In November, 1958, the United States announced a further relaxation of its own controls—freeing such items as electrical, industrial and construction machinery, machine tools, vehicles, railroad equipment, chemicals and scientific and professional instruments, ores and metals, and many rubber, paper, petroleum, glass, abrasive and iron and steel products.[152] At the same time, there was increasing American interest in the Soviets' expressed desire to hire large numbers of Western technicians and purchase entire plants for the manufacture of chemical products and synthetic materials.

It also soon became apparent that Communist China would receive the same benefits from the second "breathing space" for the "revolution" which the Soviet Union had received from the first. Although the United States continued to maintain its original embargo on shipments to Communist China, North Korea and North Viet Nam, other states did not. For example, in November, 1957, the Parliamentary Secretary to the British Board of Trade, Frederick J. Erroll, predicted that there would be a gradual, long-range expansion of British exports to Communist China *applying particularly to machine tools and industrial and chemical products.*[153] In December he reported that the British were in a good position to fill such needs:

China is proceeding with a large program of industrialization. The more successfully she industrializes, the more likely she is to import the specialized products of other countries.

Britain is well placed to meet these needs and to supply goods, particularly plant machinery and industrial raw materials which China will need to fill the gap in her own growing industrial production.[154]

It was thus made clear that Stalin's "contemporary movement for peace," launched at the Nineteenth Party Congress in 1952, would accomplish a very successful repetition of what Lenin had planned in 1920—a "respite in war" to "procure the last word in technology in the matter of equipment"—and that the free peoples were repeating the mistakes of the past—mistakes which led to the abandonment of the subject peoples and the replacement of "tattered" Red Army soldiers with "sputniks" and ballistic missiles. In the picturesque jargon of the Bolsheviks, the "foreign capitalists" were still "digging their own grave":

Without them we cannot rearm ourselves; this is the dialectic of history. . . . But while strengthening Soviet Russia, developing her productive forces, foreign capital will fulfill the role Marx predicted for it when he said that capital was digging its own grave. With every additional shovel of coal, with every additional load of oil that we in Russia obtain through the help of foreign technique, capital will be digging its own grave.[155]

CHAPTER XIII

THE BOLSHEVIK PLAN FOR WORLD PEACE

". . . to deceive, if possible, even the elect" (Matt. xxiv:24).

The Soviets make no effort to conceal the fact that they have been calling for "peace" ever since the day on which their policy of violence first proved successful. For example, in May, 1953, when President Eisenhower and Prime Minister Churchill were talking about the Soviet "change of attitude" evidenced by "recent statements and gestures" of the "new leadership," *Kommunist*, the tri-weekly organ of the Central Committee, called attention to the fact that similar statements and gestures had been made frequently in the past by Lenin and Stalin.[1] Three of such statements were cited—the Decree on Peace (November 8, 1917), which described war as "the greatest crime against humanity";[2] the appeal to All Mohammedan Workers in Russia and the East (December 7, 1917), which called for an "honest, democratic peace";[3] and Stalin's interview with Roy Howard (March 1, 1936), in which he stated that "Exported revolution is nonsense."[4]

Many other examples could have been given, because, as Lenin affirmed, "the whole history of Bolshevism, both before and after the October Revolution, is *full* of instances of manoeuvring, temporising and compromising."[5] In Lenin's view, any other course would have been "ridiculous in the extreme," and he so stated[6] in a vigorous attack upon those "left-wing Communists" who were "unable to combine illegal forms of struggle with *every* form of legal struggle"[7]:

To carry on a war for the overthrow of the international bourgeoisie, a war which is a hundred times more difficult, prolonged and complicated than the most stubborn of ordinary wars between states, and to refuse beforehand to manoeuvre, to utilise the conflict of interests (even though temporary) among one's enemies, to refuse to temporise and compromise with possible (even though transient, unstable, vacillating and conditional) allies—is not this ridiculous in the extreme? Is it not as though, in the difficult ascent of an unexplored and heretofore inaccessible mountain, we were to renounce beforehand the idea that at times we might have to go in zigzags, sometimes retracing our steps, sometimes abandoning the course once selected and trying various others?[8]

Lenin put these rhetorical questions before the Second Congress of the Communist International (July-August, 1920) in a tract urging the German Communists to accept the Peace of Versailles. By that time the German armies had been withdrawn from Russia, and nearly all of the "white" armies had been defeated; but two years before, when the Germans were threatening Petrograd, Lenin had employed the same arguments in his *Theses on Conclusion of a Separate Peace* [with Germany]:

We never committed ourselves to wage a revolutionary war without being able to choose the right moment. We must prepare for a revolutionary war. . . .

· · · · · · · ·

Let the others fight between themselves. We will make a separate peace and use this time strengthening the revolution.[9]

In their *Manifesto* of 1848, Marx and Engels had maintained that Communists would "openly declare" their violent views and intentions:

The Communists disdain to conceal their views and aims. They openly declare that their ends can be attained only by the forcible overthrow of all existing social conditions. Let the ruling classes tremble. . . .[10]

Lenin, on the other hand, asserted that when "manoeuvring, temporising and compromising" were called for, it was "stupidity and not revolutionariness" for any Communist "openly to tell the enemy . . . whether and when we shall fight him." He so advised the Communists of Germany:

If Russia, by herself, could endure the Brest-Litovsk Peace for several months to the advantage of the revolution, it is not impossible for a Soviet Germany, in alliance with Soviet Russia, to endure an even longer existence of the Versailles Peace to the advantage of the revolution.

The imperialists of France, England, etc., are trying to provoke the German Communists, they are laying a trap for them: "Say that you will not sign the Versailles Peace!" And the Left Communists childishly fall into the trap laid for them, instead of manoeuvring skilfully against the crafty and, *at the present moment*, stronger enemy, instead of telling him: "Today we shall sign the Versailles Peace." To tie one's hands beforehand, openly to tell the enemy, who is at present better armed than we are, whether and when we shall fight him, is stupidity and not revolutionariness. To accept battle at a time when it is obviously advantageous to the enemy and not to us is a crime; and those political leaders of the revolutionary class who are unable "to tack, to manoeuvre, to compromise," in order to avoid an obviously disadvantageous battle, are good for nothing.[11]

In Lenin's book the "ruling classes" were not to be made to "tremble," but to be lulled into a false sense of security; and the German "Left Communists" were accordingly censured for their "stubborn insistence on non-recognition of the Versailles Peace."[12]

In November, 1920, after the defeat of the Red Army at Warsaw, Lenin called for "peace" again, once more citing his own earlier example:

As long as we have not conquered the whole world, as long as, from the economic and military standpoint, we are weaker than the capitalist world, we must adhere to the rule that we must know how to take advantage of the antagonisms and contradictions existing among the imperialists. Had we not adhered to this rule, every one of us would have long ago been hanging from an aspen tree. . . .[13]

After Lenin's death in 1924, these tactics were explained by Stalin in a series of lectures at the University of Sverdlov. At this time, Stalin stated that there were three "phases" of the "revolution": the first "phase," from 1903 to March, 1917, when the aim was the "overthrow of tsarism" in Russia; the second "phase," from March 1917 to the October uprising, when the aim was the "overthrow of imperialism in Russia"; and the current "phase," from the October uprising onwards, in which the aim was "the consolidation of the dictatorship of the proletariat in one country, where it could be used as a fulcrum for the overthrow of imperialism in all countries."[14] In each "phase," according to Stalin, there was only one appropriate strategy but there were "frequent changes in tactics," depending upon whether the "revolutionary movement" was in a period of "advance" or "retreat." "In a given phase of the revolution," he said, "tactics can change repeatedly, according as the revolutionary tide is ebbing or flowing, according as the revolutionary movement is advancing or receding."[15]

In the third or current phase, according to Stalin, the "revolution transcends the limits of one country, and begins the epoch of the world revolution."[16] For this and every phase he listed four appropriate "tactics," of which we might consider three:

1. The main forces of the revolution must, at the decisive moment, be concentrated for an attack on the enemy's most vulnerable spot, at a moment when conditions are ripe for revolution, when a general offensive can go ahead with full steam, when armed insurrection is imminent, and when the calling of all the reserves into the fighting line is an indispensable preliminary to success. . . .

.   .   .   .

2. The moment for the decisive blow, for raising the standard of revolt, must be carefully chosen. . . .

.   .   .   .

4. The reserves must be handled in such a way as to safeguard an orderly retreat should the enemy be very powerful, should a withdrawal be inevitable, should it be obviously undesirable to accept the enemy's offer of battle, should retreat be the only way whereby (in the circumstances) the vanguard can escape destruction and keep the reserves at its disposal. . . .

The object of such strategy is to gain time, to scatter the forces of the enemy while consolidating our own for a future advance.[17]

At the Seventh World Congress of the Communist International (July-August, 1935), these tactics were explained again by Georgi Dimitrov, leader of the Bulgarian Communist Party and future "Premier" of that unfortunate country:

Comrades, you remember the ancient tale of the capture of Troy. Troy was inaccessible to the armies attacking her, thanks to her impregnable walls. And the attacking army, after suffering many sacrifices, was unable to achieve victory until with the aid of the famous Trojan horse it managed to penetrate to the very heart of the enemy's camp.[18]

Calling for "united fronts" against war and facsism, which would "exert a powerful influence on the ranks of the *Catholic, anarchist and unorganized workers*," and upon "*all other strata of the toiling people,"* upon "the peasantry," the "urban petty bourgeoisie" and "the intelligentsia,"[19] Dimitrov predicted that the free world would soon assume that the Communists had abandoned their aims. But at the same time, he assured the delegates that nothing could be further from the truth:

> There are wiseacres who will sense in all this a digression from our basic positions, some sort of turn to the Right of the straight line of Bolshevism. Well, in my country, Bulgaria, they say that a hungry chicken always dreams of millet. (*Laughter, loud applause.*) Let those political chickens think so. (*Laughter, loud applause.*)
> This interests us little. For us it is important that our own Parties and the broad masses of the whole world should correctly understand what we are striving for.
> We would not be revolutionary Marxists, Leninists, worthy pupils of Marx, Engels, Lenin, and Stalin, if we did not reconstruct our policies and tactics in accordance with the changing situation and the changes occurring in the labor movement.[20]

As Dimitrov pointed out, "the experience of the victory of the great October Revolution on the one hand, and, on the other, the bitter lessons learned in Germany, Austria and Spain during the entire postwar period" had "confirmed once more that the victory of the proletariat is possible only by means of the revolutionary overthrow of the bourgeoisie...."[21]

This was the "tactic" which the Soviets pursued prior to World War II, and again after it. It led them into repeated protestations of their peaceful intentions, numerous nonaggression pacts, and all kinds of proposals for disarmament and the banning of extreme forms of warfare. Thus, in March, 1920, after the defeat of Kolchak and Denikin, the Assistant Commissar for Foreign Affairs, Maxim Litvinov, asserted:

> ... we do not wish to attack anyone. We shall disarm as soon as freed from menace.
> We are convinced pacifists.[22]

In its comment on this statement, an editorial in *The New York Times* asserted skeptically:

> ... they said a few months ago that Bolshevism could not succeed in Russia without a worldwide revolution. Now worldwide revolution

has been forgotten and we are merely to contemplate a peaceful experiment.[23]

In May, 1920, the Soviets entertained a delegation of the British Trades Union Congress and the British Labour Party, insisting that the members work for peace with Russia. At the same time, the Red Army was invading Persia and the Trans-Caucasus.

In March, 1921, a trade agreement was signed with Great Britain, and the All-Russian Central Executive Committee proposed a similar accommodation to the President and Congress of the United States. There would be no interference in the "internal affairs of America," it said:

The Soviet Republic, absorbed in the gigantic labour of internal reconstruction and of re-creating its economic life, has not the slightest intention of interfering in the internal affairs of America, and the All-Russian Central Executive Committee addresses to you a categorical declaration in this sense.[24]

The proposal was rejected, but the "peace" campaign continued. In August, 1921, after the failure of the invasion of Persia, and on the eve of the first anniversary of the Red Army's defeat at Warsaw, the Soviet Commissar for Foreign Affairs, Grigori Chicherin, asserted:

It is absolutely impossible, so long as we are Bolsheviki and Communists, that we shall try to precipitate wars among peoples. On the contrary, we beseech the workers of all countries to oppose the war being prepared by the capitalist States.[25]

In October he called for "the convocation of an international conference . . . to examine the claims of other powers against Russia, and the claims of the Russian government against other powers." "This proposal," he said, "is the best proof of the Russian government's desire for peace with all states and for economic relations that nothing can disturb."[26]

In 1922, at the Genoa Conference for the Economic and Financial Reconstruction of Europe, Chicherin proposed "the general limitation of armaments," including "abolition of the most barbarous methods of warfare . . . poison gas, aerial warfare, and in particular the destruction of peaceful populations."[27] He also called for an "international congress" in which "all peoples" would have "equal status" and in which "their right to determine their own destinies" would be "recognized." The Soviets, he said, were willing "to participate in revising the statutes of the League of Nations, so as to transform it into a true union of all peoples without the domination of some over the others, without the present division into victors and vanquished," and he suggested the appointment of "technical commissions to outline and elaborate a program for the economic reconstruction of the world."[28]

Further proposals for the limitation of armaments were made to Poland, Finland and the Baltic States at the Soviets' own disarmament conference, held at Moscow (December 3-13, 1922), and to the major powers at the Rome Conference, convened by the League of Nations in 1923.

In September, 1922, the Soviets called for another "conference of all interested powers," to "end the Near Eastern crisis" over the Dardanelles Straits and the long-delayed Turkish peace treaty:

The Russian government believes that some powers' separate efforts to end the Near Eastern crisis by a mutual agreement, but without the participation of the interested peoples, can neither bring positive results nor prevent the threat of a new war.[29]

This appeal was directed to the governments of Great Britain, France, Italy, Yugoslavia, Bulgaria, Rumania, Greece and Egypt. The "interested peoples," of course, were those of Russia and the so-called Soviet Socialist Republics of Georgia and the Ukraine.

During the period from 1925 to 1927, nonaggression pacts were made with Turkey, Germany, Afghanistan, Lithuania and Persia, and similar pacts were offered to Poland, Finland, Latvia and Estonia. *Izvestia*, the official publication of the Soviet Central Executive Committee, asserted that such treaties "solve the coexistence problem so satisfactorily that we might be led to ask why they have not been thought of before."[30]

In May, 1927, the Soviets attended the World Economic Conference sponsored by the League of Nations. They saw "only one way out" of the "contradictions in world economy"—"to change over from the capitalist system . . . to the socialist system," but they denied the necessity of "actual conflict." "A peaceful foreign policy," the Soviet delegate said, "is a permanent feature and forms an organic part of the policy of the Soviet State." Like Khrushchev he conceded that "dissimilarity exists between two economic systems, which are forced for a given period to exist side by side," but this, he said, "by no means precludes the possibility of a practical understanding between them."[31]

In November, 1927, the Soviets participated in the proceedings of the Preparatory Commission on Disarmament, proposing the "complete abolition of all land, naval and air forces," as well as "bacteriological" warfare. Litvinov asserted that the government of the Soviet Union was "ready to participate in any and every discussion of the question of the limitation of armaments whenever practical measures . . . are proposed" and "fully subscribes to the Convention on the prohibition of the application to military purposes of chemical and bacteriological substances and processes. . . ."[32] Three days later, Stalin said, at a Congress of the Communist Party:

. . . the maintenance of peaceful relations with the capitalist world is an obligatory task for us.

Our relations with the capitalist countries are based on the assumption that the coexistence of two opposite systems is possible. Practice has fully confirmed this.[33]

In August, 1928, the Soviets signed the Kellogg-Briand Anti-War Pact. They complained that their own offers of "total" and "partial" disarmament had been rejected; that many powers had ignored their proposals—made "long before the idea of the pact now signed in Paris arose"—for "bilateral pacts renouncing not only war . . . but any and every kind of aggression and armed conflict"; and that the Soviet government and other powers "genuinely interested in securing peace" had not been invited to participate in "conversations preceding the pact, or in drawing up its text." But they signed the pact, nevertheless, because it "objectively contains certain obligations on the part of the Powers towards public opinion and gives the Soviet Government a further opportunity of putting . . . the question of disarmament."[34]

In June, 1930, at the Sixteenth Congress of the Communist Party, Stalin protested a number of "provocative attacks upon the U.S.S.R.": ". . . the rupture of relations . . . by the British Conservative Cabinet; the seizure of the Chinese Eastern Railway by the Chinese militarists; the financial blockade . . .; the clerical 'crusade,' headed by the Pope . . .; the organization by agents of foreign states of the wrecking activities of our specialists; the organization of explosions and incendiarism . . .; the attempt on the lives of representatives of the U.S.S.R. . . .; faultfinding with our exports . . . and so forth."[35] Nevertheless, he said, in spite of such "adventurist attacks on the part of the warmongers," we "have succeeded in maintaining peace, in not allowing the enemy to draw us into conflicts." And, he added, "We will continue to pursue this policy of peace with all our might and with all the means at our disposal. We do not want a single foot of foreign territory. . . ."[36]

In 1931, the Soviet Union proposed an economic nonaggression pact to the League of Nations Commission of Enquiry for European Union. In the following year, 1932, a new series of military nonaggression pacts was made—with Finland (January 21), Latvia (February 5), Estonia (May 4), Poland (July 25) and France (November 29). Litvinov, now a full-fledged Commissar for Foreign Affairs, asserted: "We don't make a fetish of these pacts and similar international agreements, but we believe no step that may lead to the maintenance of peace in the present alarming world situation should be neglected by us."[37]

In 1933, Litvinov offered a draft definition of military aggression to the Disarmament Conference of the League of Nations, and a protocol on economic nonaggression to the World Economic Conference. A "Convention for the Definition of Aggression" was made with all the neighboring states of Europe and the Middle East— Afghanistan, Czechoslovakia, Estonia, Finland, Iran, Latvia, Lithuania, Poland, Rumania, Turkey and Yugoslavia. On this occasion, Litvinov asserted: "The signing of the convention represents a new link in the chain of measures taken by the Soviet Government systematically directed to strengthening its peaceful relations with its neighbors. At the same time it serves as an example and a stimulus to other countries."[38] In September, 1933, a nonaggression pact was made with Italy.

In 1934, Stalin complained of "a number of negative occurrences," such as the "refusal" of Japan to conclude a pact of nonaggression, "of which Japan stands in no less need than the U.S.S.R."; but he reported enthusiastically upon the occurrence of two "main" events "which reflect the successes of the Soviet peace policy." One of these was the "change for the better" in relations with France and Poland. The other was the "restoration of normal relations" with the United States. This, Stalin said, was an act of "great significance for the whole system of international relations," not only because "it improves the chances of preserving peace" but also because "it is a landmark between the old position, when in various countries the U.S.A. was regarded as the bulwark for all sorts of anti-Soviet trends, and the new position, when this bulwark has been voluntarily removed, to the mutual advantage of both countries."[39] Finally, after summing up the "Continuing Crisis of World Capitalism and the Position of the Soviet Union in International Affairs," Stalin said:

> Our foreign policy is clear. It is a policy of preserving peace and of strengthening commercial relations with all countries. The U.S.S.R. does not think of threatening anybody—let alone of attacking anybody. We stand for peace and champion the cause of peace.[40]

Within a few months after this report, the Soviet Union was admitted to the League of Nations. Litvinov proudly asserted that "the advocates of the policy of ignoring and isolating the Soviet Union are no longer to be met among broad-minded statesmen."[41] He added that the Soviet Union was itself a League of Nations of the finest type:

> The Soviet Union is itself a League of Nations in the best sense of the word, uniting over 200 nationalities. . . . I will make so bold as to claim that never before have so many nations coexisted so peacefully within a single State, never before have so many nations in one State had such free cultural development and enjoyed their own national culture as a whole and the use of their own language in particular. In no other country are all manifestations of race and national prejudice so resolutely put down and eradicated as in the Soviet Union.
> Here, as regards equality of rights, are neither national majorities nor minorities. . . . Many nationalities which seemed to have been doomed to die out altogether have received a fresh lease of life and begun to develop anew. . . .[42]

This reference to "peaceful coexistence," at the peak of the Stalinist period, should have indicated clearly enough what the Soviets mean by that term.

In 1936, Stalin had his interview with Roy Howard, chairman of the board of the Scripps-Howard newspapers. It was in all respects comparable to Khrushchev's television interview in 1957. "We Marxists," Stalin asserted, "believe that revolution will occur in other countries, but only at a time when it will be considered possible or necessary by the revolutionists in each specific country." "To attempt to export revolution is nonsense," he said. "Without desire within a country there will be no revolution. . . . to presume that we want to bring about revolution in other countries by interference with their national life is unwarranted."[43]

In 1937, still another nonaggression pact was made, with China; and the Soviets were invited to the Nine-Power Conference on the Far Eastern Situation (Brussels, November 3, 1937). Litvinov expressed his assurance that "the proposals we all anticipate will pursue the aim not only of restoring peace in the Far East, but of establishing a just peace, a peace which will not untie, but, on the contrary, will bind the hands of aggressors, also for the future and in other parts of the world."[44]

In 1938, the Soviet Union vigorously condemned the Nazi aggressions in Austria and Czechoslovakia, as well as the recognition by some free powers of the Italian conquest of Abyssinia. In the following year, 1939, at the Eighteenth Congress of the Communist Party, Stalin described such aggressions as "overriding the elementary principles of international law" and putting in doubt "the value of international treaties and obligations." "The foreign policy of the Soviet Union," he said, "is clear and explicit":

1. We stand for peace. . . .
2. We stand for peaceful, close and friendly relations with all the neighboring countries which have common frontiers with the U.S.S.R. . . .
3. We stand for the support of nations which are the victims of aggression and are fighting for the independence of their country.[45]

Further Soviet condemnation greeted the new Axis aggressions in Czechoslovakia, Albania and Lithuania. And in August, 1939, even after the execution of the Nazi-Soviet nonaggression pact, Molotov claimed that this was done in the interests of "universal peace." "The Soviet Union signed a pact with Germany," he said, "fully assured that peace between the peoples of the U.S.S.R. and Germany is in the interests of all peoples, in the interests of universal peace. Every sincere supporter of peace will realize the truth of this."[46]

He was still making such claims after the joint invasion of Poland

and the conclusion of "mutual assistance" pacts with the Baltic States. "We stand for the scrupulous and punctilious observance of the pacts," Molotov asserted, "on the basis of complete reciprocity, and we declare that all the nonsensical talk about the Sovietization of the Baltic countries is only to the interest of our common enemies and of all anti-Soviet provocateurs."[47]

In the meantime, however, the Soviets had persevered in their aims of world conquest, and in their own congresses had stated as much—while the free nations increasingly allowed themselves to be convinced by the more palatable and highly publicized statements to the contrary. Thus, in 1919, even while the Allied powers, acting under the influence of Lenin's persistent "peace" offers, had been endeavoring to negotiate with the Bolsheviks, Lenin himself had made the statement most frequently quoted to demonstrate their warlike intentions:

We are living not merely in a state but in a system of states and the existence of the Soviet Republic side by side with imperialist states for a long time is unthinkable. One or the other must triumph in the end. And before that end supervenes, a series of frightful collisions between the Soviet Republic and the bourgeois states will be inevitable. That means that if the ruling class, the proletariat, wants to hold sway, it must prove its capacity to do so by its military organization.[48]

It was at this time (March, 1919) that William C. Bullitt, the leader of the President's secret peace mission, reported that he "found Lenine, Tchitcherin, and Litvinov full of a sense of Russia's need for peace, and therefore, disposed to be most conciliatory."[49] Another member of the mission, W. W. Pettit, cited the "friendship that the Soviet Government has for the United States."[50]

Others, already wise to the Soviet tactics, warned that the policies of the free world should not be guided by such impressions, but their warnings were ignored until it was too late. One such warning appeared in the *London Daily Chronicle*, shortly after the Bullitt mission's recommendation of a "proposal following the general lines of the suggestion of the Soviet Government":

Lenine frequently has changed his tactics but he never swerved from his main purpose, which is to bring about a world revolution. If the rulers of the world send to him envoys to ask him his terms he will grasp the opportunity. . . . He will give concessions. . . . He may even welcome economic aid . . . but he will do all this with one fixed object to open up connection with the allied countries and work for the overthrow of society in Western Europe and America.[51]

Later in the year, when Admiral Kolchak was in full retreat, this analysis was confirmed by the Department of State: "When the Bolsheviks say they want peace and give assurance that they wish simply to be let alone in order to work out their experiment in Russia, such offers to compromise are, it has been shown, purely tactical."[52] In the following year (1920), after the defeat of the principal anti-Bolshevik Russian forces, a new Soviet "peace" offer was rejected and the United States refused even to give it publicity.[53]

In 1921, after having negotiated treaties of "peace" with Poland, the Baltic States and Finland, treaties of "friendship" with Persia, Afghanistan and Turkey, and a trade agreement with Great Britain, the Bolsheviks convened the Third World Congress of the Communist International (June-July, 1921). On this occasion they adopted Lenin's proposals for a "Thesis on Tactics," which described neither postponement nor abandonment of the "revolution" but a more "prolonged period of revolutionary struggle";

The world revolution, i.e., the decay of capitalism, and the concentration of the revolutionary energy of the proletariat, its organization into an aggressive, victorious power, will require a prolonged period of revolutionary struggle. The variations in the sharpness of the social antagonisms and in the social structures of the various countries, and therefore in the obstacles to be overcome, the high degree of organization of the bourgeoisie in the capitalist countries of Western Europe and North America prevented the immediate victory of the world revolution as a result of the world war. *The Communists were therefore right in declaring, while the war was still raging, that the period of imperialism was developing into the epoch of social revolution, i.e., of a long series of civil wars in a number of capitalist countries, and of wars between the capitalist states on one side and proletarian states and exploited colonial peoples on the other side.*[54]

In the meantime, the United States became what Stalin called "the bulwark for all sorts of anti-Soviet trends." In 1921, the United States refused to invite the Soviet Union to the nine-power Washington Conference. In 1922, it refused to participate in the Soviets' international debut—the thirty-four-power conference at Genoa—or, as Secretary of State Charles Evans Hughes asserted, in any subsequent discussion "which merely furnishes a stage for declarations ill-adjusted to the objects sought."[55] Although Chicherin complained that such demonstrations of the "policy of coercion and injustice" introduced an "unnecessary factor" of "distrust, suspicion and complication,"[56] several requests for the exchange of diplomatic relations and the execution of a trade agreement were also rejected.

In 1923, however, when still another Soviet offer was rebuffed, senatorial wrath was aroused. Secretary of State Hughes announced that the United States did not propose to "barter away its principles" for the lure of trade, and he pointed out that it required "no conference or negotiations to accomplish" the "results which can and should be achieved at Moscow as evidence of good faith";[57] but some Senators maintained that the Soviet government had already given such evidence—that it had long since ceased to promote revolt in other countries. An investigation was demanded as to why the Soviet Union should not be recognized, and the State Department was attacked for its lack of confidence in Chicherin's assurance "that we do not and will not ever give support to revolutionary parties in the United States."[58]

Senator Norris declaimed:

I am saying that there has been no evidence produced to show that there is any truth in this so-called claim that the Russian Government is engaged in a conspiracy to overthrow our Government.[59]

Senator Borah argued that the Soviet Union was no more responsible for the activities of the Communist International than any other country in which there was a Communist Party with international affiliation, including the United States:

I do not believe that the Soviet Republic is responsible for this miserable stuff which is being circulated. . . .

   .   .   .   .

What I undertake to say is that the Soviet Government, neither directly nor indirectly, in my opinion, for the last three years has in any way countenanced or urged or promulgated or indorsed or connived at any attempt to overthrow the American Government.

   .   .   .   .

The Third International is a wholly different institution from the Soviet Government.[60]

The Soviets themselves, however, soon gave the lie to such assertions, as well as to those of their own Foreign Minister. In the very next month, January, 1924, Lev Kamenev, acting Premier, President of the Moscow Soviet, and a member of the Central Committee, made a revealing explanation of operations within the Soviet Union:

> We know our Government machinery is quite worthless. Lenin taught our Central Committee this ... we must gather taxes, and this we cannot do without a party machine, because with the Government organization it is impossible.[61]

A few weeks later, after Lenin's death, the chairman of the Communist International, Grigori Zinoviev, added another link to the chain of admissions. Speaking at a meeting of the second All-Union Congress of Soviets (the "supreme organ of power" of the government of the U.S.S.R.), he stated:

> The Russian Communist Party guides the Soviet Government. The Party is the Government's head. Our party finds things difficult without Lenin; nevertheless, it can manage with the Third International and the trade union International.[62]

Finally, when *Pravda* reported that "the Russian Communist Party conducts the affairs of all the world's proletarian organizations," *The New York Times* commented that the Soviets were themselves doing the work of the Senate investigating committee.[63]

It was not long, however, before Kamenev, Zinoviev and Trotsky were purged in the post-Lenin struggle for power. As in the case of the post-Stalin purges of Beria, Molotov, Malenkov and Kaganovich, this development was interpreted as new evidence that the Soviets had moderated their views. In October, 1926, when Zinoviev was removed as chairman of the Communist International, it was reported that his efforts to hasten the revolution had been "officially disavowed."[64] Another Soviet leader whose purge was yet to come, Nikolai Bukharin, was quoted to the effect that "world revolution" had "failed."[65] An editorial in the formerly skeptical *New York Times* now commented that "Russian nationalism" was "conquering Bolshevik internationalism":

A completed stage in the evolution of Bolshevism, before this clearly perceptible, is thus formally avowed. Russian nationalism is conquering Bolshevist internationalism. To Lenin Russia was only the springboard into Western Europe. Then, as the prospects of world revolution dimmed, Russia became the hearth, on which the spark of revolution was to [be] kept alive. To that formula Stalin still clings in the interest of consistency. But at heart he is aware that the temporary stabilization of capitalism is not so very temporary.[66]

This comforting analysis appeared on October 31, 1926. On the very next day, however, November 1, Stalin asserted that the "victory of socialism in our country" was not to be confused with the "final victory of socialism in our country." The former, he said, "means the establishment of the dictatorship of the proletariat," and the latter "means to solve the contradictions between the country of socialism and the countries of capitalism." These contradictions, he continued, could only be overcome "by the forces of the proletarian revolution in several countries," and those who confused "victory" with "final victory" were "either hopeless muddleheads or incorrigible opportunists"[67] (an accurate description upon which it is impossible to improve).

In 1927, the British police raided the premises of Arcos, Ltd., a branch of the Soviet trade delegation. They found conclusive evidence of Soviet espionage and subversion, and as a result, the trade agreement and diplomatic relations with Russia were terminated. *The New York Times* predicted that this action would add impetus to the "process of Bolshevist evolution" and away from "the famous world revolution,"[68] but according to Stalin it only marked "the revival of interventionist tendencies" on the part of the capitalists. In his report to the Fifteenth Congress of the Communist Party, Stalin warned the delegates that they must not permit themselves to be drawn, at the wrong time, into the resumption of open hostilities. The "inevitable" war with the capitalist world must be postponed "by 'buying off' the capitalists" until after the ripening of the conditions described by Lenin:

We must not forget what Lenin said about very much in our work of construction depending upon whether we succeed in postponing war with the capitalist world, which is inevitable, but which can be postponed either until the moment when the proletarian revolution in Europe matures, or until the moment when the colonial revolutions have fully matured, or, lastly, until the moment when the capitalists fight among themselves over the division of the colonies.[69]

This was the same report in which Stalin asserted that the maintenance of peaceful relations with the capitalist countries was an "obligatory task."

Several days after Stalin's report, Litvinov explained to the Congress the real Soviet position on disarmament. He did this scarcely two weeks after making his proposal to the League of Nations Preparatory Commission for the "complete abolition of all land, naval and air forces." At the party congress, he asserted: "... the proposal for complete disarmament and the end of wars can only come from the soviet state, and can be accepted and carried out only when the soviet system has spread to other states of the world, because then the principles that now guide the U.S.S.R. will form the basis of the policy of these states as well."[70] Here was the basis for Secretary Dulles' statement, twenty-eight years later, that "If that system of conformity can be made worldwide, then, they argue, there will be an end to war."[71]

In September, 1928, in a program adopted at the Sixth World Congress of the Communist International, the Soviets defined the "conquest of power by the proletariat":

The conquest of power by the proletariat does not mean peacefully "capturing" the ready-made bourgeois state machinery by means of a parliamentary majority. The bourgeoisie resorts to every means of violence and terror to safeguard and strengthen its predatory property and its political domination. Like the feudal nobility of the past, the bourgeoisie cannot abandon its historical position to the new class without a desperate and frantic struggle. Hence, the violence of the bourgeoisie can be suppressed only by the stern violence of the proletariat. The conquest of power by the proletariat is the violent overthrow of bourgeois power, the destruction of the capitalist state apparatus (bourgeois armies, police, bureaucratic hierarchy, the judiciary, parliaments, etc.) and substituting in its place new organs of proletarian power, to serve primarily as instruments for the suppression of the exploiters.[72]

This warlike resolution was adopted less than a week after Soviet adherence to the Kellogg-Briand Anti-War Pact, and while the Soviet Foreign Office was contending that British reservations to that pact were an attempt to "justify war" and "to use the pact itself as an instrument of imperialist policy."[73]

In 1929, diplomatic relations with Great Britain were resumed; and by the end of 1933, the Soviet regime had been recognized even by the United States. In a letter to Litvinov, President Roosevelt expressed his gratification at the "restoration of normal relations between our peoples" and the "co-operation of our governments in the great work of preserving peace."[74] *Izvestia* described the event as "the greatest victory of our peace policy."[75]

The first American ambassador to the Soviet Union was the same William C. Bullitt who had led the secret American peace mission in 1919. Upon his arrival in Moscow in 1933, he told President Kalinin that his new mission was "to create not merely normal but genuinely friendly relations between our two great peoples."[76] By 1935, however, he had concluded that diplomatic relations were "not regarded by the Soviet Government as normal friendly relations but 'armistice' relations." In a message to the Secretary of State, he reported that in the Soviet view such relations "can not possibly be ended by a definite peace but only by a renewal of battle":

I have yet to converse with a single leader of the Soviet Union who has not expressed his belief in the necessity of world revolution.

. . . .

. . . I am sure that the present restraint of the Soviet Government with regard to world revolution does not mean abandonment of this aim, but is merely tactical policy *"reculer pour mieux sauter."*

. . . .

The present strength of the Soviet Union is, in the eyes of the Soviet Government, weakness compared to the strength which will be the Soviet Union's at the end of a decade. Everything possible, therefore, is being done to postpone the conflict which is regarded as inevitable. It is the primary object of the Soviet Foreign Office to maintain peace everywhere until the strength of the Soviet Union has been built up to such a point that it is entirely impregnable to attack and ready, if Stalin should desire, to intervene abroad.[77]

The effects of Soviet propaganda, however, were stronger than the professional opinion of an ambassador, and Bullitt found it necessary to preface his remarks with the assertion that his convictions might "seem ill-founded." "I feel sure," he wrote, "that the Department must have received many reports that the Soviet Government has abandoned the idea of world revolution and that the convictions I have expressed ... may seem ill-founded. I can only say that my own observations, without exception, have convinced me of the accuracy of my statements."[78] He concluded his report with what amounts to one of the most accurate and disregarded prophecies of modern times:

To summarize: The aim of the Soviet Government is and will remain, to produce world revolution. The leaders of the Soviet Union believe that the first step toward this revolution must be to strengthen the defensive and offensive power of the Soviet Union. They believe that within ten years the defense position of the Soviet Union will be absolutely impregnable and that within 15 years the offensive power of the Soviet Union will be sufficient to enable it to consolidate by its assistance any communist government which may be set up in Europe. To maintain peace for the present, to keep the nations of Europe divided, to foster enmity between Japan and the United States, and to gain the blind devotion and obedience of the communists of all countries so that they will act against their own governments at the behest of the Communist Pope in the Kremlin, is the sum of Stalin's policy.[79]

Within a few days of this report, the Soviets convened the Seventh Congress of the Communist International (July 25-August 20, 1935), fully confirming Bullitt's timely observations. On the last day of the congress, new resolutions were adopted on "united front" tactics and the "transformation of the imperialist war into civil war." They stated in part:

The struggle for the establishment of the united front, the unity of action of the working class ... charges every Communist Party to wage an irreconcilable struggle ... against the illusion that it is possible to bring about socialism by peaceful, legal methods, against any reliance on *automatism* or *spontaneity* ... against belittling the role of the Party and against the slightest *vacillation of the moment of decisive action*.[80]

.   .   .   .

Should a new imperialist world war break out, despite all efforts

of the working class to prevent it, the Communists will strive to lead
the opponents of war, organized in the struggle for peace, to the
struggle for the transformation of the imperialist war into civil war
against the fascist instigators of war, against the bourgeoisie, for the
overthrow of capitalism.[81]

These resolutions were adopted less than two years after the Soviet
Union had solemnly agreed, as a price of recognition, "Not to permit
the formation or residence on its territory of any organization or
group ... which has as an aim the overthrow or the preparation for
the overthrow of, or the bringing about by force of a change in, the
political or social order of the whole or any part of the United
States."[82]

There were many representatives at this congress from the Communist Party of the United States, including William Z. Foster, party
chairman; Earl Browder, then secretary general; Sam Darcy, a district
organizer from California; and Gil Green, then secretary of the Young
Communist League. Foster and Browder were included in the Presidium of the Congress, together with Stalin and other Soviet leaders.
During the proceedings, Browder, Green and Foster were elected to
the executive committee of the Communist International, and
Browder reported on progress made in the United States:

In 1930 native American-born citizens constituted less than 10
percent of the Party, now they constitute more than 40 percent. In
1930 there was less than 100 negroes in the ranks of our Party, now
there are over 2,500. The number of active working factory cells totals
more than 500 and numbers 4,000 members (that is, about one-third
of all working members of the Party). Moreover, the cells are
functioning in enterprises embracing more than 1,000,000 workers.

        .   .   .   .

We developed the movement against war and Fascism, drawing
into the struggle more and more of the wide masses. . . .

        .   .   .   .

In a few of the more important strike battles, particularly in the
general strike of workers in San Francisco, to the Communist Party
belonged the leadership, the decisive influence.

        .   .   .   .

The Party actively led the movement of youth. . . .[83]

After the close of the congress, the Ambassador reported that the

United States would be "juridically and morally justified" in severing diplomatic relations. He recommended, however, that such action not be taken and that in the public announcement a statement should be made to the effect that the United States "must hesitate to shake the unstable structure of international peace by withholding diplomatic relations with any other government."[84]

As a result, the activities of the Comintern were minimized, and the popular delusion of a peaceful Bolshevism continued. By 1936, when Stalin had his interview with Roy Howard, many people were as convinced of his sincerity, as was the author of the following report in *The New York Times*:

... though Communist parties are active in many countries, and indisputably under the inspiration of the Comintern, whose headquarters are just outside the Kremlin wall, responsible Communists have long ago given up the idea of directly fomenting revolutions in other countries. Joseph Stalin was speaking the truth when he told Roy W. Howard in a recent interview that the idea of exporting revolutions was nonsense.[85]

By January, 1938, the Counselor for the Soviet Embassy in Washington, Constantin Oumansky, was able to state—with more than a semblance of truth—that he did "not think there" were "people left in the world today who doubt or deny the sincerity of our interest in the maintenance of peace."[86]

The deception was in fact so complete that in February, 1938, Stalin found it possible to reconfirm publicly the real Soviet aims without interfering with the relaxation of international tension in any way. He did this through the medium of what was described in *Pravda*, official newspaper of the Communist Party Central Committee, as a reply to an inquiry by "Comrade Ivanov" as to whether the "victory of socialism" could yet be considered "definitive." Stalin asserted that the "victory" would not be "definitive" until all the "capitalist" states had been destroyed:

Leninism answers these problems negatively. Leninism teaches that "the definitive victory of socialism in the sense of a complete guarantee against the restoration of bourgeois relations is possible only on the international scale".…

This is what Lenin said concerning this matter:

"We live not only in a state, but in a *system of states*, and the existence of the Soviet Republic alongside of imperialistic states for a prolonged period of time is unthinkable. In the end of ends, either the one or the other will be victorious. And while this end approaches, a number of most terrible clashes between the Soviet Republic and the *bourgeoisie* are inevitable. This means that the ruling class, the proletariat, if only it wants to and will rule, should prove this in its military organization."[87]

In thus repeating Lenin's much quoted statement at the highpoint of "peaceful coexistence," Stalin completely frustrated those who maintained that it was being cited out of context by experts who failed to mention that Lenin spoke against the background of civil war, when he was still gravely threatened by the combined attacks of "white" forces and Allied "interventionists."

In spite of Stalin's pronouncement, the illusions of the free nations were not destroyed until the following year, 1939, when the Soviet Union invaded Poland and Finland. Because of the Soviet action in Poland, and its threats to Finland and the Baltic States, the United States then declined to send the customary presidential "message of felicitation" on the twenty-second anniversary of the Bolshevik seizure of power. The chief of the Division of Protocol warned that such a message might provoke "more adverse comment than usual," and the chief of the Division of European Affairs suggested that we "confine ourselves to having cards left at the Embassy."[88]

The Soviets, however, were undismayed, and they continued their "peace" campaign right through the period of the Nazi-Soviet "nonaggression" pact, the war, and the years of postwar aggression. In 1943, when the Comintern was "dissolved," the Presidium of its Executive Committee described the "ceaseless and tireless" exposure of Nazi villainy, which it claimed to have accomplished even during the period of the Nazi-Soviet alliance:

The Communist International from the first exposed the real meaning of the Anti-Comintern Pact as a weapon for the preparation of war by the Hitlerites. Long before the war it ceaselessly and tirelessly exposed the vicious, subversive work of the Hitlerites, who marked it by their screams about so-called interference of the Communist International in the internal affairs of these states.[89]

In 1947, when the Comintern was revived, in the form of the "Communist Information Bureau" (Cominform), it was also done in

DECEMBER 3, 1939.

IN FINLAND THE SOVIETS REVEAL THEIR REAL AIMS

By G. E. R. GEDYE
Wireless to THE NEW YORK TIMES.

MOSCOW, Dec. 2—The events of this week lifted a tiny corner of the veil hiding the policy of the inscrutable Kremlin. The invasion of Finland, which outwardly might seem to conform sickeningly to the familiar Nazi pattern, reveals on closer inspection fundamental differences.

The Kremlin's program for Finland—announced quite unconvincingly as an "appeal to the Finnish Communist Party"—is for entirely different ends. It shows aggression being pursued in the name of a liberating revolution, while the program of revolutionary socialism is being modified by the familiar weapons of an ordinary imperialist or fascist aggressor. The week's events seem to furnish some answer to the fundamental question the world has been ask g since the Soviet Union made its first pact with the Nazis: "Is it imperialism or camouflaged world revolution?" That answer is "Both."

Few Commit Selves

Observers inside Russia today mostly have refused to commit themselves to dogmatic interpretations of this. "riddle wrapped in mystery inside an enigma," as Winston Churchill has called it. It is, of course, extremely easy—also irresistibly tempting for those able to say "I told you so"—to declare the socialism of the Soviet Union always has been a mask for the unchanging fundamental Russian imperialism.

Similarly with those people who in 1918 sententiously warned the world not to believe in the sham of German revolution or the smoke screen of the Weimar Democratic Republic. When Hitlerism finally overthrew German democracy they could say: "I told you so," having themselves by mistrust and harsh treatment of the Weimar Republic done most to destroy it. "The old Adam" is insufficient to explain this latest Russian development as it was the earlier changes and develo ents in Germany.

The New Methods

Common sense suggests that it was only on the breakdown of the whole system of collective security that the Soviet Union turned to new plans of securing itself, finally adopting in the case of Finland the cynical, ruthless methods of fascist aggressors.

Deciding some time in the Summer that war was inevitable, the Soviet decided to exploit Nazi fears of a two-front war. Disregarding its earlier diplomatic stand, the Soviet concluded the German pact,

Imperialism of the Old Order Is to Be Combined With World Revolution

which has proved the starting point of a new policy.

First developments were simple enough: A third of Poland, populated mainly by two minorities whose majorities belonged to Russia, was occupied. Thus the Soviet destroyed the specter, long haunting it, that Chancellor Hitler would realize his oft-proclaimed aspirations of using some conquest of the Polish Ukraine as a stepping-stone to invasion and annexation of the fertile plains of the Soviet Ukraine for colonization by his expanding population. Then the Kremlin handled three Baltic States so adroitly that new bases were occupied without war.

Then came Finland—another State

STALIN REVOLUTIONIZES THE DRAMA

AHA, VILLAIN! TRYING TO ATTACK ME, EH?

Herblock in The Wilmington News

One cartoonist's way of looking at Russia's attack on Finland.

that had blocked the peace front— which refused to accept Russian protection against Germany. Unlike the Baltic States, however, Finland stuck to her guns and, although she offered considerable cessions of territory to Russia, for which the latter offered certain compensations, resolutely refused as her obvious right the other demands, which she decided, rightly or wrongly, would have compromised her independence. For this decision to stick to her own territory, and for no other reason, she is today being bombed and invaded by Russia's gigantic army.

Very probably the Russian decision to substitute violence for a plan of economic pressure by keep-

be fairly safely assumed, will not be regarded as suitable for her alone. The new policy is revealed as one of promoting the overthrow of anti-Soviet regimes by the promotion of revolt at home and still more by aggression from without by the Soviet Union's huge, well armed and well-equipped forces.

This blend of revolutionary with typically fascist, imperialist methods apparently is not a prelude to annexation on the capitalist model nor yet to the revolutionary aim of establishing a dictatorship of the proletariat as a prelude to a Soviet economic and political system. The imperialist trend is shown in the demand to surrender naval, military and air bases that would put the whole country in these respects in the hands of the Soviet, denying the use of its territory to any other great power.

Revolutionary Trend

A revolutionary trend in Soviet policy is maintained in the demand for a new type of popular front to include not only workers and peasants but small tradesmen and followers of intellectual professions. The future government is to be based on this bloc. This demand seems to combine the imperialistic motive of seeking satisfaction through domination and the Socialist motive of seeking abolition of the control of big capital.

To be consistent the sentence that

tates are to be confiscated and distributed among the peasants. The State administration will be "democratized." Finally a "popular" army is to be established, obviously to prevent any attempt by the big bourgeoisie to regain control.

Whatever specific modifications applicable particularly to Finland this program contains, one surely is justified in seeing outlined in it at least the main principles of Russia's new policy. Nor would one be far wrong in forecasting that it is toward such a goal that the three Baltic States sooner or later will find they have got to march.

Future Policy

Whether the whole program is intended merely as a screen under cover of which Sovietization will be quietly forwarded is doubtful. Probably the Soviet Union has no particular wish to see this. Whether the plan conceals a shame-faced feeling that the Soviet method has failed to establish socialism and it would be well to experiment on different lines and watch the results, or whether, as many will conclude, the whole plan is nothing but a cynical mask for war and naked imperialism, must be left to the dogmatists to fight out.

It is overeasy to say exactly that this plan is intended for application also to great non-neighboring States such as France and Britain, though it seems probable. One thing is certain—the program is far more significant than the insignificant label of the almost nonexistent Finnish Communist party attached to it. It is a program that all immediate neighbors of the Soviet Union, among whom is Nazi Germany, should study with the greatest attention.

A Subtle Blend

It can be summed up as extension of Soviet power neither by outright annexation nor by establishment of a dictatorship of the proletariat but by a subtle blend of both.

Preceded by friendly negotiations —so far it has stopped there in Germany's case—in the event of resistance the policy will be continued by staging a regular circus of fascist aggression-allegations, "incidents," one-sided tearing up of agreements followed by undeclared war, by invasion according to the latest convention, destruction by bombing of the nearest airdromes. Simultaneously it is sought to promote, with propaganda, an internal revolution, not in accordance with Marxist tenets as an aim in itself, but primarily as an instrument to secure the domination of the Soviet Union.

In Finland, the Soviets Reveal Their Real Aims

MARCH 25, 1921.

LENIN'S "NEW COURSE."

A Serious Mistake to Believe That the Bolsheviki Have Abandoned Their Aims.

By WILLIAM ENGLISH WALLING.

"Lenin Gives Up Communism for Trade." Under this headline a metropolitan daily prints a story that the Bolshevist chief has "frankly abandoned the theories of communism and world revolution and discarded his program of confiscation and terror." Indicated that he is "ready and willing to begin with the payment of Russia's debts." Lenin, it seems, has announced a "new policy" and the Russian revolution is at a turning point.

Nor is it Lenin alone that has undergone the amazing transformation. It is pointed out that the reddest of the "Reds," were enthusiastic in support of the small as to be ridiculous; it included only the well-known New York Commissary, Mme. Kollontai and a certain Syndicalist named Shalpuloro?

All the leading Russian Reds have become more enthusiastic, Arthur Ransome, the foremost extremist of Bolshevism now writing in the English language, is given as authority for the proposition that the Moscow Government has changed its immediate tactics, first, with regard to the rest of the world, and second, with regard to the Russian peasants. "Lenin," this unbiased authority declares, "not only recognizes the need of bringing big capitalists to the head of Russian industries at home. The evolution of this revolution is taking its natural course as the organization of the peasants in the country with a necessary recognition of the town concomitantly working for the needs of the peasants.

Fortunately, the supposed foundation for all these interpretations of the latest phase of Bolshevism is given, namely the propositions offered by Lenin and

MAY 4, 1921.

LENIN DIDN'T SCRAP WORLD REVOLUTION

Text of Famous Speech Shows He Reported Its "Great Step Forward."

CONCESSIONS TO PEASANTS

These Recommended Apparently Only Exceptions to His General Policy of Communism.

The text of the speech delivered by Nikolai Lenin, the Russian Premier, before the Tenth Congress of the Communist Party, as printed in the official Bolshevist newspaper Pravda of March 10, was made public yesterday by A. J. Sack, Director of the Russian Information Bureau in the United States, representing in this country the Russian democratic anti-Bolshevist forces. This speech shows that the Russian Premier Lenin had repudiated a world revolution and communism for Russia.

Lenin said:

"In regard to the question of world revolution, Lenin said:

"We can not count on it. It is not coming as fast as we should like it, but it is coming nevertheless, and is gathering strength. Of course, the world revolution has made a great step forward, in Russia, Italy, the Communist party in every country, in Germany the Communist International has become not only the centre of the labor movement but the centre of all the economic and political life of those countries. This is our conquest, and no one can deprive us of it.

"... But, at any rate, here we are to draw

JUNE 18, 1931.

STALINISM SHELVES WORLD REVOLT IDEA; TO WIN RUSSIA FIRST

Success of Socialism at Home Held Best of Propaganda for Conversion of Others.

VIEW IS DEEMED ORTHODOX

Huge Extent of Country Cited as Giving Possibility for Full Development of Marxism.

CAPITALISM HELD DOOMED

So Stalinists Feel They Are Not Violating Ideals in Diverting Efforts to One Nation.

This is the third of a series of articles on Russia today by The New York Times Moscow correspondent, who is at present in Paris.

By WALTER DURANTY.

Special Cable to The New York Times.

PARIS, June 17. The essential feature of "Stalinism," which sharply defines its advance and difference

NOVEMBER 17, 1944.

SOVIET DENIES AIM TO DICTATE ABROAD

Non-Intervention in Nations' Internal Affairs Declared a Basic Moscow Tenet

PEACE IS MAIN OBJECTIVE

Article in Embassy Bulletin Supports Coexistence of Two Political Systems

Special to The New York Times.

WASHINGTON, Nov. 16.—The Soviet Union desires peaceful relations with all nations regardless of their political systems and has no desire to intervene in their internal affairs, a spokesman says in an official publication.

An article in the Nov. 16 Information Bulletin published by the Soviet Embassy, signed by Col. A. Galin, lists six basic principles of foreign policy that he said the Soviet Union relies consistently upon and has followed consistently over the twenty-seven years of its existence:

1. Peaceful relations of all states irrespective of their political systems.

2. Economic and political cooperation with all states on the basis of sovereign equality and independence of the contracting parties and the co-existence of two systems.

Reproduced from *The New York Times*

The "Abandonment" of World Revolution, 1921, 1931, 1944

THE NEW YORK TIMES, SUNDAY, MARCH 15, 1925.

IRON RULE OF SOVIET LOOSENED IN RUSSIA

"Bloodless Political Revolution" of Last Two Months to Give More Power to the Peasants—People Told to Be More Industrious

By WALTER DURANTY.

AUGUST 13, 1921.

LENIN ABANDONS STATE OWNERSHIP AS SOVIET POLICY

Official Decree Retains Control of Only a Few of the Big National Industries.

TO LEASE TO INDIVIDUALS

Payments for Postal, Railroads and Other Public Services Are Re-established.

BROWN MEETS LITVINOFF

No Damage Protection for American Food and Personnel of Relief Bodies.

By WALTER DURANTY.

MONDAY, MARCH 24, 1930.

SOVIET TO RESTORE RIGHTS TO MILLIONS

Stops Expropriating of Private Traders, Kulaks and Others Arbitrarily "Deprived."

COURTS TO HEAR APPEALS

Many Facing Starvation to Regain Bread Cards and Others in Exile Camps Will Get Trial.

PENALTY FOR OPPRESSORS

Factory, Farm and Other Committee That Have Acted With Fierce High-Handedness Are Reviewed.

By WALTER DURANTY.

"Attack" and "Retreat" in Bulgaria, 1958

MONDAY, JANUARY 27, 1958

BULGARIA LENIENT TO HER DISSIDENTS

Writer Guilty of Deviation Remains Union Secretary and Literary Editor

By ELIE ABEL
Special to The New York Times

SOFIA, Bulgaria, Jan. 25—It is a sign of the new, milder climate in Bulgaria today that Communist writers guilty of deviation from the party line are getting off with reprimands.

The most prominent offender against the principles of Socialist realism, Emil Manov, remains a secretary of the Bulgarian Writers Union and editor of a Sofia literary review. All 5,000 copies of his controversial novelette, "An Authentic Case," sold out in a few days. This was a large printing by Bulgarian standards.

"Everyone was curious to see what all the fuss had been about," said Khristo Radevski, secretary general of the Writers Union and one of Mr. Manov's sharpest accusers, a commercial success.

The Bulgarian regime, which refuses to be as liberal as its neighbors abroad in the recent literary tempest here, readily proved the orthodox Mr. Radevski in an interview.

It was less accommodating about interviews with dissenters from the party line. Mr. Manov, too, had been approached through the Bulgarian Foreign Ministry and the Writers Union, but did not keep the appointment.

The word at the author's home, after an hour's fruitless waiting, was that he had been called away suddenly to the country, so suddenly in fact that he had no time to send his regrets. Mr. Manov's confession of error, incidentally, did not wholly satisfy the party. He is allowed to be more aggressive.

In the case of Vladimir Tenchanarov, a well-known Bulgarian journalist recently dismissed as assistant editor of the Daily newspaper Otechestven Front, the authorities were less lenient. According to the Foreign Ministry's Press Department, Mr. Topencharov, who happened to be out of the city.

Mr. Radevski denied that the Bulgarian party was trying to picture the themes of its authors. All it wants from them is "a truthful description of life," he said.

Of Traicho Kostov, the Deputy Premier executed as a traitor in 1950 on what the Bulgarian regime has now termed trumped-up charges of Titoist deviation.

But the writer who isolates a single poverty-ridden family from the rest of life in his country is likely to give the foreign reader a false impression.

That apparently, was the essential error of Mr. Manov's recent book. The hero is an architect and a party member, a father as well as a husband. After years of marriage he meets a woman with whom he had an affair in the past. He leaves his wife and children, becomes an alcoholic and in the end loses his mind.

The crux of the issue, according to Mr. Radevski, is the position from which a writer approaches social problems. To escape official criticism, he must find an affirmative solution, one that is "in favor of our society."

The case of Mr. Topencharov was more obviously political. He is a brother in law of Traicho Kostov, the Deputy Premier executed as a traitor.

They were stopped by the police.

The city workers were told they would be allowed to get on the buses at any city on production of documents showing they

Continued on Page 4, Column 4

THURSDAY, JANUARY 30, 1958

BULGARS FORCED INTO COLLECTIVES

Policemen Besiege Villages, Halt City-Bound Workers to Spur Farm Program

By ELIE ABEL
Special to The New York Times

SOFIA, Bulgaria, Jan. 25—In a drive to achieve 100 per cent collectivization the Bulgarian regime has now resorted to siege methods against the peasantry.

While the use of force has long been suspected, the latest indications on the outskirts of Sofia provide solid confirmation. They took place during the last week in the relatively prosperous villages of Dragolevtsi and Semyonovo.

During the night of Jan. 22-23 both villages were surrounded by squads of Communist party leaders and policemen armed with machine pistols. At daybreak some of the villagers members of the party were told to board buses for the capital.

BULGARS FORCED INTO COLLECTIVES

Continued From Page 1

had enrolled in a collective farm.

Protests were of no avail. When one city-bound worker explained he earned no land, a policeman replied: "In that case, go back home and influence your father, who does own land, to enroll. When he has joined, you will be allowed to leave for Sofia."

Similar gates of persuasion by siege have been reported from the villages of Simeonovo and Zheleznitsa. These reports, however, have not been so fully substantiated as those from Dragolevtsi and Semyonovo.

When foreign observers visited Semyonovo on Friday afternoon persuasion patrols were still moving from house to house. A sign at the edge of the village read: "T. K. Z. S. collectivization) is the road to happiness and a rich life."

Nowhere in Eastern Europe has collectivization been pushed more dogmatically than in Bulgaria. By the end of Bulgaria 87 per cent of the country's arable land belonged to the so-called working Peasant Cooperative.

Almost daily the Sofia newspapers report that in this village or that a hundred or more families have enrolled "voluntarily" in new collective.

At the same time, in Poland and in Hungary the independent peasant has enjoyed a breathing spell for the first time in a decade, with encouraging over-all results in the form of increased agricultural production.

The last redoubt of the Bulgarian smallholder is in the mountainous regions and on the perimeter of Sofia.

Communist party workers acknowledge that the small stony mountain-farms do not lend themselves to mechanization, an element of collectivization. They concede that the formation of collectives would add little or nothing to the national food supply.

There have been suggestions within the party that it would be wiser to encourage handicrafts and cottage industries in the mountain villages than to herd the smallholders into collectives that cannot support themselves.

the name of "peace." A manifesto was issued condemning the "imperialist desire to unleash a new war," and calling upon the "antiimperialistic democratic camp" not to underestimate its own strength: "The forces who align themselves with peace are so numerous and powerful that if they defend hard and without flinching the cause of peace, if they show perseverance and grit then the plans of the aggressors are doomed to bankruptcy."[90] The delegates at the organizing conference were told by Andrei Zhdanov, a member of the Politburo, that of "the six so-called great imperialist powers" only two remained—"the United States and Great Britain"—and that "the position of one of them, Great Britain, has been undermined."[91] Nevertheless, he still spoke of "coexistence," and for a "long period" of time. "Soviet foreign policy," he said, "proceeds from the fact of the co-existence for a long period of the two systems—capitalism and socialism. From this it follows that co-operation between the U.S.S.R. and countries with other systems is possible. . . ."[92]

On the thirtieth anniversary of the Bolshevik seizure of power (November 6, 1947), Molotov again confirmed the "possibility" of such co-operation:

All real friends of peace—and they constitute the majority of people of any country—can rely on the fact that the Soviet Union will defend to the end the interests of universal peace.

In accordance with that peaceful policy, the Soviet Union stands for the all-embracing development of international cooperation.

Comrade Stalin profoundly elucidated our foreign policy in his talk with the well-known American, Harold Stassen. They (the Soviet Union and the United States) can, of course, cooperate with each other, said Stalin. The difference between them was not important as far as collaboration was concerned.[93]

Subsequently, the "Partisans of Peace" were organized to demand the abolition of atomic weapons, the convocation of high-level conferences, and the adoption of a "Five-Power Peace Pact." "World Congresses" for "peace" were held in Paris, Warsaw and Vienna, and hundreds of millions of signatures were solicited or claimed for the "Stockholm World Peace Appeal."

The free powers, however, confronted by the postwar renewal of Soviet aggression, remained impervious to such demands. Shortly after the invasion of South Korea, Mr. Dulles, who was at that time Consultant to the Secretary of State, pointed out that to the Com-

himself did not deny that "one can conceive" (only "conceive"!) of He spoke at a meeting of the Colgate University Conference on American Foreign Policy:

Hitler felt that his whole program had to be achieved in short order, during his own lifetime. That required intensive and sustained offensive action. In the case of the Communist program, there is no such time urgency. It is anticipated that full realization of the Communist conquest may take what Stalin refers to as "an entire historical era." And, he teaches, that "tactics of retreat" are as important as tactics of attack. Also, he teaches, the necessity of compromise when, as he puts it, this is necessary "to buy off a powerful enemy and gain a respite."[94]

In 1951, after the Soviets suggested an armistice in Korea, Secretary of State Dean Acheson warned that the "strategy of the Kremlin is still the same." In a statement to the Senate Committee on Foreign Relations, he said:

I need not remind this Committee that we have had periods of relative quiet before. There was an easing of tension for a while after the Soviet failure to dominate Iran in 1946. There was a lull in Soviet pressure after the Soviet success in Czechoslovakia. There was an easing of tension after the defeat of the Communists in Greece and after the lifting of the Berlin blockade. There may be a period of comparative quiet if there is an armistice in Korea. If so, we must not let ourselves be pulled off balance by a shift in tactics.
. . . until there is a fundamental change in Soviet policy—we must recognize temporary easings of tension for what they are—as tactical moves intended to weaken and to divide us.[95]

Even after the termination of the wars in Korea and Indochina, the adoption of "parliamentary methods" by the Communist parties of India and Indonesia, the failure of the guerrillas in Malaya and the Philippines, and the hopes for at least a temporary relaxation of tension which were aroused by the Geneva Conference, there was still no conviction that the Communists had made any fundamental changes in their "doctrine" or "creed." Secretary Dulles continued to advise that, regardless of the death of Stalin, "Stalinism" remained; and in a public address made on December 8, 1955, called attention to the persistent Soviet tactics of "zigzag" and "retreat":

... we should remember that one of the doctrines taught by Lenin and constantly emphasized by Stalin was the need for "zigzag." Repeatedly Stalin drove home the idea that it is as important to know when to retreat as when to attack, and that when blocked in one course it is necessary to find another.

Stalin is dead. But for 30 years his writings have been the Communist creed, and Stalinism in fact, though not in name, is still a potent influence in Russia. In prudence, therefore, we must act on the assumption that the present Soviet policies do not mark a change of purpose but a change of tactics.[96]

In 1956, however, simply because Khrushchev asserted at the Twentieth Congress of the Communist Party that the Communists are not "advocates of violence always and everywhere," the convictions of many in the free world appeared to be shaken. Secretary Dulles immediately concluded that the Soviets had been forced to "review their whole creed, from A to Z,"[97] and to make at least an "effort to eliminate violence from their doctrine." In a press conference held in April, 1956, he stated that they were "apparently" trying to get away from the Stalinist "point of view":

... there is an effort to eliminate from their doctrine, and perhaps to some extent from their practice, the Stalin thesis that only violence would serve. As I perhaps have quoted or paraphrased here before, Stalin said that anybody who believed that communism, Soviet communism, can achieve its goal without resort to violence has either gone out of his mind or else does not understand the basic fundamentals of Communist philosophy. Well, now apparently they are trying to get away from that point of view, both doctrinally and to some extent, I believe, in practice. And it's necessary and appropriate that we should, I think, adapt our tactics to the changes in Soviet Communist tactics.[98]

Secretary Dulles subsequently modified this statement considerably by asserting that the "Soviet rulers now *profess* to renounce the doctrine that violence is a necessary part of their foreign policy."[99] (Italics added.) But even a profession of such a change in belief would be significant, if made in a report to the Party Congress, and it is therefore worthwhile to compare the statements of the three Communist leaders (Lenin, Stalin and Khrushchev) to ascertain if there really has been such a change.

The comparison, unfortunately, gives no cause for joy. Lenin himself did not deny that "one can conceive (only 'conceive'!)" of peaceful revolution "in republican or very free countries";[100] and Stalin maintained that "a 'peaceful' course of development" could occur in the event of a "socialist encirclement" of the capitalistic nations.[101] Both indicated, like Khrushchev, that the use or non-use of violence depends entirely upon the extent of the resistance of the free world—the "bourgeoisie"—and that if it is willing to submit voluntarily to Soviet domination there will be no need for Soviet violence. Thus, in 1916, Lenin stated that "we cannot reject the possibility that in certain cases by way of exception, for example in some small state after its great neighbor has already accomplished a social revolution, a peaceful surrender of power by the bourgeoisie is possible, if they have convinced themselves of the hopelessness of resistance and prefer to keep their heads fastened to their necks."[102] And in 1924, Stalin wrote that "in the remote future, if the proletariat is victorious in the most important capitalist countries and if the present capitalist encirclement gives way to a socialist encirclement, a 'peaceful' course of development is quite possible for some of the capitalist countries whose capitalists, in view of the 'unfavorable' international situation, will consider it advisable 'voluntarily' to make substantial concessions to the proletariat."[103] This possibility was actually fulfilled in the Baltic States at the beginning of World War II—after the fall of Poland, and when the governments of those small nations saw no further hope of effective support from the Allied powers. The danger of its further fulfillment, even in the United States, was reflected, in 1958, in the excitement over studies allegedly dealing with "contingencies" that "might force the United States to choose surrender" and the "possibility of 'surrender without fighting.' "[104]

A careful analysis of Khrushchev's statement in 1956 shows no departure from the views expressed by Lenin and Stalin. Like them he asserted that "the greater or lesser degree of intensity which the struggle may assume, the use or the non-use of violence in the transition to socialism, depends on the resistance of the exploiters, on whether the exploiting class itself resorts to violence, rather than on the proletariat." Although he indicated that there were greater possibilities for the use of "parliamentary means" in the existing "historical situation," this was only because the "forces of socialism and democracy," meaning communism, had "grown immeasurably" and capitalism had "become much weaker." "In countries where capitalism is still strong," he said, "and has a huge military and police apparatus at its disposal, the reactionary forces will of course inevitably offer serious resistance. There the transition to socialism will be attended by a sharp class, revolutionary struggle."[105]

There is small comfort in the fact that Khrushchev found "capitalist encirclement" giving way to "socialist encirclement," or in his apparent belief that "parliamentary means" were succeeding in such countries as India, where the Communists later won elections in the state of Kerala, and Indonesia, where they became the major party in east and central Java. What happens after control is thus won was indicated by reports from Kerala of "cold-blooded" political murders, Communist inflation of the electoral rolls, beatings, "terrorizing" of the people by roaming Communist bands and the general "deterioration of law and order."[106] And it is safe to say that in spite of the popular opposition subsequently shown by mass demonstrations, strikes and passive resistance, Kerala would still be Communist if it were not for the intervention of the central government of India.

If the Soviets should succeed, without violence, in gaining control of the world, the victory would be due to their continuing ability to convince the free nations that violence is not intended. And if the free nations *are* so convinced, this in turn will be largely the result of their failure to remember that the Soviets have always called for peace. As one philosopher has stated (George Santayana): "Those who do not remember the past are condemned to repeat it."

Many statesmen in the free world are inclined to believe they remember the past at the very time when they are most prone to be forgetful. For example, in January, 1958, when Prime Minister Harold Macmillan reciprocated the Soviet demand for a "solemn pact of nonaggression," he mentioned the fact that in 1945 all nations were "hoping for a period of prolonged peace and friendship," even with the Soviet Union, and "were confident" they "could live in harmony together" with it.[107] Apparently, however, he did not remember the past beyond that date, because he added: "If we had thought of the phrase then we should have said 'peaceful coexistence.' "

Actually, if the free world had not thought of this phrase before 1945, it was no fault of the Soviet Union. As Litvinov said, in 1934, the Soviets had "advocated it again and again at international conferences," and had even "managed to get it recognised by inclusion in some of the resolutions of these conferences":

As to the first condition which we have named, the peaceful co-existence of different social-political systems at a given historical stage, we have advocated it again and again at international conferences. We have managed to get it recognised by inclusion in some of the resolutions of these conferences.... The invitation to the Soviet Union to join the League of Nations may be said to represent the final victory of this principle.[108]

In the course of its long history, the term "peaceful coexistence" had been given many meanings, but none augured any good for the free nations. In 1922, for example, upon the organization of the so-called Union of Soviet Socialist Republics, the term was used to describe the new relationship of the subjugated nations. According to the declaration then issued, "the new Union state" would "be a worthy expression of the basic principles of peaceful coexistence and fraternal cooperation laid down in October 1917."[109] At the same time, Stalin contrasted the "peaceful coexistence" of these nations with the "imperialist wars, national differences, oppression, colonial slavery, and chauvinism" in the "camp of capitalism." "In the camp of the soviets," he said, "we have, on the contrary, mutual trust, national equality, peaceful coexistence, and fraternal co-operation among the peoples."[110]

In 1925, Stalin used the phrase to describe the "temporary equilibrium of forces" between the Soviet Union and the free world—"an equilibrium," he said, "which has determined the present phase of 'peaceful coexistence' between the land of Soviets and the capitalist lands":

That which we at one time thought of as a brief breathing space after the war has changed into an entire period of respite. Hence a certain equilibrium of forces and a certain period of "peaceful coexistence" between the world of the bourgeoisie and the world of the proletariat.[111]

Two years later, in 1927, Stalin opined that "the period of 'peaceful coexistence'" was "receding into the past, making way for the period of imperialist raids and preparation for intervention against the U.S.S.R."[112] This, of course, was soon rectified, but not before the Communist International had met, in 1928, and made reference to the "simultaneous existence" of the two economic systems. This phrase was presumably intended to indicate that "coexistence" was no longer "peaceful." In any event, the real meaning of "peaceful coexistence" was indicated by the description given, at the same congress, of the "dictatorship of the world proletariat":

... the dictatorship of the world proletariat is an essential and vital condition precedent to the transition of world capitalist economy to socialist economy. This world dictatorship can be established only when the victory of socialism has been achieved in certain countries or groups of countries, when the newly established proletarian republics enter into a federative union with the already existing proletarian republics, when the number of such federations has grown and extended also to the colonies which have emancipated themselves from the yoke of imperialism; when these federations of republics have finally grown into a World Union of Soviet Socialist Republics uniting the whole of mankind under the hegemony of the international proletariat organized as a state.[113]

Stalin, no doubt, had the same meaning in mind when he said, in 1922:

Five years ago the Soviet government successfully laid the foundation for peaceful coexistence and fraternal co-operation. ... We have before us the task of erecting a new edifice, a new, powerful, unified toilers' state. ... Let us hope, comrades, that our Union republic will be both a true bulwark against international capitalism and a decisive step toward unifying all the toilers of the world into a World Soviet Socialist Republic.[114]

CHAPTER XIV

THE "IRREVERSIBLE" TREND

". . . the last state of that man becomes worse than the first"
(Luke xi:26).

While the post-Stalin "new look" in Soviet foreign policy revived the hopes of "peaceful coexistence" in the free world, the promises and concessions made to the subject peoples were accepted as sure signs of a new and better life behind the iron curtain. Secretary of State Dulles regarded the domestic "new look" as "even more significant" than the "new look" abroad, "because," he maintained, "while Soviet foreign policy is readily reversible, it is not so easy to erase the consequences of internal liberalization."[1] After the Twentieth Congress of the Communist Party, in February, 1956—while the Soviets were still denouncing the "cult of J. V. Stalin and its consequences"—he became convinced that this domestic policy was actually "irreversible."

This belief—that a taste of freedom, once given, is impossible to withdraw—was based on the assumption that the demands of the subject peoples, or the "inherent weakness" of the Communist system, or the inevitable "softening" of the Communists themselves, would lead to a never-ending series of increasing political and economic concessions until freedom and the ultimate abolition of terror were attained. There would thus be produced a "peaceful," "evolutionary" and "irreversible" trend to freedom. Although similar trends and predictions had failed to produce any real change in the Soviet system for more than forty years, during the eighteen-month period following Khrushchev's "secret" denunciation of "Stalinist" oppression this theory became the stated primary source of hope for the subject peoples. Its development at this time was clearly reflected in the statements of Secretary Dulles.

In July, 1956, the Central Committee issued a new pronouncement, "On Overcoming the Cult of the Individual and Its Consequences." This document asserted that "Soviet democracy not only

proclaims but also materially guarantees" the fundamental freedoms
—"the right to work, education and leisure," the right to "participation in state affairs," the right to "freedom of speech, of the press
and of conscience," and the right to a "real opportunity for the free
development of personal abilities and all other democratic rights and
freedoms for all members of society without exception."[2] In his comments on this sweeping challenge to credulity, Secretary Dulles pointed out that "these things were already promised by the Soviet State
Constitution adopted in 1936." The promises then made, he said, "did
not prevent the policies of violence and the massive terrorisms, tor-
tures, enforced confessions and judicial murders which Khrushchev
described in his originally secret and now revealed speech of last
February." Nevertheless, he was unwilling to exclude the possibility of
their current fulfillment, and he took a position on both sides of the
fence:

> I would say that the current [new look] policies of the Soviet
> Union can still be reversed at any time because they don't yet depend
> upon the consent of the governed. I believe that there are processes at
> work which will require Soviet policies to become responsive to the
> will of the governed, and at that point they cease to be suddenly
> reversible.[3]

In October, 1956, there appeared to be a more tangible response
to these "processes"—in Poland, where a state of near-revolt induced
the acceptance of the "liberal" Communist Wladyslaw Gomulka as
party leader—and in Hungary, where open rebellion brought another
"liberal" Communist, Imre Nagy, back to the post of Premier. Secretary Dulles then seemed convinced of a change. In an address to the
Dallas Council on World Affairs, October 27, 1956, he promised the
captive peoples assistance, not for the re-establishment of freedom in
their countries but for their "economic readjustment" *after they had
obtained it.* "They must know," he said, "that they can draw upon our
abundance to tide themselves over the period of economic adjustment
which is inevitable as they rededicate their productive efforts to the
service of their own people, rather than of exploiting masters." At the
same time, he also detected "some response" in the Soviet Union,
where he spoke of "an irreversible trend":

> Let me add a word about future relations with the peoples who
> compose the Union of Soviet Socialist Republics. They, too, can have

hope. The spread of education and industrial development create growing demands for greater intellectual and spiritual freedom, for greater personal security through the protection of law, and for greater enjoyment of the good things of life. And there has been some response to those demands.

There is ground to believe that that trend will prove to be an irreversible trend.[4]

The hopes aroused by the revolt in Hungary were quickly disappointed by its suppression. Nevertheless, on July 2, 1957, Secretary Dulles asserted that he was "almost certain" there would be an "evolutionary change" in the Soviet system, and that its occurrence should be made a "working hypothesis" of the policies of the free world:

We believe that it is almost certain that there will be an evolutionary change—probably evolutionary. Conceivably it could be revolutionary, but it does not seem likely. And indeed, already there is a trend in the Soviet Union to somewhat greater personal freedom, somewhat greater freedom of expression, somewhat greater enjoyment by the people of the fruits of their labor.

One can see evidence of that already. And I believe that that kind of trend is going to prevail, and I think that the United States should accept, as I say, as a working hypothesis underlying its policies, the assumption that that kind of trend is going to prevail.[5]

On the following day it was announced that Molotov, Malenkov and Kaganovich had been expelled from the Central Committee—for opposing its efforts to "do away with the consequences of the personality cult." Secretary Dulles then asserted that the existence of a trend to greater freedom had been confirmed, and that it *was* "irreversible":

The whole affair showed how powerful must be the forces for change which are at work within Russia and how perplexed the rulers must be as to how to cope with these forces and at the same time maintain absolute power.

What has happened confirms the existence in Russia of what I have called an irreversible trend.[6]

These predictions were a source of constant irritation to Khrushchev, the victorious party leader, but a comparable "evolution" is "foreseen" by the Communists themselves. It is almost as likely to occur. According to Lenin,[7] and the program of the Communist International,[8] the "evolution" of communism will lead to a "higher phase of Communism" in which the "state will be able to wither away completely" and in which there will be no more "exploitation of man by man." "Want and economic inequality will disappear," the "monopoly of education" will be "abolished" and culture "will become the acquirement of all." The "new culture" will "bury forever all mysticism, religion, prejudice and superstition," and the "class ideologies of the past will give place to scientific materialist philosophy." Under such circumstances, the "domination of man over man" in any form will be "impossible," the "organs of class domination" will "disappear" and "all measures of coercion will expire."

In August, 1917, only a few months before the Bolshevik seizure of power, Lenin wrote a tract in which he denounced the "bourgeois 'savants' " for describing his goal as "pure Utopia." But he was himself unwilling to predict when, or even whether, it would ever be attained:

... how rapidly this development will go forward ... we do not and *cannot* know.

Consequently, we have a right to speak solely of the inevitable withering away of the state, emphasising the protracted nature of this process and its dependence upon the rapidity of development of the *higher phase* of Communism; leaving quite open the question of lengths of time, or the concrete forms of withering away, since material for the solution of such questions is *not available*.

.   .   .   .

... it has never entered the head of any Socialist to "promise" that the highest phase of Communism will arrive; ... the great Socialists, in *foreseeing* its arrival, presupposed both a productivity of labour unlike the present and a person not like the present man in the street, capable of spoiling, without reflection ... the stores of social wealth, and of demanding the impossible.[9]

On the other hand, Lenin was quite willing to dictate the means by which the Communist goal was to be reached. He accordingly left the Communists a number of texts—all making clear that it could only be attained by the most severe repression employed against every class, including even the proletarians themselves. Thus, he wrote in the same tract, *State and Revolution*, that to reach the "highest phase of Communism" it was necessary for the "present man in the street" to be "reeducated" and "remoulded" by a "special machinery for suppression"[10]—the "dictatorship of the proletariat." And in *"Left-Wing" Communism*, written in April, 1920, he asserted:

The abolition of classes not only means driving out the landlords and capitalists—that we accomplished with comparative ease—it also means *abolishing the small commodity producers*, and they *cannot be driven out*, or crushed; . . . they can (and must) be remoulded and reeducated. . . .[11]

And after his death, Stalin wrote (quoting him) in *Foundations of Leninism* (April, 1924):

Under the dictatorship of the proletariat we will have to reeducate "millions of peasants and petty proprietors, hundreds of thousands of employes, officials and bourgeois intellectuals"; to subordinate "all these to the proletarian state and to proletarian leadership"; to overcome "their bourgeois habits and traditions . . ." just as much as it will be necessary ". . . to reeducate in a protracted struggle, on the basis of the dictatorship of the proletariat, the proletarians themselves. . . ."[12]

This process of "remoulding" of course precluded any thought of personal freedom or self-government. As Lenin said, the very "concept" of the "dictatorship of the proletariat" was inconsistent with freedom:

The class which has seized political power has done so conscious of the fact that it has seized power alone. This is implicit in the concept of the dictatorship of the proletariat. This concept has meaning only when one class knows that it alone takes political power into its own hands, and does not deceive either itself or others by talk about popular, elected government, sanctified by the whole people.[13]

"While the state exists," Lenin said, "there is no freedom. When there is freedom, there will be no state."[14]

At one time, Lenin apparently believed that the oppression required during the period of "transition from capitalism to Communism" would be less severe than the exertion of police power required in an ordinary "bourgeois" state. Thus, he wrote, in *State and Revolution*, that "the suppression of the minority of exploiters . . . is a matter comparatively so easy, simple and natural that it will cost far less bloodshed than the suppression of the risings of slaves, serfs or wage labourers, and will cost mankind far less. . . ." "The exploiters," he explained, "are, naturally, unable to suppress the people without a most complex machinery for performing this task; but *the people* can suppress the exploiters even with very simple 'machinery,' almost without any 'machinery,' without any special apparatus, by the simple organisation of the armed masses. . . ."[15]

Lenin's views changed, however, after the seizure of power. He discovered that the "landlords and capitalists" could not be driven out as easily as he had thought, and that even the "proletarians themselves" were not anxious to be "remoulded." Accordingly, in *"Left-Wing" Communism* he described the "dictatorship of the proletariat" as "war" against the people—a "ruthless" war against a *"more powerful* enemy":

The dictatorship of the proletariat is a most determined and ruthless war waged by the new class against a *more powerful* enemy, the bourgeoisie, whose resistance is increased *tenfold* by its overthrow (even if only in one country) . . . . victory over the bourgeoisie is impossible without a long, stubborn and desperate war of life and death, a war demanding perseverance, discipline, firmness, indomitableness and unity of will.

I repeat, the experience of the victorious dictatorship of the proletariat in Russia has clearly shown even to those who are unable to think, or who have not had occasion to ponder over this question, that absolute centralisation and the strictest discipline of the proletariat constitute one of the fundamental conditions for victory over the bourgeoisie.[16]

But at the same time, just as in the case of the "war" with the capitalist states—it was necessary for the Communists to make concessions, to use economic inducements as well as armed force, peaceful means as well as violent, and to be able to "retreat" as well as to "attack." "The transition from capitalism to communism," Lenin said, would require "an entire historical epoch."[17] It called for "very prolonged, slow, cautious organisational work," and "a party capable of watching and influencing the mood of the masses"—of "taking advantage of every, even the smallest, opportunity of gaining a mass ally, even though this ally be temporary, vacillating, unstable, unreliable and conditional."[18] Compromise would therefore have to be mixed with compulsion, and the party program, even though in-exorable, could not be pushed beyond the point of maximum endurance.

Lenin's definition of the "dictatorship of the proletariat" thus became a mixture of opposites. It was to be "a persistent struggle—sanguinary and bloodless, violent and peaceful, military and economic, educational and administrative—against the forces and traditions of the old society."[19] "We have got to understand," Lenin wrote, " (and a revolutionary class learns this by bitter experience) that victory can only be won by those who have learned the proper method both of advance and retreat."[20]

Lenin denounced the desire of the "Left" German Communists to "leap" from the "eve of the collapse of capitalism" to the "highest phase of Communism." The Bolsheviks themselves, he pointed out, even after three years of "revolution" in Russia, were still struggling in the "first steps" of the "lowest stage":

From the standpoint of Communism, the repudiation of the party principle means leaping from the eve of the collapse of capital-ism (in Germany), not to the lowest or intermediate, but to the highest phase of Communism. We in Russia (in the third year since the overthrow of the bourgeoisie) are taking the first steps in the transition from capitalism to Socialism, or the lowest stage of Com-munism.[21]

Likewise, Stalin, in his lectures on the *Foundations of Leninism,* ridiculed those who sought to attain the "highest phase" with " 'super-revolutionary' deeds and decrees":

It need hardly be emphasised that there is not the slightest pos-sibility of accomplishing these tasks in a short period of time, within a few years. We must, therefore, regard the dictatorship of the proleta-riat, the transition from capitalism to communism, not as a fleeting period replete with "superrevolutionary" deeds and decrees, but as an entire historical epoch full of civil wars and external conflicts, of persistent organisational work and economic construction, of attacks and retreats, of victories and defeats.[22]

In a pamphlet on *Problems of Leninism* (January, 1926), Stalin sought to draw the balance between the "coercive aspect of the dictatorship" and its "peaceful, organisational and cultural work":

During the period of civil war, the coercive aspect of the dictatorship is especially conspicuous. But it by no means follows from this that no constructive work is carried on during the period of civil war. The civil war itself cannot be waged without constructive work. On the contrary, during the period of socialist construction, the peaceful, organisational and cultural work of the dictatorship, revolutionary law, etc., are especially conspicuous. But here again it by no means follows that during the period of construction, the coercive side of the dictatorship has fallen away, or can fall away. The organs of suppression, the army and other organisations are as necessary now in the period of construction as they were during the civil war period.[23]

This statement, almost six years after the termination of the "civil war period," was Stalin's explanation of the "zigzag" Soviet policy of unending civil war—the "persistent struggle—sanguinary and bloodless, violent and peaceful, military and economic." Like the others, it would seem to demonstrate clearly enough that so long as the Communists remain in power the subject peoples can no more count upon liberation by an apparently "irreversible trend" toward "more personal freedom," or to "more enjoyment of the fruits of their labor," than the free world can rely for its security on such moderating "trends" in the "readily reversible" Soviet foreign policy. Every "retreat"—every period of temporary relaxation—must inevitably be followed by a new period of repression—a further "advance" along the difficult "road to Socialism."

If this was not sufficiently evident from the statements of the Communists themselves, it has been proven by experience. Ever since their first seizure of power, the use of intermittent "soft" policies and "concessions" has been as much a deliberate part of the Communists' internal policy as the use of terror and repression, and, together with the "inherent weakness" of their system, has been evoking perennial prophecies of their early demise. During that period they have made innumerable benevolent gestures to the subject peoples, repeatedly granting "new" freedoms and periodically "relaxing" internal as well as international "tensions." Just as they have always been abandoning their aims of world revolution, and renouncing the use of violence against the free nations, so have they also been "terminating" every form of domestic oppression, "democratizing" their dictatorial regime and even "discarding" the harsh and impractical economic theories of strict Marxian communism. But each Soviet concession was only introduced, as Stalin said, to "ensure" the ultimate "victory of Socialism."[24] It has been aptly stated by a Soviet specialist in the United States Department of Agriculture that every "tightening of the collective screw" is bound to increase discontent; and that the Kremlin "has usually been willing to open the safety valve just enough to prevent an explosion, resuming the collectivist offensive as soon as the danger of open revolt has passed."[25]

And in the meantime, just as in the case of every Soviet demand for "peace," there has been a corresponding renewed expectation—in the free world—of a "change" in the Soviet system. But over the years the only real or lasting change has been the gradual, inexorable closing of the Socialist vice, and the slow, determined eradication of every nonconforming custom, thought, emotion, institution, and source of inspiration.

Political and Economic "Concessions"

One of the first openings of the safety valve occurred in November, 1918, at the height of the first Red terror. At that time, on the first anniversary of the Bolshevik seizure of power, the Sixth All-Russian Congress of Soviets ordered an "amnesty" for hostages and other persons held without charge, adopted a decree "On Revolutionary Legality," and reportedly curbed the excesses of the Cheka with orders for "strict observance" of law. In February, 1919, the power of the Cheka was further "restricted"; and in April, 1919, there was still another "amnesty." At the same time, the Bolsheviks assumed a more placatory attitude toward the less hostile factions of two opposition parties, the Mensheviks and Social Revolutionaries. Decrees excluding these parties from the All-Russian Central Executive Committee were annulled, and in November, 1919, they were admitted to the Seventh All-Russian Congress of Soviets.

The illusion of change was at this time so great that in March, 1919, the secret American peace mission reported that the "destructive phase of the revolution" was "over." "All the energy of the Government" had been "turned to constructive work," it said, and the "terror" had "ceased." In further amplification of this, the report continued: "All power of judgment has been taken away from the Extraordinary Commission for Suppression of the Counter-Revolution [the Cheka], which now merely accuses suspected counter-revolutionaries who are tried by the regular, established, legal tribunals. Executions are extremely rare. Good order has been established. The streets are safe."[26]

No "irreversible" trend occurred, however, and the concessions made were illusory. In the Congresses of Soviets the two opposition groups were given only nominal representation, without the right to vote; and in 1921, they were subjected to mass arrests which soon made them virtually extinct. In 1922, the leaders of the Social Revolutionary Party were publicly tried and sentenced—fourteen of them to death. In the meantime, the activities of the Cheka persisted. As Lenin said, nine months after the peace mission's report, "both terror and the Cheka are absolutely indispensable."[27] They continued to be "indispensable," moreover, in spite of the fact that the Cheka and its successors were many times thereafter "eliminated" or "curbed" with official professions of "return" to "revolutionary legality."

Thus, in February, 1922, the Cheka was "abolished," only to be replaced, in the same decree, by the G.P.U. This action was taken pursuant to a resolution of the Ninth All-Russian Congress of Soviets calling for "strengthening" of "the principles of revolutionary legality."[28] In 1934, the G.P.U. was in its turn abolished in favor of the N.K.V.D. *Izvestia* then reported that "the proletarian dictatorship" could "change its methods of struggle and turn in a large degree to legal methods."[29] It was the "new" organ, however, which was responsible for the Great Purge in 1934-38; and according to Khrushchev, that episode was "the most brutal violation of socialist legality":

... Stalin had sanctioned in the name of the Central Committee of the All-Union Communist Party (Bolsheviks) the most brutal violation of socialist legality, torture and oppression, which led as we have seen to the slandering and self-accusation of innocent people.[30]

The Great Purge was followed in turn by the Great Change. The head of the N.K.V.D., Nikolai Yezhov, was executed along with many more of its high officials, and Lavrenti Beria was appointed in his place to "purge the purgers." Thousands of prisoners were released, and prison conditions were vastly improved, but none of the "changes" made prevented the "monstrous" acts and "rude violations of the basic Leninist principles" which the Communists themselves assert were committed during World War II.[31] Neither did they preclude the mass deportation of Poles and Baltic peoples, or the deportation of hundreds of thousands of repatriated war prisoners, refugees and other persons "tainted" by their wartime contacts with the western European nations.

There were further retreats in the economic field. Like the "end" of the terror and the "reconciliation" with the Mensheviks and Social Revolutionaries, the first of such concessions to capitalism also found its way to mention in the report of the Bullitt peace mission. In this case it was asserted (even in 1919!) that Lenin was making "compromises" and "concessions" in the matter of profits and private property, and executing a general "retreat" from the Communist "theoretical" position "all along the line":

> Lenin, indeed, as a practical matter, stands well to the right in the existing political life of Russia. He recognizes the undesirability, from the Socialist viewpoint, of the compromises he feels compelled to make; but he is ready to make the compromises. Among the more notable concessions he has already made are: the abandonment of his plan to nationalize the land and the adoption of the policy of dividing it among the peasants, the establishment of savings banks paying three percent interest, the decision to pay all foreign debts, and the decision to give concessions if that shall prove to be necessary to obtain credit abroad.
>
> In a word, Lenin feels compelled to retreat from his theoretical position all along the line.[32]

At the end of 1920, however, the land was still nationalized and the right to use it was exercised at state direction. It was neither transferable nor subject to lease, and the hiring of labor was prohibited. Other decrees had nationalized all business enterprises employing more than ten persons (five if mechanical power was used). Work was compulsory, strikes were out of the question, and labor unions had become another "organ" of "state power." At the same time, forced requisitions and restrictions on private trading had so discouraged the farmers that only half the prewar area was under cultivation. Consumer goods were unavailable, and the farmers refused to produce beyond their own needs. The result was famine and a new "retreat" in 1921.

This retreat was introduced by Lenin at the Tenth Congress of the Communist Party (March, 1921), and bore a strong resemblance to the "new look" introduced by Malenkov and Khrushchev in 1953. It was called the "New Economic Policy" (N.E.P.) and was sometimes referred to as the "New Course"—a term later applied to the economic phases of the "new look." Just as it is now believed that there is "a trend in the Soviet Union" to "somewhat greater enjoyment by people of the fruits of their labor,"[33] the decree which launched the New Economic Policy promised a "freer use by the farmer of the products of his labor and of his economic resources." The "requisition" was "replaced" with a "tax in kind," and it was stated that all "reserves of food, raw material and fodder which remain with the peasants after the tax has been paid are at their full disposition...." These could be used "for improving and strengthening their holdings, for increasing personal consumption and for exchange for products of factory and hand industry and of agriculture."[34] Even the "tax in kind" would eventually be decreased—"as our industry... makes progress"[35]—and consumerism was a principal feature of the plan. According to the decree, "a steady state reserve fund" of "objects of general consumption" was "being created." It included "both domestic products and goods purchased abroad."[36] Pursuant to a further decree, issued in May, 1922, each community was to adopt its own form of land tenure, and the members of the collective farms were allowed to withdraw. Within prescribed limits the leasing of land and hiring of labor were also permitted.[37]

For the "small commodity producers," the New Economic Policy had even more startling concessions. Formerly, these harbingers of "disunity" and "individualism" had been condemned by Lenin as "encircling" the proletariat "with a petty-bourgeois atmosphere, which permeates and corrupts" and "causes constant relapses among the proletariat into petty-bourgeois spinelessness...."[38] Now he looked to them for assistance in the restoration of "state Socialist production." "Our poverty and ruin are so great," Lenin explained, "that we cannot restore large-scale, factory, state Socialist production *at one stroke* ... it is necessary, to a certain extent, to help to restore *small* industry, which does not need machines, does not need either state reserves or large stocks of raw material, fuel and food, and which can immediately render some assistance to peasant farming and increase its productive forces." "We must not be afraid," he added, "of Communists 'learning' from bourgeois specialists, including merchants, small capitalist cooperators and capitalists; of learning from them in the same way as we learnt from the military experts.... Do not begrudge the price for 'tuition'; no price for tuition will be too high if only we learn intelligently."[39]

Private enterprise in small industry and in the marketing of consumer goods was accordingly encouraged. Establishments not yet taken over by the state were declared to "belong to the former owners,"[40] and many rights of private property were confirmed. These included the "right to the possession of buildings," "moveable property connected with factories, workshops, commercial and industrial undertakings," "tools and the means of production," the "products of agriculture and industry," "articles of domestic utility and articles of personal use"; the "right" of "building upon urban and country sites for a period fixed by law"; the "right to mortgage or pledge"; the "right to inventions, copyright, trade marks," "industrial models and drawings"; the "right of inheritance, by testament or law, by husbands or wives or direct offspring, to the limit of 10,000 gold rubles"; and the right to "conclude all manner of contracts."[41] Nationalized concerns were leased for private operation, and foreign capital was eagerly solicited. In order to relieve the famine-stricken areas, foreign agencies, including the American Relief Administration and even a Papal Relief Mission, were admitted.

In the light of these events, it was easy to assume, outside the Soviet Union, that communism had finally come to its predicted and timely end. *The New York Times* reported that Lenin had "thrown communism overboard."[42] The official reaction was more restrained, but it was almost identical with the reaction to the "new look" thirty years later. President Coolidge stated, in December, 1923: "Already encouraging evidences of returning to the ancient ways of society can be detected. But more are needed."[43]

The "ancient ways," however, did not return completely, and the policy of "liberalization" soon ended. Lenin did not hesitate, in fact, even while making these concessions, to announce his real purpose—frequently and openly asserting that the New Economic Policy was only a retreat. He thus explained, at the Eleventh Party Congress (April, 1922), the decision which had been made at the Tenth:

When, during the spring of 1921, the vanguard of the revolution was in danger of becoming isolated from the masses of the people, from the masses of the peasants, whom it must skillfully lead forward, we unanimously and firmly decided to retreat. And on the whole, during the past year, we retreated in good revolutionary order.[44]

He was even more specific at a plenum of the Moscow Soviet in November, 1922. Stalin quotes him as follows:

We are now retreating, going back as it were; but we are doing this in order first to retreat and then to get a better run for a bigger leap foward. This was the only condition on which we agreed to retreat in pursuing our New Economic Policy. We do not yet know where and how we must regroup, adapt and reorganize our forces in order to start our persistent advance after our retreat. In order to carry out all these operations in proper order we must, as the proverb says, measure not ten times, but a hundred times before we decide.[45]

At the time these statements were made, they were not taken very seriously in the free world. Many regarded them merely as transparent efforts to cover up the "failure" of communism. But there was more inclination to take them seriously when the policy which they decribed was confirmed—sixteen years later—in the "official" history of the Communist Party:

Neither the delay of the revolution in the West, nor the partial stabilization of capitalism in the non-Soviet countries could stop our advance—to Socialism. The New Economic Policy could only make this task easier, for it had been introduced by the Party with the specific purpose of facilitating the laying of a Socialist foundation for our economic system.[46]

By that time the New Economic Policy had been replaced by two Five-Year Plans of Economic (Socialist) Development, the vast majority of peasants had been driven into collective farms, and Lenin's intentions as well as his shrewdness had been thoroughly vindicated.

In the meantime, however, the belief that communism was abandoned had been further confirmed by the events which followed Lenin's death. The "liberal" policies of his successor, J. V. Stalin, were even more extravagantly "democratic" than those of Stalin's successors, Malenkov and Khrushchev; and as in their case, they also featured heavily in the transitional struggle for power. Almost the only difference in the tactics used was that in those days the "hard" Communists were called "leftists" instead of "rightists," and the "soft" Communists were called "rightists," "opportunists" and "deviationists," instead of "leftists" or "revisionists."

As Stalin moved against the "leftists," of whom Trotsky was the principal figure, the New Economic Policy was continued and even expanded. Taxes were reduced or annulled, and a temporary return of land to private ownership was announced. An "amnesty" was granted to those who had opposed the Bolsheviks in the Civil War.

In the effusion of his "moderation," Stalin even rejected proposals for Trotsky's expulsion from the party. Instead he demanded strict adherence to the principle of "collective leadership," stating (December, 1925) that the death of Lenin had made this imperative. "The Party cannot be led except collectively," he said. "Now that Ilyich [Vladimir Ilyich Lenin] is not with us it is silly to dream of such a thing. . . ." "Collective work, collective leadership, unity in the Party, unity in the organs of the Central Committee on the condition that the minority submits to the majority—that," Stalin said, "is what we need now."[47]

The free world reaction to these events was mirrored in the press. *The New York Times* described the "promised reforms" as the "greatest step" away from Marxism since the creation of the Bolshevik regime:

These promised reforms, which are expected on account of the recent concessions granted to private capital, are considered the greatest step the Soviet Government has made toward the abolition of Marxist dreams since the Government was formed in 1917.

Great importance is attached to the promises as coming from Stalin, who is the Communist Party chief and successor to the power formerly held by Lenin.[48]

The *London Daily Express* called these "steps" the greatest since the adoption of the New Economic Policy:

. . . the slogan in Russia today has become "State capitalism." Not since the acceptance of Lenin's new economic policy three years ago have the Soviet leaders taken such a decided step on the road away from militant communism.[49]

In January, 1926, Stalin published his pamphlet on *Problems of Leninism*, in which he quoted at length from Lenin's writings and speeches to show the need of alliance with the "non-proletarian strata of toilers," the "petty bourgeoisie, the small masters, the peasantry, the intelligentsia, etc." He singled out the peasants in particular. *"Nothing but an agreement with the peasants,"* Stalin insisted, "can save the socialist revolution in Russia until the revolution has taken place in other countries."[50]

In the following year, however, at the Fifteenth Congress of the Communist Party, Stalin called for a return to collectivization, war against the kulaks ("rich" peasants) and the adoption of the First Five-Year Plan. He indicated, moreover, that the New Economic Policy was already drawing to a close. In particular, the "new bourgeoisie," or "NEPmen," he said, had "no reason to be pleased with the Soviet regime." "Thousands" of "small manufacturers" had already been "proletarianized"; other "thousands" of "small and medium shops" had been "closed"; and "tens of thousands of small and medium capitalists" were "being ruined." The "discontent" of such people, Stalin said, was definitely not "accidental"—it "has its roots in life":

Progress in our industry, progress in our trading and cooperative organizations, and improvement of our state apparatus is progress and improvement for the benefit of the working class, for the benefit of the bulk of the peasantry, but to the detriment of the new bourgeoisie, to the detriment of the middle strata generally and of the urban middle strata in particular. Is it to be wondered at that discontent with the Soviet regime is growing among these strata? Hence the counterrevolutionary moods among these people.[51]

At the same time, Stalin regarded as a "favorable factor" the "passing of hundreds and thousands" of these "new bourgeoisie" to "the side of the Soviet regime."

In the case of the peasants, the Soviets announced a "crisis in grain production," and began the drive for collectivization with the confiscation of accumulated surpluses. In July, 1928, an editorial in *The New York Times*, captioned " 'Zigzag' Soviet Policy," commented: "Last Winter and again in the late Spring, when grain collections fell off disastrously, the authorities resorted to 'extraordinary measures' against the peasants, so that Stalin's agrarian policy was quite as severe as Trotsky himself could have asked for."[52]

This, however, was only the beginning. By June, 1930, when Stalin reported to the Sixteenth Congress, more than half of the peasants were in collective farms, and he asserted that the "dictatorship of the proletariat" had passed "to the decisive offensive along the whole front":

The bulk of the peasant masses has definitely turned towards the kolkhozes [collective farms]. The resistance of the kulaks has been broken.

.   .   .   .

In passing to the offensive along the whole front, we do not yet abolish NEP, for private trade and the capitalist elements still remain, "free" trade still remains—but we are certainly abolishing the initial stage of NEP, while developing its next stage, the present stage, which is the last stage of NEP.[53]

Stalin himself subsequently related that the drive against the peasants was a more "terrible struggle" than the war with the Axis powers,[54] and in this statement at least there can be little doubt of his sincerity. Before the drive was completed, ten million lives had been lost by murder and famine,[55] hundreds of thousands of people had been deported to Siberia and northern Russia, and whole villages had been bombed, burned and besieged by tanks. Yet even at the height of these outrages, Stalin counseled against "Dizziness from Success."

In this new warning against "superrevolutionary deeds and decrees" (published in *Pravda*, March 2, 1930), Stalin stated that "Collective farms cannot be set up by force." Claiming that the "success" of the "collective-farm movement" was due to its "voluntary character," he called in effect for another respite:

It is a fact that by February 20, this year, 50 per cent of the peasant farms of the U.S.S.R. had been collectivized. This means that by February 20, 1930, we had fulfilled the estimates of the Five-Year Plan more than twice over.

.   .   .   .

But successes also have their seamy side; especially when they are achieved with comparative "ease," "unexpectedly," so to speak. . . . People are often intoxicated by such successes, they become dizzy with success, they lose all sense of proportion, they lose the faculty of understanding realities, they reveal a tendency to overestimate their own strength and to underestimate the strength of the enemy. . . . In such cases care is not taken to consolidate the successes achieved and systematically to utilize them for the purpose of advancing further.[56]

Within a few days, decrees were issued calling for a "change":

All cases of enforced entry into collectives must immediately be revised and measures taken to punish persons responsible for such deviation from Communist party policy.[57]
Revise the cases of persons deprived of land and civil rights and

correct the errors in this respect committed upon middle peasants and former fighters for the Red cause. . . .[58]

As a result there was a mass exodus from the collective farms, and *The New York Times* reported that "tension among the non-proletarian elements has eased."[59] There was the usual speculation as to "whether Stalin's pronunciamento implies a genuine change of policy."[60] This time, however, such doubts were quickly set at rest. The drive was soon resumed, and three months later, at the Sixteenth Party Congress, Stalin said that "Only people who have lost their heads can seek a way out in Bukharin's childish formula about the capitalist elements peacefully growing into Socialism."[61] (Bukharin was the recently ousted leader of the "soft" Communists.)

This apparent inconsistency was a conscious application of the tactics of attack and retreat, as Stalin himself stated very clearly. In his treatise on "Dizziness from Success," Stalin had made plain his annoyance with "overzealous 'socializers'" who were "irritating the peasant" by socializing items of secondary importance. There was even some complaint about a "number of districts in Turkestan," where the use of "military force" and other Communist forms of coercion had been threatened. But Stalin was not opposed in principle to either force or speed. He was only interested in what he regarded as the most practical means of attaining his ends—the tested Leninist formula of "manoeuvring, temporising and compromising." In the same article he explained: "One must not lag behind the movement, because to do so is to become isolated from the masses. But neither must one rush ahead, for to rush ahead is to lose contact with the masses. He who wants to lead a movement and at the same time keep in touch with the vast masses must wage a fight on two fronts—against those who lag behind and against those who rush on ahead."[62]

Stalin was even more explicit in his report to the Sixteenth Party Congress (June, 1930):

Some comrades think that the chief thing in the offensive of Socialism are measures of repression, that if there are no increasing measures of repression there is no offensive.

Is this true? It is not true, of course.

Measures of repression in the sphere of socialist development are a necessary element of the offensive, but an auxiliary, not the chief element. The chief thing in the offensive of Socialism under our present conditions is to speed up the rate of development of our industry, to speed up the rate of sovkhoz [state farm] and kolkhoz [collective farm] development, to speed up the rate of the economic elimination of the capitalist elements in town and country, to mobilize the masses around socialist development, to mobilize the masses against capitalism. You may arrest and deport tens and hundreds of thousands of kulaks, but if you do not at the same time do what is necessary to speed up the development of the new forms of farming, to substitute the new forms of farming for the old, capitalist forms, to undermine and liquidate the production sources of the economic existence and development of the capitalist elements in the rural districts—the kulaks will revive and grow.

Others think that the offensive of Socialism means just pushing forward, without proper preparation, without regrouping forces in the course of the offensive, without consolidating positions already captured, without utilizing reserves to develop successes, and that if signs have appeared of, say, an efflux from the kolkhozes of a section of the peasantry it means the "ebb of the revolution," the decline of the movement, the cessation of the offensive.

Is this true? It is not true, of course.

Firstly, no offensive, even the most successful, can proceed without some checks and breaches of the line on individual sections of the front. To argue, on these grounds, that the offensive has stopped, or has failed, reveals failure to understand the essence of an offensive.

Secondly, there has never been, nor can there be, a *successful* offensive without a regrouping of forces in the course of the offensive, without the consolidation of captured positions, without the utilization of reserves for developing success and for carrying the offensive through to the end. Just pushing forward, i.e., without abiding by these conditions, the offensive must inevitably peter out and fail. Just pushing forward means death to the offensive. This is proved by the wealth of experience of our Civil War.[63]

For the benefit of the delegates Stalin described what would have happened if he had followed either the too-slow policies of the "rightists" or the too-fast policies of the "leftists":

What would have happened had we heeded the Right opportunists in the Bukharin group, had we refrained from launching the offensive, had we slowed down the rate of development of industry, had we retarded the development of kolkhozes and sovkhozes and had we based ourselves on individual peasant farming?

We would certainly have wrecked our industry, we would have sealed the doom of the socialist reconstruction of agriculture, we would have been left without bread, and we would have cleared the way for the predominance of the kulaks. We would have been stranded.

What would have happened had we heeded the "Left" opportunists in the Trotsky-Zinoviev group and have launched the offensive in 1926-27, when we had no means whatever of substituting kolkhoz and sovkhoz production for kulak production?

We would certainly have met with failure in this matter, we would have demonstrated our weakness, we would have strengthened the position of the kulaks and of the capitalist elements generally, we would have pushed the middle peasants into the embrace of the kulaks, we would have disrupted our socialist development and would have been left without bread. We would have been stranded.[64]

Certainly, there was nothing here to indicate that "concessions" were "irreversible," or even difficult to "erase." On the contrary, Stalin's tactics were eminently successful, and the "zigzag" continued. In January, 1931, another speed-up was ordered, to advance the collectivization of the "poor middle class peasants" and "to realize the liquidation of the kulaks as a class."[65] In June, 1931, there was a new decree permitting withdrawal from the collective farms. Subsequent decrees formalized the right of collective farmers to maintain small private garden plots, to own a limited number of cattle, and even to sell their returns, if any, on a free market.[66] But in 1933, withdrawal from the farms was again forbidden; and by 1936, approximately 90% of all peasant households had been collectivized.

After World War II there was a new drive—to collectivize the collective farms. By the end of 1952, a total of 252,000 collective farms had been merged into 97,000 giant ones, and in the process many of the "private plots" were reduced or lost altogether. The prime mover in this second-stage campaign was the well-known "liberal" Communist Nikita S. Khrushchev, who now maintains that it was the "anti-party group" of Molotov, Malenkov and Kaganovich who deprived the Russian peasant of his incentive to increase production.[67] After the consolidation of his own power as Stalin's successor, Khrushchev proposed even a third stage. This included the "voluntary" collectivization of the limited amount of livestock and garden plots which were still privately owned,[68] and other advances in so-called "communal" living. As he told the Central Committee in December, 1958, the time had come to "organize, not only in towns but also in collective farms, communal dining halls, laundries, bakeries and nurseries."[69]

The same mixture of coercion and "persuasion" has also been used successfully in the collectivization of farms in Communist China[70] —where "soft" Communists are still called "rightists" instead of "leftists." In 1955, when the Chinese drive was intensified, the Seventh Central Committee condemned the "rightist tendency within the Party" of "allowing capitalism to develop freely in the rural areas," but at the same time asserted that "No attempt should be made to violate the principle of voluntariness. . . ." Going either "too fast" or "too slow," it said, was not Marxism but "opportunism":

The working method of the leadership should be to learn from the mass movement, become familiar with the real circumstances, sum up experiences, and guide the movement with flexibility. Ignorance coupled with unwillingness to learn, issuing orders at random, and sometimes going too fast and sometimes too slow—all these violate the law of the actual development of the movement. . . .

The task of the leadership should be to respect and elicit the masses' creativeness and initiative and protect the growing forces. To impede and hit out against the growth of new things in society when they first emerge instead of giving them wholehearted help, or to try to bring about the new things artificially, in an impetuous and rash way, before the conditions are ripe, rather than taking appropriate measures to promote their natural birth—both measures will injure the tender buds. They are opportunism, not Marxism. There can be no leadership without fighting against such opportunism.[71]

By April, 1956, some 56% of peasant households in China had been collectivized. The 90% figure was reached in 1957. Thus, China was apparently able, within eight years, to "leap" to the same stage of communism which it took nineteen years to attain in the Soviet Union. In 1958, the year of the "great leap forward," it was reported that the Soviet Union was being surpassed by the creation of giant *communes* in which agricultural labor was to be organized "along military lines," the peasants deprived of their small garden plots and remaining livestock, and even private households were "apparently destined to disappear." And by the end of that year, it was asserted, 99% of the rural households had been organized into such communes.[72]

Nevertheless, the Chinese "cadres" and "activists," like their Soviet counterparts, had been warned frequently against acting in the "absence of free will of peasants."[73] Prior to the organization of the communes, they had been enjoined "to apply strictly the principles of voluntarism";[74] and, as in the case of the Soviet Union, "free markets" were organized for the sale of Chinese peasant surpluses, if any. Members of the Chinese collective farms were also for some time permitted to retain their small plots of garden land, poultry, livestock and small tools.[75]

After the decision to organize communes, similar tactics were employed. This drive had scarcely begun when the cadres were cautioned not to be too hasty,[76] and after six months the Central Committee issued a long directive calling for a slowdown.[77] This included temporary postponement in the urban areas and Tibet, "consolidation" in the rural areas, and a repetition of Stalin's warning that "over-eager" Communists were prone to become "dizzy with success." It was necessary, the committee said, to dispel the fear that *all* private property, such as houses, clothing, furniture and bank deposits would have to be surrendered.

In the Soviet Union, when the main collective-farm drive was nearing completion, new "concessions" were made in the field of civil rights. In spite of Lenin's injunction that the new ruling class should not "deceive either itself or others by talk about popular, elected government," a new Soviet "Constitution" was adopted (December 5, 1936), described by Stalin as "the only thoroughly democratic Constitution in the world."[78] It guaranteed not only the "right to work" but also "the right to rest and leisure," and it provided that "all citizens" should have the right to vote, "irrespective of race or nationality, sex, religion, education, domicile, social origin, property status or past activities." There was so much talk abroad about the new departure from Bolshevism that even Stalin complained:

The fourth group of critics attacking the Draft New Constitution describes it as "swing to the right," as "renunciation of a dictatorship of the proletariat," as "liquidation of the Bolshevik regime." "The Bolsheviks have swung to the right, it is a fact," they say in various voices. Certain Polish and some American newspapers display a particular zeal in this respect. What can be said about these critics, if they can be so styled?[79]

The only thing that Stalin could say was that these critics did not "know the difference between left and right." For those seeking peace and freedom, this "Stalinist" joke was devoid of humor, but it was an expression of truth nevertheless—a harsh truth cutting off even the hope of assistance from the free world.

There was also a "group of critics" who were unable to see any departure from Bolshevism. They put "the charge that the draft makes no change in the existing position . . . that it leaves the dictatorship of the working class intact" and that it "does not provide for the freedom of political parties." For this group Stalin had a ready answer—the "charge" was correct:

I must admit that the Draft New Constitution really does leave in force the regime of the dictatorship of the working class and also leaves unchanged the present leading position of the Communist Party. . . .

. . . Several parties, and consequently freedom of parties, can only exist in a society where there are antagonistic classes whose interests are hostile and irreconcilable, where there are, say, capitalists and workers, landlords and peasants, kulaks and poor peasants, and so on. But in the U.S.S.R. there are no longer such classes as capitalists, landlords, kulaks and so on. There are only two classes in the U.S.S.R., workers and peasants, whose interests are not only not antagonistic, but on the contrary, are amicable. Consequently, in the U.S.S.R. there is no ground for the existence of several parties, nor therefore, for the existence of freedom for such parties.[80]

The liquidations had apparently been completed. As Stalin might say, this was clear, "one would think"—except for the fact that the Great Purge had already begun. In his own account of this purge, Khrushchev credibly asserts that "the number of arrests based on charges of counterrevolutionary crimes" grew "10 times between 1936 and 1937."[81]

In the meantime, however, Stalin set about to prove his point that only one party was necessary, and, in 1937, conducted a nationwide "election" under the procedures prescribed in the new "Constitution." There was no choice of candidates, and "write-ins" were invalid, but ballots were cast by 96% of the eligible voters. More than 98% were valid and affirmative. Similar results were obtained in 1938, 1939 and 1946. Finally, in the "elections" of 1950, ballots were cast by 99.98% of the eligible voters, and 99.72% of these were valid and affirmative. For some reason, no one argued that such "elections" were a sign of a "trend" to "democracy."

Stalin, however, put on a real "democratization" campaign. In preparation for the 1937 "elections," he even ordered the party to "democratize" itself, and to "establish the closest contact" with "the people, the masses." Personal adulation was disapproved, and Stalin, the arch-villain of the "cult of personality," stated: "We the leaders should not be conceited. We should not think that if we are members of the Central Committee or people's commissars we possess all the knowledge necessary to give correct leadership. Rank in itself gives neither knowledge nor experience."[82] More of the same took place during World War II, with the effects on world opinion described in Chapter VII. One official visitor reported in 1943: "If they keep going as they are you'll find Russia coming out of this war the greatest democracy in the world. . . ."[83]

"Collapse" Through Internal Dissension

Hopes of effortless liberation have also been inspired by the frequent purges of high party officials and other evidence of internal dissension which might lead to the collapse of Communist power. But according to Stalin, who ought to know, "the weeding out of spies, assassins and wreckers" from the "Soviet organizations was bound to lead, and did lead," not to their self-destruction but to their "further strengthening."[84]

Dissension was not, in fact, unusual among the Bolsheviks. There were disagreements over the seizure of power itself, which was opposed, and even prematurely exposed, by Kamenev and Zinoviev—two of the leading members of the Central Committee. (Zinoviev subsequently became chairman of the Communist International.) As Stalin told the Central Committee in 1927, these two aspirants to "the privileged position of nobles in the Party" were "driven to the insurrection with a stick." "You know," he said, "that Kamenev and Zinoviev were driven to the insurrection with a stick. Lenin drove them with a stick, threatening them with expulsion from the Party (*laughter, applause*) and they were forced to hobble to the insurrection. (*Laughter, applause.*)"[85] Kamenev resigned from the Central Committee, but he returned the day before the seizure of power.

There was further disagreement among the party leaders on the composition of the Commissariat of People's Commissars (the cabinet). Many insisted upon coalition with the Mensheviks and Social Revolutionaries, even if it meant the exclusion of Lenin and Trotsky. When the Central Committee decided in favor of Lenin, five members resigned, including Kamenev, Zinoviev and Rykov, a future Premier. All were threatened with expulsion from the party, and soon recanted.

In the dispute on peace with Germany, even Lenin threatened to resign. His proposals were defeated several times in the Central Committee, and he prevailed (by the narrow vote of seven to six) only when the Germans seemed ready to wipe out the "revolution" entirely. When the German terms were accepted (by a vote of seven to four, with four abstaining) another member of the Central Committee resigned, openly attacking the majority decision in his own newspaper. This was Nikolai Bukharin, also a subsequent chairman of the Communist International.

Bukharin was reinstated, however, within a month, and the internal rifts appeared to heal. But Stalin and Trotsky were soon feuding over the defense of Tsaritsyn (Stalingrad), and there were myriads of other disputes. These related even to questions considered vital to the existence of the Bolshevik regime, such as the "right of secession" of the non-Russian nations, the suppression of the liberal party newspapers, the use of Czarist officers in the Red Army, the employment of "bourgeois" specialists, "one-man management" in industry, the status of the trade unions and, finally, the question of party "discipline" itself.

In August, 1918, Lenin was wounded by an assassin, and there were many reports thereafter of other plots against him, even by his closest associates. It was reported in 1919 that Trotsky had ordered Lenin to be arrested—because of his "moderation";[86] and in 1921, that a plot for his removal was being prepared by Trotsky, Bukharin and Dzerzhinsky.[87] Trotsky, on the other hand, suggested that Lenin's eventual death in 1924 was due to poisoning under Stalin's direction.[88]

Most of these early dissidents were later blamed by Stalin for everything that happened:

The trials [of the Great Purge] showed that these dregs of humanity, in conjunction with the enemies of the people, Trotsky, Zinoviev and Kamenev, had been in conspiracy against Lenin, the Party and the Soviet state ever since the early days of the October Socialist Revolution. The insidious attempts to thwart the Peace of

Brest-Litovsk at the beginning of 1918, the plot against Lenin and the conspiracy with the "Left" Socialist-Revolutionaries for the arrest and murder of Lenin, Stalin and Sverdlov in the Spring of 1918, the villainous shot that wounded Lenin in the summer of 1918, the revolt of the "Left" Socialist-Revolutionaries in the summer of 1918, the deliberate aggravation of differences in the Party in 1921 with the object of undermining and overthrowing Lenin's leadership from within, the attempts to overthrow the party leadership during Lenin's illness and after his death, the betrayal of state secrets and the supply of information of an espionage character to foreign espionage services, the vile assassination of Kirov, the acts of wrecking diversion and explosions, the dastardly murder of Menzhinsky, Kuibyshev and Gorky —all these and similar villainies over a period of twenty years were committed, it transpired, with the participation or under the direction of Trotsky, Zinoviev, Kamenev, Bukharin, Rykov and their henchmen, at the behest of espionage services of bourgeois states.[89]

It is difficult to imagine any more serious forms of dissension among top Communists, but the party survived nevertheless.

When these feuds were manifested in the post-Lenin struggle for power, the free nations were even more surprised than they were by the similar struggle during the post-Stalin period. Thus, in January, 1925, the *London Daily Express* reported:

> The quarrels of the "Big Seven"—Stalin, Kameneff, Zinovieff, Bukharin, Rykoff, Trotsky and Tomsky—of the Political Bureau were made public with a rush, and the gods of the Communist masses have been rudely torn from their pedestals and not by the enemies of government, but by these comrades.
>
> The result is that the brilliant teamwork of the last eight years has come to an end.
>
> The opposing leaders openly accuse each other of hypocrisy, falsehood, selfish personal ambition, intriguing against their colleagues and, most heinous of all, distortion of the doctrines of Lenin.[90]

One would certainly suppose that with all these troubles, the Communist system, if it were going to disintegrate at all, would have done so at this time. But nothing of the sort occurred. Within seven years after Lenin's death, all of these leaders except Stalin had been discredited. In 1927, Trotsky, Zinoviev and Kamenev were expelled from the party, along with a great many of their followers. Trotsky was sent to Alma-Ata, capital of remote Kazakhstan. In 1929, he was deported from the Soviet Union, and Bukharin was ousted from the Politburo. Rykov and Tomsky were reprimanded. In 1930, Rykov was replaced as Premier by Molotov.

None of these purges weakened the Soviet regime. With the exception of Trotsky, all of the ousted leaders were permitted to "recant" their errors, and were "rehabilitated." Likewise with the exception of Trotsky, all of them were subsequently shot, or committed suicide, in the Great Purge. Trotsky was murdered in exile.

The period of the Great Purge was another likely time for Communist self-destruction. Khrushchev asserts that 70% of the members and candidates of the Central Committee were arrested and shot, and "decidedly more than a majority" of the delegates to the Congress which elected it were arrested.[91] In 1925, Stalin himself had rejected such methods as "fraught with grave danger." Speaking in the Central Committee, he defended his lenience to Trotsky the year before: ". . . we knew that the lopping policy was fraught with grave danger for the Party, that the lopping method, the blood-letting method . . . was dangerous, contagious: today you lop off one, tomorrow another, the day after tomorrow a third—what will we have left in the party?"[92]

The party rule, however, did not appear to suffer from such methods, and in 1939 Stalin laughed at those who predicted weakening and "demoralization":

Certain foreign pressmen have been talking drivel to the effect that the purging of Soviet organizations of spies, assassins, and wreckers like Trotsky, Zinoviev, Kamenev, Yakir, Tukhachevsky, Rosengoltz, Bukharin and other fiends has "shaken" the Soviet system and caused its "demoralization." All this cheap drivel deserves is laughter and scorn. How can the purging of Soviet organizations of noxious and hostile elements shake and demoralize the Soviet system? . . . who needs this miserable band of venal slaves, of what value can they be to the people, and whom can they "demoralize"? In 1937, Tukhachevsky, Yakir, Uborevich and other fiends were sentenced to be shot. After that, the elections to the Supreme Soviet of the U.S.S.R. were held. In these elections, 98.6 per cent of the total vote was cast for the Soviet power. At the beginning of 1938 Rosengoltz, Rykov, Bukharin and other fiends were sentenced to be shot. After that, the elections to the Supreme Soviets of the Union Republics were held. In these elections, 99.4 per cent of the total vote was cast for the Soviet power. Where are the symptoms of "demoralization."

we would like to know, and why was this "demoralization" not reflected in the results of the elections?[93]

"Freedom" of Religion

The "tactics of retreat" were also employed in the "struggle against religion." According to Emelyan Yaroslavsky, president of the "League of Militant Atheists," the true Leninist was opposed to "rightist" and "leftist" trends in the promotion of atheism as well as in the development of other fields of communism—he "fought against the opportunist attempts to liquidate antireligious work on the pretext that religion is dying in the U.S.S.R. anyway"; and he also "fought resolutely against the theory that religion can be wiped out in no time. . . ."[94]

The result was what a French expert has aptly described as "a continuous and relentless campaign" carried on between "waves of extremism and outright persecution."[95] In between the waves there were the usual temporary "breathing spaces," in which "freedom of religion" was "restored," and atheistic "gains," like economic ones, were "consolidated." In such periods, although the drive slackened and visitors to the Soviet Union invariably reported that "the churches were crowded," there were few restorations of those already destroyed or converted to "state" uses, rarely any modification of the restrictions on moral and religious education, and never the release and "rehabilitation" of *all* the bishops, priests and teachers jailed or killed in the most recent "offensive."

It is reported that in 1920 many priests were released from prison and allowed to return to their parishes. By that time, however, all church property had been nationalized, lands confiscated and schools and seminaries turned over to the "Commissariat for Education." Religious instruction had been prohibited "in any state, public or private educational institution where general educational subjects are taught."[96] Many churches, monasteries and convents had already been destroyed or converted, and clergymen were deprived of the right to vote. Twenty-three bishops and twelve hundred priests had already been "liquidated."[97]

All of this was accomplished under decrees in which "liberty of conscience" was most strictly "guaranteed." One of these was the "Decree on the Separation of the Church from the State, and of the School from the Church." It provided in part:

2. It is unlawful to pass any local law or issue any decree whatsoever ... which will restrict or limit the liberty of conscience. ...
3. Every citizen may profess any religion he desires or profess no
religion; all laws disfranchising any citizen by reason of his profession
or non-profession of faith are hereby repealed.[98]

The first Soviet "Constitution" (adopted July 10, 1918) similarly
provided that: "For the purpose of insuring real freedom of conscience to the laboring people, the church is separated from the state
and the schools from the church, and all citizens are permitted the
liberty of religious or antireligious propaganda."[99]

A new campaign against the Church began in 1921. Any kind of
organized religious instruction for children under eighteen years of
age was prohibited; and in 1922, ostensibly "for the benefit of the
famine," the Soviets ordered the seizure of "the riches of churches of
all denominations in gold, silver and jewels whose requisition cannot
really injure the interests of the cult itself. ..."[100] Consecrated as well
as unconsecrated objects were taken, and more priests were arrested
for resisting. There were 231 public trials, among them the highly
publicized trial of Archbishop John Cieplak, leader of the Catholic
Church in Russia, who was first sentenced to death, then imprisonment, and finally expelled, and the Vicar-General, Msgr. Constantine
Budkiewicz, who was shot on Good Friday (March 30), 1923.

The Orthodox Church was attacked by the promotion of a schism
—the so-called "Living Church." The patriarch, Tikhon, was arrested, and the "Living Church" leaders summoned a conclave to deprive
him of his orders and office. "Reformist" priests and bishops were installed in the place of dissenters.

The people, however, did not accept this program and rejected
the schismatic clergymen. The "Living Church" itself was split into
various dissenting groups, such as the "Church Regenerate" and the
"Union of the Ancient Apostolic Churches."

As a result, the Bolsheviks were forced into a new "retreat."
Pravda announced that religion was "rooted in the peasantry much
deeper than Czarism," and that "great caution and wisdom" were required to "eradicate it."[101] Tikhon was released with a "confession"
and statement of "repentance," but still remained as patriarch. He
thereupon condemned the "Living Church," excommunicated its
leaders, and the actions of its bishops and priests were invalidated.

In May, 1924, the Central Committee announced its intention to revise the methods of combating "religious prejudices,"[102] and at the Thirteenth Congress of the Communist Party antireligious propaganda among the peasantry in any form was prohibited.[103] In July, Maxim Litvinov, then chief of Soviet legations abroad, sought an agreement with the papal nuncio in Germany, Msgr. Eugenio Pacelli (later Pope Pius XII).[104]

In the meantime, however, the Soviets were disorganizing church administration and exiling or imprisoning the hierarchy. After Tikhon's death, in April, 1925, his designated successor, the Metropolitan Peter, was exiled and an alleged "Testament" was published condemning "all association with the enemies of the Soviet government and all open or secret agitation against it."[105] Peter's designated successor, the Metropolitan Sergei, and a great number of other bishops were arrested. In the case of the Catholic Church, all of the episcopal sees had been rendered vacant by the end of 1923.

In spite of these continuing attacks upon the hierarchy, the illusion of religious freedom persisted for several years after Lenin's death. In 1926, an editorial in *The New York Times* asserted:

> Apparently we are witnessing, in the non-economic field, the after effects of the victory of the Stalin moderates over the Zinovieff militants at the recent Communist Congress. It was a victory for the policy of conciliation. . . . Stalin is ready to compromise with the facts of Russian life all along the line.[106]

Two days later, the *Times* had to report that a crowd of worshippers were fired upon by the O.G.P.U. In this single case nine persons were killed and fifteen wounded, because they resisted attempts to remove an ikon.

In March, 1927, Sergei was released from prison, apparently on the strength of his agreement to issue a declaration requiring all Russian Orthodox clergy, inside and outside the Soviet Union, to give their complete loyalty to the Soviet regime.[107] Many of the hierarchy protested and resigned, rather than co-operate, but they were imprisoned, exiled or shot for their pains. Still, there was plenty of evidence of "religious freedom." In December, 1927, it was even reported that one of the Protestant sects was permitted to print a new edition of the Bible,[108] a fact to be compared with the statement made by Secretary Dulles in 1956:

This year, for the first time since the Bolshevik revolution, the Christian Bible is being printed and sold in Russia.[109]

In 1928, a new drive began. All forms of "religious propaganda" were now prohibited. By 1930, all previous records for the use of open violence against priests, churches and congregations had been broken. In Odessa, for example, the local Soviet ordered the closing of *all* churches, chapels, meeting houses, and synagogues,[110] and it was reported in Minsk that *almost every rabbi* was arrested.[111] This campaign was indirectly aided by the simultaneous drive to collectivize the farms. In the process of collectivization, the peasants were deprived of the means to support the churches, and many of the priests were forced into collectives. Apparently, some of the "over-zealous 'socializers' " thought they could help the program more directly by desecrating the churches themselves, because this practice was also a subject of Stalin's withering ridicule in "Dizziness from Success." "And what," he said, "about those 'revolutionaries'—save the mark—who begin the work of organizing an artel by removing the church bells? Remove the church bells—how r-r-revolutionary indeed!"[112]

As in the case of collectivization, this caustic remark brought another temporary "retreat." The "All-Union Congress of Atheists" proclaimed that religion could not be terminated "overnight," and that excesses must cease. Yaroslavsky urged the use of peaceful argument, persuasion and propaganda.[113] As a result, there was, according to *The New York Times* account, another "lively debate" in Moscow "concerning the precise nature of the Kremlin's new attitude toward the Russian peasant in matters of land policy and religion." An editorial, captioned "Russia Changes," stated: "One school of opinion holds that the change to moderation ordered by Stalin is only a change in tempo. Others insist it is an entirely new policy."[114]

Twenty-six years later, after the denunciation of Stalin at the Twentieth Party Congress, Secretary of State Dulles was still pondering this question: "The essential question is this," he said. "Are the Soviet rulers now attacking the basic causes of this domestic discontent and foreign distrust, or is their purpose merely to allay this discontent and distrust by blaming them on the past?"[115]

But in 1930, the question was quickly solved. The same issue of *The New York Times* also carried the report of an "apparent" new drive on religion. It turned out to be real; and by 1934, at least half the churches in Russia had been closed. Nevertheless, in 1935, Stalin was seen leading a procession from the Kremlin to a reconverted Moscow cathedral. It included members of the Politburo, the Young Communist League, and factory workers—all intoning psalms, carrying icons, and bearing banners with the following inscription:

Religion is the life-blood of the people!
Unbelief is the nation's opium and the ally of foreign imperialists.[116]

In 1936, Yaroslavsky admitted that half the population was still religious, and called for the grant of suffrage to priests. On this occasion, *The New York Times* reporter seemed convinced. "Eleven years ago," he said, "Mr. Yaroslavsky stood out against ruthless destruction of church edifices and the outlawing of church services. . . ." His current stand, the report continued, "in view of his great influence in the Communist party, indicates that the destruction of churches will be carried out with restraint."[117]

In 1937, however, a new period of violence began. It coincided with the adoption of the new constitution, which restored the voting rights of the clergy and purported to guarantee freedom of religious worship. At the same time, it was reported that the party was "halting excesses," such as "the dismissing of believers from jobs" and the closing of churches "without the consent of local residents."[118] The "riotous raids" of "earlier periods" were "sternly forbidden."[119] But in 1939, *The New York Times* correspondent reported that it was doubtful if twelve churches remained in Moscow. "Naturally, therefore," he stated, "such churches as were open . . . were crowded."[120]

World War II brought a new period of "moderation." Two patriarchal elections were permitted, the election of Sergei in 1943 and the election of his successor, the Patriarch Alexei, in 1945. The "revived" Church, however, was one which demanded not only loyalty to the Soviet regime, but which supported it in all the devolutions of its propaganda directed against the free nations. Its administration was controlled by a State Council on Orthodox Affairs, headed by a former member of the secret police. For other sects, a corresponding agency, the Council on Affairs of Religious Cults, was created. By 1948, it was reported that a "strong new drive" had begun "to extirpate or at least discourage religion."[121]

In the meantime, the campaign had spread through the captured areas of eastern Europe and Asia. As in the case of the

Orthodox Church in Russia, an attempt was made to promote schism in the Catholic Church by the organization of national "independent Catholic" churches, and associations of "patriotic priests" and "progressive Catholics." An effort was made to control Church appointments in all denominations.[122]

In China the Communists also promoted the "Chinese Buddhist Association," and a "National Christian Council" which would be more amenable to their control. Members of the Taoist societies were executed as "counterrevolutionaries." Practically all foreign missionaries were expelled.

As in the case of the Soviet Union, "freedom of religious belief" was everywhere "guaranteed," while, at the same time, churches, temples, lands, monasteries, schools and orphanages of all denominations were subject to seizure; and nonco-operating clergymen were exiled, imprisoned, tortured and killed. The illusion of religious freedom was so well nurtured that, in 1954, after a visit to Communist China, the former British Prime Minister, Clement R. Attlee, reported:

. . . there was no real evidence of any desire to eradicate the religions of the West or to undo the work of western missions . . . the Christian religion was still practiced without restraint.[123]

Yet new campaigns and new measures of repression against religion are continually being announced.

Accordingly, while the future is certain to no one, it can safely be said that reports of Communist grants of "freedom," no matter how persistent, and no matter how much they appear to be based on "real concessions," do not reflect any real or permanent hope of improvement in the lot of the subject peoples. Certainly there is nothing to support the conclusions arrived at by the late Secretary of State Dulles that "it is almost certain that there will be an evolutionary change," or "that the United States should accept" as a "working hypothesis underlying its policies" the "assumption" that "a trend in the Soviet Union to somewhat greater personal freedom" is "going to prevail."[124]

It is quite impossible to believe, as Secretary Dulles did, even on the basis of the most startling concessions, that "the new Soviet tactics of increased tolerance and less dependence upon violence required a basic change in Soviet Communist doctrine," or that they "can, in the long run, have major internal consequences and set up within

Russia powerful liberalizing trends."[125] It is likewise impossible to believe as he did that "the fact that the Soviet rulers now denounce much of the past gives cause for hope," or that "it demonstrates that liberalizing influences from within and without can bring about peaceful change."[126]

Simply because the Soviets are now "debasing Stalin" and indulging in "extraordinary exertions" to "make it seem that they are offering a change," we cannot believe that "there are signs that a new day may be dawning" or that "Out of all this there may come—not this year, or next year, but some year—a government which is responsive to the just aspirations of the people. . . ."[127] Simply because the "Soviet rulers who have replaced Stalin seem to have concluded that the time had come to present a 'new look' at home," we cannot believe that we "can today see within Russia some signs of light which could mark the dawning of that new day."[128] Nor are we able to take any comfort from the fact that "Stalin, the brutal demigod, has been dethroned"; that " 'Collective leadership' now replaces one-man despotism"; that the "sway of the secret police has, it seems, been curtailed"; or even that "the heresy of 'Titoism' has been made respectable."[129]

On the contrary, we can more reasonably fear that these "concessions" are only the prelude to "a bigger leap forward," and that if the subject peoples do not receive some assistance from their more fortunate fellow-members of the human race, the "consolidation" of Khrushchev's power will be followed by new campaigns of repression, possibly even more intense than those which followed the "regrouping" and the "reorganization" of the forces led by Stalin. If there is any "evolutionary" trend in the Soviet Union, its direction is toward a more "complete stage of Communism," not toward freedom; and if the "working hypothesis" underlying the policy of the United States is to be based upon predictions, it surely should not be based on a supposed Communist desire to meet the "just aspirations" of the people "this year, or next year" or even "some year." It would be more practicable to take note of the fact that a "new look" of the same limited duration as the New Economic Policy would expire in the year 1960. When it does expire, there will most certainly be a strong new demand by the subject peoples for the help of the free world, and a new opportunity for the free world to come to their assistance. Whether it will be able to do so effectively, without launching World War III, or will have continued to assume that assistance to the subject peoples is unnecessary, because the "trend" to freedom is "irreversible," is one of the few unpredictable factors remaining in its struggle with Communist attempts at world domination—the only Soviet trend that has so far appeared to be really "irreversible."

CHAPTER XV

THE "IRRESISTIBLE" DEMAND

"The force of habit of millions and tens of millions is a most terrible force." V. I. Lenin[1]

The corollary of the theory of an "irreversible trend" to freedom is that of an "irresistible demand" which produces it. This solution of the cold war assumes that the subject peoples will become so insistent upon freedom that they will force their Soviet rulers to give it to them—and that they can do so by some form of peaceful or passive resistance rather than by violent revolt. It thus puts the onus upon the subject peoples to help themselves and at the same time rid the whole world of the Communist menace—all without disturbing the tranquillity of the free world or calling upon it for any kind of effective military assistance.

The adoption of this theory as the basis of United States policy was advocated in the Republican Party platform of 1952. It was a part of the same program which called for the repudiation of the Yalta agreements and the "end of the negative, futile and immoral policy of 'containment.' " Thus the foreign-policy section of this platform promised to give a "real function" to the Voice of America, and stated in part: "The policies we espouse will revive the contagious, liberating influences which are inherent in freedom. They will inevitably set up strains and stresses within the captive world which will make the rulers impotent to continue in their monstrous ways and mark the beginning of their end."[2]

In the course of the implementation of this pledge, President Eisenhower submitted a draft resolution to Congress which did not actually "repudiate" any of the wartime declarations, but called instead for the rejection of all "perverted" interpretations and applications.[3] This proposal clearly implied that the enslavements were not so much due to the terms of the agreements as to the free world's failure to enforce them; but at the same time no effective method of enforcement was offered. In his testimony in support of the resolution, Secretary of State Dulles maintained (February 26, 1953) that if independence for the captive peoples were clearly announced as one of the "peaceful goals" of the United States, their own "inherent longing for freedom" would be "revived" and they would "peacefully" overcome their oppressors:

If we want to maintain and stimulate the spirit of freedom which eventually will peacefully frustrate the oppressive design of Soviet despotism and disintegrate that overextended despotism, the first and indispensable step is to make clear, on the highest authority of the President and Congress, that:

One, the United States does not countenance the violations by which Soviet leadership has perverted past agreements and understandings into chains of bondage....

Two, the United States will never be a party to any international "deal" or "trade" confirming the rule of Soviet despotism over the alien peoples it dominates in Europe and Asia.

Three, the United States seeks, as one of its peaceful goals, that these enslaved national groups of Europe and Asia shall recover genuine independence.

.   .   .   .

This resolution is no call to bloody and senseless revolution .... it will, over the coming years, revive the inherent longing for freedom which persists within the captive peoples so that that longing becomes a mounting spiritual power which will eventually overcome the material power of Soviet dictatorship....[4]

Great hopes for the success of this theory were evoked a few months later by the riots in East Germany. In a letter to Chancellor Adenauer, the President stated that "repercussions of these events" would "be felt throughout the Soviet satellite empire."[5] Secretary Dulles seemed to ignore his own recent rejection of "senseless revolution," and publicly commended the "unarmed youths" who "tore up paving stones from the streets to hurl in defiance at tanks."[6] At the same time he decried "an armed revolt which would precipitate a massacre...." Short of this, he said, "the people could demonstrate an independence such that the Soviet Communist leaders would come to recognize the futility of trying to hold captive so many peoples who, by their faith and their patriotism, can never really be consolidated into a Soviet Communist world."

These declarations and statements were confined to the "captive nations"—the satellites—but after the Soviet denunciation of Stalin, the United States belatedly recognized the existence of a demand for freedom on the part of the Russian peoples as well. Thus, in April, 1956, the President was asked to comment upon a statement attributed to Secretary Dulles: that the "repudiation" of Stalin might be the "first step in the reformation of Russia." He replied that he was not convinced of any change in the intentions of the Soviet leaders, but conceded that their action might represent "the beginning of a forced reformation of some kind"—caused by "recognition of dissatisfaction among the great masses living under or behind the Iron Curtain."[7] Secretary Dulles thereafter asserted that "forces for liberalization" were "at work within the Soviet bloc" and were "powerful enough to require some response, or at least the appearance of response." "All of this," he said, "is immensely important. It is more than the free world dared hope for a few years ago."[8] And two months later, he stated: "... we can hope that the forces now at work within the Soviet Union and within the captive countries will require that those who rule shall increasingly conform to principles of freedom."[9]

In July, 1956, after the riots at Poznan, and again in 1957, after the purge of the "Stalinist" leaders in Moscow, the Secretary asserted that these forces were *irresistible*. Thus, at a news conference July 11, 1956, he stated:

I believe—although no one can be certain about the matter—I believe the forces that are now working are going to prove to be irresistible. That does not mean that will happen today or tomorrow .... no sudden transformation will come about. It is not a matter for this year or next year, but I believe this second postwar decade in which we are will see these new forces take charge of the situation and that we can really hopefully look forward to a transformation of the international scene.[10]

And at a news conference on July 16, 1957, he said:

The rulers of Russia face a rising, and in the long run irresistible, demand of the people for more personal security, more personal freedom, and more enjoyment of the fruits of their labor.[11]

THE DEMAND IN THE SOVIET UNION: 1918-1939

"Exploiters" and "Bourgeoisie," Proletarians and Peasants

As in the case of the "irreversible trend," this "irresistible

demand" had existed from the very beginning of the Soviet regime
without being able to force a change of any kind—peaceful or violent.
It was, moreover, foreseen, acknowledged and even emphasized by
the Bolshevik leaders themselves. Thus, in a pamphlet written at the
end of 1918, his first full year of rule, Lenin predicted that until the
very end of the "transition" to "communism," until the termination
of that "entire historical epoch," the "overthrown exploiters" would
"inevitably cherish the hope of restoration," and convert it "into
attempts at restoration."[12] This pamphlet, *The Proletarian Revolution and Renegade Kautsky*, is quoted by Stalin in *Foundations of
Leninism*:

> ... after their first serious defeat, the overthrown exploiters—who
> had not expected their overthrow, who never believed it possible, who
> would not permit the thought of it—will throw themselves with
> tenfold energy, with furious passion and hatred grown a hundredfold
> into the battle for the recovery of their lost "paradise" on behalf of
> their families who had been leading such a sweet and easy life and
> whom now the "common herd" is condemning to ruin and destitution
> (or to "common" work)....[13]

There would also be resistance by the "bourgeoisie," and accordingly
the quotation continues:

> In the wake of the capitalist exploiters will be found the broad masses
> of the petty bourgeoisie, to whose vacillation and hesitation the
> historical experience of every country for decades bears witness; one
> day they march behind the proletariat, the next day they will take
> fright at the difficulties of the revolution, become panic-stricken at the
> first defeat or semi-defeat of the workers; they become irritable, they
> run about, snivel and rush from one camp to the other.

The "bourgeoisie," Stalin wrote, "has reasons for making attempts at restoration, because for a long time after its overthrow it
remains stronger than the proletariat which has overthrown it." And,
he adds, the same is true of the "exploiters": "If the exploiters—Lenin
says—are vanquished in only a single country, which, of course, is the
typical case since a simultaneous revolution in a number of countries
is a rare exception, they *still remain stronger* than the exploited."[14]

Ultimately, Lenin conceded that the resistance extended even to
the "proletariat" itself. Thus, he wrote, in *"Left-Wing" Communism*
(April, 1920):

They [the "small commodity producers"] encircle the proletariat on every side with a petty-bourgeois atmosphere, which permeates and corrupts the proletariat and causes constant relapses among the proletariat into petty-bourgeois spinelessness, disunity, individualism, and alternate moods of exaltation and dejection.... The force of habit of millions and tens of millions is a most terrible force.[15]

Unless aided from abroad, however, this force was not considered "irresistible" by either Lenin or Stalin. The "strength of the overthrown bourgeoisie," they said, lies first in the strength of "international capital" and in the "strength and durability" of its "international connections."[16] They based their hopes upon the severance of these connections, and upon their ability to keep them severed until there was no longer any possibility of their being restored, i.e., until the "revolution" had succeeded in every country. And without the use of such connections—the same kind of connections which enabled the American revolutionaries to obtain extensive military and financial assistance from France, the Netherlands and Spain, technical advice and assistance from military experts of Prussia, Poland and other countries, and even the sympathetic efforts of many freedom-loving Englishmen, in the effort to enforce their demands against the despotism of George III—the subject peoples have not been able to force any change in the overextended and far more oppressive despotism of the Soviet Union. As President Eisenhower said on the occasion of the 181st anniversary of the Battle of Concord (April, 1956), even the "inevitable" comes about only through "human effort";[17] and in the case of the "inevitable" trend to freedom in the Soviet Union, it is the free world which has failed to make this effort.

The "irresistible demand" in Russia was also described by the American consul general in Moscow, Maddin Summers. In a telegraphic report made in March, 1918, shortly after the suppression of the Constitutional Assembly, he stated that "the vast masses of the peasants" were "violently opposed to the government of the Soviets":

In contradiction to reports which might reach Department regarding representative character of Congress of Soviets I am informed by prominent socialist labor and conservative leaders that the twelve hundred delegates composing the Congress represent an infinitely small proportion of the people of Russia; that the delegates were chosen by Bolshevik leaders [regardless] of the wishes of the people; that the vast [masses] of the peasants are violently opposed to the

government of the Soviets; that all the Social Revolutionary Party . . .
do not recognize the present government and that all the intelligent
classes of Russia are against the present régime. . . . I am also assured
that great dissension exists amongst the Bolsheviki themselves and
that it is merely a question of time when they must give up their
power. They have stopped the sale all over Russia of the socialist and
conservative newspapers allowing opinions their own and anarchist
literature to reach the people who are becoming greatly exercised. At
works of Chjifen factory only few hundred men out of four thousand
consented to join the Red Guard. At International Harvester Works
only fifty out of four thousand workmen volunteered to serve.[18]

Except for the prediction that the Bolsheviks would soon be
forced to give up their power, this analysis was soon confirmed by
the spread of civil war throughout the whole of Russia. Even in those
areas which were ostensibly under the control of the Bolsheviks, there
was a constant succession of violent uprisings. According to Martin
Latsis, an official of the Cheka, there were 245 separate revolts in the
areas controlled by the Bolsheviks in 1918, and 99 in the first seven
months of 1919.[19] Nevertheless, the Bolsheviks survived.

In June, 1918, a decree was issued calling for the distribution to
the poor of grain surpluses "requisitioned from the kulaks and the
rich."[20] One would think that this would be a matter of great
rejoicing for the allegedly downtrodden peasants, but in the next
three months, according to Bolshevik sources, there were 108 *peasant*
uprisings—twenty-six in July, forty-seven in August and thirty-five in
September.[21]

The revolts continued even after the defeat of the White armies
and the close of the civil war. In the summer of 1920, there were
successful uprisings in the provinces of Tambov, Saratov, Penza, and
in the North Caucasus. These persisted until the spring of 1921. In
February, 1921, there was a revolt in Armenia which was not completely suppressed until August. In these outbreaks the Soviet
"authority" was completely overthrown in wide areas. In other areas
there was extensive guerrilla resistance by the so-called green armies.
This continued for many years.

In March, 1921, there was a revolt at Kronstadt, the Russian's
island naval base in the Gulf of Finland. The "mutineers"—sailors
and civilians—organized a Provisional Revolutionary Committee and
greatly embarrassed the Bolsheviks with precisely that kind of peaceful pressure which the free world apparently now contemplates.

There were mass meetings and resolutions, a spate of arguments with Bolshevik leaders, and a long list of "irresistible" demands—including freedom of speech and assembly, new and secret elections, free trade unions, liberation of political prisoners, and the rectification of many other grievances. Moreover, the committe resolved to use arms *only in self-defense*.

The timing of this action was also most propitious. It followed closely upon a wave of strikes and demonstrations by workers of Petrograd—the first of the "victorious" proletarians. All parts of the country were in a restive mood, and the resistance of the peasants was at this time so great that grain collections had been suspended in thirteen provinces.[22] The gravity of the situation was indicated by Lenin in his opening address to the Tenth Congress of the Communist Party:

> In speaking of the internal situation in Soviet Russia, it is necessary to dwell upon the events at Kronstadt. The rising organized by France in conjunction with the Social-Revolutionaries will be crushed in the next few days. Nevertheless, it forces us to consider most seriously the internal situation of Soviet Russia.[23]

France's role of chief villain, since assumed by the United States, was the result of its advocating a policy similar to "containment"—the defensive "cordon sanitaire" around the Soviet Union—and its recent moral support of General Wrangel. But the French could no more have organized the Kronstadt revolt than they had organized the resistance in the Ukraine (from which they had been forced to withdraw two years before). The Kronstadt garrison was one of the original sources of Bolshevik strength, and many of the "mutineers" were themselves Communists.

Several regiments of the Red Army refused to move against the rebellious garrison, but in spite of Lenin's claim to the contrary there was no foreign assistance, and the revolt was "crushed" as he predicted. An estimated 18,000 Kronstadt defenders were killed in the battle, others were subsequently shot or imprisoned, and in the mutinous regiments every fifth man was shot.[24]

Nevertheless, the demand for freedom continued—still unaided. In April, 1921, there was a revolt in western Siberia.[25] It was followed by a rebellion in eastern Karelia. There were organized Cossack uprisings from 1922-26, and still more reports of revolts by the peasants during the same period.[26]

In January, 1924, Lenin died. As in the case of the death of Stalin, twenty-nine years later, this event was followed by numerous reports of rebellion. In February, 1924, the Chinese were accused of assisting a new provisional government in eastern Siberia.[27] In December it was reported that Trotsky's dismissal as commissar of war had touched off bloody riots in Moscow.[28] Throughout the year there were many accounts of extensive guerrilla fighting, with partisan units or "bands" operating in Turkestan, the Caucasus, the Ukraine and even in the vicinity of Nizhni Novgorod (250 miles from Moscow).[29] In Byelorussia, according to the Communists, there were forty of such "bands" in operation at this time.[30]

In August, 1924, the long-planned revolution broke out in the State of Georgia, quickly spreading into neighboring Armenia, Azerbaijan and Daghestan. The strength of this movement was indicated by the report that, in one week alone, 60,000 Soviet reinforcements were sent into the Caucasus.[31] This can be compared with estimates ranging from 75,000 to 200,000 as the *total* number of Soviet troops deployed in Hungary on November 2, 1956—two days before the final Red Army assault.[32] As in the case of Hungary, the revolt in Georgia was crushed in about two weeks' time, and in spite of renewed revolts in 1927, 1931, 1932, 1933, 1947 and 1956,[33] Georgia, like Hungary, continued to remain under the domination of the allegedly over-extended, overrigid and ill-founded structure of the Communist Soviet empire.

Also as in the case of Hungary, the 1924 revolt in Georgia was the subject of embarrassed and unproductive discussion in the world peace organization. The Assembly of the League of Nations simply readopted the same resolution which it had passed in 1922, after the original Soviet subjugation of Georgia, calling upon the Council to "follow attentively the course of events in this part of the world," so that it might be able "to seize any opportunity which may occur to help in the restoration" of "normal conditions" by any "peaceful means."[34]

During the next four years, while Stalin was supposed to be turning away from communism, there were at least annual reports of revolts somewhere inside the Soviet Union: in 1925, rebellion by a Byelorussian army of 60,000;[35] in 1926, new revolts at Kronstadt,

Leningrad and other parts of Russia;[36] anti-Communist infiltration of the government, and threatening messages placed on the desks of Soviet leaders by the "Brothers of the Black Star";[37] in 1927, a new revolt in Byelorussia and grave disorders and clashes with the Red Army in south Russia and the Ukraine.[38]

After Stalin turned to a "hard" policy, the reports of revolt continued with unchanging frequency. In 1928, there was the exposure of the "technicians' plot," at Shakhta, against the coal industry. This was followed by reports of similar "counterrevolutionary activity" in the chemical, munitions and metallurgical industries.[39] In 1929, fighting was reported between the Red Army and rebel bands in the Ukraine,[40] Byelorussia, and Azerbaijan.[41] In 1930, there was a resurgence of the Basmachi (nationalist) movement in Turkestan. New revolts were reported in Azerbaijan in 1931,[42] and in Byelorussia in 1934.[43]

None of these developments brought a "forced reformation" of any kind. Stalin was well aware of the continuing demand for freedom, but he was not worried so long as it received no more than the *moral* support of the free world. On the contrary, he often referred to the unrest, the strains and stresses, and even the revolts within the Soviet Union to prove his own points—sometimes as evidence of the need for vigilance against the "interventionist tendencies" of the capitalist states, and at other times as evidence of his own success in speeding up the "transition to communism."

Thus, in November, 1927, Stalin asserted that in the absence of stimulation from abroad, there would be no resistance at all—it would even be possible to abolish the secret police:

... I do not mean to say that the internal situation in the country is such as to call for punitive organs of the revolution. From the viewpoint of the internal situation, the revolution is so firm and invincible that we could well do without the G.P.U. But the trouble is that the internal enemies are not isolated individuals. The trouble is that they are connected in a thousand different ways with the capitalists of all other countries who assist them in every way and by all means.[44]

It is unfortunate that such assistance was not given, for millions of lives might have been saved. It was not given, however, and in December, 1927, when Stalin announced his new "offensive" in a report to the Fifteenth Party Congress, he more honestly attributed the "discontent" and "counterrevolutionary moods" to the natural vexation of the "bourgeoisie":

> Progress in our industry, progress in our trading and cooperative organizations, and improvement of our state apparatus is progress and improvement for the benefit of the working class, for the benefit of the bulk of the peasantry, but to the detriment of the new bourgeoisie, to the detriment of the middle strata generally and of the urban middle strata in particular. Is it to be wondered at that discontent with the Soviet regime is growing among these strata? Hence the counterrevolutionary moods among these people. Hence the Smena-Vekh ideology, a fashionable article in the new bourgeoisie's political market.[45]

As in the case of China today, there were also "contradictions" among the peoples of the Soviet Union:

> After all, our development is not proceeding smoothly, not in an all-round, ascending curve. No, comrades, we have classes, we have contradictions within the country, we have a past, we have a present and a future, we have contradictions between them, and we cannot advance in the manner of a smooth and gentle rocking on the waves of life. We are advancing in the process of struggle, in the process of development of contradictions, in the process of overcoming these contradictions, in the process of bringing these contradictions to light and liquidating them.[46]

In his report to the Sixteenth Party Congress (June, 1930), at the peak of the Socialist "offensive," Stalin again pointed out that resistance was inevitable:

> ... we must bear in mind the circumstance that our work on the socialist reconstruction of our national economy, in breaking up the economic connections of capitalism and turning all the forces of the old world topsy-turvy, cannot but rouse the desperate resistance of these forces. This is what is happening, as you know. The malicious wrecking activities of the upper stratum of the *bourgeois intelligentsia* in all branches of our industry, the brutal struggle the *kulaks* are waging against the collective forms of farming in the rural districts, the sabotage of the Soviet government's measures by the *bureaucratic elements* in the state apparatus who are the agents of our class enemy—such, so far, are the chief forms of the resistance put up by the moribund classes in our country.[47]

But in spite of these "wrecking activities," the Soviet system, according to Stalin, continued to "thrive." The "Soviet system," he boasted, "which was to have 'degenerated' (or 'had already degenerated') continues to thrive and to build Socialism, successfully breaking the backbone of the capitalist elements in our country and their petty-bourgeois toadies."[48]

Stalin derided the assumption that a forced reformation could be induced with the aid of foreign *moral* support, even when it took the form of economic boycott. In the same report (June 27, 1930) he dealt with what he called "fictitious 'obstacles,'" or "stumbling blocks," raised by free nations to the resumption of "normal" economic relations:

It is also said that another stumbling block is our Soviet system, collectivization, the struggle against the kulaks, antireligious propaganda, the struggle against wreckers and counterrevolutionaries among "men of science," the banishment of Besedovskys, Solomons, Dimitrievskys, and other lackeys of capital. But this is becoming quite amusing. It appears that they don't like the Soviet system. But we don't like the capitalist system. (*Laughter, applause.*). . . . It is our duty to abide by the Constitution of the U.S.S.R. with the utmost consistency, and we will do so. It goes without saying, therefore, that whoever refuses to reckon with our Constitution can pass on, can go wherever they please. As for the Besedovskys, Solomons, Dimitrievskys and their ilk [who opposed the Soviet system], we will in future, too, kick out such people like damaged goods that are useless and harmful for the revolution. Let them be made heroes of by those who have a special predilection for offal. (*Laughter.*)[49]

In 1934, Stalin reported that the "majority" of adherents to "antirevolutionary groups" had been "defeated and scattered." These included the "anti-Leninist Trotskyite group"—now to be found "in the backyards of the bourgeois parties abroad," the "anti-Leninist group of the Right deviationists"—whose "organizers" had "long since renounced their views" and were now trying "to expiate the sins they committed against the Party," and the "groups of nationalist deviators"—whose "organizers" had "either completely merged with the interventionist émigrés, or else recanted."[50] Nevertheless, according to Stalin, the demand for freedom still persisted. It was not yet possible to "relax the class struggle," and he denounced the mistakes of a new group of "soft" Communists who thought the time had arrived to "get rid of the state altogether":

They dropped into a state of moon-calf ecstasy, in the expectation that soon there will be no classes, and therefore no class struggle, and therefore no cares and worries, and therefore we can lay down our arms and retire—to sleep and to wait for the advent of classless society.[51]

Such people needed to be reminded that a "classless society cannot come of itself, spontaneously, as it were":

It has to be achieved and built by the efforts of all the working people, by strengthening the organs of the dictatorship of the proletariat, by intensifying the class struggle, by abolishing classes, by eliminating the remnants of the capitalist classes, and in battles with enemies both internal and external.[52]

The fact was, as Stalin said, that the "survivals of capitalism" had not yet been eliminated, either in "economic life" or in "the minds of the people." There still existed "certain intermediary strata of the population" to breed "unhealthy moods" which penetrated even "into the Party."[53]

The Red Army

These "unhealthy moods" were also to be found in the Red armed forces, where it might be expected that the demand for freedom would be most dangerous. But even here it was impotent without effective aid from abroad. This had been proven long ago by the mass defections of the civil-war period. It is estimated that one-half of all those taken into the Red Army during this period went over to the side of the anti-Bolsheviks. The number of deserters *recaptured* during 1919 to 1920 has been put at 2,846,000.[54]

There were further reports of "mutiny" and "treason" in later years. In 1923, several officers of high rank were arrested on charges of having conspired to promote a general insurrection.[55] In 1924, there was a rebellion of 20,000 recruits in Turkestan.[56] In 1926, it was reported that 20% of the officers were regarded as hostile to the Soviet regime.[57] In 1928, there was a report of revolt by four Moscow regiments, officially denied.[58] At various times it was reported that parts of the armed forces had gone over to the "left" or "right" opposition. One such report, in 1926, stated that the Navy had sided with Zinoviev and was attacking.[59]

All of these reports were overshadowed, however, by the charges made by the Communists themselves—during the Great Purge of the late 1930's. In this mass elimination of suspected harborers of the demand for freedom, the Red Army was a chief target of attack. More than half of the officers, including Marshal Tukhachevski, Assistant Minister of Defense and the Army's real leader, were liquidated. The toll included three of the five marshals, thirteen of fifteen army commanders, fifty-seven out of eighty-five corps commanders, 110 out of 195 division commanders, and 220 out of 406 brigade commanders. Also included were all of the vice-commissars of war, nearly all members of the Supreme Military Council, 90% of the generals, and 80% of the colonels.[60] Even their demands, obviously, were not "irresistible."

The "Great Patriotic War" and Its Aftermath

Still further proof of the army's demand for freedom was provided during the first eight months of the Nazi invasion. During this brief period, it is reported, the German forces took some 3,600,000 prisoners,[61] an unprecedented number, which clearly implies the refusal of large numbers to fight for the Soviet system. It is probable, moreover, that a much larger number would have *openly* defected if the Nazis had offered more than a mere exchange of one tyranny for another. According to a study made by the United States Army, this was confirmed by the testimony of the prisoners themselves, defecting Red Army officers and native intelligence agents. As this study relates, all agreed that the German propaganda "was based too much on the German viewpoint...." "The Russian People," it says, "and probably a good portion of the Red Army, could have been won over, they believed, if definite promises had been made and a definite program outlined for the political and economic future of the USSR."[62]

This probability was even confirmed by Stalin. In an order issued during the first month of fighting, he complained that the number of firm and steady commanders and commissars was "not very great." There are many, he said, *"on all fronts,"* who are "given to panic and *even oriented toward the enemy."*[63] (Italics added.) This was only a short time after the purge of all who were even suspected of dis-affection.

The Nazis, unfortunately, were not interested in aiding the oppressed. Many of the original Russian prisoners were allowed to starve, freeze and die from illness before the eyes of their own people. Nevertheless, when the Germans decided to use the prisoners, large numbers volunteered for service (estimates range up to 2,500,000). Somewhere between 500,000 and 1,000,000 were actually permitted to serve,[64] but they were scattered on all fronts, and many of them were forced to fight against the free nations.

Another manifestation of the demand for freedom occurred at the end of the war, when large numbers of Soviet troops deserted, or attempted to desert, to the Western Allies. But in this case the demand was suppressed by a free-world policy even more cruel and im-practical than that of the Nazis—prompt and forcible return to Soviet control. In this connection, a report prepared in 1953 for the Senate Committee on Foreign Relations is pertinent. "The disaffections were many," it says, "particularly after the war. And they would, probably, have been much greater had not the Western Powers been convinced immediately after the end of hostilities that their duty lay in sending back to the Soviet authorities those Red Army soldiers who tried to make their way over to the Allies. . . ."

"Since that time of overzealous international amity," the report continues, "many Red army deserters have made their way to either the British or American zones of occupied former enemy countries."[65] Unfortunately, however, when the Allies changed their policy, the best opportunities for defection had passed, and with them another opportunity for the free world to support the demand for freedom.

There were similar expressions of this demand by the civilian populations. Their feelings were best revealed by the tone of the Com-munists' own wartime propaganda. According to the same United States Army study referred to above, this propaganda put the defense of communism in a definite second place after the defense of free Russia:

Following the initial German attack, the Soviet propagandists had quickly dropped the standard Communist slogans and placed heavy emphasis on patriotism, playing up "The Great Patriotic War" and the "fatherland." The masthead on *Pravda* was changed from

"Workers of the World, Unite!" to "Death to the German Invader!" The *old czarist heroes* were dragged out and the Russian victory over Napoleon in 1812 was given wide play.[66] (Italics added.)

According to Alfred Rosenberg, Reich Minister for the Occupied Eastern Territories, and head of the Nazi Party's Office for Foreign Policy and Ideology, the people's aversion to communism was so great that, in spite of their love of the "fatherland," they would have willingly co-operated with a less inhuman invader. His report is credible, because it is a severe criticism of the policies of his own party and of the Führer, and because it was corroborated by the testimony of many other Nazis.[67] "It was apparently completely ignored," he related, "in the treatment of prisoners of war, that Germany found, in contrast to the West (France, Belgium, the Netherlands, Norway), a people who went through all the terror of Bolshevism, and who now, happy about their liberation, put themselves willingly at the disposal of Germany. . . . But instead of accepting this gift, the people of the East are being treated more contemptibly and worse than the people of the West, who do not hide their enmity. . . ." "All propaganda will be useless," he wrote, "if there is more fear of captivity than of death and wounds on the battlefield."[68]

Even behind the Soviet lines there was extensive guerrilla fighting. It is reported, for example, that in August, 1943, there were more than a hundred partisan groups operating in areas never reached by the German armies.[69] But in the regions where Soviet control was broken by German occupation, the anti-Soviet movement was, of course, more successful. Thus, in the Ukraine there was a highly organized struggle against both Nazis and Soviets, led by the Organization of Ukrainian Nationalists (OUN), the Ukrainian Insurgent Army (UPA), and other underground groups. Many of the Red Army troops showed their sympathy with this movement by refusing to fight against it,[70] and two years after the end of the war the struggle still continued. At that time the Soviets were forced to seek assistance from their puppet regime in Poland and the ostensibly free government of Czechoslovakia, making a pact of mutual aid on May 12, 1947.

In spite of this effort, however, the struggle was still going on in 1950, when the U.P.A. leader was killed by troops of the M.V.D. It had not yet been completely suppressed in June, 1952, when the secretary of the Ukrainian Communist Party complained of the "serpent's sting of Ukrainian bourgeois nationalist ideology." The

"Ukrainian bourgeois nationalists," he said, "have always been spies, saboteurs and agents of imperialist espionage. Now they have sold themselves to new masters, the Anglo-American imperialists."[71] These were the same Ukrainian "nationalist deviators" who, in 1933, had "merged with the interventionist émigrés," and who, according to Stalin, had at that time become the "major danger."[72] Nevertheless, because the "interventionists" did not wish to merge with them, they were "defeated and scattered" then,[73] and they have been forced to suspend their activities now.

There was similar organized resistance in the Baltic States. A first hand account of the struggle in Lithuania was given to Congress by one of those who helped suppress it—Grigori S. Burlitski, a former lieutenant colonel of the M.V.D. According to Burlitski's testimony, the "so-called bandits" were supported by the "majority of the Lithuanian population," and they were induced to discontinue operations only when they saw "how the Lithuanian people were being exterminated, how villages were burned" and cattle "destroyed." Thereupon they "made a decision to go and leave the underground ... to give up some of their units" and "temporarily abandon any kind of active operations ... in order to preserve the people, the leadership and the population for a future fight."[74]

In Poland the resistance was led by the "Home Army," which the Communists now concede was overcome only with great difficulty. In May, 1956, a Polish newspaper revealed that action against "enemies of the people" since 1945 had cost the lives of more than 30,000 party members, soldiers and security police.[75] Five months later, in October, 1956, the rehabilitated leader of the "liberal" Communists, Wladyslaw Gomulka, asserted that "hundreds of thousands of our Party members, soldiers, and civil servants were killed."[76] The "underground organization" in Poland, he said, had been "really widespread." Nevertheless, the Communists prevailed, and most of the members of the "Home Army" were themselves eventually killed or captured.

The major postwar resistance was thus effectively suppressed, but the demand for freedom was unabated and the spirit of unrest continued. In 1951, John F. Dulles, who was then Consultant to the Secretary of State, asserted:

The Party itself is shot through with distrust and suspicion, and there are periodic purges as between Party factions. No one, even in high authority, feels personally safe. In the case of the satellite countries, the situation is even more precarious. For example, there is much unrest on the China mainland, and, in Poland and Czechoslovakia, the people are forced to accept officials of Russian nationality because the Russian masters cannot find any Poles or Czechs they are willing to trust.

When a few men rule despotically 800 million, that is bound to be a vulnerable position.[77]

The accuracy of this report was demonstrated by subsequent events. Guerrilla fighting continued in Bulgaria, Rumania and the mountains of Czechoslovakia.[78] A nonmilitary, but active, Czech underground was heard over the "Free Homeland Radio" and through such publications as the "Voice of the Free Republic" (at Prague) and the "Voice of the Underground" (at Brno).[79]

THE DEMAND IN THE SOVIET EMPIRE

Post-Stalin Resistance in the Soviet Union and the Satellites

After the death of Stalin there was a new surge of open rebellion, as predicted by the Eisenhower administration. In the Czech uprising of June, 1953, unorganized crowds seized the city hall in Pilsen and demanded free elections. This was followed by the ten-day series of strikes and uprisings in East Germany. Sit-down strikes continued in East Germany for a month.

In the Soviet Union there were repeated outbreaks in the prison camps: in 1953, in Kazakhstan and at Karaganda; in 1954, at Norilsk, Karaganda, Revda and Churba Nura; in 1955, at various camps in the Ural Mountains. Vorkuta was the scene of annual uprisings, the one in 1953 involving 150,000 prisoners. In the Red Army there were also new disaffections as Russian soldiers balked at orders to fire on the rioters in East Germany and at Vorkuta. Elsewhere they mutinied, and in East Germany at least one complete battalion attempted to flee to the west.

Further evidence of resistance to the Communist regime was furnished by repeated Soviet efforts to destroy the National Alliance of Russian Solidarists (NTS), an exile organization engaged in the development of a new and less vulnerable type of anti-Soviet underground. One phase of the Soviet attack, an attempt to "liquidate" the NTS leaders, was exposed in 1954 by an MVD officer assigned to direct the assassination of Georgi S. Okolovich, a member of the NTS executive board in charge of its underground activities. Instead of carrying out this mission, the officer, Nikolai E. Khokhlov, surrendered himself to his intended victim at Frankfurt, Germany, and created a wave of adverse publicity for the Soviet Union by his display of the cloak-and-dagger murder weapon—an electrically operated pistol which was disguised as a cigarette case and designed to fire pellets of poison. Khokhlov revealed that an earlier attempt to assassinate Okolovich was made in 1951, and that his own assignment was part of a plan for the murder of several NTS leaders initiated shortly after Stalin's death.[80]

In addition to Okolovich, the intended victims included Dr. Alexander Trushnovic, founder and chairman of the West Berlin Rescue Committee, and Dr. Vladimir Poremsky, the president of NTS. The previous attempt on the life of Okolovich had failed because of defection by two of the three agents assigned, and Poremsky's intended assassin gave himself up in December, 1955. Trushnovic, however, was kidnapped in April, 1954; and in June, 1954, another member of NTS, Valery Tremmel, was kidnapped by Soviet agents in Linz, Austria.

Other attacks were made through diplomatic channels. In May, 1954, the Soviets demanded that the British Government "put an end" to activities of the London branch of NTS because it was plotting "diversion, sabotage and hostile-provocative work against the Soviet Union."[81] In 1956, they complained about "provocative leaflets" scattered on the grounds of the Soviet Embassy in London. In 1957, they opined that "large quantities of anti-Soviet publications in Russian were placed in places of public use"—near Soviet ships. According to this protest, "groups of unknown persons with hostile feelings towards the Soviet Union also made a nuisance of themselves by pestering Soviet seamen with provocative questions and offers of a criminal nature, making attempts to place stealthily with the seamen, as well as to disseminate on board the Soviet ships, publications of a hostile character issued by the above-mentioned organization." NTS, the Soviets asserted, "still continues its hostile and subversive activities with regard to the Soviet Union."[82] Similar protests were made at various times to the governments of Austria, Belgium, France, Germany, Greece, Sweden and Switzerland.[83]

In February, 1957, an attempt was made to discredit NTS in the Soviet Union itself, by branding it as a tool of American "aggression." Four captured members were displayed on a Moscow television broadcast, after two years of imprisonment and, presumably, the usual methods of Soviet "indoctrination."[84] Appearing with Leonid F. Ilyichev, chief of the press department in the Soviet Foreign Office, they were described by *Pravda* as "former agents of American intelligence." Ilyichev charged that a "secret war" was being "inspired" by "aggressive circles of the United States,"[85] and *Pravda* reported that it was "proved and substantiated" that "the spy group 'NTS' is in the service of and fully supported by American Intelligence."[86]

In the meantime, the reports of revolts continued. In 1955, there was an "armed incursion" in central Asia, in which Soviet border guards "fought the enemy fearlessly and destroyed all the diversionists."[87] In March, 1956, there was an uprising in Tiflis, Georgia, which the Soviets tried to pass off as a demonstration of resentment of the "defamation" of Stalin. It was soon discovered, however, to have been a genuine revolt, aimed at independence, and suppressed only by the overwhelming force of Soviet guns and tanks.[88]

Further unrest in Kazakhstan, where 3,000 workers and young Komsomols stood up against successive attacks by the security police, militia, and airborne troops of the Red Army,[89] was undoubtedly responsible for the repeated shakeups in the party and government leadership of that area[90] and even the ouster from the Presidium, in May, 1960, of Nikolai I. Belyayev, erstwhile party chief of the Kazakh Soviet Socialist Republic. In April, 1960, there were reports of strikes and protest meetings at the industrial center of Kemerovo and other parts of Siberia.[91] Reports of the opening of new slave-labor camps in the Ural Mountains, for deportees from the Baltic States— at Spassk, Dalinka and Karabash[92]—confirmed the announcement of growing unrest in that area.[93]

Resistance in China

In Communist China the reports were similar. According to Secretary Dulles (July, 1957), there were even "more revolutionary elements" present in China "than seem to be present within the Soviet Union."[94] In 1952, the Communists reported an open rebellion in the province of Kangsu, involving more than 20,000 persons, and lasting from April until July. According to these reports, three districts passed to the control of the rebels, and 3,000 Communist leaders and military officials were killed.[95] On another occasion, in February, 1954, they reported the successful liquidation of 13,000 guerrilla fighters,[96] but in the following month announced that more than ten times this number (140,000) were active in the single province of East Kwangtung.[97]

Very extensive resistance was disclosed in 1955 and 1956, at the conventions of the "National People's Congress" in Peiping. At the convention held in July, 1955, it was reported that there were at least 210 anti-Communist organizations operating on the Chinese mainland, and that during the seventeen-month period from January, 1954 to May, 1955, the so-called "people's courts" had dealt with a total of 1,179,217 cases of anti-Communist activity. This was an average of 69,360 cases per month.[98] At the convention held in July, 1956, it was reported that new uprisings had occurred in sixteen different provinces, one involving 50,000 guerrillas in the province of Kiangsu.[99]

During the rest of 1956, there were numerous further accounts of the suppression of anti-Communist activities. Thus, in one two-week period there were reports of action against six "counterrevolutionary" organizations in seven provinces.[100] A series of student demonstrations culminated in a riot of 1,000 at Hanyang, in which government and Communist headquarters were wrecked and several officers beaten.[101] In one province of Manchuria, it was reported that forty thousand "politically and ideologically unreliable" persons were "hiding in all government agencies," and even "penetrating into the party and policy-making organizations."[102]

In November, 1956, the Communists revealed the suppression of a rebellion of "reactionary bands" in North Viet Nam. President Diem of South Viet Nam stated that thousands of anti-Communists were "massacred."[103]

In Tibet, by 1957, the resistance appeared to be taking effect. The Communists reported that troops were being withdrawn from the eastern areas,[104] and Mao Tse-tung asserted: "It has now been decided not to proceed with democratic reform in Tibet during the period of the second five-year plan, and we can only decide whether it will be done in the period of the third five-year plan in the light of the situation obtaining at that time."[105]

Many thought that the Chinese Communist regime was then ready to topple, as perhaps it was. In Taipei the National Association of Youth Organizations asserted that conditions were ripe for open revolt.[106] It was reported on Quemoy, the embattled offshore island outpost of the free Chinese Republic, that preparations were being made for an ultimate return to the mainland.[107] Nevertheless, the free powers stood idly by and the Communists remained in control. They "retreated" a little, but then moved to consolidate their positions.

In October, 1957, the Communists reported that they had withdrawn more than 90% of their "cadres" and "workers" in Tibet, but at the same time they announced that the army would remain—to deal "firm and telling blows to rebellious elements."[108] These blows succeeded only after a protracted struggle culminating in the Lhasa uprising in 1959, during the course of which only the free government of the Republic of China endeavored to provide any assistance to the people—with wholly inadequate equipment.

In China proper hundreds of thousands of Communist officials and approximately 3,000,000 students were sent to farm work,[109] either as a punishment designed to fit the "crime," or as a means of filling the void created by the boycott of the co-operative state farm system by 15,000,000 farmers.[110] In February, 1958, the Communist Premier Chou En-lai reported that the "frenzied attacks of the bourgeois rightists" had been successfully "repulsed" in the "latter half of 1957," and that the "rectification campaign" was continuing with "growing intensity."[111] According to the Minister of Public Security, more than 100,000 "counterrevolutionaries" and "rightists" had been "ferreted out" of the party, the government, the Communist Youth League and other organizations.[112] Another "official" report stated that 1,300,000 persons had been "transferred" from their homes for "training" in "labor" or "basic-level units."[113]

The ultimate Communist response to the "irresistible demand" in China was the decision, made in July, 1958, to herd the entire population into so-called communes organized "along military lines." In these it was orginally announced that all significant vestiges of private property would be eliminated, and that all cooking, eating, child care, and even sleeping, would be done in central mess halls and community housing facilities—so as to make "full use of labor power" and to "enable women to play their full part in field work."[114] In the meantime, however, the unrest continued to grow; and in December, 1958, at its sixth plenary session, the Eighth Central Committee of the Chinese Communist Party called for a new slowdown. "Over-eager" party members, it said, were getting "dizzy with success."[115]

But the drive continued, nevertheless—and so did the resistance. In the same month the Nationalist Chinese reported extensive revolts in Tibet, Szechwan, Tsinghai, Sikang and Kansu, surpassing in some cases, they said, the intensity of the revolt in Hungary.[116] In January, 1959, they reported that local incidents were being transformed into "an over-all revolution," with 60% of the mainland, including Inner Mongolia, Kansu, Ningsia, Tsinghai, Sinkiang, Yunnan, Kweichow, Szechwan, Sikang and Tibet in open revolt. In Outer Mongolia, they said, 90,000 had been executed and 110,000 imprisoned by the Soviets.[117]

In Tibet these reports were confirmed by the outbreak of bloody civil war, in which 80,000 were killed, and by the flight of the Dalai Lama to India. Elsewhere on the mainland they were confirmed by announcements of the Communists themselves. In Sinkiang orders were issued to step up the struggle against "chauvinism and localism."[118] Outcroppings of "nefarious activity" were reported to have occurred in Hopei, where "counterrevolutionaries and bad elements" had committed "large-scale poisoning," "arson" and "murder." Similar reports were made in Kiangsi—and in Shansi, during a six-month period, 11,352 counterrevolutionaries were "ferreted out" and 12,898 criminals found "among persons who roved about and elements whose background was not clear."[119]

Similar reports came from Sinkiang in April,[120] Wuhan in May,[121] and in January, 1960, the Peiping *People's Daily* reported widespread arson in north China, where 11,000 granaries were destroyed. Further, it was reported at a Shanghai "public health conference" that during eighteen months of the "great leap forward" 13,000,000 people had died of exhaustion and "accidents." The ten-year total of deaths from such causes, not including 24,000,000 disabled, was put at 31,000,000.[122]

East Europe and the Riots at Poznan

In eastern Europe, in the meantime, the demand for freedom seemed even more "irresistible." Two days of rioting at Poznan, Poland, (June 28-29, 1956) were followed by reports of outbreaks in other parts of the country[123] and in the Baltic States.[124] In July, 1956, the security police of Czechoslovakia revealed the suppression, in 1953, of a hitherto hushed-up revolt in Prague—a revelation interpreted as having been made for the purpose of discouraging an anticipated renewal of disorders in that country.[125]

Within four months the "Stalinists" were ousted from power in Poland and Hungary, in order to prevent the occurrence of more serious revolts in the former country and to placate a nationwide revolt which had already occurred in the latter. In some parts of the free world it was immediately assumed that the "inherent longing for freedom" was about to be fulfilled. President Eisenhower asserted that in Poland the people had "moved to secure a peaceful transition to a new government," which, "it seems, will strive genuinely to serve the Polish people," and that in Hungary a new nation appeared to be "rising" from the "struggle." The "fervor and the sacrifice of the peoples of these countries, in the name of freedom," he said, "have themselves brought real promise that the light of liberty soon will shine again in this darkness."[126]

This new "light," however, was quickly smothered. The "liberal" Communists in Hungary became more ruthless even than the "Stalinists," and in Poland it soon became apparent that the people were only enjoying the temporary and limited benefits of a new Soviet "retreat."

The dissidence in Poznan was at first met with brutality, and an effort was made to put the blame upon "capitalist intervention." The rioters were dispersed in the usual manner, with tanks and automatic weapons, and the official Polish news agency, P.A.P., reported that their activities had been provoked by "imperialist agents." The uprising, it said, "bore the imprint of a large-scale and carefully prepared provocative and diversionary action. . . ."[127]

This story, however, was contradicted by too many foreign visitors to be believed. Even Communists—outside the Iron Curtain—described the riots as an unfortunate expression of the "legitimate demands of the workers."[128] Accordingly, a number of startling "concessions" were soon made. To many they seemed unprecedented.

At public trials of the rioters the accused were allowed to repudiate their "confessions" and to describe freely the methods of the Communist police investigators. Witnesses openly related how they had been instructed to make false accusations, and even the prosecution asserted that the defendants had been mistreated. Testimony obtained by force was excluded.

The courtroom finally became an open forum for descriptions of the massacre, and of the demands of the rioters for free elections and elimination of the secret police. One youthful spectator exclaimed, with no apparent reprisal: "My father died fighting for Poland in 1939! My mother was killed in 1942! And now we are oppressed worse than ever."[129] This was followed by a fifteen-minute recess of the embarrassed court.

Before the trials were over, "Stalinist" Hilary Minc resigned as First Deputy Premier and the entire Central Committee of the Polish Communist (United Workers') Party followed suit. A delegation from Moscow (Khrushchev, Mikoyan, Zhukov, Molotov and Kaganovich) vainly endeavored to prevent the party machinery from falling into the hands of "liberal" Communists, but it was dissuaded by the defiance of Edward Ochab, the retiring party leader, and by mass public demonstrations of popular hatred. The "liberal" Communists, who won a majority in the new Central Committee, were allowed to take over, and their leader, Wladyslaw Gomulka, who was described by Khrushchev as a "traitor,"[130] became party first secretary.

The program of "concessions" thereafter adopted was certainly impressive. Ninety-four defendants in the Poznan trials were released, and a review was ordered for the others. Secret-police activity was curtailed, the jamming of foreign radio stations discontinued, and new "elections" held. More repatriations of exiled Polish citizens were promised and carried out. The Polish Army was freed of Soviet "advisers" and officers, and even Red Army movements were to be subject to the approval of "competent" Polish authorities.

In a burst of religious tolerance, Cardinal Wyszynsky and other jailed clergymen were released, religious instruction was authorized upon request, and it was reported that efforts to control the appointment of bishops and pastors had been abandoned.

In a new "return to capitalism," many of the collective farms were allowed to dissolve. Increased prices were paid for compulsory grain deliveries, and restrictions on the ownership, sale and rental of land were removed. Taxes were also reduced and credits made available to small business for the purchase of shops, equipment and raw materials.

None of these "concessions," however, could be considered without precedent, and they were no more substantial than others made in the past. If Gomulka and his "national" Communist followers were *reluctantly* allowed to remain in power by Khrushchev, they had been preceded long ago by "national" Communists of an earlier period—such as Mikola Skrypnik in the Ukraine, Budu Mdivani in Georgia, Zylumovic and Cherviakov in Byelorussia. All had been *willingly* tolerated, and even forced upon the non-Russian nations, by Lenin and Stalin, and all were eventually liquidated.

If in 1956 Gomulka was permitted to fill his "government" with "liberal" *Communists*, Zylumovic in 1925 had repatriated and brought to power in Byelorussia many *non-Communists*, including even members of the overthrown and exiled government of the Byelorussian National Republic. If "concessions" were made to the Catholic Church in Poland, and its prelates were to be released, there had been similar "concessions" for the Orthodox Church in Russia, and Tikhon and Sergei were in and out of prison many times. If Khrushchev cancelled debts and granted credits to Poland, Stalin had granted whole provinces to Byelorussia (Mogilev and Vitebsk) and stimulated its economic life with investments from the federal treasury. If private enterprise was restored for the Polish peasants and the small shopowners of Warsaw, their counterparts in the Soviet Union had once been granted similar privileges under the "New Economic Policy" of Lenin and Stalin.

In Byelorussia, however, and the other "national republics" of the Soviet "federation," the non-Communist and "national" Communist leaders had eventually disappeared in a series of purges which thoroughly "cleansed" the Communist parties of "nationalist conspirators," "deviators" and various types of local "chauvinists." Gomulka and his "liberal" colleagues, as well as Khrushchev, no doubt recalled that Cherviakov had shot himself to avoid torture and confession, that Skrypnik had also committed suicide under a cloud of official "criticism," that Zylumovic died in an insane asylum while awaiting his trial, and that Mdivani had been executed for "conspiracy" and "nationalist deviation."

Whether or not they did recall these events, there were, before long, many familiar signs of the inevitable return to "normalcy." The once-touted "right to criticize" was suppressed, even for "liberal" Communists, and "Stalinists" were soon trickling back into the "government."

While new freedom was promised to religion, a rigid "state" control of church appointments was still demanded.[131] Censors prohibited the publication of distasteful church communications, such as the warning against collaboration with "Pax," the Communist-sponsored organization of "progressive Catholics,"[132] and the Cardinal's Christmas message of 1957, in which he asked for "a peace not of slaves but of free children of God."[133] Finally, Gomulka announced that long-term relations with the Church were dependent upon its willingness to "march with us concerning the interests of the people's Poland."[134]

An anti-Communistic youth unit was formed in the "Democratic Party," but it was quickly dissolved. There were non-Communists on the "election" slates, and some were even "elected," but they were not so numerous as to threaten Communist control. Strikes and "workers' councils" were permitted, but the former were soon outlawed again, and the latter were taken over by a "conference of workers' self-government," more amenable to Communist control. There were "reductions" in taxes, but these were followed by a confiscatory tax on monthly incomes over 15,000 zlotys. This was equal to $150 on the free (black) market.

In February, 1957, only four months after the "victory" of "liberalized" communism, its failure was conceded by a member and official spokesman of the new Central Committee, Jerszy Putrament. The only real alternative to capitalism, he said, was the "emergency socialism of Stalin's epoch." In a rare demonstration of frankness, he also pointed out that so-called "independent" communism was completely dependent not only upon Soviet tolerance but also upon Soviet subjugation. Without this, he implied, there would be no communism in Poland at all. "Those of our columnists," he said, "who today so unconcernedly 'abolish' the foundations of Marxism-Leninism in the name of the alleged 'real' Socialist revolution should understand that their trickeries are possible thanks only to their proximity to the Soviet Union."[135] Such were the conclusions of a "liberal" Communist, recently castigated by *Pravda* for "Culling his political arsenal from the Voice of America."[136]

In October, 1957, a more formal announcement of the end of "liberal" communism was made by Gomulka himself. On this occasion, almost on the first anniversary of his rise to power, the leader of the "liberal" Polish Communists told the "Tenth Plenum" of the Central Committee that in order to overcome "dogmatism" (Stalinism) it was necessary first of all to overcome "revisionism" (liberalism). "Dogmatism," Gomulka said, "cannot be cured by revisionism .... the successful combatting of revisionism will greatly facilitate the overcoming of dogmatism. In the fight against the two ailments of our Party, you should strike first of all at the basic source of its weakness: revisionism and liquidationism."[137]

This speech was worthy of Stalin himself, who had also fought against these "two ailments of our Party," and who had made a similar speech (in 1928) at a "Plenum" of the Moscow Committee. It is "our duty," Stalin said, "without of course diminishing our vigilance in regard to the Left [Trotzkyist] danger by one jot, to lay down the most stress on the fight against the Right ["soft"] danger and to bring all efforts to bear on making this danger as apparent to the Party as the Trotzkyist danger now is."[138]

Finally, in December, 1957, *The New York Times* reported that the previous enthusiasm of the Poles had been replaced by a "mood of disillusionment."[139] The "irresistible demand" for freedom was as far from fulfillment as ever.

In the meantime, the riots and demonstrations continued. In December, 1956, there was a new, three-day demonstration by the steelworkers of Poznan, to emphasize their demands for the withdrawal of Soviet troops. In addition, there were student demonstrations in Warsaw and, finally, strikes at Poznan, Bydgoszcz, Lodz and in the coal mines. Numerous riots and "incidents" were started by "intoxicated hooligans" and "social scum" at Stettin, Bydgoszcz, Stargard, Jaroslow, Poznan and Sopot. All brought stern warnings from Gomulka that the recent fate of Hungary could only be avoided by the strictest obedience.

Rebellion in Hungary

Hungary's fate did have significance for the Poles, but not necessarily that intended by Gomulka. As a mere demonstration of Soviet repression it was hardly a revelation—of this all subject peoples had more than enough experience. But as an indication of the help to be expected from the free world—of the course to be followed by the United States after it had "stimulated" and "revived" the "inherent longing for freedom"—it was informative, to say the least.

Before the revolt in Hungary, the captive peoples still had hopes of receiving free-world assistance, at least in the event of a change in their Communist form of government. Such hopes were to a large extent encouraged by the action taken in the case of Yugoslavia, where military assistance was given, even to a totally Communist regime, for the express purpose of enabling it to defy the Soviet Union and terminate its satellite status.

It has also been asserted that the expectation of assistance, in the event of an open rebellion, was encouraged by Radio Free Europe and other private agencies organized to keep alive the demand for freedom behind the iron curtain. It hardly seems possible that such agencies would make any specific promises of assistance on their own initiative, and the "charges" thus made against them have been vigorously denied. On the other hand, the hope of assistance could not fail to be aroused by the mere repetition of official statements, made by the representatives of the United States government, abjuring and condemning the previous "betrayal" of the captive peoples. So much had been said about the failure to protect them from Soviet aggression in the past that they could hardly do otherwise than conclude that more effective assistance would be made available in the future, at least for the defense of any free government that might be successfully re-established.

Such a belief would be supported even by the previous spotty record of free-world resistance. It was true that *prior* to World War II the free nations had denied assistance to many victims of Soviet aggression, but it could be argued that in these cases the victims lay within the boundaries of the former Russian Empire. After World War II the free nations had again tolerated open Soviet aggression, but at that time, it could be asserted, the Red Army had advanced under "international warrant" in eastern Europe. On still other occasions the free powers had allowed their allies to be felled by indirect and covert aggression, but even in such instances it could be said that the aggression was not open or direct. No matter what might be stated about the past, it could not yet be said that the free nations had ever stood idly by while the Red Army was used for open, direct and naked aggression, unexcused by any "secret understanding," and beyond the confines of any previous Russian Empire.

Moreover, apart from any question of a successful restoration of freedom, it was now difficult to believe that the subject peoples would not in some way be assisted in defending themselves against reprisals brought on by those "demonstrations" of "independence" which the free world itself demanded. Although its statements were confusing, the United States in particular was now encouraging active anti-Communist resistance—regardless of the consequences. In spite of its disclaimer of any intention to promote a "senseless" armed revolt, or "precipitate a massacre," the Eisenhower administration expected the subject peoples to set up "strains and stresses within the captive world." While Secretary Dulles asserted that the captive peoples must *peacefully* frustrate the "design of Soviet despotism," he also maintained that they could give it an "acute" case of "indigestion," which "might be fatal."[140] The "independence" of the "enslaved national groups" was only a "peaceful" goal, but there was high praise, nevertheless, for each new riot and every uprising.

This praise and encouragement had continued in spite of all odds and the most indiscriminate Soviet reprisals—*mass* arrests, *mass* deportations and *mass* executions. According to the United States High Commissioner, the riots in East Germany were suppressed by the "continuous application of brutal terror methods," but they were described by President Eisenhower, nevertheless, as an "eloquent message," the "message of defiance" delivered "in the memorable June uprising."[141] Secretary of State Dulles acknowledged that the revolt in Guatemala was undertaken "in the face of terrorism and violence and against what seemed insuperable odds," but he advised the free world to be grateful to those who had "the courage and the will to eliminate the traitorous tools of foreign despots."[142] In the case of Hungary itself, the President would soon be stating that "all the world" was "watching dramatic events," in which a "brave people" had "offered their very lives for independence." "We have rejoiced," he was to say, "in these historic events."[143] If anything could have led the subject peoples to expect foreign assistance, it was statements such as these. Activities deserving of the praise and commendation which they contained were certainly also deserving of assistance, and those who were thus encouraged to provoke attacks upon themselves and upon their families could hardly be blamed for counting upon some aid for self-defense.

Finally, the President made what appeared to be a firm pledge of assistance to all enslaved peoples. On the very night the revolt in Hungary began, October 23, 1956, in a public address on "Communist Imperialism in the Satellite World," he asserted that the United States, as the "champion of human freedom," was bound to help all "those freedom-loving peoples who need and want and can profitably use our aid":

> The day of liberation may be postponed where armed forces for a time make protest suicidal. But all history testifies that the memory of freedom is not erased by the fear of guns and the love of freedom is more enduring than the power of tyrants. But it is necessary that the inspiration of freedom and the benefits enjoyed by those who possess it are known to those oppressed.
> *We, as a nation*—in that light—*have a job to do, a mission as the champion of human freedom.* This is it:
> First—So to conduct ourselves in all our international relations that we never compromise the fundamental principle that all peoples who have proved themselves capable of self-government have a right to an independent government of their own full, free choice.
> Second—So to help those freedom-loving peoples who need and

want and can profitably use our aid that they may advance in their ability for self-support and may add strength to the security and peace of the free world.

.   .   .   .

> *Working in this manner, we shall expand the areas in which free men, free governments can flourish. We shall help shrink the areas in which human beings can be exploited and their governments subverted.*[144] (Italics added.)

No similar assurance was ever more quickly put to the test. When the President made this pledge, the great Stalin statue in the Boulevard Dozsa Gyorgy had already been torn down, the unarmed students of Budapest had already been fired upon for demanding the publication of their "irresistible" demands; and even as the President spoke, the first Soviet tanks were already rumbling into the streets of the city —for when it is 10 P.M. in Washington it is 5 o'clock the following morning in Hungary.

It may be that most Hungarians were not immediately made aware of the President's pledge. Possibly there were few who heard it—even after their freedom had been partially restored. But to those who did hear, the assurance which the President thus gave could hardly fail to bring hope of assistance in the national effort to expel an army of occupation which was already hesitating to support the Soviet oppression. Within two days crowds appeared in front of the United States and British legations, shouting for assistance:

"The workers are being murdered, we want help."[145]

"Why don't you send us arms? We don't want your boys."[146]

In spite of these demands, however, no such assistance was forthcoming. Instead, the United States refused to give aid directly, and in the United Nations followed a policy of procrastination devoid of any recommendation for positive action. When the Council and Assembly were finally called into session, the other free nations were encouraged to adopt a procedure which the Soviets themselves had formerly condemned. As Litvinov had said in 1937, "They begin to concern themselves principally with the maintenance of their own existence, with the procuring of moral satisfaction for those who have initiated such conferences, and with their own superficial successes, which do not always coincide with successes for the cause on account of which the conferences were brought into existence."[147]

The original United States response to the people's appeal for aid was inspirational but noncommittal. On October 25, 1956, the second day of the revolt, the President issued a statement in which he approved the demands made against the Communist "government" of Hungary, but had nothing to say about those made upon the free government of the United States. "The demands reportedly made by the students and the working people," he said, "clearly fall within the framework of those human rights to which all are entitled, which are affirmed in the charter of the United Nations, and which are specifically guaranteed to the Hungarian people by the treaty of peace. . . ."[148] Secretary of State Dulles called attention to the Declaration on Austria. This wartime declaration, made in 1943, had promised freedom and independence, not only for Austria, but also for "those neighboring states which will be faced with similar problems." "Today," Mr. Dulles said, "there are 'those neighboring states' who await the fulfillment of the promise. . . ."[149]

On October 27, Secretary Dulles spoke of a "duty" to help. In this spirit, he said, the problem had finally been referred to the United Nations:

. . . the heroic people of Hungary challenge the murderous fire of Red Army tanks. These patriots value liberty more than life itself. And all who peacefully enjoy liberty have a solemn duty to seek, by all truly helpful means, that those who now die for freedom will not have died in vain. It is in this spirit that the United States and others have today acted to bring the situation in Hungary to the United Nations Security Council.[150]

In the meantime, however, the United States and other members of the Security Council had been indicating that effective United Nations action was not favored. In the United States it was reported that certain officials were sympathetic with Hungarian demands, but reluctant to recognize any free government unfriendly to Moscow.[151] The French Foreign Minister, Christian Pineau, maintained that any effort to "cut the links" between the satellites and the Soviet Union would be "dangerous," and provide the Communists with a "pretext to go back on de-Stalinization."[152] In Canada the Secretary of State for External Affairs, Lester B. Pearson, asserted that tangible assistance would not help the captive peoples and, indeed, might "hurt them by provoking a cruel and powerful reaction from those who may be waiting for an opportunity to move in and destroy these new liberating and national forces, using the excuse of foreign threats or interference from our side."[153]

Accordingly, when the "situation in Hungary" was finally brought before the Security Council, five days after the revolt, no resolution was offered. Instead, the United States representative, Henry Cabot Lodge, indicated his belief that the mere "decision to consider" the question would be sufficient.[154] There were reports of heavy Soviet reinforcements,[155] but the free powers were content to put the question on the agenda (by a vote of 9-1) and then permit the Council to *adjourn indefinitely*. The British representative asserted that the "Big Three" wanted to wait and see what reaction the meeting would have on the Soviet Union. Other Western sources were quoted as expressing confidence that individual condemnation of Soviet action by the majority of the Council members "would in itself have an effect on Moscow."[156]

In sharp contrast to this mild reaction to the murder of children was the entirely different attitude taken toward the Israeli invasion of the Sinai desert. When this occurred, the day after the Council's adjournment on Hungary, the United States requested an "immediate" meeting of the Security Council. The chairman of the Senate Foreign Relations Committee suggested that it might even be necessary to call a special session of Congress. On the next day, October 30, the Security Council was called into session three times (11 A.M., 4 P.M. and 9 P.M.), and the United States presented a strong resolution calling upon all members "to assist the United Nations in ensuring the integrity of the armistice agreements."[157]

When the proposed resolutions on Israel were vetoed by France and Great Britain, the General Assembly was forthwith called into special emergency session and Secretary Dulles appeared personally to assert that it was "imperative that something be done."[158] After an all-night session, a resolution was adopted in the early hours of the morning of November 2. This was the fourth day after the attack, and the resolution on Israel was thus adopted in less time than it took to convene a meeting on the "situation in Hungary."

The difference in attitude was reflected in the statements of the United States representative, Henry Cabot Lodge, at the first meeting of the Security Council in each case. On the subject of "military action by Israel" he was forthright and direct:

Failure by the Council to react at this time would be a clear avoidance of its responsibility for the maintenance of international peace and security. . . .

The Government of the United States feels that it is imperative that the Council act in the promptest manner to determine that a breach of the peace has occurred, to order that the military actions undertaken by Israel cease immediately, and to make clear its view that the Israeli armed forces be immediately withdrawn behind the established armistice lines. Nothing less will suffice.[159]

On the "situation in Hungary" he seemed to be casting about for a solution not to the problem of preventing aggression but to that of relieving the embarrassment of a government unwilling to act:

It is clear that we are not going to try to reach a vote today on anything of substance. . . .

. . . .

We fervently hope that the action in bringing this matter to the Council and the Council's decision to consider the grave events in Hungary will move those responsible for the repression of the Hungarian people to discontinue such measures. . . .

. . . .

We must consider carefully, in the light of developments, the steps this Council can appropriately take to help bring about an end to these repressions and to assist the Hungarian people in the enjoyment of their fundamental rights.

. . . .

As a member of the Security Council, the United States Government is prepared to join in considering what this Council can properly do. . . .[160]

In the case of the Soviet Union, which had, as Lodge asserted, engaged in the "violent suppression of the Hungarian people by armed force,"[161] and which had a long record of defiance of the United Nations directives, it was sufficient, four days after the attack, merely to seek "consideration" by the Security Council, and to place the question on its agenda. In the case of Israel, on the other hand, which had at least made efforts to co-operate with the United Nations, and which even now, according to Secretary Dulles, had a "legitimate" cause for "complaint,"[162] it was necessary that an "*order*" be issued immediately—"in the promptest manner."[163]

The Israeli invasion was forced to an immediate vote in the Security Council, and a consequent veto, in order that the question might be promptly submitted to an emergency session of the General Assembly. As Ambassador Lodge asserts, "an emergency session of the General Assembly cannot be called until the Security Council has finished dealing with a given question."[164] But on the subject of Hungary the Security Council was not aven asked to resume consideration until *five days* after its first adjournment. When it did meet, on November 2, 1956, Soviet forces had set up road blocks on all main highways, occupied every airfield and important railroad junction, resealed the western frontier and surrounded Budapest with armor. Imre Nagy reported that still more Soviet reinforcements were arriving.

The Council also had before it Nagy's direct appeal for the assistance of the United Nations and the "four great powers." Nagy asked that "the question of Hungary's neutrality and the defense of this neutrality" be referred immediately to the General Assembly, but the "Big Three" nevertheless permitted the Council to embark upon two days of fruitless debate, and then to adjourn pending "negotiations" for the withdrawal of Soviet troops. This was the second adjournment without action, without a resolution, and without calling for a meeting of the General Assembly.

On the first day of this second debate, ten days after Soviet intervention, the United States representative still had no resolution to offer. He simply asserted that the "next step" should be to "ascertain the facts." "We must," he said, "above all, be helpful to the Hungarian people by acting with knowledge of the facts. . . ."[165]

This assertion of a need for facts was not in conformity with the statement made by the President on the second day of the revolt. At that time the President did not appear to have any doubts about the existence of aggression. On the contrary, he flatly stated that "The United States deplores the intervention of Soviet military forces which, under the treaty of peace, should have been withdrawn and the presence of which in Hungary, as is now demonstrated, is not to protect Hungary against armed aggression from without but rather to continue an occupation of Hungary by the forces of an alien government for its own purposes."[166]

The assertion of the United States representative also did not appear to be in conformity with the views of other delegates. The Cuban delegate vainly pointed out that the facts were well known:

... none can allege that the Council has insufficient evidence at its disposal. In the first place, we have the sinister and monstrous fact that more than 20,000 Hungarians have lost their lives fighting for freedom against the troops of the Soviet Union, which are foreign troops on Hungarian soil. We also have an authentic official document [the appeal from Imre Nagy] which gives an unglossed account of what is happening in Hungary. . . .

In other words, the facts are as follows: Hungary, a Member of the United Nations whose territory is being invaded by foreign troops, which are endeavoring to prevent the Hungarian people from discarding the chains of brutal tyranny, is appealing to the United Nations for help in accordance with the clear and explicit principles of the Charter. . . .

Yesterday the Cuban delegation voted in the General Assembly in favour of the draft resolution submitted by the United States of America [on the Sinai and Suez question] despite the close ties of friendship which bind us with the Powers concerned . . . . we are again prepared to support any draft resolution designed to put an end to a state of affairs which shames the human race and cannot be accepted by the free peoples of the world.[167]

The British representative also reported upon the facts, as follows:

The information concerning the situation which we received earlier today, that is, 2 November, is that in the past few days large numbers of tanks have moved into the country, and that some of these have moved to the neighborhood of Budapest. It seems that Budapest is being ringed by Soviet concentrations of armour on the outskirts of the city.

.   .   .   .

... it is the hope of Her Majesty's Government in the United Kingdom that even at this late stage the Soviet Government will recognize that it is for the people of Hungary to order their own destiny and that the Soviet policy of armed interference in Hungary's internal affairs is a bankrupt one.[168]

The French delegate presented a statement of some facts just handed to him:

A large armoured unit has arrived in Kisvarda. At the same time, the continuous movement of Soviet troops coming from the east has been noted in Debrecen. The movement of Russian armour towards the west has been noted in Szolnok. Approximately 200 tanks which have for several days taken up positions between Szolnok and Abony have begun to move towards the west. . . . On the night of Thursday to Friday, several armoured units took up positions in the area of Gyongyos. In Transdanubya, Soviet units stationed near Dombovar have surrounded the airport at Taszar and launched spearheads as far as the suburbs of Kaposvar. No incident has been noted in that area.

About twenty lorries bearing Soviet infantrymen arrived in Nyiregyháza on Friday evening. Finally, about fifty motorized batteries crossed the Soviet-Hungarian frontier at Beregsurany.[169]

He also made the following observations:

It seems to me that, since there is proof of foreign intervention, and also of the will of the Hungarian people and Government to put an end to that intervention, the Security Council, the United Nations and the whole world find themselves faced with a violation of the United Nations Charter, of international law and of the rules of international morality.

. . . .

In the present circumstances, bearing in mind that for ten years the United Nations has all too often demonstrated its powerlessness to enforce the resolutions it adopts unanimously or by a large majority, we must take the necessary measures to ensure that the great hope which took shape after the war should not die in the hearts of the peoples of the free world. Neither in the Czechoslovak affair eight years ago, nor in the matter of the arrest of Cardinal Mind- zenty, nor in the matter of the Bulgarian Protestant ministers, was the United Nations able to take any effective action. It is high time to put an end to this powerlessness. That is why the French Government instructed me to ask for an urgent meeting of the Security Council with a view to the adoption of an appropriate resolution. If this can- not be done because of a veto, we must consider the immediate con- vening of an emergency special session of the General Assembly.[170]

The Peruvian delegate stated that he had instructions to "sup- port any motion or resolution, either in the Council or in the General Assembly, which would guarantee to Hungary the right of self- determination and the freedom to establish its own structure as an independent nation."[171]

The "facts" which the United States still sought to "ascertain" had also been the subject of almost daily news reports since the day

(October 28) on which the Council had first met and adjourned. On that day, Sunday, the morning papers had described signs of the entry into Hungary of two new armored divisions. It was reported that Soviet reinforcements had already reached Budapest and that barricades were being thrown up by the defenders.[172] On Monday, October 29, it was reported that new Soviet forces in Budapest made further resistance in the city impossible.[173] On Wednesday, October 31, a dispatch from Bucharest stated that Soviet troops had moved into Hungary from Rumania.[174] On Thursday more than two Soviet divisions arrived, according to reports from the Hungarian army.[175] On Friday, the day on which the Council reconvened, it was reported that Budapest was "ringed with Soviet steel once again" and that Soviet civilian personnel were being evacuated.[176]

Nevertheless, no formal proposal was made, and the Council adjourned after a two-hour debate. The United States finally presented a draft resolution on Saturday afternoon, November 3, but when it was learned that a new Hungarian government, in which the Communists were a minority, was *negotiating* for Soviet withdrawal, the Council adjourned until Monday. It was not until after the Soviets, with overwhelming force, had launched their massive second attack, that the Security Council was hastily reconvened, in the middle of the night, to receive the Soviet veto and refer the matter to the General Assembly. This was on Sunday, November 4, one week after the case had been presented to the United Nations, and nearly two weeks after the revolt began. The end came quickly.

On that same Sunday morning it was announced that "General" Janos Kadar had taken on the duties of Prime Minister in addition to his office as party leader; and when the General Assembly met in the afternoon there was no government left to which assistance might be given—only beleaguered fighters for freedom. The United States delegate then asserted that "drastic and decisive" action would have to be taken: "We must take drastic and decisive action here in this Assembly to answer the appeal of the Hungarian Government. The United States delegation, therefore, is submitting a draft resolution which we believe should be promptly put to the vote and which I would now like to read."[177]

When these words were heard, some wondered if now, at last, the United States was going to propose effective action. As its Ambassador continued to speak, however, it became apparent that a search for "facts" was still his main preoccupation. The "drastic and decisive" action which the United States now suggested consisted in an *affirmation* of the rights of the Hungarian people, the shipment of "food, medicine, and other similar supplies," a *call* upon the Soviet Union to desist, an *investigation* of the methods which might be used to "bring an end to the existing situation," and a *call* for the admission of observers. After reading the resolution, the United States representative continued:

We do not believe that it is sufficient only to call upon the Soviet Union to desist from any further intervention in the internal affairs of Hungary and to withdraw all its troops without delay. We urge also that the Secretary-General should investigate the situation in Hungary directly and without delay and report to the Assembly as soon as possible. We call upon the USSR and Hungary to admit representatives of the Secretary-General to Hungarian territory, and if there is nothing to hide they have nothing to fear from the visit of impartial observers.[178]

The Soviet Union obviously had plenty to hide, but when this statement was made it knew that it had nothing to fear. The Assembly subsequently called upon it to desist from attack, to withdraw its forces, to admit observers and to cease the deportation of Hungarian citizens—but all to no avail. Finally, it was cited for "violation of the Charter," but the violations were continued with impunity.

After six resolutions calling for the termination of Soviet attacks had been ignored, the Assembly created a committee to collect evidence wherever it could. This committee reported, in June, 1957, that "Soviet authorities had taken steps as early as 20 October [three days before the revolt] to make armed intervention in Hungary possible" and that evidence existed of "troop movements, or projected troop movements, from that date on."[179] Since the United Nations had not been called upon even to "consider" the problem until October 27, it could hardly be deemed to have been given a chance to prove its worth. As the Secretary General, Dag Hammarskjold, said in 1959, "it is obvious that the organization can advance no further than the intentions of the parties permit . . . . it is worth remembering that, with the exception of one or two of the smaller countries, no government in the United Nations urged measures going further than those which were actually taken."[180]

In the meantime, continued resistance in Hungary—strikes, riots and guerrilla warfare—were not met with "irreversible" concessions, but with the severest repression. As the U.N. committee reported, "Mr. Kádár has successively abandoned most of the points from the revolutionary programme which he had at first promised to the Hungarian people."[181] Martial law was reimposed in December, 1956; and six months' imprisonment without trial was formally authorized for anyone "whose activities or behaviour endangers public order, or public security, and in particular the undisturbed continuity of productive work and transport."[182] In January, 1957, strikes and every other form of interference with production in "undertakings required for defence," or in public utilities, were made subject to the death penalty.[183] Thousands were deported, and tens of thousands were sent to concentration camps in each new wave of arrests. The persecution of the Church was pursued with renewed vigor.

During these difficult days the Kadar regime continued to pay lip-service to "democratization" and "de-Stalinization," while at the same time asserting that such slogans had been used for the "disintegration" and "dissolution" of the "social order" by persons of "petty bourgeois thinking," who were "masking themselves as Marxists." Kadar's real beliefs, or those imposed by his Soviet masters, were expressed in other public statements made both during and after the revolt:

They must capitulate or we will crush them.

[October 24, 1956][184]

My opinion is that one does not fight against a counter-revolution by yielding to its demands.... We are of the opinion that a tiger cannot be tamed by bait. It can be tamed and forced to peace only by beating it to death.

[November 26, 1956][185]

The state discipline of a peoples' democracy must be secured. An iron discipline and the consistent execution of the Government decrees will bring out the democratic core of the people.

[January 6, 1957][186]

On March 27, in a "friendship" meeting with Soviet Premier Bulganin, Kadar asserted that it would be necessary "to strengthen the punitive side of the proletarian dictatorship."[187]

These are the statements of the "rehabilitated," "liberal" and "national" Communist who succeeded "Stalinist" Erno Gero as party first secretary in the middle of the Hungarian revolt. His return to power was then described as a parallel to the return of Wladyslaw Gomulka, and he was considered a "genuine homegrown Hungarian Communist, not a man who lived much of his life in Moscow and was trained there, like Mr. Rakosi and the new Premier, Imre Nagy." Furthermore, although he "showed no mercy toward communism's opponents," it was not considered impossible that "he may be moved to be tough toward Russians and Hungarians alike."[188]

In June, 1958, the other "liberal" Premier, Imre Nagy, was executed. So much for the "irreversibility" of "concessions" and the "irresistibility" of "demands."

CHAPTER XVI

The Moral Force of World Opinion

"Let them be confounded and ashamed that seek my soul: Let them be turned backward, and blush for shame that desire evils to me:" (Ps. lxix:3, 4).

Another working hypothesis of current cold-war strategy is based upon the theory that if the impetus for liberation does not come from an "evolutionary" process of voluntary Soviet reform, or through a "forced reformation of some kind" induced from within, it will be provided by the moral force of world opinion, working from without. "For," it is said, "no nation, however powerful, wishes to incur, on a steadily mounting basis, the moral condemnation of the world."[1]

This statement, which was made by Secretary Dulles in 1955, seemed to overlook the fact that the Communists are not a nation, and that they do not, properly speaking, represent any nation. They are, moreover, well aware that world opinion is different from their own, and they are consciously dedicated to changing it—by force if necessary. On the other hand, it cannot be said that they are altogether impervious to world opinion, effectively expressed. Such a conclusion would ignore their own professed tactics of attack and retreat, of "manoeuvring, temporising and compromising."

So far, however, the free nations have not been willing to employ even this force effectively, uniformly and unequivocally. As indicated by the statement of Secretary Dulles, it is almost impossible to escape the inference that it is a nation or nations, rather than a criminal ruling minority, against whom the pressure must be applied—as though the injustices whose cure is sought were attributable to those who are in fact the victims. In many cases, even when the distinction is made, it is not honored, and the free powers supinely accept as representatives of the subject peoples those whom they ask the world to condemn as their oppressors. The most effective means of expressing world opinion are thus neglected, and yet it is assumed that this force alone will compel the Communists to grant the demands of the people and restore freedom.

This assumption has been repeatedly made and expressed in statements on eastern Europe. Thus, in October, 1955, a few months after the first "summit" conference, Secretary of State Dulles asserted:

There are some skeptics who doubt that change can be brought about peacefully. History does not justify this conclusion. The recent liberation of Austria came about primarily because world opinion insistently demanded it as a step which represented elemental justice. In the same way world opinion will act as a compulsion on the Soviet Union to relax its grip upon East Germany and to permit the unification of Germany.

Also, I believe that world opinion will compel the restoration of national independence to the captive states of Eastern Europe.[2]

When this statement was made, the "spirit of Geneva" was running high and the Soviet Union had withdrawn its troops from Austria—as it had once before withdrawn them from Iran. Three years later, however, the captive states were still captive, and the Soviets still refused to discuss their status. Secretary Dulles conceded that the "agreement" on Germany had "so far, certainly been repudiated."[3]

The agreement on Germany was in fact repudiated almost as soon as it was made—at the follow-up conference of foreign ministers in October-November, 1955. In a radio-television report on that conference, Secretary Dulles asserted that the "Soviet proposals were based on preserving the Soviet puppet regime in East Germany and the indefinite division of Germany, at least unless Soviet control could be extended to all Germany."[4] Nevertheless, he still maintained that moral force was the *only* force to be applied, and he so stated in another public address (December 8, 1955):

We shall not seek to cure these injustices by ourselves invoking force. But we can and will constantly keep these injustices at the forefront of human consciousness and thus bring into play the force of world opinion which, working steadily, will have its way.[5]

In the following year, 1956, the same assumption prevailed. It survived the slaughter in Hungary, and it was encouraged by the "retreat" in Poland. This was made plain in December, 1956, by Vice-President Nixon:

The United Nations has no armies that it could send to rescue the heroic freedom fighters of Hungary. There were no treaties which would invoke the armed assistance of the free nations. Our only weapon here was moral condemnation, since the alternative was action on our part which might initiate the third and ultimate world war.

There are those who say that moral force without military action to back it up means nothing. But we should never underestimate the force of the moral judgment of the world. . . .

The fact that the men in the Kremlin are writhing in the spotlight of world criticism may have saved the equally heroic peoples of Poland from Hungary's fate. Poland at least has a limited measure of independence today.[6]

In 1957, there was no change, either in the assumptions of the free powers or in the attitude of the Soviet leaders. Asking for the adoption of the eleventh United Nations' resolution on Hungary, Ambassador Lodge asserted: "The Soviet Union has shown a great resistance to the voice of world opinion on this matter, but we cannot believe that it will be forever deaf to the voice of its own manifest interest, which is to act in harmony with the conscience of the world."[7]

The "men in the Kremlin," however, have been "writhing in the spotlight of world criticism" for more than forty years, and they are still "deaf." They have been damned, doomed, denounced and deplored by every conceivable method of moral condemnation—by friendly criticism as well as by stern rebuke, in conferences and in isolation, in joint protests, in the severance of diplomatic relations, in moral embargoes, and even by expulsion from the League of Nations. Although not always consistently employed by all of the free nations, many of these methods of expressing world opinion were more vigorous, and therefore more likely to be effective, than any now employed, but the injustices remained nevertheless.

It is certainly important to assure the subject peoples, by word as well as by deed, that the ideals, pledges and commitments of the free nations are not abandoned. To whatever extent it is possible to restrain by moral force the excesses of those who recognize no moral standard, it is essential to do so. But it is wrong to assume that these things are in themselves sufficient. Limited moral pressure has been as big a failure in the war for men's minds as limited intervention was in the struggle for freedom in Russia—it has only produced the chimera of "limited" independence.

Like the "irreversible trend" and the "irresistible demand," the use of moral persuasion in the effort to restrain the leaders in the Kremlin began immediately after the Bolshevik seizure of power. In December, 1917, a joint appeal for moderation was made by the American and Swedish consul generals, acting on behalf of the Allied and neutral nations. The United States representative, Maddin Summers, even reported an apparent success. We are "endeavoring," he wired, "to do all we can in a friendly way to influence leaders Bolsheviks to stop campaign of terrorism waged against educated classes *and are encouraged by result.*"[8] (Italics added.)

The terror, however, continued, and in the following year (September, 1918) the United States urged the free nations to protest sternly a new wave of violence. All American diplomatic missions abroad were told to urge the governments to which they were accredited to "impress upon the perpetrators of these crimes the aversion with which civilization regards their present wanton acts," and in his circular telegram of instructions, the Secretary of State explained: "... this Government feels that it cannot be silent or refrain from expressing its horror at this existing state of terrorism. Furthermore, it believes that in order successfully to check the further increase of the indiscriminate slaughter of Russian citizens all civilized nations should register their abhorrence of such barbarism."[9]

As a result, there were immediate "concessions," but over the years the terror increased not only in the number of its victims but also in the deliberateness of its systematic application. Now, in the fifth decade of such rule, it is impossible to increase the weight of the judgment which was then pronounced, and no stronger words of purely moral censure can be applied.

In the next year, September, 1919, President Wilson called attention to still another free-world objection, pointing out that the Bolsheviks had ignored every suggestion, and every challenge, to accept the results of a free election. "The men who are now measurably in control of the affairs of Russia," he said, "represent nobody but themselves. They have again and again been challenged to call a constitutional convention. They have again and again been challenged to prove that they had some kind of a mandate, even from a single class of their fellow citizens." "And," he added, "they dared not attempt it; they have no mandate from anybody."[10]

In the beginning the free world was willing to back up this opinion by refusing to accept the Bolsheviks as representative of the

Russian peoples. Now, however, these men are treated as though they represented one-third of the population of the world. Their self-styled "governments" are recognized by many of the free nations, and even their satellite regimes have won admission to the United Nations. Meetings with their leaders or representatives are almost universally conducted with the cordiality and manifestations of esteem normally reserved for those who possess the real authority of their people, rather than with the grim and less festive demeanor which might normally be expected in dealings with those who are known to be engaged in every kind of crime against humanity—in those very same crimes for which the criminals of the Axis powers were publicly tried, condemned and sentenced to death at the end of World War II.

The Policy of Nonrecognition

The most obvious way of expressing an opinion that any self-styled "government" is not representative of its people is to refuse to recognize it as such. This was the basis upon which the United States originally withheld recognition from the Bolshevik regime. Thus, in 1921, at a hearing of the House Committee on Foreign Affairs, Arthur Bullard, State Department chief of the Division of Russian Affairs, stated: "I have not seen any statement of a responsible officer of the Department of State defining under what conditions a government would be recognized, but in everything I have heard on that subject discussed it has certainly put, in the first place, the greatest emphasis on the question of whether it is a truly representative government of the Russian people."[11]

If, during the last forty years, the Soviet regime had been denied recognition on this basis by all of the other nations and peoples, it is not implausible that some form of "peaceful" change might have occurred. Such a united rejection of Communist pretensions would at least have been a most effective expression of world opinion, and if it would not have produced a change, that fact only serves to demonstrate that moral force alone is insufficient.

Such a demonstration would presuppose, however, as Bullard's statement indicated, that in stating the *reasons* for nonrecognition the "greatest emphasis" would be put upon the nonrepresentative character of the Soviet regime. As it turned out, however, the great emphasis was put upon the rights of the free nations, and instead of being employed as a means of peaceful pressure for representative government in Russia, the policy of nonrecognition became a form of protest against the direction of subversive activities, open aggression, and breaches of international good faith against other governments, outside Russia. Valid as these objections are, they have little bearing upon the authority of the Soviet regime to speak for the Russian peoples. And since in the words of President Eisenhower, and of the former British Prime Minister, Sir Anthony Eden, it "would be illusory to hope that in their foreign policies, political and economic, the Soviet rulers would reflect a concern for the rights of other peoples which they do not show towards the men and women they already rule,"[12] the policy of nonrecognition as actually employed failed to provide a solution for the problems of either. Moreover, because the rights of the free nations and their citizens could be otherwise protected, waived or even entrusted to any Soviet assurances which the governments responsible for their protection might be willing to accept, the Soviet regime was soon recognized by most of the major powers.

In the case of the United States, which withheld recognition for 16 years, the original intention was to stress the unrepresentative character of Soviet rule, but the moral influence which might have been thus exerted was dissipated by what former Ambassador George F. Kennan has described as "variations in *motivation* with the course of time."[13] There was, first of all, a long delay before any official public explanation of the reason for nonrecognition was made. This gave rise to confusion with respect to the real purpose, permitting the Bolsheviks to describe it as opposition to social reform and even as evidence of hostility toward the Russian peoples. When an official explanation was forthcoming, it was not based upon the grounds described by Bullard, but upon the other considerations mentioned above. This also aided the Soviet propaganda, which depicted the policies of the free nations as based entirely upon self-interest. In subsequent explanations, if the unrepresentative character of the Soviet regime was mentioned at all as a basis of nonrecognition, it was as a consideration of secondary importance, liable at any moment to be removed by the anticipated acquiescence of the Russian peoples in Communist rule. This only promoted the belief that the Soviet rulers could not really be so bad after all, thereby contradicting every effort made by other means to direct the force of world opinion against them.

If nonrecognition had been based upon the present belief in

growing unrest behind the iron curtain, and the impossibility of popular acquiescence in Soviet rule, a far stronger policy would have been the result. There would have been no recognition until after the desired "liberalization" and "democratization" had occurred and now, in place of stress upon the Communists' hostile *attitude* toward free nations, which evokes so little concern in many quarters, there would be a more alluring emphasis upon their hostile *actions* against nations already oppressed.

It is not without significance that this basis of nonrecognition was emphasized by Bullard, or that he had in fact been one of the first to recommend the policy. When he did so, almost immediately after the Bolshevik seizure of power, he was serving in Petrograd with the Russian Division of the United States Committee on Public Information, a capacity in which he was primarily concerned with the moulding of public opinion. Moreover, he was no "reactionary," but a champion of the "left-of-center" Social Revolutionary Party, and had studied Russian affairs at firsthand since the revolution of 1905.

In his original recommendation,[14] November 27, 1917, Bullard asserted that the "reasons" for nonrecognition should be "clearly and publicly stated" on "sound democratic grounds," i.e., upon the unrepresentative character of the Bolshevik regime. "Trotsky," he said, "is claiming that the attitude of the Entente powers is based on capitalistic fear of social revolution. Much of the disorganization of the [pre-Bolshevik] army is due to this sort of argument. It is the most serious form of antagonism our publicity work has to fight." Accordingly, he maintained, "Refusal to recognize Bolsheviki should be motivated, not on repugnance to their fantastic social experiments, but on sound democratic grounds."

In support of his proposal, Bullard pointed out that the Bolsheviks were afraid of any free expression of the will of the people. Even their name, he asserted, was unknown to many of the peoples they purported to represent:

They began their insurrection on the eve of the general elections for the Constituent Assembly, which were scheduled for the 25th, 26th and 27th [of November, 1917], because they knew there is no chance of winning. In sharp contrast to the revolution of March this is a minority insurrection. The [Bolsheviki] are only one small faction of the socialist movement and moreover their influence is limited to a few well-defined localities. There are large sections consequently where their very name is unknown. And having overthrown the Provisional Government by armed revolt, lacking a majority support, they can only hold the power by sheer terror.

Bullard therefore requested a "strong statement from Washington that the United States is entirely neutral in regard to the (protracted) internal question of social reforms but refuses to recognize an undemocratic government of violence and terror...." This, he said, "would be generally approved by all the responsible democratic elements here and would be a severe blow to the irresponsible adventurers now in power."

These suggestions were approved by the consul general in Moscow, Maddin Summers, who "strongly" endorsed them in transmittal.[15] They were also endorsed by the Secretary of State, Robert Lansing, whose own recommendation to the President was made in the form of a draft of the "strong statement" which Bullard requested, and which, according to Kennan, "closely" followed Bullard's suggestions.[16] It read in part as follows:

This government has found it impossible to recognize Lenin, Trotsky and their associates as the de facto government of Russia, since there is inadequate evidence that they are the real agents of the sovereignty of the Russian people. When the Bolshevik faction under the leadership of Lenin seized by force the public offices at Petrograd and Moscow arresting or expelling the provisional ministers and military commanders who had obtained authority through legal succession from the revolutionary body which had come into power on the abdication of the Czar, they set up in those two cities arbitrary and irresponsible authority based solely on physical control over the residents.

Dedicated as the Government of the United States is to the principle of democracy and to a special order based on individual liberty and the supremacy of the popular will operating through liberal institutions, it cannot but consider that the attempt by any class of society, whether distinguished by birth, wealth, occupation or poverty, to arrogate to itself superior political authority to be inimicable to democracy....

Holding these views, this government has watched with deep concern the overthrow by force of the provisional authority representing the revolution at Petrograd, and that on the eve of the popular election of a Constituent Assembly called to establish a constitutional government based on the principle of democracy.[17]

In accepting Bullard's recommendation, Lansing soft-pedaled some of his own views on nonrecognition, which he had set forth in a memorandum two days before. In that paper he also complained of the "brutality" of the "Russian 'Terror,'" but on the subject of recognition he had put the greatest emphasis on Bolshevik hostility to other nations. "I cannot see," he wrote, "how this element which is hostile to the very idea of nationality can claim that they are the government of a nation or expect to be recognized as such. They are avowedly opposed to every government on earth; they openly propose to excite revolutions in all countries against existing governments; they are as hostile to democracy as they are to autocracy. If we should recognize them in Russia," he maintained, "we would encourage them and their followers in other lands."[18] There were similar complaints in his draft declaration, based upon the threat of the Bolsheviks to "violate treaties made with other free peoples," and to make a separate peace with Germany, but the difference in the emphasis assigned indicated an obvious deference to the merits of Bullard's position.

According to Lansing's published memoirs, the draft declaration was in turn "approved in principle" by the President,[19] but it was never issued. Thereafter, Bullard's suggestions were largely ignored, to the detriment, as it turned out, not only of the Russian peoples but of the free peoples as well.

In 1920, the long-awaited public statement of official policy was finally made by Lansing's successor, Bainbridge Colby. It was made in a published letter to the Italian Ambassador, Camillo Avezzana, and the protection of the rights of the free nations appeared to be the *only* reason for nonrecognition. "We cannot recognize," it said, "hold official relations with, or give friendly reception to the agents of a government which is determined and bound to conspire against our institutions; whose diplomats will be the agitators of dangerous revolt; whose spokesmen say that they sign agreements with no intention of keeping them."[20]

Colby stated, clearly enough, that the "present rulers of Russia do not rule by the will or consent of any considerable proportion of the Russian people"—that they had seized the machinery of government "by force and cunning" and used it "with savage oppression to maintain themselves in power"—but these considerations were not expressed as reasons for withholding recognition. They were given only as grounds for an expression of "hope" that the people themselves would "soon find a way to set up a government representing their free will and purpose."[21] It had apparently been concluded that nonrecognition for the purpose of enforcing the right of the people to manage their own affairs constituted an "interference" in such affairs that was not involved in the use of other forms of pressure for this purpose, or in the use of the same form of pressure for other purposes based solely upon considerations of self-interest.

In 1923, another explanation of nonrecognition was given by Colby's successor, Charles Evans Hughes. This statement was made in answer to a request by Samuel Gompers, president of the American Federation of Labor, for a public and official confirmation of Bullard's statement made in 1921. Hughes included, as reasons for nonrecognition, *both* the unrepresentative character of the Bolshevik regime *and* its disregard for the rights of other nations, but the greater emphasis was put upon the latter. Gompers, on the other hand, considered that the unrepresentative character of the Bolshevik regime was the *only* sound basis of the policy. His letter of request was a profound statement of the views which were then, and ought now to be, the views of the American people:

We are confronted frequently with the statement that economic conditions in Russia are improving, that the soviet authority is proving stable, that Russian agriculture is recovering and that the American government, because of these and other similar matters, should extend recognition to the soviets.

Of course much that is reported by returning travelers is misinformation gathered during closely supervised tours, but I am not at the moment discussing the truth or falsity of reports as to Russian economic conditions. What I have in mind is that it might serve some purpose if those who are standing for American principles and for the American concept of right and justice and democracy could be given clearly to understand that the backbone of the whole situation regarding Russia is the denial to the people of Russia of any opportunity to pass judgment on their own affairs or to say by whom or in what manner they shall be governed.

It has been the consistent contention of the American Federation of Labor that the soviet power cannot be recognized because it is an autocracy forced upon the people of Russia without their consent and against their will and maintained in the same manner.

I find that Mr. Bullard, then chief of the Division of Russian Affairs of the Department of State, appearing before the House Committee on Foreign Affairs of the Sixty-sixth Congress, Third Session, and discussing House Resolution 635, said:

"The State Department is very energetically opposed, and necessarily, to the present people in control of Russia because they believe they are a tyrannical minority imposing themselves on a reluctant people."

This has been repeatedly stated to be the belief of the government of the United States, although it should be said, as you doubtless would agree, that the personnel of the present tyranny is not the point of objection; the point of objection is the tyranny itself and a change of personnel would be of no significance, so long as the tyranny remains.

While the position stated by Mr. Bullard has been put forth by the Department of State on various occasions, the statement of that fundamental policy has usually been as a portion of a statement containing other provisions, so that the essential has been more or less involved with other and less vital matters.

It has for a long time seemed to me that we should understand that this is the vital principle, the very essence of our whole point of view regarding Russia; and that other matters are secondary and of minor importance.

I have stated many times that so far as my viewpoint is concerned, I am not able to see where good crops, or an improving economic condition, or any one of a number of things, including an acknowledgement of Russia's financial obligations, could change the American position regarding recognition, as long as the principle of tyranny remains. . . .

The definition of the policy of the Department of State, as read into the record of the hearing on House Resolution 635, seems to me to put the whole question on the proper basis; to put it, indeed, upon the only sound basis. I am unable to see any other tenable basis upon which a democracy could take a position that could be maintained with consistency. . . .

. . . It will be a reassurance of great value if we may all understand clearly that the denial of freedom to the Russian people is the keystone of our position in relation to the question of recognition. To the wage earners of the United States the present tyranny in Russia is a thing despicable and intolerable in practice and beyond consideration in principle; and any thought that the United States might under any circumstance extend official recognition, even in a modified form, to such a villainous despotism is repugnant.[22]

Hughes replied (July 19, 1923) that the problem "necessarily" presented itself to the Department of State in "somewhat less general terms" than it was expressed in the "various ways in which public opinion makes itself felt in the seat of government," apparently including Gompers' letter—and he seemed to feel that recognition based on popular "acquiescence" could be anticipated—but he conceded, nevertheless, that recognition would not be extended to a government which did not represent the "will of the nation" expressed or implied:

> The fundamentals of the Russian situation are pretty generally understood in the United States and have made a profound impression upon the thought of our people. We are constantly made aware of this in the Department of State by the various ways in which public opinion makes itself felt in the seat of government. We learn of the hope of America that Russia should have the opportunity of free political expression and that she should be enabled to restore her economic life and regain prosperity and once more to take her place among the nations on the basis of mutual helpfulness and respect. There can be no question of the sincere friendliness of the American people toward the Russian people. And there is for this very reason a strong desire that nothing should be done to place the seal of approval on the tyrannical measures that have been adopted in Russia or to take any action which might retard the gradual reassertion of the Russian people of their right to live in freedom.
>
> To the Department of State, charged with the conduct of our foreign relations, in accordance with the accepted principles of international intercourse, the problem presents itself necessarily in somewhat less general terms. We are not concerned with the question of the legitimacy of a government as judged by former European standards. We recognize the right of revolution and we do not attempt to determine the internal concerns of other States. The following words of Thomas Jefferson, in 1793, express a fundamental principle: "We surely cannot deny to any nation that right whereon our own Government is founded,—that everyone may govern itself according to whatever form it pleases, and change these forms at its own will; and that it may transact its business with foreign nations through whatever organ it thinks proper, whether king, convention, assembly, committee, president or anything else it may choose. *The will of the nation is the only thing essential to be regarded*." It was undoubtedly this principle which was invoked by the representative of the Department of State, in the statement which you quote....[23] (Italics added.)

On the question of popular acquiescence, Hughes pointed out that the United States had "never insisted that the will of the people of a foreign State may not be manifested by long continued acquiescence in a regime actually functioning as a government." "When there is a question as to the will of the nation," he asserted, "it has generally been regarded as a wise precaution to give sufficient time to enable a new regime to prove its stability and the apparent acquiescence of the people in the exercise of the authority it has assumed."[24]

Twenty-seven years later, however, it was noted that the people had not yet acquiesced, and that there was still no "stability." As the future Secretary Dulles asserted in 1950, the "political prisoners" numbered "from 10 to 15 million, or twice the total membership of the Party," and even the "Party itself" was "shot through with distrust and suspicion." "No one," he said, "even in high authority, feels personally safe. In the case of the satellite countries, the situation is even more precarious."[25] In these countries, according to President Eisenhower, "the fruits of imperialism" were "discontent, unrest, riots in one place and demonstrations in another, until the tyranny exercised over them either dissolves or is expelled."[26]

Nevertheless, when the Soviet regime was recognized by the United States, ten years after the Gompers-Hughes correspondence, "acquiescence" was apparently assumed to have taken place. The result was the destruction of that strong public opinion to which Hughes had so gratifyingly referred, and which the State Department is now attempting to restore.

It is important to note, however, that in spite of the changes in motivation, nonrecognition was consistently regarded as an effective and appropriate means of exerting moral pressure for the attainment of the various objectives assigned. Thus, in December, 1919, when limited intervention had failed and the British were proposing a settlement with the Bolsheviks, Secretary of State Lansing advised his Ambassador in London, John W. Davis, that he was opposed to recognition at that time as a "moral" and "tactical mistake." "There is the possibility," he wrote, "that the Bolshevik faction never will be forcibly driven from Russia, but will gradually yield to new leaders and change into a régime with which it will be possible to establish relations." In such a case, he said, it would be necessary to "determine the exact time at which the process of change" had so far developed that recognition would "help to quicken rather than retard its evolution along rational lines." To grant "premature recognition," he maintained, "would check such development" by "giving aid and encouragement to ultra-radical and uncompromising elements which still remained."[27]

Colby, in turn, maintained that by granting recognition to the Bolsheviks the free powers would be "sacrificing moral strength" for the vain hope of "material gains," and he so advised Davis in August, 1920:

The Department sympathizes with the wish of the Allied Powers to solve peacefully the difficulties now existing in Europe, and with any justifiable steps which may be taken by them, but it has not been able to see how recognizing the Bolshevik Government can possibly promote, much less bring about, this object. For that reason the Department is opposed to any relations with the Bolshevik Government in excess of the narrowest limits within which the arranging of an armistice can be kept. . . .

It is the feeling of the American Government that recognition of the Soviet régime or negotiations with it involves sacrificing moral strength for the sake of material gains, advantages which will prove to be temporary and bought at a very high price. This Government feels that no permanent and just settlement of Eastern European affairs can be thus attained.[28]

Finally, less than two months before the act of recognition, Secretary of State Hull argued that nonrecognition was one of the United States' most "powerful weapons," and an "effective" means of "exerting pressure on the Soviet government." In a letter to the President, September 21, 1933, he wrote: ". . . at the moment, the Government of the United States has two powerful weapons [loans and recognition] which can be used to bring about a favorable settlement of some, if not all, of our outstanding problems with the Soviet government. I am convinced, from the experience of other countries, that, unless we utilize every available means of exerting pressure on the Soviet government in order to obtain a settlement of outstanding problems, there is little likelihood that such problems can be satisfactorily solved."[29]

Similarly, in a memorandum to Secretary Hull, William C. Bullitt, who was about to become the first United States Ambassador to the Soviet Union, and who was at that time Special Assistant to the Secretary of State, asserted that recognition "should not be accorded except as the final act of an agreement covering a number of questions in dispute." *"Before recognition and before loans,"* he stated, *"we shall find the Soviet Government relatively amenable. After recognition or loans, we should find the Soviet Government adamant."*[30] (Italics added.) It thus appears that recognition was actually extended, not because it was considered unappropriate as a means of exerting moral pressure, but because it was assumed that the pressure had been effective—that the Bolsheviks, in other words, had been persuaded to conduct their *foreign* affairs at least in the manner desired by the free nations.

If this was not evident from statements made in connection with recognition of the Soviet Union, it was emphasized in those made the preceding year in connection with the denial of recognition to the Japanese puppet regime in Manchuria. In this case, stimulated by the threat of a more extensive Japanese invasion of China, the United States and nearly all the members of the League of Nations employed the policy of nonrecognition for the stated purpose of exerting the strongest possible moral pressure against aggression. The decision of the United States was announced in identical notes addressed to the Japanese and Chinese governments (January 7, 1932):

... the American government ... can not admit the legality of any situation *de facto* nor does it intend to recognize any treaty or agreement ... which may impair the treaty rights of the United States or its citizens in China, including those which relate to the sovereignty, the independence, or the territorial and administrative integrity of the Republic of China ...; and ... it does not intend to recognize any situation, treaty, or agreement which may be brought about by means contrary to the covenants and obligations of the Pact of Paris [the Kellogg-Briand Anti-War Pact]. . . .[31]

The motivation for this action was explained by the Secretary of State, Henry L. Stimson, in a letter to the chairman of the Senate Committee on Foreign Relations (William E. Borah):

If a similar decision should be reached and a similar position taken by the other governments of the world, a caveat will be placed upon such action which, we believe, will effectively bar the legality hereafter of any title or right sought to be obtained by pressure or treaty violation, and which, as has been shown by history in the past, will eventually lead to the restoration to China of rights and titles of which she may have been deprived.[32]

It is worthy of note that in this effort to deter aggression no attempt was made to terminate relations with the government of the aggressor itself. Although the government of Japan was severely condemned for its misconduct in the field of foreign affairs, and for its disregard of the rights of other nations, it was still recognized—presumably because it was still considered to be more or less representative of the will of the people. Its puppet regime—"Manchukuo"—on the other hand, was denied recognition because it was the *fruit* of aggression—a regime clearly imposed upon an unwilling people by force and violence. Nonrecognition was thus based not upon its conduct of its foreign affairs but upon its unrepresentative character.

The same emphasis appeared in the pronouncements of the League of Nations. In the Council it was maintained that the covenant of the League prohibited recognition, either as "valid" or "effectual" of any territorial infringement upon, or change in the political independence of, any member; and the members of the Council other than Japan addressed a communication to Japan to that effect:

> The Twelve Members of the Council recall the terms of Article 10 of the Covenant of the League by which all members of the League have undertaken to respect and preserve the territorial integrity and existing political independence of the other Members. It is their friendly right to direct attention to this provision, particularly as it appears to them to follow that no infringement of the territorial integrity and no change in the political independence of any Member of the League brought about in disregard of this article ought to be recognized as valid and effectual by the Members of the League.[33]

In the Assembly a resolution was adopted stating that it was "incumbent upon the Members of the League of Nations not to recognize any situation, treaty or agreement which may be brought about by means contrary to the Covenant of the League of Nations or to the Pact of Paris."[34]

The free nations thus set a precedent which could have been applied not only to situations created by external aggression but also to those resulting from *internal* aggression by an armed minority. This latter concept was, in fact, the basis of Bullard's proposal that nonrecognition of the Bolshevik regime should be explained solely in terms of its dependence upon terror and violence. It was the failure to apply it to the Soviet Union, moreover, which presented the

United States at this time with an apparently unsolvable dilemma—
how to reconcile its nonrecognition of the government of Russia with
its failure to sever relations with the externally more aggressive
government of Japan.

If nonrecognition of the Soviet regime had been based solely
upon its unrepresentative character, the difference in policy could
have been explained by the assumption that the Japanese government, unlike the Soviet government, still represented the will of its
own people. But since nonrecognition of the Soviet regime was by
this time explained solely in terms of its international misconduct,
there appeared to be a discrimination against it.

For the same reason, a move in favor of the Soviet Union would
seem to be a discrimination against Japan. After all that had been
said about Soviet aggressive aims and Soviet disregard for international obligations, recognition of the Soviet regime at that time, and
without a statement as to its unrepresentative character, would
appear to be inconsistent with nonrecognition of Manchukuo and
based solely on the desire to curry the favor of a natural opponent to
Japanese expansion.

This dilemma was described by Secretary Stimson in another
letter to Senator Borah (September 8, 1932), which still further
revealed the extent to which nonrecognition was regarded as an
effective means of expressing world opinion. In reply to Borah's
renewed request for recognition of the Soviets, Stimson explained
that such an action would be "misunderstood" by the "world at
large" and "destroy much of the influence of the moral pressure
which we have been endeavoring to exert":

In the Far Eastern situation the United States was making a fight
of world-wide importance for the integrity of international obligations. We were trying to buttress the great peace treaties which had
been negotiated since the end of the war by developing in behalf of
them an international sentiment throughout the world in support of
good faith and the sacredness of keeping international promises. We
were doing this solely by pacific means, endeavoring to enlist behind
our movement the support of a world opinion and avoiding anything
which approached force or political alliances.

If under these circumstances and in this emergency we recognized
Russia in disregard of her very bad reputation respecting international obligations and in disregard of our previous emphasis upon
that aspect of her history, the whole world, and particularly Japan,

would jump to the conclusion that our action had been dictated solely by political expedience and as a maneuver to bring forceful pressure upon Japan. We should thereby lose the moral standing which we had theretofore held in the controversy with Japan. She would regard us as merely an opportunist nation, seeking to enforce a selfish anti-Japanese policy against her by the usual maneuvers of international policies. I felt that this loss of moral standing would be so important that we could not afford to take the risk of it. However innocent our own motives might be, they would certainly be misunderstood by the world at large and particularly by Japan, and that misunderstanding would destroy much of the influence of the moral pressure which we have been endeavoring to exert.[35]

The dilemma was finally resolved, not by a reference to the nonrepresentative character of the Soviet regime—and withholding recognition—but by granting recognition to the Soviet Union and at the same time creating the *impression*, based upon the agreement made at that time, that it had abandoned its plans for further external aggression. The United States thus surrendered a means of exerting peaceful pressure on behalf of the demands of the subject peoples; assisted the Soviets in their deception of the free nations; and, if Secretary Stimson's analysis was correct, dealt a severe blow to a new, world-wide approach to nonrecognition which the United States itself had initiated, and which might have prevented the subsequent appeasement of the Axis powers. This led eventually to its own recognition of many puppet regimes established by the Soviets in eastern Europe, in spite of the pledge made in 1945 not to recognize governments imposed on any nation by the force of foreign power.

The decision to recognize the Soviet Union was made in November, 1933, under the new administration of President Roosevelt. At the same time, however, the United States continued to follow the Stimson policy in all cases of victims of *external* aggression. It was even formalized in two treaties to which the United States is still a party, and which are still in force. One of these treaties, the Convention on the Rights and Duties of States, was adopted at the Seventh Inter-American Conference, at Montevideo, Uruguay (December, 1933), and provides in part as follows:

The contracting parties definitely establish as the rule of their conduct the precise obligation not to recognize territorial acquisitions or special advantages which have been obtained by force whether this consists in the employment of arms, in threatening diplomatic representations, or in any other effective coercive measure.[36]

The other, the Anti-War Treaty of Non-Aggression and Conciliation, was sponsored by the Argentine Foreign Minister, Dr. Saavedra Lamas, and adhered to by the United States in 1934. It contains a very similar provision:

> They [the high contracting parties] declare that as between the high contracting parties territorial questions must not be settled by violence, and that they will not recognize any territorial arrangement which is not obtained by pacific means, nor the validity of the occupation or acquisition of territories that may be brought about by force of arms.[37]

Although most of the other parties are Latin American countries, these treaties are of general application and invite the adherence of all states. In the case of the Anti-War Treaty of Non-Aggression and Conciliation, the parties included four eastern European states —Bulgaria, Czechoslovakia, Rumania and Yugoslavia. Therefore, in their cases at least, the subsequent recognition of Soviet puppet regimes would appear to have been a flagrant violation of treaty.

Following the execution of these treaties, the United States refused to recognize the annexations or puppet regimes produced by prewar Axis aggression in Ethiopia, Austria, Czechoslovakia, Lithuania and Albania. After World War II began, and while the United States was still neutral, it also withheld recognition from the fruits of Nazi and Soviet aggression in Poland, the Baltic States, Denmark, Norway, Belgium, the Netherlands, Yugoslavia and Greece. In the case of the partition of Poland, Secretary of State Cordell Hull issued a public rebuke in which he stated that mere loss of territory could not extinguish a government or justify the recognition of another:

> Poland is now the victim of force used as an instrument of national policy. Its territory has been taken over and its Government has had to seek refuge abroad. Mere seizure of territory, however, does not extinguish the legal existence of a government. The United States therefore continues to regard the Government of Poland as in existence, in accordance with the provisions of the Constitution of Poland, and continues to recognize Count Jerzy Potocki as its Ambassador in Washington.[38]

In the case of the Baltic States, the Soviet annexation has not even yet been recognized. The reason, as given by Secretary Dulles in 1953, is the same as that for the refusal to recognize the Japanese annexation of Manchuria in 1932: "In refusing to recognize the incorporation of the Baltic States into the Soviet Union, the Government of the United States has expressed the conviction of the American people that justice and law must govern the relations between nations, great and small."[39]

In the case of Denmark, the United States even refused to recognize the acts of the legitimate government, including the attempted recall of its Minister to Washington, on the ground that it was acting under the duress of Nazi occupation forces. In a release issued April 14, 1941, the State Department asserted:

On April 9, 1940, Denmark was invaded by the German Army. Since that date an army of occupation, understood to total 200,000 German troops, has remained in subjugation of that country, and no act of the Danish Government since that time has been taken or can be taken save with the consent of the occupying power or as a result of its dictation.

In view of the foregoing, the Government of the United States has consistently held since April 9, 1940, and now holds, that the Government of Denmark can only be regarded as a government which is patently acting under duress and which is in no sense a free agent.[40]

In the meantime, however, the other nations which had subscribed to this policy followed it erratically. Recognition of "Manchukuo" was withheld, until 1937, by all members of the League of Nations except El Salvador, and thereafter by nearly all members which were not in some way under the influence of the Axis powers. In 1935, voluntary economic sanctions were employed to deter the Italian conquest of Ethiopia. But when these sanctions failed, most of the European governments expressed a desire to be released from any corresponding stricture on recognition. It remained for the delegate of the Soviet Union—of all people—to argue the cause of principle. He did so at a meeting of the Council of the League on May 12, 1938:

It is improbable that anyone would assert that the mere threat of non-recognition may avert aggression, or that non-recognition itself might free the victim of aggression from the grip of the conqueror. . . .

It would be quite wrong, however, to assert that resolutions on non-recognition are in themselves devoid of any particular value. While such resolutions have in every case a certain moral significance, and give satisfaction to public opinion, they also cause the aggressor some preoccupations and inconveniences, as is evidenced by the efforts which aggressors usually make to obtain recognition of their conquests, if only in an indirect way.

But, according to circumstances, non-recognition may be of vast importance, not only morally, but also politically—particularly when the victim of aggression itself continues to fight for its independence and for the integrity of its territory. In such cases, the recognition of the results of acts of violent aggression, or the abandonment of the policy of non-recognition, would be equivalent to abetting the aggressor directly, and to stabbing his victim in the back by discouraging and demoralising him. We have to reckon, not only with the question whether any struggle between the aggressor and his victims has come to an end, but also—should that have occurred for the time being—whether there are chances of the struggle being renewed, and likewise we have to reckon with other circumstances which may bring about a change in the situation created by aggressive acts of violence.[41]

The delegate from New Zealand, William J. Jordan, who was in accord, argued that it "cannot be right to go back on the principles of the Covenant, or to condone acts of aggression." Pointing out that even though recognition were not so "intended," it would be "so interpreted," he added: "The proceedings in which we are engaged, however they may be disguised, will only be regarded as a stage further in the surrender to aggression. . . . The New Zealand Government cannot support any proposal which would involve, either directly or by implication, approval of a breach of the Covenant."[42]

A similar stand was taken by the delegate from China, Mr. V. K. Wellington Koo. "The question of principles," he said, "is fundamentally important and should not escape our attention. . . . The principle of non-recognition of territorial changes effected by force is implicit in the Covenant. It is the foundation upon which we hope to build a new and better world order wherein nations will be able to live in peace and security under the reign of law, and wherein political disputes and economic needs will be resolved by peaceful negotiation and amicable adjustment. . . ."[43] In the end no resolution was adopted, and the members went their separate ways not only on Ethiopia but also on Austria, Czechoslovakia and Albania, until they finally had to resist aggression, not by moral force, but by armed force.

At the present time, the policy of the United States is equally inconsistent. Recognition is withheld from some of the Communist regimes and extended to others with no valid basis for distinction, and even in those cases in which recognition is withheld the reasons advanced are often contradictory. Thus, the Communist regime in China is denied recognition because of its aggressions, its failures to live up to its international obligations, and because, as Secretary of State Dulles asserted, its "foreign policies are hostile to us,"[44] but no comparable action is taken against the Soviet Union, which is regarded as the instigator of the Chinese Communist aggressions,[45] which also ignores its international obligations, and is no less hostile to the free nations. The Soviet annexation of the Baltic States is not recognized because, as Acting Secretary Sumner Welles stated, the "people of the United States are opposed to predatory activities no matter whether they are carried on by the use of force or by the threat of force,"[46] but at the same time recognition is extended to all of the puppet regimes—all of the fruits of similar Soviet predatory activities—in eastern Europe, except Albania and East Germany.

Diplomatic relations were severed with Bulgaria, but not because its "government" was regarded as the creature of Soviet aggression, or because it is maintained in power by the mass liquidation of Bulgarians. This action was based solely upon the mistreatment of American diplomatic representatives and their staff.[47] Now, moreover, because of Bulgarian-Communist promises of reform in this matter, relations have been resumed while persecution of the Bulgarian people continues.

One of the original reasons assigned for nonrecognition of the Communist regime in China was its unrepresentative character. Thus, in 1951, the Assistant Secretary for Far Eastern affairs, Dean Rusk, stated that "We do not recognize the authorities in Peiping for what they pretend to be."[48] Comparing the so-called 'Peoples' Government' in Peiping to the former Japanese puppet regime in Manchuria, he added: "The Peiping regime may be a colonial Russian government —a Slavic Manchukuo on a larger scale. It is not the Government of China. It does not pass the first test. It is not Chinese." In the case of the Chinese National Government, now on Formosa, Rusk asserted that "even though the territory under its control is severely restricted," it is recognized because it "more authentically represents the views of the great body of the people of China."

A similar explanation was given in 1955 by Dean Rusk's successor, Walter S. Robertson. The Chinese Communists, he said, "speak not for the great Chinese people and nation but for international communism," and "come no closer to representing the true interests and aspirations of their country than do William Z. Foster and his cohorts in this country, or Palmiro Togliatti in Italy, or Maurice Thorez in France." "They are all part and parcel," he stated, "of the apparatus of the international Communist conspiracy."[49]

But in 1957, Secretary of State Dulles asserted that this was not the reason at all, and that the decision with respect to recognition depended "primarily" upon the candidate government's conduct "in the realm of foreign affairs":

Our Government's dealing with other governments depends primarily upon their conduct in the realm of foreign affairs. While we have our own beliefs and our own faiths with respect to the treatment of human beings, the nature of human beings and their right to freedom of speech and expression, and so forth, we do not primarily base our foreign relations upon that but rather upon how these nations conduct themselves in the sphere of foreign affairs. I would say that, if any regime conducts itself respectably in the field of foreign affairs, then our attitude would be responsive to that. It would be without regard, necessarily, to their own domestic policies. So long as their domestic policies are wholly domestic, we do not take them into account in deciding how we deal with them in the realm of international affairs.[50]

These inconsistencies make the policy of nonrecognition incomprehensible. Instead of focusing world opinion upon Communist injustices, they give an impression that the policy of the United States is dictated by fear of the Soviet Union on the one hand and discrimination against Asians on the other. Moreover, recognition of the Communist regimes in Russia and eastern Europe has not been followed by any of the anticipated advantages. It has not produced any greater contact with the people, nor has it improved relations with the Communists—if that were desirable. On the contrary, it has only served to discourage opposition to communism on both sides of the iron curtain, and to provide an additional source of conflict and "international tension." This is the testimony of the State Department, of the press, and of those who have actually been engaged in such relationships.

According to its own reports, the staff of the American Embassy has not been permitted to have any real contacts with the Russian peoples. Thus, in 1937, Loy Henderson, then *chargé d'affaires* in Moscow, reported that severe reprisals were being taken by the Soviet government against those Soviet citizens who sought to make such contacts, and that the Embassy had no choice, therefore, but to co-operate in its own isolation:

> . . . practically all Soviet citizens who have had occasion during recent years to have relations with members of foreign diplomatic missions or with foreigners who keep in touch with their diplomatic missions appear to be in constant fear of being arrested on charges of espionage and terrorism. This alarm extends apparently even to those Soviet citizens who, as agents for the People's Commissariat for Internal Affairs, have been specially authorized to maintain contact with foreigners.
>
> There is hardly a diplomatic mission in Moscow which does not have some story to relate regarding efforts of the Soviet Government to eliminate still further the various channels with which in the past it has come into contact with Soviet life.[51]

As a result, Henderson reported, "American members of the staff of this Embassy hesitate to continue or to develop such contacts as they already have since they do not wish to be instrumental in causing misfortune to innocent persons."

In the following year, 1938, the Assistant Secretary of State, George S. Messersmith, stated that even official contacts made in Moscow were fruitless. In a memorandum to Secretary Hull, he wrote:

> Although we have a very competent Chargé d'Affaires there and a very considerable establishment, we are, through no fault of their own but because of known conditions there, not receiving any real information concerning the situation in that country nor concerning its present or probable future policy. Our officers have only the most inadequate and ineffective contact with the Foreign Office. The Foreign Office seems to have no influence on policy and apparently little direct touch with those who are making policy. While this is true in other dictatorships as well as in Russia, it is more true there.

We at least know what the objectives and in a measure the policies of Berlin and Rome are. We do not know this of Moscow.[52]

Finally, in a description of the prewar period of Soviet-American diplomatic relations, a State Department historian recorded, in 1952, that "After 6 years of diplomatic relations with the Soviet Union ... nearly every anticipated beneficial result had failed to materialize, and their intercourse had descended to a low and uncongenial level."[53]

There was no change during the war. Admiral William H. Standley, who served as United States Ambassador from February, 1942 to September, 1943, reports that he was "almost completely isolated from the Russian people...." "We got to know the Russians not at all," he says.[54] After the war, President Truman eventually came to the conclusion that in the absence of contact with the people, "formal diplomatic negotiations" were "largely barren," and so stated in a note to the President of the Presidium of the Supreme Soviet, written in July, 1951.[55] At the same time, Ambassador Alan G. Kirk revealed, in a public address in New York, that he too knew no Russians. Explaining that foreigners in Moscow were "restricted to a distance of 50 kilometers and that only on certain roads," he flatly asserted: "I am obliged to state that, except for certain officials of the Ministry of Foreign Affairs and certain Soviet employees of my Embassy, I know no Russians. Soviet citizens are not allowed to visit, to entertain, or to know foreigners."[56]

In the following year, October, 1952, Ambassador George F. Kennan was expelled from the Soviet Union because of his published remark that the Soviets were even worse in this respect than the Nazis. According to the Soviet protest, Kennan stated that "if the Nazis had permitted us to walk along the streets without the right to converse with any kind of German that would have been exactly the same situation in which we must live today in Moscow."[57]

In the same month, the U.S. representative to the General Assembly, Senator Theodore F. Green, pointed out that under a recent Soviet decree 80% of the Soviet Union was off limits to foreign diplomatic personnel. They were even barred, he said, from the capitals of those Soviet "republics," the Ukraine and Byelorussia, which the free nations had admitted to membership in the United Nations. Speaking in the Legal Committee of the General Assembly, Senator Green added:

Another Soviet decree, the State Secrets Act of 1947, drastically limits even the possibility of spoken or written communication between Soviet citizens and foreign diplomats. The average Soviet citizen thinks twice before speaking to a foreigner, lest he run afoul of the law. Our diplomatic officers similarly hesitate to speak to a Soviet citizen for fear of rendering him a suspicious character in the eyes of the Soviet regime.[58]

The Embassy, Senator Green pointed out, was not even able to make contact with persons "of known or presumed American citizenship." In their case, he stated, "The Soviet Government refuses to permit our officials to travel to the forbidden areas to see them. They in turn are refused permission to travel to Moscow to visit the Embassy. They are afraid," he said, "to communicate with us by mail or telephone; and even when they live in the Moscow area, they are afraid to come to the Embassy in person."

The travel restrictions were subsequently modified to some extent, partly as a result of the retaliatory restrictions of the United States, but even the modifications were illusory. In May, 1957, the United States complained to the Soviet Foreign Office that actual restrictions were "far more severe" than was indicated in "official communications," and that in the so-called "open" areas movement was obstructed by temporary closings, "denial of travel facilities," "roadblocks" and "other forms of police action."[59] In August, 1957, it was announced that the Soviets had opened five cities (Riga, Lvov, Uzhgorod, Chernovtsy and Irkutsk) and a few tourist attractions around Moscow, but at the same time 120,000 square miles had been added to the closed areas. These additions included a substantial portion of the environs of Leningrad, additional sections of the Moscow district and a large part of Central Asia.[60]

In the meantime, it appeared that more effective contacts with the people could be made by unofficial and irregular visitors. This was dramatically demonstrated in 1956, when an American traveler brought to the President's attention the plight of a group of Armenians, former residents of the United States, who had elected, during the period prior to the Korean War, to return with their American-born children to the Soviet Union. Their statement, as reported in *The New York Times,* indicated deep regret for this decision, as well as the reason for their subsequent failure to contact the American Embassy. "Many among us," it read, "tried to get in touch with our ambassador since 1948, for which attempt they were arrested and exiled from 10 to 15 years, often without trial. Included were young boys of 17, young girl 18, woman and men."[61] The American Embassy stated, of course, that its personnel were not permitted to go to Armenia.[62]

In the satellites the situation was no different. In a press release in 1950, the State Department reported that "the United States cannot conduct normal diplomatic and consular functions in Czechoslovakia."[63] In 1951, a United States delegate to the General Assembly, John Sherman Cooper, reported that diplomatic relations with all the puppet regimes had become "increasingly difficult," and in the case of Albania and Bulgaria, "impossible." "Year by year," he said, "we have been forced to reduce our staffs to the point at which the maintenance of our diplomatic relations has become increasingly difficult." "Our local employees," he continued, "have been intimidated and forced to leave us. The movements of our official diplomatic representatives have been restricted. The Bulgarian and Albanian regimes made it impossible for the United States to maintain diplomatic missions at all, and we were forced to suspend relations."[64]

In 1956, the State Department complained that interference with visitors to its Embassy in Prague extended to American citizens and even to "members of other diplomatic missions."[65] In Hungary the police surveillance of diplomatic missions became so restrictive that on one occasion the Austrian Minister was halted and told to move on from the "closed territory" of his own legation.[66] In all cases staffs were gradually reduced by retaliatory expulsions of "undesirable" personnel until finally, as *The New York Times* reported (May 31, 1957), the "exchanging of expulsion for expulsion" had "become a fixed part of United States relations with states in the Soviet bloc."[67]

On the other hand, the testimony is virtually unanimous that recognition of the Communist regimes enhances their prestige, both at home and abroad. This, of course, is the opposite of mobilizing world opinion against them.

The prestige involved in recognition was clearly pointed out to President Roosevelt, prior to the United States recognition of the Soviet Union, by the then Secretary of State, Cordell Hull. "There is no question," Hull said, "but that the Soviet authorities realize that recognition would strengthen the prestige of the Soviet government not only abroad, but also at home, where it is faced with tremendous

difficulties in carrying out its industrial and agricultural programs."[68]
The same point was made by Secretary of State Dulles in connection
with the refusal to recognize the Communist regime in China. Thus,
in a public address in 1954, he stated that "Those responsible for
United States policy must ask and answer: 'Will it help our country
if, by recognition, we give increased prestige and influence to a regime
that actively attacks our vital interests?' I can find only the answer:
'No.' "[69]

In the case of the Chinese Communists, it has been pointed out
that recognition would also discourage resistance—even by neighboring free peoples. For example, in 1954 the State Department
officer in charge of Chinese political affairs, Alfred le Sesne Jenkins,
stated that "recognition and acceptance of the Peiping regime would
have the effect of substantially weakening the will to resist Communist expansion on the part of other Asian people." Under such
circumstances, he said, the "nations and people near the Chinese
mainland" might "erroneously tend to view communism as 'the
inevitable wave of the future' and more and more incline their
political leanings and economic activities to accommodate this conviction."[70] In the same vein, Secretary of State Dulles asserted (June,
1957) that the "many mainland Chinese, who by Mao Tse-tung's own
recent admission seek to change the nature of their government,
would be immensely discouraged," the "millions of overseas Chinese
would feel that they had no free China to which to look," the "Republic of China, now on Taiwan, would feel betrayed by its friend,"
and the "free Asian governments of the Pacific and Southeast Asia
would be gravely perplexed." "If we seemed to waver and to compromise with communism in China," he said, "that would in turn
weaken free Asia resistance to the Chinese Communist regime and
assist international communism to score a great success in its program
to encircle us."[71]

It may well be asked why the United States should "seem to
waver and to compromise with communism" in any nation; why it is
any more tolerable for communism in the Soviet Union and eastern
Europe to be regarded as "the inevitable wave of the future" than it
is for communism in Asia; why it is permissible for any of the subject
peoples to be "immensely discouraged" or made to "feel betrayed";
or why the millions of exiles from the Soviet Union, the Baltic States,
Poland, Hungary, Czechoslovakia, Bulgaria, Rumania, Yugoslavia

and Albania are any less entitled to have free governments to which to look than the corresponding millions of exiles from China, North Korea and North Viet Nam.

We may assert if we like that recognition does not constitute "approval" of oppression, and that it does not sanction the repeated denial of the rights of life, liberty and property—but if the hopes of the subject peoples are to be based upon success in mobilizing world opinion, the free nations cannot base their policies upon this theo-retical position. As indicated by the foregoing statements, it is simply not understood or believed by those we are most anxious to convince. It is certainly not accepted by the Communists themselves, as was so painfully made clear in a Soviet *aide-mémoire*—addressed to the United States in 1958 and delivered to its ambassador in Moscow. This plainly indicated that so long as the United States maintains diplomatic relations, all discussions of the rights of the subject peoples will be regarded only as unwarranted interference in the "internal affairs of third countries":

The Soviet Government in general cannot understand why it is addressed with proposals to discuss internal affairs of third countries that are sovereign states and with which both the Government of the Soviet Union and the Government of the United States of America maintain *normal diplomatic relations*.[72] (Italics added.)

Expulsion from the United Nations

According to Henry Cabot Lodge, speaking as United States representative to the United Nations and chief of the United States mission to the United Nations, that body is "the most effective engine in the world for influencing world opinion."[73] Yet the free nations have allowed its influence to be abused and perverted by members which they know are dedicated to the destruction of everything for which the United Nations stands.

It is not merely that membership permits the Communist regimes to use the United Nations as a forum for the dissemination of deceit-ful propaganda. Such tactics might be passed over as a necessary evil, to be tolerated in the interests of free speech. But the fact of ad-mission itself implies that Communist regimes are "peace-loving" and dedicated, as the charter provides, to the protection of "human rights" and "fundamental freedoms for all." The responsibility for this deception lies with the free nations, and the failure to undo it undermines their own effort to create a public opinion aware of the true nature and purpose of the Soviet system.

In the case of the Chinese Communist regime, this effect of membership is conceded, and even the *consideration* of its application for membership was once regarded as a weakening influence. This was indicated by the statement of the previous United States representative, Warren R. Austin, made *before* the open Chinese Communist aggression in Korea. "To consider at this time," he said, "the seating of a declared opponent to United Nations efforts to repulse aggression would weaken the support to which the United Nations forces at the front are entitled and would undermine our entire peace-making endeavor."[74]

As in the case of nonrecognition, the stated objections to admission of the Chinese Communists are equally applicable to the Soviet Union, and the moral effect of the exclusion of the former is largely destroyed by the failure to make an effort to expel the latter. In 1955, for example, it was pointed out by the Assistant Secretary for Far Eastern affairs, Walter S. Robertson, that the government in Peiping is "an arrogant, contemptuous regime of hard-core international Communists who have played a gangster role in their relations with us and other countries" and who "speak not for the great Chinese people and nation but for international communism."[75] But the Soviet regime is no more able to speak for the equally great Russian peoples. It is also arrogant and contemptuous, and its puppet regimes in eastern Europe do not represent the captive nations.

As Robertson asserted, the Chinese Communists are "part and parcel of the apparatus of the international Communist conspiracy", but, it should be noted, the Soviet Communists are the leaders and directors of that conspiracy. Robertson properly stated that the objectives of the Chinese Communists are "the antithesis of the principles which constitute the foundation of the United Nations Charter," and that they "are dedicated to the destruction of everything the United Nations stands for." But the objectives of all members of the international Communist conspiracy are identical, and they are all dedicated to the destruction of the same United Nations goals.

As evidence of the established criminal activity of the Chinese Communist regime, Robertson called attention to the fact that it "stands convicted by the United Nations of the crime of aggression" in Korea. But the Soviet Communist regime was the real author of that crime, and has since been "condemned" for its "violation of the Charter" in Hungary.[76]

As an example of how the admission of the Chinese Communist regime would discourage popular resistance, Robertson asserted that it "would undermine the real Chinese Government, now based on Formosa, . . . the one remaining hope of millions of Chinese on the mainland and scattered about the world." But the absence of a free Russian government, and of free governments in exile for the captive nations, does not make the Soviet regime or its puppets any more eligible for membership in the United Nations, or render the admission of such regimes any more acceptable to the millions of Russians and eastern Europeans behind the iron curtain and scattered in emigration.

With regard to the effect on public opinion, Robertson asserted that the United States is "opposed to any action which would strengthen the international prestige of Chinese Communism or its capability for advancing its design for further conquests in collusion with Soviet Communism." But the United States should be equally opposed to action which would increase the prestige or advance the designs of any kind of communism. Since, as Robertson asserted, "acquiescence" in the admission of one "contemptuous aggressor against the peace of the world" would have "calamitous effects," it may properly be assumed that the many existing troubles are due to the actual admission of seven.

The moral effect, propriety, and even obligation of expelling from any world peace organization those governments or groups which are opposed to its essential objectives have been generally recognized and accepted. Thus the covenant of the League of Nations provided for the expulsion of any member "which has violated any covenant of the League," and in accordance with that provision the Soviet Union was itself expelled because, as the Assembly stated, it "refused to be present at the examination of its dispute with Finland."[77] Similarly, in the case of the United Nations, the charter provides for the expulsion of any member which has "persistently violated" its principles. As Secretary Dulles once asserted, it "was not set up to be a reformatory. It was assumed that you would be good before you got in and not that being in would make you good."[78]

In the application of this principle, the government of Spain was originally excluded from the United Nations, by the agreement made at Potsdam, assertedly because of "its origins, its nature, its record and its close association with the aggressor States."[79] Similarly, five of the captive nations—Albania, Bulgaria, Hungary, Outer Mongolia and Rumania—were for a long time opposed because, as Ambassador Austin asserted, their Communist puppet regimes had not "given proof" that they were "peace-loving states, able and willing to fulfill the obligations of the Charter,"[80] and because, in the words of another United States delegate, the requirements for admission, "rudimentary as they are, are not satisfied by paper assurances...."[81] Even now, after the admission of four of these regimes, the United States still holds that they are not eligible.

Finally, after the suppression of the revolt in Hungary, even the Pope felt called upon to point out the propriety of expulsion. Thus, in his annual Christmas message, December, 1956, Pope Pius XII stated: "Although the United Nations' condemnation of the grave violations of the rights of men and entire nations is worthy of recognition, one can nevertheless wish that, in similar cases, the exercise of their rights, as members of this organization, be denied to states which refuse even the admission of observers—thus showing that their concept of state sovereignty threatens the very foundations of the United Nations."[82]

It is worthy of note that those Communist regimes which are members of the United Nations have only been admitted or tolerated because of an assumed expediency—and often in conceded violation of the charter. Thus, the Soviet Union was included as an original member because, as former President Truman asserts, we did not think the United Nations would be successful without it;[83] and the failure to expel it has been defended on the ground that "there are a number of advantages which accrue to the free world...." It was thus argued by a deputy representative to the United Nations, Ernest A. Gross, that because of their membership the Soviets can be held "legally and morally accountable for violations of their commitments"; kept available for negotiation; subjected to "psychological, moral and political pressures"; and "forced to reveal the true nature and purposes of the Soviet system."[84]

None of these alleged advantages, however, has proved to be useful to anyone. In spite of continual negotiation and numerous psychological, moral and political pressures, the Soviets have not yet accounted for any violations, there has been no change in the true nature and purpose of their system, and the "forced" revelations have been confined entirely to a demonstration of their continuing ability to obstruct the purposes of the United Nations itself.

It has also been maintained, in a report of the Senate Committee on Foreign Relations, that the inclusion of the Soviet Union is desirable because the United Nations can best serve "our interests" when it functions primarily as a "forum" for the "consideration of difficulties," and when its members include "most, if not all, of the nations with whom disputes have arisen or are likely to arise." For this reason, it is said, the "interests of the Nation" are not "best served" by seeking to "reconstitute" the United Nations into an agency "primarily able to supply collective force against Communist aggressors."[85]

This argument overlooks the fact that the charter of the United Nations contains a binding commitment to create an organization which *will* be able to supply collective force against aggressors, and that its stated first purpose is "to maintain international peace and security," and to "take effective collective measures for the prevention and removal of threats to the peace and for the suppression of acts of aggression." In this regard, it should be noted that the free nations are just as much bound to their commitments as the Soviet Union is to its own.

Finally, in 1955, in order to obtain the admission of twelve additional free nations, four new Soviet satellite regimes were admitted. Pursuant to this arrangement the free powers agreed to waive their objections to the Communist regimes in return for a Soviet agreement not to veto the admission of the free states. It was carried out in flagrant disregard of an advisory opinion of the International Court of Justice, which held that all such "package deals" are "incompatible with the letter and spirit" of the charter,[86] and in admitted reversal of the previous stand of the free powers. One delegate of the free nations frankly asserted: "It is not principle with which we are concerned here but expediency—the expediency of inexorable political circumstances."[87]

It was clear enough that the free nations were acting on the basis of expediency. What is not clear, however, is how they expected to use the United Nations effectively either as a forum for influencing world opinion, or for exerting moral pressure to hold the Soviet Union to its commitments, if they were thus willing to disregard their own. As the representative of free China, Tingfu F. Tsiang, asserted, they were destroying the only influence which they hoped to preserve: "When you base a proposition on a deal—and I will say an illegal and immoral deal—I am afraid you are destroying that very moral prestige of the Assembly which we hoped the United Nations could use for the good of all the peoples of the world."[88]

The United States, on its part, refused to support the admission of the satellite regimes. But at the same time it declined to exert any strong open influence against them. Instead of taking a firm stand in opposition to the admission of governments described as "not now independent" and deriving their status from "a violation of treaties and other international agreements," the United States representative abstained from voting for the announced reason that his government did not wish to "thwart what may be the will of a qualified majority." In the place of a vigorous defense of the principles of the charter, or the authority and opinion of the International Court, he took the position that the issues were "those about which there can be honest differences of opinion," and declared in advance that the veto would not be employed even against an action considered to be in violation of the charter. "Should this bring before the Security Council," he said, "resolutions on admission which, in our opinion, involve infractions of the charter, we shall, in accordance with the spirit of the Vandenberg resolution, abstain from voting so as not to exercise, on this question of admissions, the veto power."[89]

The Vandenberg resolution, of course, proposed a *mutual* agreement *never* to use the *veto* on membership questions. It did not contemplate *affirmative* voting by any member for an applicant which it considered ineligible, or unilateral abstention from voting or vetoing when other members voted in this way. Secretary of State Dulles subsequently sought to justify the action of the United States by asserting that an abstention in the Security Council is "just the same" as a negative vote without veto,[90] but this did not explain the similar abstention in the General Assembly, where there is no veto. Moreover, even though an abstention in the Security Council may have the same effect as a negative vote without veto in so far as the passage or defeat of a resolution is concerned, it does not have the same effect on public opinion. It is also a vote without influence for the development of moral force.

By countenancing violations of the Charter for the sake of assumed advantages to themselves, the free nations can only make

Soviet violations seem more acceptable. In the case of the seating of Communist regimes, and unauthorized changes in the purpose of the organization, they are also depriving the subject peoples of their right to real representation in that body, and of the only enforcement agency created for their protection. Such a denial of their own rights would certainly not be countenanced by any of the free powers.

This was evidenced by the prompt rejection of a proposal by the Soviet Union for its own admission to the North Atlantic Treaty Organization (NATO). That idea was speedily dismissed as "unreal" and "contrary to the very principles" of the organization. In its reply (May 7, 1954), the United States asserted:

The North Atlantic Treaty Organization, which is much more than a purely military arrangement, is founded on the principle of individual liberty and the rule of law.... There is free and full exchange of information between all its members. All its decisions are taken by unanimous consent. The Soviet Union as a member of the organization would therefore be in a position to veto every decision. None of the member states is prepared to allow their joint defense system to be disrupted in this way.[91]

It is difficult to see why the same considerations do not apply to the United Nations. In any event such considerations were also made the basis of opposition to Soviet membership in an All-European Security System. At a news conference (June 28, 1955), Secretary Dulles asserted that such an organization would be a "fraud" and would "not add to anybody's security at all." "There are nations," he said, "which believe in undermining the governments of others, nations which believe in reducing to a state of captivity other nations which have had a long record of independent existence. A joining of forces with nations who believe and act that way does not add to anybody's security at all." "That is a fraud," he said. "Therefore, that kind of security system is not acceptable."[92]

In the case of the United Nations, it is argued that there is "no way of expelling the Soviet Government, even if this should be desired,"[93] but this response to the problem is as deceptive as it is defeatist. It is true that in the Security Council the Soviet Union could veto any resolution for expulsion, but there is nothing to prevent action by the General Assembly which, even though technically ineffective, would have the same *moral* effect. Even if there were no veto power in the Security Council, the only real advantage of expulsion of a member nation would be the effect on world opinion, and this would scarcely be diminished by the veto of a resolution supported by a majority—or, perhaps, even by all of the non-Communist nations. Under such circumstances continuing membership would be at least uncomfortable, and quite probably without influence.

The only real problem, as the argument indicates, is the lack of will on the part of the free nations. If the will for expulsion existed, its moral effect could readily be obtained. Moreover, as Secretary Dulles pointed out, even though the General Assembly cannot expel a member, it has the authority to pass upon the qualifications of delegates who sit in the Assembly, and thus to deprive any delegation of many of the "normal perquisites" of members. Testifying before a subcommittee of the Senate Committee on Foreign Relations (January 18, 1953), he stated:

... it is perhaps a situation where the General Assembly can exercise a certain authority of its own, at least to deprive a nation of the right to participate in the affairs of the Assembly, even though the Assembly alone could not suspend it or expel it from all of the elements of membership because of the present veto provision, and the fact that it would probably be very difficult to get a waiver of that veto at the review conference. But, I believe that the General Assembly is, to a large extent, the master of its own procedures, and to a certain extent I believe legitimately a judge of the qualifications of those who sit in the Assembly and could take its action which, while not going all the way, would go a considerable part of the way of indicating first a strong moral disapprobation of such action, and secondly, of in fact excluding such a member from many of the normal perquisites of membership.[94]

Avoiding Fraternization

Another form of moral pressure is suggested by the methods used in necessary dealings, outside the United Nations, and outside of normal diplomatic procedures, with Communist China. As Secretary of State Dulles asserted, it "exists" and "has power," and therefore we "do not refuse to deal with it where occasion requires," but at the same time it is not flattered, cajoled or condoned. It is "one thing to recognize evil as a fact," he said. "It is another thing to take evil to one's breast and call it good."[95] Accordingly, the Communist regime in China is normally dealt with, not as if it were an authorized representative of the Chinese people, but as if it were really believed to be, as Assistant Secretary Walter S. Robertson said it was, "kept in power by bloody purges and the liquidation of some 18 millions of mainland Chinese in 7 years."[96]

In the case of the Soviet regime, however, an entirely different attitude is taken. The manner in which relations with its representatives are conducted in no way reflects the belief that it is hated and feared by its own people, or that "there are at any given time 20 million" of such people, "men, women, and children in concentration camps and political prisons."[97] On the contrary, the festivities, the honors and the extreme cordiality with which the rulers of the Soviet Union are often received in the free world, and even before the eyes of the Russian peoples themselves, would seem to indicate only that they are held in the highest esteem.

This difference in attitude was disclosed in startling contrast at two Geneva conferences, one dealing with Korea and Viet Nam, in 1954, and the other the heads-of-government conference in 1955. In connection with the former, to which the representatives of Communist China, North Korea and North Viet Nam were invited, it was made clear by Secretary Dulles that "the Communist regime will not come to Geneva to be honored by us, but rather to account before the bar of world opinion."[98] During the conference itself, he avoided all social contacts with his Chinese Communist counterpart, Premier and Foreign Minister Chou En-lai, and even declined to confer with him directly.

In the following year, however, at the conference of the heads of government, the atmosphere was one of camaraderie and festivity. Khrushchev and Bulganin, the leaders of the Soviet Union, were treated to an unending round of receptions and merrymaking. The United States delegation even gave a dinner in their "honor," and mutual toasts were exchanged. At daily afternoon buffets, President Eisenhower sought out the members of the Soviet delegation, engaging them in gay conversation; and, according to the correspondent for *The New York Times*, gave every outward appearance of "having the time of his life."[99] According to Bulganin's account, it was the President himself who introduced that erstwhile Soviet Premier to the mysteries of the martini cocktail.[100]

In this case, as the President said, the "intent" was "to conciliate, to understand, to be tolerant," and "to try to see the other fellow's viewpoint as well as we see our own."[101] This is certainly a praise-

Moment of Laughter

At the Geneva Conference, July 19, 1955. Left to right: Soviet Premier Nikolai Bulganin, President Eisenhower, French Premier Edgar Faure and British Prime Minister Anthony Eden. (Wide World Photos)

A Toast to Malenkov

On March 15, 1956, Lord Citrine, chairman of the Central Electricity Board of England, raises his glass in toast to former Premier Georgi Malenkov, then Soviet Minister of Power Stations. (Wide World Photos)

Touring British Plant
On March 20, 1956, Georgi Malenkov was surrounded by General Electric workers in the Whitton Works plant in Birmingham, England. (United Press Photo)

Moscow Was Never Like This!
In an electric plant in Stafford, England, Malenkov is kissed by two of the workers, as he signs autographs. (Wide World Photos)

worthy objective when one is dealing with those who are not opposed in principle to the worth, dignity and fundamental rights of the human person, but it is hardly appropriate when the "viewpoint" which we are called upon to understand and be tolerant of calls for the universal derogation and degradation of such rights and dignity, and the ruthless subjugation of all peoples to the dictates of a cult which even denies the existence of their Divine Source. The result in this instance was that, while the President was supposed to be showing that the "American people feel strongly" about the subjugation of eastern Europe—as he stated on the opening day[102]—he was actually renewing his wartime "friendship" with one of the leaders of the subjugating armies (Marshal Georgi K. Zhukov), entertaining him at lunch and exchanging family presents. Where there might have been some peaceful pressure against mass murder and oppression, an official of the principal organ of terror, the MVD, was put in charge of all conference security arrangements; and a reporter who sought to cover the proceedings for *Possev,* an anti-Communist Russian exile publication, was put under house arrest.[103] It thus appeared that if any moral pressure were exerted at the conference at all, it was not directed against the oppressors of peoples but against those who sought to resist them.

The effect was similarly "counter-productive" to the efforts of the free nations to defend themselves. Less than two weeks before the conference, in a vain effort to call attention to continuing Communist violation of the armistice agreement in Korea, the United States representative at Panmunjom, Major General Harlan C. Parks, had summed up for the Communist representatives what he described as "monumental evidence" of their "complete insincerity, dishonesty, and utter lack of integrity":

We have listened since last summer to the soothing music of your peaceful propaganda and your expressions for a free and independent united Korea, while at the same time contending with your continued wilful and flagrant violations of the Armistice Agreement, your hostile and aggressive actions, and your murderous and inhumane atrocities. The time has come to demand that the powers who are directing your iniquitous activities start trying to reconcile your Dr. Jekyll with your Mr. Hyde.[104]

At Geneva, however, on the third day of the conference, the President expressed his own opinion that the Communists were "earnestly desirous" for peace. "I should like to say, for my part," he said, "I have talked individually, I think, to each member of the Delegation of the Soviet Republic, which now we find differing from the other three of us on a particular point in a suggestion. *And I want to make clear,*" the President continued, "*I believe they are earnestly desirous of finding peace, as are we.*"[105] (Italics added.)

The results was that within a few months Iceland demanded the withdrawal of the United States NATO forces, Khrushchev and Bulganin were welcomed in southeast Asia as "liberators," and the governor of Bombay could welcome them with the following assertion:

That your country stands firmly for peace is not questioned seriously in any quarter.[106]

This statement was unfortunately justified by appearances, if not by the facts; and if the world preferred to listen to Dr. Jekyll at Geneva, instead of to Mr. Hyde in Korea, it was the President of the United States who had given it the lead.

In the years following this first summit conference, the contradiction continued in spite of the free world's initial reluctance to hold another. It appeared, for example, in the expressions of optimism concerning "progress" of negotiations on disarmament, with provision for effective inspection, while at the same time the Communists were condemned for violating such agreements in Korea and Indochina. Thus, the truce in Indochina called for joint and neutral "control, observation, inspection and investigation" of all restrictions on the reinforcement of the opposing armed forces. But in 1957, Assistant Secretary Robertson called attention to the fact that in "flagrant violation" of these restrictions, the Viet Minh armies had been "built up by the Red Chinese from 7 to 20 divisions and their artillery firepower increased some sixfold."[107] The agreement in Korea also provided for "supervision, observation, inspection, and investigation," but in this case the system was finally abandoned, in May, 1956, because of its frustration by the Communist members of the "Neutral Nations Supervisory Commission," and because, as the United Nations Command asserted, the Chinese and North Korean governments "consistently refused to allow any bona fide inspection of clear armistice violations...."[108] In 1958, Khrushchev himself stated that "multilateral control and inspection" were unthinkable and that those who insist upon them "do not intend to speak serious-ly either about disarmament, control or trust."[109] Nevertheless, in their constant efforts to obtain such an agreement, the free powers continue to hold out the possibility, and at times probability, of one which will provide for "effective" and "dependable" guarantees against Soviet violation.

On the other hand, the propriety of a less congenial approach to the authors of enslavement is indicated by sporadic efforts to register protest against less objectionable forms of Soviet activity. For example, during the last months of 1956, simply because of certain derisive remarks made by Khrushchev about the free powers, the Western diplomatic corps in Moscow conducted an extended boycott of Soviet official functions.[110] This occurred at a time when Soviet aggression in Hungary would have offered a much better motivation.

In June, 1956, during his official visit to Moscow, General Nathan F. Twining, then Air Force Chief of Staff, sat successfully through the toasting of a Chinese Communist general because it was accompanied by an oral denunciation of the leader of free China.[111] On a later occasion, however, he was "forced" to drink a prearranged toast to "peace and friendship" with the same Communist general in order to avoid "something of a diplomatic incident,"[112] thus proving that it is impossible to condemn the behavior of Communists while fraternizing with them, whether it is with smiles or with frowns.

If it is possible to register protests of the kind thus attempted, because the *free* world is subjected to merely *verbal* attacks, it is surely possible and appropriate to take at least comparable steps to emphasize its protests against *physical* attacks upon the subject peoples. There is, in fact, no reason why it is not possible to terminate all relationships in which a toast cannot be avoided without "diplomatic incident," or why the United States should not be guided strictly by the high standard of its own original political philosophy, as expressed long ago by Thomas Jefferson:

It accords with our principles to acknowledge any Government to be rightful which is formed by the will of the nation, substantially declared. . . . With such a government *every kind* of business may be done.[113]

CHAPTER XVII

MUTUAL ASSISTANCE BEHIND THE IRON CURTAIN

". . . it chanced that a certain priest went down the same way, and seeing him, passed by. In like manner also a Levite, when he was near the place and saw him, passed by. But a certain Samaritan being on his journey, came near him, and seeing him was moved with compassion" (Luke x:31-33).

In the light of experience—and in the case of the Soviet Union there have been more than forty years of this—it seems clear that the Communists cannot be moved by moral force alone. When there is question of the defense of the free nations this is conceded, and even insisted upon. Thus, in 1957, in an address to the Council of Ministers of the Southeast Asia Treaty Organization (SEATO), Secretary of State Dulles asserted: "We must keep indelibly clear in our minds that international communism is not regardful of legality or of humanity or of the moral force of world opinion as reflected in the General Assembly of the United Nations."[1] The same opinion was expressed, in 1952, by President Truman:

By itself, of course, this moral function of the United Nations would not be enough. The collective conscience of the world is not enough to repel aggression and establish order. We have learned that moral judgments must be supported by force to be effective.[2]

A similar conclusion was reached during the first and second world wars, but only after the initiation of holocausts greater than the world had ever dreamt of—and which might have been avoided. Whereas more timely support for the demands of subject peoples—or peoples in the process of enslavement—might have led to struggles between peoples and tyrants, ending in the overthrow of the latter, the undue reliance on merely moral pressure led to wars between nations, ending in the slaughter of peoples.

In April, 1917, after a vain attempt at neutrality, President Wilson recommended war against Germany because, as he said, "No autocratic government could be trusted to keep faith" within a partnership of democratic nations, or to "observe its covenants."[3] Although, in contrast to the Communists, the rulers of the enemy powers at that time acknowledged the existence of moral laws, the use of moral force was not considered sufficient.

When Hitler launched a new round of aggression, the European powers first tried "appeasement" and the United States again invoked "neutrality," but it was soon found that force was still the only solution. By 1942, Secretary of State Cordell Hull had harsh words for those who counted upon peaceful change. "They have become so abhorrent of force and cruelty," he said, "that they have believed the bully and the gangster could be reformed by reason and justice or be defeated by passive resistance."[4] President Roosevelt asserted (October 21, 1944) that attempts to bargain and compromise were neither realistic nor acceptable:

> Obviously, we could have come to terms with Hitler and accepted a minor role in his totalitarian world. We rejected that!
> We could have compromised with Japan and bargained for a place in a Japanese-dominated Asia by selling out the heart's blood of the Chinese people. And we rejected that!
> The decision not to bargain with the tyrants rose from the hearts and souls and sinews of the American people. They faced reality, they appraised reality, and they knew what freedom meant.[5]

"The people of the Nation," he said, "want their Government to act, and not merely to talk, whenever and wherever there is a threat to world peace."

In a pledge not to repeat past mistakes, the President also indicated that force might be necessary in the future. "For too many years," he said, "we lived on pious hopes that aggressor and warlike nations would learn and understand and carry out the doctrine of purely voluntary peace." "The well-intentioned but ill-fated experiments of former years did not work. It is my hope that we will not try them again." "If we are willing to fight for peace now," he asked, "is it not good logic that we should use force if necessary, in the future, to keep the peace?"[6]

During World War II, it was concluded that the liberation of enslaved peoples could only be accomplished through invasion. Thus, in May, 1943, the Assistant Secretary of State, Adolph A. Berle, Jr., asserted:

Nothing can be done to save these helpless unfortunates, except through the invasion of Europe, the defeat of the German arms, and the breaking, once and for all, of the German power. There is no other way.[7]

Now, however, it is asserted that "foreigners" cannot help along by "direct interference" in the "internal affairs" of others. Thus, at a news conference, July 11, 1956, Secretary of State Dulles maintained:

... the most that we can do is to adhere to the old historic American tradition of setting an example of the good fruits of freedom ...

The idea that we can help along by direct interference is, I think, a false idea. It very rarely helps to bring about changes in a foreign country to have foreigners themselves directly intervene in their internal affairs.[8]

It would seem, however, that there ought to be a middle course between invasion and the mere setting of an example, and that ways could be found to assist the people themselves with arms, equipment and money—when they request it—to enforce their own legitimate demands for freedom. Interference to impose the will of a foreign power is one thing; and intervention to assist the free expression of popular will is another. The idea that the latter is wrong conflicts with the stated purposes of the free powers in both world wars; it conflicts with the ideals of the United Nations; and it conflicts with the intended postwar policy of the United States in all free countries.

It is now acknowledged that assistance to free nations is proper and necessary, but it can hardly be said that this is less of an intervention than assistance to the subject peoples. In the former case, it is pressed upon governments which often accept it with diffidence, and sometimes over the strenuous objections of large minorities; while in the latter, it may be furnished in response to the urgent appeals of all legitimate, freedom-loving parties.

Moreover, to assert that assistance must only be denied to those whose lawful government has been overthrown is to say that assistance becomes interference only when, with disastrous results, it has been too long withheld. It would seem more consistent with the developing concepts of interdependence of peoples, as well as more realistic, to say in the words of a former assistant secretary of state (Spruille Braden), that "whatever we refrain from saying and whatever we refrain from doing may constitute intervention no less than what we do or say."[9] The one choice that is possible is to make sure that the influence of the more powerful nations is exerted for the benefit of the people rather than for the benefit of actual or potential oppressors.

In the postwar period, the United States has repeatedly intervened, or interfered, in the internal affairs of other peoples. It intervened with good effect in Iran and Greece—where it thwarted Communist aims by moral force *and* military assistance; and also in Korea—where it was forced to send troops because of its previous failure to provide arms. It interfered with ill effect in China—where it sought to "mediate" between the national government and the Communists, and to impose a policy of compromise; and in the nations of eastern Europe—where it agreed to the imposition of undemocratic "provisional" governments without reference to the will of the people. Moreover, it is now intervening with no effect in the affairs of all the Communist-dominated nations—by efforts to change their form of government through pressures described as merely "psychological, moral, and political."[10]

An invasion of these nations would hardly be recommended by anyone, but, as in the case of western Europe, it is not inconceivable that such an extreme course would be successful. In the Soviet Union even the Nazi invaders were welcomed as "liberators," and they might have overthrown the Soviet regime very quickly had they been interested in playing such a role. They failed only because they were not interested in liberation, and because their plans for the people were no less oppressive than those of the Communists.

This was the conclusion reached in a report prepared by Dr. Otto Braeutigam, deputy chief of the Central Political Department of the Nazi Ministry for Occupied Eastern Territories. "Were the war being conducted only for the smashing of Bolshevism," he wrote, "then it would have been decided long ago in our favor, for, as all experiences of this war have confirmed, Bolshevism is hated to the utmost by the Eastern peoples, above all by the great mass of peasants." But, he pointed out, "With the inherent instinct of the Eastern peoples the primitive man soon found out also that for Germany the slogan: 'Liberation from Bolshevism' was only a pretext to enslave the Eastern peoples according to her own methods." The "laborer and peasant," he said, "who were educated to the highest degree of self-consciousness by Bolshevism, soon perceived that Germany did not regard them as partners of equal rights, but considered them only as the objective of her political and economic aims. That disillusioned them unspeakably, all the more since they had placed colossal hopes on Germany."[11]

When this report was made (October, 1942), the Nazis had nearly succeeded in breaking the Communist power. By December, 1941, less than six months after the initial attack, they had reached the gates of Moscow and Leningrad. By February, 1942, they had taken 3,600,000 prisoners; and in August they were in the Caucasus. According to Khrushchev, Stalin had proclaimed: "All that which Lenin created we have lost forever."[12]

It was only when the people learned what the Nazis really had in store for them that the invasion began to fail. As Braeutigam stated, the attitude of the people then changed from welcome to fierce resistance:

The population greeted us with joy as liberators, and placed themselves at our disposal willingly and freely with body and life. Wherever Ukrainians, Russians, White Ruthenians and members of the Baltic peoples were enlisted in the German Wehrmacht or in the police they have proved themselves and fought excellently almost without exception. . . .

.   .   .   .

The resistance power of the Red Army and the strength of the partisan movement has mounted in the same degree as the population realized our true enlistment for them. . . . The Russian fights today with exceptional bravery and self-sacrifice for nothing more or less than recognition of his human dignity.[13]

Invasion, however, is not the only alternative to merely moral force. When those who threaten hostilities against others are already waging war against their own people, it should not be necessary either to launch an invasion or await attack. All that is required is a readiness to assist *all* freedom-loving peoples when, as President Eisenhower said, they "need and want and can profitably use our aid."[14] This has long been the basis of Chinese plans for return to the mainland. In a television interview, released May 25, 1958, President Chiang Kai-shek asserted:

We have never conceived the struggle with the Communists in the form of a war whereby the armed forces of one country are pitted against the armed forces of another country backed by its own people. The people on the mainland are no enemy. They are our own people, and we know definitely that they are opposed to the Communists. This is a revolutionary struggle. . . .[15]

Although President Eisenhower's pledge, made on the eve of the revolt in Hungary, was not fulfilled, it seemed to be repeated in his 1957 inaugural address, less than three months afterwards. At that time he promised assistance to all nations that are or *would be* free: "We cherish our friendship with all nations that are or would be free. We respect, no less, their independence. And, when, in time of want or peril, they ask our help, they may honorably receive it."[16]

It should therefore be possible to develop forces that would be used not for invasion, or merely for the purpose of parachuting "spies" and "saboteurs" behind the iron curtain, but that could be placed at the disposal of the subject peoples—ready, under the proper circumstances, to assist them in their struggle for freedom whenever and wherever the opportunity to do so arises—and thereby give them *real* hope, and the assurance of *effective* support by the free world in their efforts.

The Nazis had no alternative to invasion because they wished to impose their own form of subjugation upon the Slavic "untermensch," and eventually to "ensure that only people of pure German blood inhabit the East."[17] The free world, however, is anxious for the release of the subject peoples, even if only for the sake of its own security. It can therefore avoid the Nazi mistakes, and even profit by them.

Hitler was loath to give arms to those who would turn against nazism as well as communism, and he therefore sought to defeat the Soviets with German troops alone, while using several million Soviet citizens for forced labor in Germany. The democratic nations, on the other hand, can best preserve the ideal of free government, not by invading the Communist-ruled nations, or by waging war against them, but by giving their people all of the assistance required to make the demand for freedom really "irresistible." For them it is not only more humane but also more practicable to furnish the arms and the training which will enable the peoples of all Communist-dominated nations to provide their own deterrent to oppression, and thus to bring about the "forced reformation" which has so often been predicted but never realized.

There have been many precedents for such assistance to the victims of tyranny. During the First World War, the Allied powers belatedly sought to assist and obtain the support of the subject peoples of that time, and in pursuance of this policy President Wilson adopted, as parts of his "Fourteen Points" program, a promise of "the freest opportunity of autonomous development" for the peoples of Austria-Hungary; "absolutely unmolested opportunity of autonomous development" for the nationalities under Turkish rule; and an "independent Polish state" whose "political and economic independence" would be "guaranteed by international covenant." At the same time, the Allied and Associated Powers armed, equipped and gave "co-belligerent" status to the armies of exiled Czechs and Poles who were then participating in the struggle for their own independence.

It was such an army of Czechs which the Bolsheviks sought to intern in Siberia, and which first demonstrated that effective intervention in Russia was possible. There were also Polish legions in Russia which had a similar experience. Some joined the Czechs in Siberia, others the Allied expeditionary forces at Murmansk and Archangel. One of their officers, Colonel Joseph Haller, ultimately went to France, where he led the Polish "Blue Army"—six divisions recruited from Poles residing in the Allied nations or found among captured prisoners of war. Still other Polish brigades assisted the new republic of Georgia in its struggle with the Turks, or joined the armies of General Denikin and the Allied expeditionary force in south Russia.

By recognizing the "co-belligerence" of such national armies-in-exile, the free powers recognized the existence of a state of war between the peoples of these nations and the governments imposed upon them by Germany and Austria-Hungary. In the case of the Czecho-Slovaks, the United States issued a formal statement (September 3, 1918) recognizing the Czecho-Slovak National Council as a "*de facto* belligerent government clothed with proper authority to direct the military and political affairs of the Czecho-Slovaks," and praising the efforts by which they had "taken up arms against the German and Austro-Hungarian Empires" under "officers of their own nationality" and in the "prosecution of their independent purposes."[18] In a letter to the president of the Polish National Committee, Roman Dmowski, our Secretary of State similarly praised the "zeal and tenacity" with which it had "prosecuted the task of marshaling its fellow-countrymen in a supreme military effort to free Poland from its present oppressors" and "recognizing the Polish Army, under the supreme political authority of the Polish National Committee, as autonomous and co-belligerent."[19]

A pattern of assistance to such groups, *without the co-belligerence of the United States,* was established in connection with its support of the exile governments of World War II. Even before it was itself at war, the United States supported the exile armies of many occupied nations—Belgium, Czechoslovakia, Greece, France, the Netherlands, Norway, Poland and Yugoslavia. With the single exception of Czechoslovakia, all were declared eligible for lend-lease military assistance prior to the attack on Pearl Harbor. In the case of Czechoslovakia, although the declaration of eligibility did not come until later (January 5, 1942), President Roosevelt had already commended "the courage and ability of the armed forces" which "organized themselves abroad to continue the struggle for the re-establishment of liberty in their country."[20]

In the announcement of lend-lease aid to Poland, it was made clear that assistance would be given to all who opposed aggression, whether or not their countries were still free. A White House press release, September 4, 1941, read in part as follows:

This action, the President said, demonstrates our intention to give material support to "the fighting determination of the Polish people to establish once again the independence of which they were so inhumanly deprived."

Polish troops are now training in Canada for action overseas. Under the President's order, machine guns, submachine guns, rifles, artillery equipment, trucks and other supplies will be sent to these troops in the near future.

The President stressed the importance of this new aid to the [exiled] Government of Poland as a continuing expression of "the policy of the United States to extend aid to all who resist aggression."[21]

The combined contribution of these exile armies to the total war effort was very substantial. The Free French Army of General de Gaulle's Committee of National Liberation was expanded from a mere 1,200 men, in 1940, to a powerful force of more than 500,000 at the time of the Allied landings in Normandy. Its navy was built up, by the end of 1943, to a force of 300,000 tons, with a complement of 48,000 men and officers, and the air force numbered several groups.

Prior to the fall of France, the Poles created an exile army of 84,500 men, with four infantry divisions, two light brigades and one motorized brigade. When France fell, this force was dispersed and the Polish government-in-exile had to begin all over again. By the end of the war, it had created, with Allied assistance, an even larger force of 228,000 men—with three infantry divisions, two armored divisions, two armored brigades, one airborne brigade, ten air-force fighter groups, four bomber groups and a small navy.[22] This force included the army of 75,000 men brought out of Russia by General Anders, but not the second Polish army formed in Russia, which the Soviets organized and controlled with the assistance of the Communist collaborator, Lieutenant Colonel Zygmunt Berling.

In the same way, the exile governments of Belgium, Czechoslovakia, Norway and the Netherlands were also assisted in the development of their own land, sea and air forces, based in the United Kingdom. All Belgian and Dutch citizens of military age residing in the Allied or neutral nations were called to the colors. As in the case of Poland, an armored brigade of Czechs was also formed in the Soviet Union, under the command of the Communist collaborator, General Ludvik Svoboda.

The dominated nations of western and central Europe, with a total population of approximately 100 million, were thus able to contribute armed forces in exile, exclusive of the underground resistance groups, comparable in size to the present land forces of the United States. It is not difficult, therefore, to imagine the size of the forces which could be created by refugees from the Communist-dominated nations, with a population approximately ten times as great.

The experience of the German invaders indicated that the people of the Soviet Union were as anxious as any to participate in a struggle for their own freedom. Hitler, however, was opposed to the bearing of arms by those who were not German, and he destroyed the incentive of the volunteers by putting them in German uniform and under German officers—and finally by transferring them to the Balkan and western fronts, where they were forced to fight the underground movements of other enslaved peoples and the armies of the free powers. For a long time, he even prohibited the assignment of Slavic peoples to combat duty, and put severe restrictions on such use of the non-Slavs.

Even so, it is estimated that citizens of the Soviet Union eventually comprised one-tenth of the German army.[23] Nazi reports of the number assigned to noncombatant service—as ammunition carriers, drivers, medics, translators, and in a multitude of housekeeping duties —range as high as 1,400,000.[24] Hundreds of thousands more were actually assigned to combat duty, either at the front or behind the lines, often in conscious violation of Hitler's personal directives.[25]

Shortly before the end of the war, the Nazis permitted the formation of an independent, free, provisional Russian Government, with its own army, its own uniform and its own general staff. It was known as the "Committee for the Liberation of the Peoples of Russia," and dedicated, under the terms of its manifesto, to the "overthrow of Stalin's tyranny, the liberation of the peoples of Russia from the Bolshevik system, and the restitution of those rights to the peoples of Russia which they fought for and won in the people's revolution of 1917."[26] It was not organized in time for any effective action, and it had only a brief, ill-fated existence, but the potential value of this exile force was clearly demonstrated by its tremendous appeal to the Russian peoples, and by the final, desperate, reluctant approval of those Nazi Party leaders who had originally tolerated such activities only for propaganda purposes.

As leader of the captive Russians, the Nazis had selected an experienced Red Army general, Andrei A. Vlasov, who was taken prisoner in July, 1942. Although he appeared to enjoy the highest esteem in Soviet circles, and had won the Order of the Red Banner for his service in defense of Moscow, Vlasov asked almost immediately for the creation of a unified Russian national army which would help to overthrow the Soviet regime.[27] He was not given authority to do this, however, for almost two years, in the meantime being restricted to activities which the Nazis considered more suitable to their own objectives.

In December, 1942, the Nazis permitted the formation of a Russian National Committee, but it was intended as a fiction, and used only for propaganda. In 1943, they allowed General Vlasov to make two speaking tours in the occupied areas, but these were of brief duration, and he was thereafter excluded altogether.

Finally, when the Committee for Liberation was authorized

(November, 1944), there was no longer any real prospect of unseating the Soviets. The Allied armies were already advancing into Germany from the west, and in the east the Red Army stood in the outskirts of Warsaw and Budapest. In January, 1945, when the committee received command of its first combat units, the Nazis were hardly in a position to offer assistance to others, even if they had so desired. Equipment was difficult or impossible to obtain, the German generals were reluctant to give up any Soviet nationals in their commands, and only two divisions (50,000 men) were authorized.

Thus delayed and abused, the newborn Russian army was doomed to failure before it began. Only one division was ever committed to action, and then only a month before the German surrender. On May 7, 1945, it turned against the Germans to liberate Prague, the capital of Czechoslovakia; but, upon learning that the city was assigned to Soviet occupation, soon disappeared into the woods.

Many of those who participated in this army were forcibly repatriated by the free powers, with readily imaginable results. The exact circumstances under which General Vlasov himself fell into Soviet hands are disputed, but his execution was announced by *Pravda* on August 2, 1946.

Nevertheless, prior to this unhappy ending, the great appeal of such an army had been amply demonstrated. Two regiments of the advancing Red Army crossed the lines and expressed a desire to join, and the response among those in German captivity was tremendous. It is reported that on one day alone, November 20, 1944, there were sixty thousand applications for enlistment.[28] The total number of such applications has been put at 2,500,000.[29] This seemingly fantastic figure represents about one-half of all Soviet citizens—men, women and children—who found themselves in Germany at this time.[30]

In 1950 the United States began a modest effort of its own to enlist the escapees from Iron Curtain countries, but under many of the same limitations which handicapped the *Wehrmacht*. Such recruits were to be assigned individually to regular Army units, and after five years of honorable service would receive American citizenship. The only incentive, therefore, was the defense and adoption of an alien country. The authorizing law,[31] first introduced in 1947 by Senator Henry Cabot Lodge, Jr., was amended in 1955 to permit an increase in the number of such enlistments from 2,500 to 12,500 men, but even this was only a small fraction of the total of those available.

At the same time, all proposals for the creation of independent, or even separate, units of escapees were rejected or ignored. One such proposal was made in still another bill introduced by Senator Lodge, in 1951, calling for the creation of a "Volunteer Freedom Corps" of 250,000.[32] This corps, it was suggested, could be included in a proposed European army. The bill was sponsored by Senators Brewster, Ives, Hendrickson, Hickenlooper and Mundt, but it was not passed.

Another bill, proposed by Representative Charles J. Kersten, provided for the creation of national units, to be attached to NATO.[33] It was adopted as an amendment to the Mutual Security Act of 1951, and has been brought up to date by several amendments, but it has never been implemented.

In support of his first bill, and an increase in the authorized enlistments, Senator Lodge related many facts which argued strongly for the adoption of his second proposal, or for the implementation of the "Kersten Amendment." Citing the "glaring errors" made by Hitler, and his "stupid handling of millions of anti-Communist Russians," Senator Lodge pointed out that the United States could find as many recruits among the subject peoples as it could "clothe and equip." Part of his statement, on the floor of the Senate, was as follows:

There is one more category, and that is the great mass of anti-Communist freedom-loving young men from behind the iron curtain. Estimates of the number of these men having an effective potential of military service run as high as 2,000,000. One of the greatest living authorities on the subject told me that in case of war the United States could recruit as many of these young men as we could clothe and equip, provided—and he stressed this proviso—we have professional officers in sufficient numbers who spoke their language and knew their customs to organize them into effective military formations and lead them in combat.

One of Hitler's most glaring errors in World War II was his stupid handling of the millions of anti-Communist Russians who hated their Russian rulers so much that they welcomed the German conquerors with open arms. One of the most famous Russian anti-Communist leaders was General Vlasov, who organized an army of non-Communist Russians to fight on the German side.... There were several millions of anti-Communist men available, but Hitler did not have enough professional officers who spoke their language and knew their customs to organize them into effective military formations and lead them in combat.

These considerations, added to personal experiences of my own in World War II, impelled me upon my return to the Senate to introduce legislation, co-sponsored by Representative Philbin in the House, authorizing the enlistment of aliens in the United States Army. After much argumentation and delay, the bill was signed by the President on June 30, 1950, authorizing the enlistment of only 2,500 men. When this bill originally passed the Senate, about a year ago, it had an authorization of 25,000 men, and it appears today that the Senate was right in voting the higher figure. The bill which became law provided for 2,500. The bill that passed the Senate last September provided for 25,000. The number was cut down in the House. What I am saying is that it appears the Senate was right.

General Collins, Chief of Staff of the Army, gave effective support to this legislation through thick and thin. This bill authorizes the Army to enlist young aliens wherever it chooses. It is hoped that among these young enlisted men there would be those who would qualify as officers and non-commissioned officers. They would join regular United States Army units—and not be organized into a separate "legion." It is hoped that many of them would have the merit to qualify as professional infantry, artillery and tank officers, and noncommissioned officers, and that after 5 years of good service they would become American citizens. There is no doubt, judging merely from the letters which I have received resulting from the slight publicity which this has had in the press abroad, that we could obtain some of the cream of the young men abroad; and that if 3 years ago we had embarked on the policy which this bill authorizes there would be today, both in Europe and in the Far East, foreign troops of great combat effectiveness.[34]

Senator Lodge, however, was thinking only in terms of the development of cadres for the future use of the United States, or for the defense of western Europe. Kersten, on the other hand, sought "cadres of armies of liberation"—an objective which would seem to be far more attractive to the intended recruits. It seems obvious that most victims of the Communists would be more interested in the liberation of their own nations than in acquiring citizenship in a foreign land, and it is doubtful that incorporation into the army of the United States, or even into a European army, would be an appealing prospect in the absence of such a goal.

Moreover, there is no reason why the subject peoples should devote their energies to preparing for the defense of the free nations while their own homes are made the scene of oppression and devastation. In 1952, Mr. Kersten stated that his own provision was designed to give them "military units of their own nationality," which would be "catalysts in the liberation of their own countries," and which would "in no sense" be acting to carry out "merely the will of some other country." The "ultimate objective," he said, was liberation of the subject peoples, not the defense of the free:

This amendment contemplates the setting up of national military units from the escapees that come from behind the iron curtain. . . .

They should be formed into these military units of their own nationality, with the uniforms and flags of their own country, symbolizing its ultimate freedom, under their own freely chosen leadership.

Free battalions of Poles, Czechs, Slovaks, Hungarians, Rumanians, Bulgarians, Albanians, Chinese, and of Russian and of the non-Russian peoples of the Soviet Union will be catalysts in the liberation of their own countries.

Such military units should in no sense be foreign legions acting to carry out merely the will of some other country. Such military units should be the cadres of armies of liberation to reestablish freedom in Poland, Czechoslovakia, Hungary, Rumania, Bulgaria, Albania, and China, and even in the Soviet Union.

.   .   .   .

. . . in the implementation and direction of these free military units, representatives of the major political parties of each of these countries should participate, except, of course, the Communist and pro-Communist Parties.

The ultimate objective is the liberation of each of these countries from Communist tyranny so that the people of Poland and the other captive nations may of their own free choice set up a government that to them shall seem most likely to secure the blessings of liberty.[35]

A further request for implementation of this law was made in 1954, by the Select Committee to Investigate Communist Aggression. This committee recommended:

That the President immediately establish the national military units authorized under Section 101 (a) (1) of the Mutual Security Act of 1951, as amended. Such national military units will demonstrate by deed to the millions of people held captive within the Communist empire that we are firmly allied with them in their hopes and struggles to attain freedom and national independence. This includes large numbers of men conscripted into the Red Army and other military establishments under Communist control.[36]

It should be noted, however, that the Kersten Amendment ostensibly provides for the attachment of such units to NATO, which is organized solely for the defense of free nations. So long as the United Nations is subject to the obstructive tactics of the Communists it may well be that some such arrangement is the best possible. But if the United Nations were really representative of the peoples of all nations, including the peoples of those which are Communist-dominated, that organization would appear to be the best guardian of such interests. Attached to a really free United Nations, these armies would not be used to "invade" the Communist empire, but at the same time they would be available for more positive action than the defense of the free world. Their very existence would increase the weight of United Nations resolutions; they would be a strong deterrent to continuing Soviet repression; and, in the event of further uprisings, they could be used to support the "irresistible" demands of their own peoples.

The creation of a Russian national army for this purpose was urged, in 1954, by the defecting MVD officer, Lieutenant Colonel Grigori S. Burlitski. Burlitski stated that such an army would encourage defection from the Red Army, and in the event of another revolt would be a rallying point for millions:

We should create a Russian national army which will increase the number of defection from the Soviet army. If such Russian national army abroad exists the ranks of this army will rapidly increase by the defectors coming over. This army, in case of uprise in the Soviet Union, would cross the border and it will become in a short while a 1 million or 2 million army which will help the Soviet people to get rid of the Communist regime. The existence of this political Russian center or organization and the existence of this Russian Army in the exile will prove to the Russian people that they are not alone, it will be a symbol of their eventual liberation, it will prove to them that they can depend on some sort of help coming from the free world.[37]

The accuracy of this prediction, in so far as the actions of the people are concerned, was demonstrated by the revolt in Hungary. During the brief period of that uprising, there were many requests for arms, ammunition and other forms of material assistance—some of which were broadcast over the free Hungarian radio stations:

We absolutely need guns, ammunition and food to be dropped through parachutes in the area of Dunapentele![38]

We are asking for immediate armed help for Hungary. . . .

We will continue to fight a partisan war. We are asking for urgent very urgent help, we are asking for armed help for Hungary![39]

According to Major General Bela Kiraly, commander of the freedom fighters of Budapest, the revolt failed only because of the absence of such assistance. "Finally," he relates, "we were forced to give up hope for help from the world outside. It was then that I left our country."[40]

Such assistance is also urged by the peoples of the Far East. At the thirteenth regular session of the United Nations General Assembly (1958), the Chinese delegate, Tingfu F. Tsiang, asserted that this was his government's program for recovery of the mainland:

. . . when our people on the mainland rise in revolt as the Hungarian people did two years ago and call for our help, we will fight side by side with them for their freedom. This is our program of recovery of the mainland, no more and no less.

When our people on the mainland rise in revolt and call for our help, we cannot sit idly by and turn a deaf ear. Under that circumstance we cannot entrust the fate of our people on the mainland to United Nations debate or to special committees or to a special representative of the United Nations, as we did here two years ago with the fate of the Hungarian nation. Under that circumstance, we are morally bound to rush to the aid of our brethren with all that we have and are.[41]

The Chinese statement was in full conformity with the declaration adopted the year before by the Asian People's Anti-Communist League. This organization was formed in Korea, in 1954, by delegates from Free China, Korea, Viet Nam, the Philippines, Hong Kong, Macao and the Ryukyu Islands. According to the declaration referred to, "material as well as moral help should be given to freedom fighters behind the Communist lines, as well as to those of the Free World. This," it stated, "can be one of the most effective ways of destroying Communism quickly."[42] This declaration was adopted at the third annual conference of the League, held at Saigon in 1957, and attended by additional representatives from Turkey, Pakistan, Australia, New Zealand, Burma, Laos and Singapore.

The opportunities for the use of exile national armies have been many and varied. Such armies already exist in the divided nations—Germany, China, Korea and Viet Nam—and are obviously essential for the defense of those parts which are still free. Prior to the division of Viet Nam, the United States insisted long and often that the Communists could only be defeated by the creation of a strong and independent national army of free Vietnamese. By the same token, if, in 1950, there had been a strong Korean national army in the south, there would have been no Communist invasion from the north. It may also be surmised that if the free Chinese armies had been in a position to give effective assistance to the people on the mainland, there would have been no effective intervention in Korea by the Communist Chinese armies. Finally, when the proper opportunity arises, there could be, in the words of General Chiang Kai-shek, a merger of "the forces of national revolution outside the Iron Curtain and of anti-Communist revolution inside the Iron Curtain."[43] Such a use of national forces in both Hungary and China was openly suggested by Secretary of State Dulles at a press conference on September 30, 1958:

If you had on the mainland a sort of unrest and revolt, like, for example, what broke out in Hungary, then the presence of a free China with considerable power a few miles away could be a very important element in the situation. I think that we would all feel that, if there had been a free government of Hungary in existence within a few miles of Hungary at the time when that revolt took place, the situation might have developed in a different way from what it did.[44]

It can only be asked why there was no such free government in close proximity to Hungary, and capable of providing the required assistance; why the free government of China is not provided with the means of giving effective assistance in similar uprisings on the mainland—as in the case of Tibet; and, finally, why action along these lines has not been taken for all of the Communist-dominated nations.

If the peoples of every Communist-dominated nation could count upon the support of a free national army of their own, even though in exile, all of the Communist armies would have to be kept at home, where they might be as likely to side with the cause of freedom as to aid in suppressing the revolt of their own people. This was what the Hungarian Communist army did, and what the Polish Communist army appeared to be ready to do when the Soviets were forced to make a tactical "retreat" in that country. There would at least be no further possibility of employing Communist troops of one nationality to suppress the people of another, such as the use of Russian Communist troops to suppress Germans, Mongolian Communist troops to suppress Hungarians, and Chinese Communist troops to suppress Koreans and Tibetans.

As Senator Lodge indicated, the number of escapees and refugees is already great enough to provide for many large armies of freedom fighters. Moreover, it is apparent that the number is vastly increased when there is hope of participating in a national liberation movement, or at least of living under a free national government. At the beginning of hostilities in Korea, 2,500,000 persons fled from north to south, ultimately to swell the ranks of the then tiny army of the republic. The total number of Korean escapees now exceeds 3,000,000. Since 1949, more than 4,000,000 people have fled from mainland China. Of these, 1,600,000 are on Formosa and 1,300,000 are in Hong Kong. Nearly a million persons fled from North to South Viet Nam within a few months after the partition of that country, and over 3,000,000 have escaped from East to West Germany.

Without effective assistance, however, neither the escapees nor those who remain behind are able to make any practical effort to remove the Communists from power. As Secretary Dulles stated, in his book *War or Peace*, "The people have no arms, and violent revolt would be futile."[45] General Bor, the leader of the Polish underground army, who headed the Warsaw uprising against the Nazis, has testified that it was "impossible" to build an underground in Soviet-occupied areas. "We tried again and again," he said, "to build under Russian occupation our home army units but we never succeeded in building a real underground there. . . . They immediately recognize what is going on and then they arrest all of the people that are working, and not only them, but also their friends, their families."[46]

This was the same reason that was assigned by Lieutenant Colonel Burlitski for the suspension of resistance in Lithuania (see Chapter XV).

The only cases of the successful ouster of a Communist regime have been those in which there was an armed intervention from outside, as in the case of Hungary in 1919, and Guatemala in 1954. The collapse of Bela Kun's regime in Hungary, in spite of intense popular hatred, did not occur until after invasion by Rumania. In Guatemala, several internal efforts failed prior to the successful "invasion" by Colonel Castillo Armas' army of exiles. Colonel Armas was himself wounded and imprisoned in one of these unaided and unsuccessful attempts; and in a statement made for a congressional committee of investigation, asserted that he had worked for three years after escape to obtain the foreign assistance he required:

... I went to Colombia, and then to Honduras, where we organized the revolution.

For 3 years my comrades and myself worked to obtain arms and equipment and to build up an organization both inside and outside of the country. We knew that our next effort must be successful.

At times the outlook was discouraging. Not many people were willing to help us, and many of those who were, lacked the means. But we kept our faith in God, and we won.[47]

It is a fact that without such help from others the United States would have failed in its own struggle for freedom. This is frankly stated in the Army's manual of *American Military History:*

Another essential ingredient was French aid—money, supplies, and in the last phase, military force. Without French aid the patriots might have fought the British indefinitely in the interior of the country, but it seems unlikely they could have won a complete and decisive victory. The bulk of the muskets, bayonets, and cannon used by the Continental Army came from France. It was the predominance of French naval power and the presence of the French army that made the final stroke of the Revolution at Yorktown possible.[48]

General Washington was emphatic and repetitive on the same point. In letters of appreciation to the French people and nation, he wrote that it was through the "kind Intervention" of that country that the United States had been "led by the Hand to Independence and a Station among the Nations," and that the aid of the French Navy had "rendered practicable those enterprizes, which without it could not with any probability of success, have been attempted."[49] Moreover, during the course of the Revolutionary War, Washington wrote a number of letters earnestly requesting such assistance. These plainly stated, in dignified but firm language, that without such assistance the United States of America would have had to throw in the sponge. For example, in October, 1780, he wrote to Benjamin Franklin, the American Minister Plenipotentiary in France, that "our present situation makes one of two things essential to us," either a "Peace, or the most vigorous aid of our Allies particularly in the article of money."[50] In November, 1780, he wrote to Arthur Lee, another member of the American diplomatic mission in Europe: "I am so entirely convinced of the absolute necessity of a large and immediate foreign aid of money, to the continuance of the war, that I should be happy to do any thing I could with propriety to promote it."[51] And in January, 1781, he wrote to Lieutenant Colonel John Laurens, his own aide-de-camp, who was being sent on a special mission to France by the Continental Congress:

But if the sending so large a succour of troops, should necessarily diminish the pecuniary aid, which our allies may be disposed to grant, it were preferable to diminish the aid in men; for the same sum of money, which would transport from France and maintain here a body of troops with all the necessary apparatus, being put into our hands to be employed by us would serve to give activity to a larger force within ourselves, and its influence would pervade the whole administration.

        .   .   .   .

... there is still a fund of inclination and resource in the country equal to great and continued exertions, provided we have it in our power to stop the progress of disgust, by changing the present system and adopting another more consonant with the spirit of the nation, and more capable of activity and energy in public measures; of which a powerful succour of money must be the basis.

        .   .   .   .

A large majority are still firmly attached to the independence of these states, abhor a reunion with Great Britain, and are affectionate to the alliance with France, but this disposition cannot supply the place of means customary and essential in war, nor can we rely on its duration amidst the perplexities, oppressions and misfortunes that attend the want of them.[52]

Any effective aid to the subject peoples involves, of course, the *risk* of a third world war, but it is also just possible that the assumption of this risk is the only way to *prevent* such a war. If the Soviet rulers may be tempted to unleash their vaunted intercontinental ballistic missiles upon those nations willing to supply arms for the defense of subject peoples, they may be equally tempted, when they are ready, to unleash them upon every nation co-operating in the defense of the free world. And they will be in a position to do so as long as the peoples under their rule can be held in subjection.

It is also noteworthy that the United States has not been disturbed by the risks involved in aid to the free nations. There was risk of World War III in aid to Greece and Turkey, in the defense of South Korea and in aid to the French in Viet Nam, yet the United States was not deterred. It was acknowledged by President Eisenhower, in 1958, that direct intervention in Lebanon might have "serious consequences," but he asserted nevertheless that "despite the risks involved" such action was "required to support the principles of justice and international law."[53]

The Soviets have also been "provoked" by innumerable other decisions—by the declarations of the "Truman Doctrine" and the "Eisenhower Doctrine," by the establishment of NATO, SEATO and the Baghdad Pact, and by the decision to rearm the republic of West Germany. Khrushchev has gone to great lengths to make it plain that they are "provoked" by the establishment of any American military bases in other free countries. Yet all of these risks have been incurred to prevent war, not to precipitate it; and as of this date, at least they have not precipitated it.

Similarly there does not appear to be any great fear of the risk involved in giving *moral* assistance to the subject peoples, even though this is also a source of "tension between East and West," and therefore presumably of the risk of war. The Soviet Union and its puppet regimes have been aggravated by the "provocative" statements of Secretary Dulles and President Eisenhower; by the use of balloons to scatter leaflets; by the "inflammatory" broadcasts beamed across the iron curtain by the Voice of America, Radio Free Europe, Radio Liberation, Radio in the American Sector (RIAS) and similar agencies whose very titles are suggestive of "subversion" and "diversionary action"; and even by the prayers of the free world. "The American leaders," Khrushchev complained in December, 1955, "declare that they are praying for a change of the existing order . . . and openly promise the 'support' of the United States of America in this matter." "All this," he said, "goes to foment passions and consequently to a new arms race and the threat of a new war." "We do not want to frighten anybody and we do not brag of our military strength but we must cool off the more rabid arms race supporters and remind them of the results of the recent tests of the latest Soviet hydrogen bomb."[54]

The risk involved in aid to the free nations has been accepted because it is realized that the risk incurred by not taking such action is even greater. From a purely selfish point of view, it would be no less advisable, and for the same reason, to accept the risk involved in aid to the subject peoples. From a humanitarian viewpoint, it would seem more desirable to help the subject peoples in a war which already exists—a war in which all peoples could be joined in the struggle against tyrants—than to await an atomic one in which the free nations may be forced to fight, and perhaps to destroy, not only the Communists but also their victims. From the point of view of duty and adherence to principle, if the free nations were not prepared to incur the risk of war for the assistance of "all the men in all the lands," they should never have attempted to form the United Nations, or have undertaken the obligations of its charter.

The greater danger of war arises not from the measures that might be taken to oppose aggression or the suppression of freedom but from actions based upon a more selfish or less appealing motivation, such as the desire to retain control of foreign dependencies, to manage the Suez Canal, to restrain "Arab nationalism," or even to defend the exponents of "national communism." In such a war it would be far more difficult to secure the co-operation of the peoples behind the Iron Curtain, or to convince them that a war thus begun would be fought for their freedom, especially if the free powers had never in the meantime lifted a finger in their defense.

Moreover, it is a travesty of justice that the free world was willing to incur the risk involved in supplying extensive military assistance to the Communist government of Yugoslavia, and yet withheld the same assistance from the free government that was briefly established in Hungary. Because the Communist government of Yugoslavia was "opposed" to the Communist government of the Soviet Union, the

United States considered a "guarantee" of its territorial integrity, and two members of NATO, Greece and Turkey, were encouraged to make an agreement which bound them to come to the aid of Yugoslavia in the event of attack. Eventually, more than $750,000,000 worth of military equipment was sent to Marshal Tito. Yet no free power is willing to give arms to those who oppose the Soviets, not with other "brands" of communism, but with the principles of freedom. In their case, it is protested that the "weapon of moral condemnation" is "the only alternative to action which might well bring on the third world war."[55]

It would actually be far less dangerous to defend the cause of freedom than the cause of "national communism"; to make of the United Nations the "general security organization" which it was intended to be, rather than a place where words are substituted for actions; and to face the *risk* of war instead of its assurance. The free nations have been forced to this conclusion twice, and it was the stated belief of President Eisenhower, even though not consistently applied. Speaking, in 1955, on "The Peace We Want," he said:

Eagerness to avoid war—if we think no deeper than this single desire—can produce outright or implicit agreement that injustices and wrongs of the present shall be perpetuated in the future.... In the judgment of history, we would have sold out the freedom of men for the pottage of a false peace. *Moreover, we would assure future conflict!*[56] (Italics added.)

As President Wilson said, the "world's peace ought to be disturbed if the fundamental rights of humanity are invaded, but it ought not be disturbed for any other thing that I can think of...."[57] This thought was more recently reflected in a statement of the United States representative, Henry Cabot Lodge, during the United Nations debate on Hungary. It only needs to be implemented:

We think that it is humanitarian to take a step which may free a man from being oppressed. We think it is just as humanitarian to take steps to provide people with international law, justice, and morality as it is to take steps which will put food in their stomachs and give them medicines to cure their illnesses.[58]

CHAPTER XVIII

THE VOICE OF EIGHT HUNDRED MILLION

"And the light shineth in the darkness: and the darkness did not comprehend it" (John i:5).

It has been said, often enough, that the cold war is a struggle between all of the people of the world on the one hand, and only a few men on the other. In the words of Secretary Dulles, "Some dozen people in the Kremlin are seeking to consolidate their imperial rule over some 800 million people, representing what *were* nearly a score of independent nations."[1] As President Eisenhower put it, "only relatively small numbers—only a handful even in Russia itself—are fixed in their determination to dominate the world by force and fraud." With the exception of such groups, he said, "mankind everywhere hungers for freedom, for well-being, for peace." And he asked, "Now, how can a few men thwart the will of hundreds of millions?"[2]

When the free nations stop asserting that it is impossible for a few men to thwart the will of millions, and spend more time seeking the answer to this question of how they do it, the cold war will soon be won. One answer may be found in the fact that while it is Moscow which deprives the subject peoples of free speech and representative government behind the iron curtain, it is the democratic nations which have taken away their voice in the free world. The "will of hundreds of millions," which finds no outlet in the "Presidiums" and "Politburos" of the Communist-dominated nations, is also denied expression in the United Nations. Neither does it obtain a hearing in the exchange of diplomatic relations between the free governments and the dummy "governments" which these Communist bodies have established. It is not only that the seats of these nations in the world body and elsewhere must be vacated by those who wrongfully occupy them; they must actually be filled by others, who can properly speak for the people of these nations and make their real voices heard.

The right to freely express their will is one of the principal demands of the subject peoples, as was painfully made clear during

459

the uprising in Hungary, and the subsequent investigation of that episode by a committee of the United Nations. In the course of debate on the report of this committee, the Australian member, and rapporteur, asserted: "They want a free society, with free political parties, a free press, and government by popular will. They want to be able to express themselves freely in political and intellectual fields and not to be forced into the monotonous mould of dreary one-party dogma."[3]

During the same debate, the United States representative pointed out that this right is just as completely denied in the General Assembly of the United Nations as it is behind the iron curtain. "The suffering and suppressed people of Hungary," he said, "have no free voice, since Moscow has taken that away from them—certainly they have no free voice in this Assembly."[4] Yet he had himself refused to insist upon such representation the year before—when Miss Anna Kethly, the one escaping member of Hungary's free government, was refused permission to address that body. In reply to widespread criticism of this action, Ambassador Lodge indicated that in his view Anna Kethly had no greater standing before the General Assembly of the United Nations than a defeated "political" candidate. "No one," he asserted, "is permitted to address the Assembly in his *private capacity*. There is not a chance in the world that a majority of the Assembly would allow the *political 'outs'* of a country, however meritorious their case may be, to use the United Nations General Assembly as a platform."[5] (Italics added.)

This attitude, of course, negates the whole purpose of the United Nations, which was originally conceived and organized to defend and give a hearing to just such meritorious cases. To exclude as a "political 'out,' " having only a "private capacity," the representative of a government which has been overthrown by aggression is to deny the use of the United Nations' platform to those for whom it was primarily intended; and whether that body is to be regarded as an organization for general security against aggression or merely as a forum for the expression of world opinion against it, such an exclusion of its victims is nothing more than open, abject acceptance of the doctrine that "might makes right."

As a result of this attitude on the part of free nations, the forces of aggression enjoy the maximum use of the United Nations forum, while the injured parties—the subject peoples—have no effective means for stating their case. They do not even have the opportunity of making an appeal on their own behalf. In the place of this natural right, the free powers have substituted an abnormal system of one-way intercourse—by radio, pamphlet, balloon and similar means—in which they bombard the subject peoples with *their* ideas, *their* plans and *their* solutions, but do not appear to be concerned with the ideas, plans and solutions of the subject peoples. Instead of allowing the subject peoples to plead for freedom in the only forum which is presently available, they insist upon describing the advantages of freedom for their alleged edification, and urging them to press their demands in places where it is impossible to do so.

It has been asserted, for example, by President Eisenhower, that "the inspiration of freedom" and even "the benefits enjoyed by those who possess it" must be made "known to those oppressed";[6] by former President Truman that the subject peoples must "awaken to the fact that they and they alone ought to have direct power and control over their government";[7] and by Secretary of State Dulles that they must be encouraged "to want themselves to strive more to get such freedoms and liberties, opportunities and enjoyments."[8] But it is rarely suggested that those who have never had to "strive" for their freedom—and who have comfortably inherited and always enjoyed its benefits—have anything to learn about the lack of them, or must themselves be awakened to the real needs and desires of those who are less fortunate.

If the subject peoples are to demand and obtain a voice in their own governments, under conditions of grave oppression, the free nations should at least be willing to demand and obtain a hearing for them in the international councils and assemblies of democracy. If they are to themselves "peacefully frustrate" the "oppressive design of Soviet despotism," their representatives *must* be admitted to the United Nations, and they *must* be recognized and dealt with by all free governments as the real spokesmen of their people. It is no solution merely to have a high-kilowatt Voice of America, Voice of Great Britain, and so on; there must be a loud Voice of the Subject Peoples. For this purpose, we could, as Secretary Dulles once suggested, "welcome the creation in the free world of political task forces to develop a freedom program for each of the captive nations." Each group, as he said, "would be made up of those who are proved patriots who would have the practical resourcefulness, and who command confidence and respect at home and abroad." Then, as he added,

"We could end diplomatic relations with present governments which are in fact only puppets of Moscow, if and when that would promote the freedom programs."[9]

As in the case of other means of assistance, there have been many precedents for such action. As Secretary Dulles asserted on another occasion, "Nations often maintain diplomatic relations with governments-in-exile."[10] They did so for example during the last years of World War I, when the subject peoples of Poland and Czechoslovakia were represented at the Allied capitals by national committees or councils of their own exiled political leaders. Although at that time these nations had no independent existence, having been dominated for many years by the Central Powers and Russia, these exile groups were recognized and given official standing by the Allied nations as the nuclei of free future governments. Thus, the Polish National Committee was recognized and supported as the "official Polish organization" by France (September 20, 1917), Great Britain (October, 15, 1917), Italy (October 30, 1917) and the United States (November 10, 1917). On June 30, 1918, the Czecho-Slovak National Committee was recognized by France as "the first step toward a future government." On August 9, 1918, it was recognized by Great Britain as "the present trustee of the future Czecho-Slovak Government," and, on September 2, by the United States as a "de facto belligerent government." Early in October, the Czech National Council organized a provisional government, with Professor Thomas G. Masaryk as President and Dr. Eduard Benes as Foreign Minister. Chargés d'affaires were sent to, and received by, London, Paris, Rome, Washington and Omsk (the capital of the free Provisional All-Russian Government in Siberia).

The right of other subject peoples to similar representation was also recognized. Thus, in April, 1918, a Congress of Oppressed Nationalities—Czechs, Yugoslavs, Serbs, Poles, Ukrainians and Rumanians—was invited to meet in Rome. Its delegations were welcomed by the Italian Prime Minister, Vittorio Orlando, and its resolutions calling for freedom, self-determination, independence and struggle against the "common oppressors" (Germany and Austria-Hungary) were not only heard but also published officially by the Italian government. They were also endorsed by the Secretary of State, Robert Lansing, and by the Allied Supreme War Council at Versailles.[11] This action stirred great enthusiasm among the oppressed peoples, and sympathetic demonstrations and assemblies were thereafter held in the subject nations themselves. A second gathering was held in Prague, under the very noses of the Central Powers, at which the subject peoples of that time openly demanded independence and democratic government.[12]

During the Second World War, a similar procedure was followed. Even before it became a belligerent, the United States not only refused to recognize the Axis and Soviet annexations of conquered nations but also continued to recognize their exiled governments and to maintain diplomatic relations with them. On October 2, 1939, after the fall of Poland, Secretary of State Cordell Hull asserted:

> More than 20 years ago the United States recognized and has since maintained diplomatic relations with the Polish Government. ... The United States ... continues to regard the Government of Poland as in existence. . . .[13]

In July, 1940, after the forced incorporation of the Baltic States, no exile governments of these nations existed. Nevertheless, the United States continued, and still continues, to recognize the diplomatic officials of the governments that were then overthrown.

In July, 1941, the United States recognized the exile provisional government of Czechoslovakia. On that occasion it was asserted, in a published note to the exiled government, that the forcible suppression of a free government could not deprive its representatives of their official capacities, or the people of their right to be represented in the outside world. "The American Government," this note advised, "has not acknowledged that the temporary extinguishment of their liberties has taken from the people of Czechoslovakia their rights and privileges in international affairs, and it has continued to recognize the diplomatic and consular representatives of Czechoslovakia in the United States in the full exercise of their functions."[14] Subsequently, all of the exiled governments of the Nazi-dominated nations were included in the original group of subscribers to the Declaration by United Nations, and thus incorporated into the free world's alliance against Axis oppression.

There is no reason why a similar procedure should not be adopted, in the cold war, for *all* of the Communist-dominated nations, including the Soviet Union. The peoples of the Baltic States, even though they have *no* government, are still represented in many free capitals by the diplomatic officials of the last ones. Free governments are recognized by many nations for South Korea, South Viet Nam, West Germany and China, and few would argue that they are not more truly representative of their enslaved compatriots than the corresponding Communist regimes established under the aegis of the Soviet Union. At the present time, however, the only such government represented in the United Nations is that of China—which therefore sometimes finds itself a lone defender in that body of the principles of the charter.

If we really wish to support the cause of freedom everywhere, and if we wish to apply the principles of the charter of the United Nations universally, then the right of all peoples to be thus represented and heard must be recognized. The propriety and advantages of such a procedure were clearly indicated in a statement made in 1954 by Edwin W. Martin, Deputy Director of the State Department's Office of Chinese Affairs. "The Chinese Government on Formosa," he said, "provides the Chinese people with a representative voice in the United Nations and in other international forums, and with a channel of continuing contact with the peoples of the free world. It has consistently supported the objectives of the United Nations and other international bodies to which it belongs, and thereby has assumed a posture in world affairs more truly representative of the desires of the Chinese people than the defiant and aggressive regime in Peiping."[15]

For the other Communist-dominated areas there are many exile organizations which could speak effectively on behalf of their peoples and form the nuclei of future free governments, if only given the opportunity. But without funds, without effective moral support from the free nations, and confronted by the almost certain assurance that they cannot hope for diplomatic recognition, admission to the United Nations or acceptance by any other free world body, there is little that they can do to sustain even the hopes of their own members. As a result, many of them have been abandoned, others have been hopelessly split into competing factions and small dissident groups, and the rest are given scant attention.

There remains, for example, the government-in-exile of Poland —abandoned by the "Great Powers" at Yalta. Now largely ignored by its former friends and allies, its continued existence is little more than a reproachful reminder that the Yalta policies have not yet been reversed. Its own warning, given shortly prior to that now infamous conference, has proven to be only too correct. Expressing the hope that the British would not consent to recognize a puppet government, the Polish memorandum stated, January 22, 1945: "The recognition of such a 'government' in Poland would be tantamount to the recognition of the abolition of the independence of Poland, in the defence of which the present war was begun."[16]

An effort has also been made by the National Yugoslav Committee to continue the wartime government-in-exile of that country. The oppressed peoples of this multinational state are also represented in the free world by the Serb National Committee, the Slovene National Committee and other corresponding national groups.

The peoples of the Soviet Union have many exile organizations, such as the All-Russian Committee for Liberation (VKO), the National Alliance of Russian Solidarists (NTS), the Union of Struggle for the Liberation of the Peoples of Russia (SBONR), the Central Union of Post-War Emigrés, the United Committee of Vlasovites, the Russian Political Committee and the World Cossack Association. Some of these organizations—such as the Ukrainian National Council, the Byelorussian National Council and the Georgian National Council—also have the character of governments-in-exile, tracing their origins to free and independent governments established after the Bolshevik seizure of power in 1917. The Armenian Revolutionary Federation (Dashnakzoutyoun) is the party which created the provisional government of the republic of Armenia in 1918, and which won the parliamentary elections in the following year by taking seventy-two out of eighty elected seats. Others, such as the Supreme Liberation Council (UHVR), and NTS, are active in the leadership or organization of underground resistance.

Beginning in 1951, an attempt to co-ordinate the efforts of these groups was made by a private organization of American citizens, the American Committee for the Liberation of the Peoples of Russia (now the American Committee for Liberation from Bolshevism). This effort was not successful, partly because of the lack of any effective free-world support, and partly because of disputes which still exist between the Russian and non-Russian nationalities. Many of the former insist upon maintaining the political unity of all parts of the pre-Soviet empire, while the desire of the non-Russians for complete independence has been aggravated and confirmed by the oppressive domination of the Soviets.[17] It seems probable, however, that if there was any hope of effective moral and material support by the free governments, these difficulties could be promptly overcome and millions of exiled Russian and Soviet citizens rallied in a great unified movement for the restoration of freedom.

In spite of the existing handicaps, a large degree of unity has already been achieved by various organizations representing the non-Russian peoples of the Soviet Union. This has been accomplished through the medium of the League for the Liberation of the Peoples of the USSR (The Paris Bloc), which includes the Azerbaijan National Union, the Armenian Revolutionary Federation (Dashnakzoutyoun), the Byelorussian National Council, the Georgian National Council, the North Caucasian National Organization, the Ukrainian National Council, the Committee for the Liberation of Turkestan, and the Idel-Ural National Committee (Volga Tartars).

A similar movement toward united action has been made by organizations representing the captive peoples of eastern Europe. The unified organization in this case is called the Assembly of Captive European Nations (ACEN), which includes a national committee or council for each of the satellite nations—the Baltic States, Poland, Czechoslovakia, Hungary, Rumania and Bulgaria. Formed in 1954, upon the pattern of the United Nations itself, ACEN combines the efforts of its members in order, as its charter resolution states, the "more effectively to voice and promote the common rights and interests of our peoples"[18]—rights and interests which its statement of "Purpose and Organization" asserts are at the present time "either unrepresented or misrepresented" in the existing "world organization."[19] Its roster of officials and delegations is certainly more illustrious than the corresponding roster of eastern European delegations in that body, and includes the names of some of the most eminent European statesmen—former prime ministers, cabinet ministers, members of parliament, political party leaders, diplomats, government officials, clergymen, and cultural, professional, labor and business leaders—many of whom are members or representatives of their last freely elected governments, and all of whom are forced to lead a life of exile because of Soviet occupation of their homelands.

In 1956, two proposals were made, in the United States Senate, for public financial assistance to such émigré organizations. But they were never adopted. One, introduced by Senator Dirksen, would have authorized the use of up to $5,000,000 of Mutual Security funds for "grants to private non-profit organizations engaged in keeping alive the will for freedom."[20] Another, by Senator Douglas, would have provided "aid and support to those groups which are actively engaged in maintaining, inspiring, and instilling" the "spirit and hope" of freedom.[21]

Under Senator Douglas' proposal, the grants would be made through a specially created "Freedom Administration." In arguing for its adoption, he asserted:

There are numerous nationality groups—in the United States as well as in Europe—who are working day and night to aid their countrymen who are now in chains. For the most part, these groups have little money and their activities are limited by the small amount of private funds which are available to them. It is true that we are providing $7 million in the present appropriation for the escapee program, which my amendment would aid and abet. It is also true that, under Section 401 of the Mutual Security Act of 1954, the President has a special fund which he may use for certain programs; $100 million may be used for any selected persons who are residing in, or are escapees from, the Soviet Union and the conquered satellites. I wish to stress those words, "selected persons," for the amendment I propose would go beyond selected persons to nationality groups who are already organized and who are fighting by peaceful means to gain freedom for their countrymen.[22]

This latter plan, however, was opposed by the Department of State. In a letter to the chairman of the Committee on Foreign Relations,[23] the Assistant Secretary for Congressional Relations, Robert C. Hill, opined that the proposed Freedom Administration would "offer a prime target for Soviet-inspired attacks" and ambiguously asserted that "certain activities" can "best be undertaken by agencies of the United States Government," while "other steps" can "be most properly carried out through private, non-governmental groups." Apparently oblivious to the billions of dollars in public funds which are being granted to the governments of the free nations, he also expressed the fear that grants of money to an exile government or council of the subject peoples would destroy its popular appeal:

If by grants of public funds the Freedom Administration publicly recorded direct Government interest in certain anti-Communist organizations, there would be the danger that such organizations would immediately take on the character and limitations of official operations, thereby impinging upon similar activities currently being carried out by governmental agencies. Moreover, the appeal which such activities offer as representative national and private groups to the people of the captive nations would thereby be sacrificed.

This type of argument actually deprives these organizations of that which they most need—the public, open, moral support of the governments of the free world. If it is a valid argument then the United States is doing the greatest harm to those free nations which it endeavors to assist, and is giving its most effective aid to those "neutral" nations which receive the least support. On the same basis, it might be said that the United States gave its greatest assistance to the national government of China when it was still on the mainland —by declaring an embargo upon the shipment of military supplies, withholding economic assistance pending the termination of "fratricidal warfare," and engaging in public, hostile criticism of its "almost overwhelming suspicion" of the Chinese Communist Party.

So long as the United States stands for freedom, it will always be the target of Soviet-inspired attacks, regardless of whether and to whom any effective material assistance may be given. Moreover, the appeal of the exile groups is already being "sacrificed" by sporadic moral support in the form of official statements approving and commending their activities. For example, in a message to the Assembly of Captive European Nations, Secretary of State Dulles asserted that its "thoughtful deliberations" were "illustrative of the Free World's just concern with the problems of the captive countries and reflect as well that unity of spirit among free men which is an indispensable element of a happier future."[24]

In 1953, he wrote a letter to Hasan Dosti, chairman of the Executive Committee of the National Committee for a Free Albania, in which he likewise commended this committee's efforts and pledged the continuing support of the United States government:

Isolated as they are and unable to speak for themselves, the people of Albania desperately need the support and assistance of those of their compatriots who are now outside Albania and free to speak in behalf of their people. As the National Committee for a Free Albania has recognized, Albanians in the free world, through unity of purpose and effort, can perform an invaluable service in supporting the morale of their countrymen and in keeping alive their faith in ultimate independence.

To the United States, which has traditionally supported the right of all oppressed peoples to freedom and liberty, the tragic plight of the Albanian people is a matter of deep concern. This Government shall continue its efforts to support the Albanian people in their endeavors for the establishment of a free and representative government.[25]

In the same way, he commended the activities of the Council of Free Czechoslovakia:

> You are now meeting to honor the democracy which was destroyed 5 years ago and to express again the world's condemnation of that act and the means by which it was brought about. . . .
>
> .   .   .   .
>
> So long as the historic antipathy of your people to foreign domination continues and the national traditions are kept alive by those abroad and by the silent millions at home, there is sustaining hope that the Czechs and Slovaks will once again take their rightful place as a constructive force in the community of free peoples.[26]

Even though few and far between, such statements can be just as "compromising" as effective material assistance. If they do not produce the suspicion of more positive forms of aid, given secretly or indirectly through other "private" organizations, they at least confirm a certain identity of purpose. They also serve to show, of course, that the efforts of these organizations are praiseworthy, and that by failing to give them more effective assistance the United States is neither showing the courage of its convictions or fulfilling its pledges of assistance to all those "freedom-loving peoples who need and want and can profitably use our aid."

To make such statements, while, at the same time, withholding material assistance, is only to create in the minds of the subject peoples an impression of insincerity; and in the minds of others, the belief that Soviet charges of subversion and "diversionary" activity are not entirely groundless. Such charges, moreover, are already extensive. No matter how attentively the exile organizations are left to shift for themselves, without recognition and without funds, there is no escape from accusations of complicity with capitalist "enemies of the people." Thus, the Soviets claimed, in 1954, that the Ukrainian National Council and other Ukrainian national organizations were operating under the "unceremonious" orders of President Eisenhower, General Ridgway and Admiral Leslie C. Stevens (then president of the American Committee for Liberation from Bolshevism).[27] In 1957, one of the major Russian exile organizations, the Union of Struggle for the Liberation of the Peoples of Russia (SBO NR), was included along with the Central Intelligence Agency, the Free Europe Committee, the Crusade for Freedom and the American Committee in a long list of "spy and saboteur" organizations allegedly financed by the United States.[28] At the same time, the Ukrainian (Communist) delegate to the United Nations, L. E. Kyzia, asserted that American intelligence had taken "into its hands all the refuse of reactionary organizations of Ukrainian émigrés."[29] Similar charges were made in Moscow with respect to NTS, which was described as "in the service of and fully supported by American Intelligence."[30]

In addition, every uprising is described as the result of foreign provocation, and the principal figures are inevitably convicted of conspiring not only with "reactionary fascists" within but also with the "imperialists" and "capitalists" abroad. For example, in the case of Imre Nagy, the unfortunate Prime Minister of the revolutionary government of Hungary, it was "proven" at his trial that the British military attaché in Budapest "took a direct part in the military direction of the uprising" and that the entire program was "worked out" by an "American Intelligence Organization."[31] Similar "proofs" have been adduced at the trials of many other purged Communists, popular democratic party leaders, and even clergymen.

It would appear, therefore, that there is little likelihood of saving any "appeal" which patriotic national groups might have, either as "private" organizations abroad or as independent political or religious institutions at home, by merely withholding American assistance. They are already being described as American *agents*.

Such objections, moreover, do not apply to the question of representation. Whether or not it is considered desirable for the free nations to furnish individual financial assistance, there is no reason why they should not at least recognize a representative national council for each subject nation, admit them all to the United Nations and otherwise assist them to perfect their representation of the subject peoples in the free world. If these things were done, a new and more powerful voice of freedom would be created—and at no expense; *real* moral pressure would be brought to bear upon the Communist governments; and it would be far more difficult for any nation to remain "neutral" in the face of Soviet aggression.

If the leaders of all the free nations were brought into more direct personal contact with the victims of communism, they would very likely lose all inclination to "neutralism" or appeasement. When the Ceylonese member of the United Nations Special Committee on Hungary, who personally interviewed many of the freedom fighters, was required by his government to abstain from voting on the censure of Soviet aggression and to deliver a speech in support of the abstention, he was, according to *The New York Times*, "clearly upset" and read the speech "with obvious distaste."[32]

Moreover, if the subject peoples were given real representation in the United Nations, the free world would have an opportunity to learn of solutions to the cold war which are based on bitter experience rather than upon the improvident desire for peace at any price—or fatuous efforts to present new and different cold-war remedies that are less designed to restore freedom than to attract votes. It would thus hear, and be more likely to act upon, proposals which have bite, which would really affect the Communist rulers, and which, while not invoking a third world war, would be more likely to produce the "forced reformation" behind the iron curtain which has been so long awaited. The free nations, in short, would find themselves acquiring that initiative in the cold war which they have so often sought in vain.

If the free world would listen to the subject peoples, it would hear proposals for the substitution, in the United Nations and elsewhere, of true representatives of the vast mass of freedom-loving peoples behind the iron curtain for those Communist delegations and diplomatic plenipotentiaries who, as Woodrow Wilson said, "have no mandate from anybody" and "represent nobody but themselves." They would also hear the demands of the subject peoples for armed assistance when open revolt occurs, the training of "liberation armies of the enslaved peoples," and many more proposals for effective "military, political and economic pressures" of all kinds.[33] They would hear proposals for the effective implementation of all those carefully drafted provisions of the United Nations charter which the free nations themselves have devised but failed to employ.

Thus, the major goal of the Assembly of Captive European Nations, as expressed in chapter I, article I, of its charter, is to affirm the right of the captive peoples "to be represented in the United Nations only by their own legitimate governments, responsive to the will of the respective peoples."[34] In a declaration "On the Occasion of the Tenth Anniversary of the United Nations Charter," issued on June 20, 1955, the Assembly pointed out that because of the "triple representation" of the Soviet Union and the exclusion of the recognized government-in-exile of Poland, the principles of the United Nations had been "violated" at its "very inception." It was further stated that these violations were compounded by the subsequent acceptance of the Communist delegate from Czechoslovakia and the failure to provide proper representation for any of the other eastern European captive nations.[35]

When the United Nations admitted the Soviet puppet regimes of Albania, Bulgaria, Hungary and Rumania, ACEN spoke up again. Pointing out that these "illegitimate governments" neither "truly represent" their nations "nor fulfill as yet the conditions for membership set forth in the United Nations Charter," the Assembly stated that because they had been "accorded international recognition" and "thus received a kind of new confirmation," Soviet aggression "is in effect condoned by the free world."[36]

In comparable declarations, the leaders of the All-Russian Committee for Liberation, the Russian Political Committee and other representative Russian organizations point out that the Communists have never been "responsive or responsible representatives of the Soviet peoples," and they urge the democratic nations to indicate "in every dealing with the Soviet Government" that "they deal with it as the *de facto* but not the *de jure* regime of the Russian people. . . ." The Russian people, they state, "do not and cannot . . . recognize the usurpers of the Kremlin whose right to rule has never been tested by a free election as the legitimate government of the nation."[37]

In November, 1950, the Byelorussian National Council submitted a memorandum to the United Nations in which it opposed the seating of Soviet-named delegates for that nation,[38] and a similar stand is taken by the Supreme Ukrainian Liberation Council. "We believe," it says, "that this representation should continue, but that the representatives themselves should be changed. The present stooges of the Kremlin should be replaced by the true representatives of the Ukrainian and Byelorussian peoples."[39]

Even before the United States recognition of the Soviet Union, the people of Armenia, through the legal representative of the Delegation of the Armenian Republic in Paris, Vahan Cardashian, called attention to the imminent disregard of the rights of that nation. In a memorandum submitted September 12, 1933, he reminded the State Department that the United States, having previously recognized the republic of Armenia, was in duty "bound, under international law, to reserve its recognition of Armenia and to insist upon the restoration of the Armenian Republic, if and when it, America, should treat with Russia." "Failure so to do," he said, "would clearly constitute a constructive trespass upon Armenian soil, as also an acquiescence in the invasion of the Armenian Republic by the Turks and the Bolsheviks, and a negation and contradiction of the doctrine of non-aggression. . . ."[40]

In its recommendations of additional forms of action, the Assembly of Captive European Nations has been very specific. Thus, on December 20, 1954 it issued an "Appeal to the Nations of the Free World" in which it called not only for the withdrawal of recognition from all Communist governments but also for a firm demand by the United Nations for the creation of conditions required for free elections and the designation of the Soviet Union as an aggressor:

. . . in the name of our subjugated nations, we, the Assembly of Captive European Nations, appeal for the support of the free nations of the world. We call upon them:

1. To withdraw the recognition from and cease all relations with the so-called governments imposed by force and fraud on our countries by Soviet Russia, and declare these so-called governments illegitimate and not representative of the will of our peoples.

2. To urge the United Nations to recognize the fact that our peoples are without legitimate governments and to decide that under its supervision be held free and unfettered elections; and, therefore, to create in our countries the conditions necessary for such elections.

3. To demand that the government which prevents the realization of decisions taken in accordance with point 2 be considered guilty of endangering world peace and security and be declared an aggressor by the United Nations.[41]

In 1955, the Assembly asked for an international investigation of the *real* conditions of forced labor in iron-curtain countries. It was pointed out that the United Nations had "investigated forced labor only from the legal point of view, studying labor legislation behind the Iron Curtain," and that this was "a method which cannot reveal the true nature of the Communist reality to the world."[42] Communist *laws* are not the same as Communist *deeds*. Although a public study of actual conditions, like the investigation of Soviet aggression in Hungary, would obviously be a potent means of mobilizing world opinion, and although there are millions of refugees available to give firsthand testimony, the free nations have so far been unwilling to follow this suggestion.

Further pleas for more effective action were made in 1956. These were transmitted to the governments of the free nations, to their delegates in the United Nations, and to the United Nations Secretariat, but they were all ignored. Thus, on June 29, 1956, after the Polish uprising at Poznan, the Assembly of Captive European Nations issued a public appeal for international action that would go beyond the usual "expressions of sympathy":

We hope, first of all, that the free world will not confine its reaction to expressions of sympathy, as was the case in 1953, but will avail itself of all means of international action to condemn the regime responsible for the crimes perpetrated in Poznan, to institute an international investigation of Soviet aggression, domination and colonial exploitation which are at the root of these and many other crimes against the captive nations, and to bring about the restoration of the God-given rights of these nations to freedom and genuine national independence.[43]

Subsequently, a direct appeal for action was made to the Security Council, and a supporting memorandum was delivered to the permanent delegations of the free nations. In the event the Security Council was unable to act, the United States, Great Britain and France were asked to convoke an international conference at which there would be "genuine Polish representation both from Poland and exiles."[44] The negative response to this appeal was proof only of the fact that the demands of the subject peoples are not even "irresistible" in the free world.

Thereafter, when Gomulka was restored to power, the Assembly gave a clear warning against growing free-world confidence in "liberal" and "national communism":

The Assembly of Captive European Nations welcomes the developments in Poland insofar as they portend a loosening of Soviet control and a step toward national independence. The Assembly wishes to stress, however: first, that the people of Poland alone and not any group of Polish Communists, deserve credit for whatever progress has been achieved in this direction; second, that the faction which has so far emerged the winner in the struggle for power within the Polish Communist Party has been successful only because, in an attempt to save, for the Communists, a situation which was rapidly getting out of hand, it had ostensibly espoused some of the popular demands; third, that neither the Polish people nor any other of the captive nations will rest until their demands are fully met.[45]

Continual appeals were made during the revolt in Hungary. On October 24, the first day of Red Army intervention, a request for "positive measures" was directed to the Security Council and to the heads of each free government represented in it—the United States, the United Kingdom, France, China, Australia, Belgium, Cuba, Peru and Iran. Two days later, it was necessary to make another appeal, and a telegram to President Eisenhower pointed out that there had as yet been no "positive response" to the previous request.[46] In a public statement, ACEN expressed its disappointment over the free world's failure to act and pointed out that a similar appeal had been made by the freedom fighters themselves:

It [the Assembly of Captive European Nations] also feels in duty bound to voice the disappointment of the captive peoples for the failure of the free nations to take speedy action in order to stop the Soviet armed intervention in Hungary. Two days have elapsed since the Assembly of Captive European Nations asked for such action. In the meantime its plea was echoed by a delegation of the Hungarian fighters for freedom which, according to trustworthy report, has presented a request for urgent UN action to the British Legation in Budapest.[47]

After five more days passed with no "positive measures" taken, another appeal was cabled, on October 31, to the "Big Three." This suggested a call for Soviet withdrawal and the creation of a commission of observers:

... we respectfully ask you to insist on an urgent meeting of the Security Council for the purpose of considering the measures required by the situation as it has developed. In the view of our Assembly such measures should comprise 1) a call for the immediate withdrawal of Soviet armed forces from Hungary 2) the affirmation of the unqualified right of Hungarian people to determine through free elections the system of government under which they want to live and 3) the establishment of a United Nations Commission to watch and report upon the faithful observance of all measures taken by the Security Council with the view of securing national independence and political freedom to Hungarian people.[48]

A resolution to this effect was not adopted by the United Nations until November 4, after the Red Army had unleashed its second massive attack. By that time it was no longer possible to send *observers,* and ACEN requested more effective measures, urging the United Nations:

> To establish forthwith a U.N. truce commission and an emergency international U.N. force to secure and supervise the cessation of hostilities and the withdrawal of Soviet troops from the territory of Hungary:
> To recommend to all member nations to deny recognition to the government set up in Hungary as a result of Soviet armed aggression:
>
> .   .   .   .
>
> Make appropriate recommendations to members of the United Nations for collective measures under Article 41 and 42 of the Charter should the Soviet Union fail to comply forthwith with the recommendations of the General Assembly.[49]

But, as in the previous instances, this request was also unheeded.

Perhaps it was by this time too late to use a United Nations force without invasion, but it was certainly not too late to adopt the other suggestions made. It was not too late then, and it is not too late even now, to deny recognition or to provide for the "complete or partial interruption of economic relations and of rail, sea, air, postal, telegraphic, radio, and other means of communication, and the severance of diplomatic relations," all as provided by Article 41 of the charter.

The failure to take such measures in this case and elsewhere cannot be excused by unsupported assertions that they would not be effective. They are all part and parcel of that "moral force of world opinion" which we have been endeavoring to exert, and they are all part of the prescribed United Nations machinery of enforcement. Moreover, if the subject nations had been adequately represented prior to the Hungarian revolt, the United Nations would not have been permitted to procrastinate until it was too late for such action to be immediately effective.

On November 7, 1956, ACEN cables were sent to sixty-eight free nations represented in the United Nations, calling attention to the fatal delay which had been allowed to occur:

> The Assembly of Captive European Nations feels in duty bound to recall that the Soviet aggression against Hungary was clearly in the

making on October 28 when the Security Council first considered the situation in Hungary. Still the Council adjourned then and again on November 2 and 3 without taking any decision. A decision was taken only on November 4 after the Soviets had launched a new attack on the Hungarian people.

In recalling these frustrating developments which have already produced a shattering effect on the morale of the Central Eastern European peoples, our Assembly directs an urgent appeal to your excellency. We beg all the free nations to realize that their failure to take effective measures to stop Soviet aggression and to put an end to Soviet brutality will have the most far-reaching and damaging consequences for them.[50]

The United States, on the other hand, which holds itself out as the present champion of the rights of the subject peoples in the United Nations, has claimed that "we took every step short of war . . . we left no stone unturned."[51] When such a relaxed attitude is taken by the free powers, and when those who would more actively promote the rights of the subject peoples are excluded as "political 'outs,' " it may well be asked whether it is really the "few men" in the Kremlin who "thwart the will of hundreds of millions."

According to a Ukrainian nationalist who died fighting for freedom, it is the free world itself which is actually destroying the "last hope" of "the Soviet masses"—intensifying the "apathy in which they live" and breaking their will to resist. This report, written in August, 1950 by Major Petro Poltava of the UPA, who was also chief of the Information Bureau of the Supreme Ukrainian Liberation Council (UHVR), was submitted to the State Department but apparently received little consideration. Major Poltava himself was killed by the Soviets during the winter of 1951-2, but his message still applies. It was, in part, as follows:

The main leitmotif of the policy and propaganda of foreign states towards the Soviet Union is well known. It is based on the assumption that the Bolshevik regime in the USSR is an internal problem of the peoples of the Soviet Union. Hence, the Western states, including the USA, should not interfere with these conditions. It is not difficult to imagine the effect which this policy of the foreign powers, and especially of the USA, has on the Soviet masses. Such a policy kills the last hope which the Soviet masses can have in the amelioration of their lot. It creates among them a feeling of utter loneliness in the world, of complete defenselessness before the

Bolshevik regime; it only helps to intensify the apathy in which they live. Such an attitude exemplified in official policy and propaganda, utterly breaks the will of the people in the Soviet Union to resist their Bolshevik oppressors. . . .

.   .   .   .

It is of the utmost importance that the peoples within the USSR realize that the Americans are clearly opposed always and everywhere, even within the territory of the USSR, to the existence of the Bolshevik usurping, totalitarian, and terrorist regime, that they are openly on the side of the peoples of the USSR in their just struggle for national and social liberation.[52]

Another point made by Major Poltava was the same as that made by Arthur Bullard more than thirty years before—that the United States should be "entirely neutral in regard to the (protracted) internal question of social reforms."[53] Poltava made it plain that the subject peoples are interested in assistance in *self-determination,* not in listening to encomiums upon the virtues of capitalism and the "American way of life":

The Soviet masses cannot be successfully stirred to fight Bolshevism in the name of capitalism, nor even in the name of the American way of life, which no doubt has many positive values. Criticism of the Bolshevik regime must be expressed from the point of view of those prominent political forces within the nations of the USSR which wish to destroy Bolshevism, not in order to restore the old system, but in order to create a new, just and progressive social and economic system.[54]

It is likewise not the desire of the subject peoples to have rash actions urged upon them by the free nations, to be incited to engage in premature uprisings—without arms or effective aid from outside —or to be made the butt or alleged explanation of a third world war. The most desirable form of assistance would prepare them— morally, politically and materially—to take due advantage, by whatever action may then seem appropriate, of the next opportunity to restore freedom; whether it be an unpremeditated uprising—as occurred in Hungary; a new wave of mass persecutions—such as the "liquidation of the kulaks" and the "Great Purge" of the 1930s; or war produced by other causes—as in the case of the Nazi invasion of World War II.

This strategy is suggested by the president of NTS, Dr. Vladimir Poremsky, who sees the subject peoples as the "strongest deterrent to a third world war":

We do not incite revolution. We try to be prepared for it, so that when it does break out its goal can be accomplished as quickly as possible. We know that a revolutionary climate exists, and that the next explosion is likely to occur at any time. This fact is well known to the communist rulers also, and it is the strongest deterrent to a third world war.[55]

In an interview with *U.S. News and World Report,* Poremsky even maintained that if sufficient preparatory work is done "it may be possible to achieve the transfer of authority without any bloodshed."[56]

It is high time that some of the suggestions of the subject peoples were acted upon, and that their demands, allegedly "irresistible" behind the iron curtain, are given some consideration by the free world.

CHAPTER XIX

THE MIRACLE OF THE SUN

And a great sign appeared in heaven: A woman clothed with the sun, and the moon under her feet, and on her head a crown of twelve stars" (Apoc. xii:1).

The history of the cold war is one of human failure. In spite of every means adopted by the free nations to limit or prevent the spread of Communist influence—even in spite of the "inherent weakness" of communism itself—the power of the Communist state increases, expands and is even emulated by others. The Communist system itself has suffered many reverses, having been frequently "abandoned" or "reformed" pursuant to the zigzag tactics prescribed by Lenin. But each time it has risen again, or "returned," stronger and more oppressive than before. Every apparent defeat and every shift to "moderation" or "softness" has been followed by new purges, new persecutions, and new "gains" in the "offensive of Socialism."

Under Lenin communism became a "corpse," but "no one" had "the courage to bury" it. The United States, the Allied powers and even the League of Nations feared to oppose it. Lenin soon died, but Stalin took his place, and in his name carried on the work of "Socialist construction." Under Stalin the free nations sought friendship with the Communist state. They regarded it as an indispensable ally—which the Nazis would not dare attack. When the Nazis did attack it, the free nations saved it; and because they did not dare oppose it, they permitted other nations, which had once repelled the strongest Communist assault, to be made captive. Eventually, however, Stalin also died; but he in turn was replaced by Khrushchev.

Under Khrushchev Stalin was denounced, and "Stalinism" was "repudiated." But, as "Leninism," the Communist system remained. Because of its economic development, its "sputniks" and its intercontinental ballistic missiles, it has come to be regarded as invincible, inevitable, and even by some as socially desirable.

Communism thus seems to fulfill, in many respects, the baneful prophecies of St. John the Apostle, whose apocalyptic visions have found application to many troubled periods in man's history:

> And I saw a beast coming up out of the sea, having seven heads and ten horns. . . . And one of its heads was smitten, as it were, unto death; but its deadly wound was healed. . . .

.   .   .   .   .   .

> And I saw another beast coming up out of the earth . . . . and it made the earth and the inhabitants therein to worship the first beast, whose deadly wound was healed. And it did great signs, so as even to make fire come down from heaven upon earth in the sight of mankind. And it leads astray the inhabitants of the earth, by reason of the signs which it was permitted to do in the sight of the beast, telling the inhabitants of the earth to make an image of the beast which has the wound of the sword, and yet lived.[1]

There are further similarities. For example, there is communism's professed opposition to social injustice, greed, selfishness, immorality and war, and St. John's description of the struggle between the beast and the harlot—"with whom the kings of the earth have committed fornication." Like the admitted faults and deficiencies of the pre-Communist world, the harlot was hated and destroyed by the beast while "the inhabitants of the earth were made drunk with the wine of her immorality":

> And the ten horns that thou sawest, and the beast, these will hate the harlot, and will make her desolate and naked, and will eat her flesh, and will burn her up in fire. For God has put it into their hearts to carry out his purpose, to give their kingdom to the beast, until the words of God are accomplished.[2]

St. John further stated that the beast itself would be destroyed by God, who is described as a warrior seated upon a white horse, leading the "armies of heaven," and having upon His garment a name written, "King of kings and Lord of lords":

> And I saw the beast, and the kings of the earth and their armies gathered together to wage war against him who was sitting upon the horse, and against his army. And the beast was seized, and with it the false prophet who did signs before it wherewith he deceived those who accepted the mark of the beast and who worshipped its image.[3]

It does not seem proper, therefore, to conclude this work without an allusion to the need for prayer—the only weapon with respect to which the non-Communist world can still assert a monopoly. For the power of prayer is the one cold-war weapon to which the Communists make no claim—and which, of course, they do not have. They cannot possibly have it because they are waging war *against* God—perhaps the only war in the history of humanity in which divine assistance has been thus rejected. In the words of Pope Pius XI (1937): "For the first time in history we are witnessing a struggle, cold-blooded in purpose and mapped out to the least detail, between man and 'all that is called God.' "[4]

Lenin and Stalin themselves insisted that the Communists could not expect divine assistance. In the "struggle" to "reeducate and remould," in their own pattern, the "millions of peasants," the "petty-bourgeois strata" and even the "proletarians themselves," there was no place for "miracles" or heavenly aid. It "will be necessary," Stalin said (quoting Lenin), " 'to reeducate in a protracted struggle, on the basis of the dictatorship of the proletariat, the proletarians themselves, who do not abandon their petty-bourgeois prejudices at one stroke, *by a miracle, at the behest of the Virgin Mary*, at the behest of a slogan, resolution or decree, but only in the course of a long and difficult mass struggle. . . .' "[5] (Italics added.)

With such assistance, however, it is possible for the free nations to win the cold war, recreate the conditions of freedom and restore peace. This is particularly true of the peoples of Russia, whose capacity for freedom was described, long ago, by President Wilson's Special Diplomatic Mission (the Root mission):

The Russians have natural self-control and kindly consideration and respect for the rights of others; they are naturally law-abiding and they have extraordinary capacity for united action. That capacity has been shown in their local self-government, in the Zemstvo Unions, in the success of the Narodny or People's Banks, and in many cooperative organizations for manufactures and for the sale of products. When they have once learned to apply their qualities in the field of national government, we have little doubt that they will be able to establish and maintain successfully free self-government on a great scale.[6]

The Russian peoples failed, nevertheless, to preserve their freedom. Some malign influence seemed to make it impossible for them to take strong and effective measures against the Bolsheviks, or to solve the many political disagreements which in 1917 redounded so greatly to Bolshevik advantage.

The first major crisis of the Russian Provisional Government was precipitated by the resignation, on May 13, 1917, of Alexander I. Guchkov, Minister of War and Navy. He had formerly been a president of the Duma, and chairman of its Military and Naval Committee. He was described by the American consul in Petrograd as the "biggest" man in the temporary government,[7] and by the American Ambassador as an "Excellent" man whose resignation was "deplorable."[8] Most of his political life had been devoted to army reforms. Yet in his letter of resignation, Guchkov professed his inability to cope with conditions "which threaten the defense, freedom and even the existence of Russia":

Seeing the condition in which the power of the Government is now placed, and particularly the power of the Minister of the Army and Navy [himself] over the army and fleet, conditions which I am unable to change and which threaten the defense, freedom and even the existence of Russia with fatal consequences, I can no more conscientiously continue my duties as Minister of War and Navy and share the responsibilities for the heavy sin which is being carried on against the fatherland.[9]

Thereafter, other Russian democratic leaders sought vainly to halt the continuing disintegration of the army, to strengthen the Provisional Government and to resolve their dissensions. But as each compromise failed, and every newly appointed ministry fell in its turn, it became increasingly apparent that there was no man, and indeed no political party, that could solve the problems of Russia. Human effort seemed inadequate, prayer the only recourse, and a miracle the only solution.

Such a solution, for those who would accept it, was at that time offered in another part of Europe, where it was recorded that there *were* miracles—a series of miracles—in which a "beautiful lady," a lady "more brilliant than the sun," appeared to three small children of the village of Fatima, Portugal. We report them here not only because we ourselves believe in them but also because, whether one believes in them or not, the record of their occurrence is an integral part of the history of international communism and the world's struggle against it, and because they indicate the same solution—

prayer and penance—which has been suggested to the people of America, in every time of crisis, by its own political and secular leaders of many faiths.

These visions, which occurred monthly from May to October, 1917, coincided with some of the most critical events of the struggle taking place in Petrograd. The last, which occurred on October 13, 1917—less than a month before the Bolshevik seizure of power—was accompanied by an extraordinary physical phenomenon, promised earlier and witnessed by some 70,000 expectant and awe-stricken people. It was described by one of the skeptical Lisbon newspapers, *O Seculo,* as a "preannounced sign"—"beyond all cosmic laws":

... The miraculous manifestation, the visible, preannounced sign, is about to show itself—many pilgrims insist. And then a spectacle, unique and incredible to one who is not a witness, is observed. From the top of the road, where the vehicles have been parked and where there are many hundreds of people who were not inclined to trod in the muddy earth, the whole immense crowd is seen to turn toward the sun which, free of clouds, is now at the zenith. The sun reminds one of a disk of dull silver, and it is possible to look straight at it without the least effort. It doesn't burn nor does it blind. One has the impression that an eclipse is taking place. But now a tremendous shout goes up from the spectators, and from those who are close by is heard the cry of, "Miracle, miracle! Wonderful, wonderful!"

To the astonished eyes of that people, whose attitude brings us back to biblical times and who, ashen with terror, with heads un-covered, look into the blue of the sky, the sun trembles, the sun makes brusque movements, never seen before, and beyond all cosmic laws—the sun "danced" as the typical expression of the peasants puts it.[10]

Another Lisbon newspaper, *O Dia,* reported that the sun "was seen to rotate and wander" while thousands "fell to their knees":

At one o'clock, the hour of the sun, the rain stopped. The sky had a certain greyish tint of pearl and a strange clearness filled the gloomy landscape, every moment getting gloomier. The sun seemed to be veiled with transparent gauze to enable us to look at it without difficulty. The greyish tint of mother-of-pearl began changing as if into a shining silver disc, that was growing slowly until it broke through the clouds. And the silvery sun, still shrouded in the same greyish lightness of gauze, was seen to rotate and wander within the circle of the receded clouds! The people cried out with one voice, the thousands of the creatures of God whom faith raised up to Heaven, fell to their knees upon the muddy ground.

Then as if it were shining through the stained glass windows of a great cathedral, the light became a rare blue, spreading its rays upon the gigantic nave. . . . Slowly the blue faded away and now the light seemed to be filtered through yellow stained glass. Yellow spots were falling now upon the white kerchiefs and the dark poor skirts of coarse wool. They were spots which repeated themselves indefinitely over the lowly holmoaks, the rocks and the hills. All the people were weeping and praying bareheaded, weighed down by the greatness of the miracle expected. These were seconds, moments, that seemed hours; they were so fully lived.[11]

Still another newspaper, *O Ordem* of Oporto, related that "The sun was sometimes surrounded by blood-red flames, at other times it was aureoled with yellow and soft purple; again it seemed to be possessed of the swiftest rotation and then seemed to detach itself from the heavens and give forth a tremendous heat."[12]

Although the visions of the lady were witnessed only by the children, the truth of their accounts was confirmed by the best possible proof. There was not only the "preannounced sign," which all had witnessed, but also the steadfast refusal of the children to deny, under constant pressure, what they alone had seen and heard— even in the face of threats. These threats occurred in August, 1917, when the children were interrogated by the chief magistrate of Ourem, Arturo Santos. He literally threatened to boil them in oil, and even convinced them, separately, that this had been done to the others—but to no avail. Moreover, the miracles continued in subsequent years, through many healings of the sick. Thus, *The New York Times* relates that on May 13, 1958, at the dedication of a fifteen-ton statue of Our Lady of Fatima, "Maria Augusta Borges, paralyzed for five and a half years and recently afflicted by a stroke, rose and walked during a blessing of the sick."[13]

At the last vision, the "beautiful lady" revealed herself to the children (Lucia de Jesus Dos Santos, and Francisco and Jacinta Marto) as the "Lady of the Rosary"—the same Virgin Mary, Mother of Christ, who had appeared to Bernadette of Lourdes some sixty years before, and at whose "behest" Lenin later admitted that the "proletarians" would not "abandon their petty-bourgeois prejudices." There was also a similarity between the messages of Lourdes and Fatima— prayer and penance. At Fatima, however, these means of moral and spiritual regeneration were specifically described as necessary for the defeat of war and communism. In her third and fourth memoirs,[14] written in 1941, Lucia records the instructions given to her on July 13, 1917, when the three children were shown a vision of hell. It counseled a return to God—without which there would be more wars and great Communist victories:

You have seen hell—where the souls of poor sinners go. To save them God wants to establish throughout the world the devotion to my Immaculate Heart.

If people will do what I tell you, many souls will be saved, and there will be peace. The war is going to end.

But if they do not stop offending God, another and worse war will break out in the reign of Pius XI. When you see a night illumined by an unknown light, know that it is the great sign that God gives you, that He is going to punish the world for its crimes by means of war, hunger, persecution of the Church and of the Holy Father.

To forestall this, I shall come to ask the consecration of Russia to my Immaculate Heart and the Communion of Reparation on the First Saturdays.

If they heed my request, Russia will be converted, and there will be peace. If not, she shall spread her errors throughout the world, promoting wars and persecutions of the Church; the good will be martyred, the Holy Father will have much to suffer, various nations will be annihilated; in the end, my Immaculate Heart shall triumph. The Holy Father will consecrate Russia to me, which will be converted, and some time of peace will be given to the world.

In Portugal, the dogma of the faith will be kept always.[15]

Before the coming of World War II, and the second round of Communist aggression, there was indeed an "unknown light." On the night of January 25, 1938, a light, described as the aurora borealis, was visible over Europe and the Atlantic from Scotland to Gibraltar and as far west as Bermuda. *The New York Times* reported that it "brought thousands of telephone calls to Swiss and French authorities asking whether it was a fire, war or the end of the world."[16] In Great Britain, police stations, fire brigades and newspapers all over the country were "inundated" by calls asking, "Where is the fire?" Scientists at the University of Grenoble stated that a similar aurora had not been seen in western Europe since 1709. In Portugal, villagers "rushed in flight from their homes, fearing the end of the world."[17]

Whether or not this light was the aurora, it was admittedly "unknown." A *New York Times* editorial commented that "There will always be mystery in the aurora, always mystery in the magnetic disturbances that annoy communication companies." It also indicated that the phenomenon was clear evidence of God's power: "If we needed any evidence," the editorial said, "that the sun and its attendant planets constitute more than a mechanical system we have it here."[18] Even in 1957, after the launching of the first two Soviet earth satellites, the aurora borealis was still "An Unsolved Mystery."[19]

In the meantime, two of the children, Francisco and Jacinta, had died (1919 and 1920), and Lucia entered the Order of Our Lady of Mount Carmel—in which she is now known as Sister Maria of the Immaculate Heart. She experienced further visions in 1925, 1926, 1927, 1929 and 1943. Other parts of the message received at Fatima have been recorded by her in part as follows:

First vision, May 13, 1917 (the day Guchkov resigned):

Do you want to offer yourselves to God to endure all the sufferings that He may choose to send you, as an act of reparation for the sins by which He is offended and as a supplication for the conversion of sinners?

Yes, we want to.

Then you are going to suffer a great deal, but the grace of God will be your comfort.

Say the Rosary every day to earn peace for the world and the end of the war.[20]

Second vision, June 13, 1917 (the day the Root mission arrived in Petrograd):

I want you to come here on the thirteenth of the next month. Say the Rosary, inserting between the mysteries the following ejaculation—"O My Jesus, forgive us. Save us from the fire of Hell. Bring all souls to Heaven, expecially those in most need."

I will take Jacinta and Francisco soon. You, however, are to stay here a longer time. Jesus wants to use you to make me known and loved. He wants to establish the devotion to my Immaculate Heart in the world. I promise salvation to those who embrace it and their souls will be loved by God as flowers placed by myself to adorn His throne.[21]

Third vision, July 13, 1917 (shortly before the July uprising):

I want you to return here on the thirteenth of next month. Continue to say the Rosary every day in honor of Our Lady of the Rosary to obtain peace for the world and the end of the war; for she alone can save it.

Continue to come here every month. In October, I will say who I am and what I desire and I will perform a miracle all shall see so that they believe.

Sacrifice yourselves for sinners; and say often, especially when you make some sacrifice: "My Jesus, it is for love of You, for the conversion of sinners, and in reparation for sins committed against the Immaculate Heart of Mary."[22]

On August, 13, 1917, the children were taken to Ourem for questioning. A few days after their release, the fourth vision occurred, on August 19, 1917. (This was shortly after the conclusion of the Sixth Bolshevik Congress, at which it was resolved that "The correct slogan at the present time can only be complete liquidation of the dictatorship of the counter-revolutionary bourgeoisie."[23]):

I want you to continue to come to the Cova da Iria on the thirteenth and to continue to say the Rosary every day.

In the last month, in October, I shall perform a miracle so that all may believe in my apparitions. If they had not taken you to the village [Ourem, where the questioning took place], the miracle would have been greater. St. Joseph will come with the Baby Jesus to give peace to the world. Our Lord also will come to bless the people. Besides, Our Lady of the Rosary and Our Lady of Sorrows will come.

Pray! Pray a great deal and make sacrifices for sinners, for many souls go to Hell for not having someone to pray and make sacrifices for them.[24]

Fifth vision, September 13, 1917 (after the collapse of the Kornilov coup):

Let the people continue to say the Rosary every day to obtain the end of the war.[25]

Sixth vision, October 13, 1917, at which the miracle of the sun occurred:

I want to tell you that they must build a chapel here in my honor; that I am the Lady of the Rosary; that they continue to say the Rosary every day. The war will end soon and the soldiers will return to their homes soon.

Offend not Our Lord any more. For He is already much offended.[26]

The requests thus made were more fully explained in subsequent visions. In December, 1925, the Communion of Reparation on the First Saturdays was explained to Lucia during a vision in which the Child Jesus appeared with His Blessed Mother and said:

Have pity on the Heart of your Most Holy Mother. It is covered with the thorns with which ungrateful men pierce it at every moment, and there is no one to remove them with an act of reparation.[27]

At the same time, the Blessed Mother said:

My Daughter, look at my Heart encircled with the thorns with which ungrateful men pierce it at every moment by their blasphemies and ingratitude. Do you at least try to console me and announce in my name that I promise to assist at the hour of death with the graces necessary for salvation all those who, on the first Saturday of five consecutive months, go to Confession and receive Holy Communion, recite the Rosary and keep me company for a quarter of an hour while meditating on the mysteries of the Rosary with the intention of making reparation to me.[28]

In the vision of 1929, the Blessed Virgin appeared again to ask the consecration of Russia to her Immaculate Heart, by the Pope in union with all the bishops of the world.

In 1943, the sacrifice required was explained in a vision of Christ. On this occasion, Sister Maria wrote to the Bishop of Gurza:

This is the penance which the good Lord now asks: the sacrifice that every person has to impose upon himself is to lead a life of justice in the observance of His Law. He requires that this way be made known to souls. For many, thinking that the word penance means great austerities and not feeling in themselves the strength or generosity for these, lose heart and rest in a life of lukewarmness and sin.

Last Thursday, at midnight, while I was in chapel with my superiors' permission, Our Lord said to me, "The sacrifice required of every person is the fulfillment of his duties in life and the observance of My law. This is the penance that I now seek and require."[29]

It was not until 1930, after many years of investigation, that the Roman Catholic Bishop of Leiria formally pronounced the manifestations of Fatima to be worthy of belief, but the basic intent of their message was neither strange nor new to those of other faiths. In America it has been the advice of political leaders of many denominations. Thus, in his *History of Plimouth Plantation,* Governor William Bradford wrote that only prayer and the grace of God had sustained the Pilgrims in their hour of danger and loneliness—on the frontier of a new freedom:

What could now sustaine them but ye spirite of God & his grace? May not & ought not the children of these fathers rightly say: *Our faithers were Englishmen which came over this great ocean, and were ready to perish in this willdernes; but they cried unto ye Lord, and he heard their voyce, and looked on their adversitie, &c. Let them therefore praise ye Lord, because he is good, & his mercies endure for ever. Yea, let them which have been redeemed of ye Lord, shew how he hath delivered them from ye hand of ye oppressour. When they wandered in ye deserte willdernes out of ye way, and found no citie to dwell in, both hungrie, & thirstie, their sowle was overwhelmed in them. Let them confess before ye Lord his loving kindnes, and his wonderfull works before ye sons of men.*[30]

Similarly, in his first inaugural address, George Washington asked for the blessing of God—the "Almighty Being who rules over the universe, who presides in the councils of nations, and whose providential aids can supply every human defect...." "No people," he said, "can be bound to acknowledge and adore the Invisible Hand which conducts the affairs of men more than those of the United States. Every step by which they have advanced to the character of an independent nation seems to have been distinguished by some token of providential agency; and," he continued:

in the important revolution just accomplished in the system of their united government the tranquil deliberations and voluntary consent of so many distinct communities from which the event has resulted cannot be compared with the means by which most governments have been established without some return of pious gratitude, along with an humble anticipation of the future blessings which the past seems to presage...."

During the Civil War, the North was thrown into a panic by the rout of the Union army at Bull Run. The capital itself was nearly taken by Confederate troops. Within a few weeks, President Lincoln proclaimed a national day of "humiliation, prayer and fasting." It is "peculiarly fit," he wrote, "for us to recognize the hand of God in this terrible visitation, and in sorrowful remembrance of our own faults and crimes as a nation and as individuals, to humble ourselves before Him and to pray for His mercy,—to pray," he added:

that we may be spared farther punishment, though most justly deserved; that our arms may be blessed and made effectual for the reestablishment of law, order and peace, throughout the wide extent of our country; and that the inestimable boon of civil and religious liberty, earned under His guidance and blessing, by the labors and sufferings of our fathers, may be restored in all its orginal excellence. . . .[31]

Lincoln was shot, but his prayers were certainly answered. His example, moreover, has been followed in the cold war by Congress, by President Truman, and by President Eisenhower. In a joint resolution approved in April, 1952,[32] Congress authorized the President to "set aside and proclaim a suitable day each year, other than a Sunday, as a National Day of Prayer." In the first proclamation issued under this resolution,[33] President Truman designated Friday, July 4, 1952, as the day in which all Americans might "beseech God to grant us wisdom to know the course which we should follow, and strength and patience to pursue that course steadfastly." "May we also," he stated, "give thanks to Him for His constant watchfulness over us in every hour of national prosperity and national peril."

By similar proclamations, President Eisenhower designated an annual Day of Prayer in each succeeding year—July 4, 1953, September 22, 1954, October 26, 1955, September 12, 1956, October 2, 1957 and October 1, 1958.[34] Thereafter, he provided for its observance in every year on the first Wednesday in October. In his proclamation designating a National Day of Prayer for 1953, President Eisenhower referred to it as a "National Day of Penance and Prayer," following the example of President Lincoln, whom he quoted:

. . . it is the duty of nations as well as of men to own their dependence upon the overruling power of God, to confess their sins and transgressions in humble sorrow, yet with assured hope that genuine repentance will lead to mercy and pardon.

In 1957, he again pointed out that "The price of peace, our ultimate objective, is unceasing sacrifice and prayer."[35]

Another joint resolution of Congress, approved in May, 1950,[36] authorized the President to designate Memorial Day as a day of nationwide prayer for peace—and this has been done.

Such prayers have always been answered in the past, and there is no reason to believe that they will not be answered now. Certainly, there is the need. As Secretary of State Dulles said, in an address to the congregation of the First Presbyterian Church in Watertown, New York, October 11, 1953, "The terrible things that are happening in some parts of the world are due to the fact that political and social practices have been separated from spiritual content." And he added:

If ever the political forces of this country become irreligious, our institutions would change. The change might come about slowly, but it would come surely. Institutions born of faith will inevitably change unless they are constantly nurtured by faith.[37]

Similarly, in April, 1955, at the Fifth Annual All-Jesuit Alumni Dinner in Washington, he stated: "It was said by Jesus that material things will be added unto those who seek first the Kingdom of God and His righteousness. But when that happens, then comes the great trial. For, as Jesus warned, those material things can readily become the rust that corrodes men's souls."[38]

After receiving the Japanese surrender, at the end of World War II, General MacArthur asserted that the problem of peace is basically "theological." In an address broadcast from the deck of the battleship *Missouri,* he stated:

Military alliances, balance of power, Leagues of Nations all in turn failed leaving the only path to be by way of the crucible of war. The utter destructiveness of war now blots out this alternative. We have had our last chance. If we do not devise some greater and more equitable system Armageddon will be at our door. The problem basically is theological and involves a spiritual recrudescence and improvement of human character that will synchronize with our almost matchless advance in science, art, literature and all material and cultural developments of the past two thousand years. It must be of the spirit if we are to save the flesh.[39]

We are not lacking therefore in testimony, human as well as divine, that a spiritual and moral effort must be made. In applying it to the cold war we could not do better than to adopt that form of penitence prescribed by the prophet Isaiah—not "sackcloth and ashes" or cries intended to be "heard on high," but generous aid to the oppressed:

Is not this rather the fast that I have chosen? Loose the bands of wickedness, undo the bundles that oppress, let them that are broken go free, and break asunder every burden. Deal thy bread to the hungry, and bring the needy and the harborless into thy house; when thou shalt see one naked, cover him, and despise not thy own flesh. Then shall thy light break forth as the morning, and thy health shall speedily arise, and thy justice shall go before thy face, and the glory of the Lord shall gather thee up. (Isaias lviii:6-8)

CHAPTER XX

FINITA LA COMMEDIA!

"I think we would win a hot war, and I do not know if we will win this cold war or not; it depends on whether we have an adequate program." John F. Dulles[1]

In their efforts to deal with communism, the free nations are floundering in a morass of shifting policies and contradictory attitudes. There is scarcely an issue of the cold war upon which they have not at one time or another adopted both sides of the question—often through the same spokesmen.

In the case of China, for example, it was, in 1946, the expressed desire of the United States that Communists be included in the national government. Thus, a State Department press release, June 28, 1946, asserted that "Too much stress cannot be laid on the hope of this Government that our economic assistance be carried out in China through the medium of a government fully and fairly representative of all important Chinese political elements, *including the Chinese Communists*."[2] (Italics added.) But in 1948, the Secretary of State, George C. Marshall, advised that there should not even be an implication of such a desire. "The United States Government," he said, "must not directly or indirectly give any implication of support, encouragement or acceptability of coalition government in China with Communist representation."[3]

In January, 1950, after the flight of the national government to Formosa, President Truman asserted that the United States still did not intend to furnish military assistance, or to "interfere" in any way in this "civil conflict":

The United States has no desire to obtain special rights or privileges or to establish military bases on Formosa at this time. Nor does it have any intention of utilizing its armed forces to interfere in the present situation. The United States Government will not pursue a course which will lead to involvement in the civil conflict in China.

Similarly, the United States Government will not provide military aid or advice to Chinese forces on Formosa.[4]

Within six months, however, interference in the Chinese "civil conflict" had already taken place, as a result of the outbreak of another "civil war" in Korea. In a statement released to the press on June 27, 1950, President Truman asserted: ". . . I have ordered the Seventh Fleet to prevent any attack on Formosa. As a corollary of this action, I am calling upon the Chinese Government on Formosa to cease all air and sea operations against the mainland. The Seventh Fleet will see that this is done."[5] Today, in spite of earlier statements, there *are* "military bases on Formosa," and "military aid" and "advice" *are* being supplied.

The United States was thus forced, in China and Korea, to recognize that assistance to other peoples in so-called "civil strife" is sometimes appropriate and necessary. On other cold-war issues, however, the inconsistencies are more indicative of an absence of fixed purpose than of any real change of attitude. For example, it was sometimes said by Secretary Dulles that the United Nations should be open to the "bad" nations as well as to the "good," but at other times he appeared to concede that it should be restricted to those which are "peace-loving." Thus, in his book *War or Peace,* first published in early 1950 and republished in 1957, he maintained that "we ought to be willing that all nations should be members without attempting to appraise closely those which are 'good' and those which are 'bad.' "[6] But in a public address in 1957, he asserted that "The United Nations is not a reformatory for bad governments. It is supposedly an association of those who are already 'peace-loving' and who are 'able and willing to carry out' the charter obligations."[7]

On one occasion, he would concede that a "customary" test for diplomatic recognition is "whether, as Thomas Jefferson put it, the recognized government reflects 'the will of the nation, substantially declared.' "[8] But on another, he would say that our dealings with foreign nations are not affected by such considerations—that "So long as their domestic policies are wholly domestic, we do not take them into account in deciding how we deal with them in the realm of international affairs."[9]

According to a statement made by Secretary Dulles in 1953, "our creed does not call for exporting revolution or inciting others to violence."[10] But according to the Republican Party platform (1952), it was nevertheless supposed to be setting up "strains and stresses" which would "make the rulers impotent."

Those who doubted that change can be brought about "peacefully" were described by Secretary Dulles as "skeptics,"[11] yet he could himself assert that "There is not, in the world as a whole, any adequate assurance of peaceful change."[12]

Where the captive peoples were concerned, Secretary Dulles was wont to rely upon the "force of world opinion which, working steadily, will have its way."[13] But when it came to the defense of free nations, he grimly warned: "We must keep indelibly clear in our minds that international communism is not regardful of legality or of humanity or of the moral force of world opinion. . . ."[14]

It was asserted by President Eisenhower that an "awesome" deterrent power is essential to the preservation of peace.[15] But he also maintained that "the more any intelligent man thinks about the possibilities of war today, the more he should understand you have got to work on this business of disarmament."[16]

President Roosevelt asserted, in the case of Spain, that the United States could "see no place in the community of free nations for governments founded on fascist principles."[17] But eleven years later, in the case of Yugoslavia, Secretary of State Dulles maintained that "the nature of another nation's regime is of no official concern to the United States Government. . . ."[18]

In spite of its "tendencies" toward "rapprochement with the Soviet Union," the Communist government of Yugoslavia was deemed eligible for extensive military and economic assistance (over a billion dollars by 1957), because, in the words of Secretary Dulles, its policies were "made in Belgrade and not in Moscow," and "account" must be taken of the "weakness of the Yugoslav economy . . . which cannot afford to pass up the relatively generous offers of credits and trade from the Soviet orbit."[19] But in the case of Egypt, which also has a weak economy, and in which the Communist Party was outlawed, significant economic assistance was withheld, because, as he said, it tries to "play both sides":

. . . the Egyptians, in a sense, forced upon us an issue to which I think there was only one proper response: That issue was, do nations which play both sides get better treatment than nations which are stalwart and work with us?[20]

After the strikes and riots in East Germany, Secretary Dulles pointed out that "All rulers, however absolute, depend on the productivity of the ruled. You cannot dig coal with bayonets."[21] But after the strikes and riots in Poland, he gave its Communist rulers a credit of $4,000,000 for the purchase of coal-mining machinery.[22]

There is one issue, however, upon which the free nations have been most consistent—the denial to the victims of communism of that assistance which has been traditionally offered to others. Whenever such help has been sought by peoples under Communist domination, or proposed on their behalf, the response has always been completely negative. There are no promises which we can honorably make, no armies that we can send, and no treaties which would invoke our assistance.

Thus, in 1924, the British delegate to the League of Nations asserted: "It is perfectly clear that we must not make promises which we cannot fulfill; it is clear that it would be cruel to encourage hopes which will not be realized."[23] In 1956, it was still impossible to fulfill such promises or encourage such hopes. As Vice President Nixon said, "The United Nations has no armies that it could send to rescue the heroic freedom fighters. . . . There were no treaties which would invoke the armed assistance of the free nations. Our only weapon here was moral condemnation. . . ."[24]

For the protection of Communists, however, there have been a number of treaties and much assistance, military as well as financial —and the "weapon" of moral condemnation has been blunted by the repeated acceptance of their so-called governments as friends of peace and freedom.

A more appropriate attitude toward such governments was suggested at the end of World War II, when an international tribunal was established, with jurisdiction of crimes against peace, crimes of war, and crimes against humanity. The governing statute provided in particular for the investigation, prosecution and punishment of such crimes as "murder, extermination, enslavement, deportation, and other inhumane acts committed against any civilian population"; and also of "persecutions on political, racial or religious grounds . . . whether or not in violation of the domestic law of the country where perpetrated."[25] After sentence had been passed upon the Nazis, the late Justice Robert H. Jackson, chief of United States counsel in the preparation of war-crimes trials, asserted that "it was the universal feeling of our people that out of this war should come unmistakable rules and workable machinery from which any who might contemplate another era of brigandage would know that they would be held *personally* responsible and would be *personally* punished."[26] (Italics added.)

Although these feelings have suffered from neglect, they still remain. Thus, in 1950, after the United Nations had stood up against Communist aggression in Korea, a deputy United States representative asserted in the Economic and Social Council that some action must be taken against Communist criminality. "The United Nations," he said, "has found the will and the means, through collective action, to deal with military aggression. We must also find the will and the means to deal with large-scale planned aggression against the individual. We cannot stand by silently while the Charter of the United Nations is violated by some of its own members."[27] As a result of the war crimes committed in that conflict, a Senate subcommittee recommended the creation of a commission of investigation to work out "means of subjecting the criminals responsible to just and lawful punishment";[28] and in 1954, a more general and permanent program was recommended by the Select Committee on Communist Aggression:

That an International Juridical Commission be established within the framework of the North Atlantic Treaty Organization so that Communist crimes perpetrated against humanity may be fully recorded and officially noted for prosecution.[29]

It is in this spirit that our actions in the cold war must be guided, and if we cannot immediately put the Communist leaders on trial, we can at least force them "to account before the bar of world opinion" by rejecting their fraudulent offers of "peaceful coexistence." Instead of making our own attempt at "rapprochement with the Soviet Union," we can give timely and effective assistance to its victims; and if this may foment passions, increase international tension, or add to the risk of further hostilities, it will at least ensure that any future war will really be a war between peoples and tyrants and not a war between nations.

Such a course would conform to the doctrine, announced by President Roosevelt, that the "right of self-determination included in the Atlantic Charter does not carry with it the right of any government to commit wholesale murder or the right to make slaves of its own people,"[30] and to the growing awareness that the world cannot ignore the violation of the rights of peoples merely because there has been no violation of formal state frontiers—that it has a responsibility to prevent internal as well as external aggression.

The existence of such a responsibility is recognized and provided for in Articles 55 and 56 of the United Nations charter. Under these articles the members of that organization have pledged themselves "to take joint and separate action in cooperation with the Organization" to promote "universal respect for, and obervance of, human rights and fundamental freedoms for all without distinction as to race, sex, language, or religion." And as the United States has maintained in that body, when the policy of a particular government runs counter to this, it cannot take refuge in its "right to regulate its own internal affairs." Neither the members nor the organization itself can avoid responsibility.

Thus, in March, 1960, during the discussion of a complaint against South Africa, Ambassador Lodge stated that "we think there is an important distinction between situations where governments are actively promoting human rights and fundamental freedoms for all ... and situations where governmental policy runs counter to this." Even though, as he said, the question then under discussion had "its own particular background of geography, racial composition, cultural diversity, and economic relationships ... difficulties of this sort do not relieve a government of its obligations, nor can they relieve the United Nations of its responsibilities."[31] And by a vote of 9-2, with two abstentions (France and the United Kingdom), the Security Council adopted its resolution calling upon the offending government to abandon such policies.

In the case of the Soviet Union, there are obviously many difficulties, but the violations of the rights of humanity are also much greater. As General Eisenhower once asserted (July 3, 1951), it is not always the easiest or seemingly safest course that is the best course. "The negative," he said, "is always the easy side, since it holds that nothing should be done. The negative is happy in lethargy, contemplating, almost with complacent satisfaction, the difficulties of any other course."[32] Such a happiness, of course, can never be permanent, and the only "peace" that the free nations will ever attain in this manner will be a false one—an ill-begotten, unwarranted and temporary peace of mind obtained at the expense of others and of an ultimate disastrous ending for themselves.

If we must adopt a Communist slogan, let it not be "peaceful coexistence" with tyrants, but rather one suggested after the failure of the first two "East-West" conferences, at Genoa and The Hague, in 1922. At that time, the official organ of the Supreme Soviet, *Izvestia,* launched a tirade against the "impudent demands" of the free nations, and stated that it would waste no tears over the results. "The inglorious end of the Hague Conference has come," it said. "It dies unnoticed, and actually it has been dead for some time. At least we have ceased to expect anything from it long ago."[33] In what might be called the "spirit of Genoa," the article was captioned in Italian, "Finita la Commedia!"—the comedy is over.

Let the free nations now declare a real end to this comedy—a tragi-comedy, in which gangsters and murderers have been masquerading as statesmen, and puppets dealt with as representative governments, while the victims of their crimes have been presented as mere "political 'outs,' " with no right to a hearing even in the United Nations. Now let the free nations themselves say, "Finita la Commedia!"—and mean it.

AMERICAN PLEDGES MADE BEFORE THE BOLSHEVIK SEIZURE OF POWER

Address of Elihu Root to the Council of Ministers of the Russian Provisional Government, June 15, 1917

> Telegram, June 17, 1917, from the Ambassador on Special Mission to Russia (Root) to the Secretary of State. *Foreign Relations, 1918, Russia,* vol. I, 118-20.

Mr. President and members of the Council of Ministers, the mission for which I have the honor to speak is charged by the Government and the people of the United States of America with a message to the Government and the people of Russia.

The mission comes from a democratic Republic; its members are commissioned and instructed by a President who holds his high office as Chief Executive of more than one hundred million free people by virtue of a popular election in which more than eighteen million votes were cast and fairly counted pursuant to law by universal, equal, direct and secret suffrage.

For one hundred and forty years our people have been struggling with the hard problems of self-government. With many shortcomings, many mistakes, many imperfections, we have still maintained order and respect for law, individual freedom and national independence.

Under the security of our own laws we have grown in strength and prosperity but we value our freedom more than wealth. We love liberty and we cherish above all our possessions the ideals for which our fathers fought and suffered and sacrificed that America might be free. We believe in the competence and power of democracy and in our heart of hearts abides a faith in the coming of a better world in which the humble and oppressed in all lands may be lifted up by freedom to a heritage of justice and equal opportunity.

The news of Russia's new-found freedom brought to America universal satisfaction and joy. From all the land sympathy and hope went out towards the new sister in the circle of democracies and this mission is sent to express that feeling. The American democracy sends to the democracy of Russia greeting, sympathy, friendship, brotherhood, and Godspeed.

Distant America knows little of the special conditions of Russian life which must give form to the Government and to the laws which you are about to create as we have developed our institutions to serve the needs of our national character and life. So we assume that you will develop your institutions to serve the needs of Russian character and life. As we look across the sea we distinguish no party and no class; we see great Russia as a whole, as one mighty striving and aspiring democracy; we know the self-control, the essential kindliness, the strong common sense, the courage and noble illustrations of Russian character; we have faith in you all; we pray for God's blessings upon you all; we believe that you will solve your problems, that you will maintain your liberty, and that our two great nations will march side by side in the triumphant progress of democracy until the old order has everywhere passed away and the world is free.

One fearful danger threatens the liberty of both nations—the armed forces of military autocracy are at the gates of Russia and of her allies. The triumph of German arms will mean the death of liberty in Russia. No enemy is at the gates of America but America has come to realize that the triumph of German arms means the death of liberty in the world; that we who love liberty and would keep it must fight for it and fight now when the free democracies of the world may be strong in union and not delay until they may be beaten down separately in succession.

So America sends another message to Russia; that we are going to fight and have already begun to fight for your freedom equally with our own and we ask you to fight for our freedom equally with yours. We would make your cause ours and our cause yours and with common purpose and the mutual helpfulness of firm alliance make sure the victory over our common foe.

You will recognize your own sentiments and purposes in the words of President Wilson to the American Congress, when, on the 2d of April last, he advised the declaration of war against Germany. He said:

We are accepting this challenge of hostile purpose because we know that in such a government (the German Government) following such methods we can never have a friend; and that in the presence of its organized power always lying in wait to accomplish we know not what purpose there can be no assured security for the democratic governments of the world. We are now about to accept the gage of battle with this natural foe to liberty and shall if necessary spend the whole force of the nation to check and nullify its pretensions and its power. We are glad, now that we see the facts with no avail of false pretense about them, to fight thus for the ultimate peace of the world and for the liberation of its peoples, the German peoples included; for the rights of nations great and small and the privilege of men everywhere to choose their way of life and of obedience. The world must be made safe for democracy. Its peace must be planted upon the tested foundations of political liberty. We have no selfish ends to serve. We desire no conquest, no dominion. We seek no indemnities for ourselves; no material compensation for the sacrifices we shall freely make. We are but one of the champions of the rights of mankind. We shall be satisfied when those rights have been made as secure as the faith and the freedom of nations can make them.

And you will see the feeling towards Russia with which America has entered the great war in another clause of the same address. President Wilson further said:

Does not every American feel that assurance has been added to our hope for the future peace of the world by the wonderful and heartening things that have been happening within the last few weeks in Russia? Russia was known by those who knew it best to have been always in fact democratic at heart, in all the vital habits of her thought, in all the intimate relationships of her people that spoke their natural instinct, their habitual attitude towards life. The autocracy that crowned the summit of her political structure, long as it had stood and terrible as was the reality of its power, was not in fact Russian in origin, character, or purpose; and now it has been shaken off and the great, generous Russian people have been added in all their native majesty and might to the forces that are fighting for freedom in the world, for justice, and for peace. Here is a fit partner for a league of honor.

That partnership of honor in the great struggle for human freedom the oldest of the great democracies now seeks in fraternal union with the youngest.

The practical and specific methods and possibilities of our allied cooperation the members of the mission would be glad to discuss with the members of the Government of Russia.

ROOT

AMERICAN POLICY AFTER THE BOLSHEVIK SEIZURE OF POWER

1. *Aide-Mémoire* of the Secretary of State to the Allied Ambassadors, July 17, 1918.

Foreign Relations, 1918, Russia, Vol. II, 287-90.

The whole heart of the people of the United States is in the winning of this war. The controlling purpose of the Government of the United States is to do everything that is necessary and effective to win it. It wishes to cooperate in every practicable way with the Allied Governments, and to cooperate ungrudgingly; for it has no ends of its own to serve and believes that the war can be won only by common counsel and intimate concert of action. It has sought to study every proposed policy or action in which its cooperation has been asked in this spirit, and states the following conclusions in the confidence that, if it finds itself obliged to decline participation in any undertaking or course of action, it will be understood that it does so only because it deems itself precluded from participating by imperative considerations either of policy or of fact.

In full agreement with the Allied Governments and upon the unanimous advice of the Supreme War Council, the Government of the United States adopted, upon its entrance into the war, a plan for taking part in the fighting on the western front into which all its resources of men and material were to be put, and put as rapidly as possible, and it has carried out that plan with energy and success, pressing its execution more and more rapidly forward and literally putting into it the entire energy and executive force of the nation. This was its response, its very willing and hearty response, to what was the unhesitating judgment alike of its own military advisers and of the advisers of the Allied Governments. It is now considering, at the suggestion of the Supreme War Council, the possibility of making very considerable additions even to this immense program which, if they should prove feasible at all, will tax the industrial processes of the United States and the shipping facilities of the whole group of associated nations to the utmost. It has thus concentrated all its plans and all its resources upon this single absolutely necessary object.

In such circumstances it feels it to be its duty to say that it cannot, so long as the military situation on the western front remains critical, consent to break or slacken the force of its present effort by diverting any part of its military force to other points or objectives. The United States is at a great distance from the field of action on the western front; it is at a much greater distance from any other field of action. The instrumentalities by which it is to handle its armies and its stores have at great cost and with great difficulty been created in France. They do not exist elsewhere. It is practicable for her to do a great deal in France; it is not practicable for her to do anything of importance or on a large scale upon any other field. The American Government, therefore, very respectfully requests its associates to accept its deliberate judgment that it should not dissipate its force by attempting important operations elsewhere.

It regards the Italian front as closely coordinated with the western front, however, and is willing to divert a portion of its military forces from France to Italy if it is the judgment and wish of the Supreme Command that it should do so. It wishes to defer to the decision of the Commander in Chief in this matter, as it would wish to defer in all others, particularly because it considers these two fronts so closely related as to be practically but separate parts of a single line and because it would be necessary that any American troops sent to Italy should be subtracted from the number used in France and be actually transported across French territory from the ports now used by the armies of the United States.

It is the clear and fixed judgment of the Government of the United States, arrived at after repeated and very searching reconsiderations of the whole situation in Russia, that military intervention there would add to the present sad confusion in Russia rather than cure it, injure her rather than help her, and that it would be of no advantage in the prosecution of our main design, to win the war against Germany. It can not, therefore, take part in such intervention or sanction it in principle. Military intervention would, in its judgment, even supposing it to be efficacious in its immediate avowed object of delivering an attack upon Germany from the east, be merely a method of making use of Russia, not a method of serving her. Her people could not profit by it, if they profited by it at all, in time to save them from their present distresses, and their substance would be used to maintain foreign armies, not to reconstitute their own. Military action is admissible in Russia, as the Government of the United States sees the circumstances, only to help the Czecho-Slovaks consolidate their forces and get into successful cooperation with their Slavic kinsmen and to steady any efforts at self-government or self-defense in which the Russians themselves may be willing to accept assistance. Whether from Vladivostok or from Murmansk and Archangel, the only legitimate object for which American or Allied troops can be employed, it submits, is to guard military stores which may subsequently be needed by Russian forces and to render such aid as may be acceptable to the Russians in the organization of their own self-defense. For helping the Czecho-Slovaks there is immediate necessity and sufficient justification. Recent developments have made it evident that that is in the interest of what the Russian people themselves desire, and the Government of the United States is glad to contribute the small force at its disposal for that purpose. It yields, also, to the judgment of the Supreme Command in the matter of establishing a small force at Murmansk, to guard the military stores at Kola, and to make it safe for Russian forces to come together in organized bodies in the north. But it owes it to frank counsel to say that it can go no further than these modest and experimental plans. It is not in a position, and has no expectation of being in a position, to take part in organized intervention in adequate force from either Vladivostok or Murmansk and Archangel. It feels that it ought to add, also, that it will feel at liberty to use the few troops it can spare only for the purposes here stated and shall feel obliged to withdraw those forces, in order to add them to the forces at the western front, if the plans in whose execution it is now intended that they should cooperate should develop into others inconsistent with the policy to which the Government of the United States feels constrained to restrict itself.

At the same time the Government of the United States wishes to say with the utmost cordiality and good will that none of the conclusions here stated is meant to wear the least color of criticism of what the other governments associated against Germany may think it wise to undertake. It wishes in no way to embarrass their choices of policy. All that is intended here is a perfectly frank and definite statement of the policy which the United States feels obliged to adopt for herself and in the use of her own military forces. The Government of the United States does not wish it to be understood that in so restricting its own activities it is seeking, even by implication, to set limits to the action or to define the policies of its associates.

It hopes to carry out the plans for safeguarding the rear of the Czecho-Slovaks operating from Vladivostok in a way that will place it and keep it in close cooperation with a small military force like its own from Japan, and if necessary from the other Allies, and that will assure it of the cordial accord of all the Allied powers; and it proposes to ask all associated in this course of action to unite in assuring the people of Russia in the most public and solemn manner that none of the governments uniting in action either in Siberia or in northern Russia contemplates any interference of any kind with the political sovereignty of Russia, any intervention in her internal affairs, or any impairment of her territorial integrity either now or hereafter, but that each of the associated powers has the single object of affording such aid as shall be acceptable, and only such aid as shall be acceptable, to the Russian people in their endeavor to regain control of their own affairs, their own territory, and their own destiny.

It is the hope and purpose of the Government of the United States to take advantage of the earliest opportunity to send to Siberia a commission of merchants, agricultural experts, labor advisers, Red Cross representatives, and agents of the Young Men's Christian Association accustomed to organizing the best methods of spreading useful information and rendering educational help of a modest sort, in order in some systematic manner to relieve the immediate economic necessities of the people there in every way for which opportunity may open. The execution of this plan will follow and will not be permitted to embarrass the military assistance rendered in the rear of the westward-moving forces of the Czecho-Slovaks.

Washington, July 17, 1918.

2. *Note of the Secretary of State to the Italian Ambassador, August 10, 1920.*

Foreign Relations, 1920, Vol. III, 463-68.

Excellency:

The agreeable intimation, which you have conveyed to the State Department that the Italian Government would welcome a statement of the views of this Government on the situation presented by the Russian advance into Poland, deserves a prompt response, and I will attempt without delay, a definition of this Government's position not only as to the situation arising from Russian military pressure upon Poland, but also as to certain cognate and inseparable phases of the Russian question viewed more broadly.

This Government believes in a united, free and autonomous Polish State and the people of the United States are earnestly solicitous for the maintenance of Poland's political independence and territorial integrity. From this attitude we will not depart, and the policy of this Government will be directed to the employment of all available means to render it effectual. The Government therefore takes no exception to the effort apparently being made in some quarters to arrange an armistice between Poland and Russia, but it would not, at least for the present, participate in any plan for the expansion of the armistice negotiations into a general European conference which would in all probability involve two results, from both of which this country strongly recoils, viz, the recognition of the Bolshevist regime and a settlement of Russian problems almost inevitably upon the basis of a dismemberment of Russia.

From the beginning of the Russian Revolution, in March, 1917, to the present moment, the Government and the people of the United States have followed its development with friendly solicitude and with profound sympathy for the efforts of the Russian people to reconstruct their national life upon the broad basis of popular self-government. The Government of the United States, reflecting the spirit of its people, has at all times desired to help the Russian people. In that spirit all its relations with Russia, and with other nations in matters affecting the latter's interests, have been conceived and governed.

The Government of the United States was the first government to acknowledge the validity of the Revolution and to give recognition to the Provisional Government of Russia. Almost immediately thereafter it became necessary for the United States to enter the war against Germany and in that undertaking to become closely associated with the Allied Nations, including, of course, Russia. The war weariness of the masses of the Russian people was fully known to this Government and sympathetically comprehended. Prudence, self-interest and loyalty to our associates made it desirable that we should give moral and material support to the Provisional Government, which was struggling to accomplish a two-fold task, to carry on the war with vigor and, at the same time, to reorganize the life of the nation and establish a stable government based on popular sovereignty.

Quite independent of these motives, however, was the sincere friendship of the Government and the people of the United States for the great Russian nation. The friendship manifested by Russia toward this nation in a time of trial and distress has left us with an imperishable sense of gratitude. It was as a grateful friend that we sent to Russia an expert commission to aid in bringing about such a reorganization of the railroad transportation system of the country as would reinvigorate the whole of its economic life and so add to the well-being of the Russian people.

While deeply regretting the withdrawal of Russia from the war at a critical time, and the disastrous surrender at Brest-Litovsk, the United States has fully understood that the people of Russia were in no wise responsible.

The United States maintains unimpaired its faith in the Russian people, in their high character and their future. That they will overcome the existing anarchy, suffering and destitution we do not entertain the slightest doubt. The distressing character of Russia's transition has many historical parallels, and the United States is confident that restored, free and united Russia will again take a leading place in the world, joining with the other free nations in upholding peace and orderly justice.

Until that time shall arrive the United States feels that friendship and honor require that Russia's interests must be generously protected, and that, as far as possible, all decisions of vital importance to it, and especially those concerning its sovereignty over the territory of the former Russian Empire, be held in abeyance. By this feeling of friendship and honorable obligation to the great nation whose brave and heroic self-sacrifice contributed so much to the successful termination of the war, the Government of the United States was guided in its reply to the Lithuanian National Council, on October 15, 1919, and in its persistent refusal to recognize the Baltic States as separate nations independent of Russia. The same spirit was manifested in the note of this Government, of March 24, 1920, in which it was stated, with reference to certain proposed settlements in the Near East, that "no final decision should or can be made without the consent of Russia."

In line with these important declarations of policy, the United States withheld its approval from the decision of the Supreme Council at Paris recognizing the independence of the so called republics of Georgia and Azerbaijan, and so instructed its representative in Southern Russia, Rear-Admiral Newton A. McCully. Finally, while gladly giving recognition to the independence of Armenia, the

Government of the United States has taken the position that the final determination of its boundaries must not be made without Russia's cooperation and agreement. Not only is Russia concerned because a considerable part of the territory of the new State of Armenia, when it shall be defined, formerly belonged to the Russian Empire: equally important is the fact that Armenia must have the good will and the protective friendship of Russia if it is to remain independent and free.

These illustrations show with what consistency the Government of the United States has been guided in its foreign policy by a loyal friendship for Russia. We are unwilling that while it is helpless in the grip of a non-representative government, whose only sanction is brutal force, Russia shall be weakened still further by a policy of dismemberment, conceived in other than Russian interests.

With the desire of the Allied Powers to bring about a peaceful solution of the existing difficulties in Europe, this Government is of course in hearty accord, and will support any justifiable steps to that end. It is unable to perceive, however, that a recognition of the Soviet regime would promote, much less accomplish this object, and it is therefore averse to any dealings with the Soviet regime beyond the most narrow boundaries to which a discussion of an armistice can be confined.

That the present rulers of Russia do not rule by the will or the consent of any considerable proportion of the Russian people is an incontestible fact. Although nearly two and a half years have passed since they seized the machinery of government, promising to protect the Constituent Assembly against alleged conspiracies against it, they have not yet permitted anything in the nature of a popular election. At the moment when the work of creating a popular representative government based upon universal suffrage was nearing completion the Bolsheviki, although, in number, an inconsiderable minority of the people, by force and cunning seized the powers and machinery of government and have continued to use them with savage oppression to maintain themselves in power.

Without any desire to interfere in the internal affairs of the Russian people, or to suggest what kind of government they should have, the Government of the United States does express the hope that they will soon find a way to set up a government representing their free will and purpose. When that time comes, the United States will consider the measures of practical assistance which can be taken to promote the restoration of Russia, provided Russia has not taken itself wholly out of the pale of the friendly interest of other nations, by the pillage and oppression of the Poles.

It is not possible for the Government of the United States to recognize the present rulers of Russia as a government with which the relations common to friendly governments can be maintained. This conviction has nothing to do with any particular political or social structure which the Russian people themselves may see fit to embrace. It rests upon a wholly different set of facts. These facts, which none dispute, have convinced the Government of the United States, against its will, that the existing regime in Russia is based upon the negation of every principle of honor and good faith, and every usage and convention, underlying the whole structure of international law; the negation, in short, of every principle upon which it is possible to base harmonious and trustful relations, whether of nations or of individuals. The responsible leaders of the regime have frequently and openly boasted that they are willing to sign agreements and undertakings with foreign Powers while not having the slightest intention of observing such undertakings or carrying out such agreements. This attitude of disregard of obligations voluntarily entered into, they base upon the theory that no compact or agreement made with a non-Bolshevist government can have any moral force for them. They have not only avowed this as a doctrine, but have exemplified it in practice. Indeed, upon numerous occasions the responsible spokesmen of this Power, and its official agencies, have declared that it is their understanding that the very existence of Bolshevism in Russia, the maintenance of their own rule, depends, and must continue to depend, upon the occurrence of revolutions in all other great civilized nations, including the United States, which will overthrow and destroy their governments and set up Bolshevist rule in their stead. They have made it quite plain that they intend to use every means, including, of course, diplomatic agencies, to promote such revolutionary movements in other countries.

It is true that they have in various ways expressed their willingness to give "assurances" and "guarantees" that they will not abuse the privileges and immunities of diplomatic agencies by using them for this purpose. In view of their own declarations, already referred to, such assurances and guarantees cannot be very seriously regarded. Moreover, it is within the knowledge of the Government of the United States that the Bolshevist Government is itself subject to the control of a political faction, with extensive international ramifications through the Third Internationale, and that this body, which is heavily subsidized by the Bolshevist Government from the public revenues of Russia, has for its openly avowed aim the promotion of Bolshevist revolutions throughout the world. The leaders of the Bolsheviki have boasted that their promises of non-interference with other nations would in no wise bind the agents of this body. There is no room for reasonable doubt that such agents would receive the support and protection of any diplomatic agencies the Bolsheviki might have in other countries. Inevitably, therefore, the diplomatic service of the Bolshevist Government would become a channel for intrigues and the propaganda of revolt against the institutions and laws of countries, with which it was at peace, which would be an abuse of friendship to which enlightened governments cannot subject themselves.

In the view of this Government, there cannot be any common ground upon which it can stand with a Power whose conceptions of international relations are so entirely alien to its own, so utterly repugnant to its moral sense. There can be no mutual confidence or trust, no respect even, if pledges are to be given and agreements made with a cynical repudiation of their obligations already in the mind of one of the parties. We cannot recognize, hold official relations with, or give friendly reception to the agents of a government which is determined and bound to conspire against our institutions; whose diplomats will be the agitators of dangerous revolt; whose spokesmen say that they sign agreements with no intention of keeping them.

To summarize the position of this Government, I would say, therefore, in response to your Excellency's inquiry, that it would regard with satisfaction a declaration by the Allied and Associated Powers, that the territorial integrity and true boundaries of Russia shall be respected. These boundaries should properly include the whole of the former Russian Empire, with the exception of Finland proper, ethnic Poland, and such territory as may by agreement form a part of the Armenian State. The aspirations of these nations for independence are legitimate. Each was forcibly annexed and their liberation from oppressive alien rule involves no aggressions against Russia's territorial rights, and has received the sanction of the public opinion of all free peoples. Such a declaration presupposes the withdrawal of all foreign troops from the territory embraced by these boundaries, and in the opinion of this Government should be accompanied by the announcement that no transgression by Poland, Finland or any other Power, of the line so drawn and proclaimed will be permitted.

Thus only can the Bolshevist regime be deprived of its false, but effective, appeal to Russian nationalism and compelled to meet the inevitable challenge of reason and self-respect which the Russian people, secure from invasion and territorial violation, are sure to address to a social philosophy that degrades them and a tyranny that oppresses them.

The policy herein outlined will command the support of this Government.

Accept, Excellency, the renewed assurance of my highest consideration.

BAINBRIDGE COLBY

His Excellency
    Baron Camillo Romano Avezzana
        Ambassador of Italy

APPENDIX C

ALLIED PLEDGES OF WAR II

1. *The Atlantic Charter, August, 1941.*

Press Release, August 14, 1941. Department of State, *Bulletin,* September 16, 1941, 125-6.

The following statement was signed by the President of the United States and the Prime Minister of Great Britain:

"The President of the United States and the Prime Minister, Mr. Churchill, representing His Majesty's Government in the United Kingdom, have met at sea.

"They have been accompanied by officials of their two Governments, including high-ranking officers of their Military, Naval, and Air Services.

"The whole problem of the supply of munitions of war, as provided by the Lease-Lend Act, for the armed forces of the United States and for those countries actively engaged in resisting aggression has been further examined.

"Lord Beaverbrook, the Minister of Supply of the British Government, has joined in these conferences. He is going to proceed to Washington to discuss further details with appropriate officials of the United States Government. These conferences will also cover the supply problems of the Soviet Union.

"The President and the Prime Minister have had several conferences. They have considered the dangers to world civilization arising from the policies of military domination by conquest upon which the Hitlerite government of Germany and other governments associated therewith have embarked, and have made clear the stress which their countries are respectively taking for their safety in the face of these dangers.

"They have agreed upon the following joint declaration:

"Joint declaration of the President of the United States of America and the Prime Minister, Mr. Churchill, representing His Majesty's Government in the United Kingdom, being met together, deem it right to make known certain common principles in the national policies of their respective countries on which they base their hopes for a better future for the world.

"First, their countries seek no aggrandizement, territorial or other;

"Second, they desire to see no territorial changes that do not accord with the freely expressed wishes of the peoples concerned;

"Third, they respect the right of all peoples to choose the form of government under which they will live; and they wish to see sovereign rights and self-government restored to those who have been forcibly deprived of them;

"Fourth, they will endeavor, with due respect for their existing obligations, to further the enjoyment by all States, great or small, victor or vanquished, of access, on equal terms, to the trade and to the raw materials of the world which are needed for their economic prosperity;

"Fifth, they desire to bring about the fullest collaboration between all nations in the economic field with the object of securing, for all, improved labor standards, economic advancement, and social security;

"Sixth, after the final destruction of the Nazi tyranny, they hope to see established a peace which will afford to all nations the means of dwelling in safety within their own boundaries, and which will afford assurance that all the men in all the lands may live out their lives in freedom from fear and want;

"Seventh, such a peace should enable all men to traverse the high seas and oceans without hindrance;

"Eighth, they believe that all of the nations of the world, for realistic as well as spiritual reasons, must come to the abandonment of the use of force. Since no future peace can be maintained if land, sea, or air armaments continue to be employed by nations which threaten, or may threaten, aggression outside of their frontiers, they believe, pending the establishment of a wider and permanent system of general security, that the disarmament of such nations is essential. They will likewise aid and encourage all other practicable measures which will lighten for peace-loving peoples the crushing burden of armaments.

FRANKLIN D. ROOSEVELT
WINSTON S. CHURCHILL".

At his press conference on August 14, the Secretary of State, when asked for comment upon the joint declaration of the President of the United States and the Prime Minister of Great Britain, said:

"It is a statement of basic principles and fundamental ideas and policies that are universal in their practical application. They have heretofore been generally accepted by all civilized nations and were being strongly supported until certain countries decided to launch a universal movement to destroy the whole structure of civilized relations between nations and to establish a system of rule over peoples who would be conquered, based, as I said some days ago, largely on barbarism and savagery. That interruption is still going on.

"As I said, they are the basic doctrines and policies that have received the support of all civilized nations and should continue to receive their support until they are completely restored throughout the world."

2. *The Declaration on Liberated Europe, February 11, 1945.*

The Conferences at Malta and Yalta 1945, 977-8.

The following declaration has been approved:

"The Premier of the Union of Soviet Socialist Republics, the Prime Minister of the United Kingdom and the President of the United States of America have consulted with each other in the common interests of the peoples of their countries and those of liberated Europe. They jointly declare their mutual agreement to concert during the temporary period of instability in liberated Europe the policies of their three governments in assisting the peoples liberated from the domination of Nazi Germany and the peoples of the former Axis satellite states of Europe to solve by democratic means their pressing political and economic problems.

"The establishment of order in Europe and the re-building of national economic life must be achieved by processes which will enable the liberated peoples to destroy the last vestiges of Nazism and Fascism and to create democratic institutions of their own choice. This is a principle of the Atlantic Charter—the right of all peoples to choose the form of government under which they will live—the restoration of sovereign rights and self-government to those peoples who have been forcibly deprived of them by the aggressor nations.

"To foster the conditions in which the liberated peoples may exercise these rights, the three governments will jointly assist the people in any European liberated state or former Axis satellite state in Europe where in their judgment conditions require (a) to establish conditions of internal peace; (b) to carry out emergency measures for the relief of distressed peoples; (c) to form interim governmental authorities broadly representative of all democratic elements in the population and pledged to the earliest possible establishment through free elections of governments responsive to the will of the people; and (d) to facilitate where necessary the holding of such elections.

"The three governments will consult the other United Nations and provisional authorities or other governments in Europe when matters of direct interest to them are under consideration.

"When, in the opinion of the three governments, conditions in any European liberated state or any former Axis satellite state in Europe make such action necessary, they will immediately consult together on the measures necessary to discharge the joint responsibilities set forth in this declaration.

"By this declaration we reaffirm our faith in the principles of the Atlantic Charter, our pledge in the Declaration by the United Nations, and our determination to build in co-operation with other peace-loving nations world order under law, dedicated to the peace, security, freedom and general well-being of all mankind.

"In issuing this declaration, the Three Powers express the hope that the Provisional Government of the French Republic may be associated with them in the procedure suggested."

APPENDIX D

AMERICAN POLICY AFTER WORLD WAR II

1. *Exhange of Notes with the President of China, August, 1946.*

U.S. Relations with China, 652-4.

a. President Truman to President Chiang Kai-shek.

Washington, August 10, 1946.

I have followed closely the situation in China since I sent General Marshall to you as my Special Envoy. It is with profound regret that I am forced to the conclusion that his efforts have seemingly proved unavailing.

In his discussions with you, I am certain that General Marshall has reflected accurately the overall attitude and policy of the American Government and of informed American public opinion also.

The rapidly deteriorating political situation in China, during recent months, has been a cause of grave concern to the American people. While it is the continued hope of the United States that an influential and democratic China can still be achieved under your leadership, I would be less than honest if I did not point out that latest developments have forced me to the conclusion that the selfish interests of extremist elements, both in the Kuomintang and the Communist Party, are obstructing the aspirations of the people of China.

A farsighted step toward the achievement of national unity and democracy was acclaimed in the United States when the agreements were reached on January 31st by the Political Consultative Conference. Disappointment over failure to implement the agreements of the PCC by concrete measures is becoming an important factor in the American outlook with regard to China.

In the United States, there now exists an increasing school of thought which maintains that our whole policy toward China must be re-examined in the light of spreading strife, and notably by evidence of the increasing trend to suppress the expression of liberal views among intellectuals as well as freedom of the press. The assassinations of distinguished Chinese liberals at Kunming recently have not been ignored. Regardless of where responsibility may lie for these cruel murders, the result has been to cause American attention to focus on the China situation, and there is increasing belief that an attempt is being made to resort to force, military or secret police rather than democratic processes to settle major social issues.

American faith in the peaceful and democratic aspirations of the Chinese people has not been destroyed by recent events, but has been shaken. The firm desire of the people of the United States and of the American Government is still to help China achieve lasting peace and a stable economy under a truly democratic government. There is an increasing awareness, however, that the hopes of the people of China are being thwarted by militarists and a small group of political reactionaries who are obstructing the advancement of the general good of the nation by failing to understand the liberal trend of the times. The people of the United States view with violent repugnance this state of affairs.

It cannot be expected that American opinion will continue in its generous attitude towards your nation unless convincing proof is shortly forthcoming that genuine progress is being made toward a peaceful settlement of China's internal problems. Furthermore, it will be necessary for me to redefine and explain the position of the United States to the people of America.

I earnestly hope that in the near future I may receive some encouraging word from you which will facilitate the achievement of our mutually declared aims.

b. The Chinese Ambassador (Koo) to President Truman.

Washington, August 28, 1946.

My Dear Mr. President: Referring to my acknowledgement of

August 12 of your letter dated August 10 containing a message to President Chiang Kai-shek, I have the honor to transmit to your excellency, in accordance with instructions, the following reply:

"Referring to your message of August 10, I wish to thank you cordially for your expressions of genuine concern for the welfare of my country.

"General Marshall has labored most unsparingly to achieve our common objective; namely, peace and democracy in China, since his arrival. Despite all obstacles, I, too, have done my utmost to cooperate with him in the accomplishment of his task.

"The desire for peace has to be mutual, therefore, it means the Communists must give up their policy to seize political power through the use of armed force, to overthrow the government and to install a totalitarian regime such as those with which Eastern Europe is now being engulfed.

"The minimum requirement for the preservation of peace in our country is the abandonment of such a policy. The Communists attacked and captured Changchun in Manchuria and attacked and captured Tehchow in Shantung after the conclusion of the January agreement. In June, during the cease-fire period, they attacked Tatung and Taiyuan in Shansi and Hsuchow in northern Kiangsu. They have opened a wide offensive on the Lunghai railway in the last few days, with Hsuchow and Kaifeng as their objectives.

"Mistakes have also been made by some subordinates on the government side, of course, but compared to the flagrant violations on the part of the Communists, they are minor in scale. We deal sternly with the offender whenever any mistake occurs on our Government side.

"In my V-J Day message on August 14, I announced the firm policy of the government to broaden speedily the basis of the Government by the inclusion of all parties and non-partisans, amounting to the effectuation of the program of peaceful reconstruction adopted on January 13 by the political consultation conference. It is my sincere hope that our views will be accepted by the Chinese Communist party. On its part, the Government will do the utmost in the shortest possible time to make peace and democracy a reality in this country.

"I am cooperating with General Marshall with all my power in implementing that policy which has as its aim our mutually declared objective. Success must depend upon the sincerity of the Communists in response to our appeals. I am depending on your continued support in the realization of our goal. (Sgd.) Chiang Kai-shek."

I again offer my highest respects.

Yours most sincerely,

V. K. WELLINGTON KOO

c. President Truman to President Chiang Kai-shek

Washington, August 31, 1946

Dear President Chiang: Your message was transmitted to me by letter on August 28 by the Chinese Ambassador Dr. Koo. I note with gratification your references to General Marshall. The strenuous efforts, indicated in the concluding paragraphs of your message, being made to effect the settlement of the internal problems now confronting you are greatly welcomed by me. It is earnestly hoped by me that a satisfactory political solution can soon be reached to bring about a cessation of hostilities, thereby making it possible for the great and urgent task of reconstruction to be continued by you and the Chinese people. With reference to the final paragraph of my policy statement of 15 December 1945, I hope it will be feasible for the United States to plan for assisting China in its industrial economy and the rehabilitation of its agrarian reforms. This can be rendered feasible, I believe, through the prompt removal of the threat of widespread Civil War in China.

With my best wishes and highest regards.

Sincerely,

HARRY S. TRUMAN

2. *Excerpts from the President's Message to Joint Session of Congress, March 12, 1947* (*Statement of the Policy of "Containment"*)

Department of State, *Bulletin,* Supplement, May 4, 1947, 830-1.

One of the primary objectives of the foreign policy of the United States is the creation of conditions in which we and other nations will be able to work out a way of life free from coercion. This was a fundamental issue in the war with Germany and Japan. Our victory was won over countries which sought to impose their will, and their way of life, upon other nations.

To insure the peaceful development of nations, free from coercion, the United States has taken a leading part in establishing the United Nations. The United Nations is designed to make possible lasting freedom and independence for all its members. We shall not realize our objectives, however, unless we are willing to help free peoples to maintain their free institutions and their national integrity against aggressive movements that seek to impose upon them totalitarian regimes. This is no more than a frank recognition that totalitarian regimes imposed upon free peoples, by direct or indirect aggression, undermine the foundations of international peace and hence the security of the United States.

The peoples of a number of countries of the world have recently had totalitarian regimes forced upon them against their will. The Government of the United States has made frequent protests against coercion and intimidation, in violation of the Yalta agreement, in Poland, Rumania and Bulgaria. I must also state that in a number of other countries there have been similar developments.

At the present moment in world history nearly every nation must choose between alternative ways of life. The choice is too often not a free one.

One way of life is based upon the will of the majority, and is distinguished by free institutions, representative government, free elections, guaranties of individual liberty, freedom of speech and religion, and freedom from political oppression.

The second way of life is based upon the will of a minority forcibly imposed upon the majority. It relies upon terror and oppression, a controlled press and radio, fixed elections, and the suppression of personal freedoms.

I believe that it must be the policy of the United States to support free peoples who are resisting attempted subjugation by armed minorities or by outside pressures.

I believe that we must assist free peoples to work out their own destinies in their own way.

I believe that our help should be primarily through economic and financial aid which is essential to economic stability and orderly political processes.

The world is not static, and the *status quo* is not sacred. But we cannot allow changes in the *status quo* in violation of the Charter of the United Nations by such methods as coercion, or by such sub-terfuges as political infiltration. In helping free and independent nations to maintain their freedom, the United States will be giving effect to the principles of the Charter of the United Nations.

RECOMMENDATIONS OF THE BOLSHEVIKS

1. *Excerpt from Statement of Maxim Litvinov, Soviet Commissar of Foreign Affairs, at the Opening Session of the Brussels Conference, November 3, 1937*

Conference of Brussels, 33

Recent years have added extremely valuable experience to international life, and that experience obliges me to draw attention to those dangerous ruts and pitfalls which lie in the path of international conferences. The experience I have in mind teaches us that international conferences, committees, and other organizations, which are called upon to serve a particular end, sometimes are inclined, particularly in the event of a protracted existence, to forget their direct purpose and the technical part they have to play, and begin to live their own life, with their own peculiar interests. They begin to concern themselves principally with the maintenance of their own existence, with the procuring of moral satisfaction for those who have initiated such conferences, and with their own superficial successes, which do not always coincide with successes for the cause on account of which the conferences were brought into existence. Moreover, there sometimes even arises a divergence between those various interests; there even comes a moment when a conference or committee which should be striving to eliminate and overcome the phenomena of aggression, itself becomes imperceptibly a tool of the aggressor, who utilizes it as a screen and an auxiliary for his aggressive activities.

This happens when international organizations come into contact with the aggressors themselves in an attempt to persuade them to alter their attitude. In the course of negotiations, leading to systematic concessions to the aggressor, it is possible to cross the boundary beyond which people who are undoubtedly inspired with the best intentions slip, without noticing it, over to the point of view of the aggressor and begin to talk his language, substantially justifying and encouraging his activities.

When it is a question of an aggressive attack by one state against another, and if that attack has been in some measure successful, there is nothing easier than for an international organization, in order to gain a momentary success, to say to the aggressor: 'Take your plunder, take what you have seized by force, and peace be with you', and to say to the victim of aggression: 'Love your aggressor; resist not evil'. But while that may constitute a superficial success for the Conference, it does not represent the victory of peace or the victory of the peace-loving countries. That kind of success can only provoke new cases of aggression, giving rise to new conferences and so on without end. The encouragement and multiplication of acts of aggression is moreover facilitated by the circumstance that when international organizations leave their direct path in the manner I have indicated, there quite inevitably arises friction between the peace-loving countries, leading to divisions among them which are skilfully utilized in their turn by the aggressors. Yet the unity of all peace-loving countries is particularly necessary at the moment when aggressive countries are more and more uniting and consolidating their forces, thereby creating a menace to an ever-increasing number of states.

Having uttered this warning, which seems to me essential, against the perils which may confront any international conference in present conditions, I desire to express my sincerest good wishes for the success of the Brussels Conference and of those proposals which we shall probably hear from the inviting powers. I am certain that the new Conference will manage to avoid the perils I have mentioned, and that the proposals we all anticipate will pursue the aim not only of restoring peace in the Far East, but of establishing a just peace, a peace which will not untie, but, on the contrary, will bind the hands of aggressors, also for the future and in other parts of the world.

2. *Statement of Maxim Litvinov, Soviet Commissar of Foreign Affairs, in the Council of the League of Nations, May 12, 1938, on Recognition of the Conquest of Ethiopia*

League of Nations Official Journal, 1938, 344

The question before us has to be considered from two points of view. The first is whether it is practicable and expedient to continue the action which the League undertook in defence of the territorial integrity and political independence of one of its Members, in accordance with Article 10 of the Covenant. The second is the bearing which our decision may have on the prestige, authority and further efficiency of the League.

Among the means for combating aggression and defending its Members which the League of Nations has at its disposal, non-recognition does not by any means play a conspicuous part. It is improbable that anyone would assert that the mere threat of non-recognition might avert aggression, or that non-recognition itself might free the victim of aggression from the grip of the conqueror. It was also my view that non-recognition should be accompanied by other more effective methods of combating the aggressor, provided by Article 16 of the Covenant. Unfortunately we have to recognise that the League of Nations has in some cases adopted resolutions on non-recognition without at the same time applying other means, more capable of arresting or repelling aggression. One might go as far as to say that resolutions on non-recognition were adopted when it became obvious that Members of the League were unwilling to inflict more telling blows on the aggressor, or when other action undertaken against him was being brought to an end. There must even be reasonable ground for the impression that resolutions on non-recognition were intended, as it were, to make up for failure to fulfil the other obligations imposed by the Covenant on League Members, in regard to the victims of aggression, and, so to speak, thereby to clear their conscience.

It would be quite wrong, however, to assert that resolutions on non-recognition are in themselves devoid of any particular value. While such resolutions have in every case a certain moral significance, and give satisfaction to public opinion, they also cause the aggressor some preoccupations and inconveniences, as is evidenced by the efforts which aggressors usually make to obtain recognition of their conquests, if only in an indirect way.

But, according to circumstances, non-recognition may be of vast importance, not only morally, but also politically—particularly when the victim of aggression itself continues to fight for its independence and for the integrity of its territory. In such cases, the recognition of the results of acts of violent aggression, or the abandonment of the policy of non-recognition, would be equivalent to abetting the aggressor directly, and to stabbing his victim in the back by discouraging and demoralising it. We have to reckon, not only with the question whether any struggle between the aggressor and his victim has come to an end, but also—should that have occurred for the time being—whether there are any chances of the struggle being renewed, and likewise we have to reckon with other circumstances which may bring about a change in the situation created by aggressive acts of violence.

In attempting to apply what I have said to the Ethiopian problem, we should obviously find ourselves in a difficult position. There is information that the struggle in Ethiopia has never ceased and is now even increasing in its intensity, if not in its extent. There are also assertions to the contrary. The material at our disposal does not permit us to arrive at a final conclusion. The despatch of a Commission of investigation would be an obvious way out, but there are apparently enormous obstacles to such a course.

On the other hand, we cannot ignore the fact that there have already been breaches by some League Members of the resolution adopted by the League Assembly in 1936 as to the non-recognition of the conquest of Ethiopia, and also the obvious intention of others not to reckon any longer with that resolution for the future, whatever the Council or the Assembly may decide. At all events, I can assure the Council that the Government of the Union of Soviet Socialist Republics, for its part, would be ready to solve this problem, not from the standpoint of its national interests, but in the spirit of the Covenant of the League of Nations, of international solidarity, of the principles of collective security and the indivisibility of peace.

But whatever the decision on the question before us, and whatever the conclusions which individual States will think it necessary to draw, on their own responsibility, from our discussion, one thing must be clear. The League of Nations has not changed its view of those actions which resulted in an Ethiopian problem arising within the League, and none of the condemnations of such activities adopted by the League is withdrawn. It must be made even more clear that the League of Nations has not changed its opinion on the general principle of non-recognition of the accomplished fact produced by aggression, and on the appropriate resolutions adopted by the League in other cases. The latter particularly applies in cases where the States which have been the victims of attack have aroused the amazement and admiration of the world by the valiance of their citizens, who continue to fight the aggressor with unweakening energy, obstinacy and fortitude. It must be clear that the League of Nations has no intention of changing its attitude, whether to the direct seizure and annexation of other people's territory, or to those cases where such annexations are camouflaged by the setting-up of puppet "national" governments, allegedly independent, but in reality serving merely as a screen for, and an agency of, the foreign invader.

I have still to remark briefly on the other aspects of the question which I have mentioned. When the United Kingdom Government puts forward its motion to grant freedom of action to all League Members, it bases its principal argument on the fact that many Members of the League, in violation of League resolutions, have already taken steps towards recognising the annexation of Ethiopia, and therefore the same opportunity should be afforded to others. This may be fair from the standpoint of equality of obligations, but equality at such a low level can hardly be an ideal of the League. If we once admit that principle, we may expect that it will be sufficient for one or a few Members of the League to break one of its decisions— and that may easily happen, in the present state of international morality—for all other Members of the League, one by one, to follow them.

We cannot admit that breaches of international obligations are examples to be followed. The League of Nations and its individual Members have made mistakes, errors and blunders: they have not always fulfilled their obligations. We should recognise and condemn such failures and take measures to prevent their repetition in future, but on no account must we legalise them, or lower the collective responsibility of the League of Nations to their level. Of course, the League's decisions are not eternal, and can always be reviewed and corrected by the League, at the request of individual League Members, but it is the League collectively which has to recognise such decisions as being out of date and invalid, not its individual Members, when they think it required, or when it seems to them to be required, by their national interests at the time. The League Council should leave no room for doubt that it not only does not approve such anarchic activities, or erect them into a virtue, but severely condemns those of its Members who are the first to set the example of engaging in them.

If we had before us any resolution or résumé of our discussion, I should insist on its reflecting the considerations I have laid before you. To neglect them will not allow the League to remain in existence much longer, and I should like to think that its preservation answers to the interests of peace and to the wishes of the vast majority of States.

APPENDIX F

THE APOCALYPSE
of St. John the Apostle

(Chapters 13, 17, 18, 19)

CHAPTER 13. *The Beast of the Sea.*

And I saw a beast coming up out of the sea, having seven heads and ten horns, and upon its horns ten diadems, and upon its heads blasphemous names. 2. And the beast that I saw was like a leopard, and its feet were like the feet of a bear, and its mouth like the mouth of a lion. And the dragon gave it his own might and great authority. 3. And one of its heads was smitten, as it were, unto death; but its deadly wound was healed. And all the earth followed the beast in wonder. 4. And they worshipped the dragon because he gave authority to the beast, and they worshipped the beast, saying, "Who is like to the beast, and who will be able to fight with it?"

5. And there was given to it a mouth speaking great things and blasphemies; and there was given to it authority to work for forty-two months. 6. And it opened its mouth for blasphemies against God, to blaspheme his name and his tabernacle, and those who dwell in heaven. 7. And it was allowed to wage war with the saints and to overcome them. And there was given to it authority over every tribe, and people, and tongue, and nation. 8. And all the inhabitants of the earth will worship it whose names have not been written in the book of life of the Lamb who has been slain from the foundation of the world.

9. If any man has an ear, let him hear. 10. He who is for captivity, into captivity he goes; he who kills by the sword, by the sword must he be killed. Here is the patience and the faith of the saints.

The Beast of the Earth.

11. And I saw another beast coming up out of the earth, and it had two horns like to those of a lamb, but it spoke as does a dragon. 12. And it exercised all the authority of the former beast in its sight; and it made the earth and the inhabitants therein to worship the first beast, whose deadly wound was healed. 13. And it did great signs, so as even to make fire come down from heaven upon earth in the sight of mankind. 14. And it leads astray the inhabitants of the earth, by reason of the signs which it was permitted to do in the sight of the beast, telling the inhabitants of the earth to make an image to the beast which has the wound of the sword, and yet lived. 15. And it was permitted to give life to the image of the beast, that the image of the beast should both speak and cause that whoever should not worship the image of the beast should be killed. 16. And it will cause all, the small and the great, and the rich and the poor, and the free and the bond, to have a mark on their right hand or on their foreheads, 17. and it will bring it about that no one may be able to buy or sell, except him who has the mark, either the name of the beast or the number of its name.

18. Here is wisdom. He who has understanding, let him calculate the number of the beast, for it is the number of a man; and its number is six hundred and sixty-six.

CHAPTER 17. *The Woman on the Scarlet Beast.*

And there came one of the seven angels who had the seven bowls, and he spoke with me, saying, "Come, I will show thee the condemnation of the great harlot who sits upon many waters, 2. with whom the kings of the earth have committed fornication, and the inhabitants of the earth were made drunk with the wine of her immorality."

3. And he took me away in spirit into a desert. And I saw a woman sitting upon a scarlet-colored beast, full of names of blasphemy, having seven heads and ten horns. 4. And the woman was clothed in purple and scarlet, and covered with gold and precious stones and pearls, having in her hand a golden cup full of abominations and the uncleanness of her immorality. 5. And upon her forehead a name written—a mystery—Babylon the great, the mother of the harlotries and of the abominations of the earth. 6. And I saw the woman drunk with the blood of the saints and with the blood of the martyrs of Jesus. And when I saw her, I wondered with a great wonder.

The Angel's Explanation.

7. And the angel said to me, "Wherefore dost thou wonder? I will tell thee the mystery of the woman, and of the beast that carries her which has the seven heads and the ten horns. 8. The beast that thou sawest was, and is not, and is about to come up from the abyss, and will go to destruction. And the inhabitants of the earth—whose names have not been written in the book of life from the foundation of the world—will wonder when they see the beast which was, and is not. 9. And here is the meaning for him who has wisdom. The seven heads are seven mountains upon which the woman sits; and they are seven kings; 10. five of them have fallen, one is, and the other has not yet come; and when he comes, he must remain a short time. 11. And the beast that was, and is not, is moreover himself eighth, and is of the seven, and is on his way to destruction.

12. "And the ten horns that thou sawest are ten kings, who have not received a kingdom as yet, but they will receive authority as kings for one hour with the beast. 13. These have one purpose, and their power and authority they give to the beast. 14. These will fight with the Lamb, and the Lamb will overcome them, for he is the Lord of lords, and the King of kings, and they who are with him, called, and chosen, and faithful."

15. And he said to me, "The waters that thou sawest where the harlot sits, are peoples and nations and tongues. 16. And the ten horns that thou sawest, and the beast, these will hate the harlot, and will make her desolate and naked, and will eat her flesh, and will burn her up in fire. 17. For God has put it into their hearts to carry out his purpose, to give their kingdom to the beast, until the words of God are accomplished. 18. And the woman whom thou sawest is the great city which has kingship over the kings of the earth."

CHAPTER 18. *The Fall of Babylon.*

And after this I saw another angel coming down from heaven, having great authority, and the earth was lighted up by his glory. 2. And he cried out with a mighty voice, saying, "She has fallen, she has fallen, Babylon the great; and has become a habitation of demons, a stronghold of every unclean spirit, a stronghold of every unclean and hateful bird; 3. because all the nations have drunk of the wrath of her immorality, and the kings of the earth have committed fornication with her, and by the power of her wantonness the merchants of the earth have grown rich."

Her Sins and Punishment.

4. And I heard another voice from heaven saying, "Go out from her, my people, that you may not share in her sins, and that you may not receive of her plagues. 5. For her sins have reached even to heaven, and the Lord has remembered her iniquities. 6. Render to her as she also has rendered, and give her the double according to her works; in the cup that she has mixed, mix for her double. 7. As much as she glorified herself and gave herself to wantonness, so much torment and mourning give to her. Because in her heart she says, 'I sit a queen, I am no widow, and I shall not see mourning.' 8. Therefore in one day her plagues shall come, death and mourning and famine; and she shall be burnt up in fire; for strong is God who will judge her."

Dirge of the Kings.

9. And the kings of the earth who with her committed fornication and lived wantonly will weep and mourn over her when they see the smoke of her burning, 10. standing afar off for fear of her torments, saying, "Woe, woe, the great city, Babylon, the strong city, for in one hour has thy judgment come!"

Dirge of the Merchants.

11. And the merchants of the earth will weep and mourn over her; for no one will buy their merchandise any more: 12. merchandise of gold and silver, and precious stones and pearls, and fine linen and purple, and silk and scarlet, and all thyine wood, and all vessels of ivory, and all vessels of precious stone, and of brass, and of iron, and of marble, 13. and cinnamon and amomum and spices, and ointment and frankincense, and wine and oil, and fine flour and wheat, and beasts of burden and sheep and horses, and chariots and slaves, and souls of men. 14. And the fruit which was the desire of thy soul departed from thee; and all the fat and splendid things perished from thee, and men will find them nevermore. 15. The merchants of these things, who grew rich by her, will stand afar off for fear of her torments, weeping and mourning, 16. and saying, "Woe, woe, the great city, which was clothed in fine linen and purple and scarlet, and gilded in gold, and precious stone, and pearls; 17. for in one hour riches so great were laid waste!"

Dirge of the Mariners.

And every shipmaster, and everyone who sails to a place, and mariners, and all who work upon the sea, stood afar off, 18. and cried out as they saw the place of her burning, saying, "What city is like to this great city?" 19. And they cast dust on their heads, and cried out weeping and mourning, saying, "Woe, woe, the great city, wherein all who had their ships at sea were made rich out of her wealth; for in one hour she has been laid waste!" 20. Make merry over her, O heaven, and you the saints and the apostles and the prophets, for God has judged your cause upon her.

The Angel's Promise.

21. And a strong angel took up a stone, as it were a great millstone, and cast it into the sea, saying, "With this violence will Babylon, the great city, be overthrown, and will not be found any more. 22. And the sound of harpers and musicians and flute-players and trumpet will not be heard in thee any more; and no craftsman of any craft will be found in thee any more; and sound of millstone will not be heard in thee any more. 23. And light of lamp will not shine in thee any more; and voice of bridegroom and of bride will not be heard in thee any more; because thy merchants were the great men of the earth, for by thy sorcery all the nations have been led astray. 24. And in her was found blood of prophets and of saints, and of all who have been slain upon the earth."

CHAPTER 19. *The Angelic Song.*

After these things I heard as it were a loud voice of a great crowd in heaven, saying, "Alleluia! salvation and glory and power belong to our God. 2. For true and just are his judgments, who has judged the great harlot who corrupted the earth with her fornication, and has avenged the blood of his servants at her hands." 3. And again they have said, "Alleluia! And the smoke of her goes up forever and ever." 4. And the twenty-four elders and the four living creatures fell down and worshipped God who sits on the throne, and they said, "Amen! Alleluia!" 5. And a voice came forth from the throne, saying, "Praise our God, all you his servants, and you who fear him, the small and the great!"

The Song of Triumph.

6. And I heard as it were a voice of a great crowd, and as the voice of many waters, and as the voice of mighty thunders, saying, "Alleluia! for the Lord, our God almighty, now reigns! 7. Let us be glad and rejoice, and give glory to him; for the marriage of the Lamb has come, and his spouse has prepared herself. 8. And she has been permitted to clothe herself in fine linen, shining, bright. For the fine linen is the just deeds of the saints."

9. And he said to me, "Write: Blessed are they who are called to the marriage supper of the Lamb." And he said to me, "These are true words of God." 10. And I fell down before his feet to worship him. And he said to me, "Thou must not do that. I am a fellow-servant of thine and of thy brethren who give the testimony of Jesus. Worship God! for the testimony of Jesus is the spirit of prophecy."

The Divine Warrior.

11. And I saw heaven standing open; and behold, a white horse, and he who sat upon it is called Faithful and True, and with justice he judges and wages war. 12. And his eyes are as a flame of fire, and on his head are many diadems; he has a name written which no man knows except himself. 13. And he is clothed in a garment sprinkled with blood, and his name is called The Word of God. 14. And the armies of heaven, clothed in fine linen, white and pure, were following him on white horses.

King of Kings and Lord of Lords.

15. And from his mouth goes forth a sharp sword with which to smite the nations. And he will rule them with a rod of iron, and he treads the wine press of the fierce wrath of God almighty. 16. And he has on his garment and on his thigh a name written, "King of kings and Lord of lords."

Defeat of the Beast and the False Prophet.

17. And I saw an angel standing in the sun, and he cried with a loud voice, saying to all the birds that fly in midheaven, "Come, gather yourselves together to the great supper of God, 18. that you may eat flesh of kings, and flesh of tribunes, and flesh of mighty men, and flesh of horses, and of those who sit upon them, and flesh of all men, free and bond, small and great."

19. And I saw the beast, and the kings of the earth and their armies gathered together to wage war against him who was sitting upon the horse, and against his army. 20. And the beast was seized, and with it the false prophet who did signs before it wherewith he deceived those who accepted the mark of the beast and who worshipped its image. These two were cast alive into the pool of fire that burns with brimstone. 21. And the rest were killed with the sword of him who sits upon the horse, the sword that goes forth out of his mouth; and all the birds were filled with their flesh.

REFERENCES

PREFACE

1. Press conference, April 25, 1956. *The New York Times*, April 26, 1956, 16. See also remarks of the President, June 12, 1959, concerning his hope of proposing a reorganization of "the very highest echelons of the executive departments" for the purpose of curing this deficiency. Department of State, *Bulletin*, July 6, 1959, 35.
2. Livingston T. Merchant, U. S. Ambassador to Canada, Department of State, *Bulletin*, February 18, 1957, 259.
3. Ernest A. Gross, deputy U.S. representative to the United Nations, Department of State, *Bulletin*, February 23, 1953, 321.
4. *Life*, January 16, 1956, 78; John R. Beal, *John Foster Dulles, A Biography*, New York, 1957, 177-84.
5. Press conference, August 11, 1954. *U.S. News & World Report*, August 20, 1954, 81.
6. Senator William F. Knowland to the Special Political Committee of the United Nations General Assembly. Department of State, *Bulletin*, March 18, 1957, 463.
7. Editorial, *The New York Times*, February 26, 1957, 28.
8. V. I. Lenin, *"Left-Wing" Communism, An Infantile Disorder*, as partly reproduced in *The Communist Conspiracy*, Part I, Section A, 136, 141-2: Committee on Un-American Activities, *The Communist Conspiracy: Strategy and Tactics of World Communism*, Part I (in five sections, A to E), House Reports Nos. 2240-2244, 84th Cong., 2d Sess., Washington, D.C., 1956.
9. *Time*, March 5, 1956, 27.
10. *Ibid.*
11. *Izvestia*, January 10, 1919, as quoted in a report of the Department of State to the Senate Committee on Foreign Relations October 27, 1919. *International Conciliation*, March, 1920, No. 148, 87.
12. H. S. Truman, Message to Congress, July 19, 1950. 96 *Cong. Rec.*, 10627.
13. Ephes. iv:6.
14. See statement of the Belgian delegate on resolution adopted by the Third Assembly (1922) with respect to Soviet aggression in the Trans-Caucasus. *Records of the Third Assembly, Plenary Meetings, 1922*, 203.

INTRODUCTION

1. Address, January 27, 1916. Sen. Doc. 260, 64th Cong., 1st Sess.
2. Address, October 26, 1916. *The New Democracy*, vol. II, 382: Ray Stannard

Baker and William E. Dodd, ed., *The Public Papers of Woodrow Wilson*, Part 2, *The New Democracy*, New York, 1926.

3. Secretary of State, 1953-59. News conference, April 24, 1956. Department of State, *Bulletin*, May 7, 1956, 749.

4. Department of State, *Bulletin*, December 21, 1947, 1213.

5. This phrase is from the Zimmerwald Program, to which Lenin was a signatory, adopted in 1915. See below.

6. Joint Resolution to Promote Peace and Stability in the Middle East. Department of State, *Bulletin*, March 25, 1957, 481.

7. Department of State, *Bulletin*, December 17, 1956, 945.

8. Address to the Supreme State Conference, February 27, 1957. *The New York Times*, June 19, 1957, 13.

9. Reply to Debate on the Political Report of the Central Committee to the Fifteenth Party Congress, December 7, 1927, reproduced in *The Communist Conspiracy*, Part I, Sec. B, 160.

10. *Nashi Politicheskiya Zadachi*, Geneva, 1904, p. 54, as quoted in *The Changing World of Soviet Russia*, 230n: David J. Dallin, *The Changing World of Soviet Russia*, New Haven, 1956.

11. *New International*, April, 1918, as quoted in *Revolutionary Radicalism*, Part I, vol. I, 223: Report of Joint Legislative Committee, *Revolutionary Radicalism*, Albany, 1920.

12. The Zimmerwald Program, as reproduced in *Revolutionary Radicalism*, Part I, vol. II, 1765.

13. Message to Congress, February 11, 1918. 56 *Cong. Rec.*, Part 2, 1952.

14. Declaration of Independence of the United States of America.

CHAPTER I—THE COLD WAR BEGINS

1. *"Left-Wing" Communism, An Infantile Disorder*, as partly reproduced in *The Communist Conspiracy*, Part I, Sec. A, 138.

2. *Foreign Relations, 1918, Russia*, vol. I, 28-9: *Papers Relating to the Foreign Relations of the United States, 1918, Russia* (in three volumes), Washington, D.C., 1931.

3. *Foreign Relations, 1918, Russia*, vol. I, 34.

4. *Foreign Relations, 1918, Russia*, vol. I, 45.

5. *Foreign Relations, 1918, Russia*, vol. I, 66.

6. *Foreign Relations, 1918, Russia*, vol. I, 80.

7. *Foreign Relations, 1918, Russia*, vol. I, 84.

8. *Foreign Relations, 1918, Russia*, vol. I, 104.

9. *Foreign Relations, 1918, Russia*, vol. I, 204.

10. *The Russian Revolution*, 497: N. N. Sukhanov, *The Russian Revolution, 1917* (abridged), London, 1955.

11. *Foreign Relations, 1918, Russia*, vol. I, 205.

12. *Stalin, A Political Biography*, 146-7: Isaac Deutscher, *Stalin, A Political Biography*, London, 1949.
13. *The Russian Revolution*, 441.
14. *The New York Times*, October 15, 1917, 3.
15. *Foreign Relations, 1918, Russia*, vol. I, 128.
16. *Foreign Relations, 1918, Russia*, vol. I, 140. New evidence regarding the amount and nature of German support for Bolshevik activities in Russia at this time has been made available as a result of the capture of secret German archives at the end of World War II. See Z. A. Zeman, ed., *Germany and the Revolution in Russia, 1915-1918*, London, 1958, in which pertinent German documents are published, and the discussion of this subject, based on the research of a group headed by Professor Stefan T. Possony of Georgetown University, in Alan Moorehead, *The Russian Revolution*, New York, 1958.
17. *Foreign Relations, 1918, Russia*, vol. I, 245.
18. *Foreign Relations, 1918, Russia*, vol. I, 240.
19. *Foreign Relations, 1918, Russia*, vol. I, 291.
20. I. N. Steinberg, *In the Workshop of the Revolution*, New York, 1953.
21. *Foreign Relations, 1918, Russia*, vol. I, 688.
22. *Foreign Relations, 1918, Russia*, vol. I, 684.

CHAPTER II—REVOLT SUPPRESSED

1. From speech delivered at meeting of nuclei secretaries of the Moscow organization of the Russian Communist Party (Bolsheviks), November 26, 1920, as partly reproduced in *The Communist Conspiracy*, Part I, Sec. B, 74.
2. *The Aftermath*, 266: Winston S. Churchill, *The Aftermath*, New York, 1929.
3. *Foreign Relations, 1920*, vol. III, 439-40: Department of State, *Papers Relating to the Foreign Relations of the United States, 1920* (three volumes) , Washington, D.C., 1935-6.
4. Notes of a meeting at the Paris Peace Conference, *Foreign Relations, 1919, Russia*, 345: Department of State, *Papers Relating to the Foreign Relations of the United States, 1919, Russia*, Washington, D.C., 1937.
5. Undated telegram from Prime Minister Derber to the Secretary of State, rec'd. April 6, 1918. *Foreign Relations, 1918, Russia*, vol. II, 101-2.
6. *Foreign Relations, 1918, Russia*, vol. II, 121.
7. *Foreign Relations, 1918, Russia*, vol. I, 495-6.
8. *Foreign Relations, 1918, Russia*, vol. I, 553. In the published reports, Pokrovsky's name is deleted. It appears in the original telegram, in the files of the State Department.
9. *Foreign Relations, 1918, Russia*, vol. I, 554-5.
10. Telegram of John A. Ray, U.S. consul at Odessa detailed to Tomsk, *Foreign Relations, 1918, Russia*, vol. II, 342-3.
11. *Foreign Relations, 1918, Russia*, vol. II, 33-4.

12. *Foreign Relations, 1918, Russia*, vol. II, 36.

13. *Foreign Relations, 1918, Russia*, vol. II, 42.

14. *Foreign Relations, 1918, Russia*, vol. I, 490, 495-6, 507, 521, 538, 558, 565; vol. II, 16, 53, 65, 165, 167, 191, 222, 243.

15. *Foreign Relations, 1918, Russia*, vol. II, 67, 82.

16. *Foreign Relations, 1918, Russia*, vol. II, 288-9. For full text see Appendix B-1.

17. *Foreign Relations, 1918, Russia*, vol. II, 288.

18. *Foreign Relations, 1918, Russia*, vol. II, 289.

19. *Foreign Relations, 1918, Russia*, vol. II, 262.

20. *Foreign Relations, 1918, Russia*, vol. II, 398.

21. *Foreign Relations, 1918, Russia*, vol. II, 398.

22. *Foreign Relations, 1918, Russia*, vol. II, 411.

23. Telegram dated March 26, 1919. *Foreign Relations, 1919, Russia*, 200-01.

24. *Foreign Relations, 1919, Russia*, 632-3.

25. Report of the U.S. *chargé d'affaires*, Felix Cole, *Foreign Relations, 1919, Russia*, 651.

26. *Foreign Relations, 1919, Russia*, 341-2.

27. *Foreign Relations, 1919, Russia*, 345-6.

28. *Foreign Relations, 1919, Russia*, 368.

29. *Foreign Relations, 1919, Russia*, 379.

30. *Foreign Relations, 1919, Russia*, 771-2.

31. *Foreign Relations, 1919, Russia*, 770-1.

32. *Foreign Relations, 1919, Russia*, 776.

33. *Foreign Relations, 1920*, vol. III. 609-10.

34. *Foreign Relations, 1920*, vol. III, 620.

35. *The Aftermath*, 266-70.

36. *Foreign Relations, 1919, Russia*, 345.

37. *Foreign Relations, 1919, Russia*, 637.

38. *Foreign Relations, 1920*, vol. III, 439-40.

39. *Foreign Relations, 1920*, vol. III, 444.

CHAPTER III—THE FIRST SOVIET "PEACE" CAMPAIGN

1. From speech delivered at meeting of nuclei secretaries of the Moscow organization of the Russian Communist Party (Bolsheviks), November 26, 1920, as partly reproduced in *The Communist Conspiracy*, Part I, Sec. B, 73.

2. Address to Congress, April 2, 1917, 55 *Cong. Rec.*, Part I, 119.

3. *Foreign Relations, 1917*, Supp. 2, vol. I, 72-3.

4. *Foreign Relations, 1918, Russia*, vol. I, 119. For full text see Appendix A.

5. *Woodrow Wilson: Selections for Today*, A. B. Tourtellot, ed., New York, 1945, 149.

6. *Ludendorff, Memoirs*, vol. II, 300: General Erich Ludendorff, *Ludendorff's Own Story*, New York, 1919 (two volumes).

7. DeWitt C. Poole, October 1, 1918, from Christiania en route to Archangel. *Foreign Relations, 1918, Russia*, vol. II, 643. Germany agreed, in fact, in a secret protocol, to "proceed with all the forces at its disposal against General Alexeyev," as well as against the Allied forces in north Russia if "Russian action" should "not be immediately successful." *Soviet Documents on Foreign Policy*, vol. I, 96-7: Jane Degras, ed., *Soviet Documents on Foreign Policy*, London, 1951 (three volumes).

8. *The Aftermath*, 267.

9. *The Communist Conspiracy*, Part I, Sec. B, 6-8.

10. *Foreign Relations, 1918, Russia*, vol. I, 253; *The Communist Conspiracy*, Part I, Sec. B, 9.

11. *The Communist Conspiracy*, Part I, Sec. B, 9-10.

12. *The Communist Conspiracy*, Part I, Sec. B, 12.

13. *The Lansing Papers*, vol. II, 343-4: Department of State, *Papers Relating to the Foreign Relations of the United States, The Lansing Papers, 1914-1920* (two volumes), Washington, D.C., 1940.

14. *The Lansing Papers*, vol. II, 345-6.

15. *Foreign Relations, 1918, Russia*, vol. I, 331.

16. *Foreign Relations, 1918, Russia*, vol. I, 405.

17. *Foreign Relations, 1918, Russia*, vol. I, 407.

18. *The Lansing Papers*, vol. II, 348.

19. *Foreign Relations, 1918, Russia*, vol. I, 330.

20. *Foreign Relations, 1918, Russia*, vol. I, 337.

21. George F. Kennan, *Russia Leaves the War*, Princeton, 1956, 385.

22. *Foreign Relations, 1918, Russia*, vol. I, 289, 319.

23. *Foreign Relations, 1918, Russia*, vol. I, 422.

24. *Foreign Relations, 1918, Russia*, vol. I, 381, 426.

25. *Foreign Relations, 1918, Russia*, vol. I, 296.

26. Department of State, *Bulletin*, July 15, 1957, 92.

27. *Foreign Relations, 1918, Russia*, vol. I, 395-6.

28. *Russian-American Relations, Documents and Papers*, 197: *Russian-American Relations, March 1917-March 1920, Documents and Papers*, comp. and ed. by C. K. Cumming and W. W. Pettit for the League of Free Nations Association, New York, 1920.

29. *Foreign Relations, 1918, Russia*, vol. II, 157.

30. *Foreign Relations, 1918, Russia*, vol. I, 399-400.

31. *Foreign Relations, 1918, Russia*, vol. I, 517-8.

32. *Russian-American Relations, Documents and Papers*, 204.

33. *Foreign Relations, 1918, Russia*, vol. I, 530-1.

34. *The Lansing Papers*, vol. II, 368.

35. *The Lansing Papers*, vol. II, 366-7.

36. *The Lansing Papers*, vol. II, 369.

37. *The Lansing Papers*, vol. II, 370.

38. *The Aftermath*, 83.

39. *The Lansing Papers*, vol. II, 366.
40. Such was the asserted position of the U. S. Ambassador, David Francis. *Foreign Relations, 1918, Russia*, vol. I, 531.
41. Memorandum of White House conference prepared by the Secretary of State, July 6, 1918. *Foreign Relations, 1918, Russia*, vol. II, 263.
42. *The Lansing Papers*, vol. II, 360.
43. Louis Fischer, *The Soviets in World Affairs*, vol. I, New York, 1930, 374, quoting *Pravda*, November 30, 1922.
44. *Russian-American Relations, Documents and Papers*, 261.
45. Wireless message addressed to the governments of Great Britain, France, Italy and the United States. *Russian-American Relations, Documents and Papers*, 268.
46. *Foreign Relations, 1919, Russia*, 1.
47. *Foreign Relations, 1919, Russia*, 15-16.
48. The Council of Ten was composed of President Wilson, Secretary of State Lansing, and the Prime Ministers and Foreign Secretaries of Great Britain, France, Italy and Japan. It was the dominating group at the Paris Peace Conference of 1919.
49. *The Paris Peace Conference*, vol. IV, 13.
50. *Current History*, vol. IX, Part 2, 272.
51. From secretary's notes at Paris Peace Conference, *Foreign Relations, 1919, Russia*, 12.
52. From secretary's notes at Paris Peace Conference, *Foreign Relations, 1919, Russia*, 14.
53. From secretary's notes at Paris Peace Conference, *Foreign Relations, 1919, Russia*, 22.
54. *Foreign Relations, 1919, Russia*, 23.
55. *Foreign Relations, 1919, Russia*, 24.
56. *Foreign Relations, 1919, Russia*, 31.
57. *Foreign Relations, 1919, Russia*, 38-9.
58. *Foreign Relations, 1919, Russia*, 45.
59. *Foreign Relations, 1919, Russia*, 60.
60. *Foreign Relations, 1919, Russia*, 57.
61. *Ibid.*
62. *Foreign Relations, 1919, Russia*, 58.
63. *Ibid.*
64. *Ibid.*
65. *Foreign Relations, 1919, Russia*, 78-80.
66. *Foreign Relations, 1919, Russia*, 77.
67. *Foreign Relations, 1919, Russia*, 109.
68. *Foreign Relations, 1919, Russia*, 114.
69. *Foreign Relations, 1919, Russia*, 110.
70. Hearings: *Treaty of Peace with Germany*, Foreign Relations Committee, U.S. Senate, S. Doc. 106, 66th Cong., 1st Sess., 1919, 1270.

CHAPTER IV—THE FIRST ROUND OF SOVIET AGGRESSION

1. *Foreign Relations, 1918, Russia,* vol. I, 213.

2. *The Communist Conspiracy,* Part I, Sec. B, 7.

3. *The Communist Conspiracy,* Part I, Sec. B, 7.

4. *Izvestia,* November 16, 1917. Translated in *Materials for the Study of the Soviet System,* 25-6: James H. Meisel and Edward S. Kozera, *Materials for the Study of the Soviet System* (second edition), Ann Arbor, 1953.

5. *The Communist Conspiracy,* Part I, Sec. B, 10-11.

6. Constitution of the R.S.F.S.R., Sec. I, Pars. 6 and 8. *Foreign Relations, 1918, Russia,* vol. I, 588-9.

7. *Foreign Relations, 1918, Russia,* vol. I, 417.

8. *Foreign Relations, 1918, Russia,* vol. I, 415.

9. *Belorussia, The Making of a Nation,* 98: Nicholas P. Vakar, *Belorussia, The Making of a Nation,* Cambridge, 1956.

10. *Foreign Relations, 1918, Russia,* vol. I, 348-9.

11. *Foreign Relations, 1918, Russia,* vol. I, 348.

12. *Foreign Relations, 1918, Russia,* vol. I, 442-3, 599-600.

13. *History of the Peace Conference,* vol. VI, 276: *A History of the Peace Conference of Paris,* ed. by H. W. V. Temperley and pub. under the auspices of the British Institute of International Affairs, in six volumes, London, 1924; *The Cambridge History of Poland,* Cambridge, 1941, 522-4; Robert Machray, *The Poland of Pilsudski,* London, 1936, 93.

14. Association Ukrainienne pour la Société des Nations, *Application of the Ukrainian Republic for Admission to the League of Nations,* Paris, 1930, 14-15.

15. Published in *Izvestia,* December 19, 1917. Text as translated in *The Russian Revolution,* vol. I, 486-8: William Henry Chamberlin, *The Russian Revolution, 1917-21,* in two volumes, New York, 1935, and *Communist Takeover and Occupation of the Ukraine,* 8: Select Committee on Communist Aggression, Special Report No. 4, House Report No. 2684, Part 7, 83rd. Cong., 2d Sess., 1955.

16. *Experience with Russia,* 48: Vasyl Hryshko, *Experience with Russia,* New York, 1956.

17. Published in *Izvestia,* December 30, 1917. Text as translated in *The Russian Revolution,* vol. I, 490.

18. *History of the Peace Conference,* vol. I, 226-7.

19. *Experience with Russia,* 58.

20. *Foreign Relations, 1918, Russia,* vol. I, 443.

21. *Foreign Relations, 1918, Russia,* vol. I, 602.

22. *Papers Relating to the Foreign Relations of the United States, 1917,* Supp. 2, vol. I, Washington, D.C., 1932, 792-4.

23. *Memorandum Presented Officially by the Representatives of Armenia to the Peace Conference at Versailles, on February 26, 1919,* executed at Paris February 12 by A. Aharonian, president of the Delegation of the Armenian Republic to the Peace Conference, and by Boghos Nubar, president of the Armenian National Delegation.

24. *Petition to His Excellency Woodrow Wilson, President of the United States of America, by the American Committee for the Independence of Armenia, Signed by 20,000 Protestant Rectors and Ministers and Catholic Priests in Favor of the Independence of Integral Armenia, Presented at the White House, March, 1919, Washington, D.C.* Eventually 25,000 signatures were actually obtained.
25. *59 Cong. Rec.* Part 8, 7886.
26. *59 Cong. Rec.* Part 8, 7886.
27. S. J. Res. 106, 66th Cong., 1st Sess., *58 Cong. Rec.*, Part 7, 7052.
28. *The Lausanne Treaty—Turkey and Armenia*, 117: The American Committee Opposed to the Lausanne Treaty, *The Lausanne Treaty—Turkey and Armenia*, New York, 1926.
29. *The Paris Peace Conference*, vol. VII, 648.
30. *The Paris Peace Conference*, vol. IX, 857.
31. *59 Cong. Rec.*, Part 7, 6978.
32. *Communist Takeover and Occupation of Georgia*, 8: Select Committee on Communist Aggression, Special Report No. 6, House Report No. 2684, Pt. 9, 83rd Cong., 2d Sess., 1954. Italics omitted.
33. *59 Cong. Rec.*, Part 7, 7533-4.
34. *59 Cong. Rec.*, Part 8, 7968.
35. *59 Cong. Rec.*, Part 8, 8060.
36. Arthur Balfour. *Records of the First Assembly, Plenary Meetings, 1920*, 189.
37. *Records of the First Assembly, Plenary Meetings, 1920*, 187.
38. League of Nations, *Official Journal*, No. 8, Nov.-Dec., 1920, 90.
39. League of Nations, *Official Journal*, No. 8, Nov.-Dec., 1920, 92-103.
40. See Alexander G. Park, *Bolshevism in Turkestan*, New York, 1957; Walter Kolarz, *Russia and Her Colonies*, New York, 1953; Olaf Caroe, *Soviet Empire*, London, 1953, 95-130; Walter Kolarz, *The Peoples of the Soviet Far East*, New York, 1954.
41. *Records of the First Assembly, Plenary Meetings, 1920*, 590.
42. *Records of the First Assembly, Plenary Meetings, 1920*, 629.
43. *Records of the First Assembly, Plenary Meetings, 1920*, 631.
44. *Records of the First Assembly, Plenary Meetings, 1920*, 633.
45. *Records of the First Assembly, Plenary Meetings, 1920*, 633.
46. *Records of the Third Assembly, Plenary Meetings, 1922*, 102.
47. *Records of the Third Assembly, Plenary Meetings, 1922*, 203.
48. *Records of the Third Assembly, Plenary Meetings, 1922*, 203.

CHAPTER V—FROM WAR TO "PEACE"

1. Speech delivered at a meeting of nuclei secretaries of the Moscow organization of the Russian Communist Party (Bolsheviks), November 26, 1920, as partly reproduced in *The Communist Conspiracy*, Part I, Sec. B, 73.
2. *Id., The Communist Conspiracy*, Part I, Sec. B, 74.
3. Report of the Central Committee to the 20th Congress of the Communist Party, February, 1956, as reproduced in *Current Soviet Policies, II*, 55, 60, 62: Leo Gruliow, ed., *Current Soviet Policies, II*, New York, 1957.

4. Speech at meeting of nuclei secretaries, November 26, 1920, *The Communist Conspiracy*, Part I, Sec. B, 74.

5. From secretary's notes at Paris Peace Conference. *Foreign Relations, 1919, Russia*, 23. There were reports of such trouble among the British, French and American troops in north Russia (see *id.*, 620-621) and among the French troops in the south. It should be noted that while the Prime Minister here refers to the "fight against the Russians," the use of Allied troops was actually designed to help them. This failure to make a distinction between the people and their oppressors—in fact a transfer of the national designation from the former to the latter—continues to be a source of irritation and discouragement to all real Russians. See N. N. Krasnov, Jr., *The Hidden Russia*, New York, 1960, 323, 327.

6. From secretary's notes at Paris Peace Conference. *Foreign Relations, 1919, Russia*, 14.

7. Minutes of Session of the Supreme War Council. *Foreign Relations, 1919, Russia*, 57.

8. See *Origin of Communist Autocracy*, 302: Leonard Schapiro, *The Origin of Communist Autocracy*, Cambridge, 1955; and *Our Secret Allies*, 125: Eugene Lyons, *Our Secret Allies, The Peoples of Russia*, New York, 1954.

9. V. I. Lenin, speech delivered at a meeting of nuclei secretaries of the Moscow organization of the Russian Communist Party (Bolsheviks), November 26, 1920, as partly reproduced in *The Communist Conspiracy*, Part I, Sec. B, 75.

10. *Id., The Communist Conspiracy*, Part I, Sec. B, 73.

11. *Id., The Communist Conspiracy*, Part I, Sec. B, 75.

12. *The Lansing Papers*, vol. II, 367.

13. *The Communist*, official organ of the Communist Party of America, April, 1921, as reproduced in *The Communist Conspiracy*, Part I, Sec. B, 81.

14. *Luther v. Sagor and Co.*, [1921] 3 K.B. 532, cited by Hackworth, vol. I, 135-6: Green H. Hackworth, *Digest of International Law*, Washington, D.C., 1940.

15. *U. S. v. Belmont*, 301 U.S. 324 (1937), cited by Hackworth, vol. I, 136-7.

16. State Department, *Bulletin*, July 1, 1957, 14.

17. Agreement with W. A. Harriman & Co., June, 1925.

18. U.S. Dept. of Commerce, *International Reference Service*, vol. II, No. 8, June, 1945, 2.

19. *Soviet Economic Development and American Business*, 58: Saul G. Bron, *Soviet Economic Development and American Business*, New York, 1930.

20. *Soviet Economic Development and American Business*, 58.

21. *The New York Times*, May 27, 1931, 8.

22. *Handbook of the Soviet Union*, 347, 361-9: American-Russian Chamber of Commerce, *Handbook of the Soviet Union*, New York, 1936.

23. *Handbook of the Soviet Union*, 364.

24. Anastas I. Mikoyan. *The New York Times*, January 9, 1959, 4.

25. *Handbook of the Soviet Union*, 352.

26. *Handbook of the Soviet Union*, 361-2.

27. *Foreign Relations, The Soviet Union, 1933-1939*, 194: Department of State,

Foreign Relations of the United States, Diplomatic Papers, The Soviet Union, 1933-1939, Washington, D.C., 1952.

28. *The New York Times,* February 6, 1931, 12.
29. *The Communist Conspiracy,* Part I, Sec. B, 267.
30. *The New York Times,* June 19, 1933, 6.
31. *The New York Times,* May 8, 1955, 18.
32. *The Red Army,* 61: B. H. Liddell Hart, ed., *The Red Army,* New York, 1956.
33. *Foreign Relations, The Soviet Union, 1933-1939,* 620.
34. *The New York Times Magazine,* July 19, 1936, 3.
35. From address made at the Metropolitan Opera House, New York City, April 11, 1933, under the auspices of the Academy of Political Science. *The New York Times,* April 12, 1933, 14-15.
36. *Ibid.*
37. *Foreign Relations, The Soviet Union, 1933-1939,* 883, 885.
38. *Foreign Relations, The Soviet Union, 1933-1939,* 891-2.
39. 21st Report to Congress on Lend-Lease Operations, period ended September 30, 1945, 24.
40. *Foreign Relations, The Soviet Union, 1933-1939,* 745.
41. *The Paris Peace Conference,* vol. IV, 13.
42. *The Communist Conspiracy,* Part I, Sec. B, 396.
43. *The New York Times,* July 7, 1957, 1.
44. *The Communist Conspiracy,* Part I, Sec. B, 73, 74.

CHAPTER VI—ADVENT OF WORLD WAR II

1. V. I. Lenin, speech delivered at a meeting of nuclei secretaries of the Moscow organization of the Russian Communist Party (Bolsheviks), November 26, 1920, as partly reproduced in *The Communist Conspiracy,* Part I, Sec. B, 72.
2. Theses and Statutes of the Third (Communist) International, adopted by the Second Congress, July 17-August 7, 1920, as reproduced in *The Communist Conspiracy,* Part I, Sec. C, 67.
3. Political Report of the Central Committee to the 15th Congress of the Communist Party, as partly reproduced in *The Communist Conspiracy,* Part I, Sec. B, 135.
4. *Pravda,* editorial, January 21, 1939. *Foreign Relations, The Soviet Union, 1933-1939,* 733.
5. *Pravda,* January 21, 1939. *Foreign Relations, The Soviet Union, 1933-1939,* 734.
6. *Foreign Relations, The Soviet Union, 1933-1939,* 733.
7. Report to the 18th Congress of the Communist Party, as partly reproduced in *The Communist Conspiracy,* Part I, Sec. B, 393.
8. *Foreign Relations, The Soviet Union, 1933-1939,* 739-40.
9. *British Foreign Policy,* Third Series, vol. IV, 419: *Documents on British Foreign Policy, 1919-1939* (in three series), H. M. Stationery Office, London.

10. *British Foreign Policy*, Third Series, vol. IV, 449.

11. *British Foreign Policy*, Third Series, vol. IV, 612.

12. *British Foreign Policy*, Third Series, vol. V, 802.

13. *Foreign Relations, The Soviet Union, 1933-1939*, 774.

14. *British Foreign Policy*, Third Series, vol. V, 351.

15. *Foreign Relations, 1939*, vol. I, 267: Department of State, *Foreign Relations of the United States, Diplomatic Papers, 1939* (volumes 1 to 4 published), Washington, D.C., 1955-6.

16. *Foreign Relations, 1939*, vol. I, 268.

17. *British Foreign Policy*, Third Series, vol. VI, 161.

18. *British Foreign Policy*, Third Series, vol. VII, 609.

19. *Documents on German Foreign Policy*, Series D, vol. VII, 246-7: Department of State, *Documents on German Foreign Policy, 1918-1945* (Series D, ten volumes published), Washington, D.C., 1949.

20. *Foreign Relations, 1939*, vol. I, 343.

21. *The New York Times*, October 2, 1939, 6.

22. House of Lords, vol. 114, 1566.

23. *The Undeclared War*, 124: Wm. L. Langer and S. Everett Gleason, *The Undeclared War, 1940-1941*, New York, 1953.

24. *Cordell Hull, Memoirs*, vol. I, 702, 707, see also 743, 745: *The Memoirs of Cordell Hull* (in two volumes), New York, 1948.

25. *Cordell Hull, Memoirs*, vol. I, 707.

26. *British Foreign Policy*, Third Series, vol. V, 35.

27. *British Foreign Policy*, Third Series, vol. V, 47.

28. Command Papers (Session 1944-5) No. 6616, Poland No. 1, 1945, H. M. Stationery Office, London, 1945.

29. *Foreign Relations, 1939*, vol. I, 420.

30. *Foreign Relations, 1939*, vol. I, 437.

31. From report of the American Ambassador in Moscow. *Foreign Relations, 1939*, vol. I, 432-3.

32. *Foreign Relations, 1939*, vol. I, 345.

33. Address to the Supreme Soviet, August 31, 1939. *The Communist Conspiracy*, Part I, Sec. B, 410.

34. *Documents on German Foreign Policy*, Series D, vol. VIII, 4.

35. *Documents on German Foreign Policy*, Series D, vol. VIII, 35.

36. *Documents on German Foreign Policy*, Series D, vol. VIII, 34.

37. *Documents on German Foreign Policy*, Series D, vol. VIII, 44.

38. *Documents on German Foreign Policy*, Series D, vol. VIII, 61.

39. *Documents on German Foreign Policy*, Series D, vol. VIII, 69.

40. *Documents on German Foreign Policy*, Series D, vol. VIII, 77.

41. *Documents on German Foreign Policy*, Series D, vol. VIII, 77.

42. *Polish Documents Report*, 2: Select Committee on Communist Aggression, *Appendix to Committee Report on Communist Takeover and Occupation of Poland*, House Report No. 2684, Pt. 4, 82nd Cong., 2d Sess., 1955.

43. *Documents on German Foreign Policy*, Series D, vol. VIII, 166.

44. *Documents on German Foreign Policy*, Series D, vol. VIII, 199.

45. Cordell Hull, *Memoirs*, 701.

46. *Foreign Relations, The Soviet Union, 1933-1939*, 968; see also *Documents on German Foreign Policy*, Series D, vol. VIII, 212-14.

47. *Nazi-Soviet Relations*, 121-2; Department of State, *Nazi-Soviet Relations, 1939-1941*, Washington, D.C., 1948.

48. Cordell Hull, *Memoirs*, 702-3. Text of the message is published in *Foreign Relations, 1939*, vol. I, 967.

49. *Foreign Relations, 1939*, vol. I, 967.

50. *Foreign Relations, 1939*, vol. I, 975.

51. *Foreign Relations, The Soviet Union, 1933-1939*, 799.

52. Cordell Hull, *Memoirs*, 707, 741.

53. Mannerheim, *Memoirs*, 396: *The Memoirs of Marshal Mannerheim*, New York, 1954.

54. *Forced Incorporation of the Baltic States*, 243, 291, 332-3, 392-3: Select Committee on Communist Aggression, *Third Interim Report*, 83rd Cong., 2d Sess., 1954.

55. Department of State, *Bulletin*, July 27, 1940, 48.

56. *Nazi-Soviet Relations*, 257.

57. *Nazi-Soviet Relations*, 252.

58. *The Communist Conspiracy*, Part I, Sec. B, 73.

59. *Nazi-Soviet Relations*, 254.

60. *Nazi-Soviet Relations*, 240.

61. *Nazi-Soviet Relations*, 258-9.

62. *The New York Times*, February 11, 1940, 44.

CHAPTER VII—THE WINNING OF WORLD WAR II

1. *The New York Times*, June 23, 1941, 10; *The Communist Conspiracy*, Part I, Sec. B, 411.

2. *The New York Times*, June 23, 1941, 10; *The Communist Conspiracy*, Part I, Sec. B, 412.

3. *The Gathering Storm*, 365: Winston S. Churchill, *The Second World War, The Gathering Storm*, Boston, 1948.

4. *The New York Times*, June 23, 1941, 8.

5. *The Communist Conspiracy*, Part I, Sec. B, 410.

6. *The Grand Alliance*, 462-3: Winston S. Churchill, *The Second World War, The Grand Alliance*, Boston, 1950.

7. *The Grand Alliance*, 456.

8. *The Grand Alliance*, 383.

9. *The Communist Conspiracy*, Part I, Sec. B, 393, 396.

10. *The Undeclared War*, 558.

11. *Roosevelt and Hopkins*, 342-3: Robert E. Sherwood, *Roosevelt and Hopkins, An Intimate History*, New York, 1948.

12. *The Soviet Partisan Movement,* 61, 110: Department of the Army, Pamphlet No. 20-244, *The Soviet Partisan Movement, 1941-1944,* Washington, D.C., 1956. Statement of Dr. Otto Braeutigam, *Nazi Conspiracy and Aggression,* vol. III, 243: Office of the U.S. chief of counsel for prosecution of Axis criminality, *Nazi Conspiracy and Aggression* (eight volumes and two supplements), Washington, D.C., 1946-8.

13. N. S. Khrushchev, Secret Address to 20th Congress, Communist Party, *U.S. News and World Report,* June 15, 1956, 163.

14. *Documents on American Foreign Relations,* IV, 216: World Peace Foundation, *Documents on American Foreign Relations,* Boston, 1938 to date.

15. *Ibid.*

16. *Documents on American Foreign Relations,* IV, 615-6.

17. See Polish-Soviet Agreement signed in London, July 30, 1941. *Polish Documents Report,* 6-7.

18. Military agreement between the Polish and Soviet high commands, August 14, 1941. *Polish Documents Report,* 8-9.

19. Department of State, *Bulletin,* February 13, 1943, 146.

20. Department of State, *Bulletin,* April 3, 1943, 273-4.

21. Address, April 4, 1943. Department of State, *Bulletin,* April 10, 1943, 292-3.

22. *Katyn Hearings,* Part 7, 2079: Select Committee to Conduct an Investigation and Study of the Facts, Evidence, and Circumstances of the Katyn Forest Massacre, *Hearings,* House of Representatives, 82d Cong., 2d Sess., Washington, D.C., 1952.

23. *Polish Documents Report,* 52.

24. Paraphrase of report, April 28, 1943. *Katyn Hearings,* Part 7, 2068.

25. *Katyn Hearings,* Final Report, 3: House Report No. 2505, 82d Cong., 2d Sess., Washington, D.C., 1952.

26. *Katyn Hearings,* Final Report, 11.

27. *Yalta Papers,* 450: Department of State, *Foreign Relations of the United States, Diplomatic Papers, The Conferences at Malta and Yalta, 1945,* Washington, D.C., 1955.

28. Letter, May 31, 1945, to the Secretary of State, signed by John M. Coffee, Hugh De Lacy, Vito Marcantonio, William J. Greene, Jr., Ellis E. Patterson, A. J. Sabath, Samuel Dickstein, Cleveland M. Bailey, Luther Patrick, Emanuel Celler, Samuel A. Weiss, and E. H. Hedrick. Department of State, *Bulletin,* July 8, 1945, 49-50.

29. Department of State, *Bulletin,* July 8, 1945, 51.

30. Department of State, *Bulletin,* May 27, 1945, 950-52.

31. *Vandenberg Papers,* 185-6: Arthur H. Vandenberg, Jr., ed., *The Private Papers of Senator Vandenberg,* Boston, 1952.

32. *Documents on British Foreign Policy,* Third Series, vol. IV, 528.

33. *Documents on British Foreign Policy,* Third Series, vol. IV, 492.

34. *Documents on British Foreign Policy,* Third Series, vol. IV, 492.

35. *The New York Times*, October 2, 1939, 6.
36. *The Undeclared War*, 795.
37. Department of State, *Bulletin*, June 28, 1941, 755.
38. State of the Union Message, January 7, 1943. *Cong. Rec.*, vol. 89, Part I, 48.
39. *The New York Times*, June 23, 1941, 8.
40. *The New York Times*, May 25, 1944, 13.
41. Department of State, *Bulletin*, September 5, 1942, 731.
42. Department of State, *Bulletin*, April 10, 1943, 291.
43. *Triumph and Tragedy*, 111-2: Winston S. Churchill, *The Second World War, Triumph and Tragedy*, Boston, 1953.
44. Department of State, *Bulletin*, September 10, 1944, 253.
45. Department of State, *Bulletin*, February 29, 1948, 273.
46. *Triumph and Tragedy*, 292-3.
47. *Triumph and Tragedy*, 300.
48. *Triumph and Tragedy*, 295.
49. Adopted January 1, 1942. Department of State, Publication No. 4245, 3.
50. These declarations are published in Department of State Publication No. 4245, 6-9, 10-12.
51. Department of State, Publication No. 2297.
52. *The Communist Conspiracy*, Part I, Sec. B, 73.
53. State Department press release, March 8, 1946. Department of State, *Bulletin*, March 17, 1946, 443-4.
54. Administrative Memorandum Number 39 (Revised 16 April, 1945) Supreme Headquarters Allied Expeditionary Force, Sec. 23 (c). Reproduced in *European Refugees*, 445-69: Malcolm J. Proudfoot, *European Refugees: 1939-52, A Study in Forced Population Movement*, Evanston, 1956.
55. *Id.*, Sec. 30 (a).
56. Plan for the delivery through the Army Lines of Former Prisoners of War and Civilians Liberated by the Red Army and the Allied Forces, Approved May 22, 1945, par. (1). Reproduced in *European Refugees*, 208-210.
57. *Crusade in Europe*, 484: Dwight D. Eisenhower, *Crusade in Europe*, Permabooks Edition, 1952.
58. *European Refugees*, 215.
59. *Crusade in Europe*, 485; *European Refugees*, 217.
60. *European Refugees*, 217.
61. *European Refugees*, 217-8.
62. *Documents on American Foreign Relations*, III, 33.
63. Department of State, *Bulletin*, February 28, 1942, 188.
64. Department of State, *Bulletin*, February 13, 1943, 145.
65. Department of State, *Bulletin*, February 13, 1943, 148.
66. Address to White House Correspondents Association, February 12, 1943. Department of State, *Bulletin*, February 13, 1943, 145.
67. *U. S. News and World Report*, June 15, 1956, 163.

CHAPTER VIII—THIRD ROUND OF SOVIET AGGRESSION

1. *League of Nations Official Journal*, 1938, 341.

2. Address at Seventh Moscow Congress of the Communist International, *Foreign Relations, The Soviet Union, 1933-1939*, 237.

3. *Communist Takeover and Occupation of Poland*, 18-19: Select Committee on Communist Aggression, Special Report No. 1, House Report No. 2684, Pt. 3, 83rd Cong., 2d Sess., 1954.

4. Josef Swiatlo. Select Committee on Communist Aggression, *Sixth Interim Report of Hearings*, House of Representatives, 83rd Cong., 2d Sess., Washington, D.C., 1954, 120, 143; *id., Tenth Interim Report of Hearings*, 41, 51.

5. *Yalta Papers*, 265.

6. *Closing the Ring*, 404: Winston S. Churchill, *The Second World War, Closing the Ring*, Boston, 1951.

7. *Yalta Papers*, 256.

8. *Yalta Papers*, 262.

9. *Ibid.*

10. *Yalta Papers*, 265.

11. *Ibid.*

12. *Triumph and Tragedy*, 227.

13. *Triumph and Tragedy*, 233.

14. The text of the armistice agreements is contained in Dept. of State Executive Agreement Series Nos. 437, 456 and 490.

15. Yalta Conference Briefing Book Paper, *American Position on Allied Control Commissions in Rumania, Bulgaria and Hungary, Yalta Papers*, 238.

16. *Yalta Papers*, 245, 247; Cordell Hull, *Memoirs*, vol. II, 1454.

17. *Yalta Papers*, 245, 247.

18. *Yalta Papers*, 238-9, 247.

19. *Yalta Papers*, 241.

20. *Yalta Papers*, 239.

21. Annex I to Potsdam Protocol, Dept. of State Publication 4245, 37-8.

22. Statements made by James F. Byrnes and President H. S. Truman. Department of State, *Bulletin*, March 16, 1947, 487; June 22, 1947, 1214. For other official comment and protests regarding the operation of the Allied Control Commissions, see Department of State, *Bulletin*, November 3, 1946, 820-1; March 16, 1947, 495; March 30, 1947, 583-4; June 15, 1947, 1161; June 22, 1947, 1215-6; June 6, 1948, 740-2.

23. Article 15 of the armistice agreement with Rumania.

24. *Yalta Papers*, 65.

25. *Yalta Papers*, 241-2.

26. *Communist Takeover and Occupation of Bulgaria*, 9: Select Committee on Communist Aggression, Special Report No. 7, House Report No. 2684, Pt. 10, 83rd Cong., 2d Sess., 1955.

27. *Yalta Papers*, 248.

28. *Ibid.*

29. Selden Chapin, U. S. Minister to Hungary July, 1947-May, 1949. Department of State, *Bulletin,* June 26, 1949, 821.

30. *Yalta Papers,* 973-4, 984.

31. *Yalta Papers,* 980.

32. *Yalta Papers,* 257.

33. Department of State, *Bulletin,* December 23, 1945, 1021.

34. *Yalta Papers,* 980.

35. *I Saw Poland Betrayed,* 118: Arthur Bliss Lane, *I Saw Poland Betrayed,* New York, 1948.

36. *Communist Takeover and Occupation of Poland,* 26.

37. *News from Behind the Iron Curtain,* August, 1956, 9-10.

38. Dept. of State Publication No. 4245, 27.

39. *The New York Times,* May 18, 1954, 1, 9.

40. Hearings August 10, 1954, Internal Security Subcommittee, U.S. Senate, 83rd Cong. 2d Sess., *Interlocking Subversion in Government Departments,* Pt. 21, 1656; Mark W. Clark, *Calculated Risk,* New York, 1950, 367-72; Michael Balfour and John Mair, *Four-Power Control in Germany and Austria 1945-1946,* London, 1956, 295-6.

41. *Crusade in Europe,* 317.

42. Churchill, *Triumph and Tragedy,* 61-4, 721-3.

43. *Yalta Papers,* 97-100.

44. *Yalta Papers,* 569.

45. *Roosevelt and the Russians,* 89: Edward R. Stettinius, Jr., *Roosevelt and the Russians, The Yalta Conference,* Garden City, 1949.

46. *Roosevelt and the Russians,* 89; *Yalta Papers,* 569-70.

47. Department of State, *Bulletin,* October 7, 1945, 509.

48. Department of State, *Bulletin,* vol. 13, 654; 92 *Cong. Rec.* 138.

49. Department of State, *Bulletin,* July 22, 1945, 110.

50. Department of State, *Bulletin,* August 26, 1945, 281.

51. Department of State, *Bulletin,* August 19, 1945, 274.

52. Department of State, *Bulletin,* November 18, 1945, 792.

53. Report of the Meeting of the Ministers of Foreign Affairs of the U.S.S.R., the U.S., the U.K., December 16-26, 1945, Sections V and VI. Department of State, *Bulletin,* December 30, 1945, 1031.

54. Department of State, *Bulletin,* December 30, 1945, 1034.

55. Harry Truman, *Memoirs,* vol. I, 551-2: Harry S. Truman, *Year of Decisions, Volume I of Memoirs by Harry S. Truman,* Garden City, 1955.

56. Department of State, *Bulletin,* June 9, 1946, 1008.

57. Department of State, *Bulletin,* November 24, 1946, 967.

58. Department of State, *Bulletin,* November 3, 1946, 821.

59. Department of State, *Bulletin,* December 23, 1945, 1021.

60. From text of note which the U.S. representative on the Allied Control Commission for Hungary was instructed to deliver to the Soviet chairman, June,

1947. Department of State, *Bulletin,* June 22, 1947, 1215-6.

61. Department of State, press release, January 28, 1947. *The Strategy and Tactics of World Communism,* Report of Subcommittee No. 5, Committee on Foreign Affairs, House of Representatives, 80th Cong., 2d Sess., Washington, D.C., 1948, Supp. II, 72.
62. Joint Declaration, U.S., U.K., France, February 26, 1948. Department of State, *Bulletin,* March 7, 1948, 304.
63. Department of State, *Bulletin,* August 31, 1947, 410.
64. *Communist Takeover and Occupation of Albania,* 12: Select Committee on Communist Aggression, Special Report No. 13, House Report No. 2684, Pt. 2, 83rd Cong. 2d Sess., 1954.
65. *News from Behind the Iron Curtain,* January, 1956, 27.
66. Department of State, *Bulletin,* August 19, 1945, 274.
67. For full texts of the peace treaties, see *United States Code and Congressional Service,* 1947, 2429 (Hungary), 2407 (Bulgaria), 2455 (Rumania).
68. Department of State, *Bulletin,* June 22, 1947, 1214.
69. Department of State, *Bulletin,* February 10, 1946, 209.
70. Department of State, *Bulletin,* September 1, 1946, 423.
71. Department of State, *Bulletin,* January 19, 1947, 134.
72. Department of State, press release, January 28, 1947.
73. *I Saw Poland Betrayed,* 301.
74. *Ibid.*
75. Department of State, *Bulletin,* June 9, 1946, 1008.
76. Department of State, *Bulletin,* November 10, 1946, 851.
77. Department of State, *Bulletin,* July 6, 1947, 38.
78. Department of State, *Bulletin,* August 17, 1947, 329.
79. Department of State, *Bulletin,* February 15, 1948, 216-7.
80. Department of State, *Bulletin,* August 24, 1947, 392-3.
81. Department of State, *Bulletin,* June 26, 1949, 821.
82. Department of State, *Bulletin,* March 7, 1948, 304.
83. Department of State, *Bulletin,* April 25, 1948, 536-9.
84. Department of State, *Bulletin,* April 21, 1946, 669-70.
85. Department of State, *Bulletin,* October 5, 1947, 702.
86. Quoted from Michael Padev, *Dimitrov Wastes No Bullets,* 153, by Robert Lee Wolff, *The Balkans in Our Time,* Cambridge, 1956, 302-3.

CHAPTER IX—THE FOURTH ROUND OF SOVIET AGGRESSION

1. See Brookings Institution, *Major Problems of U.S. Foreign Policy, 1954,* Washington, D.C., 1954, 185.
2. See letter dated April 18, 1955 from Ass't. Sec. of State Thruston B. Morton to the chairman of the House Committee on Foreign Affairs. House Report 746, Part 2, 84th Cong., 1st Sess., June 14, 1955, *Minority Views* [to accompany H. Res. 183].

3. United Nations Charter, Chap. I, Art. 1, par. 1.

4. *Records of the First Assembly, Plenary Meetings, 1920,* 633.

5. *Review of the U.N. Charter,* Part 12, 1620: *Review of the United Nations Charter,* Hearings before subcommittee of Committee on Foreign Relations, U.S. Senate, 84th Cong., 1st Sess., 13 parts, 1954-55.

6. Department of State, *Bulletin,* Supplement, May 4, 1947, 387, 850.

7. Department of State, *Bulletin,* June 21, 1954, 937.

8. Department of State, *Bulletin,* May 7, 1956, 742.

9. Department of State, *Bulletin,* Supplement, May 4, 1947, 850.

10. In January, 1957, a court of West Berlin ruled against the claim of "Anna Anderson," after 16 years of litigation. The case was revived in a new proceeding in Hamburg, in 1958. *The New York Times,* April 2, 1958, 3. See also *I Am Anastasia, The Autobiography of the Grand-Duchess of Russia,* with notes by Roland Krug von Nidda, New York, 1959.

11. Department of State, *Bulletin,* July 5, 1954, 26-32. The Organ of Consultation here referred to is the agency provided under the Rio Pact to determine what collective measures shall be taken to resist aggression against a member state. The same pact provides that until the decision of this body, each member "may determine the immediate measures which it may individually take in fulfillment of the *obligation*" (italics added) to "assist in meeting the attack."

12. *War or Peace,* 43-44: John F. Dulles, *War or Peace,* New York, 1950.

13. *Petrogradskaia Pravda,* July 15, 1920, as quoted in *Soviet Russia and The East,* 180: Eudin and North, *Soviet Russia and The East, 1920-1927,* Stanford, 1957.

14. A. Sultan-Zade, *Persiia,* 86, as quoted in *Soviet Russia and The East,* 100.

15. Georgi V. Chicherin in *Pravda,* November 6, 1921, as quoted in *Soviet Russia and The East,* 100.

16. *Soviet Russia and The East,* 100.

17. Quoted in *The Persian Corridor and Aid to Russia,* 471-2: Department of the Army, *The Persian Corridor and Aid to Russia,* volume in Series, *The United States Army in World War II,* Washington, D.C., 1952.

18. Yalta Conference briefing paper on Iran. *Yalta Papers,* 343.

19. *The Persian Corridor and Aid to Russia,* 27.

20. *Yalta Papers,* 337.

21. Churchill to "Colleagues in London," October 12, 1944. *Triumph and Tragedy,* 233-4.

22. Briefing book paper on "Reconstruction of Poland and the Balkans," *Yalta Papers,* 235.

23. *Roosevelt and Hopkins,* 559: Robert E. Sherwood, *Roosevelt and Hopkins,* New York, 1948.

24. *The Persian Corridor and Aid to Russia,* 157.

25. *War or Peace,* 44.

26. *The Persian Corridor and Aid to Russia,* 479.

27. Department of State, *Bulletin,* August 10, 1953, 178.

28. *The New York Times,* September 14, 1954, 6; September 17, 1954, 5.

29. *Triumph and Tragedy*, 292.

30. U.N. Doc. S/360, vol. I, 167.

31. Department of State, *Bulletin*, Supplement, December 7, 1947, 1121.

32. Message to Congress, March 12, 1947. Department of State, *Bulletin*, Supplement, May 4, 1947, 830.

33. Department of State, *Bulletin*, Supplement, May 4, 1947, 837.

34. Department of State, *Bulletin*, February 29, 1948, 274.

35. Issued February 26, 1948. Department of State, *Bulletin*, March 7, 1948, 304.

36. Letter dated February 26, 1948 from the Secretary of State, George C. Marshall, to the President Pro Tempore of the Senate, Arthur H. Vandenberg, Department of State, *Bulletin*, March 7, 1948, 298-9.

37. *The New York Times*, November 14, 1957, 33.

38. *Berlin Command*, 199, 202-3: Brig. Gen. Frank Howley, *Berlin Command*, New York, 1950.

39. *War or Peace*, 56.

40. Adopted April 30, 1949. U.N. Doc. A/851. Department of State, *Bulletin*, May 15, 1949, 613.

41. Adopted November 3, 1950. U.N. Doc. A/1486. Department of State, *Bulletin*, November 27, 1950, 872.

42. Department of State, *Bulletin*, September 14, 1953, 339, 340.

43. *War or Peace*, 44.

44. Department of State, *Bulletin*, September 26, 1949, 477.

45. Department of State, *Bulletin*, January 23, 1950, 115-6.

46. Report of the Meeting of the Ministers of Foreign Affairs of the U.S.S.R., the United States, and the United Kingdom, December 16-26, 1945, Department of State, *Bulletin*, December 30, 1945, 1030.

47. U.N. Doc. A/447. Department of State, *Bulletin*, November 30, 1947, 1031.

48. U.N. Doc. A/788. Department of State, *Bulletin*, December 19, 1948, 760.

49. Department of State, *Bulletin*, September 18, 1950, 455.

50. Department of State, *Bulletin*, August 21, 1950, 286.

51. Department of State Publication No. 4245, 115-20.

52. U.N. Doc. A/1435. Department of State, *Bulletin*, October 23, 1950, 648-9.

53. U.N. Doc. A/C. 1/643. Department of State, *Bulletin*, January 15, 1951, 115-16. U.N. Document A/C. 1/653. Department of State, *Bulletin*, January 29, 1951, 165-6.

54. Department of State Publication No. 4263, 37.

55. U.N. Doc. A/1805. Department of State, *Bulletin*, May 28, 1951, 849.

56. Hearings, Senate Armed Services Committee, *Ammunition Supplies in the Far East*, 83rd Cong., 1st Sess., March, 1953, 31-32.

57. Department of State, *Bulletin*, July 8, 1957, 59.

58. Report to the Military Armistice Commission, quoted in Department of State, *Bulletin*, December 26, 1955, 1083.

59. Department of State, *Bulletin*, March 14, 1955, 429.

60. Department of State, *Bulletin*, June 11, 1956, 968.

61. Department of State, *Bulletin*, July 8, 1957, 58-9.

62. U.S. Mission to the United Nations, press release No. 2804, November 12, 1957.

63. Department of State Publication No. 5609, 192.

64. December 11, 1954, U.N. Doc. A/C. 1/L.119; November 29, 1955, U.N. Doc. A/C. 1/722; January 11, 1957, U.N. Doc. A/Res/452 (A); November 29, 1957, U.N. Doc. A/C. 1/801; November 14, 1958, U.N. Doc. A/Res/1264 (XIII); December 9, 1959, U.N. Doc. A/Res/1455 (XIV). Department of State, *Bulletin*, December 20, 1954, 949; December 26, 1955, 1085; January 28, 1957, 143; December 16, 1957, 973; December 22, 1958, 1025; January 4, 1960, 24.

65. Department of State, *Bulletin*, May 7, 1956, 742.

66. Harry Truman, *Memoirs*, vol. II, 341: Harry S. Truman, *Years of Trial and Hope* (vol. II of Memoirs) , Harry S. Truman, Garden City, 1956.

67. Harry Truman, *Memoirs*, vol. II, 359.

68. *U.S. Marine Operations in Korea*, vol. III, 5: Montross and Canzona, *U.S. Marine Operations in Korea, 1950-1953*, vol. III, *The Chosin Reservoir Campaign*, Washington, D.C., 1957. Harry Truman, *Memoirs*, vol. II, 359-60.

69. Harry Truman, *Memoirs*, vol. II, 361-2, *U. S. Marine Operations in Korea*, vol. III, 7-8.

70. U. N. Doc. A/1435. Department of State, *Bulletin*, October 23, 1950, 648-9.

71. Harry Truman, *Memoirs*, vol. II, 362.

72. U. N. Docs. A/447, A/788, and A/1039. Department of State, *Bulletin*, November 30, 1947, 1031; December 19, 1948, 760; November 7, 1949, 695.

73. Harry Truman, *Memoirs*, vol. II, 382.

74. Harry Truman, *Memoirs*, vol. II, 373-6.

75. Internal Security Subcommittee, Hearings, *Interlocking Subversion in Government Departments*, Part 22, 1718; U. S. Senate, 83rd Cong., 2d Sess., 1954.

76. *Id.* Part 21, 1698.

77. Report of the U.N. Commander for the period February 1-15, 1951. Department of State, *Bulletin*, April 16, 1951, 626.

78. Report of the U. N. Commander for the period March 1-15, 1951. Department of State, *Bulletin*, April 30, 1951, 710.

79. *Vandenberg Papers*, 179.

80. *Yalta Papers*, 52, 72.

81. *New York Herald Tribune*, April 4, 1945, 24.

82. *Vandenberg Papers*, 161.

83. Although the Foreign Minister of Czechoslovakia was not a Communist, his ministry was under the actual control of the Deputy Foreign Minister, Vladimir Clementis, who was a Communist, and the foreign relations of Czechoslovakia were conducted in accordance with the orders of the Soviet Union. This was demonstrated to the world when Czechoslovakia was forced by Stalin to reverse its decision to participate in the Marshall Plan. See statements of Jan Papanek. United Nations Security Council, *Official Records, Third year*, 261st-276th meetings, 179; 299th and 300th meetings, 23-4.

84. The vote was as follows: *For the proposal*—U.S.S.R., India, Yugoslavia;

against—United States, France, China, Cuba, Ecuador, Egypt: *abstaining*—United Kingdom, Norway.

85. Testimony of Henry Cabot Lodge, Jr. *Review of the U. N. Charter*, Part 1, 50: *Review of the United Nations Charter*. Hearings before subcommittee of Committee on Foreign Relations, U. S. Senate, 83rd Cong., 2d Sess., and 84th Cong., 1st Sess., 13 parts, 1954-5. Statement of Secretary of State John F. Dulles in Department of State, *Bulletin*, July 19, 1954, 87.

86. The admission of the nations concerned and the acceptance of delegates from the Communist regimes were considered as one question. In the General Assembly only two states (China and Cuba) voted against the "admission" of all four Communist regimes. Four nations (the Dominican Republic, the Netherlands, the Philippines and the United States) abstained ("acquiesced") in each case. One nation (Greece) voted against the "admission" of the Albanian Communist regime and abstained on the others. In the Security Council the United States and China abstained (declined to exercise the veto) on all four. With the exception of Belgium, which abstained from voting on Albania in both branches, the "admission" of the four Communist regimes was formally approved by all other states in each branch of the United Nations in which they were entitled to vote.

87. Roy P. Basler, ed., *Abraham Lincoln: His Speeches and Writings*, New York, 1946, 372-3.

CHAPTER X—THE FALL OF CHINA

1. Department of State, *Bulletin*, Supplement, May 4, 1947, 829.

2. Department of State, *Bulletin*, December 29, 1946, 1180.

3. *U.S. Relations with China*, 381: Department of State Publication 3573, *United States Relations with China*, Washington, D.C., 1949.

4. Message to Congress, March 12, 1947. Department of State, *Bulletin*, Supplement, May 4, 1947, 829-30.

5. *U.S. Relations with China*, 380, 382.

6. Department of State, *Bulletin*, October 19, 1947, 777.

7. Statement to Committees on Foreign Affairs and Foreign Relations, *U.S. Relations with China*, 380.

8. *U.S. Relations with China*, 381.

9. Department of State, *Bulletin*, October 19, 1947, 778.

10. Message to Congress, March 12, 1947. Department of State, *Bulletin*, Supplement, May 4, 1947, 830.

11. Department of State, *Bulletin*, January 19, 1947, 84.

12. Statement to Committees on Foreign Affairs and Foreign Relations. *U.S. Relations with China*, 384.

13. Department of State, *Bulletin*, January 19, 1947, 85.

14. *U.S. Relations with China*, 268.

15. Letter dated December 21, 1944, Secretary of State Stettinius to Secretary of War, as quoted in *Persian Corridor and Aid to Russia*, 471-2.

16. See Department of State, *Bulletin*, April 28, 1946, 706-7; May 19, 1946, 853; June 2, 1946, 941-2; June 9, 1946, 987. *Security Council, Official Records, First Year: First Series*, 24th to 49th meetings, 126-7, 145-6.

17. Message of the President to Congress, March 12, 1947. Department of State, *Bulletin*, Supplement, May 4, 1947, 829, 831.

18. Department of State, *Bulletin*, July 20, 1947, 149.

19. Reported by Ambassador Hurley in letter to the President, January 14, 1945. *Yalta Papers*, 349-50.

20. Theses on the National and Colonial Questions, adopted at the Second Congress of the Communist International, July-August, 1920, and Theses on Eastern Question, adopted at the Fourth Congress, November-December, 1922. *The Communist Conspiracy*, Part I, Sec. C, 66-73, 142-50. For quoted text, see p. 148.

21. A Brief History of the Chinese Communist Party, 27, as reproduced in *Documents on Communism, Nationalism, and Soviet Advisers in China*, 61: Wilbur and How, ed., *Documents on Communism, Nationalism, and Soviet Advisers in China, 1918-1927*, New York, 1956.

22. *Soviet Russia in China*, 4-5: Chiang Kai-shek, *Soviet Russia in China*, New York, 1957.

23. A Brief History of the Chinese Communist Party, 29, as reproduced in *Documents on Communism, Nationalism, and Soviet Advisers in China*, 63.

24. *Communism in China*, 23: *The Strategy and Tactics of World Communism, Supplement III, C. Communism in China*, Report of subcommittee of Committee on Foreign Affairs, House Doc. 154, Pt. 3, 81st Cong., 1st Sess., 1949. Also quoted in *Soviet Russia in China*, 81.

25. *Soviet Russia in China*, 82.

26. *The Communist Conspiracy*, Part I, Sec. B, 72.

27. *The Communist Conspiracy*, Part I, Sec. C, 149.

28. Mao Tse-tung, *China's New Democracy*, January 15, 1941, as partly reproduced in *The Communist Conspiracy*, Part I, Sec. D, 510.

29. *Communism in China*, 24. Also quoted in *Soviet Russia in China*, 85.

30. *Foreign Relations, 1940*, vol. IV, 429-430: Department of State, *Foreign Relations of the United States, 1940*, vol. IV, *The Far East*, Washington, D.C., 1955.

31. *Foreign Relations, 1941*, vol. IV, 944-5: Department of State, *Foreign Relations of the United States, 1941*, vol. IV, *The Far East*, Washington, D.C., 1956.

32. *Foreign Relations, 1941*, vol. IV, 948.

33. *Communism in China*, 26-7.

34. *Yalta Papers*, 346, 348.

35. Statement on United States Policy Toward China, December 18, 1946. *U.S. Relations with China*, 690-1.

36. *Yalta Papers*, 349-50.

37. *Yalta Papers,* 350.
38. Department of State, *Bulletin,* July 7, 1946, 34.
39. Department of State, *Bulletin,* January 19, 1947, 84.
40. *Yalta Papers,* 348.
41. *Soviet Russia in China,* 172; *Fifty Years in China,* 170-71: John Leighton Stuart, *Fifty Years in China,* New York, 1954.
42. Minutes of Meeting with Stalin, February 8, 1945, as recorded by Charles E. Bohlen. *Yalta Rapers,* 771.
43. *U.S. Relations with China,* 380.
44. *U.S. Relations with China,* 606.
45. Oral statement, September 14, 1945. *U.S. Relations with China,* 939.
46. Memorandum December 9, 1945 from Secretary of State James F. Byrnes to War Department, included with, and made a part of, the President's instructions to General Marshall. *U.S. Relations With China,* 606.
47. Department of State, *Bulletin,* July 7, 1946, 34.
48. Department of State, *Bulletin,* July 7, 1946, 34.
49. *U.S. Relations With China,* 181.
50. Report of the Meeting of the Ministers of Foreign Affairs of the U.S.S.R., the United States, and the United Kingdom, December 16-26, 1945. Department of State, *Bulletin,* December 30, 1945, 1031.
51. *Soviet Russia in China,* 65.
52. *Yalta Papers,* 351.
53. *U.S. Relations With China,* 630.
54. *U.S. Relations With China,* 315.
55. *U.S. Relations With China,* 317.
56. *U.S. Relations With China,* 810.
57. *U.S. Relations With China,* 814.
58. *U.S. Relations With China,* 984.
59. *Fifty Years in China,* 209.
60. John Leighton Stuart. *U.S. Relations With China,* 277-8.
61. *U.S. Relations With China,* 323.
62. *U.S. Relations With China,* 358.
63. Message to Congress, March 12, 1947. Department of State, *Bulletin, Supplement,* May 4, 1947, 831.
64. Testimony of Struve Hensel, Assistant Secretary of Defense for International Security Affairs. Hearings, *Mutual Security Appropriations for 1956,* Subcommittee on Foreign Operations Appropriations, House of Representatives, 84th Cong., 1st Sess., June 17, 1955, 49.
65. See *Conflict in Indo-China,* 260: Allan B. Cole, ed., *Conflict in Indo-China & International Repercussions, A Documentary History, 1945-1955,* Ithaca, 1956. Also *Americana Annual,* 1955, 355.
66. Department of State, *Bulletin,* January 19, 1947, 84.
67. Paraphrase of press conference, March 10, 1948, *U.S. Relations With China,* 272.

68. Instructions, August 12, 1948 to Ambassador in China. *U.S. Relations With China,* 279.

69. *U.S. Relations With China,* 691.

70. Paraphrase of press conference, March 11, 1948. *U.S. Relations With China,* 273.

71. *U.S. Relations With China,* 358.

72. William C. Bullitt, March 25, 1919. *Foreign Relations, 1919, Russia,* 88.

73. Assistant Secretary of State Adolph A. Berle, April 4, 1943. Department of State, *Bulletin,* April 10, 1943, 292.

74. Army Talk—Orientation Fact Sheet 66, 7 April 1945, as reproduced in Part 13 of Hearings on *Institute of Pacific Relations,* Senate Internal Security Subcommittee, 82d Cong., 2d Sess., 1952, 4686.

75. General George C. Marshall, January 7, 1947. Department of State, *Bulletin,* January 19, 1947, 84.

76. Secretary of State John F. Dulles, June 9, 1956. Department of State, *Bulletin,* June 18, 1956, 1004. Cf. similar statements made by Secretary Dulles in 1958 and 1959, Department of State, *Bulletin,* June 23, 1958, 1041; February 2, 1959, 151-2.

CHAPTER XI—PARTITION IN INDOCHINA

1. *Conflict in Indo-China,* 259.

2. Edwin F. Stanton, *Brief Authority,* New York, 1956, 279.

3. J. Stalin, Report of the Central Committee to the 15th Congress of the Communist Party. *The Communist Conspiracy,* Part I, Sec. B, 135.

4. Laos had also been divided between direct French administration in the south and a protectorate, under the nominal rule of the king, in the north. The union of the two areas was proclaimed by the Laotians at the end of World War II, and agreed to by the French on August 27, 1946. The French did not accept the reunion of the three parts of Viet Nam until 1948, in the agreement made with Nguyen Van Xuan at Ha Long Bay.

5. *The Communist Conspiracy,* Part I, Sec. B, 135.

6. Theses on Eastern Question adopted at the Fourth World Congress of the Communist International, November-December, 1922. *The Communist Conspiracy,* Part I, Sec. C, 149.

7. *The Struggle for Indochina,* 134: Ellen J. Hammer, *The Struggle for Indochina,* Stanford, 1954.

8. *Conflict in Indo-China,* 19.

9. Minutes of Charles E. Bohlen, February 8, 1945. *Yalta Papers,* 770.

10. Press Conference, February 23, 1945, as reported in *Conflict in Indo-China,* 48.

11. *The Struggle for Indochina,* 143.

12. *Conflict in Indo-China,* 101.

13. *The New York Times,* April 19, 1953, as quoted in *Struggle for Indochina,* 295.

14. *Conflict in Indo-China,* 169.

15. Department of State, *Bulletin*, June 12, 1950, 977-8.
16. *Ibid.*
17. *Conflict in Indo-China*, 5-6.
18. *Conflict in Indo-China*, 40-42.
19. *Conflict in Indo-China*, 43.
20. Ha Long Bay Agreement, June 5, 1948. *Conflict in Indo-China*, 72.
21. The Elysée Accords, March 8, 1949. *Conflict in Indo-China*, 72-6.
22. Department of State, *Bulletin*, February 20, 1950, 291-2.
23. Donald R. Heath. Department of State, *Bulletin*, February 12, 1951, 262.
24. Department of State, *Bulletin*, June 30, 1952, 1009.
25. Declaration of July 3, 1953, as reproduced in *Report of Senator Mike Mansfield on a Study Mission to the Associated States of Indochina*, printed for use of Senate Committee on Foreign Relations, 82d Cong., 1st Sess., 1953, Appendix 3.
26. Address to the United Nations General Assembly, September 17, 1953. Department of State, *Bulletin*, September 28, 1953, 405.
27. Department of State, *Bulletin*, October 5, 1953, 443.
28. Department of State, *Bulletin*, June 28, 1954, 972.
29. Department of State, *Bulletin*, June 30, 1952, 1009.
30. Department of State, *Bulletin*, February 12, 1951, 262.
31. Department of State, *Bulletin*, June 30, 1952, 1009.
32. John M. Allison, Assistant Secretary for Far Eastern Affairs. Department of State, *Bulletin*, July 21, 1952, 99.
33. *Newsweek*, January 4, 1954, 17.
34. From substance of statement as reported by *The New York Times*, April 18, 1954, 3. Quoted in *Conflict in Indo-China*, 173.
35. *The Struggle for Indo-China*, 313, citing the statement of Christian Pineau, spokesman of the Finance Committee of the French National Assembly.
36. *The Americana Annual*, 1955, 355.
37. *Conflict in Indo-China*, 260.
38. Department of State, *Bulletin*, April 27, 1953, 601.
39. Department of State, *Bulletin*, September 14, 1953, 341-2.
40. Department of State, *Bulletin*, January 25, 1954, 108.
41. Thruston B. Morton, Assistant Secretary for Congressional Relations. Department of State, *Bulletin*, March 8, 1954, 363.
42. Department of State, *Bulletin*, April 12, 1954, 540.
43. Department of State, *Bulletin*, March 29, 1954, 462.
44. Hearings: *The Mutual Security Act of 1954*, Committee on Foreign Affairs, House of Representatives, 83rd Cong., 2d Sess., April-June, 1954, 15.
45. *Ibid.*
46. Department of State, *Bulletin*, April 12, 1954, 539.
47. Hearings: *The Mutual Security Act of 1954*, Committee on Foreign Affairs, House of Representatives, 83rd Cong., 2d Sess., April-June, 1954, 9.
48. *The Inside Story*, 267: Robert J. Donovan, *Eisenhower, The Inside Story*, New York, 1956.

49. Department of State, *Bulletin,* June 28, 1954, 972.
50. *The Inside Story,* 263-4.
51. *Life,* January 16, 1956, 72.
52. From substance of statement as reported by *The New York Times,* April 18, 1954, 3. Quoted in *Conflict in Indo-China,* 174.
53. Department of State, *Bulletin,* May 17, 1954, 742.
54. Department of State, *Bulletin,* June 21, 1954, 948.
55. Department of State, *Bulletin,* June 21, 1954, 948.
56. Quadripartite Communiqué Issued at Berlin, February 18, 1954. Department of State Pub. No. 5399, 217.
57. Department of State, *Bulletin,* January 23, 1956, 123.
58. *Vital Speeches,* July 15, 1954, 579.
59. *Id.,* 580.
60. Department of State, *Bulletin,* June 28, 1954, 972-3.
61. *Report of Senator Mike Mansfield on a Study Mission to Vietnam, Cambodia, Laos,* October 15, 1954, Senate Committee on Foreign Relations, 83rd Cong., 2d Sess., 2.
62. *Vital Speeches,* May 1, 1954, 418.
63. Walter S. Robertson, Assistant Secretary of State for Far Eastern Affairs. Department of State, *Bulletin,* June 11, 1956, 972.
64. Department of State, *Bulletin,* May 30, 1955, 873.

CHAPTER XII—THE COLD PEACE

1. From statement at Tenth Inter-American Conference, Caracas, Venezuela, March 8, 1954. Department of State Publication No. 5692, 52.
2. This figure is based on the report in *Partinaya Zhizn,* No. 5 (a journal for Communist Party workers) that, as of January 1, 1960, the total membership of the Party had reached 8,017,000 (not including 691,000 candidate members). See *The New York Times,* March 17, 1960, 8. According to Khrushchev, the population of the Soviet Union had by that time increased, since the 1959 census, to approximately 212,000,000. See *The New York Times,* February 4, 1960, 5.
3. See statements of Lenin. *The Communist Conspiracy,* Part I, Sec. B, 73.
4. See Stalin's reports to the 15th and 16th Party Congresses, as partly reproduced in *The Communist Conspiracy,* Part I, Sec. B, 135, and *The Strategy and Tactics of World Communism,* Supp. I, 143-6; Khrushchev's Report to the 20th Party Congress, as partly reproduced in *The Communist Conspiracy,* Part I, Sec. A, xvi, xviii, xix, xxiv-xxvii, and Lenin's addresses, as partly reproduced in *Soviet Russia and The West,* 90 and *The Communist Conspiracy,* Part I, Sec. B, 73. The italicized intercalations are also taken from published reports, the final one appearing in Stalin's report to the 17th Party Congress, as partly reproduced in *The Communist Conspiracy,* Part I, Sec. B, 273.
5. *Economic Problems of Socialism in the U.S.S.R.,* as partly reproduced in *The New York Times,* October 4, 1952, 4. For complete text of this directive, which

was published in *Bolshevik*, September, 1952, and *Pravda*, October 3 and 4, 1952, see *Current Soviet Policies I*, 1-20: Leo Gruliow, ed., *Current Soviet Policies, The Documentary Record of the Nineteenth Communist Party Congress and the Reorganization After Stalin's Death*, New York, 1953.

6. Report of the Central Committee of the Communist Party of the Soviet Union to the 20th Party Congress. Partly reproduced in *The Communist Conspiracy*, Part I, Sec. A, xxi, and *The New York Times*, February 15, 1956, 10. For full text, see *Current Soviet Policies, II*, 29-62.

7. *The Communist Conspiracy*, Part I, Sec. A, xxiv-xxv.

8. *Id.*, xxvi.

9. *Id.*, xxvii-xxviii.

10. *The New York Times*, February 15, 1956, 10.

11. *Current Soviet Policies, II*, 50-1.

12. *U.S. News and World Report*, June 15, 1956, 40. See also *Current Soviet Policies, II*, 172-88.

13. *U.S. News and World Report*, June 15, 1956, 44.

14. Department of State, *Bulletin*, January 24, 1955, 123.

15. From Summary of the Report on International Security—The Military Aspect, made by Panel II of the Special Studies Project of the Rockefeller Brothers Fund, as published in *The New York Times*, January 6, 1958, 18. Description of panel members on p. 19.

16. The "Gaither Report."

17. *Washington Post and Times Herald*, December 20, 1957, as quoted in *Congressional Quaterly Weekly Report*, December 27, 1957, 1328.

18. Department of State, *Bulletin*, February 3, 1958, 163.

19. Letter to Bulganin, January 12, 1958. Department of State, *Bulletin*, January 27, 1958, 127.

20. The reference is to the Kersten Amendment, which authorizes the formation of national military units composed of the residents or escapees of Communist-dominated nations. It was made in a statement of A. A. Sobolev, delegate of the U.S.S.R. to the United Nations. *Records of the General Assembly, Second Emergency Special Session, 4-10 November 1956, Plenary Meetings*, 9.

21. *The New York Times*, October 10, 1957, 10-11.

22. Department of State, *Bulletin*, October 20, 1952, 596.

23. *The New York Times*, October 10, 1952, 3.

24. *Newsweek*, January 5, 1953, 14.

25. *Id.*, 24.

26. *Pravda*, January 13, 1953, 4, as quoted in *Current Soviet Policies*, I, 244.

27. Statement of General L. Smirnov (condensed text). *Current Soviet Policies*, I, 245.

28. *Current Soviet Policies, I*, 257; *The New York Times*, March 17, 1953, 6.

29. Department of State, *Bulletin*, March 30, 1953, 476.

30. Department of State, *Bulletin*, April 27, 1953, 601.

31. Department of State, *Bulletin*, April 13, 1953, 524-5.

32. *Pravda*, April 6, 1953, as quoted in *Current Soviet Policies, I,* 259-60.
33. *Pravda*, July 10, 1953, as quoted in *The New York Times,* July 11, 1953, 4.
34. *The New York Times,* July 11, 1953, 1.
35. Department of State, *Bulletin,* December 7, 1953, 786-8.
36. United States Information Agency, *Problems of Communism,* vol. IV, No. 1, 17.
37. Department of State, *Bulletin,* July 13, 1953, 40.
38. Final Communiqué, July 14, 1953. Department of State, *Bulletin,* July 27, 1953, 105.
39. Note to U.S.S.R., July 15, 1953. Department of State, *Bulletin,* July 27, 1953, 107.
40. Department of State, *Bulletin,* November 30, 1953, 748.
41. Department of State, *Bulletin,* November 30, 1953, 745.
42. Department of State, *Bulletin,* November 16, 1953, 666.
43. Department of State, *Bulletin,* September 28, 1953, 413.
44. Department of State, *Bulletin,* December 14, 1953, 813.
45. Department of State, *Bulletin,* March 8, 1954, 343.
46. *Foreign Ministers Meeting, Berlin Discussions, January 25-February 18, 1954,* Department of State Publication No. 5399, 132.
47. Department of State, *Bulletin,* March 8, 1954, 343-4.
48. Department of State, *Bulletin,* March 8, 1954, 344.
49. *The New York Times,* April 1, 1954, 8.
50. Department of State, *Bulletin,* April 12, 1954, 562.
51. Department of State, *Bulletin,* March 29, 1954, 459-60.
52. *The Korean Problem at the Geneva Conference,* Department of State Publication No. 5609, 192.
53. *Participation of the U.S. Government in International Conferences, July 1, 1953-June 30, 1954,* Department of State Publication No. 5776, 12.
54. Department of State, *Bulletin,* August 2, 1954, 163.
55. Department of State, *Bulletin,* August 9, 1954, 195.
56. Parallel notes to this effect were delivered to the U.S.S.R. by the United States, Great Britain and France. Department of State, *Bulletin,* December 13, 1954, 901-2.
57. Department of State, *Bulletin,* December 13, 1954, 894.
58. *The New York Times,* February 10, 1955, 4.
59. *U.S. News and World Report,* February 18, 1955, 75.
60. *The New York Times,* April 25, 1955, 7.
61. Department of State, *Bulletin,* May 9, 1955, 754.
62. May 5, 1955. Department of State, *Bulletin,* May 23, 1955, 855.
63. Department of State, *Bulletin,* May 30, 1955, 874.
64. Department of State, *Bulletin,* December 13, 1954, 902.
65. *The Geneva Conference of Heads of Government, July 18-23, 1955,* Department of State Publication No. 6046, 6.
66. *The New York Times,* July 16, 1955, 3.
67. *Eisenhower, The Inside Story,* 346-7.

68. *The Geneva Conference of Heads of Government, July 18-23, 1955,* Department of State Publication No. 6046, 15.

69. *Id.,* 52.

70. *Id.,* 81.

71. *Id.,* 84, 86.

72. Department of State, *Bulletin,* December 23, 1957, 989.

73. Department of State, *Bulletin,* January 27, 1958, 132.

74. August 16, 1955. Department of State, *Bulletin,* August 29, 1955, 339.

75. *The Geneva Conference of Heads of Government, July 18-23, 1955,* Department of State Publication No. 6046, 86.

76. As quoted by Gen. Alfred M. Gruenther, Supreme Commander Allied Powers, Europe. Department of State, *Bulletin,* October 17, 1955, 611.

77. Department of State, *Bulletin,* October 31, 1955, 688.

78. *The Geneva Conference of Foreign Ministers, October 27-November 16, 1955,* Department of State Publication No. 6156, 3, 8.

79. *News from Behind the Iron Curtain,* May 1955, 47.

80. *Imre Nagy on Communism,* New York, 1957, 53.

81. As quoted by Secretary of State John F. Dulles, February 26, 1956. Department of State, *Bulletin,* March 5, 1956, 365.

82. *Situation in the Middle East.* Hearing of Committee on Foreign Relations, U.S. Senate, 84th Cong., 2d Sess., February 24, 1956, 19.

83. Department of State, *Bulletin,* June 18, 1956, 1004.

84. *The New York Times,* August 6, 1956, 1.

85. *The New York Times,* January 18, 1957, 1.

86. Department of State, *Bulletin,* January 21, 1957, 90-3.

87. Department of State, *Bulletin,* January 21, 1957, 89-90.

88. *The New York Times,* May 4, 1957, 1.

89. *The New York Times,* May 19, 1957, Sec. 4, 1.

90. *The New York Times,* May 2, 1957, 16; May 5, 1957, Sec. 4, 1.

91. *The New York Times,* May 11, 1957, 3.

92. *The New York Times,* June 3, 1957, 11.

93. *The New York Times,* October 8, 9 and 10, 1957. Full text appears in the issue of October 10, 1957, 10-11.

94. *The New York Times,* May 16, 1957, 14.

95. *The New York Times,* May 23, 1957, 1, 14.

96. *The New York Times,* December 13, 1957, 11.

97. *The New York Times,* May 1, 1957, 1.

98. Department of State, *Bulletin,* September 23, 1957, 487.

99. *The New York Times,* September 2, 1957, 2.

100. Department of State, *Bulletin,* October 7, 1957, 557.

101. Department of State, *Bulletin,* November 4, 1957, 709.

102. Department of State, *Bulletin,* November 4, 1957, 712.

103. *The New York Times,* November 3, 1957, 4.

104. Address on the Correct Handling of Contradictions Among the People, February 27, 1957. *The New York Times,* June 19, 1957, 14.
105. *The New York Times,* July 21, 1957, 9. See also the quotation by Secretary of State Dulles, Department of State, *Bulletin,* July 22, 1957, 139.
106. *The New York Times,* July 4, 1957, 2.
107. Department of State, *Bulletin,* August 5, 1957, 228.
108. *The New York Times,* February 9, 1955, 2.
109. *The New York Times,* October 9, 1955, 32.
110. Resolution of the Central Committee of the Communist Party of the Soviet Union, published November 2, 1957. *The New York Times,* November 3, 1957, 4.
111. *East Europe,* January, 1958, 54-5.
112. *East Europe,* May, 1957, 53.
113. Address to the Tenth Plenum of the Central Committee, October 24-26, 1957. *East Europe,* December, 1957, 33.
114. *The New York Times,* December 25, 1957, 5.
115. *The New York Times,* November 22, 1957, 6.
116. *The New York Times,* December 14, 1957, 11.
117. *The New York Times,* June 28, 1958, 2.
118. *The New York Times,* July 8, 1958, 5.
119. *The New York Times,* March 23, 1958, 29.
120. *The New York Times,* July 17, 1958, 14.
121. See staff study, Internal Security Subcommittee, Committee on the Judiciary, U.S. Senate. *The Revival of the Communist International and Its Significance for the United States,* 86th Cong, 1st Sess., Committee Print, 1959.
122. *The New York Times,* November 7, 1957, 10.
123. *The New York Times,* December 13, 1957, 4.
124. *The New York Times,* January 10, 1958, 6.
125. Department of State, *Bulletin,* January 6, 1958, 13.
126. Department of State, *Bulletin,* January 13, 1958, 52.
127. *The New York Times,* January 5, 1958, 2.
128. *The New York Herald Tribune,* January 6, 1958, 1.
129. Eisenhower letter to Bulganin, January 12, 1958. Department of State, *Bulletin,* January 27, 1958, 122.
130. U.S. *aide-mémoire* of March 6, 1958. Department of State, *Bulletin,* March 24, 1958, 457-9.
131. See Khrushchev notes to President Eisenhower, July 9 and 23, and August 5, 1958. Department of State, *Bulletin,* August 11, 1958, 231, 234, and September 1, 1958, 342.
132. Soviet note, November 27, 1958. Department of State, *Bulletin,* January 19, 1959, 81, 87.
133. *The New York Times,* January 28, 1959, 1.
134. Remarks at U.S. Embassy, Lisbon, May 19, 1960. *The New York Times,* May 20, 1960, 2.

135. Comments at the Summit Conference, May 16, 1960. *The New York Times*, May 17, 1960, 16.

136. Statement of Walter Ulbricht, Deputy Premier and party general secretary, as reported in *The New York Times*, April 16, 1960, 2.

137. *The New York Times*, March 28, 1960, 9.

138. Department of State, *Bulletin*, September 28, 1953, 406.

139. Department of State, *Bulletin*, December 13, 1954, 894.

140. Department of State, *Bulletin*, June 18, 1956, 1004.

141. Department of State, *Bulletin*, July 22, 1957, 144.

142. *The New York Times*, December 20, 1957, 14.

143. Department of State, *Bulletin*, June 23, 1958, 1041.

144. Department of State, *Bulletin*, February 2, 1959, 151.

145. Declaration of Common Purpose, October 25, 1957. Department of State, *Bulletin*, November 11, 1957, 739.

146. Declaration and communiqué of NATO heads of government, December 19, 1957. Department of State, *Bulletin*, January 6, 1958, 12.

147. *The New York Times*, May 12, 1953, 8.

148. *The New York Times*, May 11, 1956, 2.

149. *The New York Times*, July 7, 1957, 6.

150. International Cooperation Administration, Ninth Report, *The Strategic Trade Control System, 1948-1956*, Washington, D.C., 1957, 30.

151. *The New York Times*, August 15, 1958, 2; August 16, 1958, 2.

152. *The New York Times*, November 7, 1958, 1, 3.

153. *The New York Times*, November 10, 1957, 9.

154. *The New York Times*, December 4, 1957, 14.

155. Lev Kamenev, address to the Tenth Congress of the Communist Party, March 15, 1921. *Vsesoyuznaya Komm-Partiya (B) Syezd Stenograf. Otchet*, X, 1921, 254. Translation is from *Soviet Russia and the West*, 94: Eudin and Fisher, *Soviet Russia and The West, 1920-1927*, Stanford, 1957.

CHAPTER XIII—THE BOLSHEVIK PLAN FOR WORLD PEACE

1. *Kommunist*, No. 7, May, 1953, as reproduced in *Current Digest of the Soviet Press*, June 27, 1953.

2. *The Communist Conspiracy*, Part I, Sec. B, 7.

3. *The Communist Conspiracy*, Part I, Sec. B, 11.

4. *The Communist Conspiracy*, Part I, Sec. B, 321: *The New York Times*, March 5, 1936, 16.

5. *"Left-Wing" Communism, an Infantile Disorder*, as partially reproduced in *Strategy and Tactics of World Communism*, Supp. I, 51: Committee on Foreign Affairs, *The Strategy and Tactics of World Communism*, Report of Subcommittee No. 5 on National and International Movements, House Doc. No. 619, 80th Cong., 2d Sess., 1948.

6. *Ibid.*
7. *Id.*, 60.
8. *Id.*, 51.
9. *Theses on Conclusion of a Separate Peace,* January 20, 1918, as reproduced in *Strategy and Tactics of World Communism,* Supp. I, 32-3.
10. *Manifesto of the Communist Party,* as reproduced in *The Communist Conspiracy,* Part I, Sec. A, 71.
11. *"Left-Wing" Communism, an Infantile Disorder,* as partially reproduced in *Strategy and Tactics of World Communism,* Supp. I, 55-6.
12. *Id.*, 54.
13. *The Communist Conspiracy,* Part I, Sec. B, 72.
14. *The Foundations of Leninism,* as partially reproduced in *Strategy and Tactics of World Communism,* Supp. I, 102-3.
15. *Id.*, 104.
16. *Id.*, 103.
17. *Id.*, 105-6.
18. *The Communist Conspiracy,* Part I, Sec. C, 316.
19. *The Communist Conspiracy,* Part I, Sec. C, 308.
20. *The Communist Conspiracy,* Part I, Sec. C, 335.
21. *The Communist Conspiracy,* Part I, Sec. C, 333.
22. *The New York Times,* March 24, 1920, 5.
23. *The New York Times,* March 25, 1920, 10.
24. *Soviet Documents on Foreign Policy,* I, 245: Jane Degras, ed., *Soviet Documents on Foreign Policy, 1917-1941* (three volumes), London, 1951-1953.
25. *The New York Times,* August 16, 1921, 2.
26. *Soviet Russia and the West,* 80.
27. *Soviet Russia and the West,* 132.
28. *Soviet Russia and the West,* 132-3.
29. *Soviet Russia and the West,* 142.
30. *Izvestia,* April 27, 1926, editorial, as partially reproduced in *Soviet Russia and the West,* 327.
31. Speech by the Soviet Delegate, Obolenski-Ossinski, May 7, 1927 *(World Economic Conference, Geneva, 1927,* I, 125-29), as partially reproduced in *Soviet Russia and the West,* 384.
32. Statement of Maxim Litvinov, November 30, 1927 *(Preparatory Commission for the Disarmament Conference,* Series V, 9-12), as partially reproduced in *Soviet Russia and the West,* 390-1.
33. Report on the Work of the Central Committee to the 15th Congress of the Communist Party, December 3, 1927, as partially reproduced in *The Communist Conspiracy,* Part I, Sec. B, 135.
34. *Soviet Documents on Foreign Policy,* II, 335-9.
35. *The Communist Conspiracy,* Part I, Sec. B, 215-6.
36. *The Communist Conspiracy,* Part I, Sec. B., 218.
37. *The New York Times,* January 27, 1932, 11.

38. *Soviet Documents on Foreign Policy*, III, 29.

39. Report on the Work of the Central Committee to the 17th Congress of the Communist Party, January 26, 1934. *The Communist Conspiracy*, Part I, Sec. B, 264-6.

40. *Id.,* 266.

41. *League of Nations Official Journal*, Supp. 125, 66, as reproduced in *Soviet Documents on Foreign Policy*, III, 91.

42. *Id.,* 92.

43. *The New York Times*, March 5, 1936, 16; *The Communist Conspiracy*, Part I, Sec. B, 321.

44. *Conference of Brussels*, 33, as reproduced in *Soviet Documents on Foreign Policy*, III, 264. See Appendix E-1.

45. Report on the Work of the Central Committee to the 18th Congress of the Communist Party, March 10, 1939. *The Communist Conspiracy*, Part I, Sec. B, 393-4.

46. *The Communist Conspiracy*, Part I, Sec. B, 410-11.

47. As quoted by Livingston T. Merchant, U. S. Ambassador to Canada. Department of State, *Bulletin*, February 18, 1957, 260.

48. Report on the Work of the Central Committee to the 8th Congress of the Communist Party, as quoted in State Department Publication No. 4264, *The Kremlin Speaks*, 4.

49. *Foreign Relations, 1919, Russia*, 77.

50. *Foreign Relations, 1919, Russia*, 95.

51. Dr. Harold Williams. As reported in *The New York Times*, April 3, 1919, 1, 2.

52. Report to United States Senate, October 27, 1919, as reproduced in *International Conciliation*, No. 149, April, 1920, 9.

53. *The New York Times*, February 28, 1920, 1.

54. Theses and Resolutions adopted at the Third World Congress of the Communist International, June 22-July 12, 1921, Thesis on Tactics, Section 2, On the Eve of New Battles, as reproduced in *The Communist Conspiracy*, Part I, Sec. C, 98.

55. Hackworth, *Digest of International Law*, I, 301.

56. *Soviet Documents on Foreign Policy*, I, 273.

57. Hackworth, *Digest of International Law*, I, 303.

58. *The New York Times*, December 20, 1923, I, 3.

59. 65 *Cong. Rec.*, 447.

60. 65 *Cong. Rec.*, 449.

61. *The New York Times*, January 20, 1924, Sec. I, Pt. 2, 5.

62. *The New York Times*, February 11, 1924, 3.

63. *The New York Times*, March 11, 1924, 18.

64. *The New York Times*, October 28, 1926, 6.

65. *The New York Times*, January 14, 1927, 6.

66. *The New York Times*, October 31, 1926, Sec. II, 8.

67. *Soviet Russia and the West*, 335.

68. *The New York Times,* May 29, 1927, Sec. 2, 8.
69. Report on the Work of the Central Committee to the 15th Congress of the Communist Party, December 3, 1927. *The Communist Conspiracy,* Part I, Sec. B, 135.
70. *Soviet Russia and the West,* 397.
71. Address, January 11, 1955. Department of State, *Bulletin,* January 24, 1955, 123.
72. Program of the Communist International Together with its Constitution, adopted at the 6th World Congress of the Communist International, September 1, 1928, Chapter Four, The Period of Transition from Capitalism to Socialism and the Dictatorship of the Proletariat, as reproduced in *The Communist Conspiracy,* Part I, Sec. C, 197.
73. *Soviet Documents on Foreign Policy,* II, 338.
74. *Foreign Relations, The Soviet Union, 1933-1939,* 43.
75. *Foreign Relations, The Soviet Union, 1933-1939,* 45.
76. *Foreign Relations, The Soviet Union, 1933-1939,* 50.
77. *Foreign Relations, The Soviet Union, 1933-1939,* 224-5.
78. *Foreign Relations, The Soviet Union, 1933-1939,* 225.
79. *Foreign Relations, The Soviet Union, 1933-1939,* 227.
80. Resolution adopted August 20, 1935 by the Seventh Congress of the Communist International. The Offensive of Fascism and the Tasks of the Communist International in the Fight for the Unity of the Working Class Against Fascism, Part VI, The Strengthening of the Communist Parties and the Struggle for the Political Unity of the Working Class, as reproduced in *The Communist Conspiracy,* Part I, Sec. C, 359.
81. Resolution adopted August 20, 1935 by the Seventh Congress of the Communist International, The Tasks of the Communist International in Connection with the Preparations of the Imperialists for a New World War, Part IV, From the Struggle for Peace to the Struggle for Revolution, as reproduced in *The Communist Conspiracy,* Part I, Sec. C, 365-6.
82. *Foreign Relations, The Soviet Union, 1933-1939,* 29.
83. *Foreign Relations, The Soviet Union, 1933-1939,* 230.
84. *Foreign Relations, The Soviet Union, 1933-1939,* 247. As reasons not to be announced, the Ambassador suggested that the Embassy in Moscow was useful as an "official observation post," and that the Soviet Union would still have representation in the United States, for all practical purposes, unless all Soviet citizens were expelled, including the officials of such organizations as Amtorg and Intourist.
85. *The New York Times,* March 15, 1936, Sec. IV, 5.
86. *The New York Times,* January 23, 1938, 31.
87. *Foreign Relations, The Soviet Union, 1933-1939,* 524.
88. *Foreign Relations, The Soviet Union, 1933-1939,* 790.
89. *Strategy and Tactics of World Communism,* Supp. I, 166.
90. Manifesto adopted October, 1947, by the representatives of the Communist Parties of Bulgaria, Czechoslovakia, France, Hungary, Italy, Poland, Rumania,

Yugoslavia, and the U.S.S.R. *Strategy and Tactics of World Communism,* Supp. I, 211.

91. *Strategy and Tactics of World Communism,* Supp. I, 213.
92. *Strategy and Tactics of World Communism,* Supp. I, 219.
93. *Strategy and Tactics of World Communism,* Supp. I, 230.
94. Department of State, *Bulletin,* July 17, 1950, 88.
95. Department of State, *Bulletin,* August 6, 1951, 209.
96. Department of State, *Bulletin,* December 19, 1955, 1003.
97. *Situation in the Middle East.* Hearing of Committee on Foreign Relations, U.S. Senate, 84th Cong. 2d Sess., February 24, 1956, 19.
98. Department of State, *Bulletin,* May 7, 1956, 749.
99. Department of State, *Bulletin,* June 18, 1956, 1004. Italics added.
100. Lenin, Selected Works, VII, 65. Quoted in the report of the Internal Security Subcommittee, *Documentary Proof That the Communist Party, U.S.A., Teaches and Advocates the Overthrow and Destruction of the United States Government by Force and Violence,* U.S. Senate, 82d Cong., 2d Sess., 1952, 11.
101. *The Communist Conspiracy,* Part I, Sec. A, 170.
102. Lenin, *Collected Works,* vol. XXXIII, Fourth Russian Edition, 57-8, as quoted by Bertram D. Wolfe, *Khrushchev and Stalin's Ghost,* New York, 1957, 56.
103. *The Communist Conspiracy,* Part I, Sec. A, 170.
104. *The New York Times,* August 15, 1958, 1, 2; August 16, 1958, 1, 3.
105. *The Communist Conspiracy,* Part I, Sec. A, xxviii.
106. *The New York Times,* July 28, 1958, 7; August 8, 1958, 2; August 24, 1958, 2.
107. *The New York Times,* January 5, 1958, 2.
108. Speech at the League Assembly on entry of the U.S.S.R. into the League of Nations, September 18, 1934 *(LNOJ,* Supp. 125, p. 66) as reproduced in *Soviet Documents on Foreign Policy,* III, 93.
109. Declaration Concerning the Formation of the Union of Soviet Socialist Republics, adopted at the First Congress of Soviets of the Union, December 30, 1922, as partially reproduced in *Soviet Russia and the West,* 155.
110. *Soviet Russia and the West,* 154.
111. *Soviet Documents on Foreign Policy,* II, 69.
112. *The Communist Conspiracy,* Part I, Sec. B, 134.
113. *The Communist Conspiracy,* Part I, Sec. C, 197.
114. *Soviet Russia and the West,* 154.

CHAPTER XIV—THE "IRREVERSIBLE" TREND

1. Department of State, *Bulletin,* April 30, 1956, 707.
2. *Current Soviet Policies II,* 225.
3. News Conference, July 11, 1956. Department of State, *Bulletin,* July 23, 1956, 145-6.
4. Department of State, *Bulletin,* November 5, 1956, 697.
5. Department of State, *Bulletin,* July 22, 1957, 144.

6. Department of State, *Bulletin*, August 5, 1957, 228.

7. *State and Revolution*, as partly reproduced in *The Communist Conspiracy*, Part I, Sec. A, 132.

8. As adopted at the Sixth World Congress, September 1, 1928. Partly reproduced in *Strategy and Tactics of World Communism*, Supp. I, 121-3.

9. *State and Revolution*, as partly reproduced in *The Communist Conspiracy*, Part I, Sec. A, 132-3.

10. *Id.*, 131.

11. V. I. Lenin, *"Left-Wing" Communism, an Infantile Disorder*, as partly reproduced in *The Communist Conspiracy*, Part I, Sec. A, 141.

12. J. V. Stalin, *Foundations of Leninism*, quoting Lenin in *"Left-Wing" Communism. The Communist Conspiracy*, Part I, Sec. A, 167.

13. V. I. Lenin, *Collected Works*, vol. XXVI, 286 (Russian edition), as quoted by Stalin in *Problems of Leninism. The Communist Conspiracy*, Part I, Sec. A, 196.

14. V. I. Lenin, *State and Revolution*, as partly reproduced in *The Communist Conspiracy*, Part I, Sec. A, 132.

15. *The Communist Conspiracy*, Part I, Sec. A, 131.

16. *Id.*, 136.

17. *The Proletarian Revolution and the Renegade Kautsky*, as quoted by Stalin in *Foundations of Leninism. The Communist Conspiracy*, Part I, Sec. A, 165.

18. *"Left-Wing" Communism*, as partly reproduced in *The Communist Conspiracy*, Part I, Sec. A, 141-2, 149-50.

19. *Id.*, 141-2.

20. *"Left-Wing" Communism*, as quoted by Stalin in *Foundations of Leninism. The Strategy and Tactics of World Communism*, Supp. I, 106.

21. *"Left-Wing" Communism*, as partly reproduced in *The Communist Conspiracy*, Part I, Sec. A, 141.

22. As partly reproduced in *The Communist Conspiracy*, Part I, Sec. A, 167.

23. As partly reproduced in *The Communist Conspiracy*, Part I, Sec. A, 199.

24. Report of the Central Committee to the 16th Congress of the Communist Party, June 27, 1930, as partly reproduced in *The Communist Conspiracy*, Part I, Sec. B, 222.

25. Lazar Volin, *The Turn of the Screw in Soviet Agriculture, Foreign Affairs*, January, 1952, as quoted in a study, *Tensions Within the Soviet Union* (Revised), prepared by the Legislative Reference Service, Library of Congress, for the Senate Committee on Foreign Relations, Sen. Doc. 69, 83rd Cong., 1st Sess., 1953, 75. See also David J. Dallin, *The Changing World of Soviet Russia*, New Haven, 1956.

26. *Foreign Relations, 1919, Russia*, 86.

27. This statement was made in December, 1919, at the Seventh All-Russian Congress of Soviets. Lenin, *Collected Works* (second Russian edition), vol. XXIV, 612-3, as quoted in *The Bolshevik Revolution*, I, 174: E. H. Carr *The Bolshevik Revolution, 1917-1923* (three volumes), New York, 1951-3.

28. As quoted in *The Bolshevik Revolution*, I, 180.

29. As quoted in *The New York Times*, July 12, 1934, 6.

30. Khrushchev's "secret" speech to the 20th Congress of the Communist Party. *U.S. News and World Report*, June 15, 1956, 158.

31. *Id.*, 163.

32. *Foreign Relations, 1919, Russia*, 87-8.

33. Secretary of State John F. Dulles. Department of State, *Bulletin*, July 22, 1957, 144.

34. Decree of the All-Russian Central Executive Committee, March 21, 1921, as published in *Pravda*, March 23, 1921. *The Communist Conspiracy*, Part I, Sec. B, 76-7.

35. Concurrent appeal issued by the People's Commissars and the Presidium of the All-Russian Central Executive Committee, also published in *Pravda*, March 23, 1921. *The Communist Conspiracy*, Part I, Sec. B, 78.

36. *The Communist Conspiracy*, Part I, Sec. B, 77.

37. Decree of the All-Russian Central Executive Committee, May 22, 1922, as reproduced in *Materials for the Study of the Soviet System*, 133-8: J. H. Meisel and E. S. Kozera, ed., *Materials for the Study of the Soviet System*, Ann Arbor, 1953.

38. *"Left-Wing" Communism, an Infantile Disorder*, as partly reproduced in *The Communist Conspiracy*, Part I, Sec. A, 141.

39. V. I. Lenin, *The Case for the N.E.P.*, as partly reproduced in *Materials for the Study of the Soviet System*, 129-30.

40. Decree of the Central Executive Committee and Council of People's Commissars, December 10, 1921, as reproduced in *Materials for the Study of the Soviet System*, 130.

41. Decree of the All-Russian Central Executive Committee, May 22, 1922, as reproduced in *Materials for the Study of the Soviet System*, 139-41.

42. *The New York Times*, August 13, 1921, 1.

43. 65 *Cong. Rec.*, 97, December 6, 1923.

44. As quoted in *Soviet Russia and the West*, 4.

45. Lenin, *Collected Works*, vol. XXVII, 361-2, as quoted by Stalin in the Report of the Central Committee to the 16th Congress of the Communist Party. *The Communist Conspiracy*, Part I, Sec. B, 222.

46. *History of the Communist Party of the Soviet Union (Bolsheviks), Short Course*, as partly reproduced in *The Communist Conspiracy*, Part I, Sec. B, 386. This history was first published in 1938.

47. Reply to Debate on the Report of the Central Committee to the 14th Congress of the Communist Party, December, 1925, as partly reproduced in *The Communist Conspiracy*, Part I, Sec. B, 117.

48. *The New York Times*, April 15, 1925, 6.

49. As quoted in *The New York Times*, January 19, 1926, 4.

50. *The Communist Conspiracy*, Part I, Sec. A, 198. Stalin is here quoting Lenin's *Collected Works*, vol. XXVI, 238 (Russian edition).

51. Report of the Central Committee to the 15th Congress of the Communist Party, December 3, 1927, as partly reproduced in *The Communist Conspiracy*, Part I, Sec. B, 136-7.
52. *The New York Times*, July 19, 1928, 20.
53. Report of the Central Committee to the 16th Congress of the Communist Party, June 27, 1930, as partly reproduced in *The Communist Conspiracy*, Part I, Sec. B, 218, 222.
54. *The Hinge of Fate*, 498: Winston S. Churchill, *The Second World War*, *The Hinge of Fate*, Boston, 1950.
55. Churchill records that this figure was used by Stalin himself. See *The Hinge of Fate*, 498.
56. *Materials for the Study of the Soviet System*, 185-6.
57. As quoted in *The New York Times*, March 9, 1930, Sec. III, 1.
58. As quoted in *The New York Times*, March 16, 1930, 1.
59. *The New York Times*, March 16, 1930, 1.
60. *The New York Times*, March 9, 1930, Sec. III, 1.
61. Report of the Central Committee to the 16th Congress of the Communist Party, June 27, 1930, as partly reproduced in *The Communist Conspiracy*, Part I, Sec. B, 221. Bukharin was formally ousted from the Politburo in November, 1929.
62. *Materials for the Study of the Soviet System*, 188-90.
63. Report of the Central Committee to the 16th Congress of the Communist Party, June 27, 1930, as partly reproduced in *The Communist Conspiracy*, Part I, Sec. B, 223-4.
64. *Id.*, 223.
65. *The New York Times*, January 26, 1931, 9.
66. One of the principal decrees was that of February 17, 1935. *Materials for the Study of the Soviet System*, 207.
67. *The New York Times*, December 17, 1958, 1F.
68. *The New York Times*, January 26, 1958, 1; December 18, 1958, 1G.
69. As reported in *Time*, December 29, 1958, 16.
70. *China Under Communism*, 128-53: Richard L. Walker, *China Under Communism, The First Five Years*, New Haven, 1955. Wolf Ladejinsky, *The Carrot and Stick in Rural China, Foreign Affairs*, October, 1957, 91-104. *China Handbook 1956-1957*, Taipei, 1956, 571-3.
71. Resolution of the Seventh Central Committee of the Communist Party, October 11, 1955, adopted on the basis of the report of Mao Tse-tung, July 31, 1955, at the Conference of Secretaries of Provincial, City and Area Party Committees. Hsinhua News Agency, *Daily News Releases*, October 18, 1955, 163-170.
72. *The New York Times*, September 7, 1958, 16; April 16, 1959, 5.
73. *China Under Communism*, 144.
74. *The Carrot and Stick in Rural China, Foreign Affairs*, October, 1957, 100.
75. The Model Regulations for Agricultural Producer Cooperatives, adopted

November 9, 1955, as quoted in *The Carrot and Stick in Rural China, Foreign Affairs*, October, 1957, 96.

76. *The New York Times*, September 28, 1958, 19.
77. *The New York Times*, December 19, 1958, 1H.
78. Telegraphic summary of address to the All-Union Soviet Congress, as reported in *Inprecorr*, November 1936. *The Communist Conspiracy*, Part I, Sec. B, 345.
79. *Id.*, 344.
80. *Id.*, 345.
81. Khrushchev's "secret" speech at the 20th Congress of the Communist Party. *U.S. News and World Report*, June 15, 1956, 155.
82. *The New York Times*, March 9, 1937, 22; March 29, 1937, 1, 10; April 2, 1937, 9.
83. Captain Edward V. Rickenbacker. *The New York Times*, August 18, 1943, 10.
84. Report to the 18th Congress of the Communist Party on the Work of the Central Committee, March 10, 1939, as partly reproduced in *The Communist Conspiracy*, Part I, Sec. B, 397.
85. Report of the Central Committee to the 15th Congress of the Communist Party, December 3, 1927, as partly reproduced in *The Communist Conspiracy*, Part I, Sec. B, 144, 150.
86. *The New York Times*, January 9, 1919, 1.
87. *The New York Times*, April 29, 1921, 15.
88. Isaac Deutscher, *Stalin, A Political Biography*, New York, 1949, 253n.
89. *History of the Communist Party of the Soviet Union (Bolsheviks), Short Course*, as partly reproduced in *The Communist Conspiracy*, Part I, Sec. B, 388.
90. As quoted in *The New York Times*, January 19, 1926, 4.
91. "Secret" address to the 20th Congress of the Communist Party, February 25, 1956. *U.S. News and World Report*, June 15, 1956, 153.
92. Reply to Debate on the Political Report of the Central Committee, 14th Congress of the Communist Party, December 23, 1925, as partly reproduced in *The Communist Conspiracy*, Part I, Sec. B, 114.
93. Report to the 18th Congress of the Communist Party on the Work of the Central Committee, March 10, 1939, as partly reproduced in *The Communist Conspiracy*, Part I, Sec. B, 396-7.
94. Religion in the U.S.S.R., as partly reproduced in *The Communist Conspiracy*, Part I, Sec. B, 282.
95. André Pierre in *Religion in Soviet Land. Problems of Communism*, vol. IV, No. 3, 19.
96. Decree on the Separation of the Church from the State and the School from the Church, January 23, 1918. *The Communist Conspiracy*, Part I, Sec. B, 281.
97. André Pierre, *Religion in Soviet Land, Problems of Communism*, vol. IV, No. 3, 19; *The Aftermath*, 65.
98. Decree on the Separation of the Church from the State and of the School from the Church, January 23, 1918. *The Communist Conspiracy*, Part I, Sec. B, 281.
99. Constitution of the Russian Socialist Federated Soviet Republic, adopted

July 10, 1918, Sec. II, Ch. V, par. 13, *Foreign Relations, 1918, Russia*, vol. I, 589.

100. *The New York Times*, February 28, 1922, 6.
101. *The New York Times*, June 17, 1923, Sec. VIII, 5.
102. *The New York Times*, May 21, 1924, 3.
103. *The New York Times*, June 2, 1924, 1.
104. *The New York Times*, July 5, 1924, 7.
105. *The Church in Soviet Russia*, 43: Matthew Spinka, *The Church in Soviet Russia*, New York, 1956.
106. *The New York Times*, February 16, 1926, 24.
107. See *The Church in Soviet Russia*, 65-70, App. I & II.
108. *The New York Times Magazine*, December 11, 1927, 20.
109. John F. Dulles. Department of State, *Bulletin*, June 18, 1956, 1004.
110. *The New York Times*, February 2, 1930, 3.
111. *The New York Times*, February 17, 1930, 8.
112. *Materials for the Study of the Soviet System*, 190.
113. *The New York Times*, March 21, 1930, 6.
114. *The New York Times*, April 5, 1930, 18.
115. Department of State, *Bulletin*, April 16, 1956, 637.
116. *The New York Times*, February 10, 1935, Sec. IV, 8. This almost incredible event occurred at the peak of a threat of Japanese attack in Siberia, which the Soviets feared would be immediately followed by a German-Polish attack in the west. The "procession" took place one day after reports of a Japanese landing at Vladivostok were received in Moscow. The *Times* attributed it to a desire to mobilize the people in defense of "Holy Russia," demonstrating a public awareness of Soviet motivation which should have prevented the successful deception of the free nations by similar Soviet tactics during World War II.
117. Harold Denny in *The New York Times*, September 22, 1936, 17.
118. *The New York Times*, May 9, 1937, 28.
119. *The New York Times*, October 30, 1938, Sec. IV, 4.
120. *The New York Times*, April 10, 1939, 10.
121. *The New York Times*, August 19, 1948, 4.
122. For a summary of postwar religious persecution in eastern Europe, see the Report of the Social Committee submitted to the Thirteenth Plenary Meeting of the First Session of the Assembly of Captive European Nations on April 14, 1955, ACEN R No. 17 (Soc.), ACEN Publication No. 12, 48-71. For China, see the Chart Showing Persecution of Religion By the Chinese Communists, prepared by the Asian Peoples Anti-Communist League, China Chapter, in Committee Print, *Nature of Communism in Occupied China*, Subcommittee on Internal Security, U.S. Senate, 85th Cong. 1st Sess., May 13, 1957. The fate of the Catholic Church in all of the Communist-dominated areas, including North Korea and North Viet Nam, is also covered in Albert Galter, *The Red*

   Book of the Persecuted Church, Westminster, 1957.

123. *The Tablet,* Brooklyn, September 18, 1954, 1.

124. Department of State, *Bulletin,* July 22, 1957, 144.

125. Statement of Secretary of State Dulles, Department of State, *Bulletin,* March 5, 1956, 364.

126. Statement of Secretary of State Dulles, Department of State, *Bulletin,* April 16, 1956, 638.

127. Statement of Secretary of State Dulles, Department of State, *Bulletin,* June 18, 1956, 1004.

128. Statement of Secretary of State Dulles, Department of State, *Bulletin,* April 30, 1956, 707.

129. *Ibid.*

CHAPTER XV—THE "IRRESISTIBLE" DEMAND

1. *"Left-Wing" Communism, an Infantile Disorder,* as partly reproduced in *The Communist Conspiracy,* Part I, Sec. A, 142.

2. Republican Party platform, 1952.

3. Draft Joint Declaration on the Captive Peoples, submitted to Congress February 20, 1953, but never adopted. Department of State, *Bulletin,* March 2, 1953, 354.

4. Department of State, *Bulletin,* March 9, 1953, 372-3.

5. Department of State, *Bulletin,* July 6, 1953, 10.

6. Department of State, *Bulletin,* July 13, 1953, 40.

7. *The New York Times,* April 5, 1956, 10.

8. Department of State, *Bulletin,* April 30, 1956, 707.

9. Department of State, *Bulletin,* July 2, 1956, 7.

10. Department of State, *Bulletin,* July 23, 1956, 146.

11. Department of State, *Bulletin,* August 5, 1957, 228.

12. *The Proletarian Revolution and Renegade Kautsky,* as quoted by Stalin in *Foundations of Leninism. The Communist Conspiracy,* Part I, Sec. A, 165.

13. *Id.,* 165-6.

14. J.V. Stalin, *Foundations of Leninism,* as partly reproduced in *The Communist Conspiracy,* Part I, Sec. A, 166.

15. *"Left-Wing" Communism, an Infantile Disorder,* as partly reproduced in *The Communist Conspiracy,* Part I, Sec. A, 141-2.

16. J.V. Stalin, *Foundations of Leninism,* quoting *"Left-Wing" Communism. The Communist Conspiracy,* Part I, Sec. A, 166.

17. President Dwight D. Eisenhower, April 21, 1956. Department of State, *Bulletin,* April 30, 1956, 703.

18. *Foreign Relations, 1918, Russia,* vol. I, 400.

19. See *Our Secret Allies,* 119: Eugene Lyons, *Our Secret Allies: The Peoples of Russia,* New York, 1954.

20. Decree, June 11, 1918. *Materials for the Study of the Soviet System,* 75-6.

21. See Wm. H. Chamberlin, *The Russian Revolution, 1917-1921,* New York, 1935, vol. II, 45.

22. *The Bolshevik Revolution, 1917-1923,* vol. II, 170n.

23. *The New York Times,* March 23, 1921, 2.

24. *Our Secret Allies,* 125.

25. *The New York Times,* May 4, 1921, 6.

26. *The New York Times,* April 4, 1923, 2; April 20, 1925, 2; August 8, 1926, 1; August 20, 1926, 7.

27. *The New York Times,* February 9, 1924, 3.

28. *The New York Times,* December 16, 1924, 11.

29. *The New York Times,* February 9, 1924, 3; December 16, 1924, 11.

30. *Communist Takeover and Occupation of Byelorussia,* 18: House of Representatives, Select Committee on Communist Aggression, Special Report No. 9, H. Rep. No. 2684, Pt. 11, 83rd Cong., 2d Sess., 1955.

31. *The New York Times,* September 22, 1924, 13.

32. United Nations, *General Assembly Official Records: Eleventh Session Supplement No. 18* (A/3592), *Report of the Special Committee on the Problem of Hungary,* 27.

33. Select Committee on Communist Aggression, *Summary Report,* 43: House Report No. 2684, Part 16, 83rd Cong., 2d Sess., 1955. *The New York Times,* October 8, 1956, 10.

34. Records of the Fifth Assembly, Geneva, 1924, *LNOJ Spec. Supp. No. 23,* 160, 440; *LNOJ Spec. Supp. No. 29,* 23-4.

35. *The New York Times,* May 18, 1925, 1.

36. *The New York Times,* August 8, 1926, 1.

37. *The New York Times,* August 22, 1926, Sec. II, 7.

38. *The New York Times,* April 19, 1927, 1; June 3, 1927, 3.

39. *The New York Times,* April 19, 1928, 8.

40. *The New York Times,* September 19, 1929, 10.

41. Select Committee on Communist Aggression, *Summary Report,* 43.

42. *Ibid.*

43. *Communist Takeover and Occupation of Byelorussia,* 18-19.

44. Interview with foreign labor delegates, November 5, 1927, as published in *Inprecorr,* December 31, 1930, 1259. *The Communist Conspiracy,* Part I, Sec. B, 124.

45. Political Report of the Central Committee to the 15th Congress of the Communist Party, December 3, 1927, as quoted in *The Communist Conspiracy,* Part I, Sec. B, 137. The proponents of the "Smena Vekh ideology," or "smenovekhovtsy," were those "bourgeoisie" and "intelligentsia" who favored cooperation with Bolshevism on the assumption that it would "inevitably" evolve to a more moderate form of rule. The name derived from the title of two émigré publications advancing this theory, which appeared shortly after the announcement of the New Economic Policy.

46. *Id.,* 140.

47. Political Report of the Central Committee to the 16th Congress of the Com-

munist Party, June 27, 1930, as quoted in *The Communist Conspiracy*, Part I, Sec. B, 220.

48. *Id.*, 230.
49. *Id.*, 217.
50. Report to the 17th Congress of the Communist Party, January 26, 1934, as quoted in *The Communist Conspiracy*, Part I, Sec. B, 268.
51. *Id.*, 270.
52. *Ibid.*
53. *Id.*, 269.
54. *Origin of the Communist Autocracy*, 240 n14: Leonard Schapiro, *The Origin of the Communist Autocracy*, Cambridge, 1955.
55. *The New York Times*, July 24, 1923, 12.
56. *The New York Times*, May 30, 1924, 16.
57. *The New York Times*, August 20, 1926, 7.
58. *The New York Times*, January 30, 1928, 1.
59. *The New York Times*, August 9, 1926, 1.
60. B. H. Liddell Hart, ed., *The Red Army*, New York, 1956, 69.
61. Report, February 28, 1942, of Alfred Rosenberg, Reich Minister for the occupied Eastern Territories, to Field Marshal Wilhelm Keitel. *Nazi Conspiracy and Aggression*, vol. III, 127: Office of the U.S. chief of counsel for prosecution of axis criminality, *Nazi Conspiracy and Aggression* (8 vols. plus Supps. A and B), Washington, D.C., 1946-8. See also the reports cited in *German Rule in Russia*, 69: Alexander Dallin, *German Rule in Russia, 1941-1945*, New York, 1957.
62. *The Soviet Partisan Movement*, 111-12: Department of the Army Pamphlet No. 20-244, *The Soviet Partisan Movement, 1941-1944*, Washington, D.C., 1956.
63. Stalin Order No. 0019, July 16, 1941, as quoted in *German Rule in Russia*, 64, fn. 2.
64. *Soviet Opposition to Stalin*, 45: George Fischer, *Soviet Opposition to Stalin*, Cambridge, 1952. *Our Secret Allies*, 243.
65. *Tensions Within the Soviet Union* (revised), 56.
66. *The Soviet Partisan Movement*, 112.
67. *German Rule in Russia*, 521-3.
68. Report 28 February, 1942, to Field Marshal Wilhelm Keitel. *Nazi Conspiracy and Aggression*, vol. III, 128.
69. See article by N. Galay, *The Partisan Forces*, in *The Red Army*, 167-8.
70. *Communist Takeover and Occupation of the Ukraine*, 31.
71. L. G. Melnikov, Report to the 17th Congress of the Ukrainian Communist Party, September 24, 1952, as reproduced in *Current Soviet Policies*, I, 58.
72. Report to the 17th Congress of the Communist Party, January 26, 1934, as quoted in *The Communist Conspiracy*, Part I Sec. B, 268, 273.
73. *Id.*, 268.
74. Select Committee on Communist Aggression, House of Representatives, *Fourth Interim Report*, Part 2, Hearings, 83rd Cong., 2d Sess., 1954, 1369, 1372.

75. *Glos Koszalinski,* as quoted by *the New York Herald Tribune,* May 24, 1956, 1.
76. Address before Central Committee of the Polish United Workers' Party, October 20, 1956, as reproduced in *National Communism and Popular Revolt in Eastern Europe,* Paul E. Zinner, ed., New York, 1956, 208.
77. Department of State, *Bulletin,* January 15, 1951, 87.
78. *News from Behind the Iron Curtain,* December, 1952, 9-13.
79. *Id.,* 9-10.
80. Hearings of Subcommittee on Internal Security, U.S. Senate, on *Activities of Soviet Secret Service,* May 21, 1954, 83rd Cong., 2d Sess. and on *Scope of Soviet Activity in the United States,* Part 24, May 16-22, 1956, 84th Cong., 2d Sess., 1301-11.
81. *The New York Times,* May 29, 1954, 5.
82. *The Times,* London, January 7, 1957.
83. Proceedings of the Eighth Annual Conference organized by the Russian anti-Communist weekly *Possev,* in Frankfurt am Main, Germany, September 10-12, 1956, 67.
84. *New York Herald Tribune,* February 7, 1957, 1; February 8, 1957, 4.
85. *The New York Times,* February 7, 1957, 1, 10.
86. *Pravda,* February 9, 1957, 6.
87. *The New York Times,* February 14, 1956, 4.
88. *The New York Times,* October 8, 1956, 10.
89. *Novoye Russkoe Slovo,* New York, April 4 and 6, 1960.
90. *The New York Times,* October 11, 1959, 16; October 15, 1959, 1; November 22, 1959, 3; December 8, 1959, 13; January 6, 1960, 4; January 21, 1960, 5.
91. *The New York Times,* April 24, 1960, 1.
92. *U.S. News and World Report,* November 7, 1958, 31.
93. *The New York Times,* November 26, 1959, 20.
94. Department of State, *Bulletin,* July 22, 1957, 144.
95. *China Under Communism,* 187.
96. *The New York Times,* February 8, 1954, 5.
97. *The New York Times,* March 5, 1954, 5.
98. *Nature of Communism in Occupied China,* committee print, Subcommittee on Internal Security, U.S. Senate, 85th Congress, 1st Sess., May 13, 1957. Charts show "Anti-Communist Organizations on the Chinese Mainland," and "Number of Anti-Communist Organizations and Cases on the Chinese Mainland."
99. *New York Herald Tribune,* May 13, 1956, Sec. II, 3.
100. *The New York Times,* July 25, 1957, 6; July 31, 1957, 5; August 4, 1957, 9; August 6, 1957, 5.
101. *The New York Times,* August 7, 1957, 3.
102. *Kirin Daily,* August 16, 1957, as reported by *Free China Weekly,* New York, August 27, 1957, 4.
103. *The Tablet,* Brooklyn, December 15, 1956, 1.
104. *The New York Times,* April 28, 1957, 13.
105. *The New York Times,* June 19, 1957, 14.

106. *The New York Times,* July 12, 1957, 4.
107. *The New York Times,* July 18, 1957, 5.
108. *The New York Times,* October 12, 1957, 2.
109. *The New York Times,* November 28, 1957, 11; January 9, 1958, 12.
110. *The New York Times,* December 24, 1957, 5.
111. *The New York Times,* February 11, 1958, 12.
112. *The New York Times,* February 7, 1958, 4.
113. *The New York Times,* July 16, 1958, 19.
114. *The New York Times,* September 7, 1958, 16; September 28, 1958, 19.
115. *The New York Times,* December 19, 1958, 1H; December 29, 1958, 8; January 2, 1959, 3.
116. *The New York Times,* December 24, 1958, 1M.
117. *The New York Times,* January 4, 1959, 25.
118. *The New York Times,* January 14, 1959, 2.
119. *The New York Times,* February 11, 1959, 2.
120. *The New York Times,* April 26, 1959, 1.
121. *The New York Times,* May 7, 1959, 6.
122. *Chinese News Service,* New York, January 19, 1960, 3.
123. *The New York Times,* July 5, 1956, 3.
124. *The New York Times,* June 30, 1956, 3.
125. *The New York Herald Tribune,* July 7, 1956, 2.
126. Nationwide radio and television address, October 31, 1956. Department of State, *Bulletin,* November 12, 1956, 743-4.
127. *The New York Times,* June 29, 1956, 3.
128. *The New York Times,* July 1, 1956, 10.
129. *The New York Times,* October 7, 1956, 1.
130. *The New York Times,* October 20, 1956, 6.
131. *The New York Times,* March 17, 1957, 38.
132. *The New York Times,* July 13, 1957, 2; July 15, 1957, 5; *The Catholic News,* July 20, 1957, 3.
133. *The Catholic News,* January 4, 1958, 3.
134. *The New York Times,* May 16, 1957, 8.
135. *The New York Times,* February 23, 1957, 9.
136. *Pravda,* October 20, 1956, as quoted in *The New York Times,* October 21, 1956, 28.
137. Address to the Tenth Plenum of the Central Committee of the United Workers' (Communist) Party, October 24, 1957, as quoted in *East Europe,* December, 1957, 33.
138. Address at the Plenum of the Moscow Committee and Moscow Control Commission of the Communist Party, October 19, 1928, as quoted in *The Communist Conspiracy,* Part I, Sec. B., 177-8.
139. *The New York Times,* December 30, 1957, 2.
140. Department of State, *Bulletin,* February 9, 1953, 216.
141. Department of State, *Bulletin,* August 17, 1953, 200.

142. Department of State, *Bulletin,* July 12, 1954, 45.
143. Department of State, *Bulletin,* November 12, 1956, 743.
144. Department of State, *Bulletin,* November 5, 1956, 703.
145. *The New York Times,* October 27, 1956, 2.
146. *The New York Times,* April 23, 1957, 1, 10.
147. Statement of Maxim Litvinov, Foreign Minister of the Soviet Union, made at the opening session of the Brussels Conference, November 3, 1937. See Appendix E-1.
148. Department of State, *Bulletin,* November 5, 1956, 700.
149. Department of State, *Bulletin,* November 5, 1956, 737.
150. Department of State, *Bulletin,* November 5, 1956, 697.
151. *The New York Times,* October 27, 1956, 5.
152. *Ibid.*
153. *The New York Times,* October 28, 1956, 30.
154. Department of State, *Bulletin,* November 12, 1956, 758.
155. *The New York Times,* October 28, 1956, 31.
156. *The New York Times,* October 29, 1956, 1.
157. Department of State, *Bulletin,* November 12, 1956, 750.
158. Department of State, *Bulletin,* November 12, 1956, 754.
159. Statement by Ambassador Henry Cabot Lodge in the Security Council of the United Nations, October 30, 1956. Department of State, *Bulletin,* November 12, 1956, 748.
160. Statement by Ambassador Henry Cabot Lodge in the Security Council of the United Nations, October 28, 1956. Department of State, *Bulletin,* November 12, 1956, 758-9.
161. Department of State, *Bulletin,* November 12, 1956, 758.
162. Department of State, *Bulletin,* November 12, 1956, 753.
163. Statement by Ambassador Henry Cabot Lodge in the Security Council of the United Nations, October 30, 1956. Department of State, *Bulletin,* November 12, 1956, 748.
164. Statement of Ambassador Henry Cabot Lodge, March 14, 1957, in reply to *Life* magazine editorial. 103 *Cong. Rec.* 3913.
165. Department of State, *Bulletin,* November 12, 1956, 761.
166. Department of State, *Bulletin,* November 5, 1956, 700.
167. *Security Council, Official Records,* 752d Meeting, 2 November, 1956, 10-11.
168. *Id.,* 13.
169. *Id.,* 26.
170. *Id.,* 20-21.
171. *Id.,* 14.
172. *The New York Times,* October 28, 1956, 31.
173. *The New York Times,* October 30, 1956, 15.
174. *The New York Times,* November 1, 1956, 1.
175. *The New York Times,* November 2, 1956, 1.
176. *The New York Times,* November 2, 1956, 1.

177. *General Assembly, Official Records, Second Emergency Special Session, 4-10 November 1956, Plenary Meetings and Annex,* 7.
178. *Id.,* 7-8.
179. *General Assembly, Official Records, Eleventh Session,* Supp. No. 18 (A/3592), 137.
180. *The New York Times,* May 3, 1959, 2.
181. *General Assembly, Official Records, Eleventh Session,* Supp. No. 18 (A/3592), 138.
182. Decree No. 31, 1956, Presidential Council of the People's Republic, reproduced in *Hungary Under Soviet Rule,* 36: American Friends of the Captive Nations and Assembly of Captive European Nations, *Hungary Under Soviet Rule,* New York, 1957. See also, *The New York Times,* December 21, 1956, 1.
183. Decree No. 4/1957, Presidium of the People's Republic, reproduced in *Hungary Under Soviet Rule,* 37. See also, *The New York Times,* January 14, 1957, 1.
184. *The New York Times,* October 25, 1956, 1.
185. *East Europe,* January 1957, 21.
186. From excerpts of a broadcast statement by the Hungarian government, as published in some editions of *The New York Times,* January 7, 1957.
187. *The New York Times,* March 28, 1957, 9.
188. *The New York Times,* October 26, 1956, 8.

CHAPTER XVI—THE MORAL FORCE OF WORLD OPINION

1. Secretary of State John F. Dulles. Department of State, *Bulletin,* December 19, 1955, 1005.
2. Address to American Legion, October 10, 1955. Department of State, *Bulletin,* October 24, 1955, 642.
3. News Conference, January 10, 1958. Department of State, *Bulletin,* January 27, 1958, 132.
4. *The Geneva Conference of Foreign Ministers, October 27-November 16, 1955,* Department of State Publication No. 6156, 3.
5. Department of State, *Bulletin,* December 19, 1955, 1005.
6. Department of State, *Bulletin,* December 17, 1956, 945.
7. Department of State, *Bulletin,* September 30, 1957, 523.
8. Telegram to the Secretary of State, December 12, 1917. *Foreign Relations, 1918, Russia,* vol. I, 300-1.
9. *Foreign Relations, 1918,* vol. I, 688.
10. Kansas City address, September 6, 1919. *Foreign Relations, 1919, Russia,* 119.
11. Committee on Foreign Affairs, House of Representatives, hearings: *Conditions in Russia,* 66th Cong., 3rd Sess., January-March, 1921, 116.
12. Joint declaration of the President of the United States and the Prime Minister of the United Kingdom, February 1, 1956. Department of State, *Bulletin,* February 13, 1956, 232.

13. *Russia Leaves the War*, 158: George F. Kennan, *Russia Leaves the War*, Princeton, 1956.
14. *Foreign Relations, 1918, Russia*, vol. I, 270-1.
15. *Id.*, 270.
16. *Russia Leaves the War*, 157-8.
17. *War Memoirs of Robert Lansing*, New York, 1935, 343-4.
18. *Id.*, 340.
19. *Id.*, 345.
20. Letter to the Italian Ambassador, August 10, 1920. For full text, see Appendix B-2.
21. *Ibid.*
22. Letter to the Secretary of State, July 9, 1923. *Foreign Relations, 1923*, vol. II, 758-60: Department of State, *Papers Relating to the Foreign Relations of the United States, 1923*, vol. II, Washington, D.C., 1938.
23. *Foreign Relations, 1923*, vol. II, 761-2.
24. *Foreign Relations, 1923*, vol. II, 762.
25. Department of State, *Bulletin*, January 15, 1951, 87.
26. Department of State, *Bulletin*, November 5, 1956, 703.
27. Telegram to the U.S. Ambassador in Great Britain, December 4, 1919. *Foreign Relations, 1919, Russia*, 130.
28. Telegram to the U.S. Ambassador in Great Britain, August 2, 1920. *Foreign Relations, 1920*, vol. III, 462: Department of State, *Papers Relating to the Foreign Relations of the United States, 1920*, vol. III, Washington, D.C., 1936.
29. *Foreign Relations, The Soviet Union, 1933-1939*, 13.
30. *Foreign Relations, The Soviet Union, 1933-1939*, 16.
31. Department of State, *Press Releases*, weekly issue 119 (January 7, 1932), 41-2, as quoted in Hackworth, vol. I, 334.
32. Department of State, *Press Releases*, weekly issue 126 (February 24, 1932) 205, as quoted in Hackworth, vol. I, 334-5.
33. *League of Nations Official Journal*, 1932, 383.
34. *League of Nations Official Journal*, Special Supp. 101, 87-8.
35. *Foreign Relations, The Soviet Union, 1933-1939*, 1-2.
36. Department of State Treaty Series, No. 881.
37. Department of State Treaty Series, No. 906.
38. Department of State, *Bulletin*, October 7, 1939, 342.
39. Department of State, *Bulletin*, March 2, 1953, 330.
40. Department of State, *Bulletin*, April 19, 1941, 469-70.
41. Maxim Litvinov. For full text of statement, see Appendix E-2.
42. *League of Nations Official Journal*, 1938, 345.
43. *League of Nations Official Journal*, 1938, 344.
44. Department of State, *Bulletin*, July 15, 1957, 94-5.
45. Department of State, *Bulletin*, January 29, 1951, 167; June 21, 1954, 937; February 28, 1955, 327.
46. Department of State, *Bulletin*, July 27, 1940, 48.

47. Department of State Press Release, February 21, 1950. Department of State, *Bulletin*, March 6, 1950, 356.

48. Department of State, *Bulletin*, May 28, 1951, 847.

49. Department of State, *Bulletin*, January 24, 1955, 131.

50. Department of State, *Bulletin*, July 22, 1957, 139-40.

51. *Foreign Relations, The Soviet Union, 1933-1939*, 374-6.

52. *Foreign Relations, The Soviet Union, 1933-1939*, 504.

53. Rogers Platt Churchill, reviewing State Department Publication No. 4539, *Foreign Relations, The Soviet Union, 1933-1939*, in Department of State, *Bulletin*, May 26, 1952, 826.

54. Wm. H. Standley, *Admiral Ambassador to Russia*, Chicago, 1955, 131.

55. Department of State, *Bulletin*, July 16, 1951, 87.

56. Department of State, *Bulletin*, October 29, 1951, 681, 682.

57. Department of State, *Bulletin*, October 13, 1952, 557.

58. Department of State, *Bulletin*, November 17, 1952, 786-7.

59. Department of State, *Bulletin*, June 17, 1957, 986.

60. Department of State, *Bulletin*, December 9, 1957, 934-6.

61. *The Hairenik Weekly* (Boston), August 2, 1956, 1.

62. *The New York Times*, July 20, 1956, 2.

63. Department of State, *Bulletin*, June 12, 1950, 974.

64. Department of State, *Bulletin*, December 17, 1951, 987.

65. Department of State, *Bulletin*, January 7, 1957, 11.

66. *The New York Times*, March 4, 1957, 8.

67. *The New York Times*, May 31, 1957, 11.

68. *Foreign Relations, The Soviet Union, 1933-1939*, 13.

69. Department of State, *Bulletin*, April 12, 1954, 540.

70. Department of State, *Bulletin*, April 26, 1954, 626.

71. Department of State, *Bulletin*, July 15, 1957, 92.

72. *The New York Times*, March 7, 1958, 4.

73. Department of State, *Bulletin*, November 7, 1955, 738.

74. Department of State, *Bulletin*, August 14, 1950, 246.

75. Department of State, *Bulletin*, January 24, 1955, 131.

76. Resolution of the General Assembly, December 12, 1956. Department of State, *Bulletin*, December 24 and 31, 1956, 979.

77. *League of Nations Official Journal*, 1939, 540.

78. Department of State, *Bulletin*, July 19, 1954, 87.

79. Article IX, Protocol of Proceedings of the Berlin Conference, August 1, 1945. Department of State Publication No. 4245, 35.

80. Statement in the Security Council, June 24, 1949. Department of State, *Bulletin*, July 11, 1949, 13.

81. Statement of Benjamin V. Cohen, U.S. delegate to the General Assembly, to the *Ad Hoc* Political Committee, November 22, 1948. Department of State, *Bulletin*, December 5, 1948, 695.

82. *The Catholic News* (New York), December 29, 1956, 24.

83. *Review of the United Nations Charter*, Part 12, 1620: hearings, Subcommittee of Committee on Foreign Relations, *Review of the United Nations Charter*, 83rd Cong., 2d Sess., and 84th Cong., 1st Sess. (in thirteen parts) , Washington, D.C., 1954-5.

84. Department of State, *Bulletin*, February 23, 1953, 321-2: *Review of the United Nations Charter*, Part 12, 1664-5.

85. Final report of the Committee on Foreign Relations, Subcommittee on the United Nations Charter, 84th Cong., 2d Sess., Sen. Rep. 1797, Washington, D.C., 1956, 17.

86. International Court of Justice, *Reports of Judgments, Advisory Opinions and Orders*, 1948, 57-66.

87. Sir Percy Spender, representative of Australia, as quoted in *The New York Times*, editorial, December 9, 1955.

88. *The New York Times*, December 14, 1955, 10.

89. Department of State, *Bulletin*, December 26, 1955, 1068.

90. Department of State, *Bulletin*, January 2, 1956, 13.

91. Department of State, *Bulletin*, May 17, 1954, 756-7.

92. Department of State, *Bulletin*, July 11, 1955, 54.

93. Ernest A. Gross, deputy representative to the United Nations. Department of State, *Bulletin*, February 23, 1953, 321.

94. *Review of the United Nations Charter*, Part 1, 13-14.

95. Department of State, *Bulletin*, March 8, 1954, 346.

96. Department of State, *Bulletin*, February 25, 1957, 298.

97. Hearings: *Scope of Soviet Activity in the United States*, Part 86, 4826, Subcommittee on Internal Security, U.S. Senate, 85th Cong., 1st Sess., Washington, D.C., 1958.

98. Department of State, *Bulletin*, March 8, 1954, 346.

99. James Reston, *The New York Times*, July 21, 1955, 4.

100. *New York Herald Tribune*, March 12, 1956, 1.

101. *Geneva Conference of Heads of Government, July 18-23, 1955*, Department of State Publication No. 6046, 14, 84.

102. *Id.*, 20.

103. *Behind the Communist Line*, New York, September 1, 1955, 8.

104. Department of State, *Bulletin*, August 1, 1955, 196.

105. Department of State Publication 6046, 52.

106. *New York Herald Tribune*, November 25, 1955, 3.

107. Department of State, *Bulletin*, February 25, 1957, 298.

108. Department of State, *Bulletin*, December 16, 1957, 968. The U.N. Command announced suspension of the inspection provisions of the Korean Armistice Agreement, in areas under its control, in May, 1956 (Department of State, *Bulletin*, June 11, 1956, 967; September 3, 1956, 390), and made its declaration of relief from the restrictions on importation of armaments in June, 1957 (Department of State, *Bulletin*, July 8, 1957, 58).

109. *The New York Times*, July 13, 1958, 12.

110. *The New York Times,* January 5, 1957, 1.
111. *The New York Times,* June 25, 1956, 1, 6.
112. *The New York Times,* July 1, 1956, 12.
113. Letter to Ambassador Morris, November 7, 1792, as quoted in John B. Moore, *A Digest of International Law,* Washington, D.C., 1906, vol. I, 120.

CHAPTER XVII—MUTUAL ASSISTANCE BEHIND THE IRON CURTAIN

1. Department of State, *Bulletin,* April 1, 1957, 530.
2. Department of State, *Bulletin,* July 21, 1952, 122.
3. 55 *Cong. Rec.* 119.
4. Department of State, *Bulletin,* July 25, 1942, 640.
5. Department of State, *Bulletin,* October 22, 1944, 448.
6. *Documents on American Foreign Relations,* vol. VI, 18.
7. Department of State, *Bulletin,* May 8, 1943, 396-7.
8. Department of State, *Bulletin,* July 23, 1956, 148.
9. Department of State, *Bulletin,* February 24, 1946, 296.
10. As described by Ernest A. Gross, Deputy U.S. Representative to the United Nations. Department of State, *Bulletin,* February 23, 1953, 321.
11. *Nazi Conspiracy and Aggression,* vol. III, 242-3.
12. Khrushchev's "secret" speech to the 20th Congress of the Communist Party, February, 1956. *U.S. News and World Report,* June 15, 1956, 161.
13. *Nazi Conspiracy and Aggression,* vol. III, 243, 249.
14. Department of State, *Bulletin,* November 5, 1956, 703.
15. *Chinese News Service,* May 17, 1958.
16. *The New York Times,* January 22, 1957, 17.
17. Heinrich Himmler, in *Das Schwarze Korps* (Berlin), August 20, 1942, as quoted in *German Rule in Russia,* 279.
18. *Foreign Relations, 1918,* Supp. I, vol. I, 824-5.
19. Lansing to Roman Dmowski, president of the Polish National Committee, November 1, 1918. *Foreign Relations, 1918,* Supp. I, vol. I, 881.
20. Letter to Dr. Edward Benes, President of the government-in-exile of Czechoslovakia, July 30, 1941. Benes, *Memoirs,* 177.
21. Department of State, *Bulletin,* September 6, 1941, 181.
22. *The Refugee in the Post-War World,* 74: Jacques Vernant, *The Refugee in the Post-War World,* New Haven, 1953.
23. *Our Secret Allies,* 225.
24. *German Rule in Russia,* 536n; *Soviet Opposition to Stalin,* 45.
25. *German Rule in Russia,* 541n, 596-602.
26. Prague Manifesto, November 14, 1944, as reproduced in *Soviet Opposition to Stalin,* 196.
27. *German Rule in Russia,* 554.
28. *Soviet Opposition to Stalin,* 96.
29. *Our Secret Allies,* 243.

30. Between the German surrender and September, 1945, approximately 5,200,000 Soviet citizens were repatriated. See *Europan Refugees*, 212; *The Refugee in the Post-War World*, 84; *Soviet Opposition to Stalin*, 110-11.

31. Chapter 443, P.L. 1950, 64 Stat. 316, as amended by Chapter 330, P.L. 1955, 69 Stat. 297.

32. S. 238, 82d Cong., 1st Sess., 97 *Cong. Rec.* 91-2.

33. Sec. 101 (a) (1) of the Mutual Security Act of 1951, as amended, incorporated into Sec. 401 (a) of the Mutual Security Act of 1954, and redesignated as Sec. 451 (a) of the Mutual Security Act of 1958. This section provides in part as follows:

> Not to exceed $100,000,000 of the funds available under this subsection may be expended for any selected persons who are residing in or escapees from the Soviet Union, Poland, Czechoslovakia, Hungary, Rumania, Bulgaria, Albania, Lithuania, Latvia, and Estonia or the Communist-dominated or Communist-occupied areas of Germany, or any Communist-dominated or Communist-occupied areas of Asia and any other countries absorbed by the Soviet Union, either to form such persons into elements of the military forces supporting the North Atlantic Treaty Organization or for other purposes, when the President determines that such assistance will contribute to the defense of the North Atlantic area or to the security of the United States.

34. 96 *Cong. Rec.* 14775-6.

35. 98 *Cong. Rec.* 7768.

36. Select Committee on Communist Aggression, House of Representatives, *Second Interim Report*, H. Rep. No. 2650, 83rd Cong., 2d Sess., August 9, 1954, 25.

37. Select Committee on Communist Aggression, House of Representatives, *Fourth Interim Report*, Part 2, hearings, 83rd Cong., 2d Sess., 1954, 1391-2.

38. Radio Rakoczy, November 6, 1956, as reported in *ACEN News*, September-November, 1956, 24.

39. Radio Rakoczy, November 7, 1956, as reported in *ACEN News*, September-November, 1956, 25.

40. *Life*, February 18, 1957, 129.

41. *Vital Speeches*, October 15, 1958, 10.

42. *Free China and Asia* (Taipei), vol. IV, No. 4, April 1, 1957, 15.

43. *Soviet Russia in China*, 274.

44. Department of State, *Bulletin*, October 20, 1958, 599.

45. *War or Peace*, 247.

46. Select Committee on Communist Aggression, House of Representatives, *Sixth Interim Report*, Hearings, 83rd Cong., 2d Sess., 1954, 3.

47. Select Committee on Communist Aggression, House of Representatives, *Ninth Interim Report*, Hearings, 83rd Cong., 2d Sess., 1954, 7.

48. Department of the Army, ROTC Manual 145-20, *American Military History, 1607-1953*, Washington, D.C., 1956, 101.

49. *Writings of George Washington*, vol. XXVI, 432; vol. XXVII, 402: John C.

Fitzpatrick, ed., *The Writings of George Washington from the Original Manuscript Sources, 1745-1799*, (39 volumes) Washington, D.C., 1931-1944.

50. *Writings of George Washington*, vol. XX, 143.

51. *Writings of George Washington*, vol. XX, 375.

52. *Writings of George Washington*, vol. XXI, 109-10.

53. Message to Congress, July 15, 1958. Department of State, *Bulletin*, August 4, 1958, 183.

54. *The New York Times*, December 30, 1955, 4.

55. Livingston T. Merchant, U.S. Ambassador to Canada. Department of State, *Bulletin*, February 18, 1957, 259.

56. Department of State, *Bulletin*, September 5, 1955, 377.

57. *The Public Papers of Woodrow Wilson*, Part 2, *The New Democracy*, vol. II, 382.

58. Department of State, *Bulletin*, November 19, 1956, 806.

CHAPTER XVIII—THE VOICE OF EIGHT HUNDRED MILLION

1. Department of State, *Bulletin*, March 9, 1953, 372.

2. Department of State, *Bulletin*, June 14, 1954, 900.

3. Keith C. O. Shann. *The New York Times*, September 11, 1957, 14.

4. *The New York Times*, September 11, 1957, 14.

5. Statement in Reply to *Life* editorial of March 4, 1957, as reproduced in 103 *Cong. Rec.* 3913.

6. Department of State, *Bulletin*, November 5, 1956, 703.

7. *The New York Times*, July 28, 1957, 1.

8. Department of State, *Bulletin*, January 13, 1958, 55.

9. 98 *Cong. Rec.* 5900.

10. Department of State, *Bulletin*, July 15, 1957, 94.

11. Frank P. Chambers, *The War Behind the War, 1914-1918*, London, 1939, 507.

12. *Ibid.*; R. W. Seton-Watson, *A History of the Czechs and Slovaks*, London, 1943, 300-02; S. Harrison Thomson, *Czechoslovakia in European History*, Princeton, 1953, 308-9.

13. Department of State, *Bulletin*, vol. I, 342.

14. Department of State, *Bulletin*, August 6, 1941, 88.

15. Department of State, *Bulletin*, April 12, 1954, 546.

16. *Polish Documents Report*, 162.

17. Thus, in 1952, when the American Committee organized a Coordinating Center for Anti-Bolshevik Struggle, the participants (seven Russian and eight non-Russian émigré organizations) were variously and simultaneously attacked by nonparticipants, either as "dismemberers of Russia" on the one hand, or as "Great Russian imperialists" on the other. (See *Two Sides of the Coin*, publication of the American Committee, p. 9). In 1953, when the Committee abandoned this effort, it was itself charged, by members of the Center, with "unexpected insistence" upon the inclusion of "uncompromising separatists."

(See letter of Alexander Kerensky in *The New York Times,* October 9, 1953). Similarly, NTS, which is supporting another effort at unification, through the medium of periodic conferences and congresses, has been described by various Ukrainian organizations as an "unwanted weed" dedicated to the "liquidation of the non-Russian nations," and as a "group of unscrupulous opportunists and neo-Fascists"—the "Allies We Do Not Want." (See *The Ukrainian Bulletin,* publication of The Ukrainian Congress Committee of America, December 1-15, 1957, vol. X, Nos. 23-4.)

This, too, is a problem which can only be solved with the assistance of established governments of free nations. Without such assistance, all of the exile organizations will inevitably be viewed with suspicion by at least some of the Russian peoples, and none will ever be able to command the support of a sufficient number to be effective. This was indicated, as long ago as 1919, in a statement made by President Wilson at the Paris Peace Conference:

> ... the impression had got abroad among the peasants of Siberia that the United States was the standard of a free Government which they ought to imitate. When they saw the attitude of neutrality taken up by the United States soldiers, they thought there must be something wrong with the Government of Admiral Koltchak. [Notes of meeting, May 9, 1919. *Foreign Relations, 1919, Russia,* 345].

18. Resolution on adoption of the charter, September 20, 1955. ACEN Publication No. 7, *Charter and Rules of Procedure of the Assembly of Captive European Nations.*

19. Statement of "Purpose and Organization of ACEN." Assembly of Captive European Nations, *First Session (Second Part), Organization, Resolutions, Reports, Debate, February 12, 1955-September 20,* 1955, 12.

20. 102 *Cong. Rec.,* 11339.

21. 102 *Cong. Rec.,* 11355.

22. 102 *Cong. Rec.,* 11357.

23. 102 *Cong. Rec.,* 11359.

24. Assembly of Captive European Nations, *First Session (Second Part), Organization, Resolutions, Reports, Debate, February 12, 1955-September 20, 1955,* 22; see also *The New York Times,* September 28, 1956, 3.

25. Department of State, *Bulletin,* October 19, 1953, 530.

26. Department of State, *Bulletin,* March 16, 1953, 400-1.

27. *The New York Times,* May, 20, 1954, 2.

28. *Pravda,* February 27, 1957.

29. *Radyanska Ukraina,* February 28, 1957, No. 50.

30. *Pravda,* February 9, 1957, 6.

31. *The New York Times,* June 18, 1958, 10.

32. R. S. S. Gunewardene. *The New York Times,* September 14, 1957, 4; September 15, 1957, Sec. IV, 12E.

33. See, for example, two declarations signed by Alexandra Tolstoy, Igor Sikorsky and Boris Sergievsky, *The 41st Anniversary of the Bolshevik Revolution* and *A Nucleus of Humanity, A Free Russian Affirmation for the First of May, 1959* (also signed by Leon Nicolai); and statement issued April, 1953 by Mikola Lebed, secretary general, Supreme Ukrainian Liberation Council, *The Current International Situation and the Political Aspects of the Liberation Policy.*

34. ACEN Publication No. 7, *Charter and Rules of Procedure of the Assembly of Captive European Nations.*

35. Assembly of Captive European Nations, *First Session (Second Part), Organization, Resolutions, Reports, Debate, February 12, 1955-September 20, 1955,* 42-3.

36. *ACEN News,* Nos. 11-12, February-March, 1956, 4.

37. See, for example, two declarations signed by Alexandra Tolstoy, Igor Sikorsky, and Boris Sergievsky, *The 41st Anniversary of the Bolshevik Revolution* and *A Nucleus of Humanity, A Free Russian Affirmation for the First of May, 1959* (also signed by Leon Nicolai).

38. *Belorussia: The Making of a Nation,* 221.

39. Mikola Lebed, secretary general, Supreme Ukrainian Liberation Council, *The Current International Situation and the Political Aspects of the Liberation Policy,* April, 1953, 15.

40. Files of the *Armenian Review,* Boston.

41. Assembly of Captive European Nations, *Appeal to the Nations of the Free World,* (ACEN Doc. No. 24-Gen.), December 20, 1954.

42. Resolution adopted at the Thirteenth Plenary Meeting, April 14, 1955. ACEN Document No. 28 (Soc.).

43. *ACEN News,* Nos. 15-17, June-August, 1956, 4.

44. *ACEN News,* Nos. 15-17, June-August, 1956, 4-10.

45. *ACEN News,* Nos. 18-20, September-November, 1956, 26.

46. *ACEN News,* Nos. 18-20, September-November, 1956, 29.

47. *ACEN News,* Nos. 18-20, September-November, 1956, 28-29.

48. *ACEN News,* Nos. 18-20, September-November, 1956, 31-32.

49. *ACEN News,* Nos. 18-20, September-November, 1956, 34.

50. *ACEN News,* Nos. 18-20, September-November, 1956, 35.

51. Statement of Henry Cabot Lodge, U.S. representative to the United Nations, in reply to *Life* editorial of March 4, 1957, as reproduced in 103 *Cong. Rec.* 3913.

52. *The Ukrainian Insurgent Army in Fight For Freedom,* 181-2: United Committee of the Ukrainian-American Organizations of New York, *The Ukrainian Insurgent Army in Fight for Freedom,* New York, 1954.

53. *Foreign Relations, 1918, Russia,* vol. I, 271.

54. *The Ukrainian Insurgent Army in Fight For Freedom,* 183.

55. *Behind the Communist Line* (New York), April, 1957, 3.

56. *U.S. News and World Report,* June 1, 1956, 75.

1. *Apocalypse* xiii:1, 3, 11-14. For full text of Chapter 13, see Appendix F.

2. *Apocalypse* xvii:16-17. For full text of Chapter 17, see Appendix F.

3. *Apocalypse* xix:19-20. For full text of Chapter 19, see Appendix F.

4. *Atheistic Communism.* Encyclical letter, March 19, 1937, par. 22.

5. J. V. Stalin, *Foundations of Leninism,* quoting Lenin in *"Left-Wing" Communism. The Communist Conspiracy,* Part I, Sec. A, 167.

6. *Foreign Relations, 1918, Russia,* vol. I, 143. This report was written in August, 1917.

7. *Foreign Relations, 1918, Russia,* vol. I, 61.

8. *Foreign Relations, 1918, Russia,* vol. I, 53.

9. *Foreign Relations, 1918, Russia,* vol. I, 78.

10. *O Seculo,* October 15, 1917. Translation is from *Fatima in the Light of History,* 150: Costa Brochado, *Fatima in the Light of History,* trans. and ed. by George C. A. Boehrer, Milwaukee, 1955.

11. Translation is from *The Crusade of Fatima,* 102-3: John De Marchi, I.C.M., *The Crusade of Fatima, The Lady More Brilliant Than the Sun,* arr. and ed. from the Portuguese by Rev. A. C. Branco and Rev. P. C. M. Kelly, C.S.C., New York, 1958.

12. Translation is from *The Crusade of Fatima,* 107.

13. *The New York Times,* May 14, 1958, 13.

14. Unpublished memoirs were written by Lucia in 1936, 1937 and 1941, at the instruction of the Bishop of Leiria.

15. See *The Crusade of Fatima,* 47.

16. *The New York Times,* January 26, 1938, 25.

17. *Ibid.*

18. *The New York Times,* January 30, 1938, Sec. IV, 8.

19. *The New York Times,* December 1, 1957, 70.

20. See *The Crusade of Fatima,* 17.

21. See *The Crusade of Fatima,* 34-5.

22. See *The Crusade of Fatima,* 45-6.

23. Resolutions of the Sixth Congress of the Russian Social-Democratic Labor Party (Bolsheviks), August 8-16, 1917, as reproduced in V. I. Lenin, *Toward the Seizure of Power. Collected Works,* vol. XXI, Book II, 302, 304, New York, 1932.

24. See *The Crusade of Fatima,* 74-5.

25. See *The Crusade of Fatima,* 83.

26. See *The Crusade of Fatima,* 99.

27. See *The Crusade of Fatima,* 152.

28. See *The Crusade of Fatima,* 152-3.

29. See *The Crusade of Fatima,* 159.

30. Governor William Bradford, *History of Plimouth Plantation*, Book I, Chapter IX, 47.
31. *Abraham Lincoln: His Speeches and Writings*, 610.
32. P. L. 324, ch. 216; 66 Stat. 64; 36 U.S.C., sec. 185.
33. Pres. Proc. No. 2978, June 20, 1952, 17 F.R. 5537.
34. Pres. Proc. Nos. 3023, June 27, 1953, 18 F.R. 3683; 3064, August 14, 1954, 19 F.R. 5121; 3120, October 25, 1955, 20 F.R. 7977; 3150, September 1, 1956, 21 F.R. 6593; 3194, August 13, 1957, 22 F.R. 6455; 3252, August 1, 1958, 23 F.R. 5947.
35. *New York Herald Tribune*, April 18, 1957, 21.
36. P.L. 512, ch. 182.
37. Department of State, *Bulletin*, October 19, 1953, 511.
38. Department of State, *Bulletin*, April 25, 1955, 674.
39. Public address, September 2, 1945, delivered on board the U.S.S. *Missouri* in Tokyo Bay, on the occasion of the surrender of Japan.

CHAPTER XX—FINITA LA COMMEDIA

1. Testimony before subcommittee of the Appropriations Committee, House of Representatives, April 28, 1958. Hearings, *Mutual Security Appropriations for 1959*, 85th Cong., 2d Sess., 315.
2. Department of State, *Bulletin*, July 7, 1946, 34.
3. *U.S. Relations With China*, 279.
4. Department of State, *Bulletin*, January 16, 1950, 79.
5. Department of State, *Bulletin*, July 3, 1950, 5.
6. *War or Peace*, 190.
7. Department of State, *Bulletin*, July 15, 1957, 93.
8. Department of State, *Bulletin*, July 15, 1957, 94.
9. Department of State, *Bulletin*, July 22, 1957, 139-40.
10. Department of State, *Bulletin*, September 28, 1953, 406.
11. Department of State, *Bulletin*, October 24, 1955, 642.
12. Department of State, *Bulletin*, May 7, 1956, 742.
13. Department of State, *Bulletin*, December 19, 1955, 1005.
14. Department of State, *Bulletin*, April 1, 1957, 530.
15. As quoted in *The Quest for Peace*, Department of State Publication No. 6391, 12.
16. *The New York Times*, May 23, 1957, 14.
17. Letter of President Franklin D. Roosevelt, March 10, 1945, to Norman Armour. Department of State, *Bulletin*, September 30, 1945, 466.
18. Letter of Secretary of State John F. Dulles, June 13, 1956, to the chairman of the Senate Committee on Foreign Relations, as reproduced in the report of that committee on *The Mutual Security Act of 1956*, Sen. Rep. No. 2273, 84th Cong., 2d Sess., 17.
19. *Ibid.*

20. Secretary of State John F. Dulles on United States refusal to finance construction of the Aswan Dam. *The New York Times,* April 3, 1957, 8.

21. Department of State, *Bulletin,* November 30, 1953, 744.

22. Department of State, *Bulletin,* June 24, 1957, 1008.

23. Professor Gilbert Murray. Records of the Fifth Assembly, Geneva, 1924, *LNOJ,* Spec. Supp. No. 23, 159.

24. Department of State, *Bulletin,* December 17, 1956, 945.

25. Charter of the International Military Tribunal, Article 6 (c).

26. Department of State, *Bulletin,* June 10, 1945, 1075.

27. Walter S. Kotschnig, August 15, 1950. Department of State, *Bulletin,* September 25, 1950, 510.

28. Committee on Government Operations, U.S. Senate, *Report on Korean War Atrocities,* Sen. Rep. No. 848, January 11, 1954, 83rd Cong., 2d Sess., 16.

29. Select Committee on Communist Aggression, House of Representatives, *Summary Report,* H. Rep. No. 2684, Part 16, 83rd Cong., 2d Sess., 1955, 7-8.

30. Address to the White House Correspondents' Association, February 12, 1943. Department of State, *Bulletin,* February 13, 1943, 145.

31. Department of State, *Bulletin,* April 25, 1960, 667-8.

32. Department of State, *Bulletin,* July 30, 1951, 165.

33. *Izvestia,* July 22, 1922, as reproduced in *Soviet Russia and the West,* 133.

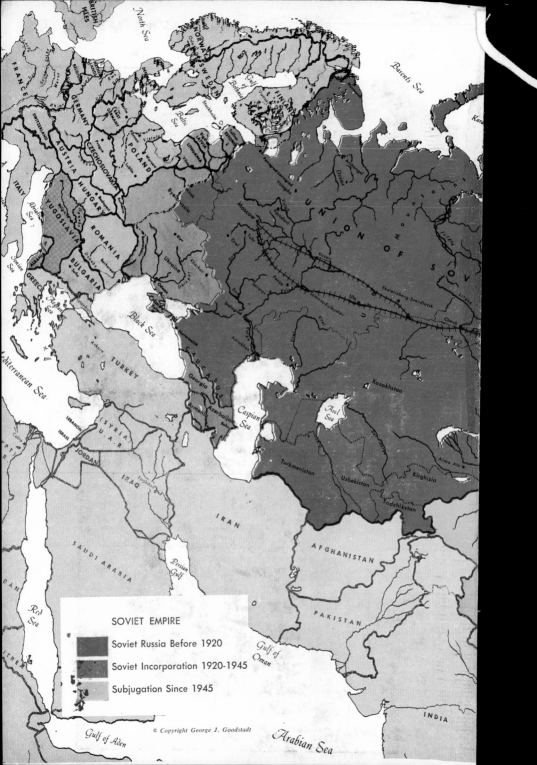

SOVIET EMPIRE

Soviet Russia Before 1920

Soviet Incorporation 1920-1945

Subjugation Since 1945

© Copyright George J. Goodstadt